A TO Z OF
AMERICAN
WOMEN
WRITERS

REVISED EDITION

A TO Z OF

AMERICAN
WOMEN
WRITERS

REVISED EDITION

CAROL KORT

An imprint of Infobase Publishing

Facts On File, Inc.
An imprint of Infobase Publishing
132 West 31st Street
New York NY 10001

Library of Congress Cataloging-in-Publication Data

Kort, Carol.
  A to Z of American women writers / Carol Kort. — Rev. ed.
    p. cm.
  Includes bibliographical references (p.   ) and indexes.
  ISBN 978-0-8160-6693-3 (acid-free paper) 1. American literature—Women authors—Dictionaries. I. Title.
  PS147.K67 2007
  810.9'9287—dc22
    [B]   2007020534

Facts On File books are available at special discounts when purchased in bulk quantities for businesses, associations, institutions or sales promotions. Please call our Special Sales Department in New York at (212) 967-8800 or (800) 322-8755.

You can find Facts On File on the World Wide Web at http://www.factsonfile.com

Text design by Joan M. McEvoy and Cathy Rincon
Cover design by Salvatore Luongo

Printed in the United States of America

VB Hermitage 10 9 8 7 6 5 4 3 2 1

This book is printed on acid-free paper.

To the Kort House: Michael, Eleza, and Tamara
and
For my mother and in loving memory of my father

CONTENTS

ACKNOWLEDGMENTS

I could not have embarked on a project of this magnitude without the assistance of many friends, colleagues, and specialists in American literature and women's studies. For helping me revise and refine my preliminary list of American women writers, I am immensely grateful to Bonnie Burt, Ronnie Friedland, Gerri Gomperts, Robin King and Darien Andreu, and Susan Morton. I would also like to thank Mary Bohlen for her expertise on women journalists; Boston University humanities professors Linda Wells and Robert Wexelblatt; Charles Capper, American history professor Boston University; Elizabeth Kean and other members of the English Department at Brookline High School for their insightful comments; Elizabeth Barnett for her expertise on Edna St. Vincent Millay, and the competent, friendly staff at Brookline Public Library's Main and Coolidge Corner branches. Simone Bloom Nathan invited me to join a freelance consulting/writers group, where members provided me with advice and encouragement and helped replenish my spirit.

I am also grateful to James Warren for initially suggesting this project. At Facts On File, I am indebted to my editor, Nicole Bowen, and to her able assistant, Liza Trinkle.

To paraphrase Emily Dickinson, my family is my estate. I grew up believing that, as Cicero said, "a house without books is like a body without a soul." For that, and for much more, I would like to thank my mother, Florence Chvat, who encouraged me at an early age and ever since to appreciate good literature. I am profoundly grateful to my wonderful daughters, Tamara and Eleza, and to Michael, my loving husband, friend, and partner of more than 35 years, who has sustained me in all my endeavors—personal and professional.

Finally, a nod to the 186 American women writers (including 36 new entries) in this book for their talent, tenacity, and inspiration. As Louisa May Alcott wrote, "Far away there in the sunshine are my highest aspirations. I may not reach them, but I can look up and see their beauty, believe in them, and try to follow where they lead."

AUTHOR'S NOTE

It was a difficult task deciding which of the myriad distinguished American women writers to include in *A to Z of American Women Writers.* Apart from space limitations, I considered several criteria. My first concern was to represent female writers from a variety of literary genres, such as fiction (including novels, short stories, mystery, science fiction, horror fiction), poetry, nonfiction (essays, letters, diaries, memoirs), drama, journalism, juvenile literature, and personal narratives. I also attempted to include notable women writers who spanned America's rich and varied history, from colonial times to the present, and who represented a panoply of geographic, cultural, and socioeconomic backgrounds. Finally, I only considered American women writers whose work is readily accessible

and about whom I could supply bibliographic material. Obviously and regrettably, not all who could be are included in this volume.

In keeping with the style of other Facts On File biographical dictionaries, the headwords in this volume list the writers by their first (original legal), middle, maiden, and last names. Exceptions are made when authors are known by pen names that differ completely from their full names (*e.g.,* MAYA ANGELOU, instead of Marguerite Johnson; ANNE RICE, instead of Howard Allen O'Brien). In some instances, I have disagreed with the use of this style (*e.g.,* LULA CARSON SMITH MCCULLERS, THEODORA SARAH ORNE JEWETT) and would have preferred to list these writers by the names under which they wrote.

INTRODUCTION

From colonial times to the present, American women have expressed themselves through the written word. Whether elucidating their personal feelings, visions, experiences, or relationships, which fiction writer Willa Cather called "the tragic necessity of human life," or delineating more universal themes relating to the human condition, American women writers, like their male counterparts, have written on every imaginable topic. Each of the notable 186 American women profiled in this book is a talented writer who was or is committed to her craft. Many of the writers have earned prestigious awards, fellowships, and prizes, including Pulitzer Prizes, O. Henry Awards, and two Nobel Prizes for literature. Some were relatively forgotten until their works were rediscovered and reissued, often by other women writers. For example, the complete works of America's first major published poet, Anne Bradstreet (1612–72), were not made available until almost 200 years after her death. A century later, the poet Adrienne Rich praised Bradstreet for writing the first good poems in America "within confines as severe as any American poet has confronted: while rearing eight children, lying frequently sick, [and] keeping house at the edge of the wilderness." Harriet Ann Jacobs's *Incidents in the Life of Slave Girl* (1861), a remarkable antebellum slave narrative about the author's seven-year struggle for freedom, was considered fiction and was largely forgotten until

the 1970s, when it, too, was rediscovered. Novelist and folklorist Zora Neale Hurston's impressive body of work from the 1930s was rediscovered in the late 1970s by scholars and promoted by esteemed writer Alice Walker, who called Hurston "the intellectual and spiritual foremother of generations of black women writers." Even the 20th-century writer Dawn Powell, whose satirical novels were critically acclaimed but went largely unnoticed during her lifetime, is enjoying a resurgence in popularity, over 40 years after her death.

Women writers have always faced obstacles. Early authors rarely had access to a formal education, as their male counterparts often did, and many had to mask their identities by using pseudonyms, or by writing anonymously, in order to get published or be taken seriously. In 1797, Hannah Webster Foster signed her popular sentimental novel, *The Coquette*, "by . . . A Lady of Massachusetts." Her real name did not appear on her books until long after she had died. Even in more recent times, for a variety of reasons, more than 30 writers in this book have used pen names. Pearl Buck, who in 1938 became the first woman to win the Nobel Prize for literature, sometimes used a male nom de plume, John Sedges, because she claimed she wanted her work reviewed on its own merits, and not as a "female" writer.

In spite of the difficulties they faced, women continued to write and to publish in a variety of genres. Mary Rowlandson dramatically described her three-month captivity in 1676 by Wampanoag Indians; this account became one of America's earliest best sellers. A century later, Abigail Adams, a preeminent letter writer, engaged in a voluminous correspondence with her husband, John, a member of the Continental Congress, and with friends such as Mercy Otis Warren, a talented political satirist and important chronicler of the American Revolution. Adams's letters, published by her grandson, reflected her astute political and business acumen, courage (she had to protect her family and homestead from British soldiers who were stationed nearby), and affection for her husband, who, while he was a delegate at the 1776 Continental Congress, she admonished to "Remember the Ladies" and their legal rights as married women. Meanwhile, Phillis Wheatley, who arrived young and sickly in Boston on a slave ship from West Africa in 1761 and was educated along with her master's children, became a highly respected poet and the first African American to publish a book.

As more opportunities were made available, including formal education and the right to sign their names to their work, American women writers began experimenting with other forms, from slave narratives to fantasy fiction. The writers in this volume represent some of America's finest novelists, short story writers, poets, nonfiction writers, playwrights, memoirists, biographers, detective novelists, diarists, food writers, essayists, literary critics, nature writers, science fiction writers, screenwriters, and writers of juvenile literature. They also are represented in every significant American literary movement, including naturalism, realism, imagism, and modernism, as well as the Harlem Renaissance of the 1920s, the Southern literary renaissance (1920 to 1950), and the American Indian renaissance. Novelist Leslie Marmon Silko, who was raised on the Laguna Pueblo reservation, explains that it is the "spoken word and reverence for tradition that are the seeds for the American Indian literary and cultural movement of the 1960s and 1970s."

Women have also created their own splinter groups. For example, the mystery writers Sara Paretsky and Sue Grafton are credited with helping establish female sleuths within the hard-boiled detective fiction genre and are among a growing number of "sisters in crime" whose works feature women private eyes.

In their works, American women writers have also introduced readers to every region in this country, from the lush, sensual Cajun country of southern Louisiana to the windswept Great Plains of the Far West; from tony Southern California to rural Georgia; and from the piney woods of Maine to the slums of New York City.

However, finding time to practice their craft has always been an issue for women writers. In the mid-1800s, the poet Emily Dickinson would steal a few moments from her chores, such as baking bread and gardening, to jot down her ideas on scraps of paper. Then, late at night, with her tasks completed and her family asleep, she would develop the fragments into poems and spend hours revising them. Although only seven poems were published during her lifetime—and those only because of prodding from her friend, novelist Helen Hunt Jackson—Dickinson apparently recognized her own self-worth. "When I die," she wrote, "they'll have to remember me."

While Dickinson and Louisa May Alcott were among a small group of women writers who never married or had children ("I'd rather be a free spinster and paddle my own canoe," Alcott wrote in her journal), for many others, parenting responsibilities often took precious time away from their work. As the great great grandmother of the biographer Catherine Drinker Bowen wrote in a diary entry in 1790, having given birth to nine children, "a woman's best years came after she left off bearing and rearing." Even then, it may be too late. "The years when I should have been writing, my hands and being were at other (inescapable) tasks," recalled fiction writer Tillie Olsen in a 1971 essay. "The habits of a lifetime, when everything else had to come before writing, are not easily broken, even when circumstances now make it possible for the writing to be first." But for others, motherhood enhanced the ability to write. "I can hardly count the ways that being a mother has broadened my writing, deepened my connection to all other women, and galvanized my commitment to the Earth and its fate," Barbara Kingsolver wrote in 1995 in *High Tide in Tucson.*

While writing is a creative endeavor, it was and remains a way to earn a living. As early as 1790, Judith Sargent Murray, a playwright and essayist who published under male pseudonyms, called upon women to become educated "sensible and informed" mothers and wives who were capable of "intellectual and economic independence." In 1845, Margaret Fuller, America's first professional literary critic and woman foreign correspondent, published a feminist manifesto, *Woman in the Nineteenth Century,* in which she emphasized the need for equality in all spheres and vocations. About 50 years later, Charlotte Perkins Gilman, a great niece of Harriet Beecher Stowe, was still arguing for female economic independence, postulating in *Women and Economics* that the "troubles of life" were mainly traceable to "the heart of the purse."

Women often turned to writing as a means of expression, which they did with eloquence and passion, in spite of restrictions placed on them. But they also turned to writing as a way to earn a living. Limited in their choice of careers, many women discovered, as Hollywood screenwriter Anita Loos put it, that "there is money in ink."

In 1822, Sarah Josepha Hale, finding herself widowed with five children and with no formal education, became a writer in order to keep her family afloat. She published some poems under a pseudonym, sold her first novel, and became the editor of one of America's first women's magazines.

The enterprising Louisa May Alcott wrote gothic romances and gruesome thrillers for children. She hated writing them, but they sold well, and she had to support her parents and sisters. Although her father encouraged his daughter to read, write, think, and be creative, he was inept at earning a living and seemed content to be known as "the grandfather of *Little Women.*"

Orphaned as a teenager, Ida B. Wells-Barnett had to support her five brothers and sisters. She was a schoolteacher for a while, and then became a prominent journalist who used her clout to protest the lynching of African Americans in the 1890s.

At the other end of the economic spectrum, women still had to contend with societal pressures. Poet Amy Lowell, who came from an illustrious, affluent family in which the men were high achievers, claimed that "one of the greatest handicaps that anyone could possibly have" was to belong to a class and a sex that were "not supposed to be able to produce good creative work." In 1925, she was posthumously awarded a Pulitzer Prize in poetry, in part for her much anthologized poem "Patterns."

The motives as to why women opt to become writers are as diverse as the women themselves. Marilyn Chin, a contemporary Chinese-American poet who writes about exile, assimilation, and loss, claims she had no choice: "You know you are a poet when you can't live without it." Acclaimed memoirist and gastronomer M. F. K. Fisher, who came from a long line of writers, claimed that becoming a writer was "just heredity, not my fault," whereas Edith Hamilton, renowned classicist, did not write her first book until she was 63 but went on to write prize-winning works about the ancient world that remain popular today. Novelist and journalist Joan Didion, who says she writes in order to find out who she is and what she fears, works seven days a week, from eleven in the morning until eight at night, while award-winning novelist Edna Ferber purportedly produced 1,000 words a day, 350 days a year. Her books, she said, were her children.

Some writers were inspired by other women. For example, short story writer Toni Cade Bambara thanks her mother, an avid reader and aspiring writer, for encouraging her to pursue a career, while Willa Cather, a Nebraskan, was influenced and encouraged by another, older writer, the regionalist Sara Orne Jewett, and dedicated her novel *O Pioneers!* to her mentor in Maine.

Yet, as fiction writer Carson McCullers observed, discipline and hard work are not enough. "There must come," she said, "an illumination, a divine spark that puts the work into focus and balance. Poet H. D. (Hilda Doolittle) felt swept away by the creative process. "Winged words make their own spiral," she explained. "To share in the making of a poem is the privilege of a poet." For novelist Toni Morrison, a Nobel laureate, fiction should be "beautiful and powerful, but it should also work. It should have something in it that enlightens."

Other American women writers have focused more on exposing social injustice and corruption. In 1861, Rebecca Harding Davis wrote a novella entitled *Life in the Iron Mills,* based on growing up in an industrial town in West Virginia, "to dig into this commonplace, this vulgar American life, and see what it is" and to expose the "soul starvation" of the nation's new mill- and factory workers. In 1887, the bold undercover journalist Nellie Bly feigned insanity to become committed at a public asylum for women in New York so she could report firsthand on its abusive, horrific conditions. Her articles helped prompt reform at mental hospitals nationwide. In 1959, Lorraine Hansberry's landmark play *A Raisin in the Sun,* the first play by an African-American woman to be produced on Broadway, changed the way white audiences viewed African-American families. "Everything is political," Hansberry insisted.

Whether describing the poor whites of Appalachia (Harriette Simpson Arnow), the horrors of the Civil War (Margaret Mitchell), the Japanese-American internment camps during World War II (Yoshiko Uchida and Hisaye Yamamoto), life in the Puerto Rican barrios of New York City (Nicholasa Mohr), the struggle of the working class to eke out a living in poverty-stricken rural Maine (Carolyn Chute), or the devastating effects of the 1992 Los Angeles race riots (Anna Deavere Smith), American women writers have used their craft as a way to voice their experiences and concerns. "I don't feel any sense of consciousness about my role as a spokesperson for Latino women in my writing, because I've taken that responsibility on from the very beginning," explained the contemporary novelist and poet Sandra Cisneros.

But not all writers agree. According to playwright and short story writer Estela Portillo Trambley, "when you inject politics into [your work], you limit its life. . . . All good literature is based on the human experience, which is nonpolitical." Rita Dove, the first African American to be appointed the country's poet laureate (1993), explained that as an artist she shunned "political considerations and racial or gender partiality" because she was more interested in "the ways in which language can change your perceptions," while novelist Rita Mae Brown is more interested in "emotional truth" than in classification by race, sex, or sexual preference, which she considers a "discreet form" of censorship. "All lives are worth concern and description," Brown asserted in 1988.

Going one step further, dramatist Lillian Hellman refused to be labeled as a "woman" playwright. The celebrated fiction writer Cynthia Ozick has stated that while women need "equal access to the greater world," she rejects the separatist classification of "women writers." Instead, Ozick wants to be judged simply as a "writer." And short story writer Jean Stafford rejected being labeled a woman writer, preferring to focus on universal themes. On the other hand, Toni Morrison has said that she has no objection to being called a black woman writer: "I really think the range of emotions and perceptions I have had access to as a black person and a female person are greater than those of people who are neither."

While they may disagree on their respective goals or motives, all the writers included in this book have something in common: they express themselves in English, and they are American citizens. After living and working in Africa for four years, poet Maya Angelou, who loved Ghana and identified with her African roots, realized that she was an American and returned home. Yet many of the women portrayed in this volume have led what Pearl Buck calls a "mentally bifocal life." They have straddled two worlds or cultures, and their experiences are reflected in their writing. Buck, who was born in West Virginia, was raised mostly in—and wrote mostly about—China. Bharati

Mukherjee came from Calcutta and most of her fiction is about Indian women who settle in New York City. Anzia Yezierska came from the small Polish village of Plinsk, and her fiction discusses Jewish immigrant struggles and concerns. Jamaica Kincaid, writing stories form her home in Vermont, often recalls her childhood experiences in Antigua through her fictional characters. Novelist Cristina García wants to pass on her extended family's history in Cuba, where she was born, to future generations. In her popular novels, Amy Tan, who was born in California, often probes the gap between Chinese immigrant women and their first-generation daughters, while the Native American poet Wendy Rose, who was raised on a reservation, attempts to depict Native Americans as multidimensional "living, working artists," rather than as literature fossils.

Many of the women mentioned in the *A to Z of American Women Writers* are famous, and a few are infamous. When it appeared in 1889, Kate Chopin's scandalous novel *The Awakening* was widely condemned, mostly by influential male critics, because it spoke openly of female sexuality, adultery, depression, and suicide. Others, such as Fannie Hurst, one of the most popular, widely read, and best-paid writers of the 1920s and 1930s, or Octavia E. Butler, whose work first appeared in the 1980s and is one of only a few popular black female science fiction writers, are less known. Some, such as Harper Lee, the author of *To Kill a Mockingbird,* have written only one major work, while other writers, such as Joyce Carol Oates, are prolific in a number of genres. However, all of the women in this volume are noteworthy.

"Nobody writes from a vacuum; writers compose from their life experiences," noted Catherine Drinker Bowen. While the backgrounds, lifestyles, and sources of inspiration of the 186 women in this book vary greatly, as a group they have created an impressive body of work and made a major contribution to America's literary canon and tradition.

Adams, Abigail Smith
(1744–1818) *letter writer*

As the matriarch of one of America's first families, Abigail Adams strongly influenced two presidents—her husband, John Adams, and her son John Quincy Adams. She is also recognized as one of the country's greatest and most prolific letter writers.

Abigail Smith was born on November 11, 1744, in Weymouth, Massachusetts. One of three daughters of a Congregational minister, William Smith, and his wife, Elizabeth, Abigail was a sickly child and was unable to attend school. Petite, quiet, and reserved, with piercing dark eyes, she was also strong-willed and had a quick and inquisitive mind.

In spite of her lack of formal schooling, Abigail was a voracious reader who took advantage of her father's well-stocked library to study literature, history, and philosophy. She taught herself French and was tutored by her maternal grandmother, whom she adored and who favored a "happy method of mixing instruction and amusement together."

John Adams, an ambitious young lawyer from Braintree (now called Quincy), Massachusetts, met Abigail Smith in 1758, when she was 14. He was struck by her wit, verve, and intelligence. After a six-year courtship, John and Abigail married in a meetinghouse on October 15, 1764. They moved to Braintree, where Abigail Adams gave birth to five children, one of whom died when she was two.

In the 1770s, John Adams became deeply involved in revolutionary politics. Abigal Adams too was a staunch revolutionary and strongly supported her husband in his commitment to colonial independence and freedom from the "tyranny of the aristocracy." When in 1774 John was called to Philadelphia as a delegate to the first Continental Congress, Abigail took complete responsibility for managing the farm and raising and educating the children. Her husband was the first to acknowledge that it was his efficient and capable marriage partner who provided the family income and enabled the Adamses to grow quite prosperous during their 10-year separation.

In spite of her many demanding responsibilities, Adams somehow managed to write a stream of animated, informative letters to her husband, keeping him abreast of important domestic, social, and political news. Her wartime letters offer a descriptive and realistic portrait of what it was like to live through the turbulent American Revolution.

Abigail Adams advised her husband to "Remember the Ladies" in 1776.
(AP/Wide World Photos)

"The constant roar of the cannon is so distressing that we cannot eat, drink, or sleep," she wrote John, adding that "the continual epidemics and sickness seem to strike nearly every household."

Left alone to protect the farm with her young children, Adams never let the British attacks intimidate her; she knew how to use a rifle, and was not afraid to do so. John correctly called his wife a "heroine" for displaying such valor as the head of the household. On Independence Day, 1776, Abigail Adams wrote: "Thus ends royal Authority in this State, and all the people shall say Amen."

For more than 40 years, Adams would continue to write to her husband, to friends such as the author Mercy Otis Warren, and to relatives, especially her sister Mary Cranch. In all, she wrote more than 2,000 letters. Together they comprise

the private and public experiences—from rearing children to befriending Thomas Jefferson—of a middle-class, self-taught woman who observed and recorded many of the pivotal events that took place during the late 18th and early 19th centuries.

Adams was a staunch advocate of equal education opportunities for women and often wrote about her own distressing lack of formal education. Although she firmly believed in family, religion, and preserving women's domestic roles, she never failed to encourage her husband to support legislation that would improve women's legal rights.

On March 31, 1776, in what is perhaps her most famous letter, Adams urged her husband, then a delegate at the Continental Congress, to "Remember the Ladies, and be more generous and favourable to them than your ancestors. Do not put such unlimited power into the hands of the Husbands. Remember all Men would be tyrants if they could."

She was unmoved when John scoffed at her proposal; she wrote him back that she hated the concept that "Men retained absolute power over Wives." She never went so far as to suggest that wives should be equal to their husbands, but she steadfastly refused to accept the intellectual inferiority of women. For that reason, Adams is considered an early champion of women's rights.

Adams also was an early opponent of slavery. For example, she defended her right to teach a black servant to read. In 1774 she wrote John that she wished "most sincerely there was not a slave in the province."

Abigail and John Adams shared an extremely close relationship; their marriage was one of mutual love and respect, and their correspondence was often amorous. "My pen is always freer than my tongue," she wrote to her husband in 1775. "I have wrote many things to you that I suppose I never could have talked."

She always addressed her husband as "Dearest Friend" and missed him terribly when they were apart. "Give me the man I love. . . . I know I have a right to your whole heart, because my own never knew another lord," she wrote to him in 1782, while he was a diplomat in France. Her letters to Europe offered her husband news, advice, encouragement, and sorely needed affection. In January 2006 Public Broadcasting Corporation (PBS) produced "John & Abigail Adams," which showed the astounding collaborative effort on paper between husband and wife.

In 1784, with the end of the Revolutionary War, Adams was finally able to arrange to join her husband in Europe. Upon hearing the news that at long last he would soon be seeing his wife, John wrote: "Your letter has made me the happiest man upon earth. I am twenty years younger than I was yesterday. Yours, and with more ardor than ever, John." After her arduous month-long voyage across the Atlantic, they were reunited.

The Adamses lived in France (1784–85) for eight months, followed by three years in England. Abigail Adams wrote detailed, gossipy letters to her friends and family in New England in which she shared her impressions of Europe, both positive and negative. "There is a rage of fashion which prevails here with despotick [sic] sway," she observed wryly, while continuing to dress as plainly as she had at home.

Adams longed for the simplicity of her life in Massachusetts. In the fall of 1784 she a wrote to a friend, "I turn my thoughts to my lovely cottage, to my rough hewn garden, as objects more pleasing than the gay and really beautiful one which now presents itself to my view."

Two years after returning to America in 1787, John Adams was elected vice president. From 1797 to 1801, he served as president of the United States. Abigail Adams split her time between the farm in Quincy and the capital cities of Philadelphia, New York, and Washington. She was the first First Lady to occupy the new official presidential residence in present-day Washington, D.C., if only for a few months. She described the White House as being a "great castle which is built for ages to come" and noted that the unfinished mansion was "cold and damp."

In spite of her deteriorating health, Adams loved being at the center of the political universe, surrounded by important statesmen and visiting diplomats. Unlike her predecessor, Martha Washington, Adams was a staunch Federalist (as was her husband) and a very involved First Lady. Some of her husband's political enemies accused "Her Majesty" of having too much behind-the-scenes influence over him, but John Adams continued to value his wife's opinions, her common sense, and her zeal for politics.

The Adamses left Washington in 1801 and returned to their beloved Quincy to live as tranquilly "as that bald old fellow, called Time" would allow. Abigail Adams resumed her farm tasks and could often be seen at the crack of dawn, skimming milk or doing the housework, accompanied by her pet dog Juno or one of her grandchildren.

Once again, Abigail Adams took complete control of managing the family's finances and properties, all the while continuing her letter writing. Although she was a master at her craft, she was self-conscious about her unrefined penmanship and poor spelling and grammar, the result of not having been formally educated. She often told her correspondents to burn her letters.

Adams died of typhoid fever on October 28, 1818, at the age of 74, six years before her son, John Quincy Adams, was elected the sixth president of the United States. She had often written to him, offering him sound political advice, some of which he heeded. According to biographer Lynne Withey, Adams was "voluble and outspoken" and was never afraid of asserting her opinions, whether in the "company of friends, family, or heads of state."

Abigal Adams was one of the most accomplished and influential women in early America, and one of the first and most important letter writers. Although she had never considered publishing her letters, her grandson, Charles Francis Adams, recognized their importance as a primary source of social history. In 1840 he published 114 of his grandmother's letters, and in 1875 he edited and published the dramatic and loving wartime correspondence between his grandparents.

Further Reading

Adams, Abigail, and John Adams. *The Book of Abigail and John: Selected Letters of the Adams Family, 1762–1784.* Edited by L. H. Butterfield. Cambridge, Mass.: Harvard University Press, 1975.

Adams, John, and Abigail Adams. *Familiar Letters of John Adams and His Wife Abigail Adams, during the Revolution.* Edited by Charles Francis Adams. Boston: Houghton Mifflin, 1875.

"First Lady Biography: Abigail Adams," The National First Ladies' Library. Available online. URL: http://www.firstladies.org/biographies/firstladies.aspx?biography2. Downloaded on January 19, 2007.

Levin, Phyllis Lee. *Abigail Adams: A Biography.* New York: St. Martin's, 1987.

Whitney, Janet P. *Abigail Adams.* Westport, Conn.: Greenwood Press, 1947.

Withey, Lynne. *Dearest Friend: A Life of Abigail Adams.* New York: Touchstone, 2001.

～ Adisa, Gamba

See LORDE, AUDRE GERALDIN

～ Alcott, Louisa May (Flora Fairfield)
(1832–1888) *novelist, young adult book writer*

Louisa May Alcott was a prolific writer best known as the author of *Little Women,* the endearing and enduring saga of the four March sisters and their mother, Marmee. Largely inspired by Alcott's own family experiences, *Little Women* was published in 1869 to great acclaim. It is considered an American classic and established Alcott as one of the premiere writers of fiction for young adults.

Louisa was born on November 19, 1832, in Germantown, Pennsylvania, the second child of Amos Bronson Alcott and Abigail (Abba) May Alcott. "I was [born] bawling at the disagreeable old world where on a dismal November day I found myself, and began my long fight," she wrote 25 years later in a letter to her father.

Alcott's "long fight" was her effort to provide her mother and three sisters with financial security, something her brilliant but impractical father seemed unable or unwilling to do. A well known educator and transcendental philosopher, Bronson Alcott introduced his daughter to his friends, some of the great literary luminaries of the day. Among them were Henry David Thoreau, who was her teacher, and Ralph Waldo Emerson, whom she greatly admired and who was the first adult to take her writing seriously.

The family often had to turn to friends to bail them out of their debts. Early in her life, Alcott became fiercely determined to support her family. Like Jo March, the central character in *Little Women,* Alcott was a tall, lanky tomboy who was a moody, rebellious adolescent, as well as a strong-willed young woman and a talented writer.

In 1834 the Alcotts moved to Boston, Massachusetts, where her father opened an experimental school for children. When it failed in 1839, the family retreated to Concord, a suburb of Boston. Although Alcott traveled to Europe twice and visited several American cities, she spent almost her entire life either in Boston or Concord, living and working in a variety of apartments and homes.

In 1843 Bronson Alcott moved his peripatetic family to Fruitlands, a utopian community he helped organize, with several other families and unorthodox believers in the "New Eden," which, like nearby Brook farm, involved communal living, farming, cold baths, singing, studying, and self-denial for the good of the community. Located in rural Harvard, Massachusetts, the experiment was a complete disaster and, after the crops failed, the Alcotts nearly starved and froze to death.

When the Alcotts moved back to Concord in 1846, 13-year-old Louisa finally had a room of her own. "It does me good to be alone," she wrote in her journal. "Now I'm going to *work really,* for I feel a true desire to improve, and be a help and comfort, not a care and sorrow, to my dear mother."

Two years later Alcott wrote her first story, "The Rival Painters: A Tale of Rome." It was published in 1852 and earned her five dollars. During her remarkable life, she would write close to 300 works.

To supplement her family's meager income—they often lived hand-to-mouth—Alcott opened a school, tutored, taught, and became a seamstress, domestic servant, physician's assistant, and traveling companion. But no matter what else she was doing, she continued to write. In 1851 she published her first poem, under the pseudonym Flora Fairfield; three years later her first book, *Flower Fables,* came out in print under her own name.

In 1857 the Alcotts purchased Orchard House, a wooden house in Concord. It was to be their home for 25 years, and it was where *Little Women* was written, at a desk built into a wall that allowed Alcott to overlook her father's colorful gardens. But a year after the move, Elizabeth Alcott, the "dear little Saint," as portrayed in the character Beth in *Little Women,* died. The family was devastated. Nonetheless, Alcott continued her quest for financial independence, while her father continued to be away from home much of the time, earning next to nothing.

In a four-week period during 1860, Alcott wrote, and later revised, a book for adults she called *Moods* (1864). It was one of her favorite novels among those she wrote, and she was disappointed by its only moderate success. However, she was pleased when, in 1862, she won a $100 prize for her short story "Pauline's Passion and Punishment." At last she was earning money by doing what she excelled at: writing. "All kinds of fun going on," she wrote in her journal. "But I didn't care if the world returned to chaos if I and my inkstand only lit in the same place."

Alcott also had a strong sense of civic duty. With friends and relatives fighting in America's bloody Civil War, she volunteered as an army nurse and spent six grueling weeks in 1862 treating soldiers at a hospital in Washington, D.C. She had hoped to stay longer but came down with typhoid fever and nearly died. Because she was treated with medications that later resulted in mercury poisoning, Alcott would suffer the effects of that illness for the rest of her life. She vividly described her experiences as a Civil War army nurse in a well-received collection of letters entitled *Hospital Sketches* (1863).

After returning in 1866 from a trip to Europe, where she had been hired as a companion to an invalid daughter of a Boston shipping merchant, Alcott threw herself into her writing. As usual, her family could not pay their bills, and publishers were clamoring for her stories. She also agreed to edit *Merry's Museum,* a popular magazine for girls.

It was at that time, in 1868, that Alcott's publisher asked her to write a "nice domestic book for girls." Alcott said she would try, and in two six-week periods she completed what would become her greatest achievement—a story that would touch the hearts of millions of readers. While even today young adults relate to the timeless dilemmas faced by the March sisters, *Little Women* was actually modeled on John Bunyon's allegory *Pilgrim's Progress,* which was written in the late 1600s. The moral lesson of Bunyon's classic tale was to "bear your burdens gladly," which both the March and Alcott families did.

With *Little Women*'s astounding success, at the age of 36 Alcott suddenly found herself wealthy and famous. She disliked the notoriety, preferring her privacy, but her father was thrilled that everywhere he went he was "adored as the grandfather of *Little Women.*"

Although in poor health, Alcott forged on to create more stories and novels for young adults, averaging a book a year. Popular sequels to *Little Women* included *Little Men* (1871) and *Eight Cousins* (1875). In between, Alcott managed to write a book for adults entitled *Work* (1873). In her journal Alcott noted that she preferred writing sensational "blood-and-thunder" tales to wholesome children's stories and that she had "grown tired of providing moral pap for the young."

But tragedy struck in 1877 with the death of Alcott's beloved mother. "My duty is done, and now I shall be glad to follow her. My only comfort is that I *could* make her last years comfortable, and lift off the burden she had carried so bravely all these years," she recorded in her journal. Abba Alcott had been the eccentric family's emotional anchor. A social worker and a dedicated advocate for the poor, even when her own family had so little, Alcott's mother had become an activist in the 19th-century feminist movement and was the first woman to register to vote in Concord when the state gave women limited suffrage in 1879.

Alcott outlived her mother by 11 years, during which time she used her wealth to help the remaining members of her family. Her father was able to successfully open and direct the Concord School of Philosophy, the crowning achievement of his old age. She also supported her widowed sister Anna and her two sons. And when her youngest sister May died of meningitis in Paris in 1879, Alcott brought May's child, Louisa May Nieriker (Lulu), to Boston, where she then raised her. Exhausted and ailing, Alcott took care of young Lulu, whom she adored, nursed her sick father, and wrote several more young adult books, including *Jo's Boys* (1886).

Louisa May Alcott died on March 6, 1888, at age 55, on the same day as her father's funeral took place. She was buried in the family plot in Concord, where she had spent her most productive and happiest years. About 100 years later, several of her early gothic thrillers were published, as well as her letters and journals. In 1997 her first romantic melodrama, *The Inheritance,* written when she was 17, was published.

"Families are the most beautiful things in all the world," Alcott had Jo March exclaim in *Little Women.* Although she had felt compelled to take care of her family's financial needs, it was also from her loving family that Louisa May Alcott was encouraged to develop her rich imagination, her independent spirit, and her enormous talent.

Further Reading

Alcott, Louisa May. *Jo's Boys.* Boston: Little, Brown, 1925, 1953.

———. *Little Men.* Boston: Little, Brown, 1901.

———. *Little Women.* Boston: Little, Brown, 1915.

Cheney, Ednah D. *Louisa May Alcott: Her Life, Letters and Journals.* New York: Chelsea House, 1981.

Myerson, Joel, and Daniel Shealy, ed, and Madeleine B. Stern, assoc. ed. *The Journals of Louisa May Alcott.* Boston: Little, Brown, 1989.

Saxton, Martha. *Louisa May Alcott: A Modern Biography.* New York: Farrar, Straus and Giroux, 1995.

Shealy, Daniel, ed. *Alcott in Her Own Time: A Biographical Chronicle of Her Life, Drawn from Recollections, Interviews, and Memoirs by Family, Friends, and Associates.* Iowa City: University of Iowa Press, 2005.

Allen, Paula Gunn
(1939–) *poet, essayist, novelist, children's book writer*

A prominent Laguna Pueblo Indian educator, social critic, and prize-winning writer, Paula Gunn Allen is the author of influential scholarly works such as *The Sacred Hoop: Recovering the Feminine in American Indian Traditions* (1986). Allen's work has been anthologized widely, and her poetry, prose, and essays have introduced many non-Indian readers to traditional American Indian literature and culture.

One of five children, Paula Gunn Allen was born in 1939 in Cubero, New Mexico, a tiny village located about 60 miles from Albuquerque between the Laguna and Acoma Pueblos. "I always knew I was Indian," wrote Allen in an autobiographical essay, despite her multicultural background: She was Lebanese on her father's side while her mother came from Laguna, Sioux, (Dakota, Lakota, Nakota) and Scottish ancestry. In *Off the Reservation* (1998), Allen asserts that in contemporary America, "we are all maverick spirits, hybrid identities."

Mostly raised by her mother and grandmother, who taught her to respect and emulate Native tribal women, especially their fortitude, Allen recalled, "I didn't know I was supposed to be silly and weak. . . . I grew up with the notion that women are strong." As a child, Paula read everything she could, from L. M. Montgomery's *Anne of Green Gables* to Shakespeare's tragedies. In her adolescent years she discovered Gertrude Stein. (She would experiment later with the modernist writer's stream-of-consciousness technique in her novel *The Women Who Owned the Shadows.*) Other influences on Allen's work include the writings of her contemporaries AUDRE LORDE, DENISE LEVERTOV, ADRIENNE RICH, and Gunn's cousin LESLIE MARMON SILKO. She was also influenced by her Catholic background: Allen attended a convent school in Albuquerque in her early years and was raised as a Catholic, although as a social activist she has criticized the role of the Church in oppressing American Indians.

Allen earned a bachelor's degree in English (1966) and two years later a master's of fine arts in creative writing at the University of Oregon. In 1975 she penned the first of eight volumes of poetry, *The Blind Lion.* "Much of her poetry explores the relationship between the individual and the spiritual realm," wrote Dacia Gentilla in an article in *American Women Writers: A Critical Reference Guide* (2000). Other poetry critics have commented on Allen's purity of language and emotional intensity. Two years after receiving a doctorate in American studies from the University of New Mexico in 1976, Allen was awarded a National Endowment for the Arts Fellowship. She also held a postdoctoral fellowship from the University of California at Berkeley (1979) to study the oral tradition elements of American Indian literature.

In 1983 Allen published her only novel, *The Woman Who Owned the Shadows,* featuring a lesbian protagonist who learns to cope with her insecurities and confusion by reconnecting with and reclaiming her tribal roots. It received a favorable review in the *New York Times Book Review.* Also in 1983 she edited a seminal resource for studying American Indian literature titled *Studies in American Indian Literature: Critical Essays and Course Designs.* Three years later Allen came out with another pivotal work, *The Sacred Hoop: Recovering the Feminine in American Indian Traditions* (1986, revised in 1992), a collection of 17 insightful essays that elucidate the multiple ways in which American Indian women and their female-based belief systems have influenced tribal history and culture.

An anthology Allen edited for a popular audience, *Spider Woman's Granddaughters: Traditional Tales and Contemporary Writing by Native American Women* (1989), won the prestigious American Book Award from the Before Columbus Foundation in 1990, the same year she received the Native American Prize for Literature. Another collection of myths and stories edited by Allen, *Grandmothers of the Light: A Medicine Woman's Sourcebook* (1991), was based on the oral tradition of a variety of tribes, and many of the stories focused on the healing power of female spirituality. In the introduction to *The Voice of the Turtle: American Indian Literature, 1900–1970* (1994), Allen describes the contributors as fashioning their work "not as individual pieces" disconnected from their heritage or ancestors, but rather "as one of the multitude of petals gracing the great flower of Native life."

In 1996 Allen published a book of verse, *Life Is a Fatal Disease,* as well as a children's book she cowrote with Patricia Clark Smith, *As Long as the Rivers Flow: The Stories of Nine Native Americans* (1996). Two years later she produced a collection of personal, political, and spiritual essays titled *Off the Reservation: Reflections of Boundary-Busting, Border-Crossing Loose Canons.* In 2001 Allen was honored with a Lifetime Achievement Award from the Native Writer's Circle of the Americas, and that same year she coedited a book of 25 short stories, *Hozho—Walking in Beauty: Native American Stories of Inspiration, Humor, and Life,* that together exemplify the richness and diversity of Indian life in America today. Allen's recent work, the biography *Pocahontas* (2003), told from an American Indian perspective, offers readers a bold new interpretation of the Indian woman's life and historical role during a "world change time," as the author describes it. According to a review in *Publishers Weekly,* Allen's Pocahontas is a "real visionary, a prodigiously gifted young woman fervently devoted to the spiritual traditions of her people."

In addition to writing, Allen has been an associate fellow at the Stanford Humanities Institute and has taught at several universities, including the University of California at Berkeley, where she was professor of Native American/ethnic studies, and San Francisco State University, where she directed the Native American studies program. She is an ardent antiwar activist, feminist, and supporter of gay and lesbian rights. Allen wrote a groundbreaking essay, which she later revised for *The Sacred Hoop,* about how lesbians are "beloved" and treated respectfully and with acceptance in American Indian culture.

In 2005, Allen, who lives in Fort Bragg, California, wrote: "I have been married to three men and partners with two women (married as I saw it). . . . I am retired from my position [in 1999, as professor of English, creative writing, and American Indian studies at the University of California, Los Angeles], but am active as a writer and speaker." Allen is the mother of four children, two of whom died—one in infancy and a son at the age of 42 in 2001; she has four grandchildren.

Paula Gunn Allen is a highly praised and influential American Indian author, intellectual, and social critic. In her work she recognizes the importance of the matriarchal tradition in Native culture and of preserving Indian literature, both past and present. As Allen once wrote, this unique body of work, with its emphasis on balance, common sense, and sacredness, "tell us of the significance of our lives within the human community."

Further Reading

Allen, Paula Gunn. "The Autobiography of a Confluence." In *I Tell You Now: Autobiographical Essays by Native American Women,* edited by Brian Swann and Arnold Krupat, 142–154. Lincoln: University of Nebraska Press, 1987.

———. *Life Is a Fatal Disease: Collected Poems, 1962–1995.* Albuquerque, N. Mex.: West End Press, 1996.

———. *Pocahontas: Medicine Woman, Spy, Entrepreneur, Diplomat.* San Francisco: HarperSanFrancisco, 2003.

———. *The Sacred Hoop: Recovering the Feminine in American Indian Traditions.* Boston: Beacon Press, 1992.

———, ed. *Spider Woman's Granddaughters: Traditional Tales and Contemporary Writing by Native American Women.* Boston: Beacon Press, 1989.

Rassett, Michelle, and David Lappen. "Paula Gunn Allen. Voices from the Gaps: Women Artists and Writers of Color, an International Website." Updated 2004. Available online. URL: http://voices.cla.umn.edu/vg/Bios/entries/allen_paula_gunn.html. Downloaded on January 19, 2007.

Sonneborn, Liz. "Paula Gunn Allen." In *A to Z of American Indian Women, Revised Edition.* New York: Facts On File, 2007, pp. 2–4.

Strom, Karen M., and Paula Gunn Allen. "Paula Gunn Allen." Updated May 2005. Available online. URL: http://www.hanksville.org/storytellers/paula. Downloaded on January 19, 2007.

Alvarez, Julia
(1950–)   *novelist, poet, children's book writer*

A distinguished Latina novelist and poet, Julia Alvarez vividly punctuates her writing with personal reflections about her childhood in the Dominican Republic and then as an immigrant in the United States. *How the Garcia Girls Lost Their Accents* (1991), Alvarez's widely acclaimed first novel, is based largely on the author's own experience as she grappled with two cultures that, as she describes it, either "collide or blend together."

Although she was born on March 17, 1950, in New York City, Julia spent her first 10 years in the Caribbean, where she was brought up by a large extended family headed by her father, a respected doctor. The Alvarezes, who were relatively wealthy, were interested in anything that came from the United States: Julia ate American food, dressed in American clothes, and attended an American school.

In 1960 Alvarez's father was accused of supporting a group opposed to the brutal regime of the Dominican Republic's dictator Rafael Leonidas Trujillo, and the family was forced to flee the country.

Julia, who spoke and read in English, was thrilled when on August 6, 1960, she arrived in New York City, her birthplace. But, her homecoming proved to be disappointing. As an uprooted 10-year-old in a new country, she felt like an outsider who was different from her peers.

Fortunately, a sympathetic English teacher asked her to write a story about herself instead of doing the regular assignment. Through writing, Alvarez discovered that although she had lost her childhood island, she could create an even better world. "I could save what I didn't want to lose—memories and smells and sounds, things too precious to put anywhere else," she said during an interview many years later.

Alvarez earned undergraduate (Middlebury College, summa cum laude, 1971) and graduate (Syracuse University, 1975) degrees in literature and writing. She went on to teach English and creative writing at the University of Vermont, George Washington University, and the University of Illinois in Urbana. In 1988 she began teaching at Middlebury College in Vermont, where she lived with her husband, Bill Eichner.

An accomplished poet, Alvarez has published three books of verse, including *Homecoming* (1984), a popular collection which she revised in 1995. Named the Robert Frost Fellow in Poetry at the 1986 Bread Loaf Writers' Conference, she also received grants from the National Endowment for the Arts (1987) and the Ingram Merrill Foundation (1990).

Alvarez is best known for her semiautobiographical novel, *How the Garcia Girls Lost Their Accents,* in which she exuberantly recounts—through 15 loosely interrelated stories—the lives of the four Garcia sisters and their parents, both before their exile from Santo Domingo and then as newcomers in New York. Much like the author and her family, the Garcias struggled financially and emotionally as they adjusted to a harsh new environment where there was neither the "smell of mangoes" nor the "iridescent, vibrating green of hummingbirds."

How the Garcia Girls Lost Their Accents won the 1991 PEN Oakland/Josephine Miles Award for excellence in multicultural literature and was designated a Notable Book by the American Library Association in 1992.

In the Time of the Butterflies (1994) is Alvarez's fictionalized account of a tragic event that took place on November 14, 1960, in the Dominican Republic: the brutal triple murders of Patricia, Minerva, and Maria Teresa Mirabal, who were known as "Las Mariposas" (The Butterflies). These brave, outspoken young women had resisted and denounced Trujillo's dictatorship; they paid for their actions with their lives. *In the Time of the Butterflies* was listed as a National Book Critics Circle Award finalist.

In 1995 Alvarez published a collection of well-crafted poems entitled *The Other Side/El Otro Lado*. It depicts the author's struggle as she attempts to live with a divided identity. The book ends with a poem describing Alvarez's mixed reactions upon returning to the Dominican Republic as a participant in an artist's colony.

Alvarez's third novel, *Yo!*, published in 1997, is the comical account of an author, Yo, who creates characters based on her relatives and friends. When she becomes a famous writer, the real-life characters on whom she has based her novel become furious with her.

Trying her hand at nonfiction, in 1998 Alvarez came out with a collection of essays titled *Something to Declare,* many of which were written to answer questions about the author's "experiences with immigration, about switching languages, about the writing life, the teaching life, the family life, about all those combined," as Alvarez explains it. In 2001 she published *In the Name of Salomé. Publishers Weekly* called the lyrical novel "one of the most moving political novels of the past century."

Turning to another new genre—writing for children and young adults—Alvarez produced several books: *The Second Footprints* (2000), a children's picture book; *How Tia Lola Came to Stay* (2001), a novel for middle readers; and two young adult novels, *Before We Were Free* (2002), which won the 2004 Pura Belpré American Library Association Award, and *Finding Miracles* (2004). Also in 2004 she came out with a bilingual cookbook called *Secrets of Salsa* and a fourth collection of verse, *The Woman I Kept to Myself.* Many of Alvarez's latest poems explore her personal and professional development as a Latina writer. Her latest novel *Saving the World* (2006) expresses her idealism and hope for a better world.

When not writing or teaching, Alvarez supervises, along with her husband, a sustainable farm-literacy center in the Dominican Republic. She wrote about their uplifting experiences in *A Cafecito Story* (2002), which she calls a modern "eco-parable green fable" and love story.

One of the outstanding contemporary Latina writers, Julia Alvarez considers herself "Dominican, hyphen, American." She is someone who is able to sensually and astutely convey both worlds. "I found myself turning more and more to writing as the one place where I felt I belonged and could make sense of myself, my life, and all that was happening to me," Alvarez explains about her dual cultural identity.

Further Reading

Alvarez, Julia. *Before We Were Free.* New York: Knopf, 2002.

———. *How the Garcia Girls Lost Their Accents.* Chapel Hill, N.C.: Algonquin Books, 1991.

———. *In the Name of Salomé: A Novel.* New York: Plume, 2001.

———. *In the Time of Butterflies.* Chapel Hill, N.C.: Algonquin Books, 1994.

———. *Saving the World.* Chapel Hill, N.C.: Algonquin Books, 2006.

———. *Something to Declare.* Chapel Hill, N.C.: Algonquin Books, 1998.

———. *The Woman I Kept To Myself.* Chapel Hill, N.C.: Algonquin Books, 2004.

Jacques, Ben. "Julia Alvarez: Real Flights of Imagination." *Américas* 53, no. 1 (2000): 22–29.

Julia Alvarez Web site. Updated July 26, 2005. Available online. URL: http://www.alvarezjulia.com. Downloaded on January 19, 2007.

Tabor, Garcia, and Maria Silvio. "The Truth According to Your Characters: An Interview with Julia Alvarez." *Prairie Schooner* (Summer 2000): 151–154.

Valerio-Holguin, Fernando. "Julia Alvarez." In *Latino and Latin Writers,* edited by Alan West-Duran, 783–799. New York: Charles Scribner's Sons, 2004.

Angelou, Maya (Marguerite Johnson)
(1928–)   *poet, autobiographer, children's book writer*

Maya Angelou overcame a difficult and traumatic childhood to become a prize-winning poet and the author of several best-selling autobiographies, including her celebrated first volume, *I Know Why the Caged Bird Sings* (1970). She was also the first African American, and the first woman, invited to read a poem at the inauguration of a president of the United States.

Born Marguerite Johnson in St. Louis, Missouri, on April 4, 1928, Maya was three when her parents were divorced. She and her four-year-old brother Bailey were sent to live with their paternal grandmother, "Momma" Anderson, who ran a grocery store in Stamps, Arkansas, where the rural black population suffered from poverty and racial oppression. Momma Anderson, a "wise, tall tree of a woman," taught her granddaughter the importance of religion, family, hard work, and standing up to bigotry. Without courage, Maya learned as a child, life's other virtues are meaningless.

Johnson would need all the courage she could muster to deal with a tragic event that occurred when she was seven-and-a-half years old. While visiting her mother, Vivian Baxter Johnson, in

Poet Maya Angelou also wrote memorable autobiographies.
(AP/Wide World Photos)

St. Louis, she was brutally raped by Vivian's boyfriend. Confused, terrified, and guilt-ridden, she retreated into silence, refusing to speak to anyone, except her brother, for five years.

When Johnson did speak again, having returned with her brother to Arkansas, it was in large part because of her friendship with Mrs. Bertha Flowers, an elegant, educated older woman who, like her grandmother, served as a role model. "It's good that you read a lot, but it's not enough. It takes the human voice to infuse words with the shades of deeper meaning," Mrs. Flowers explained to Johnson, helping the traumatized little girl regain her confidence and her speech. She also encouraged Johnson to pay attention to "the wisdom of country people" and to be proud of them and their roots.

In 1940 Johnson left Arkansas to live with her mother in San Francisco, California. She refused to be stonewalled by racist policies and eventually was hired as the city's first black woman cable car conductor. When she was 16, she graduated from high school, became pregnant, and in 1945 gave birth to a son, Clyde (Guy), who she described as "the greatest gift I've ever had."

As a teenage single mother struggling to make ends meet, Johnson had to find a job. By the time she was in her early 20s, she had worked as a cook, a cocktail waitress, a bar dancer, and even a prostitute. Yet, she refused to become a welfare recipient. "My pride had been starched by a family who assumed unlimited authority in its own affairs," she explained.

After a brief failed marriage to a sailor named Tosh Angelos, Johnson was once again on her own with a young child to support. In 1953 she landed a job as a folksinger at the Purple Onion, a popular nightclub in San Francisco. In spite of her lack of experience, the audience loved her sensual calypso-style singing and dancing routines. Suddenly Marguerite Johnson, the six-footer from the South, had become a budding cabaret star. She decided to give herself a stage name—Maya Angelou.

Much to her surprise, Angelou was invited to join an international touring company of *Porgy and Bess,* the popular Gershwin folk opera. The tour took Angelou to 22 nations. A highlight of the tour came when the troupe became the first American opera company to perform at La Scala, the renowned opera house in Milan, Italy. Angelou was impressed by the dignity and respect accorded to the all-black cast everywhere they went, and felt a new surge of pride in her heritage as a black American. But after a year of touring, during which time she had also taught modern dance in Italy and Israel, Angelou longed to be reunited with her son. "My mother had left me with my grandmother for years and I knew the pain of parting," Angelou recalled. She was overjoyed to return home.

Although she had established a reputation as a first-rate singer and could finally make a decent living, Angelou wanted to further her career as a writer, something she felt driven to do. In 1959 she moved to New York City to join the Harlem Writers Guild, an informal organization of authors. While in New York she supported herself by singing at several clubs, including the famed Apollo Theater in Harlem.

Angelou also sharpened her acting skills when in 1960 she appeared, along with James Earl Jones and Godfrey Cambridge, in Jean Genet's production of *The Blacks.* Then, she wrote, directed, and starred in an off-Broadway revue called *Cabaret for Freedom.*

In the early 1960s, Angelou became active in the civil rights movement. She served as the northern coordinator for the Southern Christian Leadership Conference for Dr. Martin Luther King, Jr., whom she met along with the charismatic Malcolm X. But she was most impressed by a visiting South African freedom fighter, Vusumzi Make, who spoke eloquently about the struggle for black self-determination. Enthralled, she married Make and left with him for Africa.

While living in Cairo, Egypt, Angelou became the associate editor of the English-language weekly *Arab Observer.* Her marriage to Make fell apart, and in 1962 she and Guy moved to "the real Africa"—Ghana. There she taught journalism and dance at the University of Ghana and wrote for various publications. "I loved Ghana," she said at an interview in 1974. "It was the first time I ever felt at home in my life."

Nonetheless, she realized that she was an American, and after four years she felt it was time for her to leave Africa. Angelou returned to the United States to resume her work in theater and to write a 10-part television series about African influences on American life.

Encouraged by friends such as the black novelist James Baldwin, Angelou decided to write the story of her life. *I Know Why the Caged Bird Sings,* the first in a series of several autobiographical volumes, was published and nominated for a National Book Award in 1970. It became an instant success. "I hadn't so much forgot as I couldn't bring myself to remember," her story begins, and goes on to poignantly chronicle her childhood experiences, ending with Guy's birth. "Her portrait is a biblical study of life in the midst of death," Baldwin said about the highly praised book, which Angelou later adapted into a film screenplay.

Angelou's other widely read autobiographies include *Gather Together in My Name* (1974); *Singin' and Swingin' and Gettin' Merry Like Christmas* (1976); *The Heart of a Woman* (1981); *All God's Children Need to Travel* (1986); *Wouldn't Take Nothing for My Journey Now* (1993), a memoir; and *A Brave and Startling Truth* (1995). She was also praised for her luminous, lyrical verse, and her first volume of poetry, *Just Give Me a Cool Drink of Water 'fore I Diiie* (1971), was nominated for a Pulitzer Prize in 1972, *Shaker, Why Don't You Sing?* (1983) and *I Shall Not Be Moved* (1990) are among her other notable collections.

Angelou married Paul Du Feu, a writer and cartoonist, in 1973, the same year her Broadway acting debut performance in *Look Away* earned her a Tony Award nomination. She then directed a film entitled *All Day Long* and became the first black woman to join the Directors' Guild. She also wrote, produced, directed, and acted in productions for stage, film, and television; her TV credits included a starring role in Alex Haley's miniseries *Roots.*

Angelou has received several prestigious fellowships and honorary degrees and has taught on numerous faculties. After divorcing Du Feu, she returned to the South, where, in 1981, she accepted a lifetime appointment as the first Reynolds professor of American studies at Wake Forest University in North Carolina.

Perhaps her crowning achievement as a writer came on January 20, 1993, when Bill Clinton, a fellow Arkansan, asked Angelou to read a poem at his presidential inauguration. Composed for the occasion, "On the Pulse of Morning" movingly celebrates and challenges America's nation of multicultural immigrants. The poet's melodious, proud voice never faltered as she read the 665-word ode to redemption, which was later published in book form. When asked why he selected Angelou, the president replied that she "embodies a spirit of hope and dignity that is quintessentially American."

Angelou has appeared in several movies and her work has been adapted for the screen, including *Poetic Justice* (1993), which incorporated her verse. In 1998, at the age of 70, Angelou directed her first Feature Film, *Down in the Delta,* about an African American family who move from Chicago to their ancestral home in Mississippi. It starred Alfre Woodard and Wesley Snipes. *Down in the Delta* was critically well received and a modest box office success, despite the fact that it had little national publicity. Angelou subsequently began directing another film, *Amen Corner,* based on a James Baldwin play.

Several of Angelou's highly acclaimed poems were published together in a gift edition titled *Phenomenal Woman: Four Poems Celebrating Women* (1995). Angelou is considered one of America's finest contemporary poets.

With the publication of *A Song Flung Up to Heaven* in 2002, Angelou returned to the autobiographical writings she had started 32 years earlier with *I Know Why the Caged Bird Sings.* The *Boston Globe* called her most recent installment "a superb account by a great woman who has embraced a difficult destiny with rare intelligence and infectious joie de vivre."

Angelou went on to publish a book for young readers, *My Painted House, My Friendly Chicken, and Me* (2003), about a South African girl and the remarkable art of her people, and *Hallelujah! The Welcome Table: A Lifetime of Memories and Recipes* (2004), a cookbook with 73 recipes gleaned from the author's childhood and world travels. From her 18-room brownstone in the Mount Morris Park section of Harlem in New York City, Angelou hosts a weekly talk show on the Oprah and Friends Channel on XM Satellite Radio. "It's the first radio show I've had," she said in an article that appeared in the *New York Times* on January 5, 2007. Topics she addresses include sex, religion, race, music, and food.

In spite of the many difficulties she faced and forced herself to remember and record, Maya Angelou achieved most of her personal and professional goals. When asked to assess her contributions, she replied, "I'd just like to be thought of as someone who tried to be a blessing rather than a curse to the human race."

Further Reading

Angelou, Maya. *I Know Why the Caged Bird Sings.* New York: Random House, 1970.

———. *Just Give Me a Cool Drink of Water 'fore I Diiie.* New York: Random House, 1971.

———. *On the Pulse of Morning.* New York: Random House, 1993.

———. *A Song Flung Up to Heaven.* New York: Random House, 2002.

Elliot, Jeffrey M., editor. *Conversations with Maya Angelou.* Jackson: University Press of Mississippi, 1989.

Joquin, Eileen O. "Maya Angelou." In *African American Autobiographers: A Sourcebook,* edited by Emmanuel S. Nelson, 10–28. Westport, Conn.: Greenwood Press, 2002.

Spain, Valerie. *Meet Maya Angelou.* New York: Random House, 1994.

➳ Antin, Mary
(1881–1949) *autobiographer, essayist*

Mary Antin is the celebrated author of *The Promised Land* (1912), one of the first great works of American Jewish literature and one of the earliest accounts of the assimilation of Eastern European immigrants. Her best-selling autobiography describes her difficult childhood in Russia and the arduous but worthwhile process of becoming Americanized.

A native of Polotsk, Russia, Antin was born on June 13, 1881. Because they were Jewish, her family suffered from religious persecution under an oppressive regime. In 1894, when she was 13, Mary emigrated to Chelsea, Massachusetts, a suburb of Boston. Determined not to let the slums in which her family lived imprison her, Mary decided early on that she was going to take advantage of America—the land of opportunity. "What real thing is this American freedom," she wrote.

Although her older sister worked in a sweatshop, Antin attended public school. Precocious and eager to learn, she completed the first five grades of school within six months. In 1899 she published her first book, *From Plotzk to Boston,* a collection of letters to an uncle still living in Russia, which she translated from Yiddish.

Encouraged by her teachers, Antin enrolled at Boston Latin School for Girls in preparation for attending college. In 1901 she married Amadeus William Grabau, a geologist and the son of a German Lutheran minister, and the couple moved to New York City. Although she took courses at Barnard and Teachers' College in New York, she never earned a college degree.

In 1907 Antin gave birth to a daughter, Josephine, whom she named after her friend and mentor, the essayist Josephine Lazarus. Lazarus had encouraged Antin to record her immigrant experiences, and after her friend's death in 1910, she was inspired to do so.

"I was born, I have lived, and I have been made over." So begins *The Promised Land,* Antin's uplifting tale of her successful assimilation into American culture and society. Although she was able to reject her Old World Jewish past, she could never forget it. "I bear the scars," she wrote in her autobiography. "But I long to forget. . . . I want now to be of today." *The Promised Land* became an immediate success: it went through 34 editions, sold

85,000 copies, and was one of the most popular immigrant autobiographies of all time.

Several of Antin's short stories appeared in the *Atlantic Monthly.* In 1914 she published her most polemical book, *They Who Knock at Our Gates,* and then spent several years lecturing on the subject of unrestricted immigration.

When Antin's husband openly supported Germany during World War I, they separated and he moved to China. Antin continued to write an occasional essay and to some extent returned to her Jewish roots. After years of struggling with depression, Mary Antin died in May 1949, at a nursing home in upstate New York. Although her popularity has declined somewhat, Antin will be remembered for recording her journey to the promised land.

Further Reading

Antin, Mary. *The Promised Land.* Princeton, N.J.: Princeton University Press, 1985.

Antler, Joyce. *The Journey Home: Jewish Women and the American Century,* 17–26. New York: The Free Press, 1997.

Mazur, Allan. *A Romance in Natural History: The Lives and Works of Amadeus Grabau and Mary Antin.* Syracuse, N.Y.: Garret, 2004.

⁓ Arnow, Harriette Louisa Simpson
(1908–1986) *novelist*

Harriette Simpson Arnow is best known for a trilogy of novels that culminated with her masterwork, *The Dollmaker* (1954). Her books sympathetically but realistically portray the hill people of southern Appalachia, where the author was born and raised. Arnow's characters, especially the women, struggle not to lose their sense of dignity in spite of the hardships they are forced to endure.

Harriette Louisa Simpson, born on July 7, 1908, in Wayne County, Kentucky, was the daughter of two schoolteachers. Her parents, descendants of original Kentuckian settlers, often recounted family stories dating back to the American Revolu-

tion. As the young Harriette listened, she hoped that one day she would become a writer and tell her own stories.

After two years at Berea College, Simpson spent a year teaching in a one-room schoolhouse in the hills of southeast Kentucky. She took a break in 1930 to complete a bachelor's degree at the University of Louisville, and then returned to teaching.

But Simpson was determined to become a writer, not a teacher. In 1934 she moved to Cincinnati, Ohio, where she published several short stories, the best-known of which was "The Washerwoman's Day" (in *Southern Review,* 1936). In 1936 she also published her first novel, *Mountain Path,* which was based largely on her experiences living with a hill family while she taught in rural Kentucky.

In 1939 Simpson married Harold Arnow, a journalist. After farming in southern Kentucky and having two children, they settled in Detroit, Michigan. In 1949 Arnow published the second novel in her country life trilogy, *Hunter's Horn.* This work was unusual in that it was written from a male point of view.

After moving to Ann Arbor, Michigan, where she lived for the remainder of her life, Arnow wrote her most successful book and the final volume of her trilogy. Published in 1954, *The Dollmaker* was critically acclaimed, and in 1955 was a runner-up for the National Book Award. It is the story of Gertie Nevels, a strong-willed Kentucky woman and gifted woodcarver who migrates with her family to Detroit, where her husband had secured a factory job. Nevels's art becomes her salvation and escape from city life. The novelist Joyce Carol Oates was deeply moved by *The Dollmaker* and called it a "brutal, beautiful novel . . . depressing yet extraordinary . . . our most unpretentious American masterpiece. . . ." The book was adapted as a television film in 1983.

Arnow's well-received regional social histories, *Seedtime on the Cumberland* (1960) and *Flowering of the Cumberland* (1963), were the result of 20 years of research on the early settlers in Kentucky and Tennessee who resided in Appalachian areas that she knew well. She also wrote two more novels: *The Weedkiller's Daughter* (1970) and *The Kentucky Trace: A Novel of the American Revolution* (1974).

Harriette Simpson Arnow, who wrote honestly about America's poor white hill people, whom she portrayed with great dignity, died of heart disease on May 11, 1986.

Further Reading

Arrow, Harriette Simpson. *Collected Short Stories of Harriette Simpson.* Edited by Sandra L. Ballard. East Lansing: Michigan State University Press, 2005.

———. *The Dollmaker.* New York: Macmillan, 1954.

———. *Mountain Path.* Lexington: University Press of Kentucky, 1985.

———. *The Weed Killer's Daughter.* New York: Knopf, 1970.

Eckley, Wilton. *Harriette Arnow.* New York: Twayne, 1974.

Oates, Joyce Carol. "Harriette Arnow's *The Dollmaker*." In *Rediscoveries,* edited by David Madden, 57–66. New York: Crown, 1971.

∾ Auel, Jean Marie Untinen
(1936–) *novelist*

Jean M. Auel was haunted by the idea of writing a short story about a young woman who lived with people very different from herself. After years of laborious research, that story evolved into a bestselling novel, *The Clan of the Cave Bear* (1980), the first of Auel's four-volume Earth's Children series. The epic series is based on the odyssey of a resourceful Cro-Magnon woman whose dangerous world is populated by horses, bears, and mammoths.

The author's own life is much more conventional than those of her characters. Born Jean Marie Untinen on February 18, 1936, in Chicago, Illinois, she attended Portland State University in Oregon, married Ray Auel when she was 18, and had five children within six years.

In 1976 Auel received a master's degree in business from the University of Portland. She landed a well-paying position as credit manager for a large company, but she was dissatisfied and eventually quit her job.

An avid reader who secretly wrote poetry, Auel's life changed dramatically in 1980 with the publication of her first novel, *The Clan of the Cave Bear.* Even though it received mixed reviews, it was extremely popular, selling over three million paperback copies and earning her an American Book Award nomination (1981). Almost overnight, Jean Auel had become a publishing superstar.

The Valley of Horses (1982), the sequel to *The Clan of the Cave Bear,* also did well, and Auel's third novel, *The Mammoth Hunters* (1985), sold a record-breaking 1,100,000 copies. *The Plains of Passage* (1990) was followed more than a decade later by the fifth entry in the Earth's Children series, *The Shelters of Stone* (2004). Auel's sagas, historical fictions depicting prehistory society, romance, and fantasy, have sold more than 34 million copies worldwide, in many translations.

In order to write knowledgeably about a clan that lived approximately 25,000 years ago, Auel did meticulous anthropological research and underwent a wilderness survival course that included the construction of an ice cave. She wanted to know how her ice-age characters felt as they struggled to survive.

Auel dispels many of the stereotypes often associated with "primitive creatures," such as that they were ignorant and brutish. For example, Ayla, the protagonist and heroine of the Earth's Children series, is both attractive and bright. She uses her inventiveness and intelligence to cope with the daunting task of living among a tribe of strangers. Auel depicts Ayla as a strong character who is capable of teaching herself to make weapons and fire, and to domesticate wild animals. When she falls in love, it is with an interesting male character the author describes as "the early equivalent of today's technical genius. . . ."

Jean Auel's prehistoric romances are more than entertaining and commercially successful "cave operas": they also provide pertinent information about the complex inhabitants of the Middle Paleolithic age. "Our distant ancestors had rich, deep, emotional lives," explains Auel in a 1985 interview in *Newsweek.* "My books are about adventure, love, danger, fear, loneliness, jealousy and belonging."

Further Reading

Auel, Jean M. *The Clan of the Cave Bear.* New York: Crown, 1980.
———. *The Mammoth Hunters.* New York: Crown, 1985.
———. *The Plains of Passage.* New York: Crown, 1990.
———. *The Shelters of Stone.* New York: Bantam, 2004.
———. *The Valley of Horses.* New York: Crown, 1982.
Lyons, Gene. "Sweet Savage Love." *Newsweek,* November 18, 1985, pp. 100–101.

∾ Austin, Mary Hunter
(1868–1934)   *nature writer, novelist*

Although Mary Hunter Austin had wide-ranging interests and wrote more than 30 books and hundreds of articles, she is best known for her nature writing and her astute observations and lyrical descriptions of the desert landscape.

Mary Hunter was born far from the desert, on September 9, 1868, in Carlinville, Illinois, where she spent the first 20 years of her life. Her childhood was unhappy: her father, with whom she had a close relationship, died when she was 10, followed shortly by the death of her favorite sister. Hunter found solace in writing mystical poetry and by immersing herself in her school work. She took only two-and-a-half years to complete a bachelor of arts degree, which she received in 1888. That same year her family moved to a homestead on the edge of the Mojave Desert in southern California, where she first became enchanted with the desert.

In 1891 Hunter married Stafford Wallace Austin. After moving to the Owens River Valley area, she worked as a teacher while she continued to write. In her regional sketches of the Southwest, such as the classic, *The Land of Little Rain* (1903), and later in *The Flock* (1906), Austin captures the remote but "intimate immensity" of the desert and presents its ecosystem as a living force.

In 1914 Austin's marriage fell apart, and tragically, her daughter, an only child who had been born mentally retarded and who had been institutionalized, died four years later.

Austin decided to escape her unhappiness by devoting herself to full-time writing and women's suffrage. She addressed the issue of reconciling work and marriage in her semiautobiographical novel *A Woman of Genius* (1912). She also wrote passionately about Native American culture in *The Basket Woman* (1904) and experimented with spiritual fiction in one of her later works, *Starry Adventure* (1931).

In 1905 Austin moved to Carmel, California, and befriended a group of established writers that included Jack London. Three years later she discovered she had breast cancer. She traveled abroad to Italy to study healing prayer techniques, and the growth eventually disappeared. While in England she met the novelist H. G. Wells, who called Austin "the most intelligent woman in America."

In 1910 she returned to the United States. That year *The Arrow-Maker,* a play about a female shaman, was produced in New York City. In 1924 Austin settled in Sante Fe, New Mexico, where she became increasingly involved in Native American rights and Hispanic culture and also worked as an ardent champion of birth control. Her home was a center for visiting luminaries, including WILLA CATHER, who wrote *Death Comes for the Archbishop* there.

Austin continued to write about mysticism—using an intuitive self, "I-Mary," to write some of her novels in a trance-like state—as well as folklore, feminism, and conservation. But her favorite subject remained the desert, with its "heart of a lonely land." Mary Hunter Austin's autobiography, *Earth Horizon,* was published in 1932, two years before she died at age 65.

Further Reading

Austin, Mary Hunter. *Earth Horizon.* Boston: Houghton Mifflin, 1932.
———. *A Mary Austin Reader.* Tucson: University of Arizona Press, 1996.
Fink, Augusta. *I-Mary, A Biography of Mary Austin.* Tucson: University of Arizona Press, 1983.
Steineman, Esther Lanigaw. *Mary Austin: Song of a Maverick.* New Haven, Conn.: Yale University Press, 1989.

B

Bambara, Toni Cade (Miltona Mirkin Cade)
(1939–1995)   *short-story writer, novelist*

Considered one of the best African-American short-story writers, Toni Cade Bambara was also a community activist who used her impressive writing skills as a way of "participating in the struggle."

Born on March 25, 1939, in New York City, Miltona Mirkin Cade grew up in two New York City neighborhoods, Bedford-Stuyvesant and Harlem. She and her brother were raised by their mother, Helen Brent Henderson Cade, an avid reader who had aspired to become a journalist; Helen Cade encouraged her daughter to pursue a career and to follow her own intuition.

Cade graduated from Queens College in New York in 1959 with a bachelor's degree in theater arts and English. That same year she published "Sweet Town," her first short story. She went on to train as a dancer in Europe, returning to America to complete a master's degree from the City College of New York in 1964.

During the 1960s Cade immersed herself in community work as a welfare investigator, recreation director in the psychiatric department of an inner-city hospital, youth counselor, and director of neighborhood programs in Harlem and Brooklyn. Those real-life experiences enabled her "to tell the truth and not get trapped" into stereotyping or simplifying characters in her fiction.

While perfecting her writing, Cade took courses in linguistics and film, and during the mid-1960s directed the Theatre of the Black Experience in New York. She also taught English and African-American studies at several colleges and universities.

Cade made a name for herself in 1970 when she edited and contributed to *The Black Woman: An Anthology,* one of the first collections of essays by black women that reflected the diversity of social and personal issues they faced. Cade dedicated the anthology to "the uptown mammas who nudged me to just set it down in print so it gets to be a habit to write letters to each other, so maybe that way we don't keep treadmilling the same ole ground."

Inspired by a signature she discovered on a sketchbook in her grandmother's trunk, Cade legally changed her name to Toni Cade Bambara in 1970, thereby linking herself to her heritage.

Hoping to stimulate interest in African-American communal traditions such as storytelling and folktales, in 1971 Bambara edited another anthology, *Tales and Stories for Black Folks.* She then turned to her own writing and in 1972 published her first volume of short stories, *Gorilla, My Love.* "Everything Bambara's characters say," observed novelist ANNE TYLER, "you feel ordinary, real-life people are saying right now on any street corner. It's only that the rest of us didn't realize it was sheer poetry they were speaking."

Bambara's second collection of short stories, *The Sea Birds Are Still Alive* (1977), was also well received. In both books, the heroic figures are mostly strong, sensible black women who become active members of their community. Although Bambara writes about humiliation, rage, and despair, she also infuses her characters with compassion, warmth, and humor. "Laughter is the most sure-fire healant I know," Bambara said in an essay.

The Salt Eaters (1980), Bambara's first novel, which won the American Book Award in 1981, begins as a journal entry and goes on to explore the complex relationship between two different black women from very different backgrounds and situations who are brought together and ultimately united by a tragic event.

Bambara, who lived in Georgia and Pennsylvania, was a founding member of the Southern Collective of African-American Writers. Alice Lovelace, coeditor of *In Motion Magazine,* a multicultural online publication, wrote an article about Bambara (February 2000) in which she praised the author for her influential role in the seminal 1984 Conference on Black Literature and Arts that took place at Emory University in Atlanta: "Toni continues to influence the focus of Southern literature. . . . Between the famous potluck gatherings at her home and her work organizing writers and artists, Bambara made a great impact on the Atlanta arts community." Her work, which has been translated into six languages, has been lauded by critics for its "rhythmic, black-inflected, sweet-and-sour language" and breezy street dialect.

In the 1980s and 1990s, Bambara increasingly became involved in media projects. Three of her short stories were adapted for film, and in 1986 *The Bombing of Osage*, a documentary about Philadelphia's use of lethal force against a group of black citizens, received honors from the Pennsylvania Association of Broadcasters and the National Black Programming Consortium.

Shortly before her death on December 9, 1995, Bambara had completed another volume of short stories and was working on a book about the troubling case of Atlanta's missing and murdered children. Throughout her career, both as a writer and political activist, Toni Cade Bambara emphasized the importance of caring about and participating in the larger community. Only by working together, she believed, could people change economic, social, and race-based policies and attitudes. "Exploitation and misery are neither inevitable nor necessary," she wrote.

Further Reading

Bambara, Toni Cade, ed. *The Black Woman: An Anthology.* New York: New American Library, 1970.

———. *Gorilla, My Love.* New York: Random House, 1972.

Hargrove, Nancy D. "Youth in Toni Cade Bambara's Gorilla, My Love." In *Woman Writers of the Contemporary South,* edited by Peggy Whitman Prenshaw, 214–232. Jackson: University Press of Mississippi, 1984.

Lovelace, Alice. "In Praise of Toni Cade Bambara." *In Motion Magazine,* February 20, 2000. Available online. URL: http://www.inmotionmagazine.com/bambara.html. Downloaded on January 19, 2007.

Perkins, Margo V. "Toni Cade Bambara." In *Notable American Women: A Biographical Dictionary, Completing the Twentieth Century,* edited by Susan Ware, 40–42. Cambridge, Mass.: Belknap Press of Harvard University Press, 2004.

Reuben, Paul P. "Chapter 10: Late Twentieth Century, 1945 to the Present—Toni Cade Bambara." PAL: Perspectives in American Literature—A Research and Reference Guide. January 9, 2003. Available online. URL: http://www.CSUStan.edu/english/reuben/pal/chap10/bambara.html. Downloaded on January 19, 2007.

Tate, Claudia, ed. *Black Women Writers at Work,* 174–187. New York: Continuum Press, 1983.

∾ Barnes, Djuna

(1892–1982) *novelist, playwright, journalist*

Djuna Barnes was a novelist, journalist, playwright, poet, and artist. She was also an expatriate who spent more than two decades living and working abroad. Barnes's place in American letters was firmly established in 1936 with the publication of *Nightwood,* an experimental novel that was a profoundly influential modernist text that the Welsh poet Dylan Thomas called "one of the three great prose books ever written by a woman."

Born on July 12, 1892, in Cornwall-on-Hudson, New York, Barnes grew up on a spacious farm. Although she had no formal education, she was tutored in a variety of subjects—from musical instruments to mysticism—by her eccentric father, Wald Barnes, and by her spiritualist, feminist grandmother, Zadel.

In 1909 Barnes moved to New York City and became part of Greenwich Village's avant-garde community. To help support her mother and three brothers, she took a job as a journalist and illustrator for the *Brooklyn Eagle* and contributed to a number of other New York newspapers and periodicals. One of her assignments was to report on imprisoned British suffragists who would sometimes die from being force-fed during hunger strikes. Barnes subjected herself to the brutal, painful procedure because she wanted to know firsthand what the suffragists had endured in their struggle for women's rights.

Barnes also wrote poetry, and in 1915 a chapbook consisting of her poems and illustrations, *The Book of Repulsive Women: 8 Rhythms and 5 Drawings,* was published. Around that time she fell in love with Ernest Hanfstaengl, the grandson of a Yankee general in the Civil War. When he broke off their two-year engagement, she was heartbroken and instead married Courtenay Lemon; they were divorced two years later in 1919.

Determined to get on with her life and her work, Barnes wrote more poetry and several plays. The Provincetown Players, a respected theatrical group founded by Eugene O'Neill, performed three of her one-act plays during its 1919–20 season.

In 1920 Barnes decided to set sail for Paris, where she wrote four of her most important books and found herself at the center of a flamboyant expatriate circle that included the writers GERTRUDE STEIN and KAY BOYLE. She hobnobbed with the likes of Samuel Beckett and Ezra Pound, and James Joyce expressed his admiration for her work.

Barnes was lauded for her magazine interviews with famous society and celebrity figures, from the designer Coco Chanel to the photographer Alfred Steiglitz. When *A Book*—a collection of Barnes's poems, short stories, plays, and drawings—was published in 1923, Barnes's reputation as a serious writer was established.

While in Paris, Barnes had several romances, including a long-term relationship with Thelma Wood, an American artist on whom Barnes based one of the central characters in *Nightwood.* Combining comedy with horror, and reality with fantasy, this early gothic novel explored the themes of sexuality, alienation, obsessive relationships, and human and animal behavior. In one passage, the author describes the cabaret performers, who act as a kind of Greek chorus, as "gaudy, cheap cuts from the beast life, immensely capable of that great disquiet called entertainment."

While *Nightwood,* with its gloomy gothic elements, was considered by some critics to be bizarre and even grotesque, others recognized Barnes as a gifted and original writer, and a master at dreamlike language. In his introduction to the novel, T. S. Eliot commented: "What I would leave the reader prepared to find is the great achievement of a style, the beauty of phrasing, the brilliance of wit and characterization, and to a quality of horror and doom very nearly related to that of Elizabethan tragedy."

Barnes's other works include *Ladies Almanack* (1928), the novel *Ryder* (1928), and *The Antiphon* (1958), an autobiographical play in blank verse. Several collections of her fiction, plays, and poetry have been published posthumously.

Although she became a recluse upon her return to New York City in 1940, refusing to grant interviews or to approve the reprinting of much of her early work, Barnes continued to write until she died on June 18, 1982, at age 90.

In his review of *What of the Night,* a one-woman show about Djuna Barnes staged in New York City in April 2005, Hilton Als, a theater critic for the *New Yorker,* asserted that "perhaps no other modernist explored the dark, twisting forces of love as deeply as Djuna Barnes." However, Als felt that the play did not capture Barnes's "famously Grand Guignol humor." The writers of the script "revere their subject too much," noted the critic, and thus "place themselves in the ranks of the scholars and feminists whom Barnes herself rejected."

Djuna Barnes once wryly observed that she had become "the most famous unknown of the century." In fact, with the passage of time, Barnes has become increasingly recognized and admired as an important and influential American novelist.

Further Reading

Als, Hilton. "The Many Faces of Jane: A One-Woman Show about the Life of Djuna Barnes." *New Yorker,* April 18, 2005, pp. 196–198.

Barnes, Djuna. *Nightwood.* New York: Harcourt, 1937.

———. *Ryder.* New York: St. Martin's, 1979.

Esposito, Carmine. "Djuna Barnes." In *American Women Writers, 1900–1945.* Edited by Laurie Champion, 20–21. Westport, Conn.: Greenwood Press, 2000.

Field, Andrew. *Djuna: The Life and Times of Djuna Barnes.* New York: Putnam, 1983.

Herring, Phillip F. *The Life and Work of Djuna Barnes.* New York: Viking, 1995.

∾ Bishop, Elizabeth
(1911–1979)   *poet, letter writer*

Elizabeth Bishop, who was held in high esteem by many of her peers, including the poets MARIANNE MOORE, Pablo Neruda, and Robert Lowell, as well as by a generation of younger poets, received the prestigious Pulitzer Prize in poetry in 1956 for *North & South* and *A Cold Spring,* and the Neus-tadt International Prize for Literature in 1976. Bishop, who refused to accept simple solutions to life's complex problems, was greatly admired for her intelligent, finely crafted, and honest poetry.

Bishop was born on February 8, 1911, in Worcester, Massachusetts. Her father died when she was eight months old. When she was five, her mother—who had been plagued by bouts of mental illness—was institutionalized and never recovered. Several of Bishop's poems, such as "In the Waiting Room," poignantly reflect her traumatic childhood.

Elizabeth was a frail and asthmatic child who did not attend school regularly until she was 16. She was raised by both sets of grandparents—first in Nova Scotia, Canada, and then in Worcester. Fortunately both families had well-stocked libraries and Elizabeth read whatever she could get her hands on. At that time her favorite poets, who would later influence her writing style, were EMILY DICKINSON, George Herbert, and Gerard Manley Hopkins.

After attending a boarding school near Boston, where she wrote and published her first poems, at age 19, Bishop enrolled at Vassar College. There she began to write in earnest. She and several other students, including the future novelist MARY MCCARTHY and the poet MURIEL RUKEYSER, founded a literary magazine called *Con Spirito.* Bishop's poetry also appeared in the more traditional *Vassar Review.*

While at Vassar Bishop met Marianne Moore, a poet 24 years her senior who became her mentor, critic, and lifelong friend. Moore encouraged Bishop to give up the idea of going to medical school and instead to make a career of writing. Thanks to a modest but steady income generated by her father's construction business, Bishop was able to heed Moore's advice.

She was also able to satisfy her quest for visiting exotic places and her fascination with geography. After receiving a bachelor's degree from Vassar in 1934, Bishop traveled extensively and reflected her experiences in three volumes of poetry: *North & South* (1946), *Questions of Travel* (1965), and *Geography III* (1976).

Bishop interrupted her nomadic lifestyle only twice. In 1938 she and Louise Crane, a classmate from college, purchased a house in Key West, Florida. For the next eight years she wrote poems that would later appear in *North & South*, the first of four volumes of poetry she published and the winner of the 1945 Houghton Mifflin Poetry Award.

The second time Bishop settled down was in 1951. During a trip to Rio de Janeiro she became ill from food poisoning. A Brazilian friend, Lota de Macedo Soares, nursed her back to health. Bishop fell in love with the Brazilian people, the beauty of the country, and with Lota; Bishop and Soares remained together in Brazil for 15 years. "I still feel I must have died and gone to heaven without deserving to," she wrote joyously in 1952 to a friend in New England. During that period Bishop translated Brazilian poetry, published *A Cold Spring* (1955)—which along with a reprint of *North & South*, garnered her a Pulitzer Prize, and wrote a travel book entitled *Brazil* (1962).

When Soares suffered a nervous breakdown and committed suicide in 1967, Bishop was shattered. She lost her desire to travel and spent most of the rest of her life in the United States. Never again would Bishop feel as secure or as content as she had in Brazil. Outwardly, however, she coped with the crushing loss.

In 1970 the acclaimed poet Robert Lowell invited Bishop to teach poetry with him at Harvard University. He praised her "unrhetorical, cool, and beautifully thought out poems," and considered Bishop "one of the best craftsmen alive." In fact, wrote British critic Andrew Motion in his review in the *Observer* of *The Letters of Robert Lowell* (2005), "Of all Lowell's poet-correspondents, no one is more important to him than Elizabeth Bishop. Lowell was quick to see her genius, and he simply and frankly admired her. 'You have more to offer, I think, than anyone writing poems in English,' he tells her in the early 1960s—and never deviates from this view."

Bishop often spent years writing and refining a single poem, even a short one. "I'm not interested in big-scale work as such," she told Lowell, adding that "something needn't be large to be good."

Bishop continued teaching at Harvard for nine years, while her reputation as a major American poet grew. *The Complete Poems* won the coveted National Book Award in poetry in 1970, while *Geography III* received the 1977 National Book Critics Circle Award in poetry.

Elizabeth Bishop, a beloved perfectionist, recognized for her powerful, carefully conceived poetry, died in Boston on October 6, 1979. "The pathos and intimacy in her work deepened until the very end of her life," wrote poet Frank Bidart, in a tribute to Bishop.

Further Reading

Bishop, Elizabeth. *The Complete Poems, 1927–1979* (an expanded version of *The Complete Poems*, 1969). New York: Farrar, Straus and Giroux, 1983.

———. *Edgar Allan Poe and the Juke-Box: Uncollected Poems, Drafts, and Fragments.* Selected and edited by Alice Quinn. New York: Farrar, Straus and Giroux, 2006.

———. *One Art: Letters.* Selected and edited by Robert Giroux. New York: Farrar, Straus and Giroux, 1994.

Costello, Bonnie. *Elizabeth Bishop: Questions of Mastery.* Cambridge: Harvard University Press, 1991.

Fountain, Gary, and Peter Brazeau. *Remembering Elizabeth Bishop: An Oral Biography.* Amherst: University of Massachusetts Press, 1994.

Lowell, Robert. *The Letters of Robert Lowell.* Edited by Saskia Hamilton. New York: Farrar, Straus and Giroux, 2005.

Miller, Brett Candish. *Elizabeth Bishop: Life and Memory of It.* Berkeley: University of California Press, 1993.

Bly, Nellie (Elizabeth Jane Cochrane Seaman)
(1865–1922) *journalist*

Nellie Bly was one of the country's first and most famous woman journalists. Her ground-breaking investigative reporting helped expose social injustice and political corruption during the late 19th century. Bly was also a flamboyant adventurer who traveled around the world on a daring solo trip in a hot-air balloon at the age of 25.

Elizabeth Jane Cochrane was born on May 5, 1865, in a small town in Pennsylvania named for her father, a mill worker who eventually became a wealthy mill owner. Elizabeth, an intelligent girl with cool gray eyes and auburn hair, was only 12 when her father died, leaving her mother to look after 13 children.

After attending a teacher's college for a year, 19-year-old Cochrane set out to find a job and earn a living. Fortunately the editor of the *Pittsburgh Dispatch* noticed a fiery letter she had written to the paper protesting an article about unmarried women and how they should hunt for husbands instead of for work. Impressed by Cochrane's spirited writing style, in 1885 the editor hired her at five dollars a week. The first woman reporter at the newspaper, she decided to call herself Nellie Bly, a name she took from a popular Stephen Foster tune.

Bly quickly made a name for herself at the *Dispatch* by taking risky undercover assignments, often disguised as a shoplifter or a factory worker. Her articles were sympathetic to Pittsburgh's large immigrant population and critical of its politicians, factory owners, and landlords.

Although the public clamored for Bly's headline-grabbing stories, corporate advertisers threatened to stop doing business with the *Dispatch* because of them, and she was reassigned to Mexico. There she again wrote about the homeless and the poor working masses. After six months, the Mexican government kicked her out of the country.

Upon her return to the United States in 1887, Bly was hired by Joseph Pulitzer, the publisher of the *New York World*. He liked Bly's willingness to get at the truth, no matter what it took. For example, in 1887 Bly became the first reporter to pretend she was insane in order to be committed to and then write about New York's notorious Blackwell Island asylum for women. For 10 days she was subjected to freezing cold baths, inedible food, and abusive nurses. After Pulitzer arranged for her release, she wrote about her degrading experiences. Her popular front-page exposés helped persuade the city to make substantial improvements at the mental facility. Bly's "sensational stunt journalism," as some labeled it,

Journalist Nellie Bly broke the record for around-the-world travel.
(AP/Wide World Photos)

provided her with material for her first book, *Ten Days in a Madhouse* (1887). Her second book, also about her experiences as an undercover reporter, was entitled *Six Months in Mexico* (1888).

But, for Bly, undercover reporting was not enough. She wanted to do something more daring and adventurous so that she would stand out from other reporters. In 1889 she persuaded Pulitzer to sponsor her on an unchaperoned trip around the world in an attempt to break the fictional record set in Jules Verne's novel *Around the World in Eighty Days.* Americans eagerly charted her daily progress, and when she completed the globe-circling journey in a record-breaking 72 days, she was welcomed back to New York with a triumphant parade down Broadway. Much to her delight, Nellie Bly had become an overnight celebrity.

After writing *Nellie Bly's Book: Around the World in 72 Days* (1890) and interviewing notable socialists such as Emma Goldman and Eugene Debs, Bly in 1895 married Robert Seaman, a 72-year-old, highly successful businessman. For a while, she stopped working and lived the life of leisure, but when her husband died in 1904, she became responsible for his steel company. Ever the reformer, Bly provided the workers with new benefits such as a medical clinic. She also initiated physical fitness by providing gymnasiums and bowling alleys, and she promoted mental fitness by opening libraries with staff trained to teach employees how to read. For almost 10 years she managed her husband's two multimillion-dollar companies.

Unfortunately, the company's finances were grossly mismanaged by unscrupulous financial associates Bly had trusted, ultimately forcing her to declare bankruptcy. In 1914 Bly fled to Europe to escape financial ruin. There she became one of the first woman journalists to report from the front during World War I, sending her dispatches to the *New York Evening Journal.* Returning to America in 1919 she continued to write for the newspaper about pressing social issues such as the plight of abandoned children.

When she died from pneumonia in New York City on January 22, 1922, at age 56, Nellie Bly, the zealous reformer and celebrated undercover journalist, was hailed by the *Journal* as "the best reporter in America."

Further Reading

Bly, Nellie (Cochrane, Elizabeth). *Nellie Bly's Book: Around the World in 72 Days.* New York: Pictorial Weekly, 1890.

Brian, Denis. "Nelly Bly Races around the World." In *Pulitzer: A Life,* 144–146. New York: John Wiley and Sons, 2001.

Hahn, Emily. *Around the World with Nelly Bly.* Boston: Houghton Mifflin, 1959.

Kroeger, Brooke. *Nellie Bly: Daredevil, Reporter, Feminist.* New York: Three Rivers Press, 1995.

"Nelly Bly." Jules Verne Web site. Available online. URL: http://www.julesverne.ca/nelliebly.html. Downloaded on January 19, 2007.

Bogan, Louise
(1897–1970)   *poet, critic, essayist*

Louise Bogan was an accomplished poet who combined traditional techniques with contemporary language. A fearless writer, "she wrestled beauty and truth of dark places," noted the English poet W. H. Auden. Bogan was also praised for her acute and influential literary criticism.

She was born on August 11, 1897, in Livermore Falls, Maine. Her family moved frequently from one small mill town to another. Her parents argued often, sometimes violently, and her mother spent long periods of time away from home. When she was 10, Bogan escaped what she later called "the horrors" of an unhappy childhood by going to a boarding school in New Hampshire. In 1909 the Bogans moved to Boston, Massachusetts, where Louise was accepted and excelled at Girls' Latin School.

The "life-saving process" of writing poetry began when Louise was 14; according to her autobiography, *Journey around My Room* (1980), she had learned "every essential of her trade" by the time she was 18. In 1915 Bogan enrolled at Boston University, where two of her poems appeared in the university's literary magazine. The following year she was offered a scholarship at Radcliffe College. Instead of accepting it, she eloped with Curt Alexander, a young army officer. It was a marriage she would later call "unfortunate," although in 1916 she gave birth to a beloved daughter, Mathilde. Alexander died in 1920, shortly after the couple had separated.

Bogan then moved to Greenwich Village in New York City. She became part of the bohemian literary community and befriended the social critic Edmund Wilson and the poet Theodore Roethke. In 1921, several of her poems appeared in *Poetry* and *The New Republic,* and two years later she published her first book of verse, *Body of This Death,* to great acclaim. In it, she used psychological analyses of love and religion.

In 1925 Bogan married Raymond Holden, a minor poet, and settled on a farm in upstate New York. Her second book of poems, *Dark Summer* (1929), with its dark lyrical force, was also well received. But that same year a devastating fire swept through the couple's farm, destroying their home and their manuscripts. After moving back to New York City in 1931, Bogan was named poetry critic for the *New Yorker,* a prestigious position she held for 38 years. Nonetheless, she suffered from depression, a condition which plagued her throughout her life. After separating from Holden, she published two collections of poetry, *The Sleeping Fury* (1937) and *Poems and New Poems* (1941), and held the Library of Congress's Chair of Poetry from 1946 to 1947.

Bogan published her last and perhaps best volume of poetry, *The Blue Estuaries: Poems 1923–1968,* in 1969. "Her language is as supple as it is accurate, dealing with things in their own tones," wrote a *New York Times* reviewer, describing the book. She garnered numerous awards, including two Guggenheim fellowships (1933, 1937) and the Bollingen Prize, which she shared with Leonic Adams in 1955.

Although best known as a prize-winning lyric poet, Bogan also published fiction and essays. A new collection titled *The Poet's Prose: Selected Writings of Louise Bogan* (2005), edited by critic Mary Kinzie, includes a selection of Bogan's best criticism, prose meditations, letters, journal entries, autobiographical essays, and published and unpublished fiction. "Bogan is a master, both in prose and poetry, a critic of singular distinction and acuity," commented fiction writer MARY GORDON.

In her review of *The Poet's Prose* for *Poetry* magazine (September 2005), Danielle Chapman asserts that in reading the collection, "one is struck by a forcefulness of character that rarely comes across in the poems. In Bogan's lyrics, as stirring and beautiful as they can be, we're often moved more by the enormity of what's being held back than by what's actually on the page. . . . Her correspondence rollicks with confidence and censures with impunity."

At a lecture at Bennington College in Vermont in 1962, Bogan stated that the best women writers are the ones who tell their own truth, both observed and suffered through. Using traditional metered, rhymed verse, Louise Bogan, who died in New York City on February 4, 1970, bravely and rigorously explored her own emotional truth through her craft.

Further Reading

Bogan, Louise. *The Blue Estuaries: Poems, 1923–1968.* New York: Farrar, Straus and Giroux, 1958.

———. *Journey around My Room: The Autobiography of Louise Bogan—A Mosaic.* Edited by Ruth Limmer. New York: Viking Press, 1980.

———. *A Poet's Prose: Selected Writings of Louise Bogan.* Edited by Mary Kinzie. Athens: Ohio University Press/ Swallow Press, 2005.

Frank, Elizabeth. *Louise Bogan: A Portrait.* New York: Knopf, 1985.

McClatchy, J. D., ed. *The Voice of the Poet: Five American Women—Gertrude Stein, Edna St. Vincent Millay, H. D., Louise Bogan, and Muriel Rukeyser.* Random House Audio Bk&Cassett edition, 2001.

～ Bombeck, Erma Louise Fiste
(1927–1996) *journalist, essayist, novelist*

Erma Bombeck is one of America's most beloved and widely read humorists, columnists, and authors. Of the 13 books she wrote, 10 appeared on the *New York Times* best seller list. From 1979 until her death in 1996, Bombeck's name appeared annually on *The World Almanac's* list of the "25 Most Influential Women in America."

Born in Dayton, Ohio, on February 21, 1927, to a 16-year-old mother and a 35-year-old father, a crane operator who died from kidney disease when his daughter was nine, Erma Louise Fiste was raised in a poor, immigrant, industrial part of Dayton. As a child, Erma felt abandoned: Her older half-sister from her father's first marriage, Thelma, whom she adored and considered her only real friend, moved away to live with her birth mother, while Erma's mother, who had left school in the sixth grade and married at 14, worked long hours at factory jobs.

To assuage her loneliness, Erma turned to the world of books; she became a voracious reader. Among the authors she most admired and whose styles she later emulated were witty, acerbic humorists like James Thurber and Robert Benchley. She published her first humor column in a junior high school newspaper, in which she made fun of bad cafeteria food and teachers. She recognized that she had a way with words and decided to become a newspaper reporter. "As a kid I spent my last nickel to hear [journalist] DOROTHY THOMPSON speak," she recalled.

Erma got her wish when, at 15, she was hired as a copygirl for the *Dayton Herald*. Although she wrote only one article—an interview with 16-year-old movie star Shirley Temple—it won her the staff award for feature of the week. (Bombeck's mother had wanted her daughter to become a famous tap dancer like Shirley Temple and tried to get her to take dance lessons, but Erma Fiste had other ideas for her future.)

Once Fiste graduated from high school—the first person in her family to do so—she returned to the *Dayton Herald*, this time as a full-time writer. She attended Ohio University in Athens but did not do well academically, barely passing freshman composition. Fiste transferred to the University of Dayton, a Catholic college where she wrote for the college magazine and graduated with a bachelor of art's degree in 1949.

Also in 1949, Fiste, by then a practicing Catholic, married Bill Bombeck. She had met him during her early years at the *Dayton Herald*, where he had worked as a copyboy. They dated before he

joined the army and was assigned to Korea. Upon his return, the couple became engaged. Bill was a high school science teacher who made extra money by working as a handyman. Eventually he would give up teaching to help manage his wife's career and finances.

After graduating from college and marrying, Bombeck returned to the *Herald*, by then the *Dayton Journal-Herald*, and wrote feature stories for the women's section. Although she did a good job, she preferred expressing her own opinions in columns to writing articles based solely on facts, especially when she had no expertise in the subject of her assignment, such as gardening.

Several years after moving to Centerville, a suburb of Dayton, Bombeck decided to give up her job at the *Journal-Herald* and stay at home as a full-time homemaker. She and Bill very much wanted children, and in 1954, believing that they were unable to have children of their own, they adopted a daughter, Betsy. Much to her surprise and delight, a year later Bombeck gave birth to a son, Andrew, followed by another son, Matthew, in 1958. It was from her experiences as a nonworking mother living in suburbia during the 1950s, when her life seemed to morph into an endless list of housekeeping chores, that Bombeck found and mined material for her future columns and books. "I hid my dreams in the back of my mind—it was the only safe place in the house," Bombeck recalled. "From time to time I would get them out and play with them, not daring to reveal them to anyone else because they were fragile and might get broken."

However, once her children were enrolled in school, Bombeck approached the *Kettering-Oakland* Times, a local suburban newspaper, to write a satirical column called "At Wit's End," about the trials and tribulations of domesticity. Impressed by the column and Bombeck's sharp eye for the common experience, in 1965 Glenn Thompson, editor of the *Dayton Journal-Herald* and Bombeck's future longtime mentor, invited her to return to the paper to produce "At Wit's End" three times a week; she was paid $15 for each column. The well-received columns were soon syndicated, first by Newsday Syndicate and then, starting in 1988, by the Universal Press Syndicate. Bombeck's wry, astute observations about the realities of being a suburban housewife were syndicated nationwide by more than 700 newspapers. She had discovered that she was not the only one who, as she put it, "did not feel fulfilled cleaning chrome faucets with a toothbrush."

With the popular column under her belt, Bombeck began to write books: Some were collections of her best-known columns (*At Wit's End*, 1967), while others were original material (*If Life Is a Bowl of Cherries, What Am I Doing in the Pitts?*, 1978).

Bombeck then carried her piquant interpretations of the lives of ordinary housewives to televi-

sion. For 11 years, beginning in 1975, she held a regular slot as a daily correspondent on ABC's *Good Morning America* show, joining celebrities such as Geraldo Rivera and David Hartman and interviewing others, including Zsa Zsa Gabor in Gabor's king-size bed.

In addition, Bombeck's best-selling novel *The Grass Is Always Greener over the Septic Tank* (1976) was adapted into a television movie starring comedian Carol Burnett. Bombeck was also a regular contributor to popular magazines such as *Reader's Digest, Good Housekeeping,* and *Family Circle,* and she lectured extensively. Two of her lectures have been recorded as *The Family That Plays Together Gets on Each Other's Nerves* (1977). In 1978 she was invited to speak to 3,500 farmers' wives in Kansas City, Missouri, but 9,000 people showed up, including several hundred men. "Though her sensibility is strictly suburban, Bombeck manages to hit everybody's funny bone," said a reporter in *Newsweek* magazine.

Bombeck strongly backed women's rights but had an ambivalent relationship with the women's movement. A pioneer of third-wave feminism, a movement that challenged former definitions of what is or is not good for women, she believed that women were entitled to the right to work or to stay at home raising children and taking care of a home; both options deserved equal respect. After hearing Betty Friedan speak, she commented that Friedan, the author of the celebrated feminist treatise *The Feminine Mystique,* and her followers had "thrown a war for themselves and didn't invite any of us. That was very wrong of them." Nonetheless, in 1978 Bombeck worked tirelessly for the passage of the Equal Rights Amendment and was bitterly disappointed when it failed to pass.

Some of Bombeck's books, including *A Marriage Made in Heaven . . . or, Too Tired for an Affair,* carried more serious messages than her earlier, lighter comedic writings did, as she wrote touchingly on subjects such as miscarriage, the loss of a close friend, and her own battle with breast cancer in 1992. *I Want to Grow Hair, I Want to Grow Up, I Want to Go to Boise: Children Surviving Cancer*

Popular columnist and humorist Erma Bombeck poses by her typewriter.
(Tom Arma)

(1989) is a collection of optimistic stories about children with cancer and how they survived the disease.

Eat Less Cottage Cheese and More Ice Cream: Thoughts on Life from Erma Bombeck (2003) is a reprint of her most famous column, "If I Had My Life to Live Over," in which Bombeck listed what she would have done had she been given an opportunity to change her life. With her hallmark good-natured sense of humor and common sense, her list included inviting friends over to dinner even if the carpet was stained and the sofa faded; sitting on the lawn with her children and not worrying about grass stains; and never saying, "Later, now go get washed up for dinner," when her kids kissed her impetuously.

Bombeck was diagnosed at age 20 with polycystic kidney disease, and by 1994 her hereditary disease had worsened and she was on dialysis treatment four times a day while waiting for a suitable transplant. Dozens of her steadfast fans offered to donate their kidneys; Bombeck was touched that strangers cared so much about her life-and-death situation. A match was found, but she suffered complications following the surgery and died on April 22, 1996, at age 69. There was an outpouring of sympathy. A tribute collection, *Forever Erma: Best-Loved Writing from America's Favorite Humorist* (1997), was published, followed in 2000 by a conference held at the University of Dayton in Bombeck's honor. Participants included such notable humorists as Art Buchwald. There is also an Erma Bombeck Writers' Workshop, which has attracted nationally syndicated columnists including Phil Donahue, Bombeck's friend and former neighbor, as guest speakers.

Erma Bombeck touched millions of American housewives through her columns, books, and appearances, because they identified with her experiences. She earned respect, even from ardent feminists like journalist Ellen Goodman, who said, "Bombeck cracked open the feminine mystique her own way: with a sidesplitting laugh." Writing in the *New York Times Book Review*, contributor Judith Viorst characterized Bombeck's musings on family life as "informed with hard-won wisdom and with love." When asked the secret to her popularity, Bombeck replied, simply: "We've all been there. We're all in this mess together. Let's get some fun out of it."

Further Reading

Bombeck, Erma. *Eat Less Cottage Cheese and More Ice Cream: Thoughts on Life from Erma Bombeck.* Kansas City, Mo.: Andrews McMeel Publishing, 2003.

———. *Forever Erma: Best-Loved Writing from America's Favorite Humorist.* Kansas City, Mo.: Andrews McMeel Publishing, 1997.

———. *I Want to Grow Hair, I Want to Grow Up, I Want to Go to Boise: Children Surviving Cancer.* New York: Harper, 1989.

Edwards, Susan. *Erma Bombeck: A Life in Humor.* New York: Avon Books, 1997.

"Erma's Life." The Erma Bombeck Online Museum. Available online. URL: http://www.ermamuseum.org/life/life.asp. Downloaded on January 19, 2007.

～ Bonfils, Martha Winifred Sweet Black (Annie Laurie)
(1863–1936) *journalist*

Winifred Black Bonfils spent much of her nearly 50-year career as a star reporter for the *San Francisco Examiner*. Considered one of the most versatile journalists of her time, Bonfils was equally comfortable interviewing presidents, investigating corruption, and covering natural disasters.

Martha Winifred Sweet was born on October 14, 1863, in Chilton, Wisconsin. By the time she was 15, both of her parents had died. Her eldest sister raised Winifred and arranged for her to receive a private-school education.

With her flare for drama, Sweet aspired to become an actress but disappointingly was cast only in minor roles for an amateur company. She described her theatrical experiences in letters to her sister, who forwarded them to the *Chicago Tribune*, which printed them. It was Sweet's first taste of journalism.

In 1890 she traveled to San Francisco, California, where she became a reporter for the *San Francisco Examiner*. The newspaper's powerful publisher, William Randolph Hearst, took a liking to Sweet; she in turn greatly admired him. Hearst encouraged her to use her acting skills in a series of undercover assignments, including pretending she was a sick indigent in order to get into the City Receiving Hospital. Written under her pen name, Annie Laurie, the resulting story documented the mistreatment and harassment of women patients and led to policy changes at the hospital.

Sweet also worked undercover in a cotton mill and a fruit cannery and got to interview President Benjamin Harrison by hiding beneath a dining table on his train and then surprising him as he sat down to eat.

In 1896 she moved to New York to cover William Jennings Bryan's presidential campaign. But she missed the West, and in 1898 went to Utah to report on polygamy among Mormon communities for the *Denver Post*. Sadly, she had two unsuccessful marriages—first to Orlow Black and then to Charles Alden Bonfils—and two of her three children died when they were young.

Bonfils found happiness in "scooping" stories for the *San Francisco Examiner*. In 1900 she was the first to report on a deadly tidal wave that crashed into Galveston, Texas. In 1906 she wrote compassionately about the great San Francisco earthquake, and her front-page articles were said to have helped boost the morale of the devastated city.

In 1907 Bonfils covered the sensational murder trial of Harry Thaw, a wealthy businessman accused of murdering the famous architect Stanford White, who was the lover of Thaw's young wife. Bonfils shared the press table with three other women reporters, all of whom were sympathetic to Thaw's vulnerable wife. A male colleague labeled the four journalists the "sob sisters"—an epithet that, unfortunately, stuck.

But Bonfils proved herself much more than a "sob sister;" she was an ace reporter with an eye for compelling stories. For example, her report on

Molokai, the Hawaiian leper colony, stirred an outpouring of public support for the inmates. She also went to Europe in 1918 to write about the effects of war on American soldiers.

Despite being severely ill and nearly blind, Winifred Black Bonfils remained an active crusading journalist until shortly before her death on May 25, 1936. She described herself as a plain, practical, all-around newspaper women. "That's my profession," she said, "and my pride."

Further Reading

Beasley, Maurine, and Sheila J. Gibbons. *Taking their Place: A Documentary History of Women and Journalism*. State College, Penn.: Strata Publishing, 2002.

Belford, Barbara. *Brilliant Bylines: A Biographical Anthology of Notable Newspaperwomen in America*. New York: Columbia University Press, 1986.

Schlipp, Madelon Golden, and Sharon M. Murphy. *Great Women of the Press*. Carbondale: Southern Illinois University Press, 1983.

Wheeler, Helen Rippier. "Celebrating California Women Who Made 'Her story,'" Berkeley Daily Planet on the Web. March 22, 2005. Available online. URL: http://www.berkeleydailyplanet.com/article.cfm?archiveDate=03-22-05&storyID=20998. Downloaded on January 19, 2007.

Bonnin, Gertrude Simmons
See ZITKALA SA

Bowen, Catherine Drinker
(1897–1973) *biographer*

Catherine Drinker Bowen was a historian and award-winning biographer widely praised for her thorough research and her flare for making her subjects—which ranged from the Russian composer Peter Ilich Tchaikovsky to the American statesman Benjamin Franklin—come alive.

Born on January 1, 1897, in the college town of Haverford, Pennsylvania, Catherine Drinker was the oldest of six children. When she was eight her father became president of Lehigh University, and the family moved with him to Bethlehem, Pennsylvania. Catherine was educated informally but traveled extensively with her mother; her exposure to other cultures provided her with a zest for history. A talented violinist, she maintained a lifelong interest in music but did not become a professional musician. Instead, she wrote articles about music.

In 1919 Catherine married Ezra Bowen, a professor of economics at Lafayette College. The couple had two children. *Rufus Starbuck's Wife* (1932), Bowen's first and only novel, was based in part on her marital problems. Four years after its publication, the Bowens were divorced. In 1939 she married a surgeon, T. McKean Downs, who died in 1960.

Bowen switched genres from fiction to nonfiction and, after doing research in the Soviet Union, wrote *Beloved Friend: The Story of Tchaikowsky and Nadejda von Meck* (1937), coauthored with Barbara von Meck; and *Free Artist: The Story of Anton and Nicholas Rubinstein* (1939), another biography based on musicians.

Bowen also wrote a meticulously researched biography of Oliver Wendell Holmes, *Yankee from Olympus: Justice Holmes and His Family* (1944). It was reviewed favorably by the distinguished historian Henry Steele Commager and was Bowen's first taste of success. Her next work, *John Adams and the American Revolution* (1950), was also well received.

The Lion and the Throne: The Life and Times of Sir Edward Coke (1957), about the eminent English jurist, is Bowen's best-known biography. The author had found her niche and, as she stated in her biography in 1969, "turned once and for all to writing biography that contained no fictional devices and documented every quotation." In 1957 it garnered a National Book Award. Her next book was a portrait of Coke's greatest rival, Sir Francis Bacon. Another book, *Miracle of Philadelphia* (1966), the story of the Constitutional Convention of 1787 and its 55 participants, became required reading for many students of American history at colleges throughout the country.

Bowen also wrote books on the art of biography. In *Biography: The Craft and the Calling* (1969),

she asserted that the novelist invents his plot whereas the biographer finds it in history "by events as they unfold . . . by the character of the biographical subject, the hero." Bowen was well aware that a biographer had to stay away from the "straight line that leads to some neat historical or moralistic pole . . . and ends up in the sterile part of history." She knew she had to keep her narrative based on fact but also lively and interesting. Bowen had a note posted in her study that read, "Will the reader turn the page?" Although Bowen's subjects were without exception prominent men, in an interview in *Atlantic Monthly* in 1970, Bowen said that she always expected to be married and have children "but not as a sole career; never, never as a sole career." Writing, she claimed, not motherhood, saved her.

Catherine Drinker Bowen, whose biographies were frequently Book-of-the-Month Club selections, died on November 1, 1973, in her hometown, while completing a biography of Benjamin Franklin, "the most dangerous man in America." That work was published posthumously in 1974.

Further Reading

Bowen, Catherine Drinker. *Biography: The Craft and the Calling.* Boston: Little, Brown, 1969.
———. *The Lion and the Throne: The Life and Times of Sir Edward Coke.* Boston: Little, Brown, 1957.
———. *Miracle at Philadelphia: The Story of the Constitutional Convention, May to September, 1787.* Boston: Little, Brown, 1966.
National Book Foundation. "Writers on their Craft and their Work: Catherine Drinker Bowen." Available online. URL: http://www.nationalbook.org/writers craft_cdbowen.html. Downloaded on January 19, 2007.
Obituary on Catherine Drinker Bowen. *Washington Post,* November 6, 1973; *Newsweek,* November 12, 1973.
Zinssen, William, ed. *Extraordinary Lives: The Art and Craft of American Biography.* New York: American Heritage, 1986.

Boyd, Nancy
See MILLAY, EDNA ST. VINCENT

⌁ Boyle, Kay
(1902–1992) *short story writer, novelist, essayist*

A versatile and prolific writer, Kay Boyle infused her finely crafted work with a passionate and life-long concern for social justice. "The older I grow," she said in a 1986 interview in the *Los Angeles Times,* "the more I feel that all writers should be committed to their times and write of their times."

Kay Boyle was born in St. Paul, Minnesota, on February 19, 1902. After moving to Cincinnati, Ohio, she studied violin and architecture. But she knew early on that she wanted to become a writer. In 1919 Boyle moved to New York City and joined the staff of *Broom,* a small avant-garde literary magazine. She remembers being awestruck to find herself working side by side with such esteemed writers as MARIANNE MOORE.

Boyle married Richard Brault in 1923 and moved with him to Paris. There she met and befriended expatriate writers, including GERTRUDE STEIN and DJUNA BARNES. Three years later her marriage failed, and she lived briefly with Ernest Walsh, a poet.

In 1929 Boyle's first collection of short stories was published, followed by eight other volumes. Many critics believe that her short stories, as exemplified by *Fifty Stories* (1980), represent her best work. In fact, according to biographer Joan Mellen, who wrote an article about Boyle in *Notable American Women* in 2004, from 1931 until the mid-1950s Boyle was "the most distinguished and consistent writer" of short stories in the esteemed *New Yorker* magazine. "Kay Boyle might even be considered the creator of what came to be known as the *New Yorker* story."

Boyle married Laurence Vail, an American painter, in 1931. They had three daughters and spent most of their time in France, England, and Austria. During that period Boyle began to write prolifically, and never stopped. *Plagued by the Nightingale* (1931) was the first of her 14 novels; she also wrote six volumes of poetry, four collections of essays, and several childrens' books.

Boyle garnered two Guggenheim fellowships (1934 and 1961) and won two O. Henry Memorial Awards for short stories (1934 and 1941). After returning to America in 1941 and divorcing Vail, Boyle married the writer Baron Joseph von Franckenstein. She wrote novels about Nazi-occupied France and the French Resistance and, while in Germany, stories about occupied Germany. She also became a foreign correspondent for the *New Yorker* (1946 to 1953).

But von Franckenstein lost his position with the American diplomatic service, supposedly as a security risk. The couple and their two young children were forced to return to the United States. Boyle spent 10 years fighting von Franckenstein's dismissal and defending him and herself against charges of being communists.

In 1962 von Franckenstein's job was reinstated, but he died a year later. Boyle turned to writing to help her cope with her loss. *Generation without Farewell* (1960) is considered one of her finest novels and *Words that Must Somehow Be Said: Selected Essays of Kay Boyle, 1927–1984* (1985), her best collection of essays.

While teaching at San Francisco University, Boyle became an outspoken critic of America's involvement in the Vietnam War. At the age of 66 she was arrested for leading a protest. Despite these obstacles, her writing never slowed down. Her last book, a collection of poetry, was published to favorable reviews a year before her death at age 90. Kay Boyle produced 50 books in a variety of genres, most of which poignantly addressed the central moral issues of our times.

Further Reading

Boyle, Kay. *Fifty Stories.* With an introduction by David Daiches. Garden City, N.Y.: Doubleday, 1980.
———. *Three Short Novels.* Boston: Beacon, 1958.
———. *Words That Must Somehow Be Said: Selected Essays of Kay Boyle.* New York: North Point Press, 1985.
Mellen, Joan. *Kay Boyle: Author of Herself.* New York: Farrar, Straus and Giroux, 1994.
———. "Kay Boyle." In *Notable American Women: A Biographical Dictionary Completing the Twentieth Cen-*

tury, edited by Susan Ware, 74–76. Cambridge, Mass.: Belknap Press of Harvard University Press, 2004.

University of Delaware Library. "Kay Boyle Papers, 1930–1991." University of Delaware Special Collections Department. Available online. URL: http://www.lib.udel.edu/ud/spec/findaids/boyle_k.htm. Downloaded on January 19, 2007.

Bradstreet, Anne Dudley
(1612–1672) *poet*

Anne Bradstreet was the first major American poet. Her work and her genius have been praised by writers from the 17th to the 20th centuries, including recent poets such as John Berryman and ADRIENNE RICH. "To have written the first good poems in America, while rearing eight children, lying frequently sick, keeping house at the edge of the wilderness," said Rich, "was to have managed a poet's range and extension within confines as severe as any American poet has confronted."

Anne Dudley was born in Northampton, England, in 1612. Her parents were prosperous, highly cultured, and devout Puritans—Protestant dissenters who adhered to strict religious discipline. Her father was chief steward to the earl of Lincoln, and during her preteen years she was allowed to use the nobleman's extensive library, where she read and was influenced by the works of Edmund Spenser and Sir Walter Raleigh. Anne was never formally educated but was tutored in religion, especially the Scriptures, and in Latin, the natural sciences, and poetry. Both she and her sister Mercy would become published poets.

At 16, Anne married a childhood friend, Simon Bradstreet, a 25-year-old college graduate who also worked as the earl's steward. Two years later, in 1630, the Bradstreets and the Dudleys joined a large group of Puritans who emigrated to America to escape religious persecution. Initially Bradstreet believed she had made a terrible mistake by leaving the comforts of civilized England for such primitive living conditions. "But after I was convinced it was the way of God," she recalled, "I submitted to it and joined to the Church at Boston. . . . [I]t was a new world and new manners."

The Bradstreets moved frequently within Massachusetts Bay Colony. They first lived in Charlestown and Cambridge, and then moved to Ipswich, where Anne was part of a community of Puritans who believed in educating women and who encouraged her to study science and write poetry.

In 1642 Bradstreet presented her father, then governor of Massachusetts Bay Colony, with several of her major poems, including what she called the "quaternions"—vivid descriptions of human and natural history and of physiology.

In 1647 the Bradstreets settled permanently in Andover, where the minister, John Woodbridge, was the poet's brother-in-law. In 1650, without Anne Bradstreet's knowledge, Woodbridge took her poems to England and arranged for them to be published as *The Tenth Muse Lately Sprung Up in America* (1650). The collection was extremely "vendible," or salable, in London. Thirty-eight years old when it appeared, and soon to give birth to the last of eight children, Bradstreet—confined by her Puritan modesty—continued to write privately, maturing as a poet, but hiding her work.

The American edition of *The Tenth Muse*—the first collection of verse produced in the New World—was published in a revised, expanded form in 1678, six years after Bradstreet's death. Entitled *Several Poems, Compiled with Great Variety of Wit and Learning, Full of Delight,* it included 18 previously unpublished poems. One of them, "Contemplations," is considered to be Bradstreet's finest. In it the poet is called upon to witness and participate in the process of perfecting Creation.

While Bradstreet's early verse was rather formal and stiff, many of her later poems, such as "Contemplations," as well as her prose, were more fluid, original, and personal. In her autobiographical letter "To my Dear Children," the "pioneer mother" was candid about how she had questioned religion during her teenage years, especially when she found her heart was "more carnal, and sitting loose from God."

Bradstreet's later poems were mostly written for her family. In "To My Dear and Loving Husband," she wrote tenderly: "If ever two were one, then surely we. / If ever man were loved by wife, then thee." She was dedicated to her children and to Simon Bradstreet, who twice served as governor of the Massachusetts Bay Colony.

Although she fully accepted the Puritan creed and her role as "First Lady," Bradstreet had a feisty spirit. Occasionally she allowed herself a flash of feminist anger, such as in her elegy to Queen Elizabeth (1643):

> Nay masculines, you have thus taxed us long.
> But she, though dead, will vindicate our wrong.
> Let such as say our sex is void of reason,
> Know 'tis slander now but once was treason.

America's first poet, who wrote in the "few hours, curtailed from sleep and other refreshment." Anne Bradstreet died at the age of 60 on September 16, 1672, in Andover. A scholarly edition of her complete works, both prose (mostly aphorisms) and poetry, was finally published in 1867, two centuries after her death.

Further Reading

"Anne Bradstreet." Celebrating Anne Bradstreet Web site. Available online. URL: http://www.annebradstreet.com/anne_bradstreet_bio_001.htm. Downloaded on January 19, 2007.

Bradstreet, Anne. *The Works of Anne Bradstreet.* Edited by Jeannine Hensley, with a foreword by Adrienne Rich. Cambridge, Mass.: Belknap Press of Harvard University Press, 2004.

Gordon, Charlotte. *Mistress Bradstreet: The Untold Life of America's First Poet.* New York: Little, Brown, and Company, 2005.

Rosenmeier, Rosamond. *Anne Bradstreet Revisited.* Boston: Twayne Publishers, 1991.

∾ Brent, Linda
See JACOBS, HARRIET ANN

∾ Brooks, Gwendolyn
(1917–2000) *autobiographer, poet, novelist*

Gwendolyn Brooks's insightful poetry reflected both her artistry and her commitment to and support of the black community. In 1950 she became the first black woman to win the Pulitzer Prize in poetry. She also held the Illinois laureateship (succeeding Carl Sandburg) and was the Consultant in Poetry at the Library of Congress. Brooks, with more than 25 books to her credit, is considered one of the finest African-American poets in America.

Gwendolyn Brooks was born on June 7, 1917, in Topeka, Kansas, but moved at an early age to Chicago. By the time she was 11 Gwendolyn was keeping a poetry notebook, and as a teenager her poems were published frequently in several magazines. In her autobiography, *Report from Part One* (1972), Brooks recalls growing up in a supportive family, with a "quick-walking, careful, duty-loving mother" and a father "with kind eyes, songs and tense recitation" for his children. Her mother, Keziah Corinne (Wims) Brooks, encouraged her daughter to read and write poetry and to attend poetry readings.

With her mother's prodding, Gwendolyn met and submitted her body of work to Langston Hughes. The renowned African-American poet told the young poet that she "must go on writing." When in 1940 she did not win a poetry contest because her poem, "The Ballad of Pearl May Lee," was considered too militant, Hughes objected, but to no avail.

As an adolescent, Gwendolyn's favorite poets were EMILY DICKINSON, Keats, and Shelley. She admired their ability to achieve "wonders with language," something she, too, was able to achieve in her carefully crafted verse. Brooks was a master at combining black idioms, jazz rhythms, and street slang with the traditional "high style" of English poetry. "I don't like suggesting that the writing of poetry is a magic process," Brooks wrote in her autobiography, "but it seems you really do have to go into a *bit* of a trance, a self-cast trance, because 'brainwork' seems unable to do it all, to do the whole job."

Although Brooks experienced a happy childhood, with "two fine parents and one brother, in a plain but warmly enclosing two-story gray house," she also recalls a dearth of celebrations for "any black glory or black greatness or grandeur" in her home or in any black household in the neighborhood. Especially in her later work, Brooks would focus on expressing and celebrating, through the "wonders of language," black greatness.

After graduating in 1937 from Chicago's Wilson Junior College, Brooks was hired as a housekeeper. She later worked as a secretary to a spiritual adviser, and for several years was the publicity director for the National Association for the Advancement of Colored People's Youth Council in Chicago. But no matter where she was employed she managed to carve out the time to work on her poetry.

In 1939 Brooks married Henry Lowington Blakely II and had two children. In 1941 she was invited by a wealthy Chicago socialite to participate in a workshop for new poets, where she was introduced to the poetry of the major modernist poets, such as T. S. Eliot and Ezra Pound. Incorporating what she learned from their rigorous techniques with her own unique sense of rhythm and style, it was not long before Brooks began to win poetry prizes, including several Midwestern Writers' Conference awards.

In 1945, when she was 28, her first book of verse, *A Street in Bronzeville* (1945), was published. That same year she was named one of the "Ten Young Women of the Year" by *Mademoiselle* magazine.

Guggenheim fellowships in 1946 and 1947 enabled Brooks to put together the 1950 Pulitzer Prize–winning book of poetry *Annie Allen* (1949), the ostensible subject of which was war but which, at a deeper level, concerned the struggle between the sexes. She then completed her only novel, *Maude Martha* (1953), a semiautobiographical story about a black woman's trying experiences as a wife and mother. But believing that "marriage should get most of a wife's attention," she "scarcely put pen to paper" for a year after her son, Henry, was born.

Her next volume of poems, *The Bean Eaters* (1960), depicts—as do other books written during the early 1960s—a vivid, realistic, and complex picture of life and racial injustice in Chicago's black neighborhoods. In 1963 her first volume of collected works, *Selected Poems,* was published. It included poetry from her first three books and several new poems.

In 1967 Brooks's personal attitudes and writing career were profoundly affected after attending the Second Black Writers' Conference at Fisk University in Nashville, Tennessee. It was there that she met a group of articulate young black poets who believed that "black poets should write as blacks, about blacks, and address themselves *to* blacks." Brooks concurred with them—"they seemed proud and so committed to their people," she told an interviewer—and pledged herself to write poetry that would successfully "call" all black people. She was determined to write poems that she could "take into a tavern, into the street, into the halls of a housing project."

In *Report from Part One* Brooks explains that at the conference she was awakened to the realization that the "black emphasis must be not *against* white but *for* black." Her next three books of poems—*In the Mecca* (1968), a lengthy poetic sequence about the diverse aspects of living in a Chicago housing project; *Riot* (1969); and *Black Steel: Joe Frazier and Muhammad Ali* (1971)—reflect a greater and more militant black consciousness than her past works.

For Brooks, the 1960s were "independent fire!", and she describes her poetic career as falling into two distinct phases: "pre-1967" and "post-1967." The later poems discuss, more directly, racial issues, and are less concerned with social themes. They use more open, less traditional poetic forms and techniques.

After publishing her books with Harper and Row for 16 years, Brooks, in 1969, in her quest to support the black community and to have more control over her career, decided to switch to black-owned independent presses in Detroit and Chicago. In 1980 she started her own publishing company, the Brooks Press, followed by David Company of Chicago, named after her father.

In 1971 Brooks traveled to East Africa to discover her roots, and in 1975 she conducted a poetry workshop for the Blackstone Rangers, a group of black teenagers from Chicago. Her goal was to encourage young people to think and write about the positive aspects of being African American.

While increasingly serving as a black activist and community leader, Brooks remained first and foremost a writer. In the 1970s, 1980s, and 1990s, she published prolifically. Her works of this period included an autobiography; several books of poetry for children; essays in a variety of magazines; and 10 more volumes of poetry, including the critically acclaimed *To Disembark* (1981); *Winnie* (1988), a paean for the South African activist Winnie Mandela; and *Children Coming Home* (1991), published by the David Company.

There were also more professional accolades: In 1968 she was appointed poet laureate of Illinois, and established the Illinois Poet Laureate Awards to encourage young students to write. In 1976 she became the first black woman to be elected to the National Institute of Arts and Letters. In honor of her 70th birthday, 70 writers paid tribute to the powerful artistic and social impact Brooks has had on the black, as well as the larger, community in a book entitled *Say That the River Turns: The Impact of Gwendolyn Brooks* (1987).

Well into her 80s, Brooks still considered herself a student who is constantly learning about herself and the world. Her work continued to reflect an awareness of current events and political oppression, from the release of the African leader Nelson Mandela to the student uprising in China's Tiananmen Square. Nora Brooks Blakely, her daughter, remarked that her mother "more than anything else . . . is a mapper . . . delineating and defining the scenery of now."

In addition to writing and her commitment to black heritage, Brooks considered family a "sustaining force in her life." She dedicated *Blacks* (1987), a collection of selected poems—mostly gleaned from her later work—to the memory of her beloved parents.

Brooks held more than 50 honorary doctorates and in 1989 was awarded a major lifetime achievement grant by the National Endowment for the Arts. She has also taught poetry at numerous colleges and universities. In the late 1990s she was a professor of English at Chicago State University, where in 1993 the Gwendolyn Brooks Center for Black Literature and Creative Writing was established.

In *Report from Part One,* Brooks said that she had "gone the gamut" from an almost angry rejection of her dark skin to "a surprised queenhood in the new Black sun." Gwendolyn Brooks, who died in December 2000, at 83, searched for and discovered a poetic and political response to her identity and her life.

Further Reading

Brooks, Gwendolyn. *Blacks.* Chicago: David Company, 1987.

———. *Report from Part One.* Detroit, Mich.: Broadside Press, 1972.

———. *Selected Poems.* New York: Harper and Row, 1963.

Bryant, Jacqueline, ed. *Gwendolyn Brooks' Maude Martha: A Critical Collection.* Chicago: Third World Press, 2002.

Gayles, Gloria Wade, ed. *Conversations with Gwendolyn Brooks.* Jackson: University Press of Mississippi, 2003.

Kent, George E. *A Life of Gwendolyn Brooks.* Lexington: University Press of Kentucky, 1990.

Muse, Daphne. "She Took Us to Our Literary Mecca: A Tribute to Gwendolyn Brooks." December 20, 2000. Available online. URL: http://www.interchange.org/msbrooks/htm. Downloaded on February 25, 2007.

Yemish, Jimoh A. "Gwendolyn Brooks (1917–2000)." *The Literary Encyclopedia.* December 27, 2001. Available online. URL: http://www.litencyc.com/php/speople.php?rec=true&UID=4931. Downloaded on January 19, 2007.

Brown, Margaret Wise (Golden MacDonald)
(1910–1952)   *children's book writer*

In a burst of creative energy that spanned approximately 15 years, Margaret Wise Brown wrote more than 100 books for children. A few, such as *The Runaway Bunny* and *Goodnight Moon,* remain best-selling classics that continue each year to delight and engross new young readers.

Born to prosperous parents on May 23, 1910, in Brooklyn, New York, Margaret moved frequently with her family. For playmates she relied on her two siblings and her menagerie of pets, including 30 rabbits. She also had her imagination and recalls "living in countries of the worlds I made up."

When Margaret was 13 she spent two years at a boarding school in Lausanne, Switzerland. She attended several other schools, including Dana Hall, a private school in Wellesley, Massachusetts. In spite of her father's reservations ("girls should just get married"), Brown enrolled at Hollins College in Virginia where she received an A.B. degree in 1932.

In 1935 Brown moved to New York City and registered at the Bank Street College of Education. She befriended the college's founder, Lucy Sprague Mitchell, who helped her understand perception as it developed in young children. Encouraged by Mitchell, Brown decided to concentrate on writing children's books instead of teaching kindergartners. In 1937 she easily sold her first book, *When the Wind Flew.* It did well, as did *The Streamlined Pig* (1938). Brown had found her vocation.

In addition to writing, she spent four years as an editor of children's books for William R. Scott, where she was responsible for signing up the illustrious modernist writer GERTRUDE STEIN. She also published her own stories with William R. Scott, including the enormously popular *Noisy Book* (1939).

In 1942 Brown gave up editing and worked full time as a writer. "I finish the rough draft in twenty minutes," she said in a 1947 interview with *Publishers Weekly,* "and then I spend two years polishing, sometimes polishing twenty-three books more or less simultaneously." She became a master at describing, as she put it, a child's reality.

The Runaway Bunny (1941), one of her most notable and touching tales, was illustrated by Clement Hurd, who was also responsible for the memorable drawings in Brown's most famous children's book, *Goodnight Moon* (1947). The comforting bedtime story begins, simply: "In the great green room. . . ." Millions of children since have joined the bunny in saying goodnight to each object in the room, and to the old lady whispering "hush." In 1947 Brown won the prestigious Caldecott Medal for *The Little Island* (1946), which was written under the pseudonym Golden MacDonald; occasionally she used other pen names. She also wrote approximately 100 songs for children.

In spite of a large circle of friends and admirers, Brown looked forward to leaving New York and spending time alone at "Only House," her rustic summer home off the coast of Maine. She needed the solitude, ocean, and woods to rekindle her imagination.

Margaret Wise Brown was only 42 when she died unexpectedly on November 13, 1952, while vacationing in France. But her simple, sensible, evocative picture books will endure in what she called "the timeless world of children."

Further Reading

Brown, Margaret Wise. *Goodnight Moon.* New York: HarperTrophy, 1975.

Greene, Carol. *Margaret Wise Brown: Author of Goodnight Moon.* Chicago: Childrens Press, 1993.

Marcus, Leonard S. *Margaret Wise Brown: Awakened by the Moon.* New York: Harper Paperbacks, 1999.

ᐃ Brown, Rita Mae
(1944–   )   *novelist, poet, screenwriter*

A comedic popular novelist, Rita Mae Brown is perhaps best known as the author of *Rubyfruit Jungle,* the picaresque, best-selling story of an outrageous, outspoken, well-adjusted lesbian. Like Brown, her fictional characters are often rebellious but successful women who know how to triumph in the face of adversity and how to enjoy life.

Rita Mae Brown was born on November 18, 1944, in Hanover, Pennsylvania. An orphan, she was adopted by Ralph, a butcher, and Julia Buckingham Brown. "I was blessed with a mother and father who did everything humanly possible to activate my mind," Brown wrote in *Starting from Scratch: A Different Kind of Writers' Manual* (1988). "I was reading when I was three. I loved Latin, especially Horace, and read it fluently. When I was eight my dad gave me a huge Underwood typewriter. He traded some meat for it."

In 1955 the Browns moved to Fort Lauderdale, Florida. "You can't imagine how beautiful Florida was then before they paved it over with concrete," Brown, who by then was a top-notch tennis player, later recalled. In 1962 she attended the University of Florida at Gainesville on a full scholarship but was forced to leave when she was accused—unjustly, she insists—of engaging in illegal civil rights activities.

In the 1960s and early 1970s, Brown became increasingly involved in radical politics and was a leader in the early women's liberation movement, especially lesbian and gay rights. She moved to New York City in 1964 and received a bachelor's degree from New York University in 1968, as well as a cinematography certificate from New York School of Visual Arts.

Brown's first book of poetry, *The Hand That Cradles the Rock* (1971), was called ribald and lewd by some reviewers. A writer with many talents, that same year she translated six medieval Latin plays for New York University Press.

Rubyfruit Jungle (1973), Brown's first and most enduring novel, was considered groundbreaking because the central character and hero was a multilayered, interesting, likeable lesbian. Described by *Ms.* magazine as "an inspiring, bravado adventure story of a female Huck Finn named Molly Bolt," the semibiographical novel was rejected by every major New York publishing company. It was accepted by a small feminist press, Daughters, Inc., where it sold unexpectedly well. Bantam Books acquired the rights to the work in 1977. Since then it has sold over a million copies and has been widely translated. Brown claims that *Rubyfruit Jungle* is so successful because it makes readers laugh, and humor is a quality rarely found in books dealing with homosexual life. "It's hard to hate people when they're funny," said Brown, who defines herself as bisexual.

During the early 1970s Brown became a research fellow at the Institute of Policy Studies in Washington, D.C. In 1973 she put together a collection of her early political essays, *A Plain Brown Rapper*. With the assistance of a grant from the National Endowment for the Arts, she was able to finish *Six of One* (1978), another semiautobiographical best-selling and upbeat novel about a clan of female relatives. "As a girl," Brown recalled, "I never saw a woman knuckle under to a man. . . . The women were dominating characters."

Working from her home in Charlottesville, Virginia, during the 1980s and 1990s, Brown produced a collection of selected poems, about a dozen novels, a mystery series (including in 1998 the fifth of the Mrs. Murphy books, *Murder on the Prowl,* which she supposedly coauthored with Sneaky Pie Brown, a cat), a memoir, and an unorthodox writers' manual. In the latter, Brown advises aspiring writers to trust their instincts. "Creativity comes from trust. Never insult your readers' intelligence nor take away the joy of discovery. . . . True fiction is always lived from within and deeply felt."

In 2005 Brown wrote, as always with her feline collaborator Sneaky Pie Brown, the 13th book in the Mrs. Murphy series, *Cat's Eyewitness*. A reviewer for *Publishers Weekly* noted that in *Cat's Eyewitness,* "the animals' wry observations on human nature and beliefs amuse as ever [in Brown's work]."

When asked by *Bookreporter.com* reviewer Bethanne Kelly Patrick in April 2004 about the origins of cowriting books with her tiger cat, Brown replied that Sneaky Pie had informed her they should work together. "She wanted to do mysteries but I was horrified, considering genre fiction the suburbs of literature. I have come to repent my original evaluation because Sneaky Pie and the mystery structure have taught me a great deal about driving forward plot. Those lessons now carry over into my own novels."

Beginning in 2000 the ever-prolific Brown added another popular series to her repertoire.

Outfoxed (2000) was the first in the Jane Arnold foxhunting novels and was described by a reporter for the *San Jose Mercury News* as a "rich, atmospheric murder mystery . . . rife with love, scandal . . . redemption, greed and nobility." The fourth novel in the series is *The Hunt Ball* (2005), again featuring Jane Arnold as the foxhound master from the Virginia countryside who solves mysteries involving human and animal characters. "Fans of the cunning animal sleuths will enjoy their antics and the spot-on descriptions of the horse-show circuit," according to *Kirkus Reviews.* In 2007 Brown published a 14th book, *Puss 'N Cahoots,* in the Mrs. Murphy Mystery Series.

As a screen and television writer, Brown received two Emmy award nominations for "I Love Liberty," a variety show; and "The Long Hot Summer," a 1985 ABC miniseries.

Although committed to depicting gay characters in a positive way, Brown is more interested in "emotional truth" than in classification by race, sex, or sexual preference. In a 1978 interview with *Publishers Weekly,* she asserted that "On the page all humans really are created equal. . . . All lives are worthy of concern and description. . . . Next time anybody calls me a lesbian writer I'm going to knock their teeth in. I'm a writer and I'm a woman and I'm from the South and I'm alive, and that is that."

Rita Mae Brown's fiction is populated by flamboyant, resilient, intelligent women who also happen to be funny, passionate, and, for the most part, happy. "Writing," she says, "makes me happy."

Further Reading

Brown, Rita Mae (and Sneaky Pie Brown). *Cat's Eyewitness.* New York: Bantam, 2005.
———. *The Hunt Ball.* New York: Ballantine Books, 2005.
———. *Puss 'N Cahoots.* New York: Bantam, 2007.
———. *Rita Will: Memoir of a Literary Rabble-Rouser.* New York: Bantam, 1997.
———. *Rubyfruit Jungle.* New York: Bantam, 1977.
———. *Three More Mrs. Murphy Mysteries in One Volume: Pay Dirt; Murder, She Meowed; Murder on the Prowl.* San Antonio, Tex.: Wings Press, 2005.
"Rita Mae Brown." Books 'n' Bytes. Available online. URL: http://www.booksnbytes.com/authors/brown_ritamae.html. Downloaded on January 19, 2007.
Ward, Carol M. *Rita Mae Brown.* New York: Twayne, 1993.

Buck, Pearl Comfort Sydenstricker (John Sedges)
(1892–1973) *novelist, biographer*

The first woman to receive the Nobel Prize in literature, Pearl S. Buck published more than 100 books and received more than 300 humanitarian awards. A prolific writer who spent the first half of her life in China and the second half in America, Buck is the author of *The Good Earth,* one of the highest selling novels ever published.

Born in Hillsboro, West Virginia, on June 26, 1892, Pearl Comfort Sydenstricker was three months old when she moved with her parents, who were Presbyterian missionaries, to China. As a child Pearl had Chinese playmates and often thought of herself as Chinese. Only when someone made fun of her light hair or blue eyes, or when her family celebrated American holidays, would she realize she was a foreigner. All her life Pearl Buck experienced the conflict of identifying with two very different cultures.

Educated at missionary schools and by a Confucian tutor, Buck learned to speak Chinese before she spoke English and to read and write in Chinese by the time she was eight. She loved listening to Chinese folktales and stories but also enjoyed philosophy, the Bible, and British and American literature, especially the novels of Charles Dickens. Grateful that her schooling was equal to that offered boys, she wrote that she was "not corrupted by home economics or cookery, or any such soft substitute for hard things."

Buck's mother, recognizing her daughter's talent, encouraged her to submit her writings for publication. By the time she was 10 she was published regularly in the *Shanghai Mercury,* an English-language newspaper, and had won several prizes for contributing the best stories and articles.

After returning to the United States in 1910, Buck attended Randolph-Macon Woman's College in Lynchburg, Virginia. An outstanding and popular student, she graduated in 1914 and planned to stay on and teach at the college. But in 1917 she rushed back to China to take care of her seriously ill mother. That same year she married John Lossing Buck, an American agriculturist employed by the Presbyterian Mission Board.

The newly married couple moved to northern China, where Buck learned firsthand about Chinese peasant farmers. "They were closest to the earth, to birth and death, to laughter and to weeping," she wrote. Many years later she would set some of her best fiction in rural China.

In 1920 Buck was elated when she gave birth to a baby girl, Carol. Using an attic room with a view of her favorite mountain, she began to write in earnest and was delighted when the *Atlantic Monthly* magazine accepted an article about China. She happily took care of Carol, taught English literature at the University of Nanking, and in her spare time wrote short stories and articles. But in 1924 the Bucks realized something was terribly wrong with Carol. Fearing that she was mentally retarded, the Bucks traveled to the United States for "certain medical care not then to be had in China." While in America, Buck managed to earn a master's degree at Cornell University, sell her first story to *Asia Magazine,* and win a Cornell-sponsored writing prize for an essay entitled "China and the West." With the prize money she bought an otherwise unaffordable warm winter coat.

After learning that Carol was, indeed, mentally retarded, Buck temporarily gave up writing to take care of her and another daughter, Janice, whom the Bucks had adopted. The China they returned to in 1927 was experiencing tumultuous civil strife; When Chiang Kai-shek's anti-Western Nationalist forces attacked Nanking, the Bucks feared for their lives and were forced to flee. A Chinese friend hid them until they could escape to Japan. Once it was deemed safe they returned to Nanking, where their home had been nearly destroyed along with one of Buck's manuscripts. This was one of several times

Pearl Buck was the first American woman to win the Nobel Prize in literature.
(AP/Wide World Photos)

Buck faced imminent danger in China, only sharpening her sense of drama, which she applied to her fiction.

In 1929 Buck returned briefly to the United States to place Carol in a special home for the mentally retarded. The good news was that her first novel, *East Wind: West Wind,* a story about the conflict between traditional Chinese and modern Western ideas in an extended Chinese family, would be published in 1930. It was the first, but far from the last, time that Buck would explain China to the West through fiction.

A year later Buck's second—considered her greatest—novel, *The Good Earth,* came out. The sympathetic and moving portrayal of the Wang Lungs, a Chinese peasant family, struck a chord with Western readers. A worldwide best seller, *The*

Good Earth won the Pulitzer Prize in 1931, sold millions of copies, and was translated into more than 60 languages. Although Buck revelled in her unexpected success and fortune, at the same time her marriage was falling apart.

In 1935 Buck divorced John Lossing Buck (she retained his last name) and married her publisher, Richard J. Walsh. In spite of her own doubts, Walsh had encouraged her to publish *The Good Earth,* believing it to be an epic of "permanent importance, one that will rank with the great novels of the soil." The couple moved to an old stone farmhouse in Bucks County, Pennsylvania, where they adopted four children.

Buck continued to write at a furious pace. Two more novels, *Sons* (1932) and *A House Divided* (1935), completed the Wang Lung family trilogy. She also translated a two-volume classic Chinese novel, *Shui Hu Chuan,* into English and wrote a compelling novel titled *The Mother* (1934) that vividly described a Chinese peasant's experiences with childbirth and abortion. In 1936 Buck published well-received biographies of each of her parents, both of whom had died. She especially admired her mother, a loving, warm, courageous, and independent woman who had supported Chinese famine refugees and who had served as her role model.

In 1938, a mere eight years after the publication of her first book, Pearl S. Buck became the first woman and, other than TONI MORRISON, the only American woman (as of 2006), to receive the Nobel Prize in literature. "You . . . cannot perhaps fully understand what it means . . . that it is a woman who stands here," she explained to the Swedish king upon being presented with the prestigious award.

Buck's longstanding advocacy for women's issues is evident in much of her work, particularly in the autobiographical novel *The Proud Heart* (1938) and a collection of essays titled *Of Men and Women* (1971). She also wrote novels with subjects as varied as the assimilation of Chinese Jews, in *Peony* (1948), and the dowager empress of China, in *Imperial Woman* (1956).

Many Americans learned for the first time about the "mysterious and exotic" Far East from Buck's books and articles. For several decades she was writing as many as five books a year, plus innumerable magazine articles, guidebooks for American servicemen in Asia, poetry, short stories, plays, and children's books, in part to help support her growing family.

She was also very involved with humanitarian causes. In 1949 Buck founded Welcome House, an adoption agency for Asian-American children located at the family's Pennsylvania farmhouse; to set a good example, she and Walsh adopted a half-dozen children of mixed races. "My mother was the first to initiate the idea of interracial adoption," noted Buck's son Edgar Walsh in 2004. "It is one of her legacies and goes so far beyond her writing." Because she openly supported feminism, tolerance, internationalism, and multiculturalism, Buck was considered controversial by some Americans. She wrote five books, all of which were set in America, under the pen name John Sedges so that her politics and gender would not influence the way her work was reviewed.

Under her own name, from 1939 to 1949, 10 more novels were published. In 1950 she decided to share the poignant account of her retarded daughter's life: Buck wrote *The Child Who Never Grew* (1950) to lend support to other parents with retarded children who might be feeling isolated or despairing. In 1954 Buck wrote an autobiography, *My Several Worlds,* in which she described her Chinese/American "mentally bifocal life." It, too, was widely read. During the last years of her life, she remained a prominent figure: a 1966 national poll showed she was among the 10 most admired American women.

When she was not writing novels, short stories, essays, and plays, she dedicated her time to issues related to civil liberties, rights for children with special needs, and women's rights. In 1964 she established the Pearl S. Buck Foundation to assist Asian-American children and their mothers.

In 2004 *The Good Earth* was selected by Oprah Winfrey, the influential and popular talk show host, for Oprah's Book Club, which claims to be the biggest book club in the world, with more than a half a million members. A paperback edition of Buck's epic tale was produced in 2004 especially for Oprah's Book Club.

The Good Earth sold 1,800,000 copies in its first year. According to Pan Jianfeng, a reporter for *Chinadaily.com,* as of October 2004 *The Good Earth* had undergone more than 800,000 reprints, "astonishing for a book over 70 years old." The Pearl S. Buck phenomenon, wrote Jiangeng, used to be controversial and rejected by both the Chinese and American literary worlds. But Buck and her books have reappeared in the spotlight in recent years as a "friendly cultural bridge between the East and the West." *The Good Earth* became the focus of news reports in June 2007, when the original 400-page manuscript, replete with Buck's handwritten edits, was recovered when one of Buck's former secretaries tried to put it up for auction. Buck had assumed the typewritten manuscript had been stolen from her home around 1966.

An enormously popular storyteller and one of the most widely translated authors in the history of American literature, Pearl S. Buck died on March 6, 1973, in Danby, Vermont, at the age of 81. She was surrounded by half-completed manuscripts, including a novel she was working on about the descendants of Wang Lung. Today, the royalties from her books continue to help fund the humanitarian programs she helped to establish.

Buck had received a Nobel Prize "for her rich and genuine epic description of peasant life in China and for her biographical masterpieces." Combining the Christianity of her missionary parents with Chinese traditions from her youth, Buck wrote "for the masses," for ordinary people who responded to the universal themes in her stories.

Further Reading

Buck, Pearl S. *The Good Earth* (Oprah's Book Club edition). New York: Washington Square Press, 2004.

———. *Imperial Woman: A Novel.* New York: J. Day, 1956.

———. *My Several Worlds: A Personal Record.* New York: John Day, 1954.

———. *Peony.* Wakefield, R.I.: Moyer Bell, 1996.

Conn, Peter J. *Pearl S. Buck: A Cultural Biography.* New York: Cambridge University Press, 1996.

Jianfeng, Pan. "Renewing the Bridge between East and West." *Chinadaily.com.* Available online. URL: http://www.chinadaily.com.cn/english/doc/2004-10/19/content_383725.htm. Downloaded on January 19, 2007.

Shiels, Barbara. "Pearl S. Buck." In *Winners: Women and the Nobel Prize,* 115–145. Minneapolis, Minn.: Dillon, 1985.

Stirling, Nora B. *Pearl Buck: A Woman in Conflict.* Piscataway, N.J.: New Century, 1983.

Butler, Octavia Estelle
(1947–2006) *science fiction, short story writer*

One of America's few black women science fiction writers, Octavia E. Butler's characters are frequently strong, independent African-American women living in a future society that is multiracial and based on sexual equality. According to *Fantasy Review* (July 1984), the author placed her protagonists in love stories that are "mythic, bizarre, exotic and heroic and full of doom and transcendence."

Born on June 22, 1947, in Pasadena, California, Octavia Estelle Butler was a quiet, shy child who was raised by her mother and grandmother in an integrated, culturally diverse neighborhood. An avid reader, by the age of 12 she was devouring every available science fiction book or magazine. She also began to write her own science fiction stories and submit them to magazines.

After graduating from Pasadena City College in 1968, and taking courses at the University of California in Los Angeles, in 1970 Butler attended the Clarion Science Fiction Writers' Workshop in Clarion, Pennsylvania. There she met and worked with established science fiction writers who offered her practical, valuable advice about the genre she had chosen as her career.

Popular among both readers and critics of science fiction who admire her chilling, well-paced, futuristic tales of despair and hope, Butler has garnered several notable awards, including the 1984 Hugo Award for her short story "Speech Sounds"

(1983); in 1985, she received three of science fiction's top honors: the Hugo, Nebula, and Locus awards, all for "Bloodchild," a story about enslavement and human males who bear children of an alien race.

Butler was best known for a series of five books set in the world of the "Patternists": *Patternmaster* (1976), *Mind of My Mind* (1977), *Survivor* (1978), *Wild Seed* (1980), and *Clay's Ark* (1984). The Patternist saga spans hundreds of years, both past and future, and depicts a society dominated by an elite group of telepaths whose 4,000-year-old leader is a tyrannical murderer. His daughter organizes the telepaths to collectively defeat her father and end his destructive reign over the Patternists. For Butler, a like-minded community can and should unite to vanquish evil individuals and to break down racial and gender barriers.

Unlike Butler's other work, her 1979 novel *Kindred* is more of a "historical fantasy" than a science fiction novel. Its heroine, Dana, is a contemporary black woman pulled back in time by her great-great-grandfather, a Southern white plantation owner. Dana must save the owner's life in order to insure her own birth in the 20th century.

Butler's second critically acclaimed series, the Xenorgensis Trilogy, is comprised of *Dawn* (1987), *Adulthood Rites* (1988), and *Imago* (1989). In the trilogy, she combined her interest in sexual and racial relationships with genetic engineering and sociobiology as nomadic aliens offer mankind a second chance at survival by mixing genes to create a new, improved species.

The Earthseed Series, Butler's latest saga about the desire to reach for the stars, as told compellingly from female perspectives, began in 1994 with the publication of *Parable of the Sower*, followed four years later by *Parable of the Talents*. In 1995 Butler was the recipient of the John D. and Catherine T. MacArthur Foundation fellowship grant, awarded to talented people who demonstrate creativity and imagination in their fields; she

was the first science fiction writer to receive this so-called genius award. In 2000 Butler received the PEN Center West Lifetime Achievement Award and two years later produced her 12th novel, *Fledgling,* about ancient, peace-loving, goddess-worshipping vampires.

During an interview on September 1, 2000, with National Public Radio's commentator Scott Simon, Butler commented that tolerance, like any aspect of peace, is "forever a work in progress, never completed, and, if we're as intelligent as we like to think we are, never abandoned." Scott introduced Butler as the first African-American woman to gain popularity and critical acclaim as a science fiction writer, who through her fictional tales "tries to understand and explain our differences as well as common traits shared by all humans."

Octavia E. Butler, one of the most admired science fiction writers of her generation, died in Seattle on February 24, 2006, at age 58, from an accidental fall outside her home. Jane Jewell, executive director of the Science Fiction and Fantasy Writers of America, called Butler a "world-class" writer. "She was one of the first and one of the best to discuss gender and race in science fiction."

Further Reading

Butler, Octavia E. *Bloodchild and Other Stories.* New York: Seven Stories Press, 1996.

———. *Fledgling.* New York: Seven Stories Press, 2005.

———. *Kindred.* Garden City, N.Y.: Doubleday, 1979.

———. *Parable of the Talents.* New York: Warner Books, 2000.

Sanders, Joshua. "Interview with Octavia Butler." *In Motion Magazine.* March 4, 2005. Available online. URL: http://www.inmotionmagazine.com/ac04/obutler. html. Downloaded on January 19, 2007.

Simon, Scott. "Interview with Octavia Estelle Butler and Essay on A World without Racism." National Public Radio. September 1, 2001. Available online. URL: http://www.npr.org/programs/specials/racism/010830. octaviabutleressay.html. Downloaded on January 19, 2007.

C

Cade, Miltona Mirkin
See BAMBARA, TONI CADE

Carson, Rachel Louise
(1907–1964) *nonfiction, nature writer, journalist*

In her celebrated books about the sea and the natural environment, Rachel Carson emphasized the importance of paying attention to the earth's fragile ecological system. Trained as a scientist, Carson, a gifted writer, was the author of two best-selling books: *The Sea around Us* (1951), a lyrical examination of the ocean and the creatures inhabiting it; and *Silent Spring* (1962), a dramatic indictment of the use of chemical pesticides such as DDT.

Rachel Louise Carson was born on May 27, 1907, in Springdale, Pennsylvania, a small rural town nestled in the Allegheny river valley, 11 miles from the industrialized steel center of Pittsburgh. A thoughtful, quiet child, she was raised on a hilltop farm that overlooked a river, where she enjoyed "the whole world of nature." When not studying or helping her two siblings with farm chores, she read every book available in her local library on her favorite topics—the ocean and wildlife.

Rachel's other childhood interest was creative writing. Her mother, Maria Carson, had high expectations for her daughter and encouraged her to submit her work for publication. In 1917, when she was 10, Rachel's first story, "A Battle in the Clouds," appeared in *St. Nicholas,* a popular magazine with a special section for young readers. Several other notable American women writers, such as EUDORA WELTY and EDNA ST. VINCENT MILLAY, had published their first stories or poems in *St. Nicholas.*

Assisted by a scholarship, Carson attended and in 1929 graduated magna cum laude from Pennsylvania College for Women (now Chatham College). There, she had switched her major from English to zoology after her biology teacher and mentor, Mary Scott Shinker, convinced her that she could combine science and writing. For the remainder of her life, Rachel Carson would pursue both career paths.

Carson went on to earn a master's degree in marine zoology in 1932 from Johns Hopkins University in Baltimore, Maryland. During the summers she studied at the Marine Biological Laboratory at Woods Hole, Massachusetts, where she was part of a scientific community that shared her passion for "discovering the sea" and the mysterious marine world. After her father died in 1935, followed by the death of her sister a year later, Carson moved to Silver Spring, Maryland, with her widowed mother and her sister's two daughters; she gave up the idea of getting a doctorate degree in zoology and instead became the family breadwinner.

In 1935 Carson was hired to write pamphlets and radio scripts for the U.S. Bureau of Fisheries (now the Interior Department's Fish and Wildlife Service), and in 1936 became one of the first women aquatic biologists at the bureau. Eventually she was appointed editor in chief of publications and insisted that her staff write accurate but lively, engaging articles. She spent more than 15 years working for the federal government, and during that time met and worked with many naturalists and conservationists. It was from them that she first learned about the ecological threat posed by chemical fertilizers.

Rachel Carson holds her influential best seller, *Silent Spring.*
(AP/Wide World Photos)

Carson continued to publish newspaper and magazine articles on the natural world. "It dawned on me," she wrote, "that by becoming a biologist I had given myself something to write about." She would often write late into the night and then put in a full day's work, having barely slept.

In 1937 Carson's first major article was accepted by the *Atlantic Monthly.* "Undersea" became the basis of her first book, *Under the Sea-Wind* (1941), a study of the life cycles of sea creatures and shorebirds. Although it was lauded as much for its scientific data as for its lyrical writing, the book did not sell well. A month after its publication, Japan attacked Pearl Harbor and America was plunged into World War II; there was little interest in anything except the war, including a book about the ocean's majesty. For the rest of her life, though, *Under the Sea-Wind* remained the author's favorite work.

A decade later, after extensive oceanographic research, Carson's second book came out. *The Sea around Us* (1951), originally serialized to much acclaim in the *New Yorker* magazine, was one of the first successful attempts at popularizing science. Translated into 32 languages, *The Sea around Us* was on the best seller list for 86 weeks, was made into an Academy Award-winning documentary, and received the National Book Award in 1951. At the National Book Award ceremony, Carson explained that "the winds, the sea and the moving tides are what they are. If there is wonder and beauty and majesty in them, science will discover these qualities. . . ."

Financially stable for the first time in her life, Carson left her civil service job in 1952 and devoted herself to full-time writing. *Under the Sea-Wind* was reissued and became a best seller, while a Guggenheim grant enabled her to do the research for *The Edge of the Sea* (1955), the final of her three "sea books." Once again, critics praised her ability to make the complex natural world both understandable and enjoyable for the average reader.

Professionally Carson was doing extremely well, but in 1957 her niece Marjorie died, leaving a five-year-old son, Roger, orphaned. Carson, who was 50 and caring for her gravely ill mother, adopted and raised Roger, and instilled in him a love of nature. He would often accompany her on trips to her summer home in Maine and to the Everglades.

Carson was becoming increasingly distressed about the effects of newly developed, poisonous chemical biocides that farmers used on their crops. "The more I learned about the use of pesticides the more appalled I became," Carson explained, adding that she realized she had the material for a book. "What I discovered was that everything which meant the most to me as a naturalist was being threatened, and that nothing I could do would be more important." The results of years of painstaking research, including 55 pages of references, were published in 1962 as *Silent Spring,* arguably Carson's most important, influential, and controversial book. An article in *Saturday Review* (September 19, 1962) described *Silent Spring* as a "devastating, heavily documented, relentless attack upon human carelessness, greed, and irresponsibility. . . ." Toxins and pesticides, warned Carson, represented the greatest threat to life on earth.

Silent Spring was a best seller that sold over 500,000 hardcover copies. It opened with a cautionary tale about a spring without the sounds of songbirds or small animals, and describes how the human race, by their own uncaring actions, brought death to a once beautiful, happy town. The explosive controversy surrounding the publication of *Silent Spring* cast Carson, who considered herself apolitical, in the role of environmental crusader. She felt compelled to respond to her critics, especially officials of the chemical industry who attempted to discredit her findings and her integrity. On April 3, 1963, she went on national television to present her carefully researched evidence to a large audience.

> For the first time in the history of the world, she explained, every human being is now subjected to contact with dangerous chemicals from the moment of conception until death. . . . These chemicals are now stored in the bodies of the vast majority of human beings, regardless of age.

Public concern created over *Silent Spring* convinced President John F. Kennedy to create the President's Science Advisory Committee, an eight-month investigation into the dangers of pesticides. The committee's report, issued in May 1963, agreed with the basic premises of Carson's book. Congress banned some of the more lethal poisons, such as DDT, and stricter controls were established. Other countries also passed laws regulating the chemical industry. *Silent Spring,* a scientifically based plea to stop poisoning the earth, became a springboard for a worldwide environmental movement.

When Carson became the first woman to be awarded the Audubon Medal, she warned that the battle was far from over. "Conservation is a cause that has no end. There is no point at which we can say 'our work is finished.'"

Carson made her last trip to her summer home in Maine in 1963, accompanied by her 11-year-old adopted son, with whom she shared "the miracles of nature." Shortly before her death she wrote, "It is good to know that I shall live on even in the minds of many who do not know me and largely through association with things that are beautiful and lovely." Carson died at age 56 from breast cancer on April 14, 1964, at her home in Silver Spring, Maryland, having successfully combined the two loves of her life, nature and writing, and having shared with millions of readers her profound concern for the fate of the earth. In 1980 President Jimmy Carter posthumously awarded Rachel Carson a Presidential Medal of Freedom, describing her as a "biologist with a gentle, clear voice who warned Americans of the dangers human beings themselves pose for their own environment." In 1999, *Silent Spring* was selected by New York University's journalism department as one of the top 10 works of journalism in the 20th century. Also in 1999, Modern Library, a division of Random House, named *Silent Spring* one of the top 100 best nonfiction books written in English during the 20th century, and *Time* magazine named Carson one of the top 100 scientists and thinkers of the 20th century.

Further Reading

Baldwin, Neil. "Rachel Carson (1907–1964), *The Sea around Us*." March 2003. Available online. URL: http://www.nationalbook.org/dirletter_rcarson.html. Downloaded on February 25, 2007.

Brooks, Paul, ed. *The House of Life: Rachel Carson at Work* (selections from her writings). Boston: Houghton Mifflin, 1972.

Carson, Rachel. *The Sea around Us*. New York: Oxford University Press, 1951.

———. *Silent Spring: 40th Anniversary Edition*. Boston: Houghton Mifflin, 2002.

Lear, Linda. *Rachel Carson: Witness for Nature*. New York: Henry Holt, 1997.

Sterling, Philip. *Sea and Earth: The Life of Rachel Carson*. New York: Crowell, 1970.

Waddell, Craig, ed. *And No Birds Sing: Rhetorical Analyses of Silent Spring*. Carbondale: Southern Illinois University Press, 2000.

Cather, Willa Sibert (Wilella)
(1873–1947)   *novelist, short story writer*

Pulitzer Prize–winning novelist Willa Cather is one of the most distinguished American women writers of the early 20th century. She is best known for her early novels, such as *O Pioneers!* (1913) and *My Ántonia* (1918), that she set in America's dusty Great Plains and which poignantly depict the difficulties and rewards of frontier life and the immigrant experience.

Born Willa (Wilella) Sibert Cather on December 7, 1873, in Back Creek Valley, Virginia, to a prosperous family, Willa spent the first nine years of her life in a large brick farmhouse in the lush Shenandoah Valley, where she and her six younger siblings frolicked in the surrounding woods, fields, and meadows. Although a tomboy, she also enjoyed listening to her grandmother read to her from the Bible or from *Pilgrim's Progress,* and became an avid reader at an early age.

In 1882 her family moved out west to frontier Nebraska, eventually settling in Red Cloud, "a bitter, dead little western town." Willa at first had a very difficult time adjusting to the sod huts and the dry, treeless prairie that was, she wrote, "naked as the back of your hand." She desperately missed the life she had known in verdant Virginia. In many of her novels and stories, Cather would explore the effects of transition and radical change on her characters.

Slowly Cather learned to appreciate the wind-swept wilderness: the splendor of willowy sunflowers that grew in profusion; the golden wheat rustling in the wind; and the coppery grass that blanketed the prairie "as if it had red wine spilled on it." She was equally impressed by the immigrant farmers she met, especially the tough-skinned pioneer women who, while doing their chores, recounted intriguing tales about the "Old Country," and who bravely endured many hardships, from failed crops to ice-encrusted winters. "They tried so hard to master the language, to master the soil, to hold their land, and to get ahead in the world," noted Cather, who took advantage of her immigrant neighbors' well-stocked libraries to study European culture and literature as well as Greek and Latin classics.

She also accompanied the town's doctor on house calls and decided, at 15, to become a surgeon. For four years she wore boyish clothes, cropped her hair, and called herself "William Cather, M.D.," or "Willie" for short. "Willie" preferred dissecting toads to playing with dolls.

After graduating from high school in 1891, Cather attended the University of Nebraska, graduating with a bachelor of arts degree in 1895. Her writing ability was so impressive that an English instructor sent one of her stories to a Boston magazine, which published it. When she saw her name in print, Cather changed her mind about studying medicine; she decided instead to become a professional writer.

Cather worked briefly as a newspaper correspondent in Lincoln, Nebraska, and then moved to Pittsburgh, Pennsylvania, in 1896, where she rented a room in a dreary boardinghouse and dutifully taught English and Latin to high school students; edited *Home Monthly,* a woman's magazine; and served as the arts and drama critic for a local newspaper, the *Daily Leader.* In her spare time she wrote short stories and poetry.

Willa Cather frequently wrote about the Nebraska prairie of her youth.
(AP/Wide World Photos)

In 1899 Cather developed a close relationship with Isabelle McClung, the daughter of a prominent Pittsburgh judge. Cather was invited to stay in the McClung's spacious home, and for five years she shared a bedroom with Isabelle and used one of the attic rooms for writing. During that productive period she traveled to Europe for the first time and, in 1905, she published her first collection of stories, *The Troll Garden.*

The next year Cather left Pittsburgh to accept a job in New York City as a staff writer and editor for *McClure's,* a popular magazine. Her first assignment took her to Boston where she befriended SARAH ORNE JEWETT, an established, older regional and early environmental writer from Maine whose work greatly influenced Cather. Jewett advised her

to give up editing and journalism, and to concentrate on writing fiction about the subject she knew best—the prairie.

Cather heeded her advice. In 1911 she took a leave of absence from the magazine and spent three months in upstate New York. There she revised the manuscript that would become her first novel, *Alexander's Bridge,* the story of an engineer torn between love for his wife and feelings for a woman from his youth. It was serialized in *McClure's* and published as a book in 1912.

Cather finally felt ready to declare herself a full-time writer. Between 1912 and 1923 she published five acclaimed novels. She dedicated the first of them, *O Pioneers!* (1913), to her mentor, Sarah Orne Jewett. Cather, who was not happy with *Alexander's Bridge,* considered *O Pioneers!* her first fully realized novel. The moving story about an independent, dynamic woman forced to head a prairie family earned Cather international recognition and has been translated into several languages.

In *The Song of the Lark* (1915), a story about ambivalent feelings toward living in a small midwestern town, Cather focused on another theme that would recur in much of her work: coping with internal conflicts. *My Ántonia* (1918), her most widely read novel, is another finely crafted saga about a strong, earthy immigrant woman who, "like the founders of early races," counts on her connections with a large, loving family to help her survive physical and emotional ordeals. As the Nobel Prize–winning novelist Sinclair Lewis pointed out, "Willa Cather made the outside world know Nebraska as no one else has done." He also said that she deserved the prestigious prize that he had won.

Yet it was *One of Ours* (1922), a World War I novel that was not critically well received, that earned Cather a coveted Pulitzer Prize. *A Lost Lady,* published a year later, was a very popular book that sold well even though it was not considered artistically equal to her "Nebraska" books.

In 1923 Cather released *April Twilights and Other Poems,* and in between a continuous stream of novels she published several notable collections of short stories, including *Obscure Destinies* (1932), and a few books of essays and criticism. In 1929 she was elected to the National Institute of Arts and Letters, and she received numerous literary awards and honorary degrees throughout her career.

When not traveling in Europe, Cather enjoyed the rich cultural life of New York City. She lived and worked in Greenwich Village, in an apartment she shared with Edith Lewis, who eventually became her lifelong companion and with whom she entertained writers, musicians, actors, and interesting people from all over the world.

In preparation for what many critics felt was artistically her most successful novel, *Death Comes for the Archbishop* (1927), Cather and Lewis made several visits to the ruins and deserts of Arizona and Mexico. The novel revolves around two French priests who move to the American Southwest in the mid-1800s, the period of the Spanish missions, and become involved with the spiritual development of New Mexico. Her next novel, *Shadows on the Rock* (1931), also explores this theme of alienation, from a world that had become increasingly materialistic and mechanized, and a longing for the past. Obviously, Cather had hit a nerve: *Shadows on the Rock* was the most widely read novel in America in 1932. Cather increasingly became disillusioned with modern life. "The American people are so submerged in machines that sometimes I think they can only be made to laugh and cry by machinery," she lamented, adding, in her 1936 collection of essays, *Not Under Forty*, that the world as she saw it had been "broken" in 1922.

Although Cather never married, she had a network of close friends that stretched from the Great Plains of Nebraska to the cosmopolitan streets of New York and Paris. For her, the most important goal in life was to find meaning through her work, friends, and religion—she joined the Episcopal Church in 1922 and wrote about spiritual rebirth in several of her short stories.

In her final novel, *Sapphira and the Slave Girl*, published in 1940, Cather returned to her early childhood by writing about the 19th-century Virginia of her ancestors. She believed that "most of the basic material a writer works with is acquired before the age of fifteen."

Willa Cather died on April 24, 1947, in New York. She had been preparing a collection of short stories, *The Old Beauty and Others,* which was published posthumously in 1948. Private and at times mistrustful, she left instructions forbidding the anthologizing of her work, and she requested that her correspondence and novel-in-progress be destroyed.

Although she had grown to love the prairie and had admired the courageous people who lived on it, she chose to be buried in the serene, bucolic town of Jaffrey, New Hampshire, where she had often retreated during autumn to write undisturbed. The epitaph on her tombstone is from *My Ántonia,* which Cather felt was her best work: ". . . This is happiness; to be dissolved into something complete and great." Cather, especially in her celebrated early works, was indeed one of America's great novelists and storytellers.

In recognition of her long-standing literary importance and influence, the Cather Project was founded in 2002 by members of the University of Nebraska–Lincoln department of English. In cooperation with the Willa Cather Pioneer Memorial and Education Foundation, the project maintains up-to-date archives on Cather scholarship, sponsors international seminars with topics related to the author and her work, and publishes the *Willa Cather Scholarly Edition* (University of Nebraska Press), the latest volume of which contained articles and commentaries about Cather's ecological imagination.

In September 2005 Public Broadcasting System's biography series *American Masters* devoted a program to Willa Cather. The notable historian David McCullough was featured on the documentary and commented that Cather "carefully avoided cloying imagery and sentimental vistas, however popular her novels became." The documentary also included numerous passages of Cather's prose that, noted a *New York Times* television reviewer, clearly inspired a century of female writers.

Further Reading

Cather, Willa. *My Ántonia.* Boston: Houghton Mifflin, 1915.

———. *The Novels and Stories of Willa Cather.* Boston: Houghton Mifflin, 1937–1941 (13 volumes).

———. *O Pioneers!* Boston: Houghton Mifflin, 1913.

"The Cather Project: The Life and Work of Willa Cather." Available online. URL: http://cather.unl.edu/cather project/index.html. Downloaded on January 19, 2007.

Lewis, Edith. *Willa Cather Living: A Personal Record.* Athens: Ohio University Press, 1989.

O'Brien, Sharon. *Willa Cather: The Emerging Voice.* New York: Oxford University Press, 1987.

Stout, Janis. *Willa Cather: The Writer and Her World.* Charlottesville: University Press of Virginia, 2000.

ᕗ Child, Lydia Maria Francis
(1802–1880) *novelist, nonfiction writer*

The author of more than two dozen books, Lydia Maria Child was a tireless social reformer, abolitionist, and suffragist, and, according to the *North American Review,* the nation's foremost woman writer in the mid-1800s.

Born on February 11, 1802, in Medford, Massachusetts, into a prosperous abolitionist family, Lydia Maria Francis was influenced by the progressive ideas of her brother, a Unitarian clergyman. She was also a close friend of the influential writer and reformer MARGARET FULLER. In 1824 Francis wrote her first historical novel, *Hobomok,* a romance about an interracial couple set in colonial Salem. Two years later she founded and edited America's first monthly magazine for children, *Juvenile Miscellany.*

In 1828 she married David Lee Child, a Boston lawyer and leader in the antislavery movement. Of the two, Child, who wrote prolifically, was the actual breadwinner. In 1829 she published *The Frugal Housewife,* one of America's earliest domestic advice manuals and an immediate worldwide best seller.

When Child published her most famous work, *An Appeal in Favor of That Class of Americans Called Africans,* in 1833, outraged antiabolitionists who had supported *Juvenile Miscellany* were offended by the book's proposal to educate blacks and cancelled their subscriptions. Child was forced to shut down the magazine in 1834. But the *Appeal* also got people thinking and talking about the negative moral and economic ramifications of slavery.

After moving to New York City in 1841, Child edited the *National Anti-Slavery Standard,* a weekly newspaper. In 1843 she published *Letters from New York,* a well-received collection of correspondence columns about topical subjects, such as women's rights. A year later, a collection of verse entitled *Flowers to Children* included "Boy's Thanksgiving," a poem that begins with the enduring lines: "Over the river and through the wood / To grandmother's house we go." Child continued to write stories, articles, a book on comparative religions, another on women's history, historical novels, and children's books.

The Childs returned in 1850 to the Boston area, where they were active abolitionists. After failing to get permission from the governor of Virginia to nurse the imprisoned abolitionist leader John Brown, Child produced in 1860 a pamphlet that included her fiery correspondence with the governor and a cogent survey of slavery. That same year she edited *Incidents in the Life of a Slave Girl* for the ex-slave HARRIET JACOBS.

After the Civil War, Child continued to write books about causes she believed in; one such book was *An Appeal for the Indians* (1868). She died on October 20, 1880, on her farm in Wayland, where she and her husband had sheltered fugitive slaves, at the age of 78. The great antislavery orator Wendell Phillips gave the eulogy. Child was, he said, "ready to die for a principle and starve for an idea. . . . We felt that neither fame, nor gain, nor danger, nor calumny, had any weight with her." Child was buried beside her husband in Wayland's historic burial ground.

According to a reviewer in the *New York Times,* Lydia Maria Child was a "genuine and literary adventurer" who courageously fought for humanitarian values and equal rights, and expressed her beliefs in an impressive body of work. The celebrated poet John Greenleaf Whittier noted that Child's writings on slavery had influenced statesmen who "availed themselves of her foresight and sound judgement. . . ."

Further Reading

Child, Lydia Maria. *An Appeal in Favor of Americans Called Africans.* Boston: Allen and Ticknor, 1883. (Reprinted by Arno Press, 1968.)

———. *The Freedmen's Book.* Boston: Ticknor and Fields, 1865. (Reprinted by Arno Press, 1968.)

———. *Over the River and through the Wood.* New York: Scholastic, 1987.

Clifford, Deborah Pickman. *Crusader for Freedom: A Life of Lydia Maria Child.* Boston: Beacon Press, 1992.

Goodwin, Joan. "Lydia Maria Child." *The Dictionary of Unitarian and Universalist Biography.* Available online. URL: http://www.uua.org/uuhs/duub/articles/lydia mariachild.html. Downloaded on January 19, 2007.

Karcher, Carolyn. *The First Woman in the Republic: A Cultural Biography of Lydia Maria Child.* Durham, N.C.: Duke University Press, 1994.

Kenschaft, Lori. *Lydia Maria Child: The Quest for Racial Justice.* New York: Oxford University Press, 2003.

∽ Chin, Marilyn (Mei Ling)
(1955–) *poet*

Marilyn Chin is an award-winning Asian-American poet. In witty, earthy, elegiac verse, she unflinchingly examines the conflicts and paradoxes of exile, assimilation, and loss, and the experiences of a family growing up in a foreign land.

A first-generation Chinese American born in Hong Kong on January 14, 1955, Marilyn Chin was raised in Portland, Oregon. Chin, whose father changed her name from Mei Ling to Marilyn, writes movingly about how she has had to live in two worlds.

Chin attended the University of Massachusetts at Amherst, where she majored in ancient Chinese literature and earned a bachelor of arts degree in 1977. She received an M.F.A. degree in poetry in 1981 from the University of Iowa and was the recipient of a Stegner Fellowship at Stanford University and of a National Endowment for the Arts

(NEA) Writing Fellowship. Chin was also one of 18 poets featured on Bill Moyers's public television series "The Language of Life," which aired in 1995.

In 1987 Chin published her first book of poems, entitled *Dwarf Bamboo,* which was nominated for the Bay Area Books Reviewers Award. Beginning in 1988, Chin taught creative writing at San Diego State University in California. Her second book of verse, *The Phoenix Gone, The Terrace Empty,* which was published in 1994, won the 1994 PEN/Josephine Miles Award. Many of the book's poems fuse the personal with the political, where the oppressed and the oppressor exist together, at least symbolically. In "Composed Near the Bay Bridge," a character poses the question, "Isn't *bondage,* therefore, a *kind* of freedom?"

Another topic Chin often writes about is the subjugation of Asian women, when she called "the forebearers of sorrow." In one of her poems, Chin recalls the cries of an elderly woman as she attempts to stop a relative from selling her daughter for a small amount of opium. Chin says that the woman represents "the true sacrificial vessel caught in the tides and vicissitudes of familial and global history."

Chin's third book of verse, *Rhapsody in Plain Yellow* (2002), is a fusion of Eastern and Western culture, high and popular culture, and Chinese (the title poem refers to the Han dynasty) and familial history. Topics range from immigration and exile to the poet's attempt to unravel the complexities of her family's past. "I always write from my subject position: which is a Chinese-American minority poet, born in the Chinese diaspora of Hong Kong . . . to a poor family . . . all roads are built from my personal experience . . . and, believe me, there is a lot to write about . . . ," said Chin during an interview in 2004 with Bryan Thao Worra of the *Asian American Press,* which was reprinted in *Voices from the Gaps: Women Artists and Writers of Color.*

In a review of *Rhapsody in Plain Yellow,* Carol Muske-Dukes of the *Los Angeles Times Book Review* says that "Chin's dazzling longing creates a past that becomes essential to our understanding of her elliptical and passionately insistent poetic statement." Another literary critic asserts that Chin's books have become Asian-American classics.

While serving as a Radcliffe Institute Fellow (2003–04) in Cambridge, Massachusetts, Chin worked on another book of poetry and continued her multilayered, multidimensional, intercultural singing. Currently she codirects the Master of Fine Arts program at San Diego University.

Chin's work is represented in numerous anthologies, including *Breaking Silence: An Anthology of Contemporary Asian-American Poets* (1984), *The Open Boat: Poems from Asian America* (1993), and *The Best American Poetry 1996* (1996). Her poems have also appeared in literary periodicals such as *Ploughshares, the Kenyon Review,* and *Parnassus.* A writer who straddles two cultures, Marilyn Chin is committed to expressing the sorrows and passions of both. She believes that her mission as a poet is to tell "many stories on many levels."

Further Reading

Chang, Victoria, ed. *Asian American Poetry: The Next Generation.* With a foreword by Marilyn Chin. Urbana: University of Illinois Press, 2004.

Chin, Marilyn. *Dwarf Bamboo.* Greenfield Center, N.Y.: Greenfield Review Press, 1987.

———. *The Phoenix Gone, the Terrace Empty.* Minneapolis, Minn.: Milkweed Editions, 1994.

———. *Rhapsody in Plain Yellow.* New York: W. W. Norton, 2002.

Hongo, Garrett, ed. *The Open Boat: Poems from Asian America,* 50–58. New York: Anchor/Doubleday, 1993.

Kafka, Phillipe. *(Un)doing the Missionary Position: Gender Asymmetry in Contemporary Asian American Women's Writing.* Westport, Conn.: Greenwood Press, 1997.

Madison, D. Sogini. *The Woman That I Am: The Literature and Culture of Contemporary Women of Color.* New York: St. Martin's, 1994.

Worra, Bryan Thao. "An Interview with Marilyn Chin." Voices from the Gaps: Women Artists and Writers of Color, An International Web site. Available online. URL: http://voices.cla.umn.edu/vg/interviews/aap/chin_marilyn.html. Downloaded on January 19, 2007.

Chopin, Katherine O'Flaherty
(1851–1904)   *novelist, short story writer*

Kate Chopin, whose acclaimed short stories are mostly set in the Louisiana bayou area, where the author had lived for several years, is considered one of the most important women writers of fiction in the 19th century. She was also a significant figure in American feminist literature. Best known for her novel *The Awakening,* she was critically lambasted at the time of its publication in 1899 for the book's frank portrayal of female sexuality, infidelity, and independence.

Born on February 8, 1851, in St. Louis, Missouri, into a prosperous family of Irish and Creole extraction, Katherine O'Flaherty attended rigorous convent schools, where she was encouraged to pursue writing as a career by a high school teacher who recognized her literary talent.

Kate's father died when she was five, and her mother became a wealthy widow who never remarried. During her school years Kate would seclude herself in the family attic and read voraciously. Besides being acknowledged as "one of the belles of St. Louis" when she made her "coming out" debut to society in 1868, she was also influenced by a household run by down-to-earth relatives—strong-willed women, all of whom were widows. They encouraged her to think for herself and to study music and French, which as a child she spoke more fluently than English. They were also slaveowners who supported the Confederacy during the Civil War, during which Kate's half-brother died.

Two years after graduating from the Sacred Heart Academy in St. Louis in 1868, O'Flaherty married Oscar Chopin, a prominent French-Creole cotton trader. The couple lived in New Orleans before moving to a plantation near Cloutierville, a small Creole village in northwest Louisiana which the author memorialized years later in her fiction. Busy raising a family of five sons and a daughter, Chopin had little time for creative writing during the early years of her marriage, although she kept journals and wrote impressionistic sketches.

Tragically, Chopin's husband died of malaria in 1882, leaving her "inconsolable" and in debt. She returned in 1884 to her mother's home in St. Louis and took up writing in earnest as a way to financially support her children. Although she wrote only one or two days a week so that she could spend time with her children, she produced more than a hundred short stories between 1889 and 1898, her most productive professional years. Her carefully crafted, lucid short fiction reflected what she knew best: Creole culture in the American deep South and the conflict between personal desire and societal obligations faced by married women during the Victorian era.

Chopin published her stories and sketches in popular magazines such as *Vogue, Atlantic Monthly,* and *Harper's.* She also wrote essays and a play as well as translations, particularly of fiction by the French naturalist Guy de Maupassant, whom she admired as having "escaped from tradition and authority, who had entered into himself and looked out upon life through his own being and with his own eyes."

Chopin, like de Maupassant, did not shy away from portraying characters who attempted to escape from tradition and authority. *At Fault* (1890), her first novel, revolved around a Louisiana widow who falls in love and eventually marries a Creole man who has left his alcoholic wife. It drew mixed reviews from literary critics but received national attention because of the daring subject matter.

Chopin's first collection of stories, *Bayou Folk* (1894), was praised for its "shrewdness of observation and . . . fine eye for picturesque situations." It includes perhaps Chopin's best known short story, "Desiree's Baby," in which a woman disappears into the Louisiana bayou with her baby after being accused of "possessing Negro blood." The second collection, *A Night in Acadie* (1897) focused even more blatantly on sexuality, passion, and the confines of conventional marriage.

Some of Chopin's best stories are about enduring friendships between women. For example, in "Odalie Misses Mass," an aging black woman befriends an adolescent white girl. Many of Chopin's characters are forced to cope with modern-day social problems, such as venereal disease, prostitution, and wife abuse. For most readers, Chopin's fiction was also their first encounter with American Cajun and Creole cultures, which she described sensually, colorfully, and sympathetically, in a style that some considered to be more French than American.

After her mother's death, Chopin bought her own home in St. Louis and hosted a weekly salon at which the city's avant-garde and literati gathered to discuss philosophical issues and the latest best sellers. The author's work evolved and matured as she became influenced by American women regionalists such as Sarah Orne Jewett and Mary Eleanor Wilkins Freeman, as well as by the European realists.

But Chopin's writing career came to an abrupt end after the publication of her infamous second novel, *The Awakening,* in 1889. It was sharply condemned for the behavior of its brazen heroine, Edna Pontellier, a dissatisfied wife and mother who experiences passion and fulfillment outside of her marriage with her Creole lover. Pontellier also experiences depression and ultimately commits suicide. Before drowning herself, she asserts that once "awakened," she would rather "ten times, die in the surf, heralding the way to a new world, than stand idly on the shore."

Most critics, including the novelist Willa Cather, considered the book "trite and immoral," and many libraries refused to carry it. Much to her chagrin, Chopin was ostracized by friends and acquaintances. For a readership accustomed to the pieties of late Victorian romantic fiction, the scandalous, psychological novel was too blunt and unsettling.

The Awakening remained mostly forgotten until it was rediscovered during the 1960s by a Norwegian scholar and Chopin's biographer, Per Seyersted. Since then, it has been lauded for its craftsmanship, artistry, and sensitive characterization of a strong woman trapped in a stifling marriage who found fleeting satisfaction and freedom in an extramarital relationship. Critics now hailed the same novel that earlier had been labeled "unwholesome and worthless" as "profound and evocative." The literary critic Edmund Wilson called it "uninhibited and beautifully written."

But Chopin did not live to see her masterpiece praised. Despondent after its disastrous reception, she decided not to publish her most graphic short story, "The Storm" which was eventually published in 1969. Her publisher cancelled her last short story collection, *A Vocation and a Voice* (1991), and she wrote only a few more short stories and poems before her death on August 22, 1904, in her native St. Louis, five years after *The Awakening* appeared.

During an interview for *Kate Chopin: A Re-Awakening,* a television show produced by Louisiana Public Broadcasting that premiered on June 23, 1999, Elizabeth Fox-Genovese, a professor at Emory University, said, "Chopin was very important as one of the earliest examples of modernism in the United States, or, if you wish, the cutting edge of modernism in American literature. . . . She was neither a feminist nor a suffragist; she said so. She was, nonetheless, a woman who took women extremely seriously."

Kate Chopin was a masterful regionalist who beautifully re-created life in America's sensual bayou country. She was also a precursor to writers of the contemporary feminist movement who skillfully wrote about Victorian women who attempted to establish their individuality and sexuality in spite of the confines of society.

Further Reading

Arima, Hiroko, ed. *Beyond and Alone: The Theme of Isolation in Selected Short Fiction of Kate Chopin, Katharine Ann Porter, and Eudora Welty.* Lanham, Md.: University Press of America, 2006.

Chopin, Kate. *The Awakening and Selected Stories.* Edited by Sandra M. Gilbert. New York: Penguin Classics, 2003.

———. *The Complete Works of Kate Chopin* (two volumes). Edited by Per Seyersted. Baton Rouge: Louisiana State University Press, 1969.

Seyerstad, Per. *Kate Chopin: A Critical Biography.* Baton Rouge: Louisiana State University Press, 1980.

Toth, Emily. *Unveiling Kate Chopin.* Jackson: University Press of Mississippi, 1999.

~ Chute, Carolyn
(1947–)   *novelist, short story writer*

A regional fiction writer whose working-class characters struggle to make ends meet in rural Maine, Carolyn Chute is the author of the best-selling novel *The Beans of Egypt, Maine* (1985), a well-crafted multigenerational saga about the backwoods, down-and-out, sometimes brutish and brutal, but always irrepressible Bean family and their eccentric neighbors.

At age 16, Chute—who was born in Portland, Maine, on June 14, 1947, dropped out of high school and married a factory worker, James Hawkes. By the time she was 24, Chute was divorced, had a daughter (a son from her second marriage died in infancy because, claimed Chute, proper health care was unaffordable and therefore unavailable), and had taken a series of menial jobs such as picking potatoes, washing floors, and plucking feathers off chickens.

In her spare time, however, Chute pursued a career in writing. She started writing stories when she was eight and came to believe that it was the only thing she was good at. As a part-time correspondent for the *Portland Evening Express* (1976–81), she honed her editing and writing skills: She considers herself a perfectionist who constantly edits and re-edits her work. In 1977 she won first prize for fiction at the Green Mountain Workshop in Vermont.

In 1978 she married Michael Chute, eight years her junior, and was hired as a columnist by the local *Courier Free Press.* Chute studied at night, eventually earning a high school diploma. Although she enrolled at the University of Southern Maine and took several courses, in an interview in *New Democracy Newsletter* (2000), she said she was proud to have escaped "institutional education" and never identified with intellectuals. On the contrary, when her first novel, *The Beans of Egypt, Maine,* was published in 1985, she was already a grandmother but had read only about 30 books.

"The ultimate white trash novel," is how one reviewer described *The Beans of Egypt, Maine.* Chute certainly did not spare readers the adverse effects of poverty and isolation. But because she identified with her characters, she also displayed compassion for the poor, rural, working-class families and drifters of western Maine, who are often cut off from the rewards, privileges, and education available to many middle- and upper-class city dwellers.

Elisabeth Sandberg, in *American Women Writers* (2000), points out that "it is the struggle, and the human dignity of those, like Chute herself, who have lived in hunger, shame, and deprivation that she wants to make known. Despite their enraged, violent, incestuous, tacky, frustrated, and ignorant ways, Chute's characters exact from the reader not only attention but also respect." They are, asserts Chute, ordinary people.

Although her books are peopled with rapists, drunken louts, ex-cons, womanizers, and liars, Chute also includes sympathetic, oddly appealing characters. In *The Beans of Egypt, Maine,* for example, there is Roberta Bean, whose many children—including those she had with a rapist who is the cousin of a wife-beater—love her. The Beans are multidimensional, as are their quirky neighbors, and the author describes them lyrically, with a wry sense of country humor. Sandberg notes that Chute's "shy, genial personality, combined with a disarmingly rumpled-looking exterior, contains a sharp mind within."

Chute says she intended *The Beans of Egypt, Maine* as a "story of defiance and occasional triumph." In that regard, critics have compared her to Erskine Caldwell, William Faulkner, and ALICE WALKER. At the other end of the cultural spectrum, the late rock star Kurt Cobain and his Hollywood actress and rock star wife, Courtney Love, named their daughter Frances Bean Cobain, in honor of the Bean clan.

When *The Beans of Egypt, Maine* was initially published, Chute realized she needed to make some changes. "Within minutes of its publication in 1985," explained Chute in a postscript to the finished version (1995), "I knew the book was far from finished." Initially it received a slew of negative reviews. "Chute felt the book had literally been taken from her and published before she was actually finished with it," explained Appalachian State University English professor Jerry Williamson. He commented that when Chute delivered a second, finished version of *Beans,* it was "indeed better and solves some of the moral dilemmas that some critics got hung up on in 1985."

The "finished" *Beans* startled the literary world: It became an immediate popular and critical success. When asked how she came to write such a stark, original portrait of a particular slice of rural life, Chute responded, "This book was involuntarily researched. I have lived poverty. I didn't choose it. No one would choose humiliation, pain, and rage." At the same time, Chute stated that the novel is not a biography.

In 1988 Chute released a second novel, *Letourneau's Used Auto Parts,* which takes place in the imaginary western Maine town of Miracle City. The protagonist, Big Lucien Letourneau, is the head of a large ragtag clan, a habitual philanderer, and the owner of a profitable business. He is also generous by nature and operates a free trailer park for down-and-outs and drifters. The book, which *Publishers Weekly* called "assured, complex, and memorable," offers the usual assortment of dislikable yet endearing Chute characters who have a strong sense of neighborliness, even as they make a mess of their lives.

Merry Men (1994), another novel set in rural Maine, with some of the same characters who appeared in her earlier books, plus a larger-than-life modern-day Robin Hood, is a "big, ambitious, satisfying novel . . . that should solidify Ms. Chute's place as one of the unique voices of her generation," wrote the book critic for the *Dallas Morning News.* It was named a *New York Times* Notable Book of the Year, and *Newsday* called it "a passionate and gorgeously written homage to Americana's poor." Also in 1994, *The Beans of Egypt, Maine* was made into a film that was nominated for several Independent Spirit awards.

A populist activist, in the early 1990s Chute became involved in what she called the "Wicked Good Militia," also referred to as "The Second Maine Militia." In a self-interview for the *New Democracy Newsletter* (2000), the author describes herself as an "uneducated redneck novelist," although she points out that the word *redneck* comes from the red neckerchiefs worn by the coal miners of the South when they, both blacks and whites, marched together by the thousands "in defiance of the atrocities and oppression caused to them by the merging of organized money and government." She also said in the self-interview that she had countless flaws. "But being redneck, work-

Regionalist Carolyn Chute sets her fiction in rural Maine.
(Phyllis Graber Jensen/Bates College)

ing class—or, more accurately, the 'tribal class'—I am proud of that."

Her novel *Snow Man* (2001) was not as well received as her others. The fast-paced story revolves around a senator who is shot by someone the media calls a member of "an ultra-right-wing militia" from Maine. Through its characters, *Snow Man* delineates the philosophy and psychology of the underground militia movement. About her own politics, Chute says she is "very patriotic and very disappointed."

Best known for *The Beans of Egypt, Maine* (the author's least favorite book), Chute has received numerous honors, including a John Simon Guggenheim Memorial Foundation Fellowship and a Thornton Wilder Fellowship. In addition to her novels, which have been published in several European countries and Japan, Chute also writes short stories. Her short fiction has appeared in prominent literary magazines and anthologies, including *Ploughshares, Agni Review, Best American Short Stories 1983,* and *Contemporary Maine Fiction: An Anthology of Short Stories* (2005).

One of Chute's interests, besides, as she puts it, "bluegrass music, bees, and sapping," is photography. Using text-word pictures, she coauthored, with the renowned photographer Olive Pierce, *Up River: The Story of a Maine Fishing Community* (1996). The novelist Peter Matthiessen said the book "conveys sharply and poignantly, in text as well as photographs, the gritty culture of a last outpost of the beleaguered commercial fishing communities on our diminished coasts."

Carolyn Chute, who lives in southwestern Maine with her husband, where she teaches creative writing courses and has known "the riches of an interdependent [extended] family," brings to contemporary American literature a powerful regional voice. In a *Washington Post* interview in 1985, Chute commented that after her divorce she befriended many people who were like the Beans: "People who work in factories, or in the woods, or maybe a dairy farm. . . . No pretensions. They just live their lives. I found them beautiful. They were all I seemed to be interested in writing about."

Further Reading

Adams, Katherine. "Chute Dialogics: A Sidelong Glance from Egypt, Maine." *National Women's Studies Association Journal* 17, no. 1 (spring 2005): 1–22.

Chute, Carolyn. *The Beans of Egypt, Maine (The Finished Version).* New York: Harvest Books, 1995.

———. *Snow Man.* New York: Harvest Books, 2001.

McNair, Wesley, ed. *Contemporary Maine Fiction: An Anthology of Short Stories.* Camden, Me.: Down East Books, 2005.

Sandberg, Elisabeth. "Carolyn Chute." In *American Women Writers: A Critical Reference Guide from Colonial Times to the Present,* 204–205. Farmington Hills, Mich.: St. James Press.

Cisneros, Sandra
(1954–)   *poet, short story writer*

In her award-winning poetry and fiction, Sandra Cisneros, one of the foremost contemporary Chicana authors, writes movingly about the diverse lives of Chicanas from a feminist perspective.

Born on December 20, 1954, in Chicago, Illinois, to a Mexican father and a Chicana mother, Sandra Cisneros was a shy, sensitive child who "retreated inside herself," especially when her six brothers ignored her. Her family was poor and moved frequently, "always in neighborhoods that appeared like France after World War II—empty lots and burned out buildings," according to Cisneros. But no matter where they lived, her parents stressed the importance of education and taking advantage of the local library.

Cisneros majored in English at Loyola University and received a bachelor of arts degree in 1976. She then attended and graduated from the prestigious writing program at the University of Iowa, though she recalls having been a misfit. "It didn't take me long to learn that nobody cared to hear what I had to say and no one listened to me even when I did speak. . . . They [her classmates] had been bred as fine hothouse flowers. I was a yellow weed among the city's rocks." Fortunately Cisneros realized that she, not the "hothouse flowers," had the material to depict the multifaceted experiences of Mexican-American women: the poverty, sexism, and racism, as well as the passion, religion, and female companionship.

In 1980 Cisneros published her first collection of poems, *Bad Boys.* Two years later, supported by a National Endowment of the Arts (NEA) fellowship, she completed her first novel, *The House on Mango Street* (1983), which garnered a Before Columbus American Book Award. The book's central character is a young Chicana from a Chicago neighborhood who strives to improve her life. "I have decided not to grow tame like the others who lay their necks on the threshold waiting for the ball and chain," she says, while recognizing that "you can't forget who you are."

In 1986 Cisneros received a Dobie-Paisano fellowship and moved to Texas. A year later, she published a critically acclaimed collection of verse, *My Wicked, Wicked Ways.* After a period of being unemployed, impoverished, and depressed, another National Endowment of the Arts fellowship enabled her to continue writing.

Cisneros became the first Chicana to receive a major book contract from a mainstream publisher when Random House published *Woman Hollering Creek* in 1991. A compelling collection of short stories about the Chicana experience in the borderlands of Texas, it was widely distributed and lauded by critics as a "choral work in which the harmonic voices emphasize the commonality of experience."

In 1994 she wrote another book of poetry, *Loose Women,* and portions of *The House on Mango Street* were republished as *Hairs/Pelitos,* a bilingual picture book for children. Her books have been translated into 10 languages and in 1995 she was named a MacArthur Fellow.

Her latest novel, *Carmelo* (2002), a widely praised multigenerational saga about a Mexican-American family of renowned *rebozo,* or shawl, makers, was selected as a notable book of the year by several major newspapers, including the *New York Times* and the *Los Angeles Times.* "Like John Dos Passos and John Steinbeck, Cisneros writes along the borders where the novel and social history intersect," commented the *Los Angeles Times* book critic.

In 2002 Cisneros received an honorary doctorate degree from Loyola University. Two years later a sampling of her best work came out. Titled *Vintage Cisneros,* it exemplified the author's versatile accomplishments as a novelist, short story writer, and poet. Sandra Cisneros is a passionate Chicana activist and an original, fresh voice in American literature.

Further Reading

The Authorized Sandra Cisneros Web site. Available online. URL: http://www.sandracisneros.com. Downloaded on January 19, 2007.

Brackett, Virginia. *A Home in the Heart: The Story of Sandra Cisneros.* Greensboro, N.C.: Morgan Reynolds Publishing, 2004.

Chavez, Andres. "Sandra Cisneros." In *Latinas! Women of Achievement,* edited by Diane Telgen and Jim Kamf, 83–88. Detroit, Mich.: Visible Ink Press, 1996.

Cisneros, Sandra. *Carmelo.* New York: Alfred A. Knopf, 2002.

———. *The House on Mango Street.* New York: Vintage, 1991.

———. *Vintage Cisneros.* New York: Vintage, 2004.

Clampitt, Amy
(1920–1994) *poet, essayist*

Amy Clampitt was 63 when her first major collection of poetry, *The Kingfisher,* was published to great acclaim in 1983. A critic in the *New York Times Book Review* said that "with the publication of her brilliant first book, Clampitt immediately merits consideration as one of the most distinguished contemporary poets." A recipient of a coveted MacArthur Fellowship in 1992, Clampitt was notable especially for shaping rhythms and patterns that were entirely her own.

Born on June 15, 1920, in New Providence, Iowa, a small agricultural community with a population of around 200, Amy Clampitt was the oldest of five children. Her father was a farmer, as was her paternal grandfather, who wrote a memoir about his experiences working the prairie.

As a child, Amy enjoyed romping around the 300-acre plot that belonged to her grandparents. Her first childhood memory was a bed of violets, suggestive of nature and art. Amy had a natural gift for observation and classifying the details of the pastoral world. But when she was 10, her parents moved to another farm located on a barren, dreary, unruly piece of land, where her father—as Clampitt would later describe in one of her poems—had to hack away "at the strangle / roots of thistles and wild morning glories." The move deeply distressed young Clampitt. Having been dislocated from her beloved prairie homestead seems to have contributed to her chronic sense of displacement, which is prominent in her poetry. Throughout her life Clampitt wrote about the natural world, always returning to her early experiences, where she had felt she was part of a community of pioneers.

After attending New Providence Consolidated School for her elementary and high school years, she graduated with honors in English in 1941 from Grinnell College, where she was elected to Phi Beta Kappa. Clampitt then moved to New York City. Although she traveled throughout Europe and to other areas of the United States and wrote movingly about a variety of landscapes, she lived in Manhattan for most of her life. Some of her most celebrated poems, such as "Manhattan Elegy" and "Times Square Water Music," use New York as a backdrop.

Clampitt attended Columbia University on a graduate fellowship and took courses at the New School for Social Research, but she never completed the work required for an advanced degree. Instead, she took a variety of jobs related to writing or books: She wrote advertising copy at a publishing company and later worked as a reference librarian for the National Audubon Society. During the 1950s, after she had become a freelance editor and researcher, she wrote three novels, none of which were published. It was then that Clampitt turned to poetry. In 1974 her first small volume of verse, *Multitudes, Multitudes,* was produced in a limited edition by a private press. She was hired as an editor at E. P. Dutton publishers and, encouraged by members of a poetry group she attended regularly, in 1978 she sent out her poems for the first time to the *New Yorker*. Howard Moss, the magazine's poetry editor, noting the elegance of her verse, accepted one of her poems, "The Sun Underfoot among the Sundews." Although considered a coup—the *New Yorker* was a highly influential magazine and mostly considered only well-known writers—she was unable to find a major press to publish her work.

In 1982 Clampitt sent her verse to Alfred A. Knopf. Alice Quinn, editor of the Knopf Poetry Series, accepted the collection. The book, Clampitt's first full-length collection, titled *The Kingfisher*, made Clampitt famous in the poetry world. It was unanimously praised and assured her a place in the canon. As critic Helen Vendler put it, "An assured and distinguished voice resembling no other has been added to the sum of American poetry." Clampitt was praised particularly for her nature-related imagery, like the kingfisher's "burnished plunge / the color / of felicity afire" or the sun that was so dazzling that when looking at it, "you start to fall upward."

During the 1980s Clampitt held positions at several visiting writer-in-residence programs, including the College of William and Mary, Amherst College, and Washington University in St. Louis. She received a poetry award from the New School for Social Research (1977) as well as a fellowship from the Academy of American Poets in 1981, followed a year later by a Guggenheim Fellowship. Perhaps the most outstanding recognition came when she was awarded a John D. and Catherine T. MacArthur Foundation Fellowship in 1992. The prestigious fellowship, granted to "talented individuals who have shown extraordinary originality and dedication in their creative pursuits," enabled Clampitt to purchase a summer home in the Berkshires in western Massachusetts, where she and Harold Korn, a law professor at Columbia and her partner of 25 years, vacationed. She kept her small apartment in Greenwich Vil-

lage, New York City, where most of her literary friends resided.

After *The Kingfisher*, Clampitt published four more well-received collections: *What the Light Was Like* (1985); *Archaic Figure* (1987), in which she evokes famous female figures such as MARGARET FULLER; *Westward* (1990); and *A Silence Opens* (1994), published the year she died. In addition, Clampitt edited *The Essential John Donne* (1988) and produced a book of critical essays and reviews, *Predecessors, Et Cetera* (1991), which included her thoughts on writers such as Henry James and MARIANNE MOORE. She also wrote an unpublished play, *Mad with Joy*, about the English prose writer and diarist Dorothy Wordsworth and her circle of friends, that was given a staged reading by the Poets' Theatre in Cambridge, Massachusetts, in 1993. In both her poetry and prose, she often praised women such as EDITH WHARTON and EMILY DICKINSON who had discovered their self-worth and talent through their writing.

Clampitt also admired English writers such as William Wordsworth, John Keats, Gerard Manley Hopkins, and George Eliot. Like them, she believed in what she called "the *livingness* of her past." Her poetry could be complex and complicated enough to warrant explanatory annotations or simple enough, though richly ornate, to describe commonplace experiences such as riding a Greyhound bus or enjoying a slice of fruit pie. Other of her poems referred to or reflected political events: Clampitt was a social activist who protested vehemently against the war in Vietnam during the 1970s.

In the spring of 1993, while teaching at Smith College, Clampitt was diagnosed with ovarian cancer. In June 1994 she and Korn, to whom she had dedicated *The Kingfisher*, were married, five days before her 74th birthday. On September 10, 1994, the late-blooming Amy Clampitt died, and her ashes were buried in the garden of her home in the Berkshires. The Amy Clampitt Foundation, formed by friend to honor Clampitt's highly regarded verse, continues to support poetry and the literary arts.

Further Reading

Clampitt, Amy. *The Collected Poems of Amy Clampitt*. New York: Alfred A. Knopf, 1999.

———. *The Selected Letters of Amy Clampitt*. Edited by William Spiegelman. New York: Columbia University Press, 2005.

Goodridge, Celeste. "Clampitt, Amy." *The Literary Encyclopedia*. January 8, 2001. Available online. URL: http://www.litencyc.com/php/speople.php?rec=true&UID=890. Downloaded on January 19, 2007.

Kaledin, Eugenia. "Amy Clampitt." In *Notable American Women*, edited by Susan Ware, 121–122. Cambridge, Mass.: Belknap Press of Harvard University Press, 2004.

Clifton, Lucille Sayles
(1936–) *poet, children's book writer, memoirist*

Winner of the 2000 National Book Award for Poetry and recipient of prestigious poetry prizes and fellowships, Lucille Clifton is considered one of the most distinguished and prolific African-American poets writing today. Her verse—she has published 10 collections—is known for its simple but intimate imagery, carefully honed language, and sharply defined rhythms that powerfully define the spectrum of human experiences, especially familial and racial history. Clifton has also written 20 popular children's books.

Born on June 27, 1936, in Depew, a small steel town near Buffalo in upstate New York, Thelma Lucille Sayles came from a home that, despite her parents' lack of any formal education, valued storytelling and African-American literature. Her mother was a poet who encouraged her young daughter to write. Lucille was the first person in her family to graduate from high school. "What I knew was true about me was that I could breathe and I made poems," Clifton recalled about her childhood in an interview in *Belles Lettres* in 1994. She never dreamed of becoming a professional poet because, she noted, the only poets she had ever heard of were "old dead white men from New England with beards."

In the early 1950s she left her working-class home to attend Howard University a historically black university in Washington, D.C., as a scholarship student; there she studied theater from 1953 to 1955. At Howard Clifton was struck by class differences, because many of her classmates came from wealthier backgrounds and were more privileged than she. Nonetheless she emphasized that while her family had been poor, they were never downtrodden. "We didn't have much money, but we had a lot of love," she later wrote.

After transferring to the State University of New York College at Fredonia, where she graduated in 1955, Clifton met important black intellectuals such as LeRoi Jones. She was greatly influenced by the Black Arts Movement of the 1960s, which emphasized using art as a way of illustrating racial oppression. She also developed her writing style by reading the works of prominent African-American writers, including James Baldwin and Toni Morrison, and, like her mentors, she believed that accepting individual responsibility is essential to creating a better life. Clifton's "lean, agile, and accurate" verse, as one critic described it, reflects her life-affirming philosophy and her respect for the lives of ordinary African Americans. In that way she resembled African-American cultural writers such as Langston Hughes and Gwendolyn Brooks.

In 1958 she married Fred Clifton and, while pursuing her writing on the side, worked as a clerk in Buffalo and then for 10 years as an assistant in the Office of Education in Washington, D.C. Her first collection of poetry, *Good Times,* was published in 1969. It was cited by the *New York Times* as one of the year's 10 best books and garnered the Discovery Award that year. She received a Creative Writing Fellowship from the National Endowment for the Arts in 1970 and 1972 and was a poet-in-residence at Coppin College, a historically black college in Baltimore, Maryland, from 1971 until 1974. During that time she wrote two more books of verse: *Good News about the Earth* (1972) and *An Ordinary Woman* (1974), volumes that question everything from "the pedestrian to the sublime," according to Dianne Johnson, in *African American Writers* (2001). "Clifton writes [lovingly] about her own family and about black communities and histories. She writes about them in very intimate ways and in very political ways, informed by an African diasporic consciousness," continued Johnson.

Clifton also is an accomplished children's book writer: In the late 1960s the poet MAXINE KUMIN encouraged her colleague to try her hand at this genre. Beginning in the early 1970s, Clifton produced 20 well-received children's books, including an award-winning series that focuses on the life of an indomitable character named Everett Anderson, a proud young African American. The series also includes white and Latino characters, as well as those from different religious and class backgrounds. One of Clifton's best-known children's books, *My Friend Jacob,* relates the friendship between a young black boy and a handicapped older white boy. It won the Access to Equality Conference Award for Children's Literature in "recognition for outstanding treatment of disabled children." Like her verse, Clifton's children's books are written passionately but without sentimentality. She drew many of her characters from her own observations as a mother. "Having six children kept me human," Clifton once observed.

In addition to writing poetry and juvenile fiction, Clifton published a poignant memoir called *Generations* (1976). In 1979 she became the first African-American poet laureate of the state of Maryland, a position she held for three years. Despite the kudos, in an essay Clifton wrote in 1984 she asserted, "I am interested in trying to render big ideas in a simple way. I am interested in being understood, not admired. I wish to celebrate and not be celebrated (though a little celebration is a lot of fun)."

Clifton was a visiting writer at Columbia University and at George Washington University. She also taught creative writing at Goucher College, American University, and the University of California at Santa Cruz. In 1985, a year after her husband died (they had been married for 27 years), she was named a finalist—the first of three times—for a Pulitzer Prize in Poetry for a volume that included both poetry and her memoir, titled *Good Women: Poems and a Memoir.* Then she returned to Maryland to teach at St. Mary's College in 1989, where she is currently a distinguished professor of humanities. Her poetry collections include *Quilting: Poems 1987–1990* (1991), *The Terrible Stories* (1996), and *Blessing the Boats: New and Selected Poems 1988–2000* (2000). Her richly emotive work has been included in more than 100 poetry anthologies.

Among her awards and distinctions, Clifton has received two National Endowment for the Arts (NEA) Fellowships for creative writing, a grant from the American Academy of Poets (where she serves as chancellor), an Emmy Award from the American Academy of Television Arts and Sciences, and honorary degrees from the University of Maryland and Townson State University. Clifton won the revered National Book Award for Poetry in 2000 for *Blessing the Boats,* a collection that examines, with empathy, the transformation of life's "boats," which carry people from one point to another. In a review of the book that appeared in *Field Notes* in 2001, Jeri Bayer wrote, "Ultimately what Clifton leaves us with—through her signature style and free-verse lines, extensive use of dramatic monologue and autobiographical anecdote, and preference for lower-case letters—is an uplifting sense that grief and evil can be transcended and that a source of rejuvenation is the essence of experience, distilled."

Clifton's latest children's book, *One of the Problems of Everett Anderson* (2001), is the eighth in the Anderson series. It addresses the issue of child abuse, when Everett notices bruises and scars on his friend's neck and asks his own mother for advice. A review in *School Library Journal* called it "useful as bibliotherapy and for opening class discussion about this sensitive topic." Clifton's 12th and most current collection of verse, *Mercy,* was published in 2004. "The only mercy," she writes, "is memory."

A survivor of breast cancer and kidney failure who also endured the death of a daughter in 2000, Clifton remains optimistic in part because of her deep spiritual beliefs. James A. Miller, a professor at George Washington University, said that "in her capacity as both witness and seer, she looks through the madness and sorrow of the world, locating moments of epiphany in the mundane and ordinary." Clifton's work is rooted in her ancestry and often is inspired by stories of survival based on what she learned about her great-great-grandmother, Ca'line, who was brought to the United States from Africa as a slave in 1830. (Ca'line's daughter was the first black woman lynched in Virginia.)

In 2007 Clifton won the lifetime achievement Ruth Lilly Poetry Prize, awarded by the Poetry Foundation. "Clifton sounds like no one else," said Christian Wiman, editor of *Poetry* magazine, while announcing the award. "And her achievement looks larger with each passing year."

Lucille Clifton's work is lyrical, accessible, and respectful of its readership. Literary critic Dianne Johnson concludes that "the world of American children's literature and the worlds of poetry and memoir and academy are all enriched by Lucille Clifton's presence at the table, by her writing about her extraordinary ordinary life."

Further Reading

Bayer, Jeri. "Clearing the Decks: A Review of *Blessing the Boats.*" *Field Notes* 11, no. 1 (Summer 2001).

Clifton, Lucille. *Blessing the Boats: New and Selected Poems 1988–2000.* New York: BOA Editions, 2000.

———. *Good Times.* New York: Random House, 1969.

———. *Mercy.* New York: BOA Editions, 2004.

———. *My Friend Jacob.* New York: E. P. Dutton, 1981.

———. *One of the Problems of Everett Anderson.* New York: Henry Holt and Company, 2001.

Johnson, Dianne. "Lucille Clifton." In *African American Writers,* edited by Valerie Smith, 123–134. New York: Charles Scribner's Sons, 2001.

∾ Cornwell, Patricia Daniels

(1956–) *mystery writer, nonfiction writer*

Renowned as a master of the American crime novel, multi–award-winning Patricia Cornwell writes best-selling mysteries that are informed by the author's extensive scientific background and expertise in forensic pathology and computer technology. Cornwell's most popular series of well-researched, well-known mysteries features protagonist Dr. Kay Scarpetta, a chief medical examiner who in many ways represents the author's fictional alter ego.

As a child, Patricia Daniels, who was born on June 9, 1956, in Miami, Florida, aspired to become an archeologist. But her life was disrupted when she was five by her parents' divorce. She and her two brothers moved with their mother, a secretary who was deeply depressed and suffered a nervous breakdown, to North Carolina. Her mother tried to give Patricia and her siblings away to their neighbors, evangelist Reverend Billy Graham and his wife Ruth, who rescued the children, housed them, and then placed them temporarily with a missionary family.

Ruth Graham became Patricia's mentor and encouraged her young neighbor to write, even providing her with a treasured leather-bound journal. (In 1983 Graham become the subject of Cornwell's first published work, *A Time for Remembering: The Story of Ruth Bell Graham,* which in 1997 she revised as *Ruth, a Portrait: The Story of Ruth Bell Graham.*) Cornwell has links to another luminary: She is a descendent of writer HARRIET BEECHER STOWE, and her favorite novel is *Uncle Tom's Cabin.*

After waging a battle with anorexia nervosa and bulimia, Cornwell transferred from King College in Tennessee to North Carolina's Davidson College, where she graduated in 1979 with a degree in English. She currently sponsors scholarships for Davidson students with exceptional abilities in creative writing. Also in 1979 she married her former English professor, Charles Cornwell, who was 17 years her senior. She took a job as a journalist for the *Charlotte Observer,* eventually becoming a crime reporter for the North Carolina newspaper and winning an investigative reporting award from the North Carolina Press Association for a series of articles she wrote on prostitution and crime in Charlotte.

In 1981 the Cornwells moved to Richmond, Virginia, where Charles prepared for the ministry and Patricia looked for work. Fortuitously, she met a medical examiner, Marcella Fierro, who encouraged Cornwell to take a job working for the Virginia chief medical examiner's office. Cornwell agreed and starting in 1984 spent six years in the office, learning the underpinnings of the morgue, first as a technical writer and then as a computer analyst. "When Fierro started talking about how you could make the body talk to you, I was just blown away," Cornwell recalled. She also volunteered in the Richmond police department, where she had experiences that would prove invaluable in writing her future thrillers. In 1989 she and her husband, by then a minister, divorced.

Cornwell's first published novel, *Postmortem* (1990), which was rejected by seven publishers before the manuscript was accepted, introduced readers to Dr. Kay Scarpetta, a smart, savvy, middle-aged detective hired to track down a serial killer who has been terrorizing women in Richmond, who finds herself one of the killer's targets. She uses her knowledge as a medical examiner and her impressive array of forensic skills to solve the case. *Postmortem* was critically acclaimed, became an international best seller, and received five major mystery awards, all in 1990, including the coveted Edgar Award from the Mystery Writers of America.

Postmortem was followed by 15 other Scarpetta mysteries (as of April 2007), including *Cruel and Unusual,* which earned Great Britain's prestigious Gold Dagger Award for the year's best novel of 1993, and *Book of the Dead* in 2007. Some of the Scarpetta books are based on homicides that took place in Virginia, often perpetuated by serial killers. All feature what literary critic Linda C. Pelzer, in an essay she wrote about Cornwell in 2000, defines as the crime writer's trademarks: "multiple murders; detailed descriptions of forensic procedures that convey the violence perpetuated against the victims, who are usually women; and her formidable heroine [Scarpetta], who must not only battle the kind of person who kills for sport, but also confront the prejudices of a male-dominated justice system."

What makes Cornwell's mysteries unusual is that instead of focusing on what she calls "aberrant people," as most thrillers do, the author turns to forensic science and technology-driven law enforcement to create a powerful and more complex sense of danger and of the evil that lurks around the corner, as well as a distinctive voice. "The Scarpetta stories are dominated by an overwhelming psychological darkness, a sense that 'it,' whatever 'it' is, never stops," asserted the *Guardian* (1999) reviewer Kasia Boddy. (Cornwell, like her heroine, carries and sleeps with a gun.) Some reviewers have criticized Kay Scarpetta as being too self-centered, serious, and unemotional. Nonetheless, Cornwell's legions of faithful readers seem to await eagerly each new thriller partly because they enjoy the way the intelligent forensic sleuth solves each bone-chilling crime, but also because they are interested in Scarpetta's life and those of the other "regulars" in the series, namely her niece and the captain of the Richmond police department. In March 1996 six of Cornwell's books were on the *USA Today* list of the 25 best-selling mystery books.

Following the Scarpetta series, in 1997 Cornwell decided to "take a break" and began working on the Judy Hammer "cop novel" series, the first book of which was titled *Hornet's Nest.* The series is written in the third person and is based on a trio of central characters, instead of one, including a young crime reporter-turned-police officer who, like the author, helps the city's deputy chief of police solve murders. The second series was not as well received as her first, and fans and critics alike demanded a return to Dr. Kay Scarpetta. Cornwell wrote only two other Judy Hammer books, the second of which was *Isle of Dogs* (2001), which sold very well despite some negative reviews. (Book reviewer Nicholas H. Allison stated that "at times the writing [in *Isle of Dogs*] strains so hard for laughs that instead it draws winces.") When Cornwell returned to the Scarpetta series, the popular main character had become a freelance consultant with the National Forensic Academy in Florida. She moves back to Richmond at the request of the new chief medical examiner, who claims he needs her help to solve the horrific murder of a 14-year-old girl.

The Scarpetta novels have sold millions of books. A writer for the *Wall Street Journal* described Scarpetta's appeal as the character's ability to continue to fascinate "with a sensibility in which clinical objectivity and human concerns coexist convincingly." Dr. Kay Scarpetta won the 1999 Sherlock Award for best detective created by an American author. A year later, Cornwell helped push a bill through the Senate that increased funding for crime labs in the United States, in order to ease the strain of backlogs.

Cornwell's most recent suspenseful best-selling novels include *The Last Precinct* (2000), *Blow Fly* (2003), *Trace* (2004), and *Predator* (2005), all part of the Scarpetta series. In November 2005, *Predator* was the number-one best seller on the *New York Times Book Review* list. *At Risk,* which is not part of the Scarpetta series, was published in 2006 and was serialized in the *New York Times Magazine.*

Trying her hand at nonfiction, Cornwell studied a landmark unsolved case and then claimed to know the identity of an infamous serial murderer. After visiting the original crime scenes and meeting with the chief investigator of Scotland Yard, Cornwell wrote *Portrait of a Killer: Jack the Ripper—Case Closed* (2002). The controversial book (Cornwell claimed the gruesome murders were executed by the British impressionist painter Walter Sickert) landed Cornwell on the *New York Times* nonfiction best seller list for the first time, although she said in an interview with CNN in September 2004 that the Ripper investigation was simply a diversion from her normal activity, which is writing fiction. "When I had a chance to work on that real case, I did, and brought it to resolution. I've simply gone back to doing what I've always done, which is my novels." What excites her more than writing about Jack the Ripper, she said, was "all kinds of very interesting research into genetics and also into the human—into the brain and why people do what they do."

Patricia Cornwell's best-selling mysteries combine suspense with forensic science.
(AP Images/Jim Cooper)

Cornwell also penned two cookbooks, *Scarpetta's Winter Table* (1998), featuring such recipes as "Bad Mood Pasta Primavera," and *Food to Die For: Secrets from Kay Scarpetta's Kitchen* (2001), as well as a children's book, *Life's Little Fable* (1999).

One of America's most successful and prolific crime writers, Patricia Cornwell, who now lives in Concord, Massachusetts, helped establish the Virginia Institute of Forensic Science and Medicine, the first forensic training facility of its kind in America, and serves as the Institute's chairman of the board. "It is important to me to live in the world I write about," says Cornwell, who has lived all over New England. "If I want a character to do or know something, I want to do or know the same things."

Further Reading

Cornwell, Patricia. *At Risk.* New York: Putnam, 2006.

———. *Book of the Dead.* New York: Putnam, 2007.

———. *Predator.* New York: Putnam, 2005.

———. *Ruth, A Portrait: The Story of Ruth Bell Graham.* New York: Bantam Doubleday Dell, 1997.

Feole, Glenn L. *The Complete Patricia Cornwell Companion.* New York: Berkley Publishing Company, 2005.

"Patricia Cornwell." Patricia Cornwell Web site. Available online. URL: http://www.patricia-cornwell.com/about_main.html. Downloaded on January 19, 2007.

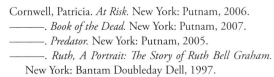 **Constantia**
See MURRAY, JUDITH SARGENT

Danticat, Edwidge

(1969–) *novelist, short story writer, children's book writer*

Edwidge Danticat is an award-winning contemporary American writer whose trenchant and often disturbing fiction is rooted in her native Haiti and the Haitian diaspora. She has been critically acclaimed for her elegant, evocative prose that often tackles complex moral dilemmas. Her debut novel, *Breath, Eyes, Memory,* published in 1994, was chosen as an Oprah's Book Club selection, and within a year her short story collection *Krik? Krak!* was a finalist for the National Book Award. Her second novel, *The Farming of Bones,* won the American Book Award, and *The Dew Breaker* became a national best seller.

Born in Port-au-Prince, Haiti, on January 19, 1969, during the brutal dictatorship of Francois Duvalier ("Papa Doc"), Edwidge Danticat was two years old when her father immigrated to Brooklyn in New York City to work as a cab driver, followed by her mother, a seamstress, two years later. Edwidge was left in Haiti with her younger brother, where she was raised by her caring aunt and strict uncle. "We were loved but not cuddled," Danticat recalled. But she was given books that she cher-

ished, and her aunt's mother would tell stories in Creole during summer vacations that the family spent in the mountains. "I loved the vibrant interaction between teller and listener," she said.

Danticat wrote her first short story, about a girl visited by a clan of women, when she was nine. An ongoing theme in her fiction is the strength and perseverance of Haitian women. When she was 12, Edwidge joined her parents, who had two more sons by then, in the United States. Because her accent and clothing were different from those of her peers at school, she felt ostracized by them. She also felt discarded by her parents, whom she hardly knew. For many years she barely spoke.

Although Danticat originally planned to study to become a nurse, she began to write stories as an undergraduate at Barnard College, where she graduated with a degree in French literature and won the 1995 Woman of Achievement Award. Some of those stories would later appear in her first-published, National Book Award–nominated collection *Krik? Krak!* (1995). Her thought-provoking stories mostly revolved around Haitian Americans or Haitians longing for political freedom and democracy. They are often based on stories she heard as a young child. "We take great pride in our past," Danticat said in an interview in *USA Today.*

Danticat attended Brown University as a scholarship student and wrote her first novel, *Breath, Eyes, Memory* (1994), about four generations of impoverished Haitian women, as the thesis for a master of fine arts degree in creative writing, which she earned in 1993. After the lyrical, well-crafted book was selected by television celebrity Oprah Winfrey as one of her coveted reading club picks in 1998, the novel became a best seller. Danticat was invited to work with Hollywood filmmaker Jonathan Demme, coproducing two documentaries about Haiti for him: *Courage and Pain* (1996), about Haitian torture survivors, and *The Agronomist* in 2003. "She is a great, new world-class writer," Demme said of Danticat, who has credited writers MAYA ANGELOU, TONI MORRISON (Danticat had a small role in the 1998 film version of Morrison's novel *Beloved*), James Baldwin, and several Haitian writers, many of whom have been jailed, exiled, or killed, as having especially influenced her work.

The Farming of Bones, Danticat's second novel, was published in 1997. It focuses, through the eyes of a Haitian housemaid, on the massacre of 1937, when the Dominican Republic's dictator Rafael Leonard Trujillo Molina ordered the murder of hundreds of Haitians who tried to flee over the border to escape racism and intolerable working conditions as cane-cutters on Dominican sugar plantations. The massacre, "just a line in my textbook," explains the author, "was still so real to people: Haitians working in the Dominican Republic in the 1970s and 1980s were afraid it could be repeated." The novel won an American Book Award in 1999 and was named one of the best books of the year by the *Chicago Tribune.*

Taking time out from writing fiction, Danticat edited two anthologies that were important to her: *The Beacon Best of 2000: Great Writing by Women and Men of All Colors and Cultures,* a collection by 26 writers of diverse ethnic and cultural backgrounds, and *The Butterfly's Way: Voices from the Haitian Dyaspora in the United States* (2001), which includes mostly autobiographical reflections by 32 writers.

Her third novel, *The Dew Breaker* (2004), composed of several interconnected stories, evokes the frightening world of a "dew breaker"—a torturer "who comes before dawn, as the dew was settling on the leaves, and . . . [takes] you away," as one character in the book explains. Dew breakers were commonplace during the 29-year period (1957–86) that Haiti was ruled by father and son dictators "Papa Doc" and "Baby Doc" Duvalier. The dew breaker (Dandicat translated the ironically poetic Creole expression into English) in the novel tries to hide his shadowy past as a former prison guard and torturer in Haiti beneath his new American reality as a working-class immigrant, but he ends up revealing his horrific past. "Your father was the hunter, he was not the prey," he confesses to his daughter. *The Dew Breaker,* a National Book Critics Circle Award finalist, attempts to look at the human face of the dictatorship, said Danticat: "We knew [dew breakers], and went to school with their children. I wanted to explore the aftermath on another generation." In his *New York Times* review of the novel, Richard Eder describes Danticat as having managed to portray the torment of the Haitian people and a Haitian truth: "prisoners all, even the jailers."

Danticat also has written a combination memoir and travelogue, *After the Dance: A Walk through Carnival in Jacmel, Haiti* (2002), and two novels for young readers: *Behind the Mountains* (2002) and *Anacaona: Golden Flower, Haiti, 1490* (2005). She has taught creative writing at New York University and the University of Miami and won the 1995 Pushcart Short Story Prize (her short stories have appeared in 25 periodicals, including the *New Yorker* magazine). She has received awards from *Seventeen* and *Essence* magazines and a James Michener Fellowship. She was named one of 21 "Best Young American Novelists" by *Granta,* one of 30 artists under 30 "likely to change the culture for the next 30 years" by the *New York Times,* and one of 20 exemplars of "American fiction of the future" by the *New Yorker.*

Soft-spoken, modest, and shy by nature, Edwidge Danticat does not welcome publicity and

Haitian-born Edwidge Danticat writes prize-winning, provocative fiction.
(AP Images/Gino Domenico)

attention. Nonetheless, the accomplished young writer, who lives with her husband, Faidherbe Boyer, in a pink stucco fixer-upper bungalow in Miami, Florida, uses her celebrity as a way to advocate for Haitian refugees. As writer PAULE MARSHALL puts it: "A silenced Haiti has once again found its literary voice."

Further Reading

Alexandre, Sandy, and Ravi Y. Howard. "My Turn in the Fire: A Conversation with Edwidge Danticat." *An International Review* 12, no. 3 (2002): 110–128.

Bell, Beverly, ed. *Haitian Women's Stories of Survival and Resistance.* With a foreword by Edwidge Danticat. Ithaca, N.Y.: Cornell University Press, 2001.

Danticat, Edwidge. *Anacaona: Golden Flower, Haiti, 1490.* New York: Scholastic, 2005.

———. *Breath, Eyes, Memory.* New York: Soho Press, 1994.

———, ed. *The Butterfly's Way: Voices from the Haitian Dyaspora in the United States.* With an introduction by Edwidge Danticat. New York: Soho Press, 2001.

———. *The Dew Breaker.* New York: Alfred A. Knopf, 2004.

———. "The Torture Debate: Does It Work?" *Washington Post.* September 22, 2006. Available online. URL: http://www.washingtonpost.com/wp/-dyn/content/article/2006/09/22/AR2006092201304.html. Downloaded on February 26, 2007.

Kerlee, Ime. "Edwidge Danticat." Postcolonial Studies at Emory University. Available online. URL: http://www.english.emory.edu/Bahri/Danticat.html. Downloaded on January 19, 2007.

Davis, Rebecca Harding
(1831–1910)   *novelist, short story writer*

A prolific author, Rebecca Harding Davis was best known for *Life in the Iron Mills,* a novella that realistically depicted the dismal working conditions in a mid-19th-century Virginia iron mill. Grimly naturalistic, it is considered a landmark in the history of American literature.

Rebecca Harding was born on June 24, 1831, in Washington County, Pennsylvania. She grew up in the steel town of Wheeling, West Virginia, where she was the oldest of five children in a middle-class family. Harding graduated with high honors from Pennsylvania's Washington Female Seminary in 1848, and she then moved back to Wheeling to tutor her siblings and help with household chores. In her spare time she took long walks through the neighborhood mills and iron foundries. Appalled by the poverty, pollution, and "soul starvation," she felt compelled to write about the workers' conditions.

Life in the Iron Mills appeared in the *Atlantic Monthly* in 1861 and was one of the first in-depth portraits of a mill worker, specifically a sculptor who attempts to escape from his harsh, alienating job as a furnace tender by creating a woman's figure out of the mill's refuse, or korl. On its publication, Harding found herself hailed as a brave new voice by such literary luminaries as LOUISA MAY ALCOTT and Ralph Waldo Emerson. They were impressed by Davis's goal, which was "to dig into the commonplace, this vulgar American life, and see what is in it."

Harding's second novel, *Margaret Howth* (1862), was also serialized in the *Atlantic Monthly,* and that same year the *Atlantic* published two of her realistic accounts of the brutality of the Civil War.

After Harding married Lemuel Clarke Davis, a Philadelphia journalist, her focus shifted to raising their three children, taking care of her sick father, and managing a home. Nonetheless she wrote more than 100 short stories, 10 novels, numerous essays for the *New York Tribune* and *Harper's Bazaar,* and children's stories.

Although Davis wrote sentimental, melodramatic potboilers, in part as a way to supplement the family's income, she also tackled serious, pressing social and economic issues. The novel *Waiting for the Verdict* (1868), for example, focused on racism in the aftermath of emancipation, while *John Andross* (1874) was one of the first fictionalized works to attack government corruption. Her last critical success was a collection of realistic short stories entitled *Silhouettes of American Life* (1892).

Rebecca Harding Davis died on September 19, 1910, at age 79. She was largely forgotten, except as the mother of the well known journalist Richard Harding Davis. TILLIE OLSEN, a writer and champion of working-class causes, rediscovered Davis and wrote a biographical afterword for *Life in the Iron Mills* when it was reissued in 1972. Olsen pointed out that Davis had "extended the realm of [American] fiction in important ways" and that her stories represented the triumph of a "housebound, class-bound, sex-bound" writer.

Further Reading

Davis, Harding Rebecca. *Life in the Iron Mills; or, The Korl Woman* (with an afterword by Tillie Olsen). Old Westbury, N.Y.: Feminist Press, 1972.

———. *Waiting for the Verdict.* New York: Sheldow & Company, 1868.

Langford, Gerald. *The Richard Harding Davis Years: A Biography of a Mother and Son.* New York: Holt, Rinehart and Winston, 1961.

"Life in the Iron Mills: Rebecca Harding Davis." Scribbling Women, a project of the Public Media foundation. Available online. URL: http://www.scribblingwomen. org/rdmills.html. Downloaded on January 19, 2007.

Dickinson, Emily Elizabeth
(1830–1886) *poet, letter writer*

Although Emily Dickinson is known as one of America's best and most beloved poets, her extraordinary talent was not recognized until after her death, with the publication of 1,775 of her poems. Known as the "Queen Recluse," Dickinson used poetry as a way to communicate with a world from which, except in her imagination, she withdrew. Today her deceptively simple verse is praised for its originality, imagery, and stylistic complexity.

Emily Elizabeth Dickinson was born on December 10, 1830, in Amherst, Massachusetts, where she spent most of her life in a stately brick mansion that her grandfather built. The Dickinson household was composed of Emily, her younger sister, older brother, semi-invalid mother, and domineering father. The latter was a pillar of the Amherst community and an ambitious politician and lawyer who, recalled Dickinson, was "too busy with his briefs" to notice his children.

A lively, curious child, Emily described herself as being "small, like the wren" with "bold hair, like the chestnut bur" and large brown eyes "like the sherry in the glass, that the guest leaves." At school she was considered a bright student whose English compositions were, according to her brother, "unlike anything ever heard—and always produced a sensation—both with the scholars and teachers—her imagination sparkled—and she gave it free reign." A voracious reader, she especially admired the craftsmanship of accomplished women writers such as Charlotte Brontë, George Eliot, and Elizabeth Barrett Browning.

After graduating from Amherst Academy in 1847, Dickinson attended Mount Holyoke Female Seminary, a boarding school in nearby South Hadley. There she challenged religious orthodoxy and was unhappy with the seminary's heavy-handed commitment to evangelicalism; she refused, under pressure, to convert and become an "established Christian." "I am standing alone in rebellion," she wrote to a friend. A year later she returned to Amherst and her family and began to write in earnest.

Although Dickinson would never marry, she had several close friendships with men. Benjamin Newton, who worked in her father's office, served as her mentor and introduced her to the works of Ralph Waldo Emerson and other notable transcendentalists. When he died in 1853, the shadow of death appeared for the first time in Dickinson's poetry, and that shadow continued to hover over it for the remainder of her life. In one of her most famous poems, "Because I could not stop for Death," death is personified as a civilized gentleman caller escorting the writer to her grave. "The carriage held but just ourselves / And Immortality." An ironic, subtle sense of humor permeates many of Dickinson's poems, which are witty rather than overtly serious, even though they often deal with the inevitably of death, the conflict between flesh and spirit, or denial and renunciation.

Dickinson seemed to enjoy her quiet life in Amherst. She left Massachusetts only once, to visit her father in Washington, D.C., in 1854, when he was serving in Congress. During that trip she met Reverend Charles Wadsworth, a married Presbyterian minister from Philadelphia. They became close friends. Many stories of a romantic connection have since circulated. But, although she was extremely fond of him and was very disappointed when he moved to California in 1861, there is no concrete evidence that they were lovers. In spite of her deeply felt, passionate love poems and letters, it remains unclear whether or not Dickinson was ever expressing feelings about a specific relationship. She once explained that in her poetry, as personal as it seemed, she was not necessarily referring to herself: "When I state myself, as the Representative of the Verse—it does not mean—me—but a supposed person."

During the mid-1860s, Dickinson wrote prolifically. In 1862 alone she produced more than 350 poems. She was a master at paring down language to its bare essentials. The majority of her poems were brief; almost all were untitled. Her writing was triggered by simple things—a bird's song, a blade of grass, a particular angle of light during winter—to which she paid unflinching attention. While doing chores, such as gardening or baking rye bread, she would quickly jot down her ideas, with both precision and haste, on scraps of paper, favoring dashes over formal punctuation. To her, dashes were a way to creativity and naturally—like a breath—separate ideas, yet still maintain the whole message of a sentence. She favored hymnal-style short lines and stanza patterns. After developing the idea into a poem, she would complete it late at night, or in spare free moments at her desk, and then revise it until she was satisfied with the results.

In 1861 Samuel Bowles, the editor of the *Springfield Republican,* agreed to publish two of her poems in his prestigious newspaper. Dickinson befriended Bowles, who was charmed both by the poet and her verse, but she was enraged when he heavily edited one of the poems.

Nonetheless, a year later she mustered up the courage to send four of her poems to Thomas Wentworth Higginson, a literary critic at the *Atlantic Monthly* who was interested in hearing from unknown writers. Unfortunately, he concluded that they were "too delicate" and that the meters—quatrains (four-lined stanzas) with an uneven rhyme scheme—were "too crude in form" for publication. Although he took Dickinson and her work seriously and encouraged her to continue writing, Higginson never fully appreciated her originality and genius.

With the death of her father in 1874, followed a year later by her mother's paralysis and her own increasingly frail health, Dickinson became even more reclusive. She insisted that her doctor examine her through a partially opened door, and she would remain upstairs in her bedroom when guests came to call, even if she had invited them. Dressed in white, she rarely left the house, which she shared with her unmarried sister Lavinia, noting: "I do not cross my father's ground to any house or town."

Yet Dickinson seemed comfortable with solitude. In fact, she felt liberated rather than trapped, having copious amounts of time to read and write, garden, and bake cookies for the neighborhood children. She was not interested in socializing or taking part in community events, and she preferred corresponding with friends to having personal contact with them. "Emily Dickinson is our great poet of inwardness," said author JOYCE CAROL OATES, "the reclusive, teasing poet, forever dressed in virginal white, in her father's house in Amherst."

At the urging of her friend and admirer, the popular novelist HELEN HUNT JACKSON, Dickinson in 1878 reluctantly agreed to let one of her poems appear in an anthology of poetry by important American poets. Unlike Higginson, Jackson recognized that Dickinson was a poet of real stature. But after the anthology's editors made five changes in the 12-line poem, Dickinson never again allowed her poetry to appear in print.

Life took a surprising turn in 1882 when Judge Otis Lord, a widowed friend of her father and 16 years her senior, proposed marriage. Dickinson was flattered but flatly refused his offer, perhaps partly because she did not want to give up her independence.

Emily Dickinson died on May 15, 1886, in Amherst, at age 55. Amazingly, only seven of her poems had been published during her lifetime. After the funeral, Lavinia Dickinson discovered a cherry-wood cabinet containing hundreds of poems by her sister, many of which were neatly arranged, carefully copied, and bound together into small booklets, or fascicles. Although Dickinson had requested that her letters and papers be burned, Lavinia felt that her sister would not have wanted her poems destroyed.

The first collection, *Poems by Emily Dickinson,* appeared in 1890 and was extremely well received by the public: it was reprinted 11 times within two years. But, the collection, and several subsequent ones, had been heavily edited, altering rhymes, shifting line arrangements, and making the language conform to conventional standards. It was not until 1955 that the scholar Thomas H. Johnson published the definitive, three-volume edition of 1,775 of her poems, maintaining the author's original punctuation. A complete collection of her letters, which supplemented her poetry, followed three years later. Only then was the magnitude and scope of Emily Dickinson's abilities revealed.

Alfred Habegger came out with a new literary biography of the elusive genius in 2001. *Publishers Weekly* praised it for its "perceptive use of feminist scholarship of the past three decades, the firsthand reports of Dickinson's intimates, and careful readings of her lyrics and letters. . . . The biographer rejects the traditional view that Dickinson's work and life were static, instead declaring: 'Her poetry shows a striking and dramatic evolution.'" Habegger also points out that Dickinson was a "noncitizen by force and custom and law, and that many doors were closed to her, and that she left behind more good hard work than any of us."

"When I die, they'll have to remember me," Dickinson once said. She had lived with her share of disappointment: her father never appreciated her intelligence; her mother was remote and unloving; editors always wanted to revise her work; and society chastised her for being so introverted. But she knew she possessed a special gift, and when Higginson advised her not to publish her poems, she admonished him by warning that "if fame belonged to me, I could not escape her."

Emily Dickinson was intensely committed to her craft. She was a highly professional, passionate, and private artist who did things her way, no matter what anyone else suggested. Above all else, she was true to herself. Who was she? She answered that in one of her poems: She was "nobody." And then she asked, "Who are you?"

Further Reading

Dickinson, Emily. *The Complete Poems of Emily Dickinson.* Edited by Thomas H. Johnson. Boston: Little, Brown, 1957.

Habegger, Alfred. *My Wars Are Laid Away in Books: The Life of Emily Dickinson.* New York: Random House, 2001.

Martin, Wendy, ed. *The Cambridge Companion to Emily Dickinson: Eleven Essays by Leading International Scholars.* New York: Cambridge University Press, 2002.

Otfinoski, Steven. "Lady of Mystery, Poet of Greatness." In *American Profiles: Nineteenth-Century Writers,* 83–92. New York: Facts On File, 1991.

Sewall, Richard B. *The Life of Emily Dickinson,* 2 vols. New York: Farrar, Straus and Giroux, 1974.

Wolff, Cynthia Griffin. *Emily Dickinson.* New York: Alfred A. Knopf, 1986.

⟶ Didion, Joan
(1934–) *novelist, essayist, journalist*

In her major work, consisting of six novels and seven nonfiction books as of 2007, Joan Didion chronicles the erosion of traditional American values. An elegant prose stylist and gifted journalist, Didion writes frankly and incisively about contemporary moral dilemmas, failed interpersonal relationships, and disintegrating societies in modern times.

Joan Didion was born on December 5, 1934, in Sacramento, California. "My first notebook," she recalled in an essay in her collection *Slouching Towards Bethlehem,* "was a Big Five tablet, given to me by my mother with the sensible suggestion that I stop whining and learn to amuse myself by writing down my thoughts."

After graduating from the University of California at Berkeley in 1956 with a bachelor of arts degree in English, Didion won first prize in *Vogue*'s Prix de Paris writing competition. She moved to New York City and eventually became an associate feature editor at *Vogue.* At the same time, influenced by novelists such as Joseph Conrad and Ernest Hemingway, she worked diligently on her fiction, constantly revising and perfecting it. "I'm not much interested in spontaneity," she wrote. "What concerns me is total control."

Didion left *Vogue* in 1963, the same year she published *River Run,* her first, and some critics say her finest, novel. Set in the Sacramento Valley in the 1940s, it was the first of numerous books and essays in which the author graphically described the boredom, decadence, and deteriorating values in her native California.

During that same period, between 1963 and 1969, she continued to write magazine articles and columns for *Vogue, Harper's, Life,* and the *Saturday Evening Post;* Didion has always considered journalist assignments an important source for her fiction.

In 1964 Didion married the writer John Gregory Dunne and returned with him to California, where they adopted a daughter, Quintana Roo. Four years later she published her first collection of essays, *Slouching Towards Bethlehem,* which was critically acclaimed and sealed Didion's literary reputation. Most of the previously published pieces, such as a sardonic portrait of "flower children" and their ingenuous hippie culture, deal with America during the turbulent late 1960s.

Slouching Towards Bethlehem also includes a popular essay entitled "On Keeping a Notebook," in which Didion explains why she jots down seemingly unimportant fragments of ideas and conversations. "The point of my keeping a notebook has never been, nor is it now, to have an accurate factual record of what I have been doing or thinking. . . . I suppose that keeping in touch is what notebooks are all about. It [the idea] is then transformed into art through the process of selectivity."

Didion's next work, *Play It as It Lays* (1970), her best-known, best-selling novel, captures the emptiness and selfishness of the glamorous life in a southern California film community. Praised for its pure, unsentimental dialogue and dramatic, spare style, it earned Didion a National Book Award nomination. In 1972 she and her husband collaborated on a screenplay version of the book, one of seven film dramatizations they worked on together.

In 1976 Didion wrote an important article for the *New York Times Book Review.* "Why I Write" begins with the statement: "I write in order to find out who I am and what I fear." The article also emphasizes the power of speech and the importance of the sound of words as they resonate from the printed page. "Grammar," she said, is "a piano I play by ear," while "the arrangement of words can be found in the picture of [the author's] mind." Discipline is also important; Didion claims that she often writes seven days a week, from 11 in the morning to eight at night.

Another national best-selling novel, *A Book of Common Prayer* (1977), takes place in a fictitious Central American country, where a female protagonist from California attempts to cope with her shattered life and desires. Didion often writes about women who in a meaningless world try to find meaning through relationships with lovers, family, and friends, but who usually fail. Some feminists have criticized Didion because she does not depict female characters as victims of male oppression, insisting on individual responsibility to resolve conflicts. In one of her essays Didion attacked feminist interpretations of literature as being "too narrow" and "obsessed with trivia."

The White Album (1979), a collection of essays that mostly focus on the "reckless, self-indulgent" age of self-discovery and spirituality during the 1960s and 1970s, was nominated for an American Book Award in nonfiction. The title essay opens with the line: "We tell ourselves stories in order to live," which is what the author seems to do. In another of the book's essays, "In the Islands," Didion describes herself as a "woman who for some time now has felt radically separated from most of the ideas that seem to interest other people."

Although Didion is considered a California writer, some of her best work is about other places—New York, Miami, and El Salvador. In 1988 she and Dunne moved to New York City, "the mysterious nexus of all love and money and power," and in subsequent years they divided their time between the East and West Coasts.

In the 1980s and 1990s Didion wrote two more novels, *Democracy* (1984) and *The Last Thing He Wanted* (1996), which was awarded the Edward MacDowell Medal, and three books of nonfiction, *Salvador* (1983), *Miami* (1987), and *After Henry* (1992). She also wrote a biographical narrative about her family's roots from 1766 to the present. *Where I Was From* (2003) represents, in Didion's words, "an exploration into my own confusions about the place and the way in which I grew up, confusions as much about America as about California, misapprehensions and misunderstandings so much a part of who I became that I can still to this day confront them only obliquely."

Then, after Didion's husband died suddenly of a massive heart attack on December 30, 2003, while they were having dinner together at home, she wrote a moving memoir, *The Year of Magical Thinking*. It described the nightmarish event and the year of mourning and grief that followed his death, while taking care of and worrying about her daughter, who had been hospitalized with a serious illness. Didion and Dunne, unofficially known as America's foremost literary couple, had shared their lives and work intimately and with extraordinary candor for 40 years. *The Year of Magical Thinking* won the 2005 National Book Award for nonfiction and the *Los Angeles Times*'s Robert Kirsch Award for lifetime achievement in 2006. "It is an utterly shattering book that gives the reader an indelible portrait of loss and grief and sorrow, all chronicled in minute detail with the author's unsavory, reportorial eye," wrote *New York Times* critic Michiko Kakutani. "It is a book that tells us how people try to make sense of the senseless and how they somehow go on." *Magical Thinking* was staged as a one-woman play starring Vanessa Redgrave in 2007.

Tragically, just weeks before *The Year of Magical Thinking* was published, Didion's daughter Quintana Roo died, less than two years after the death of her father.

John Leonard, in the *New York Times Book Review*, has called Joan Didion the best woman prose stylist in America. An acute observer of society and its illusions, she is committed to telling a good story and to telling the truth.

Further Reading

Didion, Joan. *A Book of Common Prayer.* New York: Simon and Schuster, 1977.

———. *Essays & Conversations.* Princeton, N.J.: Ontario Review Press, 1984.

———. *Play It as It Lays.* New York: Farrar, Straus and Giroux, 1970.

———. *We Tell Ourselves Stories in Order to Live.* New York: Alfred A. Knopf, 2006.

———. *Where I Was From.* New York: Alfred A. Knopf, 2003.

———. *The Year of Magical Thinking.* New York: Alfred A. Knopf, 2005.

Felton, Sharon, ed. *The Critical Response to Joan Didion.* Westport, Conn.: Greenwood Press, 1994.

Montagne, Renée. "Didion brings *Magical Thinking* to Broadway." National Public Radio. February 8, 2007. Available online. URL: http://www.npr.org/templates/story/story.php?storyId=7238970. Downloaded on February 26, 2007.

Winchell, Mark Royden. *Joan Didion.* Boston: Twayne, 1989.

🙠 Dillard, Annie Doak

(1945–) *naturalist, essayist, autobiographer*

Annie Dillard is a critically acclaimed writer whose first major publication, *Pilgrim at Tinker Creek* (1974), won a Pulitzer Prize in 1975 and has been compared to Henry David Thoreau's *Walden.* Her impressive body of work has been recognized for its finely wrought language, insightful observations, and striking imagery.

Born on April 30, 1945, in Pittsburgh, Pennsylvania, to a wealthy family, Annie Doak attended private girls' schools. In her autobiography, *An American Childhood* (1987), she described her reaction to discovering poetry.

> I dosed myself with pure lyricism; I lived drugged on sensation, as I had lived alert on sensation as a little child. . . . I wanted to swim in the stream of beautiful syllables until I tired.

In 1964 Doak married Richard Dillard, a professor and writer. They were divorced 10 years later, and Dillard remarried twice. She has a daughter and two stepchildren.

After receiving her bachelor's (1967) and master's (1968) degrees from Hollins College in Virginia, Dillard published essays, fiction, and poetry in numerous magazines, including *Harper's,* where she was also a contributing editor for several years. In 1974 she published her first book, a slim but well-received collection of verse, *Tickets for a Prayer Wheel,* about the poet's quest for spiritual knowledge.

Her next book, also published in 1974, was the best-selling, Pulitzer Prize–winning *Pilgrim at Tinker Creek.* Almost theological in tone, it was based on Dillard's astute observations on nature's contradictory forces as experienced in Virginia's Roanoke Valley and Blue Ridge Mountains, where she had spent nearly a decade living in seclusion. *Holy the Firm* (1978), a powerful metaphysical study of the author's attempt to reconcile faith in a compassionate deity with seemingly random cruelty and violence, was inspired by a neighborhood child having been badly burned in a plane crash.

After chronicling her 1982 experiences as a member of a Chinese-American cultural exchange, Dillard published her best-selling autobiography, *An American Childhood,* in 1987. Nostalgic without being sentimental, she looked deeply into her past and described growing up as a curious, intelligent, rebellious adolescent in the homogenous, middle-class urban America of the 1950s. Dillard's next book, *The Writing Life* (1989), was not a "how-to-get-published" manual with tips for hopeful writers, but rather a personalized account of the creative and practical processes involved in working at one's craft.

In 1992 Dillard wrote her first novel, *The Living,* which she set in the Pacific Northwest, where she had lived during the 1970s while teaching at Western Washington University. Critics hailed it as masterful, noting the author's impressive way with words. Three years later she attempted, somewhat successfully, an experimental volume of poetry, *Mornings Like This: Found Poems,* in which she used lines from other writers' prose works to inspire her own verse. Dillard described her next book, *For the Time Being* (1999), as comprising "scenes from a paleontologists' explorations in the deserts of China, the thinking of the Hasidic Jews of Eastern Europe, a natural history of sand, individual clouds and then moments in time, human birth defects, information about our generation, narrative bits from modern Israel and China, and quizzical encounters with strangers."

Also in 1999 Dillard came out with a collection of compelling meditations into the natural world, *Teaching a Stone to Talk: Expeditions and Encounters.* On January 6, 2005, she was asked during an interview on National Public Radio (NPR) to comment on the destruction from the recent Tsunami in Southeast Asia. She asked listeners to remind themselves that the thousands of victims were individuals with loved ones and not just faceless statistics.

Her most recent novel, *The Maytrees* (2007), is about a family living in Provincetown, Massachusetts, during the 1940s and 1950s. In a review in *Booklist,* Donna Seaman calls Dillard's book a "mythic and transfixing tale that wryly questions notions of love, exalts in life's metamorphoses, and celebrates goodness."

In much of her work, Annie Dillard, who is a professor emeritus at Wesleyan University in Middletown, Connecticut, and an American Academy of Arts and Letters Fellow, lyrically expresses her deep concern for and appreciation of nature. In one of her essays, "Sight into Insight," she writes:

> There are lots of things to see, unwrapped gifts and free surprises. . . . I open my eyes and I see dark, muscled forms curl out of water, with flapping gills and flattened eyes. I close my eyes and I see stars, deep stars giving way to deeper stars, deeper stars bowing to deepest stars at the crown of an infinite cone.

Further Reading

Dillard, Annie. *The Annie Dillard Reader.* (Includes *Pilgrim at Tinker Creek* and *An American Childhood*). New York: HarperPerennial, 1995.

———. *For the Time Being.* New York: Knopf, 1999.

———. *The Maytrees.* New York: HarperCollins, 2007.

———. *The Writing Life.* New York: Harper and Row, 1989.

Smith, Linda L. *Annie Dillard.* Boston: Twayne Publishers, 1991.

Doolittle, Hilda (H. D.)
(1886–1961)   *poet, novelist*

In the early years of her literary career, Hilda Doolittle, known as H. D., was considered the "perfect Imagist poet," producing popular short, spare, precise verse. In later years H. D. distinguished herself with longer narrative verse that was more intellectual and epic in scope.

Hilda Doolittle was born on September 10, 1886, in Bethlehem, Pennsylvania. Growing up, she was influenced by her mother's involvement in the Moravian church, a sect that identified with the "mystery which lay at the center of the world." This influence can also be detected in her later work.

Hilda attended private schools and at 15 met Ezra Pound, who would become a celebrated modernist poet. The two were twice engaged; although they never married, they became lifelong friends, and Pound introduced Doolittle to other avantgarde writers, such as William Carlos Williams and MARIANNE MOORE.

After spending only two years at Bryn Mawr College, in 1911 Doolittle decided to accompany a friend and her mother on a trip to Europe, where she permanently settled. In London she again met up with Pound, and over tea at the British Museum she showed him some of her poems. Impressed with their concrete, sharp-edged imagery, he sent them to a friend at *Poetry* magazine, signing them "H. D. Imagiste." Both the pseudonym and the name for the new poetry movement, imagism, stuck. According to Pound, an image is "an intellectual and emotional complex in an instant of time." The imagists in America attempted to rejuvenate poetic language and form through the objective presentations of visual images. They focused on precision to create a concentrated effect.

In 1913 H. D. married the British imagist poet Richard Aldington, with whom she shared a love of Greek literature. H. D. ingeniously shaped the classical world into her poetry, using myth to express the cult of the goddess, spirituality, and eternity. Her first collection of imagist poems, *Sea Garden* (1916), was well received. Having rejected Victorian norms for modern experiments, she wrote spare, chiseled verse with irregular meter; her poems, notable for its imagery, included only the essentials.

Traumatized by her older brother's death at the front during World War I, a miscarriage, and marital problems that led to her separation from Aldington (they were divorced in 1938), H. D. suffered a nervous breakdown. In her autobiographical novel *Palimpsest* (1926), she described her intense, lifelong relationship with the novelist Winifred Ellerman, known as "Bryher," as the "single bright spot" during that turbulent period.

Bryher, a young English heiress who had married twice, greatly admired H. D.'s work and became her devoted friend and companion. She adopted H. D.'s daughter Perdita and subsidized the publication her next book of verse, *Hymen* (1921). Along with *Heliodora* (1924), *Hymen* was praised for its economy of language and precision. While traveling with Bryher in Greece, H. D. had a visionary experience relating to Nike, the winged goddess of victory. This mystical vision helped her develop a kind of "woman's mythology" in which women would help save the world: Nike would merge with the god of the sun, Helios. H. D.'s interest in spiritualism and female-dominated mythology continued well into her later years.

H. D.'s reputation soared with the publication in 1925 of *Collected Poems*. It was followed by *HERmione* (1927), the first of several novels, and another popular collection of poems, *Red Roses for Bronze* (1931). H. D. also wrote plays, Greek translations, children's fiction, and short stories.

During the 1930s, however, she published relatively little and believed that her creativity was on the decline. Attempting to overcome writer's block, she underwent two years of psychoanalysis with Sigmund Freud, rejecting some of his theories and accepting others, such as the vital role played by dreams. H. D. recorded her experiences with the famous "blameless physician" in *Tribute to Freud,* which was published in 1956.

After a tense period, in which H. D. lived through the bombings of London during World War II and then suffered another nervous breakdown (in 1946), her poetry changed. Gone was the terse, pared down imagist verse. Instead she wrote intensive, lengthy epic poems, including the critically acclaimed *Triology.* Composed of three volumes of verse written between 1944 and 1946, it was based on the horrors of wartime London. In the first part, *The Walls Do Not Fall* (1944), H. D. combines classical allusions with observations of postwar England; she also combines Mary Magdalene with the Virgin Mary into a single, central woman-figure.

Imagist poet Hilda Doolittle used the pseudonym H. D.
(AP/Wide World Photos)

In *Helen in Egypt,* another epic poem, composed between 1952 and 1955, H. D. explores the divinity of the goddess through Helen as she struggles for and ultimately achieves self-definition following the Trojan War. The theme of the woman/artist as hero is prevalent throughout H. D.'s later work.

After suffering another nervous breakdown, H. D. moved from London to Kusnacht, Switzerland, where she remained at a sanitorium for 15 years; the bills were paid for by her devoted friend Bryher. Although during her lifetime she had numerous romantic relationships with men and women, H. D. continued to search beyond them for "a myth, the one reality," where she could function both as woman and artist; she was guided by the principal that, as she explained in her 1979 memoir of Ezra Pound, "the mother is the Muse, the Creator."

In 1960 H. D. returned to the United States to accept the Award of Merit Medal for poetry from the American Academy of Arts and Letters. A year later, on September 29, 1961, she died in Switzerland at the age of 75. Paying tribute to the power of the written word, she once wrote: "Winged words make their own spiral; caught up in them, we are lost, or found. . . . This winged victory belongs to the poem, not the poet. But to share in the making of a poem is the privilege of a poet."

Although her literary reputation was mainly derived from her popular and critical success as an imagist poet, her later distinguished, mythological poems, which dealt with mature themes such as death and resurrection, were recognized by and influenced contemporary poets such as LOUISE BOGAN and DENISE LEVERTOV.

Further Reading

Doolittle, Hilda (H. D.). *Collected Poems 1912–1944.* New York: New Directions, 1983.

———. *Selected Poems.* New York: New Directions, 1988.

Guest, Barbara. *Herself Defined: The Poet H.D. and Her World.* Garden City, N.Y.: Doubleday, 1984.

"Hilda Doolittle." The H.D. Home Page. Available online. URL: http://www.imagists.org/hd. Downloaded on January 19, 2007.

Robinson, Janice S. *H.D.: The Life and World of an American Poet.* Boston: Houghton Mifflin, 1982.

Dove, Rita Frances
(1952–) *poet, short story writer*

The youngest poet and the first African American appointed U.S. poet laureate (1993–94; then extended until 1995), Rita Dove has written fiction, plays, and seven volumes of verse, including her best-known collection, the Pulitzer Prize–winning *Thomas and Beulah.*

Rita Frances Dove was born on August 28, 1952, in Akron, Ohio, where both her father and grandfather were employed by the Goodyear Tire and Rubber Company; her father started working there as an elevator operator and eventually became the company's first black chemist.

Rita's parents believed strongly in the value of education and at an early age encouraged her to write plays and stories. In 1970 she was one of only 100 high school students invited to the White House in Washington, D.C., as a Presidential Scholar. In addition, to this honor, a high school English teacher took her to meet the poet John Ciardi at a writers' conference. "That day I realized . . . it was possible to write down a poem . . . in the intimate sphere of one's own room, and then share it with the world," she recalled.

After graduating summa cum laude from Miami University in Ohio in 1973, Dove spent two years at the University of Tübingen in Germany on a Fulbright fellowship. Later she would incorporate her travel experiences and expanded worldwide view into her poetry.

In 1977 Dove earned a master's degree from the University of Iowa's Writers' Workshop. Meanwhile, her poetry began to appear in major periodicals. She had decided not to limit herself to what she perceived as the narrowness of the Black Arts movement of the 1960s. "As an artist," she said in an interview in *Callaloo* magazine, "I shun political considerations and racial or gender partiality." Dove was more interested in "the ways in which language can change your perceptions."

Rita Dove was the first African-American
U.S. poet laureate.
(AP/Wide World Photos)

Dove's first two books of verse, *The Yellow House on the Corner* (1980) and *Museum* (1983), were acclaimed by critics for their impressionistic imagery, control and discipline, and the ways in which ordinary, everyday events merge seamlessly with larger historical issues.

A collection of short fiction, *Fifth Sunday* (1985), was followed by *Thomas and Beulah* (1986), a family saga told through interrelated poems. In 1987 it garnered the Pulitzer Prize in Poetry; Dove was the first African American since GWENDOLYN BROOKS to win the prestigious award. The narrative poem was based loosely on the experiences of her maternal grandparents, Thomas,

born in Tennessee in 1900, and Beulah, who hailed from Georgia. With "the kind of sweep of a novel," as Dove describes it, *Thomas and Beulah* portrays the loving relationship of a black working-class couple in middle America.

> A hanger clatters
> in the front of the shoppe.
> Beulah remembers how
> even Autumn could lean into a settee
> with her ankles crossed, sighin
> *I need a man who'll protect me*
> while smoking her cigarette down to the very
>   end.

"They are poems about humanity," explained Dove in the *Washington Post,* "and sometimes humanity happens to be black. I cannot run from, I won't run from any kind of truth."

Two more poetry books followed: *The Other Side of the House* (1988) and the largely autobiographical *Grace Notes* (1989). Dove also produced a play titled *The Siberian Village* (1991), and, in 1992, a novel, *Through the Ivory Gate*—the story of a gifted young black woman who becomes an artist in residence at an elementary school in her hometown and is forced to confront painful childhood memories.

During the fall of 1993, Dove was officially installed as poet laureate of the United States at the Library of Congress; coincidentally, almost to the day, the black novelist TONI MORRISON was announced as the winner of the Nobel Prize in literature. A year later Dove published a verse play, *The Darker Face of the Earth,* a reworking of Sophocles's *Oedipus Rex,* and in 1995 she released *Mother Love*— poems revolving around the Greek myth of Demeter and Persephone to evoke the powerful mother-daughter bond. Another collection, *On the Bus with Rosa Parks* (1999), honors Rosa Parks and other civil rights activists. According to *Publishers Weekly,* the book is filled with Dove's signature blend of masterly polished images and spare musical storytelling.

Dove has been the recipient of many awards and fellowships, including a Guggenheim and a Mellon, and several honorary doctorate degrees. She has taught writing for more than a decade, most recently as Commonwealth Professor of English at the University of Virginia. Dove and her husband, Fred Viebahn, a novelist from Germany, have a daughter, Aviva. Dove, who has been interested in music and theater since childhood, enjoys singing opera. For "America's Millennium," the White House's 1999/2000 New Year's celebration, Dove contributed—in a live reading at the Lincoln Memorial accompanied by John Williams's music—a poem to director Steven Spielberg's documentary *The Unfinished Journey.*

Dove was the editor of *Best American Poetry 2000,* and from January 2000 to 2002 she wrote a weekly column, "Poet's Choice," for the *Washington Post.* In 2001 she received a Duke Ellington Lifetime Achievement Award. Her eighth and most recent poetry collection, *American Smooth,* which, according to Janet St. John in *Booklist,* is "infused with dance rhythms and speaks through many voices to cover a broad range of thoughts and emotions," was published in 2004, the same year Dove was appointed for two years as poet laureate of the Commonwealth of Virginia.

Since her appointment as poet laureate, Rita Dove's work has received greater critical attention. She is considered by many to be one of the best young poets in the country today.

Further Reading

Dove, Rita. *American Smooth.* New York: W. W. Norton, 2004.

———. *Thomas and Beulah.* Pittsburgh, Penn.: Carnegié-Mellon University Press, 1986.

———. *On the Bus with Rosa Parks.* New York: W. W. Norton, 1999.

Georgoudaki, Ekaterini, "Rita Dove: Crossing the Boundaries." *Callaloo* 14, no. 2 (Spring 1991): 419–433.

Vendler, Helen. "Rita Dove: Identity Markers." In *The Given and the Made: Strategies of Poetic Redefinition,* 61–87. Cambridge, Mass.: Harvard University Press, 1998.

Dunbar-Nelson, Alice Ruth Moore

(1875–1935)   *short story writer, poet, diarist*

One of the first black women to distinguish herself in American literature, and a respected voice of the Harlem Renaissance, Alice Dunbar-Nelson was a versatile writer known especially for her powerful short stories and poetry. She was also an educator and a staunch advocate of racial equality, women's rights, and world peace.

Born in New Orleans, Louisiana, on July 19, 1875, the daughter of a Creole seaman and a former slave of American Indian heritage, Alice Ruth Moore was an outstanding student who attended New Orlean's Straight University when she was only 15, receiving a teaching degree in 1892. In later years she would continue her studies at Cornell University and the University of Pennsylvania.

While teaching in New Orleans, Moore began to submit poetry to the Boston *Monthly Review,* and in 1895 she published her first work, *Violets and Other Tales.* Moore described the slim collection of poems, short stories, and essays as being about "simple human beings, not the types of a race or an idea."

After moving with her family to Medford, Massachusetts, in 1896, Moore began a two-year literary correspondence with Paul Laurence Dunbar, a renowned black poet. They finally met in New York City in 1897 at a reception held in Dunbar's honor, and within hours he presented her with his mother's gold ring. They were secretly married on March 6, 1898.

Although her husband was well known, he made little money. In order to help pay their bills, Dunbar-Nelson took a job in New York City's public schools. Before joining him in Washington, D.C., she helped establish Harlem's White Rose Mission for girls. Wherever she lived or worked, she was devoted to political and social activism, while continuing to write.

In 1899 Dunbar-Nelson published a collection of 14 tales about Creole life in New Orleans entitled *The Goodness of St. Rocque, and Other Stories.* Considered her finest work, reviewers commented on the precision, richness, and complexity of the writing, as well as the clever twist endings. Some of the stories revolved around feminist issues but rarely did they directly discuss race.

Dunbar-Nelson's romantic but turbulent marriage to her celebrated husband lasted only four years. After separating in 1902 (Paul Dunbar died four years later), she moved to Wilmington, Delaware, where she taught English at Howard High School and became head of its English department. After teaching there for 18 years, she was fired for engaging in political activities; she had also made a name for herself as an impressive but controversial public speaker.

Briefly married to and then divorced from a fellow teacher, Dunbar-Nelson finally found some happiness in her third and final marriage in 1916 to Robert J. Nelson, publisher of a newspaper that championed black rights. Their two-decade relationship was fraught with financial worries, but they cared deeply about each other.

Dunbar-Nelson continued to contribute stories and poems to various periodicals, and in 1920 edited and published *The Dunbar Speaker and Entertainer.* Directed toward a black readership, it included several of her own poems and prose pieces, including the verse "I Sit and Sew," which laments the "wasted fields" of women who were not allowed to make meaningful contributions to the World War I effort. Dunbar-Nelson herself served with the Circle of Negro War Relief in 1918.

In the 1920s Dunbar-Nelson became politically active and was the first black woman to serve on Delaware's Republican State Committee. Two years later she switched to the Democratic Party in order to support anti-lynching measures. She was also appointed executive secretary of the American Interracial Peace Committee in 1928. Because of her fair skin, she could often "pass" for white, but she was proud of her Creole heritage and rarely took advantage of her light complexion.

A respected journalist, from 1926 to 1930 she wrote regular columns for the *Pittsburgh Courier* and the *Washington Eagle,* and she also reviewed books and cultural events for newspapers such as Wilmington's *Journal Every Evening,* where her last article appeared in 1932.

Alice Ruth Moore Dunbar-Nelson died on September 18, 1935, in Philadelphia. Her diary, *Give Us Each Day: The Diary of Alice Dunbar-Nelson,* was published posthumously in 1984. It incisively provides a personal, professional, and social history of an African-American working woman during the early 20th century.

Further Reading

Alexander, Eleanor. *Lyrics of Sunshine and Shadow: The Tragic Courtship and Marriage of Paul Laurence Dunbar and Alice Ruth Moore.* New York: Plume/New American Library, 2004.

Bone, Robert. *Down Home: A History of Afro-American Short fiction from Its Beginnings to the End of the Harlem Renaissance.* New York: Putnam, 1975.

Dunbar-Nelson, Alice. *Give Us Each Day: The Diary of Alice Dunbar-Nelson,* edited by Gloria T. Hull. New York: W. W. Norton, 1984.

———. *The Works of Alice Dunbar-Nelson.* Edited by Gloria T. Hull. 3 vols. New York: Oxford University Press, 1988.

Hull, Gloria T. *Color, Sex, and Poetry: Three Women Writers of the Harlem Renaissance.* Bloomington: Indiana University Press, 1987.

E

⮱ Edwards, Bronwen Elizabeth
See ROSE, WENDY

⮱ Ehrenreich, Barbara
(1941–) *nonfiction book writer,
journalist, essayist*

The author of the national best seller *Nickel and
Dimed: On (Not) Getting By in America,* Barbara
Ehrenreich is a prolific writer, having produced 13
nonfiction books and dozens of newspaper and
magazine articles and essays, including "Welcome to
Cancerland," a finalist for the National Magazine
Award in 2003. Dubbed "our premier reporter of
the underside of capitalism" by the *New York Times
Book Review,* she is a highly regarded though contro-
versial journalist and an influential social critic.

Ehrenreich was born in Butte, Montana, on
August 26, 1941. She graduated from Reed Col-
lege in 1963, where she studied physics, received a
Ph.D. in biology in 1968 from The Rockefeller
University in New York City, and is the recipient
of numerous grants and awards, including a Ford
Foundation Award for Humanistic Perspectives on
Contemporary Issues and a Guggenheim Fellow-
ship. From 1969 to 1971 she worked for the

Health Policy Advisory Center in New York City.
She and her husband, John Ehrenreich, whom she
married in 1966 (they later divorced, and in 1983
she married Gary Stevenson, whom she divorced
in the early 1990s) wrote a book together titled
*The American Health Empire: Power, Profits, and
Politics, a Report from the Health Policy Advisory
Center* (1970), exposing what Ehrenreich observed
were inequities in the health care system. She has
had firsthand experience as a breast cancer survivor.

*Witches, Midwives and Nurses: A History of
Women Healers,* cowritten with Diedre English,
was published in 1972 by The Feminist Press. It
was followed by several other provocative nonfiction works, including in 1973 *Complaints and Dis-
orders: The Sexual Politics of Sickness* (coauthored
with English), which focused on male domination
of the female health care system; *The Hearts of
Men: American Dreams and the Flight from Commitment* (1983), which Ehrenreich describes as a
study of "the ideology that shaped the breadwinner
ethic"; and *Fear of Falling: The Inner Life of the
Middle Class,* which was nominated for a National
Book Critics Circle Award in 1989. Ehrenreich
also edited a collection of her own essays, most of
which had appeared in prominent periodicals,
titled *The Worst Years of Our Lives: Irreverent Notes*

from a Decade of Greed (1990), about the consumerist 1980s. Ehrenreich was nothing if not "irreverent," when it came to exposing the nation's social ailments.

A year later she published the best-selling *Blood Rites: Origins and History of Passions of War,* in which she postulates the underlying reason for the long-standing human attraction to violence and finds it in the blood rites of early human beings. It was selected as a notable book by the American Library Association and the *New York Times* in 1997.

Although she never formally studied journalism or worked full time with a news organization, Ehrenreich wrote for many reputable newspapers and magazines and received accolades for her work. She was a columnist for *Mother Jones* magazine from 1986 to 1989 and wrote a monthly column for *Time* magazine from 1991 to 1997, in which she showcased her sardonic humor and knowledge about current social and cultural issues. She shared a National Magazine Award for Excellence in Reporting and garnered the Sydney Hillman Award for Journalism, and has been a frequent contributor to the *New York Times* (guest columnist in 2004), *Harper's,* the *Nation* (winner of the 2004 Puffin/Nation Award), the *Atlantic Monthly,* the *New Republic,* the *Progressive,* and online publications such as Salon.com.

Ehrenreich's best-known book, *Nickel and Dimed: On (Not) Getting By in America,* was published in 2001. She says she wrote it to remind readers that there is a "state of emergency" that cannot be ignored: Poverty affects millions of American low-wage workers. In 1998, while having lunch with Lewis Lapham, the editor of *Harper's* magazine, she wondered aloud how 4 million former welfare recipients would survive on $6 or $7 an hour and mentioned that someone should do the "old-fashioned kind of journalism—you know, go out there and try it for themselves." His response was "You should do it." Ehrenreich followed his suggestion.

Between 1998 and 2000, without disclosing her upper-middle-class identity, Ehrenreich took a series of low-paying jobs to support herself in three different cities. "I waited tables, cleaned the toilets of the rich . . . I sorted stock at Wal-Mart. All these were difficult, exhausting jobs, and it made me understand what a serious mistake our nation made with welfare reform," explained Ehrenreich. She continued:

No matter how carefully I pinched pennies, I couldn't get my wages to cover basic expenses. . . . Now if there's one thing that's really demoralizing, it's working hard and not making enough to live on. . . . Here's a simple theory of poverty: It's not a psychological condition. It is, above all, a consequence of shamefully low wages and lack of opportunity for anything else.

Nickel and Dimed was the result of Ehrenreich's undercover experiment and her subsequent observations. The impassioned book has sold more than 1 million copies and was a best seller for nearly two years, including 94 weeks on the *New York Times* paperback list, and seems to have struck a nerve among readers who may not have been aware of the horrific working conditions experienced by so many people on a daily basis. Scott Sherman, in an article about Ehrenreich and *Nickel and Dimed* that appeared in the *Columbia Journalism Review* in 2003, compared her to George Orwell, in that Ehrenreich wanted to "shock her readers, and shame them, and show them 'a world apart'—a beleaguered service-sector work force that, amid the sonorous reveries surrounding the New Economy, remains, as the author puts it, a smoldering tinderbox of unmet needs and desires."

In keeping with her interest in female exploitation, in 2003 she coedited, with Arlie Russell Hochschild, a collection of essays called *Global Woman: Nannies, Maids, and Sex Workers in the New Economy* that analyzes the dire consequences of globalization on a growing sector of working women. Ehrenreich's most recent book, *Bait and Switch: The (Futile) Pursuit of the American Dream,* was published in 2005. Once again the author went undercover, this time as a downsized job-hunting professional, in order to enter the world of American white-collar workers, midlevel managers,

Undercover reporter Barbara Ehrenreich's *Nickel and Dimed* sold more than 1 million copies.
(AP Images/Andrew Shurtleff)

and corporate functionaries—a group who seem to be successful and believe in the system, yet have become more vulnerable to financial failure and are no longer rewarded by the system. *Bait and Switch* was not as well received by literary critics as *Nickel and Dimed*, although it too was a best-selling book. "The problem is that the author, so comfortable as a champion of the disenfranchised, evinces such palpable disdain for this flawed but enterprising milieu," wrote Alexandra Jacobs of the *New York Times*.

In 2007 Ehrenreich wrote a nonscholarly history of collective joy, *Dancing in the Streets*, which explains and affirms the value of ecstatic communal celebrations such as carnivals and maypole festivals. Ehrenreich, who lives in Virginia and has two children from her first marriage as well as a grand-

daughter, is an honorary cochair of the Democratic Socialists of America. She has taught at several institutions, including essay-writing at the Graduate School of Journalism at University of California, Berkeley. She also has been awarded a number of honorary degrees.

When asked her reaction to Katrina, the hurricane that devastated the city of New Orleans in 2005, Barbara Ehrenreich confidently told a *Hartford Courant* reporter, "It made complete sense to me that thousands of residents wouldn't be able to evacuate the city. They don't have cars. They don't have credit cards. A single illness or injury could cost them their jobs . . . So, it didn't take 175 mile-per-hour winds—their lives already were catastrophic."

Further Reading

Ehrenreich, Barbara. *Bait and Switch: The (Futile) Pursuit of the American Dream*. New York: Henry Holt and Company, 2005.

———. *Blood Rites: Origins and History of the Passions of War*. Henry Holt and Company, 1997.

———. *Dancing in the Streets: A History of Collective Joy*. New York: Henry Holt, 2007.

———. *Nickel and Dimed: On (Not) Getting By in America*. New York: Henry Holt and Company, 2001.

———. "Nickel and Dimed in America." NOW with Bill Moyers. The Public Broadcasting System. March 19, 2002. Available online. URL: http://www.pbs.org/now/commentary/ehrenreich.html. Downloaded on January 19, 2007.

Kazin, Michael. "Barbara Ehrenreich's White Collar Blues." *The Nation*, October 3, 2005.

"Notable Writers Talk About Their Craft: Barbara Ehrenreich." Literary Nonfiction at the University of Oregon. Available online. URL: http://lnf.uoregon.edu/notable/ehrenreich.html. Downloaded on January 19, 2007.

Erdrich, Karen Louise
(1954–)   *novelist, poet, short-story writer*

Louise Erdrich, whose mother was a Turtle Mountain Chippewa, explores the complexities of contemporary American Indian life in her award-winning fiction and poetry. Erdrich's work has been praised for its mastery of language, emotional precision, humor, and shamanlike storytelling.

The daughter of a German-American father and an American Indian mother, Karen Louise Erdrich was born on July 6, 1954, in Little Falls, Minnesota. She and her six siblings were raised in Wahpeton, North Dakota, where both her parents worked for the local Indian school.

Storytelling and writing, Erdrich recalled, always played an important part of her life. "[Native Americans] just sit and the stories start coming, one after another. I suppose that when you grow up constantly hearing the stories rise, break, and fall, it gets into you somehow." In addition, Louise's father gave her a nickel for every story she wrote, while her mother wove strips of construction paper together and stapled them into book covers.

After graduating from Dartmouth College in 1976, Erdrich returned to North Dakota to conduct poetry workshops and then moved to Boston to edit the Boston Indian Council's newspaper, the *Circle*. She also held a variety of odd jobs working as a beet weeder, waitress, psychiatric aide, lifeguard, and construction flag signaler. Her "really crazy" jobs, as she described them, would provide material for her fiction in later years.

In 1978 Erdrich enrolled in a creative writing program at Johns Hopkins University. After receiving her master's degree in 1979, she returned to Dartmouth as a writer-in-residence. In 1981 she married Indian writer and anthropologist Michael Dorris, who had been her teacher at Dartmouth, where he directed the Native American Studies program. From the beginning of their relationship, the couple collaborated on their books, editing each other's work until they agreed on every word and the rhythm of each sentence. "Its a true kind at collaboration," Erdrich told *Publishers Weekly*. "We both really influence the course of the book."

In 1982 Erdrich received a fellowship from the National Endowment for the Arts (NEA). She also won the Nelson Algren fiction competition for "The World's Greatest Fisherman," a story collab-oratively composed with Dorris that would become the first chapter of their first and perhaps best-known novel, *Love Medicine*.

At the age of 30, Erdrich published a collection of poems, *Jacklight* (1984), followed the same year by *Love Medicine*. An immediate best seller, the lyrical, dreamlike novel of 14 self-contained tales, which was published under her name, garnered the 1984 National Book Critics Circle Award for fiction. *Love Medicine* was the first of Erdrich's four-volume saga about several interrelated Indian families living on the Turtle Mountain Reservation in North Dakota, and their European-immigrant neighbors, from the early 1900s until the present. Using multiple viewpoints, and a series of surreal, freestanding but related stories, the book spans 50 years and depicts the struggles of a dispossessed people grappling with the modern "white and half-breed" world and with traditions set by their Indian elders.

In 1985 Erdrich won the O. Henry Prize for *Saint Marie*. The affecting story had already appeared as the second chapter of *Love Medicine*, and its last line reads: "Rise up! I thought. Rise up and walk! There is no limit to this dust!"

Many of *Love Medicine*'s characters reappear, to a greater or lesser degree, in the saga's three other novels: *The Beet Queen* (1986), *Tracks* (1988), and *The Bingo Palace* (1994). Erdrich wrote several other novels, including *The Painted Bird* (2005), which again combined a contemporary narrative about love and loss with interconnected stories about the characters' ancestors. One critic from the *New York Times* stated that Erdrich's storytelling powers are "on virtuosic display in this novel."

Although her central focus is the Native American experience, Erdrich writes about universal themes and believes that setting American Indian literature apart from mainstream literature would be "setting Indians apart too."

In 1989 Erdrich published her second book of verse, *Baptism of Desire*. Two years later, for the first time she officially coauthored a best-selling novel with Dorris: both their names appeared on the cover. *The Crown of Columbus* raised important questions about the meaning of Columbus's voyage for both Europeans and Native Americans today. Under Dorris's name, the couple published a book about fetal alcohol syndrome (one of their adopted children was afflicted with it) entitled *The Broken Chord* (1990).

Erdrich's first major nonfictional work, *The Blue Jay's Dance: A Birth Year* (1995), is a personal memoir about the strong maternal bond between mother and daughter and the difficulty of balancing parenting with work and a public life with a private one. It was followed in 1996 by her first children's book, *Grandmother's Pigeon*.

By 1997, when Dorris committed suicide, he and Erdrich had separated and were planning to be divorced. Having collaborated personally and professionally for so many years, it was a difficult time for Erdrich and her five children. Shortly after his death, she spoke to an audience of college students at Dartmouth. In order to continue on with the mundane tasks of living, she told them, you have to "dig deep and look inside and find who's there."

Erdrich returned to her writing and had produced 11 novels as of 2005, a collection of short stories, another volume of poetry, and a second children's book, *The Birchbark House* (1999). Her novel *The Last Report on the Miracles at Little No Horse,* in which a former nun dresses as a man to serve as the priest on an Ojibwa reservation, was a finalist for a National Book Award in 2001. *Four Souls: A Novel* (2004) continues the North Dakota Indian saga, with recurring characters and themes last seen in *The Beet Queen* and *Tracks*. In *The Painted Drum* (2005), the story of a ceremonial Ojibwa drum that's magically linked to children and death, Erdrich continues the nine-volume cycle of novels revolving around an Ojibwa reservation.

Benjamin Markovits comments in the *New York Book Review* (September 11, 2005) that "assimilation, in its liveliest form, is the subject of her [Erdrich's] fiction. But its progress is neither inevitable nor one-way. . . . Her fictionalized version of the real Ojibwa tribe is a brilliant creation: it possesses the instantly persuasive strangeness of something faithful to life."

Louise Erdrich lives in Minnesota, where she set her story *The Antelope Wife,* with her daughters. She owns Birchbark Books, a small independent bookstore. "If Erdrich had been born 200 years earlier, she might have become a traditional Ojibwa storyteller," postulates Terry L. Andrews in *Critical Survey of Long Fiction.* "Her tales would have reminded her listeners of their unchanging relationship to the land and to the mythic and legendary characters who inhabited it."

Further Reading

Andrews, Terry L. "Louise Erdrich." In *Critical Survey of Long Fiction,* edited by Carl Rollyson, 1,037–1,044. Pasadena, Calif.: Salem Press, 2000.

Dorris, Michael, and Louise Erdrich. *The Crown of Columbus.* New York: HarperCollins, 1991.

Erdrich, Louise. *The Last Report on the Miracles at Little No Horse.* New York: HarperCollins, 2001.

———. *Love Medicine.* New York: Holt, Rinehart and Winston, 1984.

———. *The Painted Drum.* New York: HarperCollins, 2005.

Jacobs, Connie A. *The Novels of Louise Erdrich: Stories of Her People.* New York: Peter Lang, 2001.

Fairfield, Flora

See ALCOTT, LOUISA MAY

Fauset, Jessie Redmon
(1882–1961)   *novelist, editor*

Jessie Redmon Fauset was a leading figure and perhaps the most published novelist of the Harlem Renaissance movement. She was also the literary editor of *The Crisis,* a magazine renowned during the 1920s for publishing the works of talented young black writers. Most of Fauset's work focused on how African Americans, especially middle-class black women, handle the constraints of their heritage.

The youngest daughter of a well-educated but "dreadfully poor" family, Jessie Redmon Fauset was born on April 27, 1882, in Camden County, New Jersey. Her mother died when she was a young child and her father, an Episcopal minister, as well as her half brother, a noted anthropologist, emphasized the importance of education and literature.

Jessie graduated with honors from the Philadelphia High School for Girls in 1900 and then attended Cornell University, where she became the first black woman in the country elected to Phi Beta Kappa, and in 1905 the first black female to graduate from Cornell. After studying at the Sorbonne in Paris, she moved to Washington, D.C., and taught French to public school students for 14 years. She also earned a master's degree at the University of Pennsylvania and began to write seriously, sending out poems, essays, and short stories to magazines and journals.

In 1919, W. E. B. DuBois, the pioneering black sociologist and civil rights activist, persuaded Fauset, whose work he was familiar with, to move to New York City and become the literary editor of *The Crisis.* DuBois was editor of this influential publication sponsored by the National Association for the Advancement of Colored People (NAACP) and wanted Fauset to help "shape" it. Under her tutelage, *The Crisis* showcased and promoted aspiring young "New Negro" writers such as ZORA NEALE HURSTON and Langston Hughes, who described Fauset as one of the "mid-wives" who guided the artistic development of Harlem Renaissance writers. (The Harlem Renaissance—a movement that promoted African-American literature, art, and music during the 1920s, and was located in Harlem, a section of New York City—is sometimes considered the core of the New Negro Movement.)

Several of Fauset's poems, short stories, and essays were published in *The Crisis* both before and during her eight-year tenure as literary editor; her work also appeared in Alain Locke's landmark anthology *The New Negro* (1925).

In 1920 and 1921, Fauset edited and wrote for *Brownies' Book,* a monthly magazine for black children that featured historical biographies of notable African Americans such as SOJOURNER TRUTH. As a high school teacher, Fauset had been distressed by the dearth of role models for minority students.

In spite of the time she spent editing magazines and hosting chic multiracial literary soirees, Fauset managed to become one of the major fiction writer of the Harlem Renaissance movement. She published four novels over a nine-year period: *There Is Confusion* (1924), which sold well and was reissued in 1928; *Plum Bun: A Novel Without a Moral* (1929), which is considered her best work; *The Chinaberry Tree: A Novel of American Life* (1931); and *Comedy, American Style* (1933). In the latter story, the central character is a light-skinned black woman (as was Fauset) obsessed with being white, while minor characters surrounding her represent a strong, proud, accepting black culture.

In 1926 Fauset left *The Crisis* and returned to teaching, a more lucrative career. At the age of 47 she married Herbert Harris, a businessman, and happily became a "housewife." She continued to teach, lecture, and write—although she never again published—until she died in Philadelphia, on April 30, 1961.

Fauset's work was political, but more exploratory than dogmatic. A well-known figure in the Harlem Renaissance movement, she sensitively portrayed both the respectable world of educated, successful middle-class blacks, and what often existed just below the surface—the darker world of prejudice, bitterness, and lost opportunities. In a critical review that appeared in *African American Writers* (2001), Lois Leveen concluded that while Jessie Fauset's novels seem more "old-fashioned" than the work of her Harlem Renaissance contemporaries, her writing continues to speak to readers and interest scholars today.

Further Reading

Fauset, Jessie Redmon. *The Chinaberry Tree: A Novel of American Life.* New York: Frederick A. Stokes, 1931. Reprinted, New York: AMS Press, 1969.

———. *Comedy, American Style.* New York: Frederick A. Stokes, 1933. Reprinted, New York: AMS Press, 1969.

"Jessie Redman Fauset." The Black Renaissance in Washington, D.C. June 20, 2003. Available online. URL: http://dclibrary.org/b/kren/bios/fausetjr.html. Downloaded on February 27, 2007.

Leveen, Lois. "Jessie Redmon Fauset." In *African American Writers,* edited by Valerie Smith, 217–232. New York: Charles Scribner's Sons, 2001.

Starkey, Marion. "Interview with Jessie Fauset." *Southern Workman* 61 (May 1932): 217–220.

Sylvander, Carolyn Wedin. *Jessie Redmon Fauset: Black American Writer.* Troy, N.Y.: Whitston Publishing Company, 1981.

West, Aberjhani, and Sandra L. West. "Jessie Redmond Fauset." In *Encyclopedia of the Harlem Renaissance,* 110–111. New York: Facts On File, Inc., 2003.

∼ Ferber, Edna
(1887–1968) *novelist, journalist, playwright*

Edna Ferber is a Pulitzer Prize–winning novelist who ranks as one of the most popular women writers of the 20th century. During her prolific 50-year literary career, she penned close to 20 novels, 12 collections of short story collections, and eight plays, in addition to working as a journalist.

When Julia Ferber was expecting her second child, she hoped it would be a boy, whom she would name Edward. But the child born on August 15, 1887, in Kalamazoo, Michigan, was a girl, whom Mrs. Ferber called Edna. Petite and strong-willed as a child, Ferber later described admiring her mother for her "self-reliance, courage, fortitude, humor, and intelligence," while she recalled her father, Jacob, a Jewish immigrant from Hungary, as a "sweet decent dull [sic] rather handsome man who was a failure as a shopkeeper."

Seeking work, the Ferbers moved several times throughout the Midwest, eventually settling in Appleton, Wisconsin, where Edna excelled at high school, graduating in 1902 when she was 17. That same year she won the state declamatory contest. Her plan was to attend college and study drama.

But her father went blind and lost everything, and her mother had to run the family store while raising two daughters. Edna gave up the idea of an expensive college education. Instead, she became the first female reporter for Appleton's local newspaper, earning three dollars a week. She then landed a job that paid four times as much at the *Milwaukee Journal,* sending home most of her salary to help support her beleaguered family. Her three-year stint at the *Journal,* Ferber recalled, helped her develop a keen eye for details, a sense of how to dramatize a story, and a "vast storehouse of practical and psychological knowledge" that proved very useful in her career as a creative writer.

After her father's death in 1909, Ferber moved to Chicago with her mother and sister. She was

Edna Ferber's novel *Showboat* was made into a popular Broadway musical.
(AP/Wide World Photos)

suffering from nervous exhaustion, and, while convalescing, began to write fiction. Her first story, "The Homely Heroine," was published in 1911 in *Everybody's,* a popular magazine. During her illness she also completed the manuscript of her first novel, *Dawn O'Hara, The Girl Who Laughed,* which was, unsurprisingly, about a newspaperwoman in Milwaukee. After several publishers rejected it, Ferber angrily tossed the manuscript into the garbage. Fortunately, her mother retrieved it. When it was finally published in 1911, more than 10,000 copies were sold, and Ferber's reputation as a writer and storyteller was secured.

Ferber moved to New York City and began publishing short stories, including a widely read series revolving around a divorced, independent, resourceful traveling saleswoman named Emma McChesney. Ultimately there would be 30 Emma McChesney stories written over a five-year period. They were immensely popular: Theodore Roosevelt wrote to Ferber pleading with her to have McChesney give up her job selling petticoats and instead settle down and remarry; the author refused. "Ten years from today," wrote Ferber, "the idea that anyone ever questioned the propriety of a woman's going into business . . . will be obsolete."

In 1915 the series was turned into a book, *Emma McChesney & Co.,* and then dramatized on Broadway in New York City as *Our Mrs. McChesney,* starring Ethel Barrymore. As a New Yorker, Ferber, known for her carefully orchestrated dinner parties, became part of the Algonquin Round Table circle, a group of witty, temperamental, talented writers—among them, DOROTHY PARKER, Moss Hart, and Alexander Wollcott—who met regularly at the Algonquin Hotel.

Having become a celebrated short-story writer, Ferber returned to novels, beginning in 1917 with the semiautobiographical *Fanny Herself. The Girls,* published in 1921, was her first work to deal with several different generations—a theme that was to become her trademark. Ferber's best-selling 1924 novel *So Big* earned the author a Pulitzer Prize in fiction, sold more than 300,000 copies, and spawned two motion pictures. Selina Peake Dejong, the book's central character, is a penniless, hard-working, middle-aged farm woman who successfully makes her own way in the world, in spite of difficult circumstances. She was a classic Ferber heroine: determined, industrious, and proud.

Ferber was prophetic about women's capabilities. "If men discover how tough women actually are they'll be scared to death," she wrote. "And if women ever decide to throw away that mask, wig and ruffled kimono and be themselves, this will be another monarch—and perhaps it's about time. Certainly if this is a man's world I'll make you a present of it." In spite of its problems, Ferber loved America and its hardworking, ordinary people. "I found creative satisfaction in writing only about the people and the land I knew and, in a measure, understood," she said.

A noted playwright, in 1924 she began a long and successful collaboration writing plays with her close friend George S. Kaufman, including *Royal Family* (1928), *Dinner at Eight* (1932), and *Stage Door* (1936). She was thrilled when one of her most widely read novels, *Showboat* (1926), was adapted for the stage by Jerome Kern and Oscar Hammerstein. It became an acclaimed Broadway musical that has been successfully revived over the years. The novel follows three generations of women and, as in many of Ferber's works, the subplot discusses racist attitudes. (In *Showboat,* a mulatto showboat actress faces social prejudices because of her "mixed" heritage.) When Ferber saw the lavish Broadway production and heard for the first time the song "Old Man River," she was deeply moved. "My hair stood on end, tears came to my eyes. I knew that this . . . was a song that would outlast Kern and Hammerstein's day and my day and your day," she recalled in her autobiography.

"The name of Edna Ferber runs through twentieth-century American life," wrote Julie Gilbert in an article about Ferber that appeared in the *Lincoln Center Theatre Review* in 2003. "She is known primarily as a novelist, but her love and dedication to the theater were akin to a calling."

Three other best-selling novels followed: *Cimmaron* (1929), *Saratoga Trunk* (1941), and *Giant* (1952). All would be made into motion pictures. *Cimmaron* is a satirical novel set in the Southwest whose protagonist is a housewife and mother forced to run her incompetent husband's newspaper business; she eventually becomes a respected politician. Ferber described the book as a "malevolent picture of what is known as American womanhood and American sentimentality." *Saratoga Trunk*'s main protagonist is the illegitimate daughter of an established Creole family who sets out to make her fortune by marrying a millionaire but realizes at the last minute that love is more important than money. Ferber often wrote about monetary greed and dishonest work resulting in unhappiness. In 1952, *Giant,* Ferber's sweeping saga of a genteel Virginian adapting to a oil-rich Texas, was adopted into an Academy Award–winning movie starring Elizabeth Taylor and James Dean.

Ferber also wrote two autobiographies. In the first, *A Peculiar Treasure* (1939), she recounted painful anti-Semitic incidents from her youth and warned that even America could fall prey to the anti-Semitism that was sweeping through Europe. Her unpublished dedication to the book read: To Adolf Hitler, who has made of me a better Jew and a more understanding and tolerant human being . . . this book is dedicated in loathing and contempt.

Although her parents did not actively practice Judaism, Ferber learned about anti-Semitism early in life while living in Ottumwa, Iowa, a "Jew-hating, Jew-baiting" small coal-mining town. Edna had suffered proudly ("my other cheek was all worn out long before I grew up") and silently, escaping the taunting and the forced isolation by becoming a voracious reader and by observing, rather than participating in, the community. As a writer, she often created characters who were forced to overcome adversity.

Ferber was a master at researching a site, such as Alaska, Texas, or the Northwest, and then setting a story there. In the novel *Ice Palace* (1958), she graphically traced the emergence of America's last frontier, Alaska, using the locale as if it were a central character in the book.

In 1965 Ferber was selected as one of 20 outstanding women of the 20th century by the New York World's Fair's Women's Hall of Fame. She never married, calling her books "her children," and spent her "free time" (she wrote more than 1,000 words a day, 350 days a year) enjoying friends, family, food, walking, and traveling. In her second autobiography, *A Kind of Magic* (1963), she observed that "hundreds of millions of people never once in their lifetime reflect on the stupendous fact that they are alive. . . . To be alive, to know consciously that you are alive, and to relish that knowledge—this is a kind of magic."

Ferber had remarkable business acumen and accrued great wealth during her lifetime. She supported her sister and nieces, and described Treasure Hill, her opulent estate in Stepney Depot, Connecticut, as her "middle-aged fling" and "love affair."

Edna Ferber died in New York City on April 16, 1968, at age 82. In the obituary that appeared in the *New York Times,* she was praised for her "wholesome respect for the color and harmony of words, and precise ability at portraiture." A great believer in the American Dream, Ferber—who was more entertaining than profound, more popular than intellectual—was able to realize that dream through her work. "Life," she said, "can't ever really defeat a writer who is in love with writing."

Further Reading

"Edna Ferber: Biography." Appleton Public Library. Available online. URL: http://www.apl.org/history/ferber/edna.bio.html. Downloaded on January 22, 2007.

Ferber, Edna. *A Peculiar Treasure.* Cutchogue, N.Y.: Buccaneer Books, 1991.

———. *So Big.* Urbana: University of Illinois Press, 1995.

Gilbert, Julie. "An Appreciation of Edna Ferber." *Lincoln Center Theatre Review* 34 (Winter 2003).

———. *Ferber: Edna Ferber and Her Circle.* New York: Applause Books, 2000.

Slater, Elinor, and Robert Slater. "Edna Ferber: A Giant of an Author." In *Great Jewish Women,* 81–83. Middle Village, N.Y.: Jonathan David, 1994.

Fisher, Mary Frances Kennedy (M. F. K. Fisher, Mary Frances Parrish)
(1908–1992) *food writer, autobiographer, novelist*

In more than two dozen books, including several classics of American cookery as well as the definitive English translation of Jean Anthelme Brillat-Savarin's *Physiologie du goût,* Mary Frances Kennedy Fisher delineated how to "live well gastronomically." Praised for her wit, eloquence, and intelligence, Fisher, who wrote under the pen name M. F. K. Fisher, was an adventurer and bon vivant. According to the English poet W. H. Auden, she was also the best prose writer in America.

Mary Frances Kennedy was born on July 3, 1908, in Albion, Michigan. However, she was raised in Whittier, California, and considered herself a Californian. Even as a young child, Mary Frances was interested in food and writing. In her autobiography *To Begin Again* (1992), she recalled that when she was about five she noticed that "eating something good with good people was highly important." She decided to become a professional writer, as were both her parents, "practically from the very beginning."

After dropping out of college, Kennedy married a fellow student named Albert Young Fisher and moved with him to Dijon, France, in 1929. There she became enamored with the simple, fresh, colorful produce of the region and began to record her observations. She tried every dish, no matter what the ingredients. "There's only one thing I don't think I could eat," she said in an interview in 1989, "and that's a grilled eye."

Returning to California, Fisher published her first cookbook, *Serve It Forth* (1937), which—like so much of her writing—also contained personal anecdotes, travel notes, and culinary history. When the publishers finally met "M. F. K. Fisher," they were shocked, having assumed the author would be a man. Fisher kept the gender-ambiguous pen name throughout her life despite three marriages.

After her first marriage ended in 1938, Fisher settled in Vevey, Switzerland, with her second husband, the artist Dillwyn Parrish, with whom she cowrote a novel, *Touch and Go* (1939). After Parrish committed suicide in 1942 (her brother also took his own life), Fisher escaped to Hollywood, California, where she worked as a screenwriter and artist's model.

Under the name Mary Frances Parrish, she published *The Gastronomical Me* (1943), a popular compendium of recipes, culinary tales, and memoirs. In it she explained how life's three basic needs—food, security, and love—were intrinsically intertwined. "When I write of hunger, I am really writing about love and the hunger for it, and the warmth and the love of it and the hunger for it."

For Fisher, eating was a metaphor for life, and in her writing she attempted to provide both body and soul with nourishment. For example, she described eating Italian white beans in a story entitled "The Flaw": "They tasted delicious, so fresh and cold. . . . It was good to be eating and drinking there on that train, free forever from the trouble of life, surrounded with a kind of insulation of love. . . ."

Fisher considered her best work a 1949 translation of Jean Brillat-Savarin's 1825 French classic, *The Physiology of Taste,* in which he postulated that "only wise men know the *art* of eating," a sentiment with which Fisher completely concurred. *The Art of Eating* (1954), Fisher's most widely read book and the culmination of her early career, contained her first five food-related books, including the two classics *Consider the Oyster* and *How to Cook a Wolf,* in which she suggested ways to survive well on rations and food shortages during World War II.

Fisher's third marriage, to Donald Friede, a publisher whom she had married in 1945, ended in divorce in 1951, leaving her to care for two young daughters and her gravely ill father, who died in 1953. She moved with her children back to Provence and wrote about their adventures in France—culinary and otherwise—in *A Cordial Water* (1961) and *Maps of Another Town: A Memoir of Provence* (1964).

Fisher's later writing includes three volumes of memoirs, travel books, recollections of her marriages and romances, a volume on Japanese cuisine, articles for the *New Yorker* magazine, and reflections on living on a ranch in the wine region of California, where she spent the last 20 years of her life. She continued to write even after becoming bedridden, always recognizing that the small moments in life are the important ones. "I am," she once asserted, "basically a simple person."

In 1983, two of her best-known books were published, reviving interest, which had flagged, in her work: *As They Were,* a collection of memoirs, short stories, and journal entries; and *Sister Age,* which probes "aging and ending and living" with wit, wisdom, and empathy, despite the fact that by the end of her life she could neither see nor write and was forced to dictate.

In the last published letter to a friend before her death from Parkinson's disease at the age of 83, on June 22, 1992, M. F. K. Fisher wrote, "Transcendental is the word. I don't believe in all this stuff about grief because I think we grieve forever, but that goes for love, too, fortunately for us all."

Further Reading

Fisher, M. F. K. *The Art of Eating, Five Gastronomical Works: 50th Anniversary Edition.* New York: John Wiley and Sons, 2004.

———. *Last House: Reflections, Dreams, and Observations, 1943–1991.* New York: Pantheon Books, 1995.

Lazar, David, ed. *Conversations with M. F. K. Fisher.* Jackson: University Press of Mississippi, 1992.

Reardon, Joan, ed. *A Stew or a Story: An Assortment of Short Works by M. F. K. Fisher.* Emeryville, Calif.: Avalon Publishing, 2006.

Storace, Patricia. "The Art of M. F. K. Fisher." *New York Review of Books,* December 7, 1989. Available online. URL: http://www.nybooks.com/articles/3819. Downloaded on January 22, 2007.

Flanner, Janet (Genet)
(1892–1978) *journalist, essayist, novelist*

A respected journalist and foreign correspondent who wrote "Letter from Paris" for the *New Yorker* magazine for 50 years, Janet Flanner was recognized for her astute observations and analytic commentary on the cultural, social, and political life of Paris and much of Europe after World War I. She received the National Book Award in 1966 for her collection of essays *Paris Journal: 1944–1965.*

Janet Flanner, the second of three daughters, was born to Quaker parents on March 13, 1892, in Indianapolis, Indiana. She attended a private high school where she pursued an interest in writing. At 17, she traveled with her family to Europe, where they spent a year before returning to Indiana. Then, unexpectedly, her father, a mortician who dabbled in social causes and even founded a settlement for African Americans, killed himself. Flanner subsequently became an agnostic, firmly rejecting her family's religious beliefs.

Flanner took courses at the University of Chicago from 1912 to 1914 but had no patience for academia and dropped out. She returned to her hometown to work for the *Indianapolis Star,* first as an art critic and then, in 1918, as one of the country's first film critics.

In 1918 she married William Lane Rehm, an artist living in New York City whom she had befriended at the University of Chicago. The marriage was short lived, although the two remained on cordial terms. Flanner later admitted that she had married Rehm in order to escape Indianapolis and move to Greenwich Village, then the bohemian section of New York where many artists and writers congregated. It was while living in the Village that she met Solita Solano (born Sarah Wilkinson), a freelance journalist and drama editor for the *New York Tribune.* They became lovers and lifelong friends, even when Flanner became involved in relationships with other women. They were portrayed as plucky writers Nip and Tuck in *Ladies Almanack* (1928), a satirical novel written by DJUNA BARNES.

When Solano was sent to Greece on assignment for *National Geographic* magazine in 1921, Flanner went with her. The next year Flanner settled in Paris, France, where she would live until 1975, except for the war years of 1939–44, when she returned to New York. She lived with Solano in a small, spare apartment on the Left Bank of Paris, where many other aspiring expatriate American writers resided in the 1920s. Flanner corresponded with a friend from New York City, Jane Grant, who was married to Harold Ross, then editor of the newly published *New Yorker* magazine. She described Parisian life, culture, and politics so vividly and in such detail that Grant suggested to her husband that he publish Flanner's chatty, witty letters in his literary magazine. Flanner published her first "letter" from Paris on October 10, 1925, and continued sending them to the *New Yorker* until 1975. It was Ross's idea that Flanner use a pen name, "Genet," which sounds like a French version of "Janet," for her sophisticated columns.

During the 1930s she also wrote from other parts of Europe, contributing an occasional "Letter from London" to the *New Yorker.* Flanner also interviewed well-known European luminaries such as Edith Piaf, Jean-Paul Sartre, Maurice Ravel, Charles de Gaulle, Thomas Mann, Jean Cocteau, and EDITH WHARTON. She became close friends with the American novelist Ernest Hemingway. The insightful profiles, written with panache and authority, along with a series of essays, were published in a collection titled *An American in Paris: Profile of an Interlude between Two Wars* (1940). Extracts from the book were turned into a piece for chorus and orchestra by the composer Ned Rorem.

Flanner's reportage enabled Americans to understand what really was going on in Paris and other parts of Europe in terms of historically important or culturally interesting events and people, some of whom she befriended, including expatriate writers GERTRUDE STEIN and KAY BOYLE. Like them, Flanner felt more liberated living in open-minded Paris. She was an intense, hard-working, chain-smoking, self-critical writer who was as passionate about her work as she was about her romances. She dressed elegantly even though she often had a hard time paying her rent. In *Notable American Women,* Nancy F. Cott describes Flanner in the 1930s: "Her Chanel or Yves St. Laurent tailored suits and well-shod feet, her (prematurely) silver mass of hair and direct brown eyes, which balanced the prominent "beak" (as she called it) of her nose—[were all] consistently remarked upon, as were her skills as a raconteur and her infectiously cackling laughter."

After returning to New York City in 1939, because Paris was occupied by the Germans, Flanner produced a guide to French customs for American servicemen and -women and continued writing for the *New Yorker*. The next year she met and fell in love with Natalia Danesi Murray, an Italian-born broadcaster for the National Broadcasting Company, whose son William described her as "an explosive force of nature." William Murray, a journalist and novelist, wrote a memoir about having been raised successfully by three independent, talented women: Flanner, his mother (who was also Flanner's literary agent), and his grandmother. His admiration for Flanner's writing was "a beacon that lit his path." *Darlinghissima,* a collection of letters Flanner wrote to Natalia Murray, exemplifies Flanner's passion and vulnerability in a way her other work did not.

Flanner went back to Paris in 1944 and continued her bimonthly "Letters" in the *New Yorker* until 1975. While in France, she wrote several riveting essays about seminal war-related events such as Adolf Hitler's rise to power (she personally interviewed the dictator, which was not without controversy), the Warsaw Ghetto where Jews had been forced to live before they were taken to death camps, and the historic Nuremberg war-crime trials. She often expressed concern over the long-term damage done to Europe during the war, noting that "with the material destruction collapsed invisible things that lived within it."

She also reported on less significant topics, such as a French television show featuring the newly discovered actress Brigitte Bardot or a retrospective featuring Pablo Picasso. Whether writing about the Algerian revolution or what the designer Coco Chanel ate, Flanner never revealed her sources.

"Crime, theatre, politics, art, photography, literature, film—all are discussed with the eye of a social historian and journalist in an epigrammatic yet personable style," writes Kathy A. Fedorko in *The Oxford Companion to Women's Writing.*

In 1948 Janet Flanner was knighted by the French Legion of Honor for her "Letter from Paris" essays. She also received an honorary doctorate degree from Smith College, and *Paris Journal, 1944–1965* garnered a National Book Award. As a journalist and foreign correspondent for five decades, Flanner was lauded for her insightful, informative, and richly detailed political and cultural commentaries. Although she wrote a semiautobiographical novel, *The Cubical City* (1926; reprinted 1974), and attempted briefly to break into radio broadcast journalism, she did not succeed at either genre. In 1975 she returned from Paris to Manhattan, where she died of a heart attack on November 7, 1978, at the age of 86.

Further Reading

Flanner, Janet. *An American in Paris: Profile of an Interlude between Two Wars.* New York: Simon and Schuster, 1940.

———. *Darlinghissima: Letters to a Friend.* Edited and with commentary by Natalia Danesi Murray. New York: Harcourt Brace Jovanovich, 1985.

———. *Janet Flanner's World: Uncollected Writings, 1932–1975.* Edited by Irving Drutman. With an introduction by William Shawn. New York: Harcourt Brace Jovanovich, 1981.

———. *Paris Journal, 1944–1965.* Edited by William Shawn. New York: Harcourt Brace Jovanovich, 1965.

"Janet Flanner." The Knitting Circle: Journalism. Available online. URL: http://www.knittingcircle.org.uk/janetflanner.html. Downloaded on January 22, 2007.

Lesinska, Zofia P., and Hans H. Rudnick, eds. *Perspectives of Four Women Writers on the Second World War: Gertrude Stein, Janet Flanner, Kay Boyle, and Rebecca West.* New York: Peter Lang Publishing, 2002.

Murray, William. *Janet, My Mother, and Me: A Memoir of Growing Up with Janet Flanner and Natalia Danesi Murray.* New York: Simon and Schuster, 2000.

Wineapple, Brenda. *Genet: A Biography of Janet Flanner.* New York: Ticknor and Fields, 1989.

∾ Foster, Hannah Webster ("a Lady of Massachusetts")
(1758–1840) *novelist*

Hannah Webster Foster caused a sensation when her best-selling novel *The Coquette; or, The History of Eliza Wharton* was published in 1797. It went through 13 editions in its first 40 years.

Hannah Webster was born in Salisbury, Massachusetts, on September 10, 1758. Little is known about her childhood, although it would appear that she was intelligent, attractive, and—unlike most young women of that era—well educated. Webster enjoyed writing and published several political articles in local newspapers. These articles caught the attention of John Foster, a minister of First Church in Brighton, Massachusetts, who made it a point to meet the journalist. The couple courted and were married in 1785.

As a clergyman's wife, Foster became involved in social and literary activities at her husband's parish, while raising six children. Then, in 1797, she published one of the most important early American sentimental novels, *The Coquette; or, The History of Eliza Wharton*. Sentimental novels often served as cautionary tales, designed to show women how they could protect themselves against seductive men in a society that offered women little in the way of legal rights. Like most women writers in the 18th century, Foster felt compelled to use a pen name; she signed her book, "By a Lady of Massachusetts."

Foster claimed that *The Coquette* was "founded on fact." It closely followed the case of Elizabeth Whitman, the daughter of a minister who unwisely trusted a "gentleman," Pierpont Edwards, and who, like Foster's fictional heroine, was seduced and eventually died in a tavern in Danvers, Massachusetts, after giving birth to a stillborn child.

A number of journalists criticized *The Coquette* as not being factual and for unjustly characterizing Edwards as a rogue. Foster, however, defended herself by asserting that through her husband's distant cousin she had access to unpublished information. The epistolary narrative unfolds through a series of letters and recounts Eliza Wharton's doomed flirta-tion with the dashing, arrogant Major Peter Sanford, who tells the reader: "If she will play with a lion, let her beware the paw, I say." A morality tale about "paying for straying," the book describes how Eliza Wharton is punished because she chooses the seductive and dishonorable major over an admirable but dull clergyman.

The Coquette resembles the classic sentimental novels of the English writer Samuel Richardson, and the protagonist is warned that Major Sanford is "a second Lovelace," a reference to the seducer in Richardson's celebrated novel *Clarissa*. Foster believed that society was too lenient with seducers, and through her fiction she pleads for sympathy for their vulnerable victims.

Foster's second novel, *The Boarding School; or, Lessons of a Preceptress to Her Pupils,* was published anonymously in 1798, and was less successful commercially. It combined moral reflections with letters and was dedicated to "the young ladies of America," in the hope that they would become better educated and that they would recognize that "reformed rakes do not make the best husbands."

After her husband's death, Foster published only a few newspaper articles. She settled in Montreal, Canada, where two of her daughters, both of whom were also writers, lived. She died on April 17, 1840, but *The Coquette* lived on. It was one of the most popular novels in America prior to 1800 and was reprinted eight times between 1824 and 1828. Foster's real name did not appear on the book until 1866.

Further Reading
Finseth, Ian. "A Melancholy Tale: Rhetoric Fiction and Passion in *The Coquette.*" *Studies in the Novel* 33, no. 2 (2001): 125–159.

Fleischmann, Fritz. "Concealed Lessons: Foster's *Coquette.*" In *Early America Re-Explored: New Readings in Colonial, Early National, and Antebellum Culture,* 309–348. New York: Peter Long, 2000.

Foster, Hannah Webster. *The Coquette; or, The History of Eliza Wharton.* With an introduction by Cathy N. Davidson. New York: Oxford University Press, 1986.

Mulford, Carla, ed. *Early American Writings.* New York: Oxford University Press, 2002.

Franklin, Madeleine L'Engle Camp
See L'ENGLE, MADELEINE

Freeman, Mary Eleanor Wilkins
(1852–1930)   *short story writer, novelist*

Mary Wilkins Freeman was one of the great regionalist writers in New England in the late 19th and early 20th centuries. Best remembered for her finely crafted short stories, she was a master at describing small-town life and of portraying the constricted lives of poor, rural women coping with what Freeman perceived as the rigid, oppressive influences of Puritanism.

Mary Eleanor Wilkins was born on October 31, 1852, in Randolph, Massachusetts. Frail, sensitive, and largely self-educated, she did not have a happy childhood. When she was 15 her father moved the family to Brattleboro, Vermont, where he opened a small store. After graduating from Brattleboro High School in 1870, and briefly attending Mount Holyoke Female Seminary and Mrs. Hosford's Glenwood Seminary, Mary's life fell apart: her father's business failed, and by 1883 her younger sister, mother, and father had all died. At the age of 31, Mary Wilkins found herself homeless and impoverished.

Although she had not intended on becoming a writer, having aspired to be an artist, she discovered that she could earn money by writing. In 1882 one of her short stories garnered a $50 prize from a Boston newspaper, and the following year her first book, *Decorative Plaques,* a collection of poems for children, was published.

Still, she could not afford her own home. In 1884 she returned to her birthplace, Randolph, where she spent close to 20 years living in the household of her childhood (and lifelong) friend, Mary Wales. Liberated from housekeeping chores, she was able to earn her keep by writing, although she was plagued by nightmares.

Encouraged by Mary Louise Booth, an editor at *Harper's Bazaar* who had accepted one of her stories, Wilkins began to sell her tales of village life in rural New England to a variety of magazines, while continuing to publish juvenile short stories and

poetry. In her fiction she often focused on proud, independent unmarried women who survived in spite of appalling poverty and societal restrictions. She clearly understood the implications of living in a country town in which the hope of achievement had long since disappeared, and she did not flinch from describing these conditions.

With the publication of *A Humble Romance and Other Stories* (1887) and *A New England Nun and Other Stories* (1891), her two acclaimed volumes of short stories, Wilkins established a reputation as a first-rate "local-colorist," although she also delved into more universal themes, including rebellion. For example the protagonist in her best-known story, "The Revolt of Mother" (in *A New England Nun*), is an oppressed wife who eventually asserts her will against her husband.

Although lauded for her astute powers of observation in her short stories, only one of her novels, *Pembroke,* was considered successful. With its portrayal of greed, sexuality, heroism, and tragedy, some critics likened it to the novels of Nathaniel Hawthorne.

In 1895 Wilkins traveled throughout New England and, influenced by the renowned New England author SARAH ORNE JEWETT, established herself as a regionalist—a writer who realistically describes a locale and its people from within the culture. But she also wrote about things she had never seen and emotions she had never experienced, much like the English writer Emily Brontë, whom she admired and about whom she wrote: "How she ever came to comprehend the primitive brutalities and passions, and the great truth of life that sanctified them, is a mystery."

Mary E. Wilkins was 49 when in 1902 she married Charles Freeman, a nonpracticing physician, and moved with him to Metuchen, a wealthy suburban town in New Jersey. Although initially supportive of her writing, as an alcoholic he was frequently confined to sanitariums. In 1919 Freeman was forced to institutionalize her husband, and she was able to obtain a legal separation before he died. Later she had to contest his will, a difficult and demoralizing experience.

At last wealthy and established, Freeman at the end of her life was the recipient of numerous honors: In 1926 she received the Howells Medal for Fiction by the American Academy of Arts and Letters, and that same year she and EDITH WHARTON became the first women elected to membership in the National Institute of Arts and Letters.

When she died on March 13, 1930, at the age of 78, Mary Wilkins Freeman, a respected and prolific regionalist, had produced 230 short stories; 13 novels, including her most successful, *Pembroke* (1894); six volumes of children's stories; a play; and two volumes of verse.

Further Reading

Alaimo, Stacy. *Undomesticated Ground: Recasting Nature as Feminist Space.* Ithaca, N.Y.: Cornell University Press, 2000.

Camfield, Gregg. "Humor in the Stories of Mary Wilkins Freeman." *American Transcendental Quarterly* 14, no. 2 (June 2000): 215–232.

Freeman, Mary Eleanor Wilkins. *A New-England Nun and Other Stories.* New York: Penguin Classics, 2000.

Glasser, Leah Blatt. *In a Closet Hidden: The Life and Work of Mary E. Wilkins Freeman.* Amherst: University of Massachusetts Press, 1996.

Voller, Jack G. "Mary E. Wilkins Freeman." *The Literary Gothic.* April 13, 2006. Available online. URL: http://www.litgothic.com/Authors/freeman.html. Downloaded on February 27, 2007.

∽ Fuller, Sarah Margaret (Margaret Fuller Ossoli)
(1810–1850) *essayist, journalist, editor*

Margaret Fuller, a pioneering feminist and leading intellectual of her time, was also a prominent journalist and foreign correspondent, essayist, editor, and literary critic. In 1845 Fuller published *Woman in the Nineteenth Century,* the first major philosophical book in America to discuss feminist issues, including the advocacy of equal education for women and the elimination of gender roles.

Sarah Margaret Fuller was born on May 23, 1810, in Cambridgeport, Massachusetts. The eldest of nine children, she was influenced and educated by her father, a Harvard-educated lawyer and politician, who had hoped for a son and treated his precocious first-born daughter as if she were one. Fuller is said to have learned to read before she was two, mastered Latin and the classics at a very young age, immersed herself in the literature of several cultures, and taught herself German in order to read Goethe.

Margaret's only formal education consisted of two unhappy years, 1824 and 1825, at Miss Prescott's Young Ladies' Seminary in Groton, Massachusetts, after which she resumed designing her own studies and tutoring her younger siblings. Socially awkward with her peer group, Margaret grew up, in her own words, "bright and ugly." She was more comfortable with adults, including literary luminaries Henry David Thoreau and Ralph Waldo Emerson. "She was," said Emerson, Fuller's mentor and friend, "the most agreeable and intelligent woman in Boston."

When her father died in 1835, Fuller was forced to recognize how financially dependent women were on men. In her mid-20s, having always lived comfortably at home, she left for Boston to earn a living. Her first job was teaching at Bronson Alcott's progressive, experimental Temple School. Fuller dazzled Alcott, the father of celebrated writer LOUISA MAY ALCOTT, and the students. But in 1837 she accepted a better paying, less demanding position at a school in Providence, Rhode Island. In her spare time she translated Johann Eckermann's *Conversations with Goethe.*

In 1839 Fuller returned to Boston and became associated with the transcendentalists, a group of liberal intellectuals who believed in the importance of spirituality, intuition, and insight over logic and reason. Even among the likes of Emerson and Alcott she was a formidable force, once brashly commenting: "I now know all the people worth knowing in America, and I find no intellect comparable to my own."

The group used conversations as a way of debating and discussing important philosophical issues. Fuller, whom Bronson Alcott called "the most commanding talker of the day, of her sex," organized and led formal "Conversations with Women," which offered intellectually stimulating discussions to small groups of women and that later included men as well, in topics such as art, ethics, Greek mythology, and women's rights. From 1839 until 1844, Fuller had a devoted following among a group of "well-educated and thinking women . . . who had been trampled in the mud to gratify the brute appetites of men," as she described them in an article in the *New York Daily Tribune.*

Fuller's thought-provoking and radical analyses, and her impressive "piquant, vivid, terse, bold, luminous" criticism, as her early admirer Edgar Allan Poe described it, captivated the audience, which met weekly in private homes or at educator Elizabeth Peabody's bookstore in downtown Boston.

In 1840 a group of prominent transcendentalists invited Fuller to edit the nation's first literary journal, the *Dial.* For two years she served as editor, without pay, of the prestigious publication. Impressed by her editing and writing, Horace Greeley, editor of the *New York Daily Tribune,* asked Fuller in 1844 to move to New York to become assistant editor of his popular newspaper. As America's first professional book review editor and literary critic, Fuller argued against "books which imitate or represent the thoughts and life of Europe," and looked for "fresh currents of life" from the new nation; she brought American literature to life and became a role model for future generations of newswomen. "In some respects," said Greeley, "Fuller was the greatest woman whom America has yet known." But a highly learned woman and peer was also intimidating, even to those who admired her, such as the writer Nathaniel Hawthorne.

That same year Fuller published her first book, a travel journal entitled *Summer on the Lakes* (1843), which featured interviews with Native Americans and European immigrants, especially pioneer women, and raised disturbing questions about the exploitation of both groups.

Woman in the Nineteenth Century, Fuller's landmark manifesto in the history of American femi-

nism, created a stir when it appeared in 1845. A compilation of her early feminist philosophies, most of which appeared as articles in the *Dial,* Fuller pleads passionately and cogently for harmony between the sexes, by allowing women to become better educated and independent, and men more "God centered." She asserted that "there is no wholly masculine man, no purely feminine woman." *Woman in the Nineteenth Century* served as the first American feminist manifesto and was a model for writers of the "Declaration of Sentiments" at the Seneca Falls Women's Rights Convention three years later.

In 1846 some of Fuller's literary criticism was collected and published as *Papers on Literature and Art,* further establishing her reputation as a versatile woman of letters. That same year she became the first female foreign correspondent to report from Europe. While compiling her "letters," as the news dispatches were called, for the *Tribune,* Fuller met such venerable writers as Thomas Carlyle, who conceded that Fuller's prose was unique among women of their generation, "rare even for men."

After settling in Rome in 1847, during the Italian nationalist movement, Fuller fell in love with one of Giuseppe Mazzini's revolutionary partisans, Marchese Giovanni Angelo Ossoli, a nobleman who was 10 years her junior. She bore him a son in 1848, at the age of 38. It is unclear whether they married, although Fuller took Ossoli's last name. Meanwhile her "letters" to the *Tribune* were filled with news about the arrival of General Giuseppe Garibaldi and the French siege, during which time she ran an emergency hospital.

When the short-lived Roman Republic was overthrown in 1849, she and Ossoli fled with their son to Florence; a year later they set sail for America aboard the *Elizabeth.* Shipwrecked in a storm on July 19, 1850, just off the coast of Fire Island in New York Harbor, all three perished. As Hawthorne noted, "She proved herself a woman after all and fell like the lowest of her sisters."

Margaret Fuller Ossoli was 40 when she drowned, and her manuscript describing Italy's ill-fated revolution of 1849, which she considered her finest writing, was never found. Ironically, the last line in *Woman in the Nineteenth Century* reads: "Though many have suffered shipwreck, still beat the noble hearts." At least Fuller succeeded at her goal: "I am determined," she once said, "on distinction."

A plaque at the Margaret Fuller Memorial in Cambridge, Massachusetts, sums up her life and her invaluable contributions: "By birth a child of New England; by adoption a citizen of Rome; by genius belonging to the world. In youth an insatiable student seeking the highest culture; in riper years teacher, writer, critic of literature and art; in maturer age companion and helper of many earnest reformers in America and Europe."

Further Reading

Capper, Charles. *Margaret Fuller: American Romantic Life.* 2 vols. New York: Oxford University Press, 1992, 2007.

Clack, Randall A. *The Marriage of Heaven and Earth: Alchemical Regeneration in the Works of Poe, Hawthorne, and Fuller.* Westport, Conn.: Greenwood Press, 2000.

Dickinson, Donna. *Margaret Fuller: Writing a Woman's Life.* New York: St. Martin's Press, 1993.

Fuller, Margaret. *My Heart Is a Large Kingdom: Selected Letters of Margaret Fuller.* Edited by Robert N. Hudspeth. Ithaca, N.Y.: Cornell University Press, 2001.

———. *Women in the Nineteenth Century.* New York: Norton, 1971.

Van Mehren, Joan. *Minerva and the Muse: A Life of Margaret Fuller.* Amherst: University of Massachusetts Press, 1994.

G

Galler, Christine Quintasket Mcleod
See MOURNING DOVE

Gaitskill, Mary
(1954–) *novelist, short story writer*

Mary Gaitskill is an award-winning fiction writer who unflinchingly and with clarity takes on traditionally taboo subjects, including the darker aspects of sexual relationships. She has been lauded by reviewers for bringing a new vitality to American writing with her bracing depiction of vulnerable characters living in emotional complexity and extremity. Her most recent novel, *Veronica,* was named one of the best 10 books in 2005 by the *New York Times Book Review* and was nominated for a National Book Award.

Born on November 11, 1954, in Lexington, Kentucky, Gaitskill was raised outside of Detroit, Michigan, along with two siblings. Her father, who died in 2001, was a political science professor; he and Gaitskill shared a close relationship. Her mother, whom she describes as having a "keenly nuanced mind," was a social worker and homemaker who now lives in Chicago, Illinois. Mary also spent two months in mental institu-

tions when she was 15 and suffering from, as she describes it, "a difficult adolescence." At the age of 16, feeling stifled, Gaitskill ran away from home, first to California and then to Canada. In a *New York Times* article in 2005, she recalled that she had a "strong conviction that there was something out there in the world that was more wonderful." She ended up selling flowers on the street in San Francisco and performing as a stripper in bars, all the time keeping a journal. "I had really wanted adventure," Gaitskill said in the *Times* article.

In another interview, Gaitskill asserted that her background is of limited relevance to her writing except for one thing, as she told *Contemporary Authors:*

> My experience of life as essentially unhappy and uncontrollable taught me to examine the way people, including myself, create survival systems and psychologically "safe" places for themselves in unorthodox and sometimes apparently self-defeating ways. These inner worlds, although often unworkable and unattractive in social terms, can have a unique beauty and courage.

When she was 20, Gaitskill moved back home and attended the University of Michigan, where she won the University's Hopwood Award for a short story collection in 1981, the same year she graduated. She left home again, this time for New York City, to pursue a writer's life and took a job as a legal proofreader while continuing to write fiction on the side.

Gaitskill made her literary debut with the publication of a critically acclaimed collection of short stories titled *Bad Behavior* (1988), in which several characters deal, often unsuccessfully, with sexual degradation, drug addiction, pornography, and prostitution. Many of the stories, including "Secretary," which inspired a film by the same name in 2005, are an unsettling mixture of sadomasochism, romance, humor, and cruelty. The author's unsparing prose, wrote a reviewer for the *New Statesman* magazine, is "bold and heedless . . . with febrile intensity . . . moving and thrilling to read." Another critic describes Gaitskill's writing and her vivid portrayal of the seamy side of life as "brainy lyricism, of acid shot through with grace, which is unlike anyone else's."

After the publication of *Bad Behavior*, Gaitskill left Manhattan and moved to Northern California, in part to escape "misguided assumptions" about her: "People expected me to be this embodiment of all knowing hipness and I just wasn't," she said in the *New York Times*. She later moved to Texas where she taught creative writing at the University of Houston.

Her first novel, *Two Girls, Fat and Thin,* came out in 1991. It juxtaposes the two title characters and centers on their relationship: One is sexually promiscuous and outgoing while the other is the exact opposite. As children, however, both characters were sexually abused, and each reacts to that traumatic experience in her own way. The novel was followed by another short fiction collection, *Because They Wanted To* (1997), which was nominated for the PEN/Faulkner Award and won an online Salon Books Award. But critics also pointed out that Gaitskill's books, with their sometimes explicit and titillating sexual content, are not for everyone. In the *Washington Post,* Carolyn See wrote that "she [Gaitskill] has got a reputation as

rowdy and a reprobate whose ideas about sex are—to say the least—startlingly innovative." Gaitskill explains that her characters sometimes confuse violation with closeness and are "searching for a carnality full of honor and truth."

Veronica (2005), Gaitskill's prize-winning second novel, is set during the 1980s in Paris, Manhattan, and San Francisco and is narrated by Alison Owen, a once-beautiful fashion model who worked in haute couture in Paris and Rome. Her career crashes, and she ends up sick, poverty-stricken, and unstable: "My focus sometimes slips and goes funny," is the way Alison explains herself. Now middle-aged, she reflects on her past, including her improbable friendship with Veronica, a wisecracking, eccentric older woman who is decidedly unstylish ("From a distance her whole face looked askew, puckered like flesh around a badly healed wound") and not very appealing. But unlike Alison, Veronica, who dies of AIDS, accepts her shortcomings. A writer for *New York Magazine* noted that the novel feels different from the author's earlier work, "with a dreamy, hallucinatory quality and a new obsession with mortality and aging."

When *Veronica* was nominated as a finalist for the 2005 National Book Award, the judges' citation read, in part:

> Mary Gaitskill is an unforgiving writer, harsh, caustic and raw. With *Veronica* she is at the height of her narrative powers, evoking the indelible friendship of two women while zigzagging through time, place and the far reaches of the mind. In the process she manages the ultimate hat trick of fiction: appalling, shocking, even offensive, but at the end of the day enormously illuminating. An utterly honest book from someone who understands and evokes the cul-de-sacs of the soul.

Gaitskill's stories have appeared in the *New Yorker, Harper's Magazine, Esquire, The Best American Short Stories* (1993), and *The O. Henry Prize Stories* (1998), and she received a Guggenheim Fellowship in 2002. She teaches creative writing at

Mary Gaitskill's prize-winning fiction has been lauded for its wit and edginess.
(AP Images/Henry Ray Abrams)

Syracuse University, where she lives on campus during the week. Gaitskill, whose favorite writers include Vladimir Nabokov, Jean Genet, FLANNERY O'CONNOR and MAXINE HONG KINGSTON, offered this advice to aspiring writers: "At some point, you need to stop asking other people's opinions, especially on draft-stage work. You need to be alone, in the dark, feeling your way along as if you're on a tightrope—because you are."

Gaitskill spends weekends with her husband, Peter Trachtenberg, whom she married in 2002 and who is also a writer, in a home they rent in Rhinebeck, New York. "I often thought of marriage as rather dull," Gaitskill said, "[But] there's a deep level of support that I never knew I was missing, because I'd never really had it." The couple supports and mentors two children through the Fresh Air Fund, paying for their education at a Catholic school in Brooklyn, New York.

Mary Gaitskill writes structurally complex fiction that is witty and raw and often examines the darker sides of life with icy insight, where troubled people desperately seek intimate relationships of all varieties but mostly end up alone. According to *New York Times* critic Michiko Kakutani, Gaitskill's plots and characters are believable and not "merely perverse" because the author "writes with such authority, such radar-perfect detail, that she is able to make even the most extreme situations seem real."

Further Reading

Bellafante, Ginia. "Can a Writer of Malaise Find Happiness in Acclaim?" *New York Times,* October 30, 2005, Style Section, pp. 1, 16.

Gaitskill, Mary. *Bad Behavior.* New York: Poseidon Press, 1988.

———. *Because They Wanted To.* New York: Simon & Schuster, 1997.

———. *Two Girls, Fat and Thin.* New York: Poseidon Press, 1991.

———. *Veronica.* New York: Pantheon, 2005.

Nussbaum, Emily. "Mary, Mary, Less Contrary: Mary Gaitskill." *New York Magazine.* November 14, 2005. Available online. URL: http://newyorkmetro.com/nymetro/arts/books/14988. Downloaded on January 22, 2007.

García, Cristina
(1958–) *novelist, journalist*

Cristina García was a journalist before she wrote her first impressive novel, *Dreaming in Cuban* (1992). A finalist for the National Book Award, it portrays the tumultuous lives of four strong-willed Cuban women. In 1997 she published a second novel, *The Agüero Sisters,* that also chronicles a divided family—some members remain in Cuba after the revolution, while others make their way to America—who grapple with issues such as exile, cultural fragmentation, and patriotism.

Cristina García was born on July 4, 1958, in Havana, Cuba, and immigrated to the United States with her parents when she was two. She hoped to join the foreign service and majored in political science at Barnard College in New York City, where she earned a bachelor of arts degree in 1979. At Johns Hopkins University's School of Advanced International Studies she switched her concentration to Latin American studies, graduating with a master's degree in 1981.

In 1983 García opted to pursue a career in journalism. She landed a job as a reporter and researcher for *Time* and became a correspondent at the magazine from 1985 until 1990, often writing articles about the concerns of Hispanics. But García grew tired of "telling the truth" and decided to try her hand at fiction. In a 1992 interview with the *Ann Arbor News,* she recalled that while writing a poem about three crazy women who kill themselves, the feeling of being liberated by her own words prompted her to leave *Time,* where she had been "frustrated with the constraints of journalism." The same year she left *Time,* 1990, she married Scott Brown.

Having been bureau chief in Miami, and having lived there, she was thrust into the city's large, vibrant Cuban-American population, and "all the issues of childhood bubbled up." When *Dreaming in Cuban* appeared in 1992, it was the culmination of Cuban-related stories that had been percolating in her imagination for several years.

A finalist for the National Book Award in 1992, *Dreaming* was described by a *New York Times* book reviewer as "completely original" and its author as "blessed with a poet's ear for language, a historian's fascination with the past and a musician's intuitive understanding of the ebb and flow of emotion." *Dreaming in Cuban* chronicles three generations of feisty Cuban women, beginning in 1972 with the matriarch Celia del Pino, who remains in Havana and is a staunch believer in Castro's revolution. The saga, which moves from the past to the present and from third to first person, ends with Celia's granddaughter Pilar, a punk artist living in New York City, who is visited in her dreams by her far-

away *abuela* (grandmother), arranging a reunion at Celia's house in Cuba. "Every day," says Pilar, "Cuba fades a little more inside me, my grandmother fades a little more inside me. And there's only my imagination where our history should be." For Celia, as she skirts the familiar beach in Havana, "past the pawpaw tree," the sea beckons her "with its blue waves of light."

Writing *Dreaming in Cuban* helped García better understand her parents and their generation, which was virulently anti-Castro. By passing on her family's history, she hopes that her daughter, Pilar Akiko, will have a balanced picture of her Cuban heritage.

García published her second novel, *The Agüero Sisters,* in 1997. In richly imagined prose, it relates

Cristina García stands in front of a copy of her first novel, *Dreaming in Cuban.*
(AP/Wide World Photos)

the sometimes comic, sometimes tragic relationships between the children and parents of a Cuban family, while eloquently focusing on more universal themes such as evolution, exile, and extinction. Her third novel, *Monkey Hunting* (2003), follows a family through four generations, from China to Cuba to America. In this mini-epic, writes the literary critic for the *Atlantic* magazine, García "combines her gorgeous writing with a relentless view of history and a fierce understanding of the degree to which the individual life is at the mercy of larger forces." During an interview in 2003 with the *Los Angeles Weekly,* García describes *Monkey Hunting,* which was a *New York Times* Notable Book, as the hardest thing she had ever written, because it was so far from her own experiences. "Ultimately," she said, "the novel is a 120-year dialogue between Cuba and Asia." In 2007 she published another work of fiction, *A Handbook to Luck,* a novel about three characters over the course of several decades.

Cristina García, who resides in Santa Monica, California, with her daughter Pilar, has been hailed as an important, visionary voice in contemporary American and Latino fiction. "What I love," she says, "is the music of a sentence, the jarring juxtaposition of unexpected things."

Cristina García is, according to one critic, "a deft and supple writer" and an important, visionary voice in modern American and Latino fiction.

Further Reading

Andreassi, D. D. "Cristina García." In *Latinas! Women of Achievement,* edited by Diane Telgen and Jim Kamf, 159–162. Detroit, Mich.: Visible Ink Press, 1996.

García, Cristina, ed. *Bordering Fires: The Vintage Book of Contemporary Mexican and Chicanola Literature.* New York: Vintage, 2006.

———. *The Agüero Sisters.* New York: Alfred A. Knopf, 1997.

———. *Dreaming in Cuban.* New York: Alfred A. Knopf, 1992.

———. *Monkey Hunting.* New York: Alfred A. Knopf, 2003.

———. *A Handbook to Luck.* New York: Alfred A. Knopf, 2007.

Heredia, Juanita, and Bridget Kevane. "At Home on the Page: An Interview with Cristina García." In *Latina Self-Portraits: Interview with Contemporary Women Writers,* 69–71. Albuquerque: University of New Mexico Press, 2000.

Rivero, Eliana. "Cristina García." In *Latino and Latina Writers,* edited by Alan West-Duran, 635–652. New York: Charles Scribner's Sons, 2003.

Gilman, Charlotte Perkins
(1860–1935)   *short story, nonfiction writer*

One of America's preeminent feminist writers and social reformers at the turn of the century, Charlotte Perkins Gilman stressed the importance of economic independence and equality for women in all spheres of life. She is best known for her short story "The Yellow Wallpaper," a harrowing, semiautobiographical portrait of a woman's descent into madness that first appeared in 1892 and was out of print for almost 50 years.

Charlotte Perkins was born on July 3, 1860, in Hartford, Connecticut, and grew up in a modest home in Providence, Rhode Island. Her father abandoned her mother, leaving the family destitute and homeless. Her mother refused to display any physical affection, in part to protect her daughter from being betrayed and hurt by men, as she had been. In her posthumously published autobiography *The Living of Charlotte Perkins Gilman* (1935), Gilman explained why as a child she would pretend she was sleeping: "My mother would not let me caress her, and would not caress me, unless I was asleep." As for her father, Gilman noted only that the word father meant nothing to her.

Because she moved 19 times in 18 years, Gilman was for the most part self-educated. But she inherited the intellectual curiosity and literary skills of the novelist HARRIET BEECHER STOWE, and followed in the footsteps of feminist education activist Catherine Beecher, both of whom were her great-aunts. At age 17, she resolved to "help humanity" and develop a "noble character" while enjoying herself "like other people." Taking advantage of her artistic nature and the training she had received briefly at the Rhode Island School of Design, Gilman worked as a commercial artist and art teacher.

In 1884, at age 24, she reluctantly married the Rhode Island artist Charles Walter Stetson, but she was skeptical about combining marriage, work, and motherhood. The next year, shortly after the birth of their daughter, Katherine Beecher, Gilman felt enveloped by a terrible "dark fog." Today she probably would be diagnosed as having suffered from postpartum depression. Instead, S. Weir Mitchell, a popular "nerve specialist" and a Victorian guru of sorts, recommended complete bed rest. His advice—"live as domestic a life as possible . . . have your child with you all the time . . . and *never* touch pen, brush, or pencil as long as you live"—drove Gilman, as she described it, "near the borderline of utter mental ruin."

Realizing that her option was "not between going and staying with her husband" but between "going insane and staying sane," she left Stetson in 1888 and moved to California. When her health measurably improved, she attributed some of her problems to her marriage, and obtained a divorce. "After I was finally free," she wrote later in her autobiography, "wreck though I was, there was a surprising output of work, some of my best. . . . Made a wrong marriage—lots of people do. Am heavily damaged, but not dead."

Gilman supported herself by lecturing, teaching, editing, running a boarding house, and writing. In 1892 she published a short story in *New England Magazine* that would many years later become a classic of feminist literature. "The Yellow Wallpaper," a fictionalized version of the author's own nervous breakdown, is the gripping tale of a woman driven to madness by the destructive "rest cure" therapy of an overprotective doctor who completely ignored the heroine's intellectual and creative needs. The protagonist shreds the wallpaper of the room to which she has been confined, and becomes suicidal. "So now she servants are gone, and the things are gone, and there is nothing left but that great bedstead nailed down. . . . I am getting angry enough to do something desperate. . . . It is so pleasant to be out in this great room and creep around as I please!" The surrealistic portrayal of a mind proceeding to collapse and of the detrimental mental and physical effects of society's subjugation of women was decades ahead of its time.

In 1893 Gilman published a polemical collection of verse about the adverse effects of suffocating love entitled *In This Our World.* Her reputation as a writer was growing, but when Stetson married Gilman's close friend, the writer Grace Ellery Channing, Gilman sent nine-year-old Katherine to live with her father and his new wife. Subsequently, Gilman was publicly condemned in newspapers and by friends for being "unfeeling" and "unnatural." Nonetheless, Gilman continued to struggle to support herself, refusing to take money from her ex-husband, with whom she remained on friendly terms.

In 1895 Gilman moved to Chicago to live and study at the experimental Hull House, which was organized by her friend and colleague, the social reformer Jane Addams, with whom she would cofound the Women's Peace Party in 1925. Both Addams and Gilman believed that the education of women was integral to creating a truly democratic society. Although Gilman was a progressive writer and attended the International Socialist and Labor Congress in England in 1896, she called herself a philosopher and teacher rather than a reformer. "My business," she wrote, "was to find out what ailed society, and how most easily and naturally to improve it."

In 1898 Gilman published her first and best known nonfiction work, *Women and Economics: A Study of the Economic Relations between Men and Women as a Factor in Social Evolution,* which was hailed as the bible of the women's movement. In it she asserts: "To speak broadly, the troubles of life as we find them are mainly traceable to the heart or the purse."

Using a witty, satirical approach, Gilman analyzed women's status in society in the past and present, denouncing their economic dependence within marriage. Women, she argued, were undervalued, undereducated, and underdeveloped as social beings because they were forced to rely on their husbands instead of having the opportunity to become autonomous individuals.

In *Women and Economics* Gilman called for freeing women from domestic duties and to fostering "the will which only comes by freedom and power." She proposed that men and women share the responsibility of housework and that education, including centralized nurseries and day care centers, should become a social responsibility. These were radical notions in the late 1890s. Charlotte Perkins Gilman's *Women and Economics* was translated into seven languages and became a manifesto for the turn-of-the century women's movement. It brought its author international acclaim, as well as a fair share of criticism.

In 1900 she married her younger first cousin George Houghton Gilman, who was also a member of the Beecher family. She took his name, dropping Stetson, and with household help and his support she continued to lecture and write. For the next three decades the unconventional couple lived in New York and Connecticut. In spite of recurring bouts of depression, Gilman published seven novels, hundreds of short stories, and close to a dozen nonfiction books that included *Concerning Children* (1900), *The Home: Its Work and Influence* (1903), *Human Work* (1904), and *The Man-Made World* (1911), all of which explored alternative social organizations that would enable women to find meaningful work outside the home.

From 1909 to 1916, Gilman published, edited, and wrote for the *Forerunner,* a monthly magazine that she had founded. Largely funding it herself, she used the publication to serialize three of her utopian novels, the best known of which was *Herland* (1915). In it, a futuristic all-female society that is based on nurturing, cooperation, and caring results in a peaceful, prosperous, and ecologically sound society.

In 1920 William Dean Howells, who had encouraged Gilman as a poet and fiction written throughout her literary career, included "The Yellow Wallpaper" in *Great Modern American Stories,* which he edited. But it was not until feminist scholars rediscovered and reinterpreted it in the early 1970s that it became a best seller and that Gilman's nonfiction and feminist utopian novels became popular.

Although Gilman supported the suffrage movement, her emphasis was on practical changes, such as the establishment of child care centers and take-out restaurants that would ease the burden on working mothers. In 1934, after her husband's sudden death, she moved back to California to be near her daughter and her friend from the past, the now widowed Grace Channing Stetson. When she was diagnosed with incurable cancer, Gilman considered her career of service over. She took her own life on August 17, 1935, refusing to become a burden and calling her choice "the simplest of human rights."

In 1994 she was one of 25 women, including Zora Neale Hurston and Oprah Winfrey, inducted into the National Women's Hall of Fame in Seneca Falls, New York. A three-day international conference on Charlotte Perkins Gilman was held in England in 1995, covering all aspects of her extraordinary and influential life and work. Another conference sponsored by the Charlotte Perkins Gilman Society, which was founded in 1990 to promote scholarship and issues related to the author, took place in June 2006 in Portland, Maine.

Charlotte Perkins Gilman was named the sixth most influential woman of the 20th century in a poll commissioned by the Siena Research Institute. The celebrated suffragist Carrie Chapman Catt called Gilman "the most original and challenging mind which the [women's] movement produced."

Further Reading

The Charlotte Perkins Gilman Society. Available online. URL: http://web.cortland.edu/gilman. Downloaded on January 22, 2007.

Gilman, Charlotte Perkins. *A Nonfiction Reader.* New York: Columbia University Press, 1990.

———. *The Living of Charlotte Perkins Gilman: An Autobiography.* New York: Harper and Row, 1975.

———. *The Yellow Wall-Paper and Other Writings.* With an introduction by Alexander Black. New York: Random House, 2000.

Lane, Ann J. *To Herland and Beyond: The Life of Charlotte Perkins Gilman.* New York: Pantheon Books, 1990.

∼ Glaspell, Susan Keating
(1876–1948)   playwright, novelist

Pulitzer Prize–winning dramatist Susan Glaspell cofounded the Provincetown Players, a theater company that produced experimental works of talented young American playwrights. And in 50 short stories, 10 novels, and a dozen plays, she captured, as one of her female characters says, "the outward commonplaceness of things that were tragic."

Born on July 1, 1876, in Davenport, Iowa, where her ancestors had come as pioneers in the 1830s, Susan Keating Glaspell attended Iowa's Drake University. After graduating in 1899 she worked as a reporter for two local Des Moines newspapers, but she grew restless and became more interested in fiction than in journalism.

In 1902 she took off for Chicago and wrote short stories that appeared in magazines such as *Harper's* and *Booklovers*. Although sentimental and escapist, the stories often dealt with a theme that Glaspell would more successfully develop in her later work: the conflict between desire and personal integrity. For example, in "Contrary to Precedent" (1904), the protagonist ultimately makes the "right" choice for "her soul, herself," even though it meant giving up love, "the thing she could not do without."

Glaspell was also establishing herself as a popular novelist. In 1909 she published her first novel, *The Glory of the Conquered: The Story of a Great Love,* a conventional romance. After a trip to Europe, she met and fell in love with George Cram Cook, a writer, spiritualist, and socialist who came from her hometown in Iowa. Unfortunately he was married; not surprisingly, many of Glaspell's female characters were attracted to married men. Influenced by Cook's idealism and politics, Glaspell wrote *The Visioning* (1911), a novel that was more sophisticated than her earlier fiction. In it a privileged women "sees the light" and gives up capitalism for socialism.

Once Cook was divorced, Glaspell married him, and in 1913 the couple moved to Greenwich

Playwright Susan Glaspell won a Pulitzer Prize for *Alison's House.*
(AP/Wide World Photos)

Village in New York City to live among other free-thinking writers. They spent their summers in Provincetown, a beach community at the tip of Cape Cod in Massachusetts, where in 1915 they founded the Provincetown Players, an avant-garde theater company that fostered the work of promising new playwrights. One of their "discoveries" was the as yet unknown playwright Eugene O'Neill: the Players produced his first play.

Glaspell discovered that she enjoyed writing plays, having cowritten a satire titled *Suppressed Desires* (1915) with her husband. In 1916 the company moved to Greenwich Village, where the Provincetown Playhouse continued to operate as the Playwright's Theatre off and on for several years until 1998, when New York University purchased the space for its theater department.

Trifles (1916), a one-act play considered to be Glaspell's masterpiece, was remarkable for its frank portrayal of a woman driven to kill her abusive husband. The tacit agreement of two neighbors to conceal evidence of her guilt inspires one of them to say: "We [women] all go through the same things—it's all just a different kind of the same thing." A short-story adaptation of *Trifles*, "A Jury of Her Peers," appeared in *The Best Short Stories of 1916*.

In 1919 the Provincetown Players staged Glaspell's first full-length play, *Bernice,* in which the heroine never appears on stage. It was followed in 1921 by her most experimental play, *The Verge,* about a "new woman," who must choose between traditional comfortable relationships and personal integrity; the character tries to free herself from a man but is driven to madness and murder.

In spite of the Provincetown Players' success, Cook felt dissatisfied, and in 1922 he and Glaspell journeyed to Greece, where he was venerated as a holy man until his death two years later. Glaspell stayed in Europe and met another writer, Norman Matson. In 1925 she married him and, as she had with her first husband, collaborated with him on a play, *The Comic Artist* (1928). Meanwhile Glaspell published another novel, *Brook Evans* (1928). While portraying a failed relationship in her next novel, *Fugitive's Return* (1929), her own marriage was failing.

But in 1930 Glaspell scored her greatest career success with *Alison's House,* a play based loosely on the life of poet EMILY DICKINSON and for which Glaspell was awarded a Pulitzer Prize in 1931; the same year, she was divorced from Matson. Although she headed the Federal Theater Project's Midwest Play Bureau in the mid-1930s, Glaspell never again completed a play, and she wrote only a few more novels and short stories.

In her review of *Susan Glaspell: Her Life and Times* (2005), by Linda Ben-Zvi, J. Ellen Gainor, a professor of theater at Cornell University, calls the biography a compelling and much-needed corrective to this legacy of dismissal and neglect.

It both complements the burgeoning field of Glaspell studies and provides nuanced and fresh readings of Glaspell's oeuvre. . . . Her writing emerges as history as well—chronicles of life in the conservative American heartland, in the bohemian communities of Greenwich Village and Provincetown, and in a post-war nation grappling with competing ideologies for its future.

Susan Glaspell died in 1948 in Provincetown, near the theatrical company she had helped to create and which proved to be a seminal force in shaping American theater. An accomplished playwright, she created strong characters—especially women—tinged with modernist despair, who fought for their integrity and rights.

Further Reading

Ben-Zvi, Linda. *Susan Glaspell: Her Life and Times.* New York: Oxford University Press, 2005.

Carpenter, Martha C. *The Major Novels of Susan Glaspell.* Gainesville, Fla.: Florida University Press, 2001.

Gainor, J. Ellen. "Fruits of Anger." HotReview.org: Hunter on-line theater review. Available online. URL: http://www.hotreview.org/articles/fruitsofanger.htm. Downloaded on January 22, 2007.

———. *Susan Glaspell in Context: American Theater, Culture, and Politics, 1915–1948.* Ann Arbor: University of Michigan Press, 2001.

Glaspell, Susan. *Plays.* Edited by C. W. E. Bigsby. New York: Cambridge University Press, 1987.

The Gleaner

See MURRAY, JUDITH SARGENT

Glück, Louise Elisabeth

(1943–) *poet, literary critic*

As of 2006 Louise Glück had written nine volumes of highly acclaimed poetry, including *The Wild Iris,* which won the Pulitzer Prize in 1993. Using straightforward, spare, and lyrical language, her insightful poems often probe domestic situations, such as marriage and motherhood, that have gone awry. Glück's poetry is haunting and strong, yet beautiful and delicately crafted.

Born on April 22, 1943, in New York City, and raised on Long Island in a family in which "the right of any member to complete the sentence of another was assured," Louise Elisabeth Glück learned Greek mythology from her well-educated parents when she was three and was composing poems by the time she was five. At age 16, Glück became anorexic. "Anorexia proves not the soul's superiority but its dependence on flesh," she said. In "Dedication to Hunger," a poem written in 1980, she further explained that a woman's body is "a grave."

Renowned poet Louise Glück writes beautifully crafted verse.
(AP/Wide World Photos)

After dropping out of high school, Glück underwent seven years of psychoanalysis. She then studied poetry at Columbia University with Stanley Kunitz, whom she considered a "companion spirit" and who greatly influenced her early poetry. He admired his student's work and said that "everything she [Glück] touches turns to music and legend."

Glück graduated from Columbia in 1965 and published her first volume of poems, *Firstborn,* in 1968, when she was 24. In 1971 she moved to Vermont to teach at Goddard College. She produced another volume of poetry, *The House on Marshland,* four years later. In it, Glück finds her own voice and writes with emotional and rhetorical intensity about the pain of lost or damaged relationships. *The Garden* (1976), a series of five related but independent poems, also focuses on loss, pain, and fear. But Glück always leaves open a glimmer of hope and "radiance." In 1980, when her house burned to the ground, she said, "I watched the destruction of all that had been, all that would not be again, and all that remained . . . and it conferred on daily life an aura of blessedness . . . all that remained took on a radiance."

Glück's poems were appearing regularly in popular magazines such as the *New Yorker* and *Atlantic Monthly,* as well as in collections. The author describes the poems in *Descending Figure* (1980) as saturated with "a mother's grief and fearfulness." At the age of 30, she became a mother and experienced what she called "wild, protective, terrified love."

Her fourth book, *The Triumph of Achilles* (1985), which received the National Book Critics Circle Award for poetry, plays on allusions to Greek mythology and reflects the poet's artistic maturity and deepening mastery of language. *Ararat* (1990), a series of short lyrics with a recurrent narrative about separation and the struggle for reunion, was followed in 1992 by *The Wild Iris,* which earned Glück the Pulitzer Prize in poetry in 1993. The literary critic Helen Vendler compares Glück to the poet EMILY DICKINSON, who also used flowers as images of the soul, and describes

The Wild Iris as an "opulent, symbolic book, really one long poem: flowers talk to their gardener-poet, who is mourning the loss of youth, passion and the erotic life, and prays to a nameless God." Another book of poetry, *Vita Nova: Poems,* was published in 1999. The acclaimed collection won the *New Yorker* magazine's Book Award in Poetry; it poignantly but without sentimentality explores the interim period after love has ended and before the stirrings of new emotions. Glück's next volume of verse, *The Seven Ages,* published in 2001, was followed in 2004 by a chapbook, *October,* a six-part poem that award-winning poet Mark Strand labeled a "masterpiece."

She also has produced notable criticism: *Proofs and Theories: Essays of Poetry* (1994) won the PEN/Martha Albrand Award for Nonfiction. "Writing is not decanting of personality," the author wrote in one of the essays. "The truth, on the page, need not have been lived. It is, instead, all that can be envisioned."

Glück has received grants from the Rockefeller Foundation, the Guggenheim Foundation, and National Endowment for the Arts (NEA). She has received numerous prizes, including the Poetry Society of America's William Carlos Williams Award, the Lannan Literary Award, the MIT Anniversary Medal, and the 2001 Yale University Bollingen Prize in Poetry, which honors a poet's "lifetime achievement in his or her art."

From 1983 to 2004 Glück was a member of the English faculty at Williams College. Divorced, with a grown son, Glück currently teaches at Yale University, where she is also the judge, through 2007, for the Yale Series of Younger Poets. In 2003 Glück, a former Vermont state poet, was appointed U.S. poet laureate, joining other esteemed laureates such as Penn Warren, RITA DOVE, Robert Pinsky, and Billy Collins. Her collection of 18 poems, *Averno* (2006), demonstrates that Glück is "writing at the peak of her powers," said the *New York Times Book Review* critic in March 2006, who praised the "complex, haunting power of the poems." In 2007 Glück was awarded an L. L. Winship/PEN New England Award for *Averno.*

Considered by many critics one of America's most talented contemporary poets, Louise Glück is passionate about language and turning commonplace experiences into personal, mythical poetry.

Further Reading

Diehl, Joanne E., ed. *On Louise Glück: Change What You See.* Ann Arbor: University of Michigan Press, 2005.

Glück, Louise. *Averno.* New York: Farrar, Straus & Giroux, 2006.

———. *The First Four Books of Poems.* Hopewell, N.J.: Ecco Press, 1998.

———. *October.* Louisville, Ky.: Sarabende Book, 2004.

Vendler, Helen. "Flower Power: Louise Glück's 'The Wild Iris.'" In *Soul Says: On Recent Poetry,* 16–22. Cambridge, Mass.: Harvard University Press, 1995.

Godwin, Gail Kathleen
(1937–   ) *novelist, short story writer, nonfiction book writer*

A three-time National Book Award nominee, Gail Godwin is the author of a dozen critically acclaimed novels, two collections of short stories, a book of nonfiction, and, together with composer Robert Starer, 10 musical compositions. Her richly textured fiction is mostly about modern, literate, bright women, many of them from the South, who face difficult decisions, often because they are troubled by self-identity issues as they become enmeshed in complicated familial or romantic relationships.

Born on June 18, 1937, in Birmingham, Alabama, but raised in Asheville, North Carolina, Godwin recalled in an essay in *The Writer on Her Work* that at five she already had allied herself with "the typewriter rather than the stove," and by nine she had written her first story. Her mother was a reporter and, after divorcing, taught writing and wrote stories to help support her daughter. "I am my mother's child, weaned on shapely plot; the child of the woman who knew more about herself than she dared to put into her heroines," wrote Godwin in *The Writer on Her Work.*

Godwin began her writing career in 1959 as a general assignment reporter for the *Miami Herald* soon after graduating from the University of North Carolina at Chapel Hill with a degree in journalism. After she was fired—and after a brief marriage in 1960 to a newspaper photographer failed, she moved back to North Carolina and took a job as a waitress. Her goal was to save enough money to travel and to write, which is what she did from 1961 to 1965, while working at the U.S. embassy in London. Goodwin married an English psychiatrist named Ian Marshall in 1965 and divorced him a year later; he helped her face her debilitating fear of failure. She continued writing and ultimately returned to North Carolina. She applied for and was accepted into the competitive University of Iowa Writers Workshop.

Godwin's first published novel, *The Perfectionists* (1970), was written as her Ph.D. thesis at the University of Iowa, where she earned both her master's degree (1968) and doctorate (1971) in English. The *Saturday Review* called *The Perfectionists* "an extraordinary accomplishment," while JOYCE CAROL OATES praised it as a "most intelligent and engrossing novel" in the *New York Times Book Review.*

From 1971 to 1972 Godwin was a fellow at the Center for Advanced Studies at the University of Illinois at Champaign-Urbana. *The Odd Woman* (1974), Godwin's third novel and perhaps best-known work, about a literature professor and a married man who have an affair and metaphorically about how women retain or lose their sense of self while engaged in intimate relationships, was considered more fully developed than her two earlier books in terms of plot and character development, as well as in its exemplary use of irony and nuance.

Godwin produced her first short story collection in 1976. *Dream Children* has 15 stories. "The characters [in these stories] are people who have all gone beyond limits of some kind," wrote Jane Hill in the *Dictionary of Literary Biography.* "The resolutions are often beyond the boundaries of physical reality."

In addition to writing fiction, Godwin is a librettist of musical works by composer Robert Starer, her longtime companion. In 1978 their full-length opera, *Apollonia,* was commissioned by the Minnesota Opera Company. That same year *Violet Clay,* another thought-provoking and well-received novel, was published. One of the central characters, Violet Clay's Uncle Ambrose, was based loosely on Godwin's father, whom she did not meet until her high school graduation and who committed suicide by shooting himself.

It was Godwin's fifth novel, *A Mother and Two Daughters* (1982), nominated for a National Book Award and critically praised for its sensitive, compassionate, and multidimensional portrayal of contemporary women confronting complex emotions such as envy, anger, and loss, that put her name on the literary map. It was on the *New York Times* best seller list for three months. "It most surprised me that I could get into the head of an elderly woman," Godwin said in *Publishers Weekly,* "but in fact it was easy." Assessing the popular novel, *Washington Post Book World*'s reviewer Jonathan Yardley called Godwin a "stunningly gifted novelist of manners" who keenly observes and then expertly describes social and physical details in the Victorian tradition.

Godwin wrote about her half brother Tommy's death, during a shooting incident in 1983, in her seventh novel, *A Southern Family* (1987), another *New York Times* best seller and one of her most psychologically astute and accomplished books. Her next best-selling book was *Father Melancholy's Daughter* (1991), in which the protagonist, Margaret Gower, is conflicted about her emotional needs and her responsibilities to her father after her mother abandons the family (and then dies in a car accident), when Margaret is a young child. These novels were followed by *The Good Husband* in 1994, the "greatest accomplishment of which," wrote Penelope Mesic in the *Chicago Tribune,* "lies in capturing the sheer work of dying," and in 1999 by *Evensong,* another *New York Times* best seller in which a character from a previous novel, the motherless daughter in *Father Melancholy's Daughter,* returns.

Godwin's first nonfiction book, *Heart: A Personal Journey through Its Myths and Meanings* (2001), explores heart-related history, religion, literature, and art through historical, biological, and literary analysis. "Finding out how all these areas branched out and connected was a broadening experience," commented Godwin during an interview with *Book Page* in 2001. "I feel more and more that we spent hundreds of years perfecting our minds and our industries and our reason, and now it's time . . . to develop more consciousness of heart."

After the death of her companion and musical collaborator Robert Starer in 2001, the same year their chamber opera, *The Other Voice,* based on the life of St. Hilda of Whitby, premiered in New York City, Godwin penned a novella, *Evenings at Five* (2003), self-described as her "grief sonata" and based on her 30-year friendship with Starer. The writer Kurt Vonnegut, in commenting about *Evenings at Five,* noted that "with words alone Godwin created an important piece of music about a love which death can only increase and deepen." For Godwin, fact and fiction, and reality and fantasy, often merge, "shapelifting into one another," as she describes it.

In Godwin's novel *Queen of the Underworld* (2006), Emma Gant, the affable heroine, like Godwin, started her writing career as a journalist in Miami. "The wizardry of this novel is its pitch-perfect rendition of what it was like to be a true solo artist, a female of ambition coming out of 1950s America," writes *Boston Globe* reviewer Madeleine Blais. "The narrative [the first 10 days of Emma's career] provides a wonderful balancing act between Gant's undisputed talent and intelligence and her age-appropriate silliness and narcissism. These youthful writings provide the author with a wonderful ally," writes Blais, "as [Godwin] captures the contradictory nature of Emma, who is conniving and naïve, shy and aggressive, faltering and self-assured, all at once. . . . Like all other shining females in literature, Emma Gant is, above all and most endearingly, a woman of appetite at life's feast who refuses to nibble when she can devour." Also in 2006, Godwin chronicled her early years as a struggling writer, when she, like Gant, was a reporter in Miami, in *The Making of a Writer, Journals 1961–1963.*

Among the honors Godwin has received are a Guggenheim Fellowship, National Endowment

Gail Godwin writes revealingly about smart contemporary women coping with emotional issues.
(Beth Bliss)

for the Arts (NEA) grants for both fiction and libretto writing, and the American Academy and Institute of Arts and Letters Award in Literature. She was editor of *The Best American Short Stories* (1985) and garnered the Distinguished Alumna award from the University of North Carolina at Chapel Hill and the University of Rochester's Janet Kafka Award, both in 1988. She also has taught creative writing at various universities, including Columbia, has been awarded several honorary doctorate awards, and was inducted into the Fellowship of Southern Writers in 1997.

"More than any other contemporary writer, Gail Godwin is [reminiscent] of 19th-century pleasures, civilized, passionate about ideas, and ironic about passions," asserted Carol Sternhell in a *Village Voice* review of *The Finishing School* (1985). "Her characters—sensible, intelligent women all—have houses, histories, ghosts." Godwin is also a master at examining the conflicting needs and desires of women today and in delineating their strengths and frailties.

Gail Godwin, a resident of Woodstock, New York, since 1976, writes, swims, and draws (she keeps a jar of colored pencils next to her bed), especially when she is "baffled about some aspect of a character. Making a visual image of that character in action . . . almost always reveals something new." In *The Writer on Her Work,* Godwin reflected: "I am—thanks to the efforts of those who have loved me (and to some who have not) and thanks to the example of people who did their work well, and thanks to the efforts of myself—my own woman." That is also what Godwin's independent-minded, strong, and complex female characters seem to want to be.

Further Reading

Blais, Madeleine. "The Apprentice: Gail Godwin Reveals the Maturation of a Young, Hungry Writer." *Boston Globe.* January 8, 2006. Available online. URL: http://www.boston.com/ae/books/articles/2006/01/08/the_apprentice?mode+PF. Downloaded on January 22, 2007.

Godwin, Gail. "Becoming a Writer." In *The Writer on Her Work,* edited by Janet Sternburg, 231–255. New York: Norton, 1980.

———. *Heart: A Personal Journey through Its Myths and Meanings.* New York: William Morrow, 2001.

———. *The Making of a Writer, Journals 1961–1963.* Edited by Rob Neufeld. New York: Random House, 2006.

———. *A Mother and Two Daughters.* New York: Viking, 1982.

———. *Queen of the Underworld.* New York: Random House, 2006.

∾ Goodwin, Doris Helen Kearns
(1943–) *biographer, memoirist*

Pulitzer Prize–winning author Doris Kearns Goodwin combines a novelist's sense of drama with a reporter's eye for compelling detail. In her acclaimed biographies of the Fitzgeralds and Kennedys, Lyndon B. Johnson, Franklin and Eleanor Roosevelt, and Abraham Lincoln, she probes both the external and internal forces that have influenced their lives and political beliefs.

Born on January 4, 1943, in Rockville Centre, New York, Doris Helen Kearns grew up in a traditional Catholic neighborhood where she was steeped in history, ritual, and the Brooklyn Dodgers. In her memoir *Wait Till Next Year* (1997), she recalls:

> When I was six, my father gave me a bright-red scorebook that opened my heart to the game of baseball. By the time I mastered the art of scorekeeping, a lasting bond had been forged among my father, baseball, and me.

Goodwin graduated magna cum laude from Colby College and received a doctorate degree from Harvard University, where for many years she was a professor of government. She began her political career as an intern, first at the State Department and then at the House of Representatives.

In 1967 she met President Lyndon Baines Johnson (popularly called LBJ) at a White House dance, and although he knew she disagreed vehemently with his foreign policy, instead of arguing with her he asked her to dance. By the end of the evening, LBJ had asked Goodwin to work with him as his special assistant. They became close friends, and nine years later she would publish *Lyndon Johnson and the American Dream,* a compassionate biography, with an emphasis on the psychological forces that helped inform and shape some of President Johnson's decisions.

In 1977 Goodwin began working on a biography of John F. Kennedy, but after several years it had evolved into a multi-generational saga of two Irish-American families. "As I got into the project," Goodwin explained, "I realized I wanted to do a book about my own heritage, something different than just a biography of Jack." A national best seller, *The Fitzgeralds and the Kennedys: An American Saga* (1987) chronicles three generations of both families—from the baptism of John "Honey

Fitz" Fitzgerald in 1863 to the inauguration of his grandson and namesake, John F. Kennedy, in 1961. Goodwin, who had unprecedented access to the Kennedy family and their personal correspondence, wove a tale marked by ambition, love, and tragedy.

In 1995 Goodwin received the Pulitzer Prize in biography for *No Ordinary Time: Franklin and Eleanor Roosevelt: The Home Front in World War II,* the best-selling story of the complex relationship and partnership shared by the brilliant, courageous wartime president and his more reserved, liberal activist wife.

Goodwin's memoir, *Wait Till Next Year,* begins in 1949 and depicts her family, neighborhood, and, as she describes it, "the evolution of her sensibilities" in the suburbs of New York in the 1950s.

Doris Kearns Goodwin is a Pulitzer Prize–winning biographer.
(AP/Wide World Photos)

Ten years in the making, her next book, *Teams of Rivals: The Political Genius of Abraham Lincoln,* was published to much acclaim in 2005. "Lincoln's political genius," writes Goodwin, "was not simply his ability to gather the best men of the country around him, but to impress upon them his own purpose, perception and resolution at every juncture." The book won the 2006 Lincoln Prize, the most generous in the field of American Civil War history, administered through the Lincoln and Soldiers Institute at Gettysburg College.

In his review of the book, which focuses on Lincoln's relationship with three cabinet members—key rivals who became his allies—*New York Times* critic Michiko Kakutani points out that Goodwin's

> narrative abilities, demonstrated in her earlier books, are on full display here, and she does an enthralling job of dramatizing such crucial moments in Lincoln's life as his nomination as the Republican Party's presidential candidate, his delivery of the Gettysburg address, his shepherding of the 13th Amendment (abolishing slavery) through Congress, and his assassination, days after General Lee's surrender.

Despite having been accused in 2002 of improper attribution of several sources in *The Fitzgeralds and the Kennedys,* including borrowing passages from other books without using quotation marks, a settlement was reached and Goodwin retains her reputation as a first-rate writer of compelling, engaging biographies. She lives in Concord, Massachusetts, with her husband Richard Goodwin, a writer and political consultant; they have three sons.

Doris Kearns Goodwin, who believes you have to feel you "own" a historic period before you can write about it, has produced four highly important studies of political figures who helped shape American history.

Further Reading

Goodwin, Doris Kearns. *No Ordinary Time: Franklin and Eleanor Roosevelt: The Home Front in World War II.* New York: Simon & Schuster, 1994.

———. *Team of Rivals: The Political Genius of Abraham Lincoln.* New York: Simon & Schuster, 2005.

———. *Wait Till Next Year: A Memoir.* New York: Simon & Schuster, 1997.

Klein, Joe. "The Original Power Couple." *New Republic* (October 10, 1994): 42–47.

Gordon, Mary Catherine
(1949–) *novelist, short story writer, essayist*

Known for her precise, lyrical prose and darkly resonant fiction, Mary Gordon has earned a reputation as a gifted chronicler of the lives and mores of traditional, family-oriented Catholic women, whom she portrays from a feminist, modernist point of view.

Born on December 8, 1949, in Far Rockaway, New York, to devout Catholic parents, Mary Catherine Gordon as a young child treasured telling stories with her father. "We'd make up whole lives for the characters we encountered," she recalled. Tragically the man she loved "more than God" died when she was seven. "I've always thought that was the most important thing anyone could know about me," Gordon wrote in her memoir, *The Shadow Man* (1996). Although it was her father, a publisher and convert from Judaism, who had encouraged her to become a writer, it was her Irish-American mother, a legal secretary, who taught her how to "listen," which enabled her to write with assurance and authority. "I am the kind of writer I am because I am my mother's daughter," says Gordon.

In 1978 Gordon wrote the first of five novels, *Final Payments,* a best seller that won the Janet Heidinger Kafka Prize and was nominated for the National Book Critics Circle Award. The story follows the development of a woman ushered back into the world, with the help of a group of women friends and an alcoholic priest, following the death of her all-consuming, invalid father.

Gordon has always been willing to probe unfashionable themes. *The Company of Women* (1981), which also received the Kafka Prize, revolves around the rebellious daughter of a female disciple of a conservative priest. The young woman ends up devoting herself to an attractive liberal professor who is in his own way just as authoritarian as the priest.

Her next novel, *Men and Angels* (1985), is less concerned with overtly religious themes and focuses on the balance of power of individual members of a family.

An accomplished writer of short fiction, in 1987 Gordon produced a collection of short stories entitled *Temporary Shelter,* and won the O'Henry Award for her story "City Life" in 1996. Her next novel, *The Other Side* (1989), was unusual in that the narrative moves in and out of the minds of several generations of an immigrant family from Ireland, while exploring the limitations of love and of self-sacrifice, two themes that run throughout Gordon's work. She was again praised by critics for her 1992 provocative collection of essays, *Good Boys and Dead Girls, and Other Essays* (1992). It was followed a year later by *The Rest of Life,* a set of three novellas.

In 1996 Gordon published *The Shadow Man,* a poignant memoir that the author calls "the biography of a relationship." It delineates her painful discovery of the truth about her beloved father: he was a high school dropout, not Harvard-educated; he was a virulent anti-Semitic Jewish convert born in Ohio, not Russia; he had published right-wing Catholic magazines and pornography; and his real name was Israel, not David.

In the process of writing *The Shadow Man,* Gordon reconciles her feelings of revulsion and love for her father, and transforms them into art. After completing the book, she felt that she was finally able to stop writing about the father-daughter relationship. "That particular monster seems fed," she declared.

Spending: A Utopian Divertimento (1998) is more upbeat, noticeably un-Catholic, and less reflective than her earlier work. Its protagonist-narrator is a sensual, talented, and unapologetically ambitious artist who takes a wealthy male lover as her patron. She is determined to get everything she

Fiction writer and memoirist Mary Gordon is pictured here in 1989.
(AP/Wide World Photos)

wants in life, from becoming a successful artist to finding eternal love. In 2000, Gordon wrote a "biographical mediation," as she described it, titled *Joan of Arc,* a historic figure who was "a mirror of my own desires."

Pearl: A Novel, which came out in 2005, revolves around a strong-willed, middle-aged single mother's struggle to understand her daughter's public act of martyrdom: Pearl intends to kill herself in a self-imposed hunger strike as she sits chained to a flagpole in front of the American embassy in Dublin. "The Catholic Church, complicated family and class relationships, and current events—mainstays of Gordon's considerable body of work—play out powerfully in this riveting tale of a mother's fierce, unstoppable determination to save her daughter," says a reviewer for *Library Journal.*

The Stories of Mary Gordon was selected as a Notable Book of the Year in 2006 by the *New York Times.* The collection, written over 30 years and composed of 41 stories, primarily focuses on the emotional repercussions of childhood pain and grief. It won the $20,000 Story Prize for fiction, awarded to Gordon in 2007.

Gordon is often praised for her deep insights, lyrical writing, and what *Los Angeles Times* critic Ellen Akins called "her delicate rendering of the drama of consciousness." She is also known for her probing analysis of Catholic family life, spirituality, and mores.

In her essay "The Parable of the Cave," Mary Gordon, whose role model was Jane Austen, explains the importance of having the company of other women writers.

> I discovered that what I loved in writing was not distance but radical closeness; not the violence of the bizarre but the complexity of the quotidian. . . . My [women] writer friends . . . help me banish the dark specters.

Gordon, who has been married twice and has two children, is the recipient of a Guggenheim fellowship and the Lila Acheson Wallace-Reader's Digest Writer's Award. She has taught at several colleges and as of 1999 has been the Millicent C. McIntosh professor of English at Barnard College.

Further Reading

Bennett, Alma. *Mary Gordon.* New York: Twayne, 1996.
Gordon, Mary. *The Company of Women.* New York: Random House, 1981.
———. *Final Payments.* New York: Random House, 1978.
———. "The Parable of the Cave." In *The Writer on Her Work,* edited by Janet Sternburg, 27–32. New York: W. W. Norton & Company, 1980.
———. *Pearl: A Novel.* New York: Pantheon, 2005.
———. *The Shadow Man.* New York: Random House, 1996.
———. *The Stories of Mary Gordon.* New York: Pantheon, 2006.
Iannone, Carol. "Fiction: The Secret of Mary Gordon's Success," *Commentary* (June 1987): 62–66.

∿ Grafton, Sue Taylor
(1940–) *mystery writer*

An award-winning mystery writer, Sue Grafton has played a major role in the "New Golden Age" of hard-boiled detection fiction by women writers about female sleuths, that took hold during the 1980s. Grafton is best known for her alphabet mystery series that features one of the most fully developed female detectives in contemporary crime fiction.

Born on April 24, 1940, in Louisville, Kentucky, Sue Taylor Grafton had a troubled childhood—both her parents were heavy drinkers who mostly ignored her and her sister. Her father wrote mysteries, although he could not make a living from it, and her mother died in 1960 from an overdose of drugs. As a child, Sue escaped from her unhappiness by "telling spooky stories" until her friends "were scared half to death."

After graduating from the University of Louisville in 1961, Grafton wrote two novels and spent 15 years as a screenwriter. She published the first book in her alphabet mystery series, *"A" Is for Alibi,* in 1982; it quickly became a best seller. In it she introduces her blue collar heroine-protagonist:

> My name is Kinsey Millhone. I'm a private investigator, licensed by the state of California. I'm thirty-two years old, twice divorced, no kids. The day before yesterday I killed someone and the fact weighs heavily on my mind. I'm a nice person and have a lot of friends. My apartment is small but I like living in a cramped space. . . . Aside from the hazards of my profession, my life has always been ordinary, uneventful, and good.

By the end of the book Millhone has solved an eight-year-old murder and shot a man who had stalked her.

Like traditional male detective heros, Grafton's private eye is daring, intelligent, witty, and wisecracking. Although she has numerous romances, Millhone claims, in *"N" Is for Noose* (1998), another best seller, that she is "not that good at relationships" and keeps her distance, "thus avoid-

ing a lot of unruly emotions." According to Grafton, the unpretentious, self-deprecating character is based largely on herself, "only she's thinner, younger, and braver, the lucky so-and-so." Through Millhone, Grafton shares her humorous, and sometimes violent, vision of contemporary society with an enormous readership.

"A" Is for Alibi was followed in 1985 by *"B" Is for Burglar,* which won the Anthony and the Shamus awards for mysteries. Since then Grafton has published an A-to-Z mystery annually, selling more than eight million copies to date. Critics have noted that *"K" Is for Killer,* which received a Doubleday Mystery Guild Award in 1995, contains some of Grafton's finest and most suspenseful prose.

"Sue Grafton knows what she's doing," asserted Marilyn Stasio, the crime book reviewer for the

Sue Grafton is a best-selling mystery writer.
(AP/Wide World Photos)

New York Times, in her column on December 11, 2005:

> In the 19 alphabet-series novels she's written since 1982, the latest of which is *"S" Is for Silence* (2005), she's never bowed to fad or fashion. Instead, she's kept her whip-smart private investigator, Kinsey Millhone, focused on modestly scaled domestic crimes that have a way of expanding to galvanize an entire community. In dealing with big themes on a small canvas, her clever but unpretentious mysteries reassure us that no life is insignificant, no death inconsequential.

Along with mystery writer SARA PARETSKY, Grafton is credited with establishing believable, popular female sleuths. "I chose the classic private eye genre because I like playing hardball with the boys," Grafton explained in an interview in *Armchair Detective.* Her detective stories have been translated into two dozen languages, including Estonian and Indonesian.

Sue Grafton, who lives in southern California and Louisville, Kentucky, is married to screenwriter Steven F. Humphrey and has three children from two previous marriages.

Further Reading

Grafton, Sue. *"A" Is for Alibi.* New York: Holt, Rinehart & Winston, 1982.

———. *"M" Is for Malice.* New York: Henry Holt and Company, 1996.

———. *"S" Is for Silence.* New York: Putnam, 2005.

Kaufman, Natalie Hevener, and Carol McGinnis Kay. *"G" Is for Grafton: The World of Kinsey Millhone.* New York: Henry Holt and Company, 1998.

Pederson, Jay P., ed. *St. James Guide to Crime & Mystery Writers.* Detroit, Mich.: St. James Press, 1996.

∽ Graham, Katharine (Kay Graham)
(1917–2001) *autobiographer, editor*

The former publisher of the *Washington Post* and chairman and chief executive officer of the newspaper's parent company, as well as the author of the 1997 Pulitzer Prize–winning autobiography *Personal History,* Katharine Graham served as a role model for women who aspire to careers in business, publishing, and journalism.

Born Katharine Meyer on June 16, 1917, in New York City, she was the youngest daughter and one of five children of wealthy financier Eugene Meyer, who in 1933 purchased the *Washington Post* and became its publisher, and his artistic socialite wife Agnes. Both of Graham's parents placed great value on learning, ideas, and leadership, but they were distant and unaffectionate with their children. "We were left to bring ourselves up emotionally and intellectually," Graham wrote in *Personal History.* After graduating from Madeira, a private high school for girls in Virginia, Graham attended Vassar College for two years and then the University of Chicago, where she graduated in 1938. She took a job as a reporter for the *San Francisco News* for a year before returning to Washington to work in the editorial and circulation departments of the *Washington Post,* which by then her father owned.

In 1940 she married attorney Philip Graham, a brilliant protégé of Supreme Court Justice Felix Frankfurter and an adviser to Lyndon Johnson. Five years later Graham left her position at the *Post* in order to stay at home and raise the couple's four children. Meanwhile, her husband ran the *Post* (Graham's father, who died in 1946, left the newspaper to his son-in-law because he believed that no man should work for his wife).

According to Graham's memoir, her husband was domineering and manic-depressive. She stayed in the marriage despite his philandering and his erratic and sometimes abusive behavior: In subtle ways, she said, he destroyed her self-esteem. In 1963 Philip Graham committed suicide; his wife discovered his body. A devastated Katharine Graham, at the age of 46, found herself at the helm of the Washington Post Company. Although she had little business experience ("It's hard to describe how abysmally ignorant I was . . . and uneducated in even the basics of the working world," she wrote in *Personal History*), and was advised—as a woman in a man's world—against taking over the company, in 1969 she stepped into her role as publisher of the *Washington Post*.

With newfound strength, she learned quickly and became a savvy, competent leader. "I had very little idea of what I was supposed to be doing, so I set out to learn. What I essentially did was to put one foot in front of the other, shut my eyes, and step off the edge," recalled Graham. According to Robin Gerber, in her book *Katharine Graham: The Leadership Journey of an American Icon* (2005), with her overbearing husband gone, "the pent-up energy of Katharine's unrealized desires and ambitions began to drive her actions. Her father intended the paper to pass down through generations of his family, and Katharine wanted to fulfill his dream." Under Graham's direction and acumen, the company became a diversified conglomerate composed of newspapers, magazines (including *Newsweek*), television and cable stations, and educational services, all of which together were worth more than $1 billion.

Although Graham was not a feminist per se, she was the first woman to head a *Fortune*-500 company. She also stood up for women when she felt they were treated unfairly. Gerber writes that while visiting President Lyndon B. Johnson's Texas ranch in 1964, Graham reprimanded the president for criticizing his wife in her presence. She reminded Johnson that Lady Bird "got you where you are today." And when President Johnson persisted in criticizing Lady Bird about her plans for his birthday barbecue, Graham erupted and told the president, politely but firmly, to "Shut up."

In 1971 Graham courageously decided to publish excerpts of the secret Pentagon Papers in the *Washington Post,* after a federal judge had halted publication of them in the *New York Times.* She vigorously supported the newspaper's reporters and editors as they covered what became known as the Watergate scandal in 1973 and 1974, despite pressure on her to do otherwise from President Nixon's administration. She guided the *Post* through its groundbreaking coverage of that historic event, which ultimately helped lead to Nixon's resignation. In the process, the newspaper, with Benjamin

C. Bradlee as her hand-picked managing editor, set a new standard for investigative journalism and earned the *Post* a Pulitzer Prize for Public Service. "The truth is," wrote Graham in her memoir, "I never felt there was much choice. . . . Once I found myself in the deepest water in the middle of the current, there was no going back."

Credited with turning the *Washington Post* into one of the nation's great papers, Graham also successfully ran a multimillion-dollar communications empire. From 1973 to 1991 she served as board chairman and chief executive of the Washington Post Company and remained chairman of the executive committee until her death in 2001. But in 1975 a 139-day pressmen's strike threatened to cripple the paper. Graham's refusal to give in to the workers broke the power of the pressmen's union, but it was a bitter labor battle. Though gracious, she could be a hard-nosed, strong-willed businesswoman and did whatever she deemed necessary. During the strike, she helped wrap Sunday papers in order to get the newspaper out. Warren Buffet, a major stockholder in the Washington Post Company, described Graham's "spectacular performance—which far outstripped those of her testosterone-laden peers—and always left Kay [her nickname] amazed, almost disbelieving."

Graham was also a highly regarded writer. *Personal History* (1997), her candid best-selling autobiography, won a Pulitzer Prize in biography in 1998, when she was 80 years old. The book was praised for its honest portrayal of her husband's mental illness and is filled with stories about well-known political figures such as Robert McNamara and George Schultz. In his review of Graham's memoir in *Time* magazine, Richard Zoglin writes, "Not only does Graham chronicle her personal transformation with more honest self-analysis than probably any other media mogul ever; she also provides an invaluable inside glimpse of some of the most critical turning points in American journalism." She recognized that her upbringing affected her leadership style, citing "that good old-fashioned encumbrance of mine, the desire to please" as the reason she could get along with many cantankerous but important politicians.

Graham was a prominent philanthropist, particularly supporting charitable causes in Washington, D.C., the city where she resided for most of her life, with an emphasis on improving public education. She retired as chief executive of the Washington Post Company in 1991 and handed over the business to her son Donald. At the time, the company was worth $1.4 million. After her retirement, she continued to meet with local, national, and international prominent figures (she went to the movies with Henry Kissinger on occasion) and to introduce them to one another. She also met with *Post* and *Newsweek* editors and writers.

Katharine Graham, one of the most powerful women in American media, who had transformed herself into a publishing legend, died on July 17, 2001, at 84, from injuries suffered in a fall while attending a meeting of business executives in Sun Valley, Idaho. Posthumously, *Katharine Graham's Washington,* a collection of writings about Washington, D.C., edited by Graham, was published in 2003. The anthology included articles, essays, history, and personal remembrances about the city that had so greatly influenced her personal and professional life, written by politicians and media figures ranging from President Harry Truman to humorist Art Buchwald. Her comments as editor reflected the same acuity, candor, and insider's knowledge that were apparent in her engaging autobiography. In her review of *Personal History,* the popular contemporary writer Nora Ephron wrote that "Graham's story of her journey from daughter to wife to widow to woman parallels to a surprising degree the history of women in this century."

Further Reading

Berger, Marilyn. "Katharine Graham, Former Publisher of Washington Post, Dies at 84." The *New York Times,* July 17, 2001. Available online. URL: http://www.nytimes.com. Downloaded on January 22, 2007.

Gerber, Robin. *Katharine Graham: The Leadership Journey of an American Icon.* New York: Penguin/Portfolio, 2005.

Graham, Katharine, ed. *Katharine Graham's Washington.* New York: Vintage, 2003.

———. *Personal History.* New York: Alfred A. Knopf, 1997.

Zoglin, Richard. "Katharine Graham: The Iron Lady Speaks." *Time Magazine,* February 17, 1997. Available online. URL: http://www.time.com/time/sampler/article/0,8599,167910,00.html. Downloaded on January 22, 2007.

❧ Grobsmith, Kaila
See SIMON, KATE

H

H. D.
See DOOLITTLE, HILDA

H. H.
See JACKSON, HELEN MARIA FISKE HUNT

Hale, Sarah Josepha Buell
(1788–1879)   *editor, poet, biographer*

As longtime editor of *Godey's Lady's Book,* which was considered America's first serious magazine for women, Sarah Hale was one of the most prominent women in the literary world of the mid-19th century.

Sarah Josepha Buell was born on October 24, 1788, in rural Newport, New Hampshire, on a farm belonging to her great-grandfather. She was educated largely at home by her mother who encouraged her "predilection for literary pursuits," and by her college-educated brother, who taught her Latin and philosophy.

During her nine-year marriage to David Hale, Sarah Hale described herself as being blissfully happy. But tragedy struck in 1822 when he died suddenly, leaving Hale to raise five young children by herself. Few occupations were open to women at that time, and Hale turned to writing as a means of supporting her family.

In 1823 she published a slender volume of verse, *The Genius of Oblivion,* followed four years later by her first novel, *Northwood: or Life North and South: Showing the True Character of Both,* which sold well and attracted attention. Hale was invited to become editor of the *Ladies' Magazine,* a fledgling magazine for women based in Boston. Driven by financial need, she agreed and not only edited the new magazine but also wrote half the articles that appeared in each issue.

Hale used the *Ladies' Magazine* to promote her socially conservative views; for example, she did not support suffrage for women. But, she fervently advocated better education for women, all-women's schools that would be taught primarily by women, and property rights for married women. She also encouraged unknown women writers to submit their work to her magazine.

Meanwhile, Hale continued to write fiction and poetry. *Poems for Our Children* (1830) included "Mary Had a Little Lamb," a celebrated nursery rhyme that has become part of America's folklore despite suspicions as to the true authorship of the first stanza. Hale also worked for patriotic and benevolent causes, such as helping to organize the

Sarah Buell Hale penned the nursery rhyme "Mary Had a Little Lamb."
(AP/Wide World Photos)

Seamen's Aid Society and the completion of Bunker Hill Monument.

In 1837 Louis Godey of Philadelphia bought the *Ladies' Magazine,* incorporated it into the *Lady's Book,* and named Hale as its literary editor. Under her leadership, *Godey's Lady's Book,* as it was now called, featured popular domestic departments as well as poetry and fiction by writers such as Edgar Allan Poe. *Godey's* eventually became the single most important periodical for women in the 19th century.

Hale's most serious work was a compendium of 36 volumes of biographical sketches titled *Women's Record; or, Sketches of All Distinguished Women, from the 'The Beginning' till A.D. 1850* (1853), which contained close to 2,500 entries.

Sarah Josepha Buell Hale, the first of the great "lady editors," died on April 30, 1879, in her 90s, having provided millions of women with a magazine that was, as she described it, "a beacon-light of refined taste, pure morals, and practical wisdom."

Further Reading

Ford, Henry. *The Story of Mary and Her Little Lamb.* Dearborn, Mich.: Privately published by Mr. and Mrs. Henry Ford, 1938.

Fryatt, N. R. *Sarah Josepha Hale: The Life and Times of a Nineteenth-Century Career Women.* New York: Hawthorn Books, 1978.

Greenberg, Hope. "Godey's Lady's Book: Sarah Josepha Hale, Biography and Sample Selections." Godey's Lady's Book Web site. Available online. URL: http://www.uvm.edu/~hag/godey/hale.html. Downloaded on January 22, 2007.

Hale, Sara Josepha. *Mary Had a Little Lamb.* Illustrated by Tomie De Paola. New York: Holiday House, 1984.

———. *Northwood: or, Life North and South: Showing the True Character of Both.* New York: H. Long and Brother, 1852.

Niles, Lisa. "Sarah Josepha Hale, Domestic Goddess." Available online. URL: http://www.womenwriters.net/domesticgoddess/hale1.html. Downloaded on January 22, 2007.

Hamilton, Edith
(1867–1963)   *classical writer, translator*

Edith Hamilton, whose seven books have introduced millions of readers to the ancient world, is recognized as the greatest woman classicist. She was a master at interpreting for the modern mind Greek and Roman civilization and their ideals, as well as the Old and New Testaments.

Born in Dresden, Germany, on August 12, 1867, Edith Hamilton was raised in Fort Wayne, Indiana, in a large, close-knit family that enjoyed sharing good books and stories. Educated at home, Edith's mother taught her French while her father tutored her in Latin, when she was seven, and then Greek a year later. An avid reader with an impressive verbal memory, at an early age she could recite poetry by Percy Bysshe Shelley, John Keats, and

George Gordon, Lord Byron by heart. She was also captivated by historical novels and classical myths and fables.

In their late teens, Edith and her younger sister Alice, who would become a prominent reformer of health care for workers, attended Miss Porter's School in Connecticut. In 1895 Hamilton received her bachelor's and master's degrees from Bryn Mawr College, in Pennsylvania, having majored in Greek and Latin. Awarded a European fellowship by the college to study the classics, Hamilton was the first woman to enroll at the University of Munich, in Germany.

Upon returning to America in 1896, Hamilton became headmistress of Bryn Mawr School in Baltimore, Maryland, the country's only girls' college preparatory school. She accepted the position, which she held for 22 years, largely because her father's business had failed and she needed to support herself. Besides being a shrewd chief administrator—enrollments increased dramatically under her leadership—she taught an advanced Latin course. Hamilton recalled that she read Latin for "her own pleasure," in the same way she enjoyed reading French and German.

After retiring and moving to New York City with her lifelong companion and friend, Doris F. Reid, at the age of 63 Hamilton became a full-time writer. For inspiration she visited Greece and Egypt; the pyramids, she wrote, were "immutable, immovable, the spirit of the desert incased in granite." In 1930, when Hamilton was 63 years old, she published her first book, *The Greek Way*, a probing but highly readable study of the similarities and differences between the ancient Greek and the modern conception of life. A best seller, *The Greek Way* brought Hamilton immediate acclaim and established her reputation as a scholar. As in all of her work, it was critically praised for its vivid, graceful prose. Two years later she wrote *The Roman Way*, which described life as it existed according to ancient Roman poets such as Platus and Virgil and then applied their ideas to the modern world.

Moving to another area of interest, Hamilton wrote *The Prophets of Israel* (1936), which inter-

preted the beliefs of the "spokesmen for God" in the Old Testament. She then retold the stories of classical mythology and ancient fables in *Mythology* (1941), which sold over a half-million copies. "When one takes up a book like this," Hamilton explained, "one does not ask how entertainingly the author has retold the stories, but how close he has brought the reader to the original."

In 1942 Hamilton moved with Reid to Washington, D.C., where she continued to write with undaunted energy. At the age of 82 she provided a fresh perspective on the New Testament in *Witness to the Truth: Christ and His Interpreters* (1948), and in 1957 she produced the sequel to her popular *The Greek Way*, titled *The Echo of Greece*. Although it was to be her final book, she continued to travel and to lecture, write articles and reviews, and translate Greek plays; she also edited *The Collected Dialogues of Plato* (1961). Regarding that preeminent Greek philosopher, Hamilton stated that his thought "has never been transcended."

In 1957 Edith Hamilton was made an honorary citizen of Athens and watched her translation of

Classicist Edith Hamilton lectures in Athens, Greece, in 1957.
(AP/Wide World Photos)

125

Prometheus performed at the ancient theater of Herodes Atticus at the foot of the Acropolis. Accepting the accompanying award she said,

> This is the proudest moment in my life. . . . For Athens, truly the mother of beauty and of thought, is also the mother of freedom. . . . That is the spirit that Greece gave to the world.

Hamilton, who was elected to the American Academy of Arts and Letters and received the Constance Lindsay Skinner Award from the Women's National Book Association, died on May 31, 1963, at the age of 96. Another writer, John Mason Brown, aptly described her as a citizen of both the ancient and the modern worlds, "equally at home with the best of both."

Further Reading

Brown, John Mason. *Seeing More Things.* New York: Whittlesey House, 1948.
"Edith Hamilton." Distinguished Women of Past and Present. Available online. URL: http://www.distinguished women.com/biographies/hamilton=e.html. Downloaded on January 22, 2007.
Hamilton, Edith. *The Greek Way.* New York: W. W. Norton, 1958.
Reid, Doris Fielding. *Edith Hamilton: An Intimate Portrait.* New York: W. W. Norton, 1967.
Reid, Doris Fielding, ed. *A Treasury of Edith Hamilton* (selections). New York: W. W. Norton, 1969.

❧ Hansberry, Lorraine Vivian
(1930–1965) *playwright, essayist*

Lorraine Hansberry was an award-winning playwright and a lifelong champion of civil rights. Her best-known work, the acclaimed *A Raisin in the Sun,* was the first play by an African American woman to be produced on Broadway and has become a landmark—it was the first time the authentic voice of the black working class was captured onstage—and a classic in American theater.

Lorraine Vivian Hansberry was born on May 19, 1930, in Chicago, Illinois. The youngest of four children, she grew up in a middle-class black neighborhood on the South Side of Chicago, where her father was a prosperous and influential landlord and her mother was a homemaker and school teacher. Both were prominent members of the community and social activists.

Lorraine's parents encouraged her to develop her mind and artistic abilities. They included her when they entertained an impressive array of friends, such as W. E. B. DuBois, Duke Ellington, and Paul Robeson. She was also influenced by her uncle, a professor of African history at Howard University who introduced her to students from the African continent.

The Hansberrys' middle-class status did not protect them from racial discrimination. When she was eight, Lorraine's parents made the decision to fight housing segregation by moving the family to one of Chicago's all-white neighborhoods. She

Lorraine Hansberry wrote the celebrated hit play *A Raisin in the Sun.*
(AP/Wide World Photos)

recalled being "spat at, cursed and pummeled in the daily trek to and from school." After a mob of whites gathered in front of the house and tossed a brick through the front window, narrowly missing Lorraine, an Illinois court ruled that the Hansberrys had to leave. A long court struggle ensued, resulting with the Supreme Court upholding the family's right to live where they chose. Lorraine's father, tired of fighting, decided to move his family to Mexico. However, he died before he could do so. The events of Hansberry's tumultuous teenage years planted the seeds that, 20 years later, would grow into her celebrated play, *A Raisin in the Sun.*

While other members in her family attended black colleges, Hansberry enrolled at the University of Wisconsin. She found the traditional course offerings uninspired, but she integrated her all-white dormitory and became president of the left-wing Young Progressive League. Hansberry was profoundly affected by a university production of Sean O'Casey's *Juno and the Paycock,* a drama about the dashed hopes of Irish peasants and the universality of suffering. Of the playwright's uncompromising social conscience, she wrote admiringly:

> O'Casey never fools you about the Irish . . . and [presents] the genuine heroism which must naturally emerge when you tell the truth about people. This, to me, is the height of artistic perception and is the most rewarding kind of thing that can happen in drama.

In 1950 Hansberry moved to Harlem in New York City and worked as a reporter and editor for the progressive newspaper *Freedom,* published by Paul Robeson. At the newspaper she learned that "all racism is rotten, black or white, that everything is political, and that people tend to be indescribably beautiful and uproariously funny." She also wrote articles, essays, and poetry for the publication.

While at a civil rights demonstration at New York University, she met an aspiring songwriter, Robert Nemiroff, the son of a Jewish immigrant family, whom she married in 1953. The couple lived in Greenwich Village and became part of the "beat" movement—a group of intellectuals and artists who gathered in smoky coffeehouses to exchange and share unorthodox literary and political ideas. The bohemian movement centered in San Francisco and New York City in the latter half of the 1950s. Meanwhile, the revenues from a hit pop ballad that Nemiroff cowrote enabled Hansberry to give up odd jobs and concentrate on her writing full time.

In 1957 Hansberry completed *A Raisin in the Sun.* On March 11, 1959, after previewing throughout the country, it premiered at Broadway's Ethel Barrymore Theater, with a stellar cast that included Sidney Poitier and Ossie Davis. Critically acclaimed for the unflinching honesty of her work, Hansberry became an overnight celebrity.

A Raisin in the Sun is the poignant, powerful story of an African American family's struggle to claim its economic share of the "American Dream" by moving to a better (white) neighborhood. Black and white audiences alike identified with the Younger family and their generational and personal conflicts as each member attempted to escape the dreary life of Chicago's ghetto. Hansberry chose to portray her black characters as being both good and bad. Based on her own childhood experiences, she did not imply that it would be any easier for the working-class Youngers to live in their new white neighborhood than in their old black one. Instead, she asserts that whatever tribulations the Youngers encounter, they would grow, change, and survive together as a family.

The plays's title and theme were inspired by Langston Hughes's poem "Harlem," in which he poses provocative questions about deferred dreams either drying up like raisins in the sun or exploding. Both Hughes and Hansberry recognized that the suppression and hopeless social conditions of African Americans could only lead to bitter disappointment or violence.

A Raisin in the Sun ran on Broadway for 19 months, with 530 performances; it also toured extensively, and has been published and produced in more than 30 countries. It won the 1959 Drama Critics' Circle Award, making Hansberry the youngest playwright, the first African American, and one of only five women to receive the prestigious award. In 1961 Hansberry adapted the play into an award-winning film.

Then 29 years old, Hansberry used her fame to speak out publicly on social injustice. She believed a dialogue between the races was essential before any concrete societal changes could take place in America and that people of all colors had to stand up for their convictions. "I think that the human race does command its own destiny," she said. In 1961 she wrote a tongue-in-cheek prescient feminist essay entitled "In Defense of the Equality of Men," and a year later moved with Nemiroff to Croton-on-Hudson, a bucolic suburb north of Manhattan, where she completed her only other full-length play, *The Sign in Sidney Brustein's Window* (1964). It was promoted as a "drama of ideas," and was based on the lives of white intellectuals she had met in Greenwich Village during the 1950s and '60s. It received mixed reviews and closed on Broadway after a short run.

Despite the fact that she was in considerable pain because she suffered from cancer, Hansberry wrote the text for an influential photo documentary, *The Movement: A Documentary of a Struggle for Equality* (1964). She also delivered a speech to the winners of the 1964 United Negro College Fund's writing contest, where she coined the famous phrase "young, gifted and black," and left her sickbed to participate in a debate at Town Hall, a New York City auditorium, at which she joined other black artists in defending the growing militancy of the civil rights movement.

Although Hansberry and Nemiroff had been quietly divorced in 1964, in part because she questioned her sexual identity, they remained close friends and Hansberry designated him as her literary executor. Lorraine Hansberry died at the young age of 34 on January 12, 1965, in New York City the same night that *The Sign in Sidney Brustein's Window* closed. Nemiroff considered it his mission, until he died in 1991, to publish, produce, and promote her finished and unfinished writings. He adapted excerpts from her diaries, journals,

essays, and letters into a long-running play starring Cicely Tyson, *To Be Young, Gifted and Black*. It was also published as a book with an introduction by writer James Baldwin, who greatly admired Hansberry's work: "Never before, in the entire history of the American theater, had so much of the truth of black people's lives been seen on stage."

Nemiroff then edited an anthology that included what Hansberry believed to be her most important play, *Les Blancs*. Set in Africa and about a struggling nation and its liberation movement, it was produced posthumously on Broadway in 1970. Like her mentor, W. E. B. DuBois, Hansberry was a Pan-Africanist who believed black Americans should identify with emerging African nations. She also strongly defended homosexual rights.

Raisin, a musical version of *A Raisin in the Sun*, garnered a Tony Award in 1974. The Yale Repertory Theatre put on a 25th anniversary version of the drama in November 1983, the same year Hansberry's *Collected Last Plays* was published. This volume included *The Drinking Gourd*, a television play that was considered too controversial to produce. In 1989 *A Raisin in the Sun*, with the original material restored, was shown on national television and once again was hailed as a brilliant, timeless classic. The play received four Tony Award nominations for the 2004 Broadway production and won a Tony for best performance by a leading actress.

Despite the brevity of her theatrical career, Lorraine Hansberry made a significant contribution to American theater. Like many of her characters, she affirmed life in the face of hatred and despair. Appropriately, the inscription on her gravestone, the last line from *The Sign in Sidney Brustein's Window*, reads: "Tomorrow, we shall make something strong of this sorrow."

Further Reading

Abell, Joy L. "African/American: Lorraine Hansberry's *Les Blancs* and the American Civil Rights Movement." *African American Review* 35 (Fall 2001): 459–470.

Hansberry, Lorraine. *A Raisin in the Sun: A Drama in Three Acts*. New York: Random House, 1959.

McKissack, Patricia C., and Frederick L. McKissack. *Young, Black and Determined: A Biography of Lorraine Hansberry.* New York: Holiday House, 1998.

Nemiroff, Robert, ed. *To Be Young, Gifted, and Black: Lorraine Hansberry in Her Own Words.* With an introduction by James Baldwin. Englewood Cliffs, N. J.: Prentice Hall, 1969.

Hardwick, Elizabeth
(1916–) *essayist, critic, novelist*

Elizabeth Hardwick is a major American social and literary critic and an accomplished essayist who has also written award-winning fiction. She also edited the letters of William James and has rediscovered fiction by American women. In 1963 she helped found the *New York Review of Books.*

Born on July 27, 1916, in Lexington, Kentucky, where she was one of nine children, Hardwick earned undergraduate and graduate degrees at the University of Kentucky before leaving the South for New York City, where she has since spent most of her adult life. After two years of postgraduate studies in English at Columbia University, she became a full-time writer.

Hardwick's first novel, *The Ghostly Lover* (1945), was a feminist tale about a lonely, alienated young woman who comes to realize that she has to rely on herself, not others, to fill her longing for intimacy. Although it received mixed reviews, Philip Rahv, and editor at *Partisan Review,* was impressed enough to invite Hardwick to join established literary figures such as KATHERINE ANNE PORTER and ELIZABETH BISHOP in contributing to the avant-garde review. It was the beginning of Hardwick's long and successful career as a witty, insightful, and sometimes fearsome essayist and critic.

Hardwick continued working on her fiction, with her short stories appearing in periodicals such as *Harper's* and the *New Yorker.* Between 1945 and 1949, five of her stories were published in the annual volumes of the *O. Henry Memorial Award Prize Stories* and *The Best American Short Stories,* and in 1948 she was awarded a Guggenheim fellowship in fiction.

In 1949 Hardwick married the poet Robert Lowell, with whom she had a daughter, Harriet. Even though Lowell was mentally unstable and sometimes abusive, they remained together for more than 20 years before divorcing in 1972.

Hardwick's second novel, *The Simple Truth* (1955), about a murder trial and the opposite reactions of two onlookers, was released in 1955 to mixed reviews. She turned her hand to editing starting with *The Selected Letters of William James* (1960), and then with two well-received collections of essays: *A View of My Own: Essays on Literature and Society* (1962) and *Seduction and Betrayal: Women and Literature* (1974), a "rich, moving historical pageant in which literature's women pass before us on stage sets of art, romance, sex, and death," according to *Newsweek.* Writing about fellow author and friend MARY MCCARTHY in *A View of My Own,* Hardwick noted that "a career of candor and dissent is not an easy one for a woman; the license is jarring and the dare often forbidding." The same could be said for Hardwick, who took risks by writing frank, shrewd, often tough-minded essays and critical reviews.

After editing 18 volumes of *Rediscovered Fiction by American Women: A Personal Selection* (1977), she returned to her own fiction, after a hiatus of more than 20 years, by publishing her third novel, *Sleepless Nights* (1979). Her most critically acclaimed work, it combined autobiography and fiction through the musings of a protagonist named Elizabeth who selectively reflects on her past. It was nominated for the National Book Critics Circle Award and praised for its understated emotional power, exemplified in this passage:

> How pretty she is with her kinky head, her large, camera teeth and the diamond brooch of her Ph.D. Men have mistreated her, a mild mistreatment, as one would speak of a mild case of, say, bronchitis.

In 1963 Hardwick became one of the founding editors of the *New York Review of Books,* which became a leading intellectual journal. She produced another collection of essays, *Bartleby in*

Manhattan (1984), tackling subjects as diverse as a Rolling Stones concert and the preacher Billy Graham, and edited *The Best American Essays of 1986.*

Hardwick's long career has been recognized with a lifetime achievement citation from the National Book Critics Circle, the George Jean Nathan Award for outstanding dramatic criticism, and the Gold Medal for Belles-Lettres and Criticism from the American Academy of Arts and Letters in 1993. The *New York Times* noted that her fourth collection of essays, *Sight-Readings: American Fictions* (1998), attests to her "perspicuity as a critic, and her eloquence and wit as a writer." In the *New Republic,* the novelist ANNE TYLER said Hardwick "has a gift for coming up with descriptions so thoughtfully selected, so exactly right, that they strike the reader as inevitable."

In 2000 Hardwick wrote a brief biography of Herman Melville, the author of the great American seagoing novel *Moby-Dick.* According to *Publishers Weekly,* "Hardwick's own literary talent for metaphor and no-nonsense interpretation makes this an especially engaging critical account. Perhaps most important, Hardwick is able to convey both the complexity of the man as well as the inherent impossibility of the biographer's task to fully elucidate the life of a multifarious individual. . . . This work is a delight to read."

Elizabeth Hardwick lives in New York City, where she continues as an advisory editor and a frequent contributor to the *New York Review of Books.* She became an adjunct professor of English literature at Barnard College in 1964.

Further Reading

Gray, Janet. "Elizabeth Hardwick." In *American Writers,* edited by Lea Baechler and A. Walton Litz. New York: Charles Scribner's Sons, 1991.

Hardwick, Elizabeth. *Herman Melville.* New York: Viking Books, 2000.

———. *Seduction and Betrayal: Women and Literature.* New York: Random House, 1974.

———. *Sleepless Nights.* New York: Random House, 1979.

Harper, Frances Ellen Watkins
(1825–1911)   *poet, novelist*

Frances Ellen Watkins Harper, who was one of the preeminent African-American poets of the 19th century, combined a prolific, successful literary career as a best-selling poet, the first black novelist to depict the Reconstruction, and the first black woman to publish short stories. In all, her works represent a fervent commitment to equality between the races and the sexes.

The daughter of free black parents, Frances Ellen Watkins was born in Baltimore, Maryland, on September 24, 1825, and was orphaned by the time she was three. She lived with her uncle, a minister and antislavery activist whose school she attended. But, in order to support herself, at age 13 Frances left school to take care of a bookseller's children; there she began to write poetry and read novels. By the time she was 20 she had published her first collection of poetry, *Forest Leaves* (1845).

In 1854 Harper, who became a renowned orator, delivered her first speech, in New Bedford, Massachusetts, on a subject that became a lifelong passion: "The Education and the Elevation of the Colored Race." Described as a dignified, dramatic, and forceful speaker, she lectured widely for antislavery societies, sharing the platform with well-known abolitionists such as SOJOURNER TRUTH, and peppering her speeches with her social-reform verse.

Harper's literary reputation was launched with the publication of *Poems on Miscellaneous Subjects* (1854), a collection that went through more than 20 printings and sold thousands of copies. It contained her most popular abolitionist poem, "Bury Me in a Free Land," and others that poignantly addressed the horrors of slavery.

> She is a mother, pale with fear,
> Her boy clings to her side,
> And in her kirtle [outer skirt] vainly tries
> His trembling form to hide.
>
> —"The Slave Mother," 1854

Harper's narrative poems used rhymed tetrameter and the ballad form stanza "as a metrical extension of her life dedicated to the welfare of others," according to the author Joan R. Sherman. She dramatized the suffering endured by blacks, especially by black women whose needs, she asserted, were more pressing than those of any other class. "The Two Offers," which appeared in *The Anglo-African Magazine* in 1859 and is considered the first published short story by an African American, focused on two married women, one of whom was more satisfied than the other because she had a career and felt useful.

On November 22, 1860, she married Fenton Harper, with whom she had a daughter, Mary. Harper's husband died just four years later, leaving her widowed and penniless. She was forced to take her young child on a grueling lecture circuit through 13 states, where she addressed both black and white audiences and emphasized interracial harmony and the educational needs of freed slaves. In her spare time, she would write. Her most original and powerful poem, *Moses: A Story of the Nile* (1869) is a 40-page blank-verse biblical allegory that calls for self-sacrifice and leadership, qualities Harper felt were crucial to building moral character.

While living in Philadelphia, Pennsylvania, with her daughter during the 1870s, she wrote several more volumes of poetry. Her verse used both standard English and black dialect, and was simple, direct, and lyrical. It was oral poetry, meant to be read aloud.

In 1892 Harper wrote *Iola Leroy; or, Shadows Uplifted*—the first novel by a black author to describe the Reconstruction era. In spite of its stylistic weaknesses, it provided historical and early feminist insights. African-American scholar Hazel V. Carby described the novel as being "rooted in the authority of Harper's experience as abolitionist, lecturer, poet, teacher, feminist, and black woman."

From 1883 to 1890 Harper worked actively for organizations that promoted the rights of freed slaves and women and advocated Christian humanism and educational racial equality. She also helped found and became vice president of the National Association of Colored Women. Although Harper lectured less, she continued to write; her last collection of poetry appeared in 1895, when she was almost 70. She died when she was 85, in Philadelphia, on February 22, 1911. Three of her novels were rediscovered and published posthumously.

In an online commentary about Harper that appeared in 2004 on "BlackAmericaWeb.com," Wayne Dawkins wrote that "it is remarkably sad that women who were so highly regarded more than a century ago are almost invisible in the 21st century. Harper's body of literary work and record of social activism are an ode to freedom . . . and her legacy is worthy of celebration."

An influential and inspired writer, orator, and social activist, Frances Ellen Watkins Harper, according to legendary writer and educator W. E. B. DuBois, deserved to be remembered for "forwarding literature among colored people. . . . She took her writing soberly and earnestly; she gave her life to it."

Further Reading

Boyd, Melba Joyce. *Discarded Legacy: Politics and Poetic in the Life of Frances E. W. Harper*. Detroit, Mich.: Wayne State University Press, 1994.

Dawkins, Wayne. "Commentary: Harper's Independence Left Legacy Worth Celebrating." BlackAmericaWeb.com. July 2, 2004. Available online. URL: http://www.blackamericaweb.com/site.aspx/bawnews/harper71. Downloaded on January 22, 2007.

Harper, Frances E. W. *Complete Poems of Frances E. W. Harper*. Edited by Maryemma Graham. New York: Oxford University Press, 1988.

———. *Iola Leroy; or, Shadows Uplifted*. New York: AMS Press, 1971.

Sherman, Joan R. *Invisible Poets: Afro-Americans of the Nineteenth Century*. Urbana: University of Illinois Press, 1974.

Hellman, Lillian Florence
(1905–1984) *playwright, memoirist*

Lillian Hellman, one of America's most influential contemporary playwrights, wrote award-winning dramas about controversial topics such as homosexuality and corruption. She was also a renowned screenwriter and memoirist and a leading leftist political activist.

The only child of middle-class Jewish parents, Lillian Florence Hellman was born on June 10, 1905, in New Orleans, Louisiana. When she was six her father relocated the family to New York City. Lillian spent half of each year in urbane, money-conscious New York attending public school, and the other half in genteel, segregated New Orleans, in a boardinghouse run by relatives. In her most memorable plays she would capture, and often merge, the two disparate worlds of her childhood.

Hellman studied at New York and Columbia universities and then took a job in 1924 as a manuscript reader for a New York publishing firm. She reveled in the glamorous literary world, with its after-hours soirees. "By the time we were nineteen or twenty we had either slept with a man or pretended that we had," she recalled in *An Unfinished Woman* (1969). In 1925 she married Arthur Kober, a press agent and writer, and for the next three years she reviewed books for the *New York Herald Tribune*. After a trip to Europe with Kober, she worked briefly in Hollywood, California, reading scripts. In 1930 she met a left-wing, alcoholic mystery writer who would become the central figure in her life: Dashiell Hammett.

Playwright Lillian Hellman works on a script in London in 1945.
(AP/Wide World Photos)

After divorcing Kober in 1932, she returned to New York and worked as playreader and script reviewer for producer Harold Shulman, all the time honing her skills for her own plays. She lived with Hammett—her political mentor and lifelong friend—for "thirty-one on and off years," until his death in 1961.

Hellman's first play, *The Children's Hour*, was produced on Broadway in 1934. An instant and long-running hit, it was all the more notable because she was a woman playwright in a male-dominated theatrical world. Banned in several cities, including Boston and Chicago, the ground-breaking play portrayed two small-town teachers falsely accused by a student of having a lesbian affair. Hellman helped shape American drama by allowing her characters to deal frankly with sexual, familial, and socioeconomic issues. Both playwrights write about strong, independent women protagonists, even though Hellman refused to be labeled a "woman" playwright. "I believe in women's liberation," she said in an interview in 1974, "[but] I think it all comes down to whether or not you can support yourself as well as a man."

A year after *Days to Come* opened unsuccessfully in New York in 1936, Hellman visited the Soviet Union. A staunch antifascist, she became a supporter of Russian Communism and chose to ignore evidence that Joseph Stalin was a murderous tyrant. She then spent a month in Spain during its bloody civil war and coproduced with Ernest Hemingway a documentary entitled *The Spanish Earth*, which strongly supported the Loyalist cause.

After returning to New York, Hellman's most popular and best-known play, *The Little Foxes* (1939), opened on Broadway on the eve of World War II. A well-crafted and carefully constructed drama about good and evil, it recounted the story of the Hubbards, a predatory, turn-of-the-century nouveau riche Southern family trying to maintain its social position during the rise of the industrial South. The Hubbards ruthlessly defrauded each other in their quest for power and wealth. They were, as Hellman described them,

the "eaters of the earth," the "little foxes who spoil the vines." One of the play's characters notes that "there were people who ate the earth and other people who stood around and watched them do it." She then avers: "I'm not going to stand around and watch you do it. . . ." *The Little Foxes,* with its rich texture and profound condemnation of avarice, was considered by many critics to be Hellman's finest work. She adapted it into an Academy Award–nominated movie in 1941 starring Bette Davis.

Another of Hellman's better-known works, *Watch on the Rhine* (1941), which won the New York Drama Critics Circle Award, examined the effects of the war and fascism on an American family. It was Hellman's patriotic attempt to awaken the American conscience to the European tragedy. She and Hammett spent the war years on Martha's Vineyard, a small resort island off the coast of Massachusetts, where she wrote several minor plays, such as *The North Star* (1943) and *The Searching Wind* (1944).

After the war Hellman visited the Soviet Union on a goodwill tour and almost died in Siberia after ingesting the wrong medication. She returned to New York for the opening, to mixed reviews, of *Another Part of the Forest* (1946), which she wrote and directed. In this prequel she introduced the Hubbard clan 20 years before the events of *The Little Foxes,* again focusing on their greediness and selfishness.

Hellman then wrote three play adaptations: *Montserrat* (1949), which she also directed; *The Lark* (1955), her only successful Broadway adaptation; and *Candide* (1956), an operetta that she coauthored with the composer Leonard Bernstein and the poet Richard Wilbur. In 1955 she edited the letters of Anton Chekhov, whose dramaturgy she greatly admired. Although she was Jewish, Hellman exhibited almost no interest in her heritage and in fact was hostile to it. She played a major role in an effort to falsify *The Diary of Anne Frank* by eliminating any trace of Jewishness or the Holocaust when the book was turned into a play in the mid-1950s.

133

The late 1940s and early 1950s proved to be traumatic years for Hellman. A prominent, outspoken leftist, she was blacklisted during the McCarthy era and was unable to find work; she was forced to sell her house and suffered severe financial hardships. When summoned to testify before the House Un-American Activities Committee (HUAC) in 1952, she courageously refused to provide names of other Communist sympathizers, explaining that "to hurt innocent people whom I knew many years ago in order to save myself is, to me, inhuman and indecent and dishonorable. I cannot and will not cut my conscience to fit this year's fashion."

Hellman was also at the center of another controversy. Her personal integrity was publicly challenged on television by her literary rival, novelist MARY MCCARTHY, who called her a liar. Other writers and critics also questioned her honesty. "You have to live by your own standards," she replied, "even if you're going to be lonely and unpopular."

At age 55 Hellman wrote the most notable of her later plays, *Toys in the Attic* (1960), which won her a second New York Drama Critics Circle Award for best play. The story, set in her native New Orleans, was more psychological and less political than her previous works. It skillfully explored the effects of sudden wealth on a poor family and the relationship of a weak brother to his older, more forceful sisters.

Her last play, *My Mother, My Father and Me,* was produced in 1963 and only briefly appeared on Broadway. A year later, the National Institute of Arts and Letters honored Hellman with the Gold Medal for Drama. She later received other awards and accolades, including invitations to teach at Yale and Harvard universities.

In her mid-60s Hellman switched genres and became a memoirist, penning four accomplished autobiographies. Her first, in 1969, was *An Unfinished Woman,* which won the National Book Award. The book recounts her relationship with Dashiell Hammett, whom she called "my closest, my beloved friend." The critically acclaimed *Penti-*

mento: A Book of Portraits followed in 1973. "The pain has aged now and I wanted to see what was there for me once, what is there for me now," explained Hellman, who interwove portraits of friends with the story of Julia, a young American woman who fought fascism by joining the German underground. In 1977 *Pentimento* was adapted as an award-winning film, *Julia,* starring Jane Fonda and Jason Robards.

Two other autobiographical memoirs ensued: *Scoundrel Time* (1976), which described her frightening experiences during the investigations of the House Un-American Activities Committee; and *Maybe: A Story* (1980), which blended fact and fiction and which a *Newsweek* critic described as a "nonstory, nervy mediation on the fallibility of memory and the shivery unpredictability of malice."

Even in her 70s and suffering from a variety of illnesses, Hellman remained feisty and vibrant, feuding with friends and critics and cowriting her final work, *Eating: Recollections and Recipes,* with her young friend and biographer, Peter Feibleman.

Some of Hellman's recent biographers, such as Carl Rollyson, who wrote *Lillian Hellman: Her Legend and Her Legacy* (1988), have been more critical of the playwright. Rollyson deplored Hellman's longstanding adherence to Stalinism, which he calls her "Stalinist skewing of history." In an article in the *New York Sun* (2005), Rollyson wrote, "Hellman forces such an obsession [proving Hellman a liar] on her biographers, who are obliged to sort out her misstatements of fact and distortions of history. Her account of Whittiker Chambers in *Scoundrel Time,* for example, is a travesty of the true story." But Deborah Martinson, the author of *Lillian Hellman: A Life with Foxes and Scoundrels* (2005), is more interested in Hellman the "exceptionally full, complicated, and dramatic woman" than in her controversial political stances.

Lillian Hellman died on June 30, 1984, alone, at her beloved home in Martha's Vineyard. In a tribute to the renowned playwright, David Ansen wrote in *Newsweek,* "She remained true to her passion throughout her rich and tumultuous life. . . . The fire within lit up the cultural landscape; its heat will be deeply missed."

Further Reading

Feibleman, Peter S. *Lilly: Reminiscences of Lillian Hellman.* New York: Morrow, 1988.

Hellman, Lillian. *Collected Plays.* Boston: Little, Brown, 1972.

———. *Three.* (Including *An Unfinished Woman, Pentimento,* and *Scoundrel Time.*) New York: Bantam Books, 1979.

Kazin, Alfred. "The Legend of Lillian Hellman." *Esquire,* August 1977, pp. 28–30, 34.

Martinson, Deborah. *Lillian Hellman: A Life with Foxes and Scoundrels.* New York: Counterpoint Press, 2005.

Rollyson, Carl. *Lillian Hellman: Her Legend and Her Legacy.* New York: St. Martin's, 1988.

Wright, William. "Why Lillian Hellman Remains Interesting." *New York Times.* November 3, 1996. Available online. URL: http://www.writing.upenn.edu/~afilreis/50s/hellman_today.html. Downloaded on February 28, 2007.

∼ Henley, Elizabeth Becker (Beth Henley)
(1952–) *playwright, screenwriter*

The regional dramatist Beth Henley preserves the Southern voice of her Mississippi upbringing while portraying strong, amicable, and somewhat freakish women characters who come from dysfunctional families. At the age of 29 she was awarded a Pulitzer Prize for the play *Crimes of the Heart,* a rueful Southern gothic comedy.

Born on May 8, 1952, in Jackson, Mississippi, Elizabeth Becker Henley received a bachelor of fine arts degree from Southern Methodist University in Dallas in 1974. Her first play, *Am I Blue* (1972), was produced on campus. She also attended the University of Illinois, Urbana, where she taught acting.

Although an actress, Henley pursued a career as a playwright. In 1976 she moved to Los Angeles, and two years later submitted a three-act play, *Crimes of the Heart,* to the Actor's Theatre of Louisville's Great American Play Contest. It won the

Beth Henley's *Crimes of the Heart* garnered a Pulitzer Prize for drama.
(AP/Wide World Photos)

contest and was subsequently performed in regional theaters and off-Broadway in New York City before it opened, much to Henley's surprise and delight, on Broadway in November 1981.

What would become her most widely produced play, *Crimes of the Heart* garnered the Pulitzer Prize in drama even before it opened on Broadway; it also received the New York Drama Critics Circle Award for the best new American play. (Henley later adapted it into an Academy Award–nominated movie in 1986.) The play revolves around three eccentric sisters who reunite in the Mississippi home of the youngest after she has shot her husband because, as she explains it, "I didn't like

135

his looks." Throughout the high energy play, the sisters laugh and cry together, especially when they find newspaper clippings describing their mother's double suicide with her cat. Apparently, says one of them, she had had "a bad day. A real bad day." In spite of their own constricted lifestyles and failed relationships, the sisters remain resilient. "You may be beaten and defeated, but your spirit cannot be conquered," noted Henley in the *Dictionary of Literary Biography Yearbook: 1986.*

In 1980 *The Miss Firecracker Contest,* a grotesquely gothic comic drama about the futile attempt of an outcast to assimilate into a small Southern town, was staged off-Broadway as well as in London. (Henley adapted it into a film, as *Miss Firecracker,* in 1989). Two years later *The Wake of Jamey Foster,* in which the central protagonist is actually empowered by observing the burial of her husband, was produced on Broadway.

Henley, who lives in Los Angeles, California, with her young son, wrote several screenplays, including *True Stories* (1986) with David Byrne and Stephen Tobolowsky, and four more dramas staged in New York: *The Lucky Spot* (1987); the quirky *The Debutante Ball* (1988); perhaps her most ambitious play, *Abundance* (1990), which spans 25 years in the lives of two pioneer women who end up looking like freaks; and *Impossible Marriage* (1998), a comedy about three Southern women and their perceptions of marriage, starring Holly Hunter, an actress who has appeared in seven of Henley's productions and a few of her films based on her plays. As in all of Henley's dramas, there is no resolution to the women's horrifying problems, but they are treated seriously and with compassion. Her latest play, staged in 2000 and starring actress Carol Kane, was a quirky, clever comedy called *Family Week.*

In 2000 Beth Henley won the Richard Wright Literary Excellence Award for her playwriting skills. She garnered a Natchez Literary and Cinema Celebration's (NLCC) Horton Foote Award for Special Achievement in Screenwriting in 2006, becoming the NLCC's only multiple award winner.

Further Reading

Berney, K. A., ed. *Contemporary Dramatists.* Detroit, Mich.: St. James Press, 1994, 290–291.

Henley, Beth. *Crimes of the Heart.* New York: Viking Press, 1982.

———. *Three Plays by Beth Henley: Control Freaks, L-Play, and Sisters of the Winter Madrigal.* New York: Dramatists Play Service, 2002.

Padgett, John B. "Beth Henley." The Mississippi Writers Page. Available online. URL: http://www.olemiss.edu/depts/english/ms-writers/dir/henley_beth. Downloaded on January 22, 2007.

Pogrebin, Robin. "Sharing a History as Well as a Play: Beth Henley and Holly Hunter," *New York Times,* October 11, 1998, pp. 5, 25.

Herbst, Josephine Frey ("Josie" Herbst)
(1892–1969) *novelist, journalist, memoirist*

The major fictional achievement of Josephine Herbst's diverse literary career was the Trexler-Wendel trilogy of novels. Comparative in scope and style to John Dos Passo's *U.S.A.,* they chronicled America's turbulent social history from the Civil War through the Depression era. Herbst was also known for her compelling memoirs, which chronicled her turbulent personal and political life.

Born on March 5, 1892, in Sioux City, Iowa, "a prairie wildflower, deserted by the major railroads for more flashy Omaha," Josephine "Josie" Frey Herbst grew up in a poor but close-knit family. Her self-educated mother fostered in her four daughters the belief that they could accomplish whatever they set out to do in life; young Josie decided she wanted to become a writer.

After working at odd jobs in order to study at the University of Iowa and the University of Washington in Seattle, Herbst saved enough money to enroll at the University of California at Berkeley, where she graduated in 1918, at the age of 26, with a bachelor of arts degree. In Berkeley she met a group of writers who introduced her to radical politics. "I always knew that somewhere in the world were people who could talk about the things I wanted to talk about," she wrote to her mother.

In 1919 Herbst moved to Greenwich Village in New York City to pursue a literary career. There she became enmeshed in literary gossip and politics and had numerous romantic liaisons with both men and women writers. Three years later she traveled to Europe, living cheaply in postwar Berlin and later in Paris. At a cafe frequented by American artists and writers, she met a young novelist named John Herrmann, whom she married in 1926.

After returning to America, Herbst published her first novel, *Nothing Is Sacred* (1928), which loosely recreated her Sioux City childhood at the time of her mother's death. It was followed a year later by *Money for Love,* a dark comedy about a woman's attempts to extort money from one boyfriend in order to begin a new life with another.

Novelist and memoirist Josephine Herbst also worked as a journalist.
(AP/Wide World Photos)

Herbst also wrote a dozen short stories and, with Herrmann, who as an alcoholic was becoming increasingly difficult, purchased a secluded stone farmhouse in rural Pennsylvania. The couple spent their winters in Key West, Florida, as a guest of Ernest Hemingway, Herbst's close friend.

During the 1930s Herbst focused on journalism. She reported sympathetically on the Iowa farm strikes of the depression; was in Cuba following the general strike of 1935; and wrote about antifascist resistance to Hitler in Germany. She was one of the only female journalists allowed to report from the front line of the Spanish Civil War in 1937. After the Japanese attack on Pearl Harbor brought the U.S. into World War II, she volunteered to write anti-Nazi reports for overseas broadcasts, but she was dismissed for having left-wing affiliations.

Today Herbst's reputation rests mostly on her semiautobiographical, Depression-era trilogy about the Trexler-Wendel family: *Pity Is Not Enough* (1933), *The Executioner Waits* (1934), and *Rope of Gold* (1939). Through the probing story of generations within a single family, the sweeping fictional saga dramatizes social disintegration and rising class tensions and is interspersed with actual historical events.

After divorcing her philandering husband in 1940, Herbst wrote two more novels, *Satan's Sergeants* (1941) and *Somewhere the Tempest Fell* (1947), neither of which was critically successful. Herbst then turned to other literary genres. She wrote a biography of two 18th-century American naturalists, John and William Bartram, and a well-crafted novella, "Hunter of Doves," about a middle-aged woman who reexamines her past.

She also published her own memoirs, in the form of long essays that initially appeared in literary journals. "The Starched Blue Sky of Spain" (in *The Noble Savage,* 1960) was a passionate, frank account of the Spanish Civil War; she described "The horrible treachery involved, the sheer lack of ammunition, all of it. . . . I find it very hard . . . to live in so impersonal a world." She vehemently supported the struggle for black civil rights in the

1960s and opposed America's role in the war in Vietnam.

Josephine Herbst died in 1969, at 71, alone and impoverished. Despite her impressive body of fiction and nonfiction, she was largely forgotten until 1983 when social critic Elinor Langer wrote a popular biography about her; Herbst's absorbing memoirs were published a decade later. She was also rediscovered by feminists because of her strong, courageous protagonists, such as Vicky in the Trexler-Wendel trilogy. Overall, Herbst believed it was more important to be a humanistic, politically committed "mensch" than to be a "lady."

Further Reading

Herbst, Josephine. *Pity Is Not Enough.* New York: Harcourt, Brace, 1933.

———. *Rope of Gold.* New York: Harcourt, Brace, 1939.

———. *The Starched Blue Sky of Spain and Other Memoirs.* New York: HarperCollins, 1991.

Hubler, Angela E. "Herbst, Josephine." The Literary Encyclopedia. Available online. URL: http://www.litencyc.com/php/speople.php?rec=true&UID=2103. Downloaded on January 22, 2007.

Langer, Elinor. *Josephine Herbst: The Story She Could Never Tell.* Boston: Little, Brown and Company, 1983.

∾ Hoffman, Alice

(1952–) *novelist, children's book writer, screenwriter*

Alice Hoffman's luminous, best-selling fiction often combines surreal, magical, or mystical elements with realistic, quotidian details and reflective prose. Her impressive body of work comprises 18 novels and several short fiction collections, children's books, and screenplays. According to Maryanne O'Hara, in a profile of Hoffman that appeared in *Ploughshares* literary magazine in 2003, the author works "quietly and consistently," fusing "the mysterious and the practical, the dark with the optimistic."

Born in New York City on March 16, 1952, Hoffman was raised in a working-class town in Long Island, New York. Her parents divorced when she was eight, a traumatic event that shaped her view of relationships. As O'Hara points out in the *Ploughshares* article, many of the characters in Hoffman's books are "strong women, single women, struggling women, children facing danger," even though Hoffman has been in a stable, long-lasting marriage and has successfully raised two children. "Very often what you're writing about is what you've experienced as a child," explains the novelist.

Hoffman enrolled in night school at Adelphi University in Garden City, New York, and went on to obtain a bachelor of arts degree in English and anthropology there in 1973. She was offered a prestigious Mirrellees fellowship at the Stanford University Creative Writing Center and received a master's in creative writing degree at the university in 1975. A Stanford professor and his wife helped her get a short story published in *Fiction* magazine. Ted Solotaroff, the editor of *American Review,* was impressed with the quality of her work and asked Hoffman if she had written a novel. That inspired the burgeoning writer to produce one: She completed *Property Of* in 1977, at the age of 25, and a section of it was published in *American Review.* The critically successful novel dealt with the shady underworld of New York City. Hoffman has not shied away from tackling such thorny social issues as drugs, incest, AIDS, infidelity, and cancer, although her lyrical prose and trademark use of symbolism and magic help offset the heavy subject matter in her work. "A scrim of magic lies gently over her fictional world" is the way a reviewer in *Publishers Weekly* describes Hoffman's prose.

Hoffman's *Property Of* was followed quickly by several notable novels, including *The Drowning Season* (1979), *Angel Landing* (1980), *White Horses* (1982), and *Fortune's Daughter* (1985), which contemporary writer ANNIE DILLARD called "one of the best novels to come out of the United States in a decade." In 1987 Hoffman produced *Illumination Night,* a finely wrought tale replete with a touch of magic and a young blond giant, in which a teenager attempts to destroy a young family vacationing on Martha's Vineyard, an island off of

Cape Cod in Massachusetts: "It is terrifying how people can midjudge each other," observes a character in the disturbing novel, echoing the author's belief that it is difficult to understand the complex interior lives of other people. *At Risk* (1988) is a more realistic but equally reflective portrayal of a family in crisis, in this case one that attempts to cope when their young daughter contracts the AIDS virus. (Hoffman donated her advance from *At Risk* to AIDS research.)

Hoffman continued to write critically acclaimed popular fiction such as *Turtle Moon* (1993), a Book-of-the-Month Club main selection; *Practical Magic* (1995), which was adapted into a film in 1998 starring Nicole Kidman and Sandra Bullock; and *Here on Earth,* which is loosely based on Emily Brontë's classic novel *Wuthering Heights,* in a modernized version, and was a 1998 Oprah's Book Club selection. *Blue Diary* (2001), selected as a *New York Times* Notable Book and a best seller, features a happily married couple that has to face an ugly incident from the past: The husband was a rapist in his youth.

In *The Probable Future* (2003), the storyline revolves around three generations of women with unusual supernatural gifts living with the legacy of witchcraft. Hoffman commented in an interview in *Publishers Weekly* in 2003 that she is interested in witchcraft's symbolic essence and history more than in the "craft" itself—"what it means to be a woman in this society and an outcast." She has stated that the predominant theme of many of her novels is the search for identity and connection, especially in the face of family strife, but she is also interested in capturing ordinary, commonplace details. "Hoffman's fiction is like a Vermeer [painting]: a beautifully crafted study of the interior life," writes *Boston Review* contributor Alexandra Johnson. "She fuses fantasy and realism and is preoccupied with the way the mythic weaves into the everyday."

Blackbird House (2004) is a collection of riveting interrelated stories that all take place in the same Cape Cod farmhouse over a period of 200 years. "Fear and love seem to be the two motivat-ing forces within the book," explains Hoffman. *The Ice Queen,* published in 2005, is a dark yet life-affirming fairy tale, loosely based on a Hans Christian Andersen classic, about an emotionally frozen woman, a self-proclaimed ice queen, who when struck by lightning suddenly comes alive. Also in 2005, Hoffman wrote *The Foretelling,* a coming-of-age fantasy for young adults that features an all-female Amazon tribe and is set during the Bronze Age.

Along with her husband, Tom Martin, Hoffman has penned an average of two screenplays a year for 25 years. Her original screenplay *Independence Day,* a 1983 film starring Dianne Wiest and Kathleen Quinlan, unflinchingly examined the repercussions of the choices people make in their lives. "Sorrow defines character in fiction, just as it defines us. I do believe that the worst of times sometimes forms the best of what's inside us," said Hoffman during an interview with writer Jennifer Morgan Gray in 2005. Another film, based on Hoffman's book *Aquamarine* (2001), is a comedic magical tale for children that was released in 2006.

Dubbed by some critics as a master at "feminist magic realism," Hoffman has published her work in more than 20 translations and more than 100 foreign editions. Several of her novels have been named notable books of the year by the *New York Times, Los Angles Times,* and *Library Journal.* Hoffman's short fiction and nonfiction have appeared in *Kenyon Review, Architectural Digest,* and the *Boston Globe Magazine.* In 2004 she received the *Southwest Review*'s McGinnis-Ritchie Award for Fiction for "The Conjurer's Handbook," one of the haunting stories in *Blackbird House.*

When asked in the *Publishers Weekly* interview with Melissa Mia Hall about remaining hopeful in the face of troubling global events, Hoffman replied that she tries to take sorrow and make it into something enduring, meaningful, and beautiful. "Even in times when it's difficult to figure out, how do you go forward, art—and books—always help."

Alice Hoffman, who was diagnosed with breast cancer in 1998 and was sustained by her writing during months of treatment (she donated proceeds from her 1999 collection of interrelated short stories, *Local Girls,* to breast cancer research), lives in a Victorian house in a suburb of Boston, Massachusetts, with her husband, her sons (she cowrote *Moondog,* a children's book, with her younger son in 2004), and her dogs. She also spends time at her farmhouse on Cape Cod, which is rumored to be haunted. "On my first visit, I noticed a woman, a ghost in the parlor," said Hoffman during an interview with BookBrowse.com. "Then I looked more closely and discovered it was a mirror and that the woman was me. I knew then it was my house."

Further Reading

Gray, Jennifer Morgan. "A Conversation with Alice Hoffman." BookBrowse. Available online. URL: http://www.bookbrowse.com/author_interviews/full/index.cfm?author_number=366. Downloaded on January 22, 2007.

Hoffman, Alice. *Blackbird House.* New York: Doubleday, 2004.

———. *The Foretelling.* Boston: Little, Brown, 2005.

———. *The Ice Queen.* Boston: Little, Brown, 2005.

———. *Illumination Night.* New York: Putnam, 1987.

O'Hara, Maryanne. "About Alice Hoffman: A Profile." *Ploughshares: The Literary Journal at Emerson College* 29, no. 2 & 3 (August 15, 2003): 194–199.

Hogan, Linda Henderson
(1947–)   *poet, novelist, essayist*

Linda Hogan is a prominent American Indian writer whose work is informed by her Chickasaw background and her political and spiritual beliefs. "I am interested in the deepest questions, those of spirit, of shelter, of growth and movement toward peace and liberation, inner and outer," the author said in a 1995 interview.

Born on July 16, 1947, in Denver, Colorado, of a Chickasaw father from Oklahoma and a mother from an immigrant family who moved to Nebraska, Linda Henderson Hogan recalls that in her working-class home there were no books. The mesmerizing stories told to her by her father and uncle, how-

ever, were a literary resource that enriched her writing and her keen sense of observation.

Hogan received a master's degree in English and creative writing in 1978 from the University of Colorado at Boulder, where she later was a professor of English. She has also taught at Colorado Women's College and the University of Minnesota.

Hogan's first collection of verse, *Calling Myself Home* (1979), reflects the spare imagery of the Oklahoma landscape (because her father originated from Oklahoma, she maintained close ties there) and the rich imagery of her Chickasaw heritage. For example, in the poem "Turtle" she writes about tribal women as amber procreators with shells on their backs.

In 1980 her three-act play *A Piece of Moon* won the Five Civilized Tribes* Playwriting Award. *Daughters, I Love You,* a collection of poetry that appeared a year later, is an elegiac indictment of nuclear power by a grieving mother who feels unable to protect her daughters, or the planet, from annihilation. Like the contemporary Indian writer LESLIE MARMON SILKO, Hogan recognizes the importance of confronting the apocalyptic nuclear threat in her work.

Hogan continued to publish her provocative poetry. In 1985, *Seeing through the Sun* won an American Book Award from the Before Columbus Foundation. In one of its poems, "Daughters Sleeping," an everyday event is transformed into a mother's sensual, powerful prayer for protecting her children.

After producing two volumes of short fiction—*That Horse* (1985) and *The Big Woman* (1987)—two screenplays, and another book of poems, *Savings* (1988), Hogan tried her hand at writing a novel. In 1990 *Mean Spirit* was released to critical acclaim. A finalist for a Pulitzer Prize and recipient of the Oklahoma Book Award, *Mean Spirit* combines fact and fiction in chronicling the tragic tale of American Indians in Oklahoma who were cheated and then forced off their oil-rich tribal

---

*Historically, the Chickasaw and four other tribes traditionally from the Southeast were known as the Five Civilized Tribes.

land. The novel as well as the author's haunting language are, according to well-known Chippewa novelist LOUISE ERDRICH, "rooted in both truth and mystery." Both her verse and fiction focus on the injustice of poverty.

Hogan's verse collection *The Book of Medicines* was a finalist for the National Book Critics Circle Award in 1993. The finely crafted novel *Solar Storms* (1995) tells the story of five generations of Indian women attempting to cope with the harsh landscape between Canada and Minnesota. This work is a parable of the American Indian search for a lost, more mystical way of life. In it, Hogan writes:

> And though it was cloudless, it began to rain, a soft female rain. . . . I sang an old song. . . . It was the animal-calling song. And while I sang, the animals came to where she lay. I didn't see them with my eyes, but I knew they were there.

Hogan has also contributed to literary criticism in cogent essays on Native American early literature and the role of the oral concept of language. *Intimate Nature: The Bond between Women and Animals* (1998) is a collection of her incisive essays. The second volume in a trilogy on women and the natural world, *The Sweet Breathing of Plants: Women Writing on the Green World* (2001), which Hogan coedited with Brenda Peterson, is a meditative collection of essays that ranges from personal to scientific entries written by women from all walks of life.

In her essay "Let Us Hold Fierce," the Laguna Pueblo writer PAULA GUNN ALLEN asserts that being an Indian, Hogan is "able to resolve the conflict that presently divides the non-Indian feminist community; she does not have to choose between spirituality and political commitment, for each is the complement of the other. They are the two wings of one bird, and that bird is the interconnectedness of everything."

Linda Hogan has received numerous awards, including a 1986 National Endowment for the Arts fiction grant and a 1991–93 Guggenheim fellowship. She also won a Five Civilized Tribes Museum Playwriting Award and in 1998 received the Lifetime Achievement Award from the Native

Writers' Circle of the Americas. In 2002 she won a Worldcraft Circle Award for creative prose and also published *The Woman Who Watches Over the World: A Native Memoir,* which blends Hogan's personal history with stories about important American Indians. "I sat down to write a book about pain and ended up writing about love," says the poet and novelist. Divorced, Hogan has two adopted daughters, Sandra Dawn Protector and Tanya Thunder Horse. Her interests include wildlife rehabilitation, studying the relationship between humans and other species, and trying to create and promote global survival skills for the nuclear age.

Further Reading

Allen, Paula Gunn. *The Sacred Hoop: Recovering the Feminine in American Indian Traditions.* Boston: Beacon Press, 1986.

Green, Rayna. *That's What I Said: Contemporary Fiction and Poetry by Native American Women.* Bloomington, Ind.: Indiana University Press, 1984.

Hogan, Linda. *The Book of Medicines: Poems.* Minneapolis, Minn.: Coffee House Press, 1993.

———. *Savings: Poems.* Minneapolis, Minn.: Coffee House Press, 1988.

———. *The Woman Who Watches Over the World: A Native Memoir.* New York: W. W. Norton, 2002.

Peterson, Brenda, and Linda Hogan. *Sightings: The Gray Whales' Mysterious Journey.* Washington, D.C. National Geographic, 2002.

Sonneborn, Liz. "Linda Hogan." *A to Z of American Indian Women,* 92–94. New York: Facts On File, 2007.

Wilson, Norma C. "Linda Henderson Hogan." In *Dictionary of Native American Literature,* 449–452. New York: Garland Publishing, 1994.

Holm, Saxe

See JACKSON, HELEN MARIA FISKE HUNT

Howe, Julia Ward
(1819–1910)   *poet*

Best remembered as the author of the popular Civil War anthem "The Battle Hymn of the Republic," poet Julia Ward Howe was also a leading advocate of women's suffrage. Born into a wealthy New York City family on May 27, 1819, Julia was largely educated at home. A bright, serious student, she read *Pilgrim's Progress* at age nine, and by 12 she was writing and publishing religious verse. She taught herself German so she could study German philosophy and literature.

In 1843 she married a prominent Boston abolitionist and physician, Samuel Gridley Howe. Busy raising six children and entertaining illustrious visitors such as Oscar Wilde, Howe was nonetheless determined to pursue a literary career, even though her husband would have preferred her to sharpen her domestic skills. Her first collection of poems, *Passion Flowers* (1854), appeared anonymously, in part because they expressed Howe's unhappiness with her unsuccessful marriage, as did her next book of verse, *Words for the Hour* (1857).

Howe would probably have been forgotten as a poet—her work was undistinguished—had it not been for her one true literary success, the "Battle Hymn of the Republic." The poem first appeared in the *Atlantic Monthly* in 1862 and was immediately acclaimed and adopted as the unofficial Civil War anthem of the Union army. The words for the inspirational song came to Howe after awakening from a deep sleep, having earlier heard Union troops marching through the streets of Washington, D.C., singing "John Brown's Body." She wrote the poem in one sitting on a scrap of paper, to the tune of the dirge. Its biblical allusions and patriotic spirit even impressed President Abraham Lincoln, who asked to meet Howe and then publicly praised her work.

Using her celebrity status as a way to galvanize women into demanding more rights, Howe helped establish the American Woman Suffrage Association (AWSA) in 1869 and was named its first president. She also edited and wrote for its influential publication, the *Woman's Journal,* and became a leading supporter of the women's club movement as a way to expand the cultural horizons of women. In 1873 she helped found the Association for the Advancement of Women (AAW), serving as president from 1881. Howe had, as she put, a flair for "finding the right word," and was an effective advocate for social reforms, including coeducation and world peace. When not lecturing she wrote poetry, plays, travel books, philosophical essays, a biography of the transcendentalist writer MARGARET FULLER (1883), and her memoirs, *Reminiscences* (1899).

In a *New York Times* (April 11, 2004) review of Valarie H. Ziegler's prize-winning biography *Diva Julia: The Public Romance and Private Agony of Julia Ward Howe* (2003), reviewer Sherie Posesorksi asserts that from early childhood Howe made her "formidable intellect and drive evident, as well as the importance of writing as an emotional and creative outlet." Despite harsh criticism from her authoritarian husband and even from her children, "once Howe found a public voice, there was no turning back." She felt she had no choice: "The soul whose desires are not fixed upon the unattainable is dead even while it liveth," said Howe.

In 1908 Julia Ward Howe became the first woman elected into the American Academy of Arts and Letters. She remained gregarious and independent until her death at the age of 91 at her summer home in Newport, Rhode Island, on October 17, 1910. During Howe's memorial service at Boston's Symphony Hall, a 4,000-voice choir sang, as a fitting tribute to America's "Grand Old Lady," "The Battle Hymn of the Republic."

Further Reading

Clifford, Deborah Pickman. *Mine Eyes Have Seen the Glory: A Biography of Julia Ward Howe.* Boston: Little, Brown, 1979.

Hall, Florence Howe. *The Story of the Battle Hymn of the Republic.* New York: Harper, 1916.

Howe, Julia Ward. *Julia Ward Howe and the Woman Suffrage Movement: A Selection from her Speeches and Essays.* New York: Arno Press, 1969.

———. *Reminiscences, 1819–1889.* New York: Negro Universities Press, 1969.

Ziegler, Valarie H. *Diva Julia: The Public Romance and Private Agony of Julia Ward Howe.* Harrisburg, Pa.: Trinity Press International, 2003.

∾ Humishuma
See MOURNING DOVE

∾ Hurst, Fannie
(1889–1968) *novelist, short story writer*

Fannie Hurst, a popular and prolific writer as well as a best-selling novelist, often portrayed society's misfits and the struggles of the common people, especially indigent women, in her fiction. One of America's most highly paid writers at the time, she contributed generously to a variety of social causes and to fostering college-level creative writing programs.

Born on her grandparent's farm in Hamilton, Ohio, on October 18, 1889, Fannie was raised in St. Louis, Missouri, in an assimilated German-Jewish, middle-class family. A voracious reader and storyteller, she admired Charles Dickens, Upton Sinclair, and Edgar Lee Masters for their sharp eye for detail. When she was 14 her first manuscript was rejected by the *Saturday Evening Post*, the first of 35 rejections she would receive from the magazine.

After graduating from Washington University in St. Louis in 1909, the same year her first story "Ain't Life Wonderful" was published in a local magazine, Hurst permanently left the Midwest. Energetic and ambitious, she moved to New York City in pursuit of a literary career and to observe life on the street, as she put it, "the way Dickens did." Hurst took odd jobs as a sweatshop worker, waitress, actress, and nursemaid; visited night court sessions; and lived in poor, working-class neighborhoods, sometimes identifying too closely with the underdog figures she would later describe in her fiction. "I wrote all day from loneliness, and all evening for the same reason," she recalled in her autobiography, *Anatomy of Me*.

In 1912 the *Saturday Evening Post* finally accepted one of her stories, "Power and Horse Power," and paid her $30 for it. The *Post* and other literary magazines were soon paying Hurst 10 times that amount: all told, she would publish 300 short stories, 10 of which were listed in *Best Ameri-*

Fannie Hurst returns to New York City from a vacation in 1924.
(AP/Wide World Photos)

can Short Stories. One, "Humoresque," which won an O. Henry Prize Award, was dramatized by Hurst in 1923.

Just Around the Corner, the first of Hurst's four collections of short stories, appeared in 1914 to popular acclaim. The public loved Hurst's work, which frankly yet compassionately addressed issues such as failed relationships, wife abuse, and age discrimination. Reviewers, however, often found her writing too melodramatic and dubbed her the "sob sister" of American fiction. Still, critics praised Hurst for her ability to bring everyday characters to life.

In 1915 Hurst married a Russian-born pianist, Jacques S. Danielson. For five years the couple lived apart, with Hurst retaining her maiden name. Their unconventional marriage was loving, romantic, and respectful, and lasted until Danielson's death in 1952.

Two years after Hurst saw her first novel, *Star-Dust: The Story of an American Girl* (1921), published, she established her reputation with her first best seller, *Lummox* (1923). In it she sympathetically depicted the tribulations of a downtrodden Scandinavian servant. Of the 30 novels Hurst wrote, *Lummox* remained the author's favorite; as she noted in her autobiography, *Lummox* "symbolized a complete breakthrough. . . . from the circumscribed world in which I had been reared into a new social consciousness."

Producing nearly a title a year in the 1920s, followed by two best sellers during the 1930s—*Back Street* (1931) and *Imitation of Life* (1933), a classic rags-to-riches American success story, Hurst became one of America's most beloved and highly paid writers. She often incorporated feminist heroines or her favorite causes into her fiction, but her bittersweet stories were entertaining rather than didactic. Her books have been widely translated, and 29 films were made from her fiction, notably three Hollywood versions of *Back Street* and two of *Imitation of Life.*

Hurst, who had befriended the African-American writer ZORA NEALE HURSTON, addressed in her novels the issue of racism, became increasingly more aware of her Jewish roots, and during World War II helped Jewish refugees escape from Germany. She also promoted creative writing by donating a million dollars to Washington and Brandeis Universities to fund new professorships in creative literature. Respected by her colleagues, in 1937 she was elected president of the Authors Guild. She later received honorary doctorate degrees from two universities.

Fannie Hurst continued to write well into her 70s and in 1958 published an autobiography, *Anatomy of Me,* which documented her literary and social activist life. She died in New York City on February 23, 1968, at age 75, having captivated millions of readers with her enduring and heartfelt stories. "I'm not happy when I'm writing," she once said, "but I'm more unhappy when I'm not."

In 1999 Brooke Kroeger wrote a vividly rendered biography titled *Fannie: The Talent for Success of Writer Fannie Hurst,* in which, notes *Kirkus Reviews,* the biographer presents her heroine as an "American original and passionate hack who spoke to the masses, even if she did not number herself among them." The Feminist Press published a collection of Hurst's best stories in 2004, introduced by short story writer GRACE PALEY, in order to encourage a revival and reassessment of Hurst's celebrated and popular, yet now nearly forgotten, body of work.

Further Reading

Hurst, Fannie. *Anatomy of Me: A Wanderer in Search of Herself.* Garden City, N.Y.: Doubleday, 1958.

———. *Imitation of Life.* New York: Harper, 1933.

———. *The Stories of Fannie Hurst.* Edited by Susan Koppelman. With an introduction by Grace Paley. New York: The Feminist Press, 2004.

Kroeger, Brooke. *Fannie: The Talent for Success of Writer Fannie Hurst.* New York: Crown, 1999.

Shaughnessy, Mary Rose. *Fannie Hurst: Myths about Love and Woman.* New York: Gordon Press, 1979.

◈ Hurston, Zora Neale
(1891–1960)   *novelist, folklorist*

Perhaps one of the most highly acclaimed novels in the canon of African-American literature, Zora Neale Hurston's *Their Eyes Were Watching God* (1937) portrayed a proud, independent, passionate black woman—much like Hurston—who celebrated her heritage but did not feel victimized by it. With one of the most distinctive voices in American literature, Hurston brought to life the people she called "the Negros furthest down."

Born on January 7, 1891, in Eatonville, Florida, the first incorporated all-black township in America, Zora grew up in a warm, nonracist community. She had a happy childhood until she was 13, when her loving mother died and her father, a Baptist preacher and three-term mayor of Eatonville, remarried a woman whom Zora disliked. Throughout her life Hurston heeded her mother's advice to "Jump at de sun—and you might at least catch holt to de moon."

A voracious reader who once said that books gave her more pleasure than clothes, Zora's imagination was fueled by classic literature, such as a book of Milton's poetry she found in a garbage bin, and by the rich oral traditions of the rural African-American South. Forced to leave school at 14 to earn a living, she supported herself by taking low-paying jobs. "There is something about poverty that smells like death," she wrote later in her autobiography.

Hurston joined a traveling operetta company and then worked as a maid, manicurist, and waitress, while attending high school at night. In 1920 she received an associate's degree from Howard University and published her first story, "John Redding Goes to Sea," in the university's literary magazine. From that point on, she dreamed of becoming a professional writer.

In 1924 an autobiographical story entitled "Drenched in Light" was accepted by *Opportunity: A Journal of Negro Life,* an important publication linked to the Harlem Renaissance—a black cultural and literary movement centered in the Harlem district of New York City during the 1920s. Although African-American women during this period, in which black art, music, and literature flourished, did not receive as much support and recognition as their male counterparts, their impact was significant. The editor, impressed by Hurston's literary skills, invited her to enter the highly competitive *Opportunity* writing contest.

"Beginning to feel the urge to write I wanted to be in New York," Hurston recalled. She arrived in the metropolis in 1925 with $1.50 in her pocket and "a lot of hope." Witty, flamboyant (she once dressed as an African princess to get into a segregated tea salon), and a brilliant storyteller, Hurston had no trouble meeting the city's cultural elite. She earned money by working as a secretary and companion for, and living with, the popular novelist FANNIE HURST, and from a wealthy white patron, Charlotte V. Q. Mason, who financially supported her until 1931.

The most important event during Hurston's first year in New York occurred when she won second prize in the 1925 *Opportunity* literary contest; the gifted black poet Langston Hughes, whom Hurston befriended, won first prize. That same year she entered Barnard College as an anthropology major and scholarship student, and contributed short stories to the seminal anthology *The New Negro,* edited by her mentor and friend Alain Locke, an influential member of the Harlem Renaissance. In 1926 she helped edit *Fire!!,* a literary magazine rooted in the real-life experiences of ordinary black people.

Hurston was determined to become not only a successful writer, but also a successful folklorist. At Barnard she studied with the renowned anthropologist Franz Boas, who suggested she collect traditional African-American folklore of the South. She traveled to Florida, Alabama, and Louisiana, documenting esoteric initiation ceremonies. "Nobody knows for sure how many thousands in America are warmed by the fire of hoodoo, because the worship is bound in secrecy," she explained in *Mules and Men* (1935). In later years she would receive Guggenheim fellowships to collect folklore in Jamaica, Haiti, and Honduras, where she preserved aspects of black life that might otherwise have been lost.

In 1928, after becoming the first African American to graduate from Barnard, Hurston published an autobiographical essay, "How It Feels to Be Colored Me," in which she cogently expressed her beliefs:

> I am not tragically colored. There is no great sorrow dammed up in my soul. . . . I do not belong to the sobbing school of Negrohood who hold that nature somehow has given them a lowdown dirty deal and whose feelings are all hurt about it. . . . Sometimes, I feel discriminated against, but it does not make me angry. It merely astonished me. How *can* any deny themselves the pleasure of my company? It's beyond me.

Hurston collaborated with Langston Hughes on a play, *Mule Bone: A Comedy of Negro Life* (1930), which was based on an unpublished short story of hers. Arguments arose when Hughes accused Hurston of denying his role in its creation during the play's production; sadly, their friendship ended. Four years later she published her first novel, *Jonah's Gourd Vine,* based on a story about a black preacher modeled largely on her father. She then published her most important folklore collection, *Mules and Men,* a vivid account of African-American folklore tales and her experiences doing research in the rural South. Hughes noted that Hurston "had great scorn for all pretensions, academic or otherwise. That is why she was such a fine folklore collector, able to go among the people and never act as if she had been to school at all."

In 1937 Hurston produced her magnum opus, *Their Eyes Were Watching God.* A lyrical, poignant love story in which the central protagonist repudiates being "de mule uh de world," and returns to Eatonville, Florida, with a profound understanding of herself and her community, the novel was well received by most reviewers; the *New York Times* called it a "well nigh perfect story." Reactions from some members of the black community, however, were largely negative. The distinguished novelist Richard Wright, for example, was critical of Hurston's use of black language patterns, which could be construed as negative stereotyping. He called the novel "counterrevolutionary" and "designed to entertain white readers." Hurston, a complex figure who was politically conservative but culturally liberal, defended herself as a realist who used the language and dialogue she knew her fictional characters would have used. Her skill was in *showing* what her characters did, not in judging their actions. "My interest lies in what makes a man or a woman do such-and-such, regardless of his color," she wrote. Out of print for 30 years until it was reissued in 1978, *Their Eyes Were Watching God* is today considered one of the finest and most important novels written by and about an African-American woman.

After publishing another folklore collection, in 1939 Hurston produced *Moses, Man of the Mountain,* her third novel and fifth book in seven years. An imaginative attempt to redesign the Judeo-Christian biblical story, it was based on black folk-

lore. That same year she married Albert Price III, but her marriage fared no better than her first, to Herbert Sheen in 1927, and she and Price divorced after a few years. Like many of her characters, Hurston failed at intimate relationships and remained alone, although she did not feel lonely. In her autobiography, *Dust Tracks on a Road* (1942), the most popular book she had ever written, she emphasized her life as a southern female writer in a male-dominated world, rather than as a black writer. "Skins are no measure of what was inside people," she explained. When the book was reissued with additional material in 1985, it sold more than 200,000 copies in less than a year.

Just before the publication of her last novel, *Seraph on the Suwanee,* in 1948, Hurston was arrested on a morals charge for allegedly sexually abusing a 10-year-old boy. Although the case was dismissed, when the story was leaked to the black press by an African American, Hurston felt betrayed and humiliated and retreated from public life forever, returning to Florida. For the next 12 years she continued to publish minor pieces, but, to her disappointment, a novel about Herod the Great was rejected. Eventually she took a job as a maid in Miami and then relied on welfare assistance. Too proud to ask for help after being evicted from her home, she ended up in a country welfare home and died—sickly, alone, and poor—on January 28, 1960.

Almost 20 years later, a new generation of readers would discover the multifaceted, opinionated, and gifted writer. The African-American novelist ALICE WALKER defined Hurston's strength as "racial health—a sense of black people as complete, complex, *undiminished* human beings," and was instrumental in having Hurston's works reissued. In 1973 Walker, who considered Hurston her "spiritual antecedent," placed a headstone on her grave with the epitaph: "A Genius of the South: Novelist, Folklorist, Anthropologist." Walker, who also wrote a seminal essay entitled "In Search of Zora Neale Hurston," called her "the intellectual and spiritual foremother of generations of black women writers."

Interest in Hurston continues to grow. In 2001 a critically acclaimed second volume of her collected authentic African-American folklore, *Every Tongue Got to Confess,* appeared. It was followed in 2002 by Valerie Boyd's *Wrapped in Rainbows: The Life of Zora Neale Hurston* (2002), the first biography of Hurston in 25 years; Boyd's carefully researched book sheds new light on the writer's complex private and public lives. That same year, Carla Kaplan edited a voluminous collection of 600 recently discovered letters, which the *Los Angeles Times* called a "real contribution to the understanding of Hurston's life." And in August 2002 thousands of Hurston admirers gathered in Central Park in New York City for "Zora's Salon," a program of readings by luminaries such as Ossie Davis and Ruby Dee, to celebrate the "protean folklorist and queen of the Harlem Renaissance," as she has been called.

The media blitz continued in March 2005, when a television movie version of *Their Eyes Were Watching God,* starring Halle Berry and produced by Oprah Winfrey, was aired. The well-attended annual Zora Neale Hurston Festival of the Arts and Humanities took place for the 17th time in January 2006 in Eatonville, Florida. "She's a goddess," said one of her fans. He had traveled from Oregon to pay tribute to the "widely beloved but never easily fathomable figure," as the *New York Times*'s Ralph Blumenthal described her, adding that "Hurston is emerging as an epic literary figure as her reputation grows under a surge of new scholarship." Also in 2005, *Lies and Other Tall Tales,* a collection edited by Hurston, was published posthumously. "Although intended for school-age children, [it] is enjoyable for anyone who suspects, in a world grown rather too literal, that there is nothing so satisfying as the boundless inventiveness of the truly well-told whopper," wrote Patricia Williams in the *New York Times Book Review.*

Further Reading

Boyd, Valerie. *Wrapped in Rainbows: The Life of Zora Neale Hurston.* New York: Scribner, 2002.

Hemenway, Robert E. *Zora Neale Hurston: A Literary Biography.* Urbana: University of Illinois Press, 1977.

Hurston, Zora Neale. *The Complete Stories.* With a foreword by Henry Louis Gates, Jr. New York: HarperCollins, 1994.

———. *Dust Tracks on a Road.* With a foreword by Maya Angelou. New York: HarperPerennial, 1991.

———, ed. *Lies and Other Tall Tales,* adapted and illustrated by Christopher Myers. New York: HarperCollins, 2005.

———. *Their Eyes Were Watching God.* With a foreword by Alice Walker. New York: HarperCollins, 1990.

Kaplan, Carla, ed. *Zora Neale Hurston: A Life in Letters.* New York: Doubleday, 2002.

Walker, Alice, ed. *I Love Myself When I am Laughing. . . . And Then Again When I Am Looking Mean and Impressive: A Zora Neale Hurston Reader.* New York: The Feminist Press, 1979.

∼ Jackson, Helen Maria Fiske Hunt (H. H., Saxe Holm)
(1830–1885) *novelist, poet, essayist*

Best remembered as a crusader for American Indian rights, Helen Hunt Jackson wrote two pioneering works about their plight: an investigative essay titled *A Century of Dishonor: A Sketch of the United Government's Dealings with Some of the Indian Tribes* (1881); and *Ramona* (1885), a novel.

Born on October 14, 1830, in Amherst, Massachusetts, Helen Maria Fiske was a robust, energetic child. As with the poet EMILY DICKINSON, her neighbor and lifelong friend, Helen's father taught at Amherst College and was a strict Calvinist. After her parents died, Helen, still a teenager, lived with relatives and friends until she married an army officer, Edward B. Hunt, when she was 22. Both her husband and two young sons died from illnesses between 1854 and 1865.

As a way to assuage her grief, and to support herself financially, Hunt turned to writing. "I never write for money, I write for love, then after it is written, I *print* for money," she explained, having published her critically acclaimed verse (under the pseudonym "H. H.") in several prominent magazines such as the *Atlantic Monthly.* Ralph Waldo

Emerson, the noted transcendentalist, admired of Hunt's verse and was said to have carried it around with him.

After marrying William Jackson, a wealthy Colorado businessman, in 1875, Helen Hunt Jackson continued her literary career with a series of popular short stories penned under the pseudonym Saxe Holm. She also wrote children's books, travel articles, and more poetry.

Although Jackson was not active in the women's or antislavery movements, she was deeply distressed when in 1879 she heard about displaced American Indians such as the Ponca of Nebraska. Two years later, using her real name, she wrote the first widely read book to call attention to the mistreatment of the Indians. *A Century of Dishonor: The Early Crusade for Indian Reforms* was a passionate and carefully researched attack on the Bureau of Indian Affairs.

In 1884 Jackson fictionalized the story of Ramona Lubo, a Cahuilla woman, and the findings of an investigation of California's Mission Indians—she had been appointed a commissioner by the Interior Department—in the novel *Ramona.* She hoped that the romantic tale of forbidden love because of prejudice against Indians would evoke public sympathy for Native Americans in the same way that HARRIET BEECHER STOWE's *Uncle Tom's Cabin* had for African Americans. Although it never achieved that level of fame, *Ramona* went through numerous printings, was the basis of three movies, and is staged annually at an outdoor pageant in California.

Helen Hunt Jackson died of cancer on August 12, 1885, at age 54, never having known the impact *Ramona* and *Century of Dishonor* had in spurring legislation that helped the surviving Mission Indians. Not long before her death Jackson told a friend, "Nothing looks to me of any value except the words I have spoken for the Indians." Emily Dickinson, saddened by her friend's untimely death, lyrically noted that, "Helen of Troy will die, / but Helen of Colorado, never."

Further Reading

"Helen Hunt Jackson." Colorado Women's Hall of Fame. Available online. URL: http://www.cogreatwomen.org/jackson.htm. Downloaded on January 22, 2003.

Mathes, Valerie Sherer, ed. *The Indian Reform Letters by Helen Hunt Jackson*. Norman: University of Oklahoma Press, 1998.

May, Antoinette. *Helen Hunt Jackson: A Lonely Voice of Conscience*. San Francisco, Calif.: Chronicle Books, 1987.

Phillips, Kate. *Helen Hunt Jackson: A Literary Life*. Berkeley: University of California Press, 2003.

ᔐ Jackson, Shirley

(1919–1965)   *short story writer, novelist*

Shirley Jackson was a master of two radically different writing genres and styles. She could pen heartwarming, humorous nonfiction tales about ordinary domestic life but was best known as the creator of eerie and often gruesome gothic horror tales that explored the darker aspects of human nature. It was those tales that secured her reputation as one of the outstanding writers of her generation.

Shirley Jackson was born on December 14, 1919, in San Francisco, California. As a child she tended to be solitary, reading and writing poetry in her room for hours at a time. In 1940, the same

year in which she graduated from Syracuse University, she married Stanley Hyman, a literary critic. The couple moved to New York City and then to Vermont. They had a happy marriage—Hyman admired his wife's talent and encouraged her career—and raised four children.

Jackson's publishing career began in the early 1940s. She became a regular contributor to the *New Yorker*, where her husband was a staff member, before vaulting to prominence with "The Lottery," a short but haunting horror tale that became her most famous work. The *New Yorker* published it on June 26, 1948. It begins innocuously with the people of a small New England town who gather together for their annual lottery, which turns out to be a sacrificial rite in which the "winner" is stoned to death. The story prompted the greatest outpouring of mail in the *New Yorker*'s history: more than 450 letters from readers in 25 states and several foreign countries. The reactions ranged from fury to fascination to frustration; many letter writers were uncertain if what they had read was a good chiller or a grim commentary on humankind's essentially evil nature. "The Lottery" has since been hailed by some critics as the perfect short story and was adapted as a popular television movie.

Jackson's first novel, the semiautobiographical *The Road through the Wall*, was published in 1948, the same year as "The Lottery." Her most important fiction dealt with the supernatural and included *The Sundial* (1958), which was about a group of people who take refuge on a large estate to await the end of the world; *The Haunting of Hill House* (1959), in which a group of researchers investigate a house to see if it is haunted; and *We Have Always Lived in the Castle* (1962) a novel that focuses on two sisters who become pariahs because they are suspected of murdering other members of their family. In 1963, *The Haunting of Hill House* was adapted into a movie, *The Haunting*, which has since become a classic in the horror film genre. A new version of *The Haunting* was released in 1999 and starred Liam Neeson, Lili Taylor, and Catherine Zeta-Jones.

One reason that Jackson, whom one reviewer called a "literary sorceress," chose to write about the supernatural was because she found it "so convenient a shorthand of the possibilities of human adjustment to what seems at best to be an inhuman world." Yet she also enjoyed writing funny, touching books about her daily life, as she did in her family memoir *Life among the Savages* (1953).

"Whether the genre is domestic comedy, gothic horror, or realistic narrative," wrote Joan Wylie Hall in *The Columbia Companion to the Twentieth-Century American Short Story*, "Jackson pulls the rug from under her precariously balanced housewives and career women. Drawing on myth, ritual, and literary antecedents, these modern tales of loss and bewilderment create an atmosphere of quiet threat that was promptly recognized as the signature of a Shirley Jackson story."

Shirley Jackson never lost her zest for writing nor the joy of practicing her craft. As she put it, "I can't persuade myself that writing is honest work. It's great fun and I love it." She died on August 8, 1965, of heart failure, while at the height of her literary career. More than 30 years after her death, two of her children edited a collection of 54 of her stories, many of which had been lost until they were discovered, in fittingly gothic fashion, in a cobwed-covered box in a barn in Vermont.

Further Reading

Hall, Joan Wylie. "Shirley Jackson." In *The Columbia Companion to the Twentieth-Century American Short Story*, edited by Blanche H. Gelfant, 310–314. New York: Columbia University Press, 2000.

Hattenhauer, Darryl. *Shirley Jackson's American Gothic.* Albany: State University of New York Press, 2003.

Jackson, Shirley. *The Haunting of Hill House.* New York: Viking Press, 1959.

———. *Just an Ordinary Day: The Uncollected Stories of Shirley Jackson.* Edited by Laurence Jackson Hyman and Sarah Hyman Stewart. New York: Bantam, 1998.

———. *The Lottery and Other Stories.* With an introduction by A. M. Homes. New York: Farrar, Straus and Giroux, 2005.

Oppenheim, Judy. *Private Demons: The Life of Shirley Jackson.* New York: Putnam, 1988.

Jacobs, Harriet Ann (Linda Brent)
(1813–1897)   *autobiographer*

Harriet Ann Jacobs recorded the "true and just account," as she described it, of her seven-year struggle for freedom in *Incidents in the Life of a Slave Girl, Written by Herself* (1861). A seminal work in the canon of writings by African-American women, *Incidents* is considered to be the most highly regarded antebellum slave narrative by a black woman published in the United States.

Jacobs was born into slavery in Edenton, North Carolina, in 1813. After her mother died, when Harriet was six, her mistress, Margaret Horniblow, took her into her house to work and taught her to read and to write. In 1825 Horniblow died, and Harriet was inherited by a three-year-old child, the daughter of Dr. James Norcom, who became her master. To protect herself from Norcom's unrelenting sexual advances, Jacobs agreed to a relationship with a neighbor, a white future congressman named Samuel Sawyer. With him she bore a son in 1829 and a daughter in 1833.

Jacobs's only protector was her nurturing grandmother, who in 1828 had become a freed slave, and with whom she and her children lived. In her autobiography Jacobs movingly describes the fate that awaited her children if they were not freed:

> I once saw two beautiful children playing together. One was a fair white child; the other was her slave, and also her sister. When I saw them embracing each other, and heard their joyous laughter, I turned sadly away from the lovely sight. I foresaw the inevitable blight that would fall on the little slave girl's heart. I knew how soon her laughter would be changed to sighs. . . .

After discovering Norcom's plan to sell her children, Jacobs escaped, becoming a fugitive in the 1830s. For nearly seven years she hid from her master and his cruel wife—first in a snake-infested swamp, and then in a tiny crawl space in her grandmother's attic, where she practiced writing and read from the Scriptures. "My master had power and law on his side; I had a determined will. There is might in each," she explained in *Incidents*.

In 1835 Sawyer purchased Jacobs's children; but in spite of his promises, he did not free them. Assisted by abolitionists, Jacobs managed to escape to the North in 1842 and arranged to have her children sent to her there. "I resolved that out of the darkness of this hour a brighter dawn should rise for them."

When Norcom died in Edenton in 1850, his daughter attempted to recapture Jacobs, but an abolitionist, Cornelia Grinnell Willis, arranged for her emancipation, after 27 years of slavery, by paying for her freedom. More than 10 years after her escape, Jacobs was encouraged by another white abolitionist, novelist LYDIA MARIA CHILD, to record her life. She began *Incidents in the Life of a Slave Girl, Written by Herself* in 1853, and described the manuscript to a friend:

> I have . . . striven faithfully to give a true and just account of my own life in Slavery. I have come to you just as I am a poor Slave Mother, not to tell you what I have heard but what I have seen and what I have suffered, and if there is any sympathy to give, let it be given to the thousands of Slave Mothers that are still in bondage. . . . Let it plead for their helpless Children.

After failing to find a publisher, in 1861 Jacobs independently published her memoir under the pseudonym Linda Brent. Child edited the book but said that "with trifling exceptions, both the ideas and the language are her [Jacobs's] own."

According to Jean Fagan Yellin, the editor of the 1987 edition of *Incidents in the Life of a Slave Girl*, in order to help other "sisters in bondage," Jacobs documented the success of her heroic efforts to prevent her master from raping her, to rescue her children from him, and finally to achieve freedom. "Slavery is terrible for men; but it is far more terrible for women," wrote Jacobs. "Superadded to the burden common to all, *they* have wrongs, and sufferings, and mortifications peculiarly their own." Jacobs was the only slave to candidly describe the full extent of sexual abuse endured by female slaves.

She simultaneously presented her failure to adhere to sexual standards in which she believed, because of the degradation inflicted on slave women who were never able to exercise control over their own bodies. She also stressed the importance of familial bonds and of insuring a home and a community for the next generation of black children, and dealt forcefully with the Fugitive Slave Act of 1850, which subjected runaways in the North to deportation back to the South, as well as with slave revolts.

After the Civil War, Harriet A. Jacobs and her daughter devoted their lives to public service and to helping newly freed slaves. She died in Washington, D.C., on March 7, 1897. Her work was considered fiction and largely forgotten until the 1970s, when the most comprehensive slave narrative ever penned by an African-American woman was rediscovered by feminists and civil rights activists.

Further Reading

"Harriet Ann Jacobs." Massachusetts Hall of Black Achievement at Bridgewater State College. Available online. URL: http://www.bridgew.edu/HOBA/Jacobs.cfm. Downloaded on February 28, 2007.

Jacobs, Harriet. *Incidents in the Life of a Slave Girl, Written by Herself.* Edited by Jean Fagan Yellin. Cambridge, Mass.: Harvard University Press, 1987.

Yellin, Jean F. *Harriet Jacobs: A Life.* New York: Basic Civitas, 2004.

Jen, Gish (Lillian Gen)
(1955–)   *novelist, short story writer*

Gish Jen's debut novel, *Typical American*, was a 1991 *New York Times* Notable Book of the Year and a finalist for the National Book Critics Circle Award. Her prose has been called "bone clean yet lustrous," and she is widely praised for imbuing her characters with diverse voices, humor, quirkiness, and intelligence as they attempt to find and claim their identities. Considered one of the outstanding contemporary Asian-American writers, Jen says her Chinese heritage is inseparable from the way she perceives the creative process itself. Yet she also has stated that she hopes to define herself as an American, rather than a Chinese-American, writer.

Born Lillian Gen on August 12, 1955, in New York City, but known professionally and personally by a chosen nickname she adopted in high school, Gish Jen, the second of five children, was raised by educated immigrant parents in Queens and then in Scarsdale, an affluent suburb of New York. Gish was an avid reader as a child. Her favorite books included LOUSIA MAY ALCOTT's *Little Women,* and she wrote her first story while in fifth grade. Nonetheless, she never thought about becoming a writer: She planned to please her education-minded parents by becoming a doctor or a lawyer, but neither profession sparked her interest.

Jen took premed and prelaw courses at Harvard University, graduating cum laude in 1977 with a bachelor of arts degree in English and, after working at Doubleday Books (a Harvard poetry professor suggested she become a writer or at least work in publishing), enrolled in business school at Stanford University. She dropped out of the graduate program, later recalling that she knew immediately she was not interested in business. Jen finally found her calling, after a trip to China, at the Iowa Writers' Workshop, where she earned a master of fine arts degree in fiction writing in 1983, under the tutelage of such outstanding teachers as novelist BHARATI MUKHERJEE. "I had to become a writer or die," Jen once said in an interview.

Shortly after obtaining her degree, Jen married David O'Connor, and two years later, after living in California while O'Connor worked for Apple Computer, the couple moved to Cambridge, Massachusetts. Although Jen was ready to take a job as a typist, she was accepted as a fellow at Radcliffe's prestigious Bunting Institute in 1987. While there she began writing *Typical American,* based on her short story about the Chang family titled "In the American Society." The book revolves around three Chinese immigrants in New York who pursue the American dream while sometimes retaining and at other times rejecting their Chinese identity. Pub-

lished in 1991, it was critically acclaimed for its darkly comedic, bittersweet voice and endearing, complicated characters.

"This fractured and at times disoriented world [the immigrant experience] is hilariously depicted by Jen in *Typical American,*" write the authors of *Chinese America: The Untold Story of America's Oldest New Community* (2005). In Jen's novel, the newly Americanized Chang family rename themselves the Chang-kees, short for Chinese Yankees. "They want the best of the West for their children," says the author. In fact, as *Typical American* begins, "It's an American story. . . ."

Mona in the Promised Land (1996), Jen's next novel and another *New York Times* Notable Book of the Year, returns to the Chang family, who have now "made it" and moved to a wealthy suburb of New York that resembles Jen's adolescent hometown. In the story, the American-born younger daughter decides to convert to Judaism (her friends call her Changowitz), much to her parents' dismay. "American means being whatever you want," argues the eccentric teenager with her parents. The novel was named of one of the 10 best books of 1996 by the *Los Angeles Times.*

Jen's only published volume of short fiction, *Who's Irish? Stories,* published in 1999, includes eight tragicomic short stories about Chinese and other immigrants who do not fit into ethnic stereotypes. Reviewer Barbara Liss, in the *Houston Chronicle* (November 12, 2004), commented, "It comes as no surprise that most of Jen's protagonists, caught as they are between two cultures, suffer from an identity crisis. . . . These folks are at war with themselves." One of the short stories, "Birthmates," was included in *Best American Short Stories of the Century,* edited by John Updike. Jen said in an interview with Sarah Anne Johnson in *Conversations with American Women Writers* (2004) that she has been influenced by short fiction writer GRACE PALEY, whom she admires for "her humor, her humanity, and her interest in society."

Jen's latest novel, *The Love Wife* (2004), is "her most ambitious and emotionally ample work yet," according to *New York Times* critic Michiko

Kakutani. The fast-paced story revolves around the idiosyncratic Wong family consisting of a Chinese-American husband, a blue-eyed wife named Blondie, two adopted Asian daughters, a biological son, plus a relative, Lanlan, a mysterious survivor of the Cultural Revolution who arrives from mainland China. Disparate narratives are woven skillfully together to present, as one character puts it, "the new American family." *Love Wife*, which was a *San Francisco Chronicle* best seller, draws "to an unusual degree," says the author, on the story of many people. "Her characters are so alive," commented CYNTHIA OZICK, a writer Jen greatly admires, "that one can hardly call them 'characters.' Having lived for a time (too brief a time) with Jen's people as with one's own family, one comes to love them."

Jen's stories have appeared in the *New Yorker, Ploughshares,* the *Atlantic Monthly,* the *New Republic,* and numerous other publications and anthologies, including *The Best American Stories of the Century.* Her honors include the Strauss Living Award from the American Academy of Arts and Letters; Guggenheim, Fulbright (in China), and National Endowment for the Arts fellowships; writer-in-residence at Radcliffe (2002); and the Lannan Award for Fiction. Her three novels are widely taught at colleges and universities, and she has taught fiction at such institutions as Tufts University, University of Massachusetts at Boston, and Harvard University.

Jen, who lives in Cambridge with her husband and two children, told Sarah Anne Johnson that she does not mind "Asian American" being used as a description of her, but she does mind it being used as a definition of her. "Sorting out the differences between being Chinese, American, and Chinese American is one of the themes of my writing," said Gish Jen in an interview in Seattle in 1996. "How much are the groups learning from each other? Are we looking forward? What is my place in America? What are my responsibilities? What should we teach our children? Writing is a way of thinking about looking at ourselves."

Further Reading

Jen, Gish. *The Love Wife.* New York: Knopf, 2004.

———, ed. *Ploughshares.* Fall Fiction Issue, 26, nos. 2 and 3 (2000).

———. *Typical American.* New York: Houghton Mifflin, 1991.

———. *Who's Irish? Stories.* New York: Random House, 1999.

Johnson, Sarah Anne. "Gish Jen." In *Conversations with American Women Writers,* 88–96. Lebanon, N.H.: University Press of New England, 2004.

Kwong, Peter, and Dusanka Miscev. *Chinese America: The Untold Story of America's Oldest New Community,* 256, 304, 340. New York: New Press, 2005.

Whipple, Mary. "Gish Jen." Mostly Fiction Book Reviews. October 12, 2004. Available online. URL: http://mostlyfiction.com/humor/jen.htm. Downloaded on March 1, 2007.

Jewett, Theodora Sarah Orne
(1849–1909) *novelist, short story writer*

Sarah Orne Jewett was a regional writer who spent her literary career depicting and illuminating the residents and the landscape of southern Maine. Her best-known work is *The Country of the Pointed Firs* (1896). It is an elegiac novel composed of vignettes about characters whose lives are intertwined in a small, rural town in Maine, not unlike South Berwick, where Theodora Sarah Orne Jewett was born on September 3, 1849.

Sarah Jewett came from a wealthy, seafaring Maine family. During trips with her father, a distinguished country doctor, she grew to know and respect his patients, the "common people," and the region's harsh but striking landscape. A tall, graceful, intelligent child who considered her father the "best and wisest man" she ever knew, Sarah was strongly influenced by his love of nature and literature. She was a voracious reader with eclectic tastes ranging from George Sand to Rudyard Kipling. Although she received a high school diploma from Berwick Academy in 1865, she was largely self-educated. After reading a novel by HARRIET BEECHER STOWE that was set in Maine, she decided to write about the people and small villages she knew best.

At 18, Jewett published her first story, "Jenny Garrow's Lovers," under a pseudonym in a weekly

Boston periodical. A year later several of her poems and stories, or "sketches" as she preferred to call them, appeared in the prestigious *Atlantic Monthly,* which in 1873 printed her story, "The Shore House." It was the first of a series of related, impressionistic sketches about "things themselves," as Jewett described them, that later were published together as a book-length collection titled *Deephaven* (1877). The sketches were interrelated and revolved around the friendship of two young women vacationing on the coast of Maine. Although the reviews for this book were mixed, Jewett's next three collections of short fiction, verse, and essays were better received by the critics, and her reputation as a regional writer of "local color" was secured.

After her father's death in 1878, Jewett visited Boston more often and became a member of its intellectual literary society. In her early diaries she had mentioned forming intimate friendships with several women. One of them, Annie Adams Fields, the wife of a prominent Boston publisher, became her devoted companion. Fields was one of the city's most celebrated hostesses, as well as a writer. After her husband's death in 1881, Fields and Jewett enjoyed a lengthy, satisfying relationship. This relationship, in which they lived together as a couple, (known in the 19th century as a "Boston Marriage") may have been, although was not necessarily, sexual. It is clear that the two women shared their interests with each other and forged a deep friendship.

Fields and Jewett resided in Boston and at their home in the affluent town of Manchester-by-the-Sea, north of the city. They frequently traveled to Europe, where they befriended luminaries such as Alfred, Lord Tennyson and Henry James. After a visit to Ireland in 1882, Jewett became the first significant American writer to treat seriously the Irish immigrants and the vitality they brought to New England; she published her Irish tales in national periodicals such as *Scribner's* and *McClure's.* But Jewett always looked forward to returning to South Brunswick. It was where she had written her best works and felt most at home. "I was determined,"

she remarked to a Boston journalist, "to teach the world that country people were not the awkward, ignorant set . . . people seemed to think."

Her first and most overtly feminist novel, *A Country Doctor* (1884), is the story of a young, ambitious woman determined to become a physician in spite of sex discrimination and pressure to follow a more conventional path. After struggling with herself, her family, and her community, she decides to attend medical school instead of accepting an attractive marriage proposal. At one point Jewett herself had considered following in her father's footsteps, but she opted instead to pursue a literary career.

Jewett's next short-story collection, *A White Heron and Other Stories* (1886), was praised for its craftsmanship and maturity. In the title story, a young girl grapples with adolescence and the powerful forces of nature. Jewett sets the mood for this inner struggle by contrasting darkness and light, as is demonstrated in the opening paragraph:

> The woods were already filled with shadows one June evening, just before eight o'clock, though a bright sunset still glimmered faintly among the trunks of the trees. A little girl was driving home her cow, a plodding, dilatory, provoking creature in her behavior, but a valued companion for all that. They were going away from the western light, and striking deep into the dark woods. . . .

After producing several books for children, Jewett saw the publication of her most celebrated work, *The Country of the Pointed Firs,* in 1896. Set in an elm-shaded midcoastal harbor village in Maine, the novel (or more accurately, the collection of interrelated sketches) is unified by the relationship between the town's talkative herbalist, Mrs. Almiry Todd, who heals spiritual as well as physical problems, and the narrator.

While some critics considered *Pointed Firs* a slight and sentimental book, most acclaimed the author's subtle, finely crafted small-town character studies. The novel poignantly focuses on the temporary quality of personal relationships—nothing lasts—and on the isolation and frustration characters experience in coping with Maine's economic and social decline. At the same time, *Pointed Firs* celebrates the resilience of its characters and their ability to survive and to thwart the forces of spiritual destruction. Their weapons are knowing how to spin a good yarn, as well as their own unique brand of humor, acuity, and compassion. *The Country of the Pointed Firs* was, like all of Jewett's fiction, deeply rooted in place: a fading but still beautiful world of bitterness, dreams, and longings, where the "grey primness of rosemary was made up of a hundred colors." Jewett was one of the first American writers to subordinate the plot to setting and characterization.

After reading the novel, the American philosopher William James wrote to its author: "It has that incommunicable cleanness of the salt air when one first leaves town." His brother, the novelist Henry James, admired Jewett for her "precise observation, delicate style, and sly humor," while fiction writer WILLA CATHER rated *Pointed Firs* as one of the three enduring masterpieces of American literature. "The young student of American literature in far distant years to come will take up this book and say 'a masterpiece,'" asserted Cather.

Having firmly established her own reputation, Jewett began helping younger writers such as Cather; in 1908 she advised the prairie writer to relinquish "the masquerade" of her male narrator and write from a female point of view. Cather acknowledged her mentor and friend by dedicating *O Pioneers!* (1913) to Jewett. Jewett would also influence regionalist writers KATE CHOPIN and MARY WILKINS FREEMAN.

In 1901 Jewett published her last major work, a popular historical novel called *The Tory Lover;* it went through five printings in three months, although it was not critically well received. That same year she became the first woman to be awarded an honorary doctorate degree from Maine's Bowdoin College, her father's alma mater and, at that time, an all-male institution. "You can't think," she wrote to Annie Fields, "how nice it was to be the single sister of so many brothers."

Sarah Orne Jewett's literary career ended after she suffered from a spinal concussion in a serious carriage accident in 1902. She died seven years later, on June 24, 1909, in her beloved, stately Georgian home in South Berwick. "I was born here and I hope to die here, leaving the lilac bushes still green and growing and all the chairs in their places," she had written. Jewett's home is open to the public; most of the original decor, which had been furnished by her seafaring grandfather, remains intact, including her small writing desk, with its view of the town square, where she did much of her work.

Further Reading

Blanchard, Paula. *Sarah Orne Jewett: Her World and Her Work.* Reading, Mass.: Addison-Wesley, 1994.

Brown, Bill. "Regional Artifacts: The Life of Things in the Work of Sarah Orne Jewett." *American Literary History* 14, no. 2 (2002): 195–226.

Cather, Willa. *Not Under Forty.* New York: Knopf, 1936.

Jewett, Sarah Orne. *The Country of the Pointed Firs, and Other Stories.* New York: Signet Classic, 2000.

May, Stephen. "A Literary Tour of Small-Town Maine." *New York Times,* May 4, 1997, Travel Section, 12, p. 27.

✎ Johnson, Georgia Douglas Camp
(1886–1966)   *poet, playwright*

One of the preeminent black female writers during the Harlem Renaissance of the 1920s, Georgia Douglas Johnson was an accomplished poet and playwright who wrote about social inequality and the mishaps of romantic love.

Born in Atlanta, Georgia, on September 10, 1886, Georgia Douglas Camp attended Atlanta and Howard Universities, Oberlin Conservatory, and the Cleveland College of Music. In 1903 she married Henry Lincoln Johnson, a politician and lawyer, and moved with him to Washington, D.C. The Johnsons' home became a center of literary activity where they entertained such outstanding figures as W. E. B. DuBois, Langston Hughes, and ZORA NEALE HURSTON.

Although she had studied music, Johnson decided to pursue a literary career and published her first book of verse in 1918. *The Heart of a Woman* contained short lyrical poems that touched on romantic themes such as the loneliness women experience after a failed relationship. Although she became one of the first widely recognized black woman poets since FRANCES E. W. HARPER, she later considered *The Heart* too placid and sentimental. "It was not at all race conscious. Then someone said she [the author] has no feeling for the race. So I wrote *Bronze: A Book of Verse* [in 1922]. It is entirely race conscious."

After her husband died in 1925, Johnson had to support herself and her two teenage sons. She found work at a variety of government agencies but continued to write poetry in addition to becoming an accomplished playwright. Johnson's first play, *Blue Blood,* was produced in Harlem in 1927. It was followed by *Plumes: A Play in One Act,* which won *Opportunity* magazine's coveted first-prize award for the best new play of 1927. Her most daring social protest play, *A Sunday Morning in the South* (1928), unflinchingly examined the lynching of a young innocent black man and the collusion between southern police and the Klu Klux Klan. She also produced a play in 1940 about abolitionist Frederick Douglass at the New Negro Theatre in Los Angeles. On the stage as in life, Johnson supported the Pan-African movement and women's rights.

Johnson's third collection of poetry, *An Autumn Love Cycle* (1928), was praised by critics for its skillfully crafted form and mature treatment of love. Her much-anthologized poem "I Want to Die While You Love Me" appears in this volume. Whether dealing with a broken heart or racial discrimination, Johnson understood the disappointment of "burst bubbles" and unfulfilled dreams. Her final collection of verse, *Share My World* (1962), was autobiographical.

Considered one of the finest traditional writers of her time, in 1965 Georgia Douglas Johnson was awarded an honorary doctorate in literature from Atlanta University. She remained active until her death at age 80, on May 14, 1966. Many of her poems and plays are represented in prominent anthologies of black literature. "Her [Johnson's] Romanticism is the Romanticism of the best poetry of the Harlem Renaissance, a facing of life's difficulties through an intensification of experience and a transformation of reality, not an escape from it," asserted Ronald Primeau in *The Harlem Renaissance Remembered.*

Further Reading

Hull, Gloria T. *Color, Sex and Poetry: Three Women Writers of the Harlem Renaissance.* Bloomington: Indiana University Press, 1987.

Johnson, Georgia Douglas. *The Selected Works of Georgia Douglas Johnson.* New York: G. K. Hall, 1997.

———. *The Heart of a Woman, and Other Poems.* New York: AMS Press, 1975.

Martin, George-McKinley. "Georgia Douglas Johnson." The Black Renaissance in Washington, 1920–1930s. Available online. URL: http://www.dclibrary.org/blkren/bios/johnsongd.html. Downloaded on January 22, 2007.

Roses, Lorraine Elena. *The Harlem Renaissance and Beyond: One Hundred Black Women Writers, 1900–1950.* Boston: G. K. Hall, 1989.

∼ Johnson, Marguerite
See ANGELOU, MAYA

∼ Jong, Erica Mann
(1942–   )   *novelist, poet, memoirist*

Erica Jong is best known for her groundbreaking novel *Fear of Flying* (1973). In it she graphically depicts a woman's sexual awakening and erotic escapades as she pursues personal and professional fulfillment and selfhood.

Like *Fear of Flying*'s heroine Isadora Wing, Erica Mann Jong comes from an upper-middle-class Jewish intellectual family in New York City, where she was born on March 26, 1942. Also like Wing, Jong was educated at Barnard College and at Columbia University, where she earned a master's degree in 18th-century literature.

Jong began her prolific literary career in 1971 with *Fruits and Vegetables,* the first of seven volumes

Erica Jong wrote the famous feminist novel
Fear of Flying,
(AP/Wide World Photos)

of poetry. Critics praised her sensual, exuberant verse, and in 1971 *Poetry* magazine awarded her the Bess Hokin Prize, one of numerous awards and fellowships she has received. In her poetry and prose she tries to express "the authentic voice of woman, whether it was sweet and low like the voice of Shakespeare's Cordelia, or raging and powerful like the voice of Lady Macbeth."

Fear of Flying (1973), the first of Jong's eight novels and an instant best seller, was one of the first contemporary American novels to introduce readers to a provocative female author who was willing to explore female sexuality unashamedly and humorously and who created a bright, pas-

sionate protagonist willing to risk the unknown and do the very things that she feared the most. In *Interview* magazine (1987), Jong explained that *Fear of Flying,* which as of 2006 had sold more than 18 million copies worldwide, was not an endorsement of promiscuity, as some male critics had contended: "I wanted to create a thinking woman who also had a sexual life."

After producing another collection of poetry in 1976, Jong wrote a less successful sequel to *Fear of Flying* entitled *How to Save Your Own Life* (1977) and an 18th-century picaresque novel, *Fanny, Being the True History of the Adventures of Fanny Hackabout-Jones.* Isadora Wing, *Fear of Flying*'s protagonist, resurfaced in *Parachutes & Kisses* (1984), a wry tale of coping with middle age in the 1980s. It was followed by two more novels, *Serenissima: A Novel of Venice* (1987) and *Any Woman's Blues* (1990); a children's book about divorce; a semifictional biographical study of writer Henry Miller; in 1994, a candid midlife memoir, *Fear of Fifty,* in which she tells a "certain truth about the interior of [her] life."; and, in 1998, *What Do Women Want? bread, roses, sex, power,* a collection of "inspiration, humor, and provocation."

In an essay in *The Writer on Her Work* (1980), Jong explains that her women characters "are torn, as most of us are torn, between the past and the future, between our mothers' frustrations and the extravagant hopes we have for our daughters." Jong, who has been married four times and lives in New York City and Westport, Connecticut, has a close relationship with her daughter, Molly Jong-Fast, herself a novelist. In 1997 Jong published *Inventing Memory: A Novel of Mother and Daughter.* Her advice to Molly, and to all women, is not to tie themselves "to the mast of anger" but to "sail into the unknown" instead of becoming "paralyzed into immobility by fear."

In 1998 Erica Jong was honored with the United Nations Award for Excellence in Literature. Her novel *Sappho's Leap* (2003) is the imaginative story of Sappho, the amorous Greek poet celebrated for her candid and unapologetic sensuality.

"Jong slips into Sappho's skin, delivering glib commentary on sexual and individual freedom, romantic love power and theology," writes reviewer Jackie Pray in *USA Today*. In 2003 *Fear of Flying* was reissued in a 30th anniversary edition, with an introduction by MAYA ANGELOU. Jong's seminal best-selling modern classic, which greatly influenced the sexual revolution and feminism, has been printed in 35 languages worldwide. *Fear of Flying*, wrote Cristina Nehring in *The Atlantic Monthly* in 2006, "revolutionized the way people thought about women's erotic desire . . . and turned its thirtysomething author into a celebrity."

In *Seducing the Demon: Writing for My Life* (2006), Jong combines a freewheeling memoir with feminist thought and literary criticism. *Publishers Weekly*, in its review of the book, notes that Jong, now in her 60s, is "well-read, well-traveled, therapized, happily married, and sexually satisfied. . . . There is a fine section on women writers who pursued death (Plath, Sexton, Woolf); Jong explains why she refused to be one of them."

Further Reading

Gordon, Lois. "Erica Jong." In *Contemporary Novelists,* ed. D. L. Kirpatrick, 483–485. New York: St. Martin's, 1986.

Hyman, Paula and Deborah D. Moore, eds. *Jewish Women in America: An Historical Encyclopedia*. New York: Routledge, 1997.

Jong, Erica. *Fear of Fifty: A Midlife Memoir.* New York: HarperCollins, 1994.

———. *Fear of Flying* (30th Anniversary Edition). New York: New American Library, 2003.

———. *Ordinary Miracles: New Poems.* New York: New American Library, 1983.

———. *The Poetry of Erica Jong.* 3 vols. New York: Holt, 1976.

———. *Seducing the Demon: Writing for My Life.* New York: Penguin, 2006.

———. *Sappho's Leap.* New York: Norton, 2003.

K

Kincaid, Jamaica (Elaine Potter Richardson)
(1949–)   *novelist, short story writer*

Jamaica Kincaid is a prize-winning Caribbean-American writer whose sensual, autobiographical fiction focuses on West Indian characters and on the often ambivalent relationship between mothers and daughters.

Born Elaine Potter Richardson on May 25, 1949, in St. Johns, Antigua, in the West Indies, Kincaid attributes her keen interest in writing to her mother's early influence. (She did not know of or meet her biological father until later in her life.) "I was very bright; I was always being made fun of for it," she recalled of her childhood.

After immigrating to America at age 16, Kincaid became an au pair in New York City. She honed her writing skills by contributing stories to *Rolling Stone* and the *Paris Review* before publishing, on a regular basis, short stories in the *New Yorker.* In 1976 she became a staff writer at the prestigious *New Yorker,* a position she would hold until 1995.

Her first collection of stories, *At the Bottom of the River* (1983), was critically acclaimed for its vivid descriptions of the Caribbean as well as its surreal quality. The book, which won the Morton Dauwen Zabel Award of the American Academy and Institute of Arts and Letters, included one of Kincaid's most popular stories, "Girl." Comprised almost entirely of a catalogue of demands by a mother to her daughter—typical of the author's upbringing—the solemn repetition begins to "take on nearly mystical importance," noted novelist ANNE TYLER: "This is how you set a table for tea; this is how you set a table for dinner; this is how you set a table for dinner with an important guest." Kincaid was hailed as an important new voice in American fiction.

In 1985 Kincaid's first novel, *Annie John,* was published. Semiautobiographical and emanating a strong sense of place, it contained eight interrelated stories about an adolescent's coming-of-age in Antigua and her struggle to separate from her mother. *Library Journal* selected it as one of the best books of 1985.

Kincaid returned to Antigua after a 25-year hiatus and then published her reactions in *A Small Place*—a long, searing critical essay about the corruption of her beloved native country:

The Antigua that I knew, the Antigua in which I grew up, is not the Antigua you, a tourist, would see now. That Antigua no longer exists partly for the usual reason, the passing of time, and partly because the bad-minded people who used to rule over it, the English, no longer do.

Her next novel, *Lucy* (1990), more or less a sequel to *Annie John* but with a different protagonist, is based largely on the author's experiences as a teenage au pair working for a wealthy white couple in New York, and about her mother, whom she both loves and despises. In an article in the *New York Times Magazine,* the esteemed West Indian poet Derek Walcott called the richly detailed book "true to life, without any artificiality . . . so full of spiritual contradictions . . . extremely profound and courageous."

In 1995 Kincaid produced a third novel, *The Autobiography of My Mother,* which was a finalist for the National Book Critics Circle Award for fiction and the PEN Faulkner Award, both in 1997.

The first-person story poignantly recounts the long, difficult life of an elderly woman from the West Indies who longed for "the voices that should have come of me, the faces I never allowed to form, the eyes I never allowed to see." Much of Kincaid's work is about physical and emotional loss. In 1997 she wrote a poignant biography about her brother and his struggle with AIDS. She also is an avid gardener who in 1998 edited *My Favorite Plant,* a collection of stories, essays, and poems by gardeners and writers. A year later she published *My Garden,* a compendium of her own reflections on gardening. "Sometimes I do what suits me, sometimes I do in the garden just whatever I please," she wrote in one of the essays.

In *Talk Stories* (2001), Kincaid selected 77 of her short pieces that had appeared in the popular "Talk of the Town" column in the *New Yorker* from 1976 to 1983. And in 2005 she edited *The Best American Travel Writing 2005,* an anthology of carefully selected personal accounts by such esteemed travel writers as John McPhee and Simon Winchester, and wrote *Among Flowers: A Walk in the Himalayas,* the story of her remarkable plant-hunting expedition into the foothills of the Himalayas.

The African-American studies scholar Henry Louis Gates, Jr., in *Harper's Bazaar,* compared Kincaid's work to that of the venerated novelist TONI MORRISON.

There is a self-contained world which they explore with great detail. Not to chart the existence of that world, but to show that human emotions manifest themselves everywhere. . . . Kincaid never feels the necessity of claiming the existence of a black world or a female sensibility. She assumes them both.

Jamaica Kincaid is a naturalized American citizen. She resides in North Bennington, Vermont, with her two children, having divorced her husband, the composer Allen Shawn. She is a fervent advocate of civil rights for minorities and, as a convert to Judaism, serves as president of her local Reconstructionist synagogue.

Further Reading

Dance, D. Cumber, ed. *Fifty Caribbean Writers.* Westport, Conn.: Greenwood, 1986.

Kincaid, Jamaica. *Among Flowers: A Walk in the Himalayas.* Washington, D.C.: National Geographic Publishing, 2005.

———. *Annie John.* Farrar, Straus and Giroux, 1985.

———. *The Autobiography of My Mother.* Farrar, Straus and Giroux, 1995.

———. *A Small Place* (essays). New York: Farrar, Straus and Giroux, 1988.

———. *Talk Stories.* With a foreword by Ian Frazier. New York: Farrar, Straus and Giroux, 2001.

Simmons, Diane. *Jamaica Kincaid.* New York: Macmillan, 1994.

Kingsolver, Barbara
(1955–)   *novelist, short story writer*

With the eyes of a scientist and the vision of a poet, Barbara Kingsolver writes about family ties and life choices, using resilient, defiant characters who hail from America's Southwest.

Born on April 8, 1955, in Annapolis, Maryland, and raised in a small town in eastern Kentucky, Barbara, as a child, was by her own admission an "inordinate storyteller." She graduated magna cum laude from DePauw University in 1977 and received a master's degree in science from the University of Arizona, where she also worked as a technical writer.

In 1985 Kingsolver became a full-time writer and married Joseph Hoffman, a chemist, with whom she had a daughter, Camille. "I can hardly count the ways that being a mother has broadened my writing, deepened my connection to all other women, and galvanized my commitment to the Earth and its fate," she mused in *High Tide in Tucson* (1995).

Fiction writer and essayist Barbara Kingsolver is pictured here in 1992.
(AP/Wide World Photos)

Kingsolver's first novel, *The Bean Trees,* appeared to critical acclaim in 1988. Taylor Greer, its no-nonsense protagonist, leaves her home in rural Kentucky in search of a more fulfilling life but unexpectedly becomes the guardian of an abandoned two-year-old Cherokee girl whom she names Turtle. Praised for its sensitivity, humor, and musical quality, *Ms.* magazine noted that "from the very first page [the characters] tug at the heart and soul." Kingsolver once commented that she wanted her fiction to "pull readers into the troubles and joys of people they might otherwise not know."

On the heels of success, Kingsolver came out with another favorably reviewed book, *Homeland and Other Stories* (1989), a collection of short stories about women in the Southwest who, explains the author, are "finding a home, a place for themselves."

After completing a study of the role women played during the Arizona copper mine strike of 1983, Kingsolver wrote the PEN fiction prize–winning novel *Animal Dreams* (1990). It traces the story of a woman who returns to her rural hometown in Arizona after a 14-year hiatus. The science fiction writer URSULA K. LE GUIN described *Animal Dreams* as belonging to a "new fiction of relationship, aesthetically rich, full of bitter pain, and of great political and spiritual significance. . . ."

Turning to verse, in 1992 Kingsolver produced *Another America/Otra America,* a collection of poems in English and Spanish that deal compassionately with the experiences of Latinos. A year later, she published *Pigs in Heaven,* a sequel to *The Bean Trees,* set three years after Greer illegally adopts Turtle.

Kingsolver also has proven to be a skillful essayist. In *High Tide in Tucson* she explores topics that range from her divorce from Hoffman to the importance of preserving the natural world. In one essay she defines art as "the antidote that can call us back from the edge of numbness, restoring the ability to feel for another." *The Poisonwood Bible* (1998), a best-selling novel about a family's life-changing experiences in the Congo in 1959, was named a Best Book of 1998 by editors of the *New York Times Book Review.* The epic novel was also a finalist for the Pulitzer Prize and won the National Book Prize of South Africa.

In 2000 Barbara Kingsolver was awarded the National Humanities Medal, America's highest honor for service through the arts. Her work since then includes *Prodigal Summer* (2000), a novel that sensually weaves together three stories about love during one summer and the protagonists' relationships to one another, and even more so to the land in southern Appalachia. *Small Wonder* (2002) is a collection of 23 essays that represent the author's personal response to terrorism by celebrating nature, family, literature, and the joys of everyday life.

Nature has always served as the inspiration for Kingsolver's work. "With all due respect for the wondrous ways people have invented to amuse themselves and one another on paved surfaces," she writes in *Small Wonder,* "I find that this exodus from the land makes me unspeakably sad." Her next project, using both words and images, was *Last Stand: America's Virgin Lands* (2002), published with award-winning photographer Annie Griffiths Belt for the National Geographic Society. "In the places that call me out, I know I'll recover my wordless childhood trust in the largeness of life and its willingness to take me in," Kingsolver ponders.

In 2007 the author penned an entertaining nonfiction narrative, *Animal, Vegetable, Miracle,* that describes a year living off the land with her second husband, biologist Steven L. Hopp, and her two daughters, on a farm in Appalachia, Virginia, where they now reside.

Further Reading

"Bill Moyers Interviews Barbara Kingsolver." NOW with Bill Moyers, PBS. May 24, 2002. Available online. URL: http://www.pbs.org/NOW/transcript/transcript_kingsolver.html. Downloaded on January 22, 2007.

Butler, Jack. "The Bean Trees: She Hung the Moon and Plugged in All the Stars." *New York Times Book Review,* April 10, 1988, p. 15.

Kingsolver, Barbara, with Steven L. Hopp and Camille Kingsolver. *Animal, Vegetable, Miracle.* New York: HarperCollins, 2007.

———. *The Bean Trees.* New York: Harper & Row, 1988.

———. *High Tide in Tucson: Essays from Now or Never.* New York: HarperCollins, 1995.

———. *Small Wonder.* New York: HarperCollins, 2002.

Kingston, Maxine Hong
(1940–)   *novelist, memoirist*

Weaving together childhood memories, fiction, and oral history, Maxine Hong Kingston has written two award-winning books, *The Woman Warrior* and *China Men,* which are based largely on her cultural identity as a Chinese-American woman.

Born in Stockton, California, on October 27, 1940, to Chinese immigrants, as a child Maxine worked in her parent's laundry and listened intently to her mother's "mysterious and marvelous" stories about China. An avid reader and writer, in 1962 she received a bachelor of arts degree in English literature from the University of California at Berkeley, where she is currently a professor.

Kingston has contributed stories, articles, and poems to a variety of well-known magazines and journals, including the *New Yorker, Ms.,* and *American Heritage.* Her first book, *The Woman Warrior: Memoir of a Girlhood among Ghosts* (1976), combined autobiography and fiction and was primarily a recounting of "ghosts" that haunted Kingston's childhood: the "foreigners"— white Americans with whom she went to school but from whom she was estranged—and her Asian ancestors, whose "lessons to grow up on," both real and imaginary, were related to her by her mother, known in the book as "Brave Orchid." As a feminist, Kingston challenged Chinese culture as being patriarchal, even though she was fiercely proud of her heritage. And although she admitted to being part of it, she also lambasted the white-dominated society. "I had to make room for paradoxes," she explained.

Critics acclaimed the fictional memoir as "extraordinarily rich" and "savagely terrifying," and Kingston as one of the most poetic storytellers and interpreters of the Chinese-American experience from a woman's perspective. *The Woman Warrior* won the National Book Critics Circle Award for the best book of nonfiction published in 1976 and was cited by *Time* magazine as one of the top 10 nonfiction works of the decade. In it Kingston recreates, simply and directly, the life of a "No Name" Chinese aunt who committed "spite suicide" after bearing an illegitimate child; the adventures of a legendary Chinese woman warrior; the story of her mother's life in China as a physician and midwife and in America, where she toiled as a laundress and field hand; and her own tale of reconciling the "ghosts" of her Chinese past with her Americanized self. In the first section of *Woman Warrior,* Kingston asks:

Chinese-Americans, when you try to understand what things in you are Chinese, how do you separate what is peculiar to childhood, to poverty, insanities, one family, your mother who marked your growing with stories, from what is Chinese? What is Chinese tradition and what is the movies?

Her second book, *China Men* (1980), which also mixes fact and fiction, is the story of several generations of Chinese "founding fathers" who had come to America to find the "Gold Mountain" of Chinese legend. Although a composite of the experiences of numerous men, it specifically focuses on Kingston's father, a scholar and teacher in China who became a laundryman and gambling house manager in America; her grandfather; and her Hawaiian great-grandfather. *China Men* won the American Book Award for nonfiction in 1981 and was runner-up for a Pulitzer Prize.

While classified as nonfiction, Kingston's books are, asserted novelist ANNE TYLER in the *New Republic,* "fiction at its best—novels, fairytales, epic poems . . . edges blur, the dividing line passes unnoticed. . . . [I]t shifts between the concrete and the mythical."

In 1990 Kingston published *Tripmaster Monkey: His Fake Book* (1990), a long, richly textured, humorous novel revolving around a young Chinese American who lives in the present despite the consequences. Considered a surreal Asian-

American *Ulysses,* it received the PEN West Award for fiction.

Beginning in 1967, Kingston and her husband, Earll, an actor, and their son, Joseph Lawrence Chung Mei, lived in Honolulu, Hawaii, where she taught English at a drop-in high school, at private schools, and at the University of Hawaii. In 1980 she was named a "Living Treasure of Hawaii." After living there for 17 years, the Kingstons returned to the mainland and now reside in California; in 1998 she published a collection of essays entitled *Hawaii: One Summer.*

In 1998 President Bill Clinton selected Maxine Hong Kingston as one of 10 honorees to receive a National Humanities Medal. She has garnered four honorary doctoral degrees and numerous awards, including the American Academy and Institute of Arts and Letters award in literature in 1990.

Her most recent publication, *The Fifth Book of Peace* (2003), combines memoir, history, and culture. The poignant story of loss and reconciliation grew out of Kingston's traumatic loss of her home, all her possessions, and the manuscript of a nearly completed book in the Oakland, California, firestorm of 1991. She used that tragedy as a metaphor for war and peace and at the same time began teaching writing to Vietnam War veterans, to help them express themselves. "The only way I could regain my creativity was to write in a community," she realized.

"As she hoped, the writing became a process of healing, renewal, and hope both for Kingston and for the veterans who had experienced so much devastation," according to The National Women's History Project, which selected Kingston as a 2004 Women's History Month Honoree, noting that the author "blends her melodic and poetic storytelling ability with her rich Chinese ancestry and her cultural struggles. The result is partly autobiographical, partly fiction, but her writings are masterpieces of literature that have helped recent generations discover the fullness of their own spirit."

When asked about her distinctive writing style, during an interview with Powells.com, Kingston explained that she has various ways of melding the

Chinese and Western experiences. "My hands are writing English, but my mouth is speaking Chinese," she said. "Somehow I am able to write a language that captures the Chinese rhythms and tones and images, getting that power into English. I am working in some kind of fusion language."

Further Reading

Huang, Guiyou. "Maxine Hong Kingston." In *Asian American Novelists: A Bio-Bibliographical Critical Sourcebook,* edited by Emmanuel S. Nelson, 138–155. Westport, Conn.: Greenwood Press, 2000.

Kingston, Maxine Hong. *China Men.* New York: Alfred A. Knopf, 1980.

———. *The Fifth Book of Peace.* New York: Alfred A. Knopf, 2003.

———. *Tripmaster Monkey: His Fake Book.* New York: Vintage, 1990.

———. *The Woman Warrior: Memoirs of a Girlhood among Ghosts.* New York: Alfred A. Knopf, 1976.

"Maxine Hong Kingston." The National Women's History Project. Available online. URL: http://www.nwhp.org/resourcecenter/biographycenter.php#Kingston. Downloaded on January 22, 2007.

Sabine, Maureen. *Maxine Hong Kingston's Broken Book of Life: An Intertextual Study of the Woman Warrior and Chinese Men.* Honolulu: University of Hawaii Press, 2004.

∾ Kumin, Maxine Winokur
(1925–)   *poet, short story writer, novelist*

Maxine Kumin, whose book *Up Country: Poems of New England* (1972) received the Pulitzer Prize in poetry in 1973, lyrically weaves traditional and orderly verse from the author's everyday experiences.

Born in Philadelphia, Pennsylvania, on June 6, 1925, to Jewish parents, Maxine Winokur attended a Catholic high school, where, she recalls, she wrote "very bad late-adolescent romantic poetry." She went on to receive a bachelor's and a master's degree from Radcliffe College in Cambridge, Massachusetts.

In 1946 Winokur married Victor Kumin, an engineering consultant, and moved with him to a suburb of Boston, where they had three children. Seeking intellectual stimulation, she signed up for a poetry workshop, at which she befriended another "mother-from-the-suburbs" poet, ANNE SEXTON, with whom she would collaborate on four children's books.

The first of Kumin's many well-received volumes of poetry, *Halfway,* appeared in 1961 and was composed of 40 poems, many of which were drawn from childhood recollections and her relationship to nature. After winning several literary prizes and fellowships, in 1973 her fourth volume of verse, *Up Country: Poems of New England,* garnered the Pulitzer Prize. The book was praised for its technical expertise and meticulous observations; novelist JOYCE CAROL OATES reviewed it by acknowledging its debt to Henry David Thoreau but noting the "sharp-edged, unflinching and occasionally nightmarish subjectivity [that is] exasperatingly absent in Thoreau."

Kumin, in *To Make a Prairie* (1979), said that in her work she tries "to be true to actuality." She has been compared to Robert Frost, for paying close attention to the rhythms of rural New England without sentimentalizing it. She has also been linked with the confessional poets, her peers Anne Sexton and SYLVIA PLATH, in part because her verse is frequently autobiographical. (The confessional poets tended to emphasize their personal suffering, often related to romantic or familial relationships.) But while Kumin insists that "poetry is essentially elegiac in nature," she also celebrates life and order, as witnessed by nature, and the need to survive; as one critic explained it, "her mode is memorial rather than confessional."

Skeptical but hopeful, quirky but universal, Kumin's vivid verse, which is about ordinary things in life, has appeared in literary periodicals such as the *New Yorker, Harper's, Poetry,* and *Partisan Review.* She has taught at a number of universities, including Tufts, Brandeis, and Columbia; is the recipient of six honorary degrees; and in 1980 received an American Academy and Institute of Arts and Letters Award for excellence in literature. She has also served as poetry consultant to the

Library of Congress, was awarded the Poets Prize in 1993, and received the Aiken/Taylor Award for Modern Poetry in 1995. That same year Kumin became a chancellor of the Academy of American Poets but resigned that post four years later, along with poet Carolyn Kizer, in protest over the board's reluctance to admit poets of color. "I don't like the way the collection of chancellors sets itself apart from the mainstream," said Kumin. "I don't want to see it identified with elitism." The academy relented and restructured its bylaws.

Her more recent books include a mystery titled *Quit Monks or Die!,* published in 1999, the same year she garnered the Ruth E. Lily Prize; *Inside the Halo and Beyond: The Anatomy of a Recovery* (2000), a memoir about her torturous recovery, of body and soul, from an equestrian accident in 1998 that left her with a broken neck and serious internal injuries; *Always Beginning: Essays on a Life in Poetry* (2000); *The Long Marriage: Poems* (2001), which includes tributes to poets she admires such as MURIEL RUKEYSER, as well as two poems about the agony of having survived the suicide in 1974 of her friend Anne Sexton ("there is no oblivion," writes Kumin); and *Jack and Other New Poems*

(2005), another well-received collection. "The power that Kumin draws from and brings to literature is potent and seemingly inexhaustible," asserted a *Booklist* critic about Kumin's earthy, accessible, well-balanced verse.

Although a prolific poet, Maxine Kumin also has published short stories, a memoir, several widely praised novels, four collections of essays, and two dozen books for children. When not dealing with farm chores, friends, or family, she raises Arabian horses and takes care of a large vegetable garden on her farm in rural New Hampshire.

Further Reading

Grosholz, Emily, ed. *Telling the Barn Swallow: Poets on the Poetry of Maxine Kumin.* Hanover, N.H.: University Press of New England, 1997.

Kumin, Maxine. *Inside the Halo and Beyond: The Anatomy of a Recovery.* New York: W. W. Norton, 2000.

———. *Jack and Other New Poems.* New York: W. W. Norton, 2005.

———. *To Make a Prairie: Essays on Poets, Poetry, and Country Living.* Ann Arbor: University of Michigan Press, 1979.

———. *Up Country: Poems of New England.* New York: Harper, 1972.

Lady of Massachusetts, A
See FOSTER, HANNAH WEBSTER

Lahiri, Jhumpa
(1967–   )   *short-story writer, novelist*

The winner of a Pulitzer Prize for her collection of short stories *Interpreter of Maladies* (1999), Jhumpa Lahiri, whose distinctive, wry, deceptively spare, and empathetic literary voice has been acclaimed by critics and readers alike, also wrote the best-selling novel *The Namesake* (2003). Lahiri's varied motifs include miscommunication, loss, troubled relationships, a sense of otherness, and the eternal quest for self-identity and self-acceptance.

Jhumpa Lahiri was born in 1967 in London, England, to Bengali immigrant parents from Calcutta. Her mother is a teacher who has a master's degree in literature, and her father worked as a librarian at the University of Rhode Island, not far from South Kingston, the small New England town where the Lahiris moved when Jhumpa was three and where she was raised. She frequently traveled to Calcutta with her parents and younger sister for long visits that would have a profound effect on her later work.

Lahiri recalls creating stories and mini-novels from the time she was seven, sometimes in collaboration with her best friend during recess. Although she wrote for her high school newspaper, she had stopped writing fiction by the time she went to college. She graduated with a bachelor of arts degree in English literature from New York City's Barnard College but was rejected from several graduate English programs. While waiting to reapply, Lahiri worked as a research assistant in a non-profit organization in Cambridge, Massachusetts, and learned how to use a computer; it became her tool for writing more serious fiction when she was not working. Eventually she earned master's degrees in English, creative writing, and comparative literature and the arts before obtaining a Ph.D. in Renaissance studies, all at Boston University.

Although she had the credentials to become a professor of literature, she recognized that her true calling was creative writing. The year after she finished her doctoral dissertation, Lahiri was accepted as a fellow in writing at the Fine Arts Work Center in Provincetown, Massachusetts. "That changed everything," she said in an interview. "It was something of a miracle. In seven months I got an agent, sold a book, and had a story published in the *New Yorker.* I've been extremely lucky." In 1999 Lahiri was named by the *New Yorker* as one of the 20 best writers under the age of 40.

When Lahiri received the prestigious Pulitzer Prize for fiction in 2000 for *Interpreter of Maladies,* it surprised both the recipient (she had no idea she was a contender) and the literary community, in part because Lahiri's work was not very well known: Three of her stories had appeared in the *New Yorker* in 1998, and a few others elsewhere. In addition, it is more common for novels, rather than short fiction, to win Pulitzers. But the collection of nine stories, highlighting Lahiri's acute, penetrating observations of familial and romantic relationships and her bemused, precise writing style, was a huge success. *Interpreter of Maladies* has been translated into 29 languages, including Bengali, Hindi, and Marathiand, and became a best seller both in America and abroad. By 2005 it had sold 500,000 copies and helped earn Lahiri the American Academy of Arts and Letters, the Addison M. Metcalf, the PEN/Hemingway, and the *New Yorker* Best Debut of the Year awards.

In 1999 the title story, "Interpreter of Maladies," was selected for an O. Henry award and included in *The Best American Short Stories.* According to Lahiri, it had to be the title story of the collection because "it best expresses, thematically, the predicament of the heart of the book—the dilemma, the difficulty, and often the impossibility of communicating emotional pain and affliction to others, as well as expressing it to ourselves." That is why being a writer, she says, also can mean being an interpreter, in the attempt to articulate those emotions. "Lahiri is one of the finest short-story writers I've read," commented her contemporary AMY TAN, while *New York Times* critic Michiko Kakutani praised Lahiri's "uncommon elegance and poise. With *Interpreter of Maladies* she has made a precocious debut."

The author, who became an American citizen when she was 18, represents a new generation of Indian writers who have opted for more subtle, sensual, and finely crafted traditional fiction over magical realism, with its emphasis on sensational effects and exaggerated characters and circum-

stances. Although Lahiri's work has sometimes been described by Indian scholars as "diaspora fiction" and by American critics as "immigrant fiction," and many of her characters are immigrants, expatriates, and first-generation Americans, "her real subject is miscommunication," contends Paul Brians in *Modern South Asian Literature in English* (2003). "The relationships in her stories are a series of missed connections."

Mostly set in America and written from a second-generation Indian American point of view, Lahiri explains that her work "is less a response to her parents' cultural nostalgia and more an attempt to forge her own amalgamated domain." Some book reviewers have grouped Lahiri with so-called classic American authors, such as Ernest Hemingway, rather than so-called ethnic writers such as Amy Tan. Nonetheless, in an interview with her publisher, Lahiri observed that identity is always a difficult issue, "especially so for those who are culturally displaced, as immigrants are, or those who grow up in two worlds simultaneously. . . . The feeling that there was no single place to which I fully belonged bothered me growing up. It bothers me less now."

In January 2001 Lahiri, a soft-spoken, well-coiffed, attractive woman with large expressive eyes, married Alberto Vourvoulias-Bush, a Guatemalan Greek journalist, in a traditional two-hour Hindu ceremony held in Calcutta. The paparazzi staked out the Pulitzer Prize winner's wedding, climbing on top of neighboring rooftops with their cameras. Somehow Lahiri, desperate for privacy, managed to keep them away from the wedding.

In 2002 Lahiri received a Guggenheim Fellowship. A year later *The Namesake,* her best-selling debut novel, which focuses on the children of immigrants rather than their first-generation parents, was released. Lahiri's amusing, defiant, conflicted characters were "Calcutta-born New England transplants and other American-born children who might have crossed paths with the uprooted Bengalis of her short stories," wrote Sheila Benson in the *Seattle Weekly.* Lahiri describes *The Namesake* as, essentially, "a story about life in

Lahiri has taught creative writing at Boston University and the Rhode Island School of Design. She resides in Brooklyn, New York, with her husband and son, Octavio, a second-generation American-born Guatemalan Greek Bengali.

Further Reading

Atpe, Sudheer. "The Namesake: Jhumpa Lahiri." MostlyFiction.com. September 7, 2003. Available online. URL: http://mostlyfiction.com/world/lahiri.htm. Downloaded on January 22, 2007.

Brians, Paul. "Jhumpa Lahiri: Interpreter of Maladies." In *Modern South Asian Literature in English,* 195–204. Westport, Conn.: Greenwood Press, 2003.

Flynn, Sean. "Women We Love: Jhumpa Lahiri." *Esquire,* October 2000, pp. 172–173.

Lahiri, Jhumpa. *Interpreter of Maladies.* Boston: Houghton Mifflin, 1999.

———. *The Namesake.* Boston: Houghton Mifflin, 2003.

Selvadora, Shyam, ed. "Jhumpa Lahiri: This Blessed House." In *Story-Wallah: A Celebration of South Asian Fiction,* 391–410. New York: Houghton Mifflin, 2005.

Prize-winning Jhumpa Lahiri writes luminously about loss, identity, and alienation.
(Courtesy Houghton Mifflin/©Marion Ettinger)

the United States. . . . The terrain is very much the terrain of my own life—New England and New York, with Calcutta always hovering in the background." In her review of *The Namesake,* Teresa Wilz of the *Washington Post* asserted that "It is the complications of being a hyphenated American that informs Lahiri's work, the same challenges that face Gogol, the American-born protagonist in this coming-of-age tale." A film, *The Namesake,* adapted from Lahiri's novel, was released in 2007.

∾ Larsen, Nella
(1891–1964)   *novelist, short story writer*

A major writer of the Harlem Renaissance, Nella Larsen is known best for two short novels, *Quicksand* (1928) and *Passing* (1929). She was the first African-American woman to win a Guggenheim fellowship, in 1930. More recently, accomplished black female writers such as MAYA ANGELOU and ALICE WALKER rediscovered Larsen's work and have expressed their admiration for the enigmatic but talented writer who had the temerity, in the early 20th century, to portray candidly characters, especially women, confronting racial, sexual, and class issues.

Larsen was born Nellie Walker in 1891 in Chicago, the daughter of Mary Hansen, a Danish dressmaker, and a light-skinned African-American father named Peter Walker. It is difficult to ascertain biographical details about Larsen's life because of conflicting or obscure information she provided during interviews and in her written work: She constantly was reinventing herself. Larsen's parents separated (or her birth father died) soon after she was born, and in 1893 her mother married Peter Larsen, a white man, and raised her daughter as white, perhaps even denying that she had given birth to an African American. (In her scholarly work, Larsen's biographer, Thadious M. Davis, conjectures that Peter Walker, who "passed" as white to get a job with the Chicago railroad, and Peter Larsen may have been the same person, which would help explain why Larsen guarded and altered her family's history.)

After her stepfather enrolled her, with her mother's blessing, at Fisk University Normal School (now Fisk University), a highly regarded African-American institution in Nashville, Tennessee, 16-year-old Larsen felt that her family could no longer pretend that she was white, which is why they sent her away to a black school. Although she took her stepfather's surname, she permanently severed relationships with her family. It also marked the beginning of Larsen's lifelong identity crisis. She left Fisk for the Lincoln Hospital Training School for Nursing in New York City, graduating in 1915 and practicing nursing, first in Alabama as head nurse at John Andrew Memorial Hospital and Nurse Training School, and then back in New York City, for several years.

In 1919 she married Elmer S. Imes, a physicist, and frequently would use his last name, even after she separated from him. The couple settled in Harlem, an uptown area of Manhattan, where they befriended influential African-American figures in the burgeoning Harlem arts movement such as W. E. B. DuBois, the pioneering black sociologist and civil rights leader; writer and editor JESSIE FAUSET; and Walter White, director of the National Association for the Advancement of Colored People (NAACP), who would later read Larsen's drafts of *Quicksand* and encourage her to complete the manuscript and submit it to publishers. Many of these luminaries, including Larsen, played important roles in what became known as the Harlem Renaissance— a movement that promoted African-American literature, art, and music during the 1920s.

From the early 1920s until 1926, Larsen, who had become disillusioned with nursing, worked as a librarian at the Harlem branch of New York City's public library system while taking courses at Columbia University's library school. At the same time she began to write creatively. Her first two published articles, about Danish games, appeared in *Brownies' Book* (June 1920; July 1920), a children's magazine edited by Jessie Fauset. Six years later she published two stories in *Young's Magazine* under the pseudonymous anagram Allen Semi (her married name reversed).

Larsen, whose marriage and health were failing, gave up her job as a librarian to work full time on her landmark novels. The central protagonist of *Quicksand* (1928) is an educated, refined African American whose mother is white and whose black father was never around, who bravely attempts to cope with being a multiracial woman with middle-class aspirations. *Quicksand* won the Harmon Foundation's Bronze Award for Literature and was critically well received. The psychologically complex semiautobiographical novel sensitively tackled subjects such as illegitimacy and interracial relationships, taboo topics at that time. W. E. B. DuBois praised it as the "best piece of fiction that Negro America has produced since the heyday of [the celebrated writer Charles] Chesnutt." Decades later, Alice Walker described Larsen's fiction as "absolutely absorbing, fascinating, and indispensable."

The second novel, *Passing* (1929), focuses on two characters: African-American Clare Kendry passes for a white woman and is married to a white man unaware of her racial heritage. Her childhood friend, Irene Redfield, who also is light-skinned but opts to define herself as black and remains in the African-American community, is fearful that Kendry is trying to steal her husband from her. "Taken together, Larsen's two novels comprise the most fully developed black American female characters of any writers until that time," wrote Charles R. Larson in *The Oxford Companion to Women's Writing*. Davis, Larsen's biographer, adds, in the introduction to a recently reprinted edition of *Pass-*

ing, that Larsen depicts with trenchancy "the golden days of black cultural consciousness" and unapologetically "critiques a social insistence on race as essential and fixed."

Despite having faced disturbing accusations of plagiarism for her short story "Sanctuary," Larsen became the first African-American woman to be awarded a Guggenheim fellowship, in fiction, a grant she held in 1930–31. The coveted fellowship enabled her to do research in Europe, which is where she penned her third novel, *Mirage.* After the manuscript was rejected by several publishers, Larsen returned to America, obtained a divorce in 1933, and during the 1940s, identifying herself as Mrs. Nella L. Imes, worked in a variety of supervisory nursing positions in hospitals in Brooklyn, New York. However, she never recovered psychologically from the fallout of the plagiarism charges and the failure of her third novel. For the most part she stopped writing and had no contact with her coterie of Harlem friends.

Nella Larsen, an accomplished novelist "who wrote highly charged interior dramas of the black middle class in Harlem that were original and hugely insightful," according to a *New York Times* critic, was found dead in her New York apartment on March 30, 1964, practically in obscurity. The cause of death was listed "unspecified." During the 1970s, her fiction, like that of several other now-prominent African-American women writers, was rediscovered and reprinted.

Further Reading

Davis, Thadious M. *Nella Larsen, Novelist of the Harlem Renaissance: A Woman's Life Unveiled.* Baton Rouge: Louisiana State University Press, 1994.

Gates, Henry Louis, Jr., and Nellie Y. McKay, eds. *The Norton Anthology of African American Literature,* 2nd ed. New York: W. W. Norton, 2004.

Hutchinson, George. *In Search of Nella Larsen.* Cambridge, Mass.: Harvard University Press, 2006.

Larsen, Nella. *The Complete Fiction of Nella Larsen: Passing, Quicksand, and The Stories.* Edited by Charles R. Larson. New York: Anchor, 2001.

———. *Passing.* Reprint, with an introduction by Ntozake Shange. New York: Random House, 2002.

McLendon, Jacquelyn Y. *The Politics of Color in the Fiction of Jessie Fauset and Nella Larsen.* Charlottesville: University Press of Virginia, 1995.

Laurie, Annie

See BONFILS, MARTHA WINIFRED SWEET BLACK

Lazarus, Emma
(1849–1887) *poet, novelist*

Poet, translator, and novelist Emma Lazarus is best known as the author of the stirring words engraved on the Statue of Liberty that have for generations welcomed the "huddled masses, yearning to breathe free" to America.

A descendant of Sephardic Jews who had fled the Spanish Inquisition in the 1600s, Emma Lazarus was born in New York City on July 22, 1849, into an affluent family. A dark-eyed, shy, intelligent child who excelled at languages and literature, Emma published her first book, *Poems and Translations* (1867), when she was 18. Literary luminary Ralph Waldo Emerson admired the collection, both for its original poetry and for the astute translations of French and German writers it contained. Serving as a mentor, he encouraged Emma to continue writing. She dedicated her second book of verse, *Admetus, and Other Poems* (1871), to him.

During the 1870s and 1880s Lazarus continued to earn critical acclaim for her poetry, while her first novel, *Alide: An Episode of Goethe's Life* (1874), based on Goethe's conflicting demands as an artist and as an ordinary citizen, was praised by critics such as the Russian novelist Ivan Turgenev. Her next work, *Poems and Translations of Heinrich Heine* (1881), was considered her greatest achievement as a translator; it included the renowned German poet's verse on Jewish subjects.

Lazarus's interest in her religious and cultural heritage was rekindled after reading George Eliot's novel *Daniel Deronda,* which called for a Jewish national revival movement. She also learned about

Russian pogroms that had decimated Jewish villages in 1881 and 1882. To better educate herself, she studied Hebrew and translated the classic poetry of great literary figures of Spain's Jewish golden age such as Judah Halevi. One of her most passionate works was a verse drama that appeared in *Songs of a Semite* (1882), a collection Lazarus insisted be issued in an inexpensive edition so working-class people could afford it. She dedicated "The Dance of Death" to George Eliot; it graphically described the slaughter of medieval Jews during a 14th-century pogrom in Germany, and the redemption of the victims. "Even as we die in honor, from our death / Shall bloom a myriad of heroic lives," she wrote.

After meeting with Russian Jewish immigrants who were arriving steadily at Ellis Island, Lazarus become obsessed with their cause. She gave them money, volunteered her services at settlements on New York's Lower East Side, and defended them from anti-Semitic attacks in the press. "I'm all Israel's now," she explained "till this cloud passes—I have no thought, no passion, no desire, save for my own people." *An Epistle to the Hebrew* (1883) depicts Lazarus's Zionist belief in a national and cultural revival of Jewish life in America and Israel. Still a secular intellectual, she also wrote an essay calling for an American literature that was independent of British tradition.

Lazarus's most famous poem was "The New Colossus," a sonnet written in 1883, when she was 34, to benefit a fund for the construction of the pedestal at the foot of the Statue of Liberty. When asked by the chairwoman of the committee to submit a poem that could then be auctioned off for the fund, Lazarus replied, "I cannot write verse on order." But when the chairwoman retorted with, "Think of the Russian refugees," Lazarus wrote, in two days, a poem about America as a symbol of freedom for oppressed, downtrodden immigrants. While the title of the poem, "The New Colossus," is largely forgotten, its closing lines have represented a beacon of hope for countless immigrants entering the United States:

Give me your tired, your poor,
Your huddled masses, yearning to breathe free,
The wretched refuse of your teeming shore,
Send these, the homeless, tempest-tost to me,
I lift my lamp beside the golden door!

The "poet for the masses" died of Hodgkin's disease in New York on November 19, 1887, four years after composing "The New Colossus." Her poetry fell largely into obscurity until 1901, when her friend Georgina Schuyler led a drive to have "The New Colossus," the original handwritten version of which had been preserved, engraved on the Statue of Liberty. In 1903 Emma Lazarus's immortal words were cast in their original form—several politicians had attempted to soften the tone of the poem by changing the words—inside the pedestal building. In 1945 the bronze tablet was moved to the main entrance of the Statue of Liberty, where visitors and immigrants can readily see Emma Lazarus's impassioned testimonial to the importance of freedom.

In *Emma Lazarus* (2006), Princeton University English professor Esther Schor recasts the celebrated poet as an American iconoclast. "Her metaphor is one of deformation, that being a Jew in a society with anti-Semitism, however nuanced, is very deforming," said Schor in an interview in *Nextbook* magazine in 2006. "It warps the soul, and it warps one's ambition and one's identity."

Further Reading

Hollander, John, ed. *Emma Lazarus: Selected Poems.* New York: Library of America, 2005.

Merriam, Eve. *Emma Lazarus Rediscovered: A Biography, with Selections from her Writings.* Expanded 2nd ed. With an introduction by Morris U. Schappes. New York: Biblio Press, 1999.

Schor, Esther. *Emma Lazarus.* New York: Schocken Books, 2006.

Slater, Elinor, and Robert Slater. "Emma Lazarus." In *Great Jewish Women*, 150–152. Middle Village, N.Y.: Jonathan David Publishers, 1994.

Young, Bette Roth. *Emma Lazarus in Her World: Life and Letters.* Philadelphia: Jewish Publication Society, 1995.

∾ Lee, Nelle Harper

(1926–)   *novelist*

Harper Lee's place in American letters was secured in 1960 with the publication of her Pulitzer Prize–winning novel *To Kill a Mockingbird* (1960), the story of a young girl's encounter with fear, ignorance, and courage in a small Southern town.

Born in Monroeville, Alabama, on April 28, 1926, Nelle Harper Lee was the daughter of a lawyer similar to the widowed, upstanding attorney Atticus Finch in *To Kill a Mockingbird*. Like the novel's narrator, Scout Finch, Nelle attended a rural grammar school that served three counties, and, with her childhood friend Truman Capote, she would race by a neighbor's spooky house that resembled Boo Radley's, another character in the book. Capote later invited Lee to help him research *In Cold Blood* and based a character in one of his books on her.

After graduating from the University of Alabama in 1948 and spending a year studying law at Oxford University, Lee headed north to New York City. She took a job as an airline reservation clerk and in her spare time wrote fictitious accounts of her childhood experiences. In 1957 she submitted the manuscript to a New York publisher; one of the editors felt it had potential but was too episodic and suggested she quit her job and work full time on her book. Lee heeded her advice and after, as she put it, "a long and hopeless period of writing the book over and over again," *To Kill a Mockingbird* was finally published.

Although some critics found the novel too melodramatic and objected to having an eight-year-old narrator with a mature woman's ability to recall the past, Lee's first and only novel became an immediate best seller. The recipient of the 1961 Pulitzer Prize in fiction and the Brotherhood Award from the National Conference of Christians and Jews, *To Kill a Mockingbird* was adapted into a film, which in 1962 won two Academy Awards. Subsequently, critics reevaluated the novel's author, this time acclaiming her as a "remarkable storyteller" who possessed "wit and compassion." By 2005 the novel had sold more than 30 million copies and had been translated into 40 languages.

The story covers a three-year period during which Scout, an eight-year-old girl, and her brother observe a trial at which their father, a lawyer, defends Tom Robinson, a black man unjustly accused of raping a white woman. They come to admire their father for standing up to injustice and racism and to understand that to kill Tom would be as senseless as to destroy a mockingbird who "don't do one thing but make music for us to enjoy." The subplot revolves around the siblings's attempt to get to know Boo Radley, a strange local recluse of whom they are terrified but who ends up saving their lives. They are forced to admit that their preconceptions of Boo had been very much mistaken.

In the foreword to the 1995 edition of *To Kill a Mockingbird,* Lee said, "I associate 'Introductions'

Harper Lee's *To Kill a Mockingbird* was her only novel.
(AP/Wide World Photos)

with long-gone authors and works that are being brought back into print after decades of internment. Although *Mockingbird* will be 33 this year [1993], it has never been out of print and I am still alive, although very quiet. . . . *Mockingbird* still says what it has to say; it has managed to survive without preamble." In fact, *Mockingbird* was voted the best novel of the 20th century by librarians across the country, according to *Library Journal,* and in 2005 actress Catherine Keener portrayed Lee in the award-winning Hollywood movie *Capote,* sparking renewed interest in Lee's best-selling novel. In 2007 Lee became a member of the prestigious American Academy of Arts and Letters.

Harper Lee, who is very private and is said to be defiantly silent on the subject of her celebrated novel, travels frequently but continues to live part time in Monroeville, Alabama. Aside from a few magazine articles, she has published no new work since 1960. But *To Kill a Mockingbird* continues to be a favorite with high school and college students and Lee continues to be considered a notable American novelist. "I still plod along with books," wrote Lee in 2006. A fervent reader, she has little use for "laptops, cell phones, and iPods."

Further Reading

Johnson, Claudia D. *To Kill a Mockingbird: Threatening Boundaries.* New York: Twayne, 1994.

Lee, Harper. *To Kill a Mockingbird: The 40th Anniversary Edition.* New York: HarperCollins, 1999.

Shields, Charles J. *Mockingbird: A Portrait of Harper Lee.* New York: Henry Holt, 2006.

∿ Le Guin, Ursula Kroeber

(1929–) *science fiction, fantasy writer, children's book writer*

Ursula K. Le Guin is a prolific, award-winning science fiction and fantasy writer who creates imaginative, well-crafted fiction informed by her impressive knowledge of mythology, psychology, anthropology, and telepathy. She is also a notable writer of children's books.

Born on October 21, 1929, in Berkeley, California, Ursula Kroeber, as a child, was influenced by her father, a distinguished anthropologist who according to his daughter "preferred to find other civilizations while she preferred to invent them;" and by her mother, a writer-folklorist who helped ensure the survival of American Indian tales. After receiving degrees from Radcliffe College and Columbia University and spending a year as a Fulbright scholar in Paris, in 1953 she married historian Charles Le Guin. The couple moved to Portland, Oregon, where they raised three children.

"I always wanted to write," Le Guin recalled in an interview in 1994, "and I always knew it would be hard to make a living at it." She began her literary career in 1964 with the publication of a short story in *Amazing Science Fiction.* Her first novel, *Rocannon's World* (1966), was based on that story and was also the first book in the Hainish series which, along with Earthsea, Orsinia, and the future West Coast, comprise the four worlds the author has created in her major works.

In 1968 Le Guin published *A Wizard of Earthsea,* winner of the Boston Globe-Horn Book Award and the first of three fantasy novels in her critically acclaimed Earthsea trilogy, which takes place on an archipelago peopled by wizards, sorcerers, and dragons. The two other novels in the popular series are *The Tombs of Atuan* (1971) and *The Farthest Shore* (1972), which won the National Book Award for Children's Books, even though they are often considered adult fiction and deal with a mature issue—the importance of facing death. The trilogy reflects the author's Taoist optimistic belief in a holistic conception of the universe restored to wholeness through balance and her interest in anthropology rather than in technology.

The Left Hand of Darkness (1969), which garnered the prestigious Hugo and Nebula awards and is widely regarded as Le Guin's most important work, is one of six novels and four short stories set on a Hainish planet "seeded" with life about 1 million years ago by an ancient people. *The Left Hand* combines myth, scientific and pseudoscientific concepts, history, and fiction to depict the biologically regulated "androgynes"—bisexuals who live peacefully without sex roles. Two other books in the Hainish series, *The Word for World Is Forest* (1972), a novella, and *The Dispossessed* (1974), are also considered among the best of Le Guin's science fiction.

Besides producing a dozen children's books, Le Guin was also a successful writer of verse, essays, and short fiction. *The Word for World Is Forest,* which won the Nebula and Hugo awards for short works, is a tale about the use of force against an alien people, although many critics and readers viewed it as a trenchant critique on America's involvement in Vietnam during the early 1970s. Le Guin often used science fiction as a way of dealing with current ethical, moral, and political issues.

An anthology of short stories, *Orsinian Tales* (1976), introduced the Orsinia series, set in an imaginary but realistic Central European country. That same year Le Guin turned to another genre—conventional fiction. *Very Far Away from Anywhere Else* is a straightforward novella for young adults about conforming to peer pressure. But Le Guin always returned to science fiction. Eighteen years after publishing *The Farthest Shore,* in 1990 she added another award-winning volume to the Earthsea chronicles: *Tehanu: The Last Book of Earthsea.* A master at inventing new worlds, new cultures, and new circumstances for her characters, she used the protagonists from the original trilogy but had them age and become involved in the life of a young girl who had been raped and burned, yet survives.

Le Guin's best-known novel in the series about the future, postnuclear and reshaped northern American West Coast is *Always Coming Home* (1985). Praised by critics for its "lyrical and luminous" writing and its "high invention and deep intelligence," it describes Kesh society in great detail, including an archive of fictional anthropological data and a cassette of Kesh music and invented sounds that accompanies the book.

In addition to the five Hugo and five Nebula awards, the Kafka award, the Pushcart prize, and the American Academy of Arts and Letters award that she had already received, in 2004 Le Guin won a Margaret A. Edwards Award for lifetime achievement to young adult readers. She was honored further in 2005 with a PEN Center USA award in children's literature for *Gifts* (2004), the first full-length young adult novel she has written in 14 years and another fantasy tale filled with earthy magic and plot twists. The PEN/USA judges wrote, "*Gifts* is a novel of startling grace and mythological complexity, and it manages to be both hopeful and truthful about genetic destiny and personal will." It also garnered the *Booklist* Editor's Choice Books for Youth Award. In 2006 she earned the Maxine Cushing Gray Fellowship for Writers Award for her distinguished body of work.

Other recent Le Guin titles include *The Other Wind (The Earthsea Cycle, Book 6),* published in 2001 and described by *Publishers Weekly* as a "superb novel-length addition to the Earthsea universe"; *The Birthday of the World and Other Stories* (2002), another collection of short fiction by an author who, according to University of Missouri professor Elizabeth Cummins, "is revered for her world building, experimental structures, lyrical style, moral concerns, and character-centered stories"; *The Wave in the Mind: Talks and Essays on the the Writer, Reader, and the Imagination* (2004), which deftly explores subjects ranging from Mark Twain and Leo Tolstoy to autobiographical notes and perceptive reflections on reading and writing; *Incredible Good Fortune—New Poems* (2006), her sixth collection of verse; and *Voices* (2006), a young adult novel nominated for a Locus Award in 2007.

"Like all great writers of fiction, Ursula K. Le Guin creates imaginary worlds that restore us, hearts eased, to our own," said the *Boston Globe.* Le Guin's own metaphor for her work is a drafty house. As she said in a 1998 interview, "Opening doors in walls is the image I always go back to. If I have any particular job as a writer, it's to open as many doors and windows as possible and to leave them open. So the house gets drafty."

Further Reading

Cummins, Elizabeth. "Ursula K. Le Guin." In *The Columbia Companion to the Twentieth-Century American Short*

Story, edited by Blanche H. Gelfant, 329–332. New York: Columbia University Press, 2000.

Le Guin, Ursula. *Four Ways to Forgiveness.* New York: HarperCollins, 1995.

———. *Gifts.* New York: Harcourt, 2004.

———. *Incredible Good Fortune.* Boston: Shambhala, 2006.

———. *The Other Wind (The Earthsea Cycle, Book 6).* New York: Harcourt, 2001.

———. *Voices.* New York: Harcourt, 2006.

———. *The Wave in the Mind: Talks and Essays on the Writer, the Reader, and the Imagination.* Boston: Shambhala, 2004.

Slaughter, Jane. "Ursula K. Le Guin." *Progressive* 62 (March 1998): 36–39.

∾ L'Engle, Madeleine (Madeleine L'Engle Camp Franklin)

(1918–2007)   *children's book writer, novelist*

Considered one of America's outstanding contemporary writers of juvenile fiction, Madeleine L'Engle, who has also written popular novels for adults, was known for her family-centered, entertaining, provocative books for young readers, including her award-winning fantasy novel, *A Wrinkle in Time* (1962).

The only child of two artistic parents, Madeleine L'Engle Camp was born on November 29, 1918, in New York City, where she lived until she was 12. Shy, sensitive, and often lonely, she occupied herself by reading voraciously, writing, and retreating into her imagination. After graduating cum laude from Smith College in 1941, she returned to New York as an actress, winning a small part in a production of Chekhov's *The Cherry Orchard* and adopting her mother's Swiss-French family name. A year later she married Hugh Franklin, an actor. The couple divided their time between New York City and an old farmhouse in Connecticut, and L'Engle decided to devote herself full time to writing and raising their three children.

L'Engle's earlier books were adult novels with characters who often shared her own adolescent experiences. In the 1960s she rewrote some of them for young adults, including *Meet the Austins,* a novel about a caring suburban family whose 12-year-old daughter is forced to cope with an upsetting situation. The book was so popular that L'Engle continued the Austins' saga in two more books. She discovered that she enjoyed writing for children because they were "excited by new ideas; they have not yet closed the doors and windows of their imaginations."

A Wrinkle in Time (1962), her most highly regarded juvenile work, was initially rejected by several publishers. The novel, a futuristic, metaphysical fantasy about a close-knit family with real problems as well as a teenage heroine who must travel in space to save her father from a disembodied brain, was considered unusual and unacceptable subject matter for children. But in 1963 it won the coveted Newbery Medal "for the most distinguished contribution to American literature for children" and has been a best-selling classic of children's literature ever since.

"Even the most straightforward tales say far more than they seem to mean on the surface," L'Engle noted in her Newbery Medal acceptance speech, ". . . and this is why we turn to them again and again when we were children, and still again when we have grown up." As of 1999 she had gone on to write 10 more novels for children, including *A Wind in the Door* (1973), a sequel to *A Wrinkle in Time.* She also wrote as a witty verse biblical drama; a reflective collection of verse for adults; a trilogy of compelling autobiographical essays; three plays; and, in 1988, shortly before Franklin died of cancer, a memoir entitled *Two-Part Invention* about their extraordinary marriage of more than 40 years. "Love and prayer," she wrote in it, "are never wasted." During the 1990s L'Engle wrote several novels for adults, including *Certain Women* (1992) and *A Live Coal in the Sea* (1996).

In 1998 L'Engle was honored for her remarkable body of work by the American Library Association when she received its Margaret A. Edward Lifetime Achievement Award for writing in the field of young adult literature. In 1999 she garnered a Wisdom House Award, followed a year later by an honorary doctorate degree from Haverford College in Pennsylvania. She was also writer-in-residence at the Cathedral of St. John the Divine in New York City for many years.

Madeleine L'Engle Herself: Reflections on a Writing Life, compiled by L'Engle's biographer Carole F. Chase, was published in 2001. "I have never served a work as I would like to, but I do try, with each book, to serve to the best of my ability, and this attempt at serving is the greatest privilege and the greatest joy that I know," L'Engle said in this collection of her thoughts on her craft, creativity, and the writing life. Prize-winning nonfiction writer Thomas Cahill commented on *Madeleine L'Engle Herself,* praising its author as "one of the wise women not only of our time, but of the ages." L'Engle produced another book for young readers, *The Other Dog: Book of Wonder,* in 2001. An anthology of L'Engle's new and collected poems was published in 2005. On September 6, 2007, L'Engle died in her home in Connecticut. Near the end of her life she had focused on spending time with her friends and family.

Madeleine L'Engle, an imaginative storyteller who never condescended to her young adult audience, believed that a good book can be "a living fire to lighten the darkness, leading out into the expanding universe."

Further Reading

Franklin, Hugh. "Madeleine L'Engle." In *Newbery and Caldecott Medal Books: 1956–1962,* 124–128. Boston: Horn Book, 1965.

L'Engle, Madeleine. *Madeleine L'Engle Herself: Reflections on a Writing Life.* Compiled with Carole F. Chase. Colorado Springs: Shaw Books, 2001.

———. *The Ordering of Love: The New and Collected Poems of Madeleine L'Engle.* New York: WaterBrook Press/Random House, 2005.

———. *A Wrinkle in Time.* New York: Dell, 1973.

Levertov, Denise

(1923–1997)   *poet, essayist*

A political activist and award-winning poet, Denise Levertov believed that the written poem is at its best a record of what she calls an "inner song" and

that content and form are "in a dynamic state of interaction." A literary critic noted that her poems are "truly lyrics while speaking of political and religious affairs."

Born on October 24, 1923, in Ilford, England, Levertov recalled growing up surrounded by books in a bucolic "extraordinarily rich environment which nurtured the imagination." Her father was a converted Russian Jew who became an Anglican priest devoted to the reconciliation of Jews and Christians, while her mother came from a mining village in Wales and regaled her with colorful Welsh and English folklore. Educated at home except for ballet classes, she was introduced to poetry at an early age by her older sister, Olga.

During World War II Levertov worked as a nurse in a London hospital. Her debut volume of verse, *The Double Image,* appeared shortly after the war in 1946. She was dubbed by other more established British poets as "the baby of the new Romanticism," in that her verse was formal and somewhat sentimental, resembling Neoromantic poets of the 1940s. After the war she married the American writer Mitchell Goodman and emigrated to the United States in 1948, where she had a son, Nikolai Gregor.

Although she described herself an "independent" writer, Levertov was influenced by the Black Mountain school—poets such as Robert Creeley and Robert Duncan—and by the modernist poet William Carlos Williams, whose concrete immediacy of language she greatly admired. She also learned from the example of HILDA DOOLITTLE (H. D.), who "showed a way to penetrate mystery, which means, not to flood darkness with light so that darkness is destroyed, but to *enter* into darkness [and] mystery."

In her work Levertov preferred to focus on commonplace objects and everyday images, rather than to tackle large philosophical issues. In a poem titled "Matins," for example, she captured the essence of ordinary objects, from steaming bathrooms to horses to eggs, using the cadence of ordinary speech.

Levertov became an American citizen in 1955 and went on to publish numerous collections of verse, including the widely read *Jacob's Ladder* (1961); *O Taste and See* (1964); *The Sorrow Dance* (1966), an elegiac tribute to her sister Olga, who had died; *Relearning the Alphabet* (1970); and *The Freeing of the Dust* (1975), a collection of poems about the horrors of the war in Vietnam. A prominent antiwar activist, she traveled with poet MURIEL RUKEYSER to North Vietnam. No matter how critical she was of the destructiveness of war ("O to kill / the killers"), she also affirmed life and the power, beauty, and sensuousness of nature. In an essay in *The Poet in the World* (1973), she explains the poet's role in social activism: "People are always asking me how I can reconcile poetry and political action, poetry and talk of revolution . . . precisely because I am a poet, I know, and [those] other poets who do likewise know, that we must fulfill the poet's total involvement in life. . . . [A] poet does not *use* poetry, but is at the service of poetry."

Critically acclaimed for her lyricism, intensity, and craft, Levertov often wrote about the spiritual and erotic aspects of love, as well as of her own problems. After a long marriage, she and Mitchell were divorced in 1975. In the poem "Divorcing" she worried whether the couple could survive apart from each other after so many years together.

Levertov survived, wrote more than 30 volumes of evocative poetry, essays, memoirs, and translations, taught creative writing at numerous colleges and universities nationwide, translated works by the French poet Jean Joubert, and served as poetry editor of the *Nation* and *Mother Jones*. Among the many honors bestowed on her were the Bess Hokin Prize from *Poetry* magazine, the Elmer Holmes Bobst Award in poetry, and a Guggenheim fellowship.

Highly responsive to moral political causes, including the threat of nuclear annihilation, as well as to metaphor, she said, in a passionate speech she delivered in 1991, "the tragic and fearful character of our times is not something from which we can detach ourselves; we are *in* it, as fish are in the sea. . . ." In 1992, a well-received collection of nonfiction—*New & Selected Essays*—was published, dealing with topics such as politics, religion, and poetry.

Denise Levertov died on December 20, 1997, in Seattle, Washington. "She was a touchstone, a maintainer for our generation," eulogized poet Robert Creeley, one of her first American publishers. "She always had a vivid emotional response and also a completely dedicated sense of political and social need."

Further Reading

Bodo, Murray. *Poetry as Prayer: Denise Levertov.* With a foreword by Peggy Rosenthal. Boston: Pauline Books, 2001.

Brooker, Jewel Spears, ed. *Conversations with Denise Levertov.* Jackson: University Press of Mississippi, 1998.

Levertov, Denise. *The Letters of Denise Levertov and William Carlos Williams.* Edited by Christopher MacGowan. New York: New Directions, 1998.

———. *The Selected Poems of Denise Levertov.* Edited and with an afterword by Paul A. Lacey. Preface by Robert Creeley. New York: New Directions, 2002.

———. *Tesserae: Memoirs and Suppositions.* New York: New Directions, 1995.

O'Connell, Nicholas. "A Poet's Valediction: Denise Levertov." *Poets and Writers Magazine,* May/June 1998. Available online. URL: http://www.pw.org/mag/levertov.htm. Downloaded on March 1, 2007.

Loos, Anita
(1893–1981)   *novelist, playwright, screenwriter*

The author of the perennially best-selling novel *Gentlemen Prefer Blondes* (1925), Anita Loos was also one of the earliest and most prolific female screenwriters in Hollywood.

Born on April 26, 1893, in Sissons, California, Anita performed in her father's theatrical company when she was five years old; she was successful enough to help support her financially unstable family. By the time she was 13, she was publishing comic sketches in magazines and had become a correspondent for the New York *Morning Telegraph*.

When she was 19, Loos tried her hand at writing a script for a movie and sent it to D. W. Griffith's American Biograph Company. Two weeks later the legendary director accepted the scenario and paid Loos $25 for *The New York Hat* (1912), which when produced featured Mary Pickford and Lionel Barrymore. "As soon as I found out that there was money in ink, I dropped acting and stocked up on ink," she later told a *New York Times* reporter. By 1916 she had written more than 100 scenarios for silent films, consisting mostly of slapstick comedies and romantic melodramas, as well as the subtitles for Griffith's classic movie, *Intolerance* (1916).

In 1919 Loos married John Emerson, an actor-director, with whom she collaborated on books, plays, and movie scripts. She later described their tormented marriage as both tragic and comic "together with a thousand combinations of the two."

Petite and energetic, Loos churned out hundreds of movie scripts for the silent screen, was claimed to have invented "talking" titles for silent films and worked closely with the actor Douglas Fairbanks, whose screen persona she helped shape. Loos quickly earned a reputation as a first-rate screenwriter and was also earning an impressive salary, especially for a woman in Hollywood.

But Loos's greatest achievement was her first novel, *Gentlemen Prefer Blondes* (1925), a light-hearted satire of love and sex that originally appeared in *Harper's Bazaar.* Based on the diary of Lorelei Lee, an irrepressible, materialistic, sexy blonde who realizes that unlike romance a "diamond bracelet lasts forever," it was internationally acclaimed by writers such as William Faulkner, James Joyce, and EDITH WHARTON, who called it a "Great American novel." It was even admired by famous politicians, including such diverse figures as Winston Churchill and Benito Mussolini. The popular best seller, which has been through more than 80 editions, was intended as a spoof of Loos's close friend, H. L. Mencken, an intellectual literary critic with a penchant for beautiful blondes. (Loos was a brunette.) "I had no thought of its ever

Screenwriter Anita Loos wrote
Gentlemen Prefer Blondes.
(AP/Wide World Photos)

being printed," she once commented. "My only purpose was to make Henry Mencken laugh—which it did." Loos and Emerson adapted *Gentlemen Prefer Blondes* for the stage in a production that opened on Broadway in 1926. It was also made into a hit musical starring Carol Channing in 1949 and a movie starring Marilyn Monroe in 1953.

Loos enjoyed her newfound celebrity in social circles in New York, Palm Beach, and the capitals of Europe, mingling with writers like Ernest Hemingway and GERTRUDE STEIN, until she lost her money during the stock market crash of 1929 and had to return to Hollywood. For 18 years she worked for Irving Thalberg, the head of MGM studios; at MGM she quickly learned how to write for talking films. Among the many well-known screenplays she wrote during that period were *Red-Headed Woman* (1932), which catapulted the actress Jean Harlow into stardom; *San Francisco* (1936), starring Clark Gable; and *The Women* (1939), which was notable for its all-female cast. Meanwhile, Loos was coping with her husband's manic-depressive illness and larcenous behavior; he had controlled and misused her money. Emerson was hospitalized and remained so until his death in 1956.

Loos returned to New York and wrote a Broadway comedy—*Happy Birthday* (1946)—for her friend, the actress Helen Hayes. This was followed by two popular adaptations of novels by the French writer Colette, *Gigi* (1952) and *Cheri* (1959). She also penned three more novels; several librettos; a witty book about New York City "then and now," which was cowritten with Hayes; a memoir; and three volumes of gossipy autobiography, including *A Girl Like I,* which one reviewer called "an intriguing bit of Americana."

After a lucrative career ("I did it for the money and it was the easiest money I ever made," she once said) that spanned six decades, having written close to 200 screenplays and scenarios and a classic American novel, Anita Loos, a luminary of the silent film era, died in 1981 in New York at the age of 88.

In 2003 interest in Loos was rekindled when the well-received *Anita Loos Rediscovered* was published. According to the *New York Sun,* the "colorful and well-integrated" collection of work by the best-selling novelist is an "intriguing selection of previously unpublished film treatments, one-act plays, and short stories written over the course of Loos's career." Also in 2003, the Museum of Modern Art in New York City held a special screening of Loos's classic comedy *Red-Headed Woman.* The accompanying publicity brochure described "smart and witty" Loos as one of Hollywood's most beloved and prolific screenwriters, creating unforgettable roles for such stars as Mary Pickford, Jean Harlow, and Audrey Hepburn.

Further Reading

Beauchamp, Cari, and Mary Anita Loos, eds. *Anita Loos Rediscovered: Film Treatment and Fiction by Anita Loos.* Berkeley: University of California Press, 2003.

Carey, Gary. *Anita Loos: A Biography.* New York: Knopf, 1988.

Loos, Anita. *Gentlemen Prefer Blondes / But Gentlemen Marry Brunettes.* New York: Penguin, 1998.

———. *Kiss Hollywood Good-by.* New York: Viking Press, 1974.

∾ Lorde, Audre Geraldin (Gamba Adisa) (1934–1992) *poet, essayist*

Audre Lorde, a self-described "black lesbian feminist warrior poet," was best known for her poetry decrying racism, sexism, and homophobia in America. She also wrote movingly about black pride, erotic love, and her lengthy battle with breast cancer.

Audre Lorde was born on February 18, 1934, in New York City; her parents had emigrated to New York City from the West Indies. Audre recalled what it was like growing up in Harlem: "I was . . . a member of the human race hemmed in by stone and away from earth and sunlight." At a young age she became fascinated by word relationships and language, and began writing poetry in eighth grade. She published her first poem when she was 15.

At the Catholic schools she attended, Audre was confronted by what she called "patronizing racism." At Hunter College High School, however, she befriended other feisty young poets who called themselves the "sisterhood of rebels." Working at odd jobs to support herself, Lorde graduated from Hunter College in New York in 1959 and two years later earned a master's degree in library science from Columbia University. In 1962 she married attorney Edwin Ashley Rollins. They had two children, Elizabeth and Jonathan, but the marriage ended in divorce in 1970.

Lorde worked as a librarian from 1961 to 1968, when she received a grant from the National Endowment for the Arts grant, enabling her to write full-time. In 1968 she published her first collection of poetry, *The First Cities,* which the critic Dudley Randall described as a "quiet, introspective book," and she was invited to Tougaloo, a small black college in Mississippi, as a poet-in-residence. During her stay there she met Frances Clayton, who would become her lover and companion for many years.

After returning to New York, Lorde taught at City University and at the John Jay College of Criminal Justice, and later was appointed a professor of English at Hunter College. *From a Land Where Other People Live* (1973), her third collection of poetry, was nominated for a National Book Award in 1974. When the feminist poet ADRIENNE RICH won the award, Rich would only accept it with the two other award nominees, the celebrated black novelist ALICE WALKER and Lorde.

Coal (1976), a collection of new and old poems, was Lorde's first book produced by a major publisher. It was acclaimed for its innovative use of metaphor and its mastery of language. With her seventh and, some critics say, most successful volume of verse, *The Black Unicorn* (1978), in which she explored African matriarchal myths and claimed Africa as her homeland, Lorde became a widely known and respected poet. Her essays were also well received. In 1980, she published *The Cancer Journals,* a poignant, candid account of her reactions, including fear and anger, to having been diagnosed with breast cancer. The book, which won the American Library Association Gay Caucus Book of the Year Award in 1981, helped raise public awareness about breast cancer and its aftermath at a time when few women publicly wrote about their experiences. "The struggle with cancer now informs all my days, but it is only another face of that continuing battle for self-determination and survival that black women fight daily, often in triumph," Lorde asserted in *A Burst of Light* (1988), which garnered an American Book Award in 1989.

In *Zami, A New Spelling of My Name: A Biomythography* (1982), which combined history, biography, and fiction, Lorde delineated her devel-opment as a writer, lesbian, and militant social activist. The *New York Times Book Review* commented that the biography reflected "the evolution of a strong and remarkable character." In spite of teaching, lecturing, and coping with cancer, Lorde managed to continue to publish more poetry and prose collections. *The Marvelous Arithmetics of Distance,* her last volume of verse, appeared posthumously in 1993. "I want this book," she stated, "to be filled with shards of light thrown off from the shifting tensions between the dissimilar, for that is the real stuff of creation and growth."

A lifelong activist and outspoken lesbian, Lorde was a founding member of Kitchen Table: Women of Color Press, and Sisterhood in Support of Sisters in South Africa. In 1991, she was the recipient of the Walt Whitman Citation of Merit, establishing her as the poet laureate of New York State. Governor Mario Cuomo described her as the "voice of the eloquent outsider who speaks in a language that can reach and touch people everywhere." She also received numerous honorary doctorates and contributed to a number of influential poetry anthologies.

Lorde died on November 17, 1992, of liver cancer, in her home in the Virgin Islands. In the last years of her life, she often used her adopted African name, Gambia Adisa, which means "Warrior: She Who Makes Her Meaning Clear." Adrienne Rich once noted that Audre Lorde wrote as a black woman, a mother, a daughter, a lesbian, a feminist, and a visionary: "She refused to be circumscribed by any identity."

Lorde, whose voice "resonates now louder than ever," according to Blanche Wiesen Cook in *Notable American Women* (2004), has been the subject of several films, including Jennifer Abod's *The Edge of Each Other's Battles: The Vision of Audre Lorde* (2000) and Ada Gay Griffith and Michelle Parkerson's *A Litany for Survival: The Life and Work of Audre Lorde* (1995), produced by the Public Broadcasting System (PBS) as part of their True Lives Series. *Ms.* magazine called *A Litany for Survival* a "mesmerizing documentary tribute."

Alexis De Veaux, chair of the women's studies department at State University of New York at Buffalo, in 2004 wrote a biography of Lorde titled *Warrior Poet* that uses source material from more than 60 of Lorde's unpublished personal journals and from interviews with her family, friends, and lovers. She assesses Lorde's cultural legacy ("Poets must teach what they know, if we are all to continue being," said Lorde) and explains the sometimes contradictory facts of the writer's public and private personae, including her sense of displacement. "Lorde's work and words," writes Cook, "inspire and galvanize activists everywhere to continue the struggle for civil liberties, human rights, racial justice, the freedom to love, the right to learn."

Further Reading

"Audre Lorde, Voices from the Gaps—Women Artists and Writers of Color." Available online. URL: http://voices. cla.umn.edu/vg/Bios/entries/lorde_audre.html. Downloaded on January 22, 2007.

Cook, Blanche Wiesen, and Clare M. Coss. "Audre Lorde." In *Notable American Women*, edited by Susan Ware, 393–396. Cambridge, Mass.: Belknap Press of Harvard University Press, 2004.

De Veaux, Alexis. *Warrior Poet: A Biography of Audre Lorde.* New York: W. W. Norton, 2004.

Hall, Joan Wylie, ed. *Conversations with Audre Lorde.* Jackson: University Press of Mississippi, 2004.

Lorde, Audre. *A Burst of Light: Essays.* Ann Arbor, Mich.: Firebrand Books, 1988.

———. *The Cancer Journals.* San Francisco: Spinsters, 1980.

———. *The Collected Poems of Audre Lorde.* New York: W. W. Norton, 2000.

———. *Sister Outsider: Essays and Speeches.* Trumansburg, N.Y.: Crossing Press, 1984.

∼ Lowell, Amy Lawrence
(1874–1925) *poet*

Amy Lowell, an unconventional, prolific, Pulitzer Prize–winning poet, was America's leading exponent of the imagist movement and an influential figure in modern poetry.

Born on February 9, 1874, at Sevenels, her family's estate in Brookline, Massachusetts, Amy Lawrence Lowell grew up surrounded by wealth and high achievers. One of her brothers (Percival) became a noted astronomer while another assumed the presidency of Harvard University. A tomboy who preferred boys' toys to dolls, Amy immersed herself in her father's library, which contained 7,000 books. At 15 she noted in her diary: "I should like best of anything to be literary." But a debutante from a prominent Bostonian family was not supposed to produce "good creative work."

Nonetheless, on October 21, 1902, moved by a passionate theatrical performance by the Italian actress Eleanora Duse, Lowell felt impelled to write her first poem, which she referred to as "seventy-one lines of bad verse." She later explained that watching Duse "loosed a bolt in my brain and I found out where my true function lay." Lowell's muses would always be women and her imagery distinctly feminine.

In 1910 she published her first poem in the *Atlantic Monthly,* and two years later issued her first collection of verse, *A Dome of Many-Coloured Glass;* critics deemed the book acceptable but conventional and unexciting. Around that same time, something exciting did happen to Lowell: She met an actress named Ada Dwyer Russell who would become her devoted friend, artistic collaborator, and lifelong companion. Many of Lowell's most sensual, impressionistic poems were inspired by her loving relationship with Russell, who lived with Lowell at Sevenels until the poet's death.

Professionally, Lowell was about to discover herself. After reading an issue of *Poetry* magazine in which the poet Ezra Pound launched imagism— an avant-garde movement drawing on late 19th-century French symbolist poetry—Lowell realized that like Ezra Pound, H. D. (HILDA DOOLITTLE), Carl Sandburg, and others, she was an imagist. In her second, highly successful book, *Sword Blades and Poppy Seed* (1914), she used polyphonic, unrhymed free verse, which she renamed *vers libre,* based on the imagiste belief that "the sound should be an echo to the sense," and that language should be clear, precise, and centered on the image itself. *Sword Blades* marked the beginning of her career as an experimentalist and preeminent modern poet.

After Pound disdainfully labeled imagism as "Amygism," Lowell assumed leadership of the movement, editing a three-volume anthology entitled *Some Imagist Poets* (1915–17) and penning three imagist collections, *Men, Women, and Ghosts* (1916), *Can Grande's Castle* (1928), and *Pictures of the Floating World* (1919). In her later work she would return to more conventional forms, such as her six-sonnet tribute to her earliest muse, Eleanora Duce.

Lowell also delivered emotional readings of her long narrative poems to packed audiences and lectured across America on modern music and ancient Chinese poetry. In addition, she wrote several more poetry collections, two volumes of well-received critical essays—*Six French Poets* and *Tendencies in Modern American Poetry*—and in 1925 produced a major scholarly biography of John Keats, a poem who she had admired since childhood.

Although she considered herself a serious artist, Lowell was as famous for her eccentric behavior as she was for her poetry. Dressed flamboyantly in mannish clothes and a pince-nez, she smoked cigarillos, worked from a baronial bed festooned with exactly 16 down pillows, often covered windows and mirrors in black drapes even in hotel rooms while traveling, and subjected house guests to a pack of high-strung sheepdogs. Ernest Hemingway once commented that "she smoked cigars all right, but her stuff was no good." But, other established writers such as Robert Frost praised her strong, lyrical "clear resonant calling of things seen," and according to the editors of *No More Masks! An Anthology of Poems by Women* (1973), Lowell had helped launch 20th-century women's poetry.

In 13 years Amy Lowell published 650 poems, among which was her popular and most frequently anthologized poem, "Patterns," an anguished antiwar statement set to verse. In spite of suffering from a glandular disorder that left her severely overweight and often in pain, Lowell traveled, worked diligently, gardened seriously, entertained literati from around the world, and unabashedly promoted her work. Her goal was to "let each day pass, well ordered in its usefulness."

The celebrated poet T. S. Eliot called Amy Lowell "the demon saleswoman of poetry," while the cigar-smoking proponent of free-verse modernism said of herself, "God made me a businesswoman and I made myself a poet." Looking at the more amorous side of the poet, what strikes the modern reader is not the sophistication of Lowell's feminist or antiwar stances, suggested Honor Moore, who edited a selection of Lowell's verse in 2004, but the "bald audacity of her eroticism," referring to Lowell's beautifully crafted homoerotic love poems.

Lowell died at Sevenels on May 12, 1925, during "lilactime"; she was 51 years old. Almost a year later, she was posthumously awarded a Pulitzer Prize for *What's O'Clock* (1925). This collection featured many of her finest poems, including "Sisters," about the "strange, isolated little family" of women poets, and "Lilacs," her lovely ode to New England, which begins,

Lilacs,
False blue,
White,
Purple,
Colour of lilac,
Your great puff of flowers
Are everywhere in this my New England.

Further Reading

"Amy Lowell." Women's History. Available online. URL: http://womenshistory.about.com/library/bio/blbio_amy_lowell.htm. Downloaded on January 22, 2007.

Bevenuto, Richard. *Amy Lowell.* Boston: Twayne, 1985.

Gould, Jean. *Amy: The World of Amy Lowell and the Imagist Movement.* New York: Dodd, Mead, 1975.

Lowell, Amy. *Amy Lowell: Selected Poems.* American Poets Project. Edited by Honor Moore. New York: Library of America, 2004.

———. *Complete Poetical Works.* Boston: Houghton Mifflin, 1955.

———. *John Keats.* 2 vols. Boston: Houghton Mifflin, 1925.

～ Lurie, Alison

(1926–   ) *novelist, children's book writer, essayist*

Alison Lurie, who won the 1985 Pulitzer Prize for her novel *Foreign Affairs,* is known primarily for satirical, psychologically astute fiction that is entertaining but has a melancholic edge. Her farcical novels often are set in university towns and involve academics dissatisfied with their careers or their marriages, who then attempt to change the carefully constructed course of their lives. Lurie has also written traditional folktales for children and nonfiction books, including critical essays, memoirs, and a book on the psychology of fashion.

Lurie was born on September 3, 1926, in Chicago. Her father was a sociology professor who became a welfare administrator, and her mother was a journalist. They encouraged their daughter to be creative at an early age. For young Alison, a voracious reader who was partially deaf and thought of herself as "odd-looking," creativity was a form of escapism. "By the time I was eight or nine," she wrote in the *New York Review of Books,* "it was my belief that I would be an ugly old maid, the card in the pack that everyone tried to get rid of. Making up stories was fun. With a pencil and paper I could revise the world. I could move mountains: I could fly over Westchester [New York] at night in a winged clothes basket; I could call up a brown-and-white-spotted milk-giving dragon to eat the neighbor who had told me and my sister not to walk through her field and bother her cows."

After graduating from Radcliffe College in 1947, Lurie worked as a manuscript reader for Oxford University Press. A year later she married Jonathan Peale Bishop, a professor; the couple divorced in 1985. After sending out her own manuscripts and receiving numerous rejections (she had sold poems and a short story while at Radcliffe and privately printed a memoir of a friend), in 1962 Lurie was successful in getting her first novel, *Love and Friendship,* published. A modern-day comedy of manners set in a New England univer-

sity town, like many of Lurie's books it revolves around a marital crisis faced by a faculty member and his spouse. In this case the professor's wife realizes she no longer loves her husband, and an unexpected love affair seems to free her from her unhappiness. "One can read Lurie," said JOYCE CAROL OATES, "as one might read Jane Austen, with continual delight."

Lurie's next novel, *The Nowhere City* (1965), takes place in Los Angeles, where Lurie lived for several years, and includes among its protagonists a Harvard University couple who migrate to the West Coast, a waitress aspiring to become a movie star, and a psychiatrist. *Imaginary Friends* (1967), described by a London *Times* critic as a "classic comedy about the desire to command knowledge," is set in upstate New York, one of Lurie's favorite backdrops. It pokes fun both at academics who take themselves too seriously and at fanatics who join religious cults. The novel became the basis of a television series, also called *Imaginary Friends,* in 1987.

In 1968 Lurie joined the English department at Cornell University in Ithaca, New York. She was the Frederic J. Whiton Professor of American literature at Cornell from 1989 until her retirement in 1998, having taught creative writing, adult and children's literature, folklore, and the reading of fiction. Lurie based many of her endearing characters on her observations of highly educated, vain, middle-class academics or writers who tend to isolate themselves, and then yearn to escape their sometimes claustrophobic surroundings. It is when the characters leave their normal stultifying surroundings and take up with someone else, usually in the form of an extramarital affair, that they discover who they really are.

The War between the Tates (1974), a critically acclaimed contemporary comedy of manners, takes place at a fictional campus known as Corinth University in upstate New York. It is the story of a breakdown of a marriage during the Vietnam War. "The whole complicated pattern of alliances and strategies works itself out against the background of the other war of the late sixties," wrote Sara Sanborn in her review for the *New York Times.* The novel, whose narrative point of view alternates between the young daughter and an objective third person, was adapted as a television film.

Lurie then switched genres and wrote three children's books: *The Heavenly Zoo: Legends and Tales of the Stars* (1979), *Clever Gretchen and Other Forgotten Folktales* (1980), and *Fabulous Beasts* in 1981. That same year she wrote *The Language of Clothes,* a study of the psychology of fashion and how politics and social mores influence the way we dress. A few years later Lurie published her most celebrated novel, *Foreign Affairs* (1984). Set in London, it tells the story of a middle-aged American professor of children's literature on sabbatical in England and her unlikely love affair with a sanitation engineer from Oklahoma. "*Foreign Affairs* should help propel Alison Lurie into the forefront of American novelists, where she clearly belongs," wrote William French in the *Toronto Globe and Mail.* The novel received American Book Award and National Book Critics Circle Award nominations in addition to winning the Pulitzer Prize. It was adapted into a television movie in 1993, starring Joanne Woodward and Brian Denehy.

Lurie lives part-time in Key West, Florida, which is where *The Truth about Lorin Jones* (1989), the story of a biographer doing research on a celebrated female painter, takes place. It garnered the Prix Femina Étranger in France. A year later she published *Don't Tell the Grown-Ups: Subversive Children's Literature,* a compendium of critical essays that interpret children's literature and folklore. It was followed in 1994 by a collection of nine amusing but unsettling ghost stories called *Women and Ghosts.* In an interview with the *Chicago Tribune,* Lurie said that the short stories could be read either as realistic or supernatural, "about people in desperate situations who begin to see things that aren't there. . . . Ambiguity is part of the charm of ghost stories."

After a 10-year hiatus from fiction, Lurie produced *The Last Resort* (1998). Again set in Key West, the comedic novel revolves around a famous nature writer and his much younger spouse who

leave New England in the hope that a move to a sunnier climate will improve the depressed husband's spirits. The novel also is about, according to Lurie, "age and change and renewal and the knowledge of death. I write about people my own age and am aware of the changes men and women go through in their lives, the selves they leave behind." The writer Francine Pose, in a review of the book in the *New York Times,* comments:

> By the end of this astringently bittersweet novel, after the romantic triangles and quadrangles have been divided into suitable pairs, we are struck by how much Alison Lurie has managed to layer into this deceptively frothy romance men and women ending and renewing their lives in the

Pulitzer Prize–winning writer Alison Lurie is known for her bittersweet social satires set in academia.
(Photography by Edward Hower)

hothouse (or vacation paradise) perched on the southern tip of our country.

Lurie returned to children's literature with the retelling of the traditional Russian folktale, *The Black Geese: A Baba Yaga Story from Russia* (1999). In 2001 she wrote a memoir, *Familiar Spirits: A Memoir of James Merrill and David Jackson*. She credits the prize-winning poet, James Merrill, and his longtime companion, David Jackson, with encouraging her to continue writing in the 1950s, when she was going to give up. Lurie then published a collection of 14 penetrating essays entitled *Boys and Girls Forever: Children's Classics from Cinderella to Harry Potter* (2003), which deconstructs writers' lives and works. About Louisa May Alcott, Lurie wrote, "She was the daughter of what would now be described as vegetarian hippie intellectuals, with fringe religions and social beliefs, and spent nearly a year of her childhood in an unsuccessful commune." Lurie also coedited, with Justin G. Schiller, a 73-volume series titled *Garland Library of Classics of Children's Literature* and edited *The Oxford Book of Modern Fairy Tales*.

Lurie's most recent novel, *Truth and Consequences* (2005), returns to Corinth University, where *The War between the Tates* was set, this time honing in on a disillusioned academic whose rising star has fallen and his frustrated but reliable younger wife who increasingly resents her husband's constant demands. "The intrigues in Lurie's fiction can take several seasons or semesters to unfold," wrote Alice Traux in the *New York Times Book Review,* "thereby granting readers a delicious and exasperating intimacy with every self-serving and misguided notion of the principal players."

Alison Lurie married the writer Edward Hopper in 1995 and has three grown sons and three grandchildren. She has received fellowships from the Rockefeller and Guggenheim foundations and in 1978 won the American Academy of Arts and Letters award in literature. Lurie divides her time between Ithaca, Key West, and London, and when not writing she dabbles in gardening, needlepoint, and collecting contemporary folklore and ghost stories.

Further Reading

"Alison Lurie." It Happened in History! American Society of Authors and Writers. Available online. URL: http://amsaw.org/amsaw-ithappenedinhistory-090304-lurie.html. Downloaded on January 22, 2007.

Lurie, Alison. *Boys and Girls Forever: Children's Classics from Cinderella to Harry Potter.* New York: Penguin Books, 2003.

———. *Foreign Affairs.* New York: Random House, 1984.

———. *Truth and Consequences.* New York: Viking, 2005.

———. *The War between the Tates.* New York: Random House, 1974.

Pearlman, Mickey. *American Women Writing Fiction.* Lexington: University Press of Kentucky, 1988.

Wright, Charlotte Megan. "Adjusting the Stereotype." In *Plain and Ugly Janes: The Rise of the Ugly Woman in Contemporary American Fiction,* 52–55. New York: Garland Publishing, 2000. Reprint, Iowa City: University of Iowa Press, 2006.

Macdonald, Golden
See BROWN, MARGARET WISE

Marshall, Paule
(1929–   )   *novelist, short story writer*

Lauded for her craftsmanship and creative use of West Indian–black dialogue, Paule Marshall writes fiction about American-born women whose parents emigrated from the Caribbean and who struggle with safeguarding their heritage while assimilating into their new nation.

The daughter of immigrant parents from Barbados, West Indies, Paule Marshall was born and raised in Brooklyn, New York. As a child she was a voracious reader, favoring novelists such as Thomas Mann, Joseph Conrad, Ralph Ellison, and James Baldwin. In a *New York Times Book Review* essay in 1983, Marshall credited her storytelling skills to a group of West Indian immigrant "ordinary housewives and mothers" who sat around her mother's kitchen table chatting "passionately, poetically, and with impressive range." Their cogent discussions provided Marshall with her "first lessons in the narrative art," and she savored the "rich legacy of language and culture they so freely passed on to me in the 'wordshop' of the kitchen." From her childhood on, Marshall's goal has been to "tell a good story."

After graduating cum laude and Phi Beta Kappa from Brooklyn College in 1953, Marshall became the only female staff writer for *Our World,* a magazine for African Americans, and was sent on assignment to Brazil and the Caribbean.

Her critically acclaimed (although relatively unknown) debut novel, *Brown Girl, Brownstones* (1959), is a semiautobiographical, sexually candid, coming-of-age story about a young black woman and her Barbadian parents, who have difficulty becoming "successful" Americans. The novel, which should have been "more widely read and celebrated," according to *Ms.* magazine, is notable for its compelling and lyrical use of West Indian dialect. After *Brown Girl* was reprinted in 1981 by the Feminist Press, it was rediscovered and newly appreciated by a larger audience, in similar fashion to the way that the African-American writer ZORA NEALE HURSTON's novel *Their Eyes Were Watching God* became a classic years after its original publication.

Marshall's next work, *Soul Clap Hands and Sing* (1961), a collection of short stories about aging men who attempt to regain their youth through

Paule Marshall writes about black women in search of their cultural identity.
(AP/Wide World Photos)

relationships with women, received a Rosenthal Award from the National Institute of Arts and Letters. It was followed eight years later by what is considered the author's most ambitious novel, *The Chosen Place, The Timeless People,* a lengthy saga of a black woman who emigrates to England and travels with a group to a Caribbean island, where she confronts the consequences of being alienated from her native past.

In *Praisesong for the Widow* (1983), winner of the Before Columbus Foundation American Book Award, Marshall again creates a black heroine in search of her cultural and spiritual identity: this time a wealthy, middle-aged, middle-class widow who ultimately reclaims her West Indian–African-American roots after undergoing a spiritual rebirth.

Around the same time, Marshall published a collection of short fiction titled *Reena and Other Stories* (1983), which included the popular novella "Merle."

With nearly a 10-year span between her second and third novels, in 1991 Marshall came out with *Daughters.* "One of the reasons it takes me such a long time to get a book done," she explained, "is that I'm not only struggling with my sense of reality, but I'm also struggling to find the style, the language, the tone that is in keeping with the material." *Daughters* takes place in New York City and the West Indies, twin settings central to Marshall's work, and revolves around a successful professional African-American career woman with a dual heritage who breaks away from her father, a leading politician on a Caribbean island, and the patriarchal domination that has marked their relationship. Strong women dominate Marshall's fiction. In a 1979 interview in *Essence* magazine, she explained why: "I wanted them to be central characters. . . . I wanted women to be the centers of power."

Marshall, who won MacArthur and Guggenheim fellowships and numerous literary awards, has taught creative writing at a number of universities, including Yale, Columbia, and Cornell. She has been a professor of English at Richmond's Virginia Commonwealth University. She married Nourry Menard in 1970, and the couple has a son, Evan.

The esteemed African-American novelist ALICE WALKER described Paule Marshall's fiction as "unequaled in intelligence, vision [and] craft by anyone of her generation, to put her contributions to our literature modestly."

Further Reading

Brownley, Martine W. *Deferrals of Domain: Contemporary Women Novelists and the State (Atwood, Marshall, Drabble).* New York: Palgrave Macmillan, 2007.

Denniston, Dorothy Hamer. *The Fiction of Paule Marshall: Reconstruction of History, Culture, and Gender.* Knoxville: University of Tennessee Press, 1955.

De Veaux, Alexis. "Paule Marshall—In Celebration of Our Triumphs," *Essence* 11 (May 1980): 123–134.

Marshall, Paule. *Brown Girl, Brownstones.* New York: Random House, 1959. Reprinted by The Feminist Press, New York: 1981.

———. *Reena and Other Stories.* (Includes novella "Merle.") New York: The Feminist Press, 1983.

∾ McCarthy, Mary Therese
(1912–1989) *novelist, nonfiction writer*

An accomplished, versatile writer and prominent American social commentator and intellectual, Mary McCarthy's fiction and nonfiction were driven by her belief that "there is a truth, and that it's knowable."

Born in Seattle, Washington, on June 21, 1912, the eldest child of affluent, devoted parents, Mary Therese McCarthy, at the age of six, underwent a trauma that profoundly affected her life: Both her mother and father died during the influenza epidemic of 1918. Mary and her three orphaned brothers were then raised in Minneapolis, Minnesota, by cruel relatives, including a sadistic uncle who viciously beat her. In *Memories of a Catholic Girlhood* (1957) she recalled how surprised she was when, in 1923, her grandfather rescued her and brought her back to Seattle: "[I] thought it only natural that grandparents should know and do nothing, for did not God in the mansions of Heaven look down upon human suffering and allow it to take its course?"

After graduating Phi Beta Kappa from Vassar College in 1933, McCarthy moved to New York City and married a playwright, the first of four husbands. She wasted no time in becoming part of New York's lively intelligentsia and was soon publishing articles and reviews in noteworthy magazines such as *New Republic, Harper's Bazaar,* and *Partisan Review,* for which she served as drama critic from 1937 to 1962.

In 1938 McCarthy married Edmund Wilson, a well-known social critic who encouraged her to write fiction; in fact, some of her best short stories are based on their intense, fractious (she claimed abusive) relationship. Four years later she published her largely autobiographical and sexually explicit first novel, *The Company She Keeps,* a series of satiric sketches about a woman who forces herself to stop lying and "snatching blindly at the love of others, hoping to love herself through them, borrowing their feelings, as the moon borrowed light."

After divorcing Wilson in 1946 and remarrying that same year, McCarthy was awarded a Guggenheim fellowship that enabled her to complete her second novel, *The Oasis* (1949), which garnered the *Horizon* magazine prize. It was followed by a collection of short stories, *Cast a Cold Eye* (1950); two novels about American intellectuals, *The Groves of Academe* (1952) and *A Charmed Life* (1955); and several volumes of theater criticism, travel writing, and essays.

In *Memories of a Catholic Girlhood* (1957), which chronicled McCarthy's painful childhood and formative Catholic education, as well as in two later volumes of intellectual autobiography (*How I Grew,* 1987; and *Intellectual Memoirs,* 1992), McCarthy's goal was to be unsparingly candid. "There I was, a walking mass of lies, pretending to be a Catholic and going to confession while really I had lost my faith, and pretending to have monthly periods by cutting myself with nail scissors," she wrote in *Memories.*

McCarthy's final marriage, to James Raymond West, a State Department official with whom she moved to France in 1961, proved to be her most satisfying relationship and lasted until her death. She also blossomed professionally. In 1963, with the publication of *The Group*—a story of the careers, romances, and intrigues of eight Vassar college graduates over seven years—McCarthy became a best-selling author. Some reviewers called the popular novel little more than lightweight fodder for the "women's magazine audience," while others praised it as an important early work of the emerging feminist movement. Nonetheless, McCarthy refused to be pigeonholed as a "feminist"; she preferred to define herself as an intellectual writer, like her close friend, the political scientist and social commentator, Hannah Arendt, with whom she maintained a lengthy correspondence about ideas and politics. Their correspondence was collected and published in 1995.

McCarthy wrote astute essays, published as reportage, about current political events such as the Vietnam War, which she vehemently opposed, and the Senate Watergate hearings. Her sixth novel, *Birds of America* (1971), the coming-of-age tale of a teenage bird-watcher disillusioned by technology as it replaced and controlled nature, reflected the political unrest in America, which McCarthy had observed as an "outsider" while living in Paris. Her final novel, *Cannibals and Missionaries* (1979), dealt with the brutal ramifications of terrorism and torture.

McCarthy, who taught at several colleges and in 1984 received the National Medal for Literature, found herself engaged in a bitter literary feud with the playwright LILLIAN HELLMAN, whom she had publicly denounced as a compulsive liar. Hellman had fully intended to sue McCarthy but died in 1984 before she could do so.

Five years later, Mary McCarthy, the master of veracity, who the critic ELIZABETH HARDWICK called a "prodigy" and "master of the art of writing," and who revelled in controversy, romance, or the complex world of ideas, died on October 25, 1989, in Castine, Maine.

Two new books about McCarthy, a biography titled *Seeing Mary Plain: A Life* (2000) and a collection of essays called *Mary McCarthy: A Bolt from the Blue and Other Essays* (2002), have rekindled interest in the provocative author and her body of work. "To reread the essays is to be reminded of a singular virtue of all her writings," said Judith Shulevitz in the *New York Times Book Review.* "She knew that to hit its target, a description must be clean, precise and aimed with aggression. She revelled in her unabashed willingness to commence hostilities."

Further Reading

Kiernan, Frances. *Seeing Mary Plain: A Life of Mary McCarthy.* New York: W. W. Norton, 2000.

McCarthy, Mary. *The Group.* New York: Harcourt Brace Jovanovich, 1963.

———. *Intellectual Memoirs: New York, 1936–1938.* New York: Harcourt Brace Jovanovich, 1992.

———. *Memories of a Catholic Girlhood.* New York: Harcourt Brace Jovanovich, 1957.

Pierpont, Claudia Roth. *Passionate Minds: Women Rewriting the World,* 251–288. New York: Knopf, 2000.

Scott, A. O., editor. *Mary McCarthy: A Bolt from the Blue and Other Essays.* New York: New York Review of Books, 2002.

McCullers, Lula Carson Smith
(1917–1967) *novelist, playwright*

A prominent, controversial, southern gothic writer, Carson McCullers imaginatively portrayed the lives of eccentric, spiritually isolated characters who populated the "small, lonely, lost world" of America's southland, as McCullers described it.

Born on February 19, 1917, in Columbus, Georgia, Lula Carson Smith was a lanky, sickly, solitary child who at 15 began to write plays, emulating playwright Eugene O'Neill's works that were, as she put it, "thick with incest, lunacy, and murder." She also admired Gustave Flaubert's novels for "flowing straight from [his] pen without an interruption of thought," and she considered herself an intuitive writer. At 18 she left Georgia to study music at the Juilliard School in New York City, but after her tuition money was lost by a roommate who was holding the money for Carson, she was forced to work at a series of day jobs, while taking writing courses at night at Columbia University.

In 1937 she married a fellow southerner, Reeves McCullers. Three years later, at age 23 and having published only one short story, Carson McCullers became a critically acclaimed best-selling author. Her first novel, *The Heart Is a Lonely Hunter* (1940), which in 1998 was named by the Modern Library one of the best 100 novels of the 20th century, is a "parable in modern form" that centers around John Singer, a deaf-mute, and an assortment of misfits who gravitated to him, including an adolescent would-be musician. When Singer commits suicide, the other characters, who dreamed of a better world while confiding in him, return to their bleak, indifferent one.

McCullers became so immersed in the motives of her characters that, she claimed, they became her own: "When I write about a deaf mute, I become dumb during the time of the story." In an article in *Esquire* magazine she elaborated on her characters: "Love, and especially love of a person who is incapable of returning or receiving it, is at the heart of my selection of grotesque figures to write about—people whose physical incapacity is a symbol of their spiritual incapacity to love or receive love. . . ."

In 1937 McCullers, who was bisexual, fell in love with the beautiful Swiss writer Annamarie Clarac-Schwarzenbach. "My nature," she admit-

ted, "demanded, craved, a reciprocal love relationship with a woman." She and Reeves, who was also bisexual, divorced in 1941, the same year her second novel, *Reflections in a Golden Eye,* appeared. Although lauded for its craftsmanship, its subject matter—sadomasochism and homosexuality—was considered scandalous.

McCullers continued to publish short fiction. "A Tree, A Rock, A Cloud" was included in *O. Henry Memorial Prize Stories of 1942;* in 1942 she also received the first of two Guggenheim fellowships. Her award-winning elegiac novella, *The Ballad of the Sad Cafe,* which was serialized in *Harper's Bazaar* in 1943 and published in 1951, is perhaps her most accomplished work, with its cast of memorable southern gothic characters: a self-centered hunchback, a strong-willed, autonomous cross-eyed cafe owner, and a homeless dwarf. In 1963 it was dramatized by playwright Edward Albee. "Spiritual isolation is the basis of most of my themes," McCullers wrote in an essay in 1971.

In 1945 McCullers remarried Reeves, and a year later she produced her last major novel, *A Member of the Wedding,* which received rave reviews. At the suggestion of her friend, the playwright Tennessee Williams, she wrote a stage version of the largely autobiographical story of a motherless teenage poet who feels isolated and searches for love. When it opened in New York in 1950 it won several coveted drama awards. Delighted by its financial and critical success, McCullers wrote to a friend: "When the illumination has focused a work so that it goes limpidly and flows, there is no gladness like it."

An untreated childhood case of rheumatic fever resulted in McCullers's suffering from chronic illnesses—including a debilitating stroke, which left her partially blind and paralyzed. She also had breast cancer and suffered from bouts of pneumonia. She made an unsuccessful suicide attempt in 1948; five years later, Reeves McCullers ended their tumultuous relationship by killing himself.

McCullers's second play, *The Square Root of Wonderland,* which was produced in 1957, was poorly received by critics, as was her last novel,

Clock without Hands (1961), about a man facing premature death in the moribund South.

On September 29, 1967, McCullers died in upstate New York. A posthumous collection of her short storis, *The Mortgaged Heart,* was published in 1971. Tennessee Williams called her the greatest prose writer that the South had produced. "Her heart was often lonely," he wrote, "and it was a tireless hunter for those to whom she could offer it, but it was a heart that was graced with light that eclipsed its shadows."

Further Reading

Clark, Beverly Lyon, and Melvin J. Friedman, eds. *Critical Essays on Carson McCullers.* New York: G. K. Hall, 1996.

McCullers, Carson. *Carson McCullers: Complete Novels: The Heart Is a Lonely Hunter, Reflections in a Golden Eye, The Ballad of the Safe Café, The Member of the Wedding, Clock without Hands.* Edited by Carlos L. Dews. New York: Library of America, 2001.

———. *Collected Stories.* Edited by Virginia Spencer Carr. Boston: Houghton Mifflin, 1987.

———. *Illumination and Night Glare: The Unfinished Autobiography of Carson McCullers.* Edited by Carlos L. Dews. Madison: University of Wisconsin Press, 2001.

Savigneau, Josyane. *Carson McCullers: A Life.* Translated by Joan E. Howard. Boston: Houghton Mifflin, 2001.

～ McDermott, Alice

(1953–)   *novelist, short story writer*

Alice McDermott's critically acclaimed novels, including *Charming Billy,* which won the 1998 National Book Award, are written from the perspective of her decidedly middle-class, suburban, Irish American, Roman Catholic background. Praised for their richly textured, detailed, lyrical prose, her six novels and dozens of short stories revolve around the ups and downs of close-knit family members, while poignantly and honestly probing the role faith, morality, and human frailty plays in their lives.

Born on June 27, 1953, in Brooklyn, New York, McDermott grew up with her two older brothers among other Irish Americans in suburban Elmont, Long Island, where McDermott later would set of many of her novels. During her childhood, to compensate for her "uninteresting life," she kept diaries, recalling that "writing was a way for me to make my own world and work out my own thoughts. . . . I filled up notebooks and wrote a novel on loose-leaf paper when I was 11 or 12." It was not easy, she pointed out in *The Book That Changed My Life,* being a shy child with two older brothers in a patriarchal, Irish Catholic family, but her mother, a secretary and housewife, encouraged her to write down anything that was bothering her. Educated at parochial grammar and high schools, McDermott then attended the State University of New York in Oswego, where she received a bachelor of arts degree in 1975.

After working for a year as a typist for a vanity publishing company and writing short stories during her free time, she was offered a teaching assistantship in English at the University of New Hampshire, which is where she obtained a master's degree in English in 1978. McDermott planned to go to law school (both her brothers became lawyers), but while at New Hampshire, under the guidance and encouragement of an English professor who recognized her talents as a writer, McDermott published short stories in *Redbook, Mademoiselle, Seventeen,* and *Ms.* magazines. She began with short stories, she explained in *Publishers Weekly,* because "I felt I had to apologize for wanting to write fiction for a living, and with a short story there was this sense, of, well, it's just a little bitty thing."

In 1982, *A Bigamist's Daughter,* McDermott's first novel, was published. The manuscript, about an editor employed by a vanity press who falls in love with an author, had been accepted only months after she submitted it, even though she had not completed it. Reviewer Jean Strouse described the author's debut novel as a "wise, sad, witty novel about men and women, God, hope, love, and fiction itself." Although writing did not come easily to her, and she thought that it should if she were to make it her life's career, McDermott gave up her plans to become an attorney and committed herself to creative writing. In addition, she taught creative writing at schools such as the University of California at San Diego and American University. She has also served as writer-in-residence at Lynchburg and Hollins Colleges in Virginia.

McDermott won a Whiting Writers Award in 1987, and her next novel, *That Night* (1987), a penetrating portrait of suburban adolescence, was a *New York Times* best seller and a finalist for the Pulitzer Prize, the National Book Award, the *Los Angeles Times* Book Prize, and the PEN/Faulkner Award for Fiction. The essence of the story, according to McDermott, was that "even places we think are safe and happy aren't really that way." Set in Irish-Catholic suburbia, and recalled through the selective memories of a woman who witnessed the events during the early 1960s, when she was 10, *That Night* tells the coming-of-age story of two alienated teenagers in love and the violent ramifications of their separation. "Both mythic and personal" is the way the *New York Times* described *That Night*, which was adapted into a film in 1992.

Her third novel, *At Weddings and Wakes* (1992), also a finalist for the Pulitzer Prize, is another immigrant Irish Catholic family-oriented novel, this time revolving around a dysfunctional family and focusing on the four grown sisters but seen through the perspective of the children in the story. "You only see relatives at weddings and wakes," says one of the characters, which is what happens (the wake comes shortly after the wedding of a middle-aged aunt and former nun). A *New York Times* best seller, the elegiac novel was described as a "haunting and masterly work of literary art" in the *Wall Street Journal*.

Charming Billy, the author's most popular book, garnered the 1998 National Book Award for fiction, much to McDermott's surprise. The chairman of the judging panel hailed the book as having "a voice like nothing we could recall. . . . It found us. It was what we kept hearing. . . . McDermott evokes the subtle yet fierce links between family and community." *Charming Billy*, which also won a Before Columbus Foundation Award, chronicles Billy Lynch's life when his Irish Catholic friends and family come together at his wake and try to make sense out of their loss by sharing their memories. In an interview with the *Sacramento Bee*, McDermott explained that she did not want to portray Billy as a stereotypical Irish drunk. "I wanted to individualize the character," she said. "It is ultimately a novel about faith, and what we believe in, and above all what we choose to believe in."

McDermott's next novel, the affecting coming-of-age tale *Child of My Heart* (2004), takes place during a summer spent away from New York City in East Hampton, Long Island. Its protagonist is a smart, middle-class, literary teenager hired as a caretaker for, as she tells it, "four dogs, three cats, the Moran kids, Daisy, my eight-year-old cousin; and

Alice McDermott earned a National Book Award for her finely crafted novel *Charming Billy*.
(Eames Armstrong)

Flora, the toddler child of a local artist." The story arises from the voice of a girl "who refuses to be reconciled to some simple truths about relationships and how we live and die," said McDermott during an interview with Dave Welch (Powells.com). "The world as Theresa sees it is not acceptable to her. In her own way, she remakes it." McDermott's novel *After This* (2006) features another family living on Long Island during the Vietnam War era. "*After This* is really about suffering," said McDermott in the *Johns Hopkins* magazine (November 2006). "It is about the forces that work on us, both those that are in our control and those that are not."

In April 2006, McDermott's short story "Enough" was selected as be staged as part of Stories on Stage, a program of dramatic readings of short fiction read by prominent actors, in Denver, Colorado. Also in April 2006 McDermott was a guest speaker at the Festival of Faith and Writing at Calvin College in Grand Rapids, Michigan.

Alice McDermott, who lives in Bethesda, Maryland, with her husband, David Armstrong, a neuroscientist she married in 1979, and their three children, is the Richard A. Macksey Professor in the Writing Seminars at Johns Hopkins University in Baltimore, where she teaches graduate writing seminars. McDermott suggests to her students to "write about what you know" and has followed her own advice. Through her wry, heartbreaking novels, she creates deceptively simple and compelling family portraits that surprise the reader with their impact. "Such wonderful things happen deep inside the sentences," asserted a critic from *Newsweek* magazine, while the Canadian writer Margaret Atwood, in the *New York Review of Books,* commented on McDermott's ability to explore "subtly but ruthlessly the angry, ruined, melancholy, occasionally hopeful lives of second- and third-generation emigrant Irish."

McDermott, who views herself chiefly as a storyteller, offers this advice to aspiring writers of all ages:

> Read everything, write all the time. And if you can do anything else that gives you equal pleasure

and allows you to sleep soundly at night, do that instead. The writing life is an odd one, to say the least. . . . For writers, it's a matter not so much of deciding you will write fiction with the hope that you will publish fiction, but rather writing fiction because there is nothing else you can do that will give you a satisfying sense of yourself or of life.

Further Reading

McDermott, Alice. *After This.* New York: Farrar, Straus and Giroux, 2006.

———. *Charming Billy.* New York: Farrar, Straus and Giroux, 1998.

———. *Child of My Heart.* New York: Farrar Straus and Giroux, 2002.

"Off the Page: Alice McDermott." Washingtonpost.com, with host Carole Burns. October 2, 2003. Available online. URL: http://www.washingtonpost.com/ac2/wp-dyn/A31756-2003Aug22?language+printer. Downloaded on January 22, 2007.

Osen, Diane, ed. "Interview with Alice McDermott." In *The Book That Changed My Life,* 109–129. New York: Random House, 2002.

McMillan, Terry
(1951–) *novelist, screenwriter*

The critically acclaimed contemporary novelist Terry McMillan writes popular, breezy fiction about professionally successful African-American women and their less successful relationships with black men.

Born on October 18, 1951, in Port Huron, Michigan, where she was one of five children raised by her mother, a domestic and automobile factory worker, Terry became an avid reader at an early age, devouring the works of Thomas Mann, Henry Thoreau, and Ralph Waldo Emerson. "I had not yet acquired an ounce of black pride," she explained in the *Washington Post.* That changed after she read Alex Haley's *Autobiography of Malcolm X* and realized there were also black authors whom she could emulate.

McMillan received a bachelor of science degree from the University of California at Berkeley in

1979 and a master of fine arts degree from Columbia University that same year.

In 1987 she published her first novel, *Mama.* Humorous, authentic, and semiautobiographical—hallmarks of McMillan's fiction—it portrayed a black woman "as tired an old workhorse" from raising five children alone, who "hated never having enough of anything." To promote the book McMillan sent out 3,000 letters and gave 39 readings. Her efforts paid off. *Mama* was lauded by reviewers for its "touching, tough, believable characters" and went into its third printing six weeks after being released.

After teaching at the Universities of Wyoming and Arizona, McMillan published her second novel, *Disappearing Acts* (1989), which is narrated from alternating points of views of two star-crossed lovers: Zora is a strong-willed, educated music teacher with a "weakness for black men and food," while Franklin is an uneducated, sometimes abusive construction worker who is tired of women who "start hearing wedding bells . . . and want you to meet their damn family. . . ." Both characters learn to compromise without giving up their independence.

In 1990, frustrated by a dearth of anthologies of emerging African-American fiction writers, McMillan edited such an anthology, *Breaking Ice.* Two years later she published her third novel, *Waiting to Exhale,* about four professional African-American "sistuhs" searching for the love of "good men." Praised for its exuberance, although criticized for its excessive use of profanity, *Waiting to Exhale* became a best seller and was adapted by McMillan as one of the first major films to depict African-American life outside an urban ghetto.

McMillan's next book, *How Stella Got Her Groove Back* (1996), was another best seller and another love story about an unlikely couple: a 42-year-old investment analyst and single mother, and a 20-year-old soft-spoken Jamaican man. McMillan also cowrote the script for a film adaptation of the book; the result was a 1998 Hollywood hit starring Angela Bassett and Whoopi Goldberg.

During an interview in 2002 with the editor of SeeingBlack.com, McMillan explained that she writes about people and situations that are causing us harm. "Somebody needs to say it or show it—and if it's embarrassing, then it should be." Her sixth novel, *The Interruption of Everything,* is about an African-American wife and mother of three grown children who is weary of living for everyone but herself and plunges into a midlife crisis, and then is helped out of it by her two supportive girlfriends. It was published in 2005 and became a *New York Times* best seller. A Book-of-the-Month selection, it was praised for its sharp, irreverent, pitch-perfect dialogue and realistic writing.

Also in 2005, McMillan left her husband, Jonathan Plummer, who is 23 years her junior, after six years of marriage. She based *How Stella Got Her Groove Back* on their romance, having met Plummer while vacationing in Jamaica. A three-time fellow at Yaddo Artist Colony and the MacDowell Colony, McMillan is the recipient of a National Book Award by the Before Columbus Foundation and fellowships from the National Endowment for the Arts (NEA) and the New York Foundation for the Arts.

McMillan, who lives in northern California with her son Solomon, is proud to have achieved celebrity status as an author of popular novels about today's African Americans. But she is also aware that "a house and a car and the money in the bank won't make you happy. People need people. People crave intimacy."

Further Reading

McMillan, Terry, ed. *Breaking Ice: An Anthology of Contemporary African-American Fiction.* New York: Viking, 1990.
———. *The Interruption of Everything.* New York: Viking, 2005.
———. *Waiting to Exhale.* New York: Viking, 1992.
Smith, Wendy. "Terry McMillan," *Publishers Weekly* (May 11, 1992): 50–51.

Millay, Edna St. Vincent (Nancy Boyd)
(1892–1950) *poet, playwright*

A prolific and highly esteemed American poet and early feminist, Edna St. Vincent Millay wrote

Esteemed lyric poet Edna St. Vincent Millay
was an early feminist.
(AP/Wide World Photos)

popular lyrical and dramatic verse and was the first woman to garner the Pulitzer Prize in poetry.

Born on February 22, 1892, in Rockland, Maine, and raised in nearby Camden, Vincent—as she was called by family and friends—began writing poetry when she was five. She was encouraged by her mother; her parents divorced when she was eight, and her mother supported her three daughters by becoming a practical nurse. At 14 Vincent published her first poem in *St. Nicholas*, a prominent children's magazine.

Although the Millays struggled to make ends meet, Vincent had a happy, culturally rich childhood. At age 20 she submitted a poem entitled "Renascence" to a contest sponsored by *The Lyric Year*, an anthology of contemporary poetry. The

poem was acclaimed nationally in literary circles, and today "Renascence" is considered one of her most memorable and moving poems. Like much of her verse, it is accessible and personal, yet intensely reflective:

> But, sure, the sky is big, I said:
> Miles and miles above my head.
> So here upon my back I'll lie
> And look my fill into the sky.
>
> . . .
>
> The soul can split the sky in two,
> And let the face of God shine through.

With financial assistance Millay attended Vassar College, where she excelled as a poet, actress, and playwright. She graduated in 1917 and moved to the artists' community of Greenwich Village in New York City. There, noted the literary critic Edmund White, red-haired, green-eyed, flirtatious Millay "had an intoxicating effect on people," especially on male poets.

Her first book of verse, *Renascence and Other Poems,* appeared in 1917 and was well received by critics and the public alike. Over the next three years Millay acted, wrote and directed her own plays and, in order to earn a living, published stories and articles in magazines under the pseudonym Nancy Boyd. But she never stopped writing poetry and in 1920 published her second book, *A Few Figs from Thistles,* a witty, direct plea, in verse, for women's rights.

Unwilling to be dominated by men, Millay dedicated herself to her work instead of to any of her suitors, but noted in "First Fig" the pleasure of passion:

> My candle burns at both ends;
> It will not last the night:
> But ah, my foes, and oh, my friends—
> It gives a lovely light!

In 1920 Millay published *Aria de capo,* an expressionistic play in verse staged in New York in 1919. She would go on to write six more plays, including an acclaimed opera libretto, and to publish a total of 16 books of poems and a translation, with George Dillon, of Charles Baudelaire's *Les Fleurs du mal.*

While Millay was traveling in Europe on assignment for *Vanity Fair* magazine, *Second April* (1921), a third collection of poems, appeared, and Millay was praised for having matured as a poet. In 1923 she returned to America to discover that she had become something of a literary celebrity: her poetry was selling well, and her nationwide poetry readings were well attended. During the 1920s Millay was at the height of her popularity and productivity, and in 1923 she became the first woman to receive the prestigious Pulitzer Prize, awarded for her collection *The Ballad of the Harp-Weaver and Other Poems.*

That same year she married Eugen Jan Boissevain, a widowed Dutch businessman who was supportive of her work. The couple moved to Steepletop, a wooded farmstead in Austerlitz, New York, where Millay continued to write and to fight for women's rights and other social causes; in 1927 she was arrested for protesting against the execution of anarchists Sacco and Vanzetti. During World War II, she wrote antifascist "propaganda" verse. Unnerved by the horrors of war, and with her health declining, she suffered a nervous breakdown in 1944.

Boissevain died in 1949, followed by Edna St. Vincent Millay on October 19, 1950; she had been working through the night on a set of galley proofs. As for the inevitability of death, in "Dirge without Music" she had complained: "I know. But I do not approve. And I am not resigned." *Mine the Harvest* (1954), said by many to contain some of her best and most technically original verse, was published posthumously in 1954 by her sister Norma Millay.

With the predominance of modernist poets like Ezra Pound, T. S. Eliot, and William Carlos Williams, Millay's reputation diminished. However, during the 1970s, she began to be recognized as a gifted romantic poet and admired for openly defending women's rights. As Edmund Wilson noted, she "stood forth as a spokesman for the human spirit."

Several new books about Millay and her life have pointed out her darker side, such as her addiction to morphine and alcohol and her self-destructive promiscuity with men and women. Nonetheless, she continues to be lauded as a "defiant, passionate, fearless, talented genius," albeit a troubled one. In a national poll in 1931, Millay was named one of the 10 most famous people in America, and the great British writer Thomas Hardy once said of Millay, "America has two great attractions: the skyscrapers and the poetry of Edna St. Vincent Millay."

Further Reading

Epstein, Daniel M. *What Lips My Lips Have Kissed: The Loves and Love Poems of Edna St. Vincent Millay.* New York: Henry Holt and Company, 2001.

Meade, Marion. *Bobbed Hair and Bathtub Gin: Dorothy Parker, Zelda Fitzgerald, Edna St. Vincent Millay and Edna Ferber.* New York: Random House, 2004.

Milford, Nancy. *Savage Beauty: The Life of Edna St. Vincent Millay.* New York: Random House, 2001.

Millay, Edna St. Vincent. *Collected Poems of Edna St. Vincent Millay.* Compiled by Norma Millay. New York: Harper, 1981.

———. *The Selected Poetry of Edna St. Vincent Millay.* Edited and with an introduction by Nancy Milford. New York: Modern Library, 2002.

Miller, Sue
(1943–) *novelist, memoirist, short story writer*

The author of several best-selling novels, a poignant memoir of her father, and a well-received collection of short stories, Sue Miller is a celebrated chronicler of contemporary family life, particularly when relationships unexpectedly fall apart or tragedy strikes. She is a virtuoso storyteller who weaves deceptively simple tales slowly, quietly, and in great emotional and physical detail, "through a domestic prism," as she describes it.

Born in Chicago, Illinois, on November 29, 1943, the second of four children, Miller grew up in Hyde Park, on the South Side of Chicago. Her father was an ordained minister and church historian who taught at the University of Chicago and Princeton University. Her mother was a housewife who felt that staying at home was her proper role, but she also wrote poetry. "My parents were very judgmental," recalled Miller in a *Ploughshares* author's profile. "You had to be able to defend your standing in the universe against theirs. If you wanted to be bad, you had to have a rationale for being bad." However, even though her mother could be "difficult and demanding," and her father distant, she observed that her parents "had a very intensely loving relationship." Miller also has said that she inherited a "tendency towards self-examination and examination in others—intention, meanings, scruples, ethics—that seems to connect directly to that [her parents'] tradition," which has served her well as a writer.

Shy, solitary, and overachieving, as a child Miller was, by her own account, "an obsessive reader, the sort of kid who wants to be excused from the table to go read more of a book." She also enjoyed painting and writing poetry and short stories. A precocious student, she skipped her senior year at a small private girls' high school and was accepted at Radcliffe College when she was 16. Two months after graduating in 1964 with a bachelor's degree in English literature, Miller married and then supported her husband, while he attended medical school, by waitressing, modeling, and working as a research assistant in psychology. Miller became a mother in 1968, when she gave birth to a son, Ben. "I didn't write more than a few pages of fiction a year for the next seven or eight years," she said. After separating from her husband in 1970 and divorcing him several years later, she worked in day care centers and parent cooperatives in the Boston area.

Although she had written two novels, both unpublished, Miller never envisioned herself as a professional writer until 1977, when she took a creative writing course through Harvard University's extension program. She began to feel more confident and recognized that she had something to say. In 1979 Miller was awarded a fellowship to

Boston University's creative writing program and was able to stop working. Meanwhile, her short stories were published for the first time in two notable literary magazines, *Ploughshares* and the *North American Review,* and later a story appeared in the *Atlantic Monthly.* She ultimately earned three master's degrees: in English from Boston University, in teaching from Wesleyan University, and in education from Harvard University. From 1981 to 1989, she taught writing at various institutions, including Boston University, Emerson College, Tufts University, Massachusetts Institute of Technology, and the Harvard Summer School Writing Program.

In 1983 Miller received a fellowship at the Bunting Institute at Radcliffe College, which is where she began to write her first published novel, *The Good Mother.* Assisted the following year by a grant from the Massachusetts Artists Foundation (she also has received a Henfield Foundation Award and a Guggenheim fellowship), she was able to give up her part-time teaching positions and work full time on her fiction.

The Good Mother (1986) is a powerful, unsettling, intense novel that earned Miller widespread acclaim and became a surprise international best seller. "I was startled by the success of my first novel. It changed my life quite literally," Miller observed in an interview in 1998. Her compassionate but realistic rendering of the story's central protagonist was lauded for its complexity and depth. A single mother, Anna belatedly discovers her sensuality when she embarks on a passionate love affair, but at a tremendous cost: She accepts defeat in a courtroom for something that never happened, involving her lover, and loses custody of her young daughter in order to spare her child further trauma. Describing Anna's role in the novel, Miller said: "I was trying . . . to establish what I regard as a very female notion of heroism and, I think, a very feminist notion of heroism."

In addition to being adapted into a Hollywood film starring Diane Keaton in 1988, *The Good Mother* became a popular book group selection among women who were drawn to a well-written, accessible novel that focused on a female character who was appealingly real—a sexual, vulnerable, caring mother who had unmet desires and needs. Readers often comment that they feel as if they intimately know Miller's meticulously drawn characters. Although many of them, such as Anna in *The Good Mother,* are frustrated or seem to pay a high price for finding love, Miller says that she believes it is possible, although difficult, to find complete emotional and sexual fulfillment within a permanent relationship, according to an article about her in Bloomsbury.com.

Miller remarried in 1984, to writer Douglas Bauer. Three years later she published *Inventing the Abbotts,* a collection of short stories that Miller had been working on before and while she was writing *The Good Mother.* The stories demonstrated, wrote Ellen Lesser in the *Village Voice,* that Miller "doesn't need the breadth of a novel to chart the complex and confusing topography of families after divorce." The collection was adapted as a motion picture in 1997.

Family Pictures (1990), Miller's second novel and another best seller, is a wrenching saga of a wealthy family from the Midwest, from the end of World War II through the mid-1980s. When one of the Eberhardt's six children is diagnosed with autism, the other family members are affected at many levels and the family dynamic is irrevocably altered. The husband, a psychiatrist, blames his wife for their son's autism, and the guilt-ridden, strong-willed, angry wife struggles to prove otherwise. *Family Pictures* was a finalist for a National Book Critics Circle Award and in 1993 was made into a television movie starring Anjelica Huston.

Other critically acclaimed novels followed, including *For Love* (1993); *The Distinguished Guest* (1995); *While I Was Gone* (1999), a *New York Times* best seller and Oprah's Book Club selection described in the *New York Times* as a "beautiful and frightening book"; and *The World Below* (2001). A year later Miller served as editor of *The Best American Short Stories, 2002.* Her only nonfiction work is a memoir titled *The Story of My Father* (2003) about her relationship with her father while he struggled with Alzheimer's disease (he died in 1991). She wanted to write about what her father's life and death meant to her and what it felt like to "live through the illness with someone whom you love," Miller said during an interview with *Book-Page.* "There was a kind of softening of my very dark anger. That is something I learned from my father, and from writing about him." The memoir was a *New York Times* Notable Book.

In *Lost in the Forest,* published in 2005, the author, who has been called a "doyenne of domesticity," delineates the interior lives of her characters as a family in upheaval dissolves and then eventually comes back together again, although forever changed by betrayal and a series of uncontrollable events and emotions. "When their lives are altered by missteps and tragedies, Miller explores the fallout, taking us deep into their most intimate moments," writes Tricia Brick in *Bostonia* magazine. A literary critic in London's *Sunday Telegraph* further explained, "William Thackeray, Charles Dickens and T. S. Eliot found in domestic life evidence of humanity at its noblest, its most depraved, its most complicated and interesting, and so in her elegant and clear-eyed way, does Sue Miller. She misses nothing about love, and the gnawing griefs that go with it."

When asked what role autobiography plays in her fiction, Sue Miller, who lives in Boston, replied, in *Conversations with American Women Writers:* "When I'm writing fiction, my sense is very much of letting myself invent anything, while also using things that I know from my own life, or things that I've lived through. But I feel that at their cores my stories are completely invented in every case."

Further Reading

Brick, Tricia. "The Good Author." *Bostonia* (Summer 2005): 26–28.

Johnson, Sarah Anne. "Sue Miller: The Hot Dramas of the Domestic Scene." In *Conversations with American Women Writers,* 140–154. Lebanon, N.H.: University Press of New England, 2004.

Miller, Sue. *The Good Mother.* New York: HarperCollins, 1986; Reprint, Delta, 1994.

———. *Inventing the Abbotts and Other Stories.* New York: HarperCollins, 1987.

———. *Lost in the Forest.* New York: Knopf, 2005.

———. *The Story of My Father.* New York: Knopf, 2003.

———. *While I Was Gone.* New York: Knopf, 1999.

"Sue Miller." BookBrowse. Available online. URL: http://www.bookbrowse.com/biographies/index.cfm?author_number279. Downloaded on March 3, 2007.

Mitchell, Margaret Munnerlyn (Peggy Mitchell)
(1900–1949) *novelist*

Margaret Mitchell is the author of the best-selling novel of all time, *Gone with the Wind* (1936). Her Pulitzer Prize–winning, semiautobiographical Civil War and Reconstruction saga sold more than 20 million copies and was adapted into an Academy Award–winning film.

Margaret (Peggy) Munnerlyn Mitchell spent almost her entire life in Atlanta, Georgia, where she was born on November 8, 1900, and where *Gone with the Wind* mostly took place. Like the novel's heroine, Scarlett O'Hara, Peggy was a rebellious, attractive, pampered, redheaded tomboy, born into one of Atlanta's most prominent and progressive Irish Catholic families. A voracious reader who had an early interest in the Civil War, she also excelled at writing and wrote two novels and several adventure plays while still a teenager.

After graduating from Atlanta's Washington Seminary in 1918, Mitchell attended Smith College. But after her mother died from the flu in

Margaret Mitchell reads congratulatory messages when *Gone with the Wind* won a Pulitzer Prize in 1937. (AP/Wide World Photos)

1919, she returned to Atlanta to help her father and brother. In 1922 she landed a job writing for the *Atlanta Journal* and that same year married Red Upshaw, who is believed to have been the model for Rhett Butler, the dashing, roguish, boorish, and passionate central male character in *Gone with the Wind*. After a stormy relationship and an attempted rape, Mitchell's marriage to Upshaw was annulled. In 1924 she married a public relations executive, John Marsh, a "true gentleman" whom she loved deeply. It was Marsh who encouraged her to write fiction.

In 1926, after abandoning a novel set in World War I Atlanta, Mitchell gave up journalism and began working on her epic Civil War tale, writing thousands of pages in no particular chronological order, based on stories she had heard from relatives who remembered the war. Ambivalent about showing the manuscript to anyone, especially because several characters closely resembled friends and relatives, she finally agreed in 1935 to deliver it to an editor at Macmillan, who described it as "the worst-looking manuscript he had ever been given in his long career in publishing." But he quickly became absorbed in the sweeping saga of romance, war, and the triumph of hope over despair, and eventually agreed to publish it.

When *Gone with the Wind* appeared in 1936, almost overnight Mitchell became an international celebrity and her book a literary and publishing phenomenon. "Alas," she wrote to a friend in 1937, "where has my quiet peaceful life gone?" A record-breaking 1 million copies sold in the United States within six months, and it was translated into more than two dozen languages in 37 countries. While it was never considered serious literature, the colorful 1,000-page story of romance and adventure struck a chord with the weary, financially strapped American public, and in 1937 Mitchell won the Pulitzer Prize in fiction.

With David O. Selznick's 1939 Academy Award–winning film adaptation of the blockbuster, which starred Vivien Leigh and Clark Gable, Scarlett O'Hara and her lover-antagonist Rhett Butler became household names. And some of the novel's

memorable dialogue entered the American lexicon, such as Rhett's reply to Scarlett when she wondered what she would do after he left her: "Frankly, my dear, I don't give a damn."

Feisty and independent, like the heroine she had created, Mitchell fought inequities imposed on writers and helped set important precedents in copyright and tax laws. Baffled by her extraordinary success, she was also realistic enough to know that she was incapable of repeating it. Mitchell never wrote another novel. Instead she did charity work and answered her voluminous fan mail; she is said to have written at least 10,000 letters, many of them lengthy.

In 1949 Mitchell was fatally injured in an automobile accident in Atlanta. An estimated 100 million readers throughout the world have read *Gone with the Wind,* and it continues to sell 250,000 paperback copies annually. A recently written sequel has proved unsuccessful; only Mitchell's original novel—one of the best-loved classics of all time—has endured.

Further Reading

Allen, Patrick, ed. *Margaret Mitchell: Reporter.* Athens, Ga.: Hill Street Press, 2002.

Harwell, Richard, ed. *Margaret Mitchell's Gone with the Wind Letters.* New York: MacMillan, 1976.

Mitchell, Margaret. *Gone with the Wind.* New York: Macmillan, 1936.

Pyron, Darden Asbury. *Southern Daughter: The Life of Margaret Mitchell.* New York: Oxford University Press, 1991.

Walker, Marianne. *Margaret Mitchell and John Marsh: The Love Story behind Gone with the Wind.* Atlanta: Peachtree Publishing, 2002.

‿ Mohr, Nicholasa Golpe
(1938–   ) *children's book writer, novelist*

Nicholasa Mohr is the author and illustrator of several award-winning novels and stories for children and adults that realistically portray life in New York City's Puerto Rican neighborhoods.

Born in New York City on November 1, 1938, to Puerto Rican immigrant parents, Nicholasa

Golpe was raised in a barrio (Spanish-speaking neighborhood) in the Bronx. After her father died, her mother encouraged her gifted *hijita* (little daughter) to develop her artistic talent. Although she greatly admired her mother's "strength and independence," Mohr could find no Puerto Rican Latina role models outside the barrio.

By supporting herself as a waitress, clerk, and factory worker, Mohr was able to afford art schools such as the Art Students League in New York. She also studied in Mexico, where she was influenced by the colorful, ethnically inspired murals of Diego Rivera and the paintings of Frida Kahlo. After returning to the United States she met Irwin Mohr, a clinical psychologist, whom she married in 1957; they have two sons.

Mohr had already earned a reputation as a successful artist and printmaker when she decided, after submitting some vignettes to a publisher, to take up writing full time. "I am learning a new craft," she noted, "but the artistic growth I achieved as a graphic artist is all transferable." She wrote and illustrated her first novel, *Nilda* (1973), an autobiographical coming-of-age story for young adults about an unhappy, poverty-ridden Puerto Rican girl who escapes reality through her vivid imagination. Widely acclaimed, *Nilda* earned the *New York Times* Outstanding Book Award in juvenile fiction in 1973 and was named Best Book of the Year by *Library Journal.* She also won the Jane Addams Children's Book Award in 1974.

El Bronx Remembered, Mohr's second book, consists of a novella and a dozen short stories depicting the lives of Puerto Rican immigrants in postwar New York. This work provided more insights into what it is like "being poor and belonging to a despised minority" but also revealed universal emotions. It also received a *New York Times* Outstanding Book Award and was a National Book Award finalist for "most distinguished book in children's literature" in 1976.

Mohr's next work, *In Nueva York* (1977), a collection of interrelated short stories set in New York's Lower East Side, portrays eccentric, resilient characters within a Puerto Rican community who,

in spite of difficult and sometimes tragic circumstances, maintain their self-respect, and survive. *In Nueva York* deals sensitively with mature subjects such as homosexuality and teenage violence, and won Mohr the best book award in young adult literature from the American Library Association.

Felita (1979), written for younger readers, describes an eight-year-old Puerto Rican girl growing up in a caring, close-knit family that experiences discrimination and harassment after moving "up in the world"; eventually they move back to their old neighborhood.

After teaching at several universities, coproducing and writing the television series *Aqui y Ahora* ("Here and Now"), and dealing with the untimely deaths of her husband and brother, Mohr moved to Brooklyn. She published her next book, written for adults, in 1985; *Rituals of Survival: A Women's Portfolio* was a well-received story collection.

Mohr returned to writing books for young adults, including *Going Home,* a popular novel; a biography of social activist Lopez Antonetty; *Growing Up inside the Sanctuary of My Imagination* (1994), an autobiographical account of the author's life until age 14; *The Magic Shell* and *The Song of El Coqui and Other Tales of Puerto Rico,* both of which appeared in 1995; and *Old Letivia and the Mountain of Sorrow,* an original fairytale, in 1996. Her fiction has been translated into Spanish and Japanese.

In 1997 Mohr published a collection of seven short stories set in New York City and the Caribbean entitled *A Matter of Pride and Other Stories.* The same year, she received the Hispanic Heritage of Literacy Award. "Aside from its strength of characterization, Mohr's work is also noteworthy in terms of its language. Inspired by the Puerto Rican culture's respect for the art of storytelling, Mohr seeks to document daily life among mainland Puerto Ricans in a realistic manner previously unknown to mainstream audiences," writes Maria Elena Cepeda in an essay about Mohr published in 2000. "As part of one of the first waves of widely published Nuyorican [members of the Puerto Rican diaspora in New York City or their descendents] authors," continues Cepeda, "her willingness to address 'taboo' issues while faithfully portraying the daily lives of her characters has made Mohr a key predecessor of current American Latina/o literature."

"My work incorporates a strong social statement," explained Mohr in an interview. "Using art, the universal language of humanity, I bring forth the point of view of a sub-culture in America, the Puerto Rican people with all their variety and complexity."

Further Reading

Cepeda, Maria Elena. "Nicholasa Mohr." In *The Columbian Companion to the Twentieth-Century American Short Story,* edited by Blanche H. Gelfant, 380–383. New York: Columbia University Press, 2000.

Garcia-Johnson, Ronie-Richele. "Nicholasa Mohr." In *Latinas! Women of Achievement,* ed. Diane Telgen and Jim Kamp, 247–254. Detroit, Mich.: Visible Ink Press, 1996.

Mohr, Nicholasa. *Growing Up inside the Sanctuary of My Imagination.* New York: J. Messner, 1994.

———. *In Nueva York.* New York: Dial Press, 1977.

———. *A Matter of Pride and Other Stories.* Houston: Arte Publico Press, 1997.

———. "Puerto Rican Writers in the United States, Puerto Rican Writers in Puerto Rico: A Separation Beyond Language." *America Review* 15 (Summer 1987): 87–92.

Moore, Lorrie
(1957–)   *short story writer, novelist*

Lorrie Moore is admired by critics for infusing her widely read fiction with sardonic humor, irony, and pathos. She is best known for insightful short stories that show off her supple, pitch-perfect prose, her finely honed observation skills, and her carefully crafted characters, especially frustrated or disillusioned modern female protagonists, as they search for fulfillment and companionship.

Born Marie Lorena Moore on January 13, 1957, in Glens Falls, New York, Lorrie (nicknamed by her parents), the second of four children, grew up in a comfortable household surrounded by books and music. She was encouraged by her "culturally alert,"

parents, as she described them, to develop her talents in both areas. Lorrie was an excellent pianist whose writing ability became apparent in 1976, at the age of 19, when she won first prize for "Raspberries" in a short story contest sponsored by *Seventeen* magazine. A shy, precocious adolescent, Lorrie skipped grades in school. She attended St. Lawrence University in Canton, New York, where she tutored on an Indian reservation and was editor of the university literary magazine, graduating with a bachelor of arts degree summa cum laude in 1978. She received the university's Paul L. Wolfe Memorial prize for literature.

After moving to New York City, where she worked for two years as a paralegal, Moore enrolled at Cornell University and earned a master of fine arts degree in 1982, the same year she was awarded the A. L. Andrews prize for three of her short stories. While a student at Cornell, she gave up one of her great passions, piano playing, because it had become a distraction. "I wasn't getting any writing done, so I had to choose," recalled Moore. *Self-Help* (1985), her first collection of stories, based mostly on what she had written for her master's thesis, was published while she was employed as a writing instructor at the University of Wisconsin, Madison. ALISON LURIE, an English professor at Cornell, recommended a literary agent to her talented student. Even though Moore did not know exactly what an agent was or did, she heeded Lurie's advice and sent her manuscript to the agent. It was accepted quickly by a major publishing company.

Six of the nine stories in *Self-Help* were written in the unusual second-person voice, mostly as stylistic experiments, said Moore. "Let's see what happens," she explained during an interview with *Contemporary Authors,* "when one eliminates the subject, leaves the verb shivering at the start of a clause; what happens when one appropriates the 'how-to' form for a fiction, for an irony, for a 'how-not-to.'" Moore was hailed by reviewers as a new "voice of her generation," and they compared the 28-year-old author to much better-known writers such as GRACE PALEY and Woody Allen. Meanwhile, Moore was teaching at the University of

Wisconsin, Madison, but she missed the East Coast. She returned to New York City whenever she could, even though she remained a professor of English at the university.

Self-Help was followed by Moore's first novel, *Anagrams,* in 1986. It was not well received by literary critics. Attempting another genre, she wrote a children's book, *The Forgotten Helper,* in 1987, before winning a National Endowment for the Arts Award and a Rockefeller Foundation fellowship, both in 1989. Her second collection of short fiction, *Like Life* (1990), received very positive reviews and was considered her most accomplished, affecting work to date. It is notable for its clever repartee about love and loss and confirmed the author's reputation as a comedic master of contemporary American fiction. Moore once commented that being funny is "a kind of generosity between people. And I'm interested in that, those little moments of generosity." On the other hand, she has also said that she considers the essence of her work to be sad. It is that juxtaposition of the horrific and the hilarious and their constant interplay that makes her fiction both edgy and entertaining. One of the stories in *Like Life,* "You're Ugly, Too," was her first to be published in the *New Yorker,* in 1989, and at that time was considered a controversial piece for the prestigious magazine. "I could not say 'yellow light,' I had to say 'amber light,'" recalled Moore.

In 1991 Moore was awarded a Guggenheim fellowship. She also has received a Lannan Foundation Literary Fellowship (2001) and the *Irish Times* International Prize for Fiction. She has served as editor for such literary magazines as *Ploughshares* and *Tri-Quarterly* and has edited an anthology of stories about childhood by contemporary writers, *I Know Some Things* (1992). In 1994 she produced a novella, *Who Will Run the Frog Hospital?,* which focuses on adolescence and takes place in Paris and an amusement park in New York State's Adirondacks. "It is unacceptable, all the stunned and anxious missing a person is asked to endure in life," says a protagonist. "It is not to be endured, not really."

Moore's third short fiction collection, *Birds of America* (1998), a *New York Times* bestseller, is her longest, "almost three hundred pages," she says, proudly. "Unbelievable, you could keep a small door open with this [book]." It is also her first publication since becoming a mother, and it impressed critics with what they perceived as a "new assurance" and "full maturity" in her writing. *Birds of America* was named by the *New York Times Book Review* as one of the best books of 1998. The wide-ranging collection, mostly about parents or characters contemplating parenthood, was also nominated for the National Book Critics' Circle Award. One of the most celebrated and frequently anthologized stories, "People Like That Are the Only People Here," is about a mother's reaction to her one-year-old baby's having cancer, necessitating chemotherapy treatments. "She [the baby] has already started to wear sunglasses indoors, like a celebrity widow," comments the horrified narrator/mother.

Though Moore remains a master at portraying the sublimely darker sides of her characters and their disconnections with each other, some of the stories in *Birds of America* are more hopeful and life-affirming than her earlier work, says Janet R. Raiffa, in an essay she wrote about Moore in 2000. The female protagonists are not always victims, and more of the male characters care about someone other than themselves, namely, their children. Raiffa concludes, "The hope of romance and true companionship makes Lorrie Moore's often bleak observations on the hazards of the modern world more embraceable, and gives her long-time readers the satisfaction of finding a light at the end of her long, dark tunnel."

Moore's short stories continue to be lauded and have been included in *The Best American Short Stories* in 1997 (she edited the anthology in 2004) and *Prize Stories: The O. Henry Awards* (1998). They have appeared in the *New Yorker,* which published "The Juniper Tree" in 2005; the *New York Review of Books; Harpers;* and the *Paris Review,* and have been anthologized in *The Best American Short Stories of the Century* in 1999, the same year Moore served as a judge for the O. Henry Awards. Returning to juvenilia, in 2002 Moore wrote *The Forgotten Helper* and two years later edited *The Best American Short Stories 2004,* received Cornell University's Distinguished Alumni Artist Award (she was a visiting professor there in 1990), and was the recipient of the Rea Award for achievement in short story writing. The Rea Award jurors, including EDWIDGE DANTICAT, said that Moore had "earned a place among the finest writers in the country by exploring the lives of modern women" and that her short stories "charted this territory with unfailing intelligence, an almost miraculous wit, and a remarkable depth of feeling." Moore also was the 2005 winner of the PEN/Malamud Award for excellence in short fiction.

Lorrie Moore lives with her husband, Mark, and their son in Madison, where she continues to write and currently is the University of Wisconsin's Delmore Schwartz Professor of the Humanities. Commenting on why she has gravitated toward short fiction, Moore replied, in *Women Write* (2004), "The short story is one of the most beautiful, limber and rewarding art forms there is. . . . [It's] a very emotional enterprise, like a song. It can be a single emotion pursued and interrogated, and in that way has a sustained intensity."

Further Reading

Cahill, Susan, ed. *Women Write: A Mosaic of Women's Voices in Fiction, Poetry, Memoir and Essay.* New York: New American Library, 2004.

Lee, Don. "About Lorrie Moore: A Profile." *Ploughshares.* Fall 1998. Available online. URL: http://www.pshares. org/issues/article.cfm?prmArticleID-4504. Downloaded on March 3, 2007.

Moore, Lorrie. *Birds of America.* New York: Alfred A. Knopf, 1998.

———. *Like Life.* New York: Alfred A. Knopf, 1990.

———. *Self-Help.* New York: Alfred A. Knopf, 1985.

∾ Moore, Marianne Craig
(1887–1972) *poet*

One of the most distinguished modern American poets, during her six-decade, multi-prize-winning career Marianne Moore was praised for her originality, wit, and keen sense of observation. She was, by her own definition of a good poet, a first-rate "literalist of the imagination" with a "burning desire to be explicit."

Born on November 15, 1887, in Kirkland, Missouri, near St. Louis, shy, red-haired, nine-year-old Marianne Craig Moore moved with her mother and brother—her father having abandoned the family—to Carlisle, Pennsylvania, where she was raised. She graduated in 1909 from Bryn Mawr College, where she concentrated on the sciences but published poems and short stories in the college's periodical, *Tipyn o'Bob.*

After attending Carlisle Commercial College and traveling to Europe with her mother, Moore taught secretarial and business courses at the United States Indian School in Carlisle. She continued to submit her verse to literary magazines, and in 1915 several of her poems were accepted by *Poetry* in Chicago and the *Egoist* in London.

In 1918 Moore and her mother, with whom she lived until her mother's death, moved to the Greenwich Village area of New York City. There Moore felt at home, mingling with avant garde writers and artists—she had briefly considered a career as an artist and was considered an accomplished watercolorist. To earn a living she took a job at a branch of the New York Public Library; meanwhile, in 1921, without her knowledge, her friend and former Bryn Mawr classmate, the poet H.D. (HILDA DOOLITTLE), along with another friend, brought out Moore's first collection of verse, *Poems,* in London. Three years later the critically acclaimed collection was published in the United States, with additions, as *Observations.*

There was more good news for Moore. The *Dial* accepted a number of her poems, including some of her major ones such as "A Grave," and in 1924 she received the *Dial*'s prestigious annual award for *Observations.* Moore was named editor of the important literary magazine in 1925, a position she held until it ceased publication in 1929. Under her leadership it showcased the works of such controversial modernists as James Joyce, D. H. Lawrence,

Hart Crane, and Ezra Pound. In her own verse Moore increasingly followed "the new order" by incorporating jagged stanza forms and "disruptive" language. A prolific writer, in each of the three decades between 1921 and 1952 Moore published two volumes of poetry.

Having moved with her mother from Manhattan to Brooklyn, where her brother, a Presbyterian minister, lived, in 1935 Moore published one her best-reviewed volumes, *Selected Poems,* which included a laudatory introduction by the poet T. S. Eliot. For the most part Moore had returned to syllabic meter and rhyme.

Moore excelled at fastidiously accurate observations of exotic animals—for example turning a jerboa into a small, nocturnal desert rat that is "not famous." Whether Moore was writing about "Smooth Gnarled Crape Myrtle" or "Four Quartz Crystal Clocks," she believed that aesthetic expression was "a kind of doctrine of existence," and as a perfectionist she constantly rewrote previously published poems. "Omissions are not accidents," she once said. Like T. S. Eliot, Moore frequently quoted from other sources—obscure poets, scientists, Greek philosophers, and Russian mystics. Unlike Eliot, however, she used quotation marks, as she was "trying to be honorable and not steal things."

In 1947 Moore's mother, with whom she had shared a very close relationship, died. Sadly she did not live to see her daughter receive the Pulitzer Prize and National Book Award in 1952, or the Bollingen Prize and the National Institute of Arts and Letters Gold Medal in 1953—all of them for her seventh book of verse, *Collected Poems* (1951). Moore's poetry began to focus on more accessible subjects, such as the "Carnegie Hall: Rescued," the Brooklyn Bridge in "Granite and Steel," and, as an avid Brooklyn Dodgers' fan, on baseball in "Baseball and Writing."

A Francophile, Moore spent a decade translating all of La Fontaine's *Fables* (1954). She was also a notable essayist and reviewer and collected her prose, which covered a broad range of subjects from herbal medicine to sculpture, first in a volume entitled *Predilections* (1955) and later in *The Complete Prose of Marianne Moore* (1986). In addition, she wrote a comedy, retold three French fairy tales, and penned more than 33,000 letters that were often lengthy; occasionally she wrote as many as 50 a day. One of her correspondents was Ezra Pound, whose work she admired but whose misguided anti-Semitism and fascist beliefs she rejected. She preferred to write to him about the intricacies of language: "Lemon-yellow-black was my idea of the underwing of the grasshopper but carmine in connection with the sunset is better."

Another well-received collection, *Tell Me, Tell Me* (1966), was followed, in 1967, by *The Complete Poems of Marianne Moore,* which marked her 80th birthday and contained one of her best-known poems, about disliking poetry but finding truth in it.

"I never knew anyone with a passion for words who had as much difficulty in saying things as I do," Moore explained in a *New York Times* interview. "Each poem I think will be the last. But something always comes up and catches my fancy."

In her later years Moore became something of an American icon. Dressed in her trademark long cape and three-cornered hat ("to hide my face somewhat," she once commented), she was the subject of photo essays in popular magazines such as *Life* and *Look.* She faithfully attended baseball games and was praised by sports figures such as Muhammad Ali and Joe Garagiola. In 1967 America's "greatest modern poet," as the contemporary poet John Ashbery called her, even appeared on television's *Today* show, and thoroughly enjoyed it. As an elder statesman she earned six honorary degrees and lent advice to an array of younger poets such as Allen Ginsberg, urging him to focus on "one's struggle with what is too hard." She also helped launch the careers of younger poets, including ELIZABETH BISHOP, a college student at Vassar who subsequently became a lifelong friend and correspondent; Bishop considered Moore her mentor and "not in the least intimidating."

In 1967 Moore was named a Chevalier des Arts et Lettres by the French Republic and in 1968 she received the National Medal for Literature, America's highest literary honor. Near the end of her life Marianne Moore, one of the major poets of the modernist era, still writing and revising poems, moved from Brooklyn back to Greenwich Village, where she and her impressive literary career had begun. She died at 84 in New York City, on February 5, 1972, having for more than 60 years produced what T. S. Eliot called "part of the small body of durable poetry written in our time."

Further Reading

Miller, Cristanne. *Marianne Moore: Questions of Authority.* Cambridge, Mass.: Harvard University Press, 1995.

Molesworth, Charles. *Marianne Moore: A Literary Life.* New York: Atheneum, 1990.

Moore, Marianne. *The Complete Poems of Marianne Moore.* New York: Macmillan, 1967.

———. *In Her Own Image.* New York: New York Center for Visual History, 1988. (Videorecording.)

Reuben, Paul. "Marianne Moore." PAL: Perspectives in American Literature. March 7, 2004. Available online. URL: http://www.csustan.edu/english/reuben/pal/chap7/moore.html. Downloaded on January 23, 2007.

ᗌ Morrison, Toni (Chloe Anthony Wofford)
(1931–) *novelist, essayist*

A Nobel laureate, Toni Morrison lives up to her own definition of what it means to be a good writer: she combines the "irrevocably beautiful and unquestionably political." Using precise, richly textured prose and compelling characters driven by a moral vision, Morrison deftly explores America's most troubling issues, from racism to cultural identity.

Toni Morrison was born Chloe Anthony Wofford on February 18, 1931, in the small, multiracial town of Lorain, Ohio, which she described in an essay in *Black Women Writers at Work* as "neither plantation nor ghetto," and in which she set her first novel, *The Bluest Eye.* "No matter what I write," she explained in the essay, "My beginnings [in the Midwest] are always there. . . . It's the matrix for me."

Critically acclaimed Tony Morrison won the Nobel Prize for literature in 1993.
(AP/Wide World Photos)

Chloe grew up in a "story-telling" house where she listened to African-American folklore and was surrounded by people who "talked about their dreams with the same authority that they talked about what 'really' happened." Several of Morrison's fictitious characters, such as Pilate in *Song of Solomon,* reflect her childhood interest and belief in the supernatural. Others, such as Sethe, the proud and tortured heroine in *Beloved,* reflect the sense of self-confidence instilled in her by her parents, who in spite of being poor put a high value on education. Chloe was the only pupil in her class who entered first grade already knowing how to read. She also graduated high school with honors.

209

"The world back then didn't expect much from a little black girl, but my father and mother certainly did," Morrison recalled.

After receiving a bachelor's degree in English from Howard University in 1953, and changing her name to Toni, Wofford attended Cornell University, earning a master's degree in 1955. She returned to Howard as an English instructor in 1957, and a year later she married Harold Morrison, a Jamaican architect, with whom she had two sons, Harold Ford and Slade Kevin.

In 1964, having divorced her husband and given up her position at Howard, Morrison and her sons moved to Ohio, then to Syracuse, New York, and finally to New York City, where from 1965 until 1985 she served as a senior editor at Random House and was responsible for editing the works of such prominent black authors as Angela Davis and TONI CADE BAMBARA. In addition, she taught at several colleges and universities, including the State University of New York at Purchase and at Albany, Yale, Bard, and Princeton, where in 1989 she was named to a university chair in the Humanities. Whether editing or teaching, she has continued to write fiction.

In Morrison's first novel, *The Bluest Eye* (1969), a young black girl convinced of her ugliness is raped by her father. She desperately wants to have blue eyes, as her definition of beauty is defined entirely by the dominant white culture. "I hadn't seen a book in which black girls were center stage," Morrison said during a 1993 television interview about *The Bluest Eye*. She explained that she wanted to provoke readers into thinking about what it means to have virtually no self-esteem:

> How does a child learn self-loathing? Who enables it? And what might be the consequences? [Without self-esteem] you never have the opportunity to develop what's really valuable, which is grace, balance, health—all those good things that each of us can be.

Morrison's second book, *Sula* (1973), was critically acclaimed for its controlled writing and its imaginative, soulful characters. It vividly portrays, from childhood to death, the unlikely friendship and emotional development of two African-American women in a small Midwestern black community. One of them is the title character, Sula, a rebellious, unconventional "woman-for-self." In the novel, as in all of Morrison's work, the quest for selfhood is a motivating factor.

Combining fantasy, fable, song, allegory, and mythology (that Africans could fly), *Song of Solomon* (1977), which sold a million copies and won the National Book Critics Circle and the American Academy and Institute of Arts and Letters Awards, focuses on a character's painful journey as he discovers and celebrates his African-American ancestry and heritage, with the help of his aunt, a strange but wise spiritual guide. *Song of Solomon* transcends ethnic identity by exploring universal themes: the discovery of self and the importance of communal and familial values, as opposed to individualism and materialism.

Morrison's next best-selling, widely praised novel, *Tar Baby* (1981), the title of which comes from an African-American folktale about a trickster who escapes his fate by outsmarting his captors, depicts a passionate affair in the Caribbean set against a background of racial and class tensions. Turning to other genres, in 1983 Morrison published a short story in *Confirmation,* an influential anthology; an essay entitled "Rootedness: The Ancestor as Foundation" in *Black Women Writers* (1984); and a play, *Dreaming Emmett* (1986), about a 14-year-old African-American boy from Chicago who was murdered in Mississippi in 1955 for whistling at a white woman.

Morrison's best-known novel, *Beloved* (1987), brought her worldwide recognition and, in 1988, the Pulitzer Prize for fiction. Based on the true story of an escaped slave who kills her own child, known only as "Beloved," rather than having her sold into slavery, it delineates the devastating effects of slavery and its aftermath, and how the past impinges on the present. Set in rural Ohio a few years after the Civil War, *Beloved* is also the story of a mother-daughter relationship, and the feelings of guilt, anger, grief, and love that they feel for each other. The novel opens abruptly and violently: "124 was spiteful. Full of baby's venom." Morrison noted that she wanted readers to feel disoriented, as if they were "snatched just as the slaves were from one place to another, from any place to another, without preparation and without defense." In 1998 *Beloved,* which is considered the author's greatest work to date, was adapted as a Hollywood film starring the talk show hostess Oprah Winfrey, who said she wanted to play Sethe because the book had profoundly moved her.

In 1992 Morrison saw three of her books published. *Jazz* is a "prose poem" novel in which the rhythms of Harlem during the 1920s form the backdrop of the story of a man from the rural South who is driven to violence by the dazzling music of jazz, jealousy, and passion. *Playing in the Dark: Whiteness and the Literary Imagination* is a collection of essays that critically analyzes American authors from Edgar Allan Poe to WILLA CATHER to Ernest Hemingway within the context of how they were influenced and shaped by what Morrison calls "the African presence." And *Racing Justice, En-Gendering Power: Essays on Anita Hill, Clarence Thomas, and the Construction of Social Reality* is a collection of essays that Morrison edited.

In 1993 Toni Morrison won the Nobel Prize in literature, followed in 1996 by the National Book Foundation Medal for Distinguished Contribution to American Letters. Toward the end of the decade she published *Paradise* (1998), a novel that, like *Beloved,* deals with the loss of innocence, the legacy of slavery, and the possibility of redemption by letting go of the past. It is set in Ruby, an imaginary small, idyllic black Oklahoma town founded by former slaves, where no one went hungry, there was no crime, and "freedom was not entertainment that you can count on once a year." One of the characters expresses their sense of contentment: "How exquisitely human was the wish for permanent happiness." During the 1970s, at a time when the town is confronted with racial, generational, and political problems, in a futile attempt to return to "paradise" a group of men violently attack a scapegoated all-female household of misfits and fugitives, with tragic and violent results. Although *Paradise* sold well, it received mixed reviews. *Time* magazine called it "one of the great novels of our day," while a *New York Times* reviewer found it "thoroughly lacking in the novelistic magic the author has wielded so effortlessly in the past."

But Morrison, who has no objection to being called a black woman writer, does not write to please critics. She is more interested in accurately and compassionately describing the African-American "pariah community" in white America, especially its resilient, proud, loving women. Her goal, she has said, is to create fully realized characters coping with loss and rediscovery. "Fiction," she wrote in *Black Women Writers at Work,* should be "beautiful, and powerful, but it should also work. It should have something in it that enlightens; something in it that opens the door and points the way. . . . [Writing] is discovery; it's talking deep within myself."

Turning to another genre, in 1999 Morrison published a children's book, *The Big Box.* It was followed by four others, all produced in collaboration with her son, Slade. *The Poppy or the Snake? (Who's Got Game?)* came out in 2004 and is the third title in an extended series of modern retellings of Aesop's famous fables. She also wrote another novel, *Love* (2003), as well as the nonfiction work *Remember: The Journey to School Integration* (2004). In 2005 the opera *Margaret Garner,* for which Morrison wrote the libretto, based largely on her novel *Beloved,* was first performed; it later toured the country.

In February 2006 Toni Morrison turned 75 years old. She was feted by critics and readers as "the closest thing the country has to a national writer," according to the *New York Review of Books.* Also in 2006, her novel *Beloved* was chosen by a select group of writers and critics as the best work of American fiction published since 1980. Throughout her successful career as a writer, editor, professor, public speaker, mentor, mother, and grandmother, Morrison has attempted to study "how and why we learn to live this life intensely well." One of America's foremost contemporary novelists, Toni Morrison has had a profound influence on America's national literature.

Further Reading

Beaulieu, Elizabeth Ann, ed. *The Toni Morrison Encyclopedia*. Westport, Conn.: Greenwood Press, 2003.

Duvall, John Noel. *The Identifying Fictions of Toni Morrison: Modernist Authenticity and Postmodern Blackness*. New York: St. Martin's (Palgrave), 2000.

Furman, Jan. *Toni Morrison's Fiction*. Columbia: University of South Carolina Press, 1995.

McKay, Nellie Y., ed. *Critical Essays on Toni Morrison*. Boston: G. K. Hall, 1988.

Morrison, Toni. *Beloved*. New York: Knopf, 1987.

———. *Love*. New York: Knopf, 2003.

———. *Playing in the Dark: Whiteness and the Literary Imagination*. Cambridge, Mass.: Harvard University Press, 1992.

———. *The Poppy or the Snake? (Who's Got Game?)*. New York: Scribner, 2004.

O'Reilly, Andrea. *Toni Morrison and Motherhood: A Politics of the Heart*. Albany, N.Y.: State University of New York Press, 2004.

Tate, Claudia, ed. *Black Women Writers at Work*. New York: Continuum, 1983.

∾ Mourning Dove (Christine Quintasket McLeod Galler, Humishuma)
(ca. 1888–1936) *novelist*

One of the first American Indians to publish a novel, Mourning Dove helped preserve and record the experiences, folklore, and rich culture of her tribal people and ancestors.

In her autobiography, Christine Quintasket McLeod Galler, who was known by her pen name Mourning Dove (a translation of her tribal name, Humishuma), described her birth:

> I was born in a canoe on the Kottenay River, near Bonner's Ferry, Idaho, during the Moon of the Leaves [April] in 1888. My mother and grandmother were being ferried across the river when I arrived. The Indian who was paddling their canoe was kind enough to pull off his shirt and hand it to my grandmother, who swaddled me.

According to Mourning Dove's account, her father was part Indian and part Scottish or Irish, so like the protagonist in her novel, *Cogewea,* she was a half blood. She was raised on the Colville Reservation in northeastern Washington State; her people were the Okanagan and the Colville. According to Jay Miller, who edited her autobiography in 1990, at an early age she recognized the importance of education in terms of achieving her goals and left the reservation to attend government-sponsored schools and Catholic mission boarding schools. But because she had missed several years of schooling, she was older and taller than most of her classmates and felt like an outcast; in addition, she was often reprimanded for speaking her tribal language, Salish, instead of English.

Nonetheless, she was determined to improve her English and typing skills and enrolled in a business school. She took a job teaching at an Indian school in Montana, where she often visited her grandmother, who was living nearby among the Kottenay. There she would listen to, and later record, the stories of the elderly tribal women. Mourning Dove was deeply impressed by their traditions and their courage. "It is all wrong, this saying that Indians do not feel as deeply as whites," she wrote. "We do feel, and by and by some of us are going to be able to make our feelings appreciated, and then will the true Indian character be revealed."

In 1908, after witnessing the roundup of one of the last free-ranging wild bison herds in America, Mourning Dove decided to be a writer so that she could describe what was really happening to Indians and their culture. She began working on a novel in 1912. Two years later she met Lucullus Virgin McWhorter, an Indian-rights activist, who offered to help her develop her manuscript, which blended familial events, western romance, and Salishan folklore, into a publishable novel. Much to her dismay, he also rewrote much of it. With few options available, she agreed to his changes, but the project remained stalled for nearly a decade.

In 1919, Mourning Dove and her second husband, a Wenatchee named Fred Galler, settled on the Colville Reservation. They supported themselves by picking apples or hops for $1.50 a day. After 10-hour days spent in the blazing sun, living out of tents and makeshift cabins, Mourning Dove would take out a battered typewriter and write until she dropped from exhaustion.

In 1927, after Mourning Dove agreed to help pay for the printing of her novel by putting in extra shifts as a migrant worker, *Cogewea the Half Blood: A Depiction of the Great Montana Cattle Range,* the story of a half-blood woman on the Flathead Reservation at the turn of the century and her conflict with assimilation, finally appeared. It was, in spite of being melodramatic, a popular and critical success. Meanwhile, Mourning Dove turned to recording folklore and spent several years traveling around the Pacific Northwest listening to, collecting, and translating folktales that would form the basis of *Coyote Stories,* which was published in 1933. The traditional Indian myths she wrote about revolve around a mischievous, powerful character, Coyote, one of the "Animal People" used by the "Spiritual Chief" to improve the world.

Toward the end of her life, Mourning Dove became increasingly involved in defending the rights of American Indians. She was the first woman elected to the Colville Tribal Council and reported on the reservation's slow but steady loss of territory. She also wrote an autobiography, *Mourning Dove: A Salishan Autobiography* (1990), which was heavily edited posthumously and chronicled her life as well as the varied roles played by, and the exploitation of, Indian women. It also provides an historical account of the Okanogan as their reservations were opened to white miners and settlers.

After suffering from nervous exhaustion and illness, Mourning Dove died on August 8, 1936, having worked tirelessly, both as a writer and an activist. She had succeeded in her lifelong goal: to help preserve and celebrate American Indian traditions from a woman's point of view through her writing, and to encourage other Indian women to record their stories.

Further Reading

Mourning Dove. *Cogewea the Half Blood: A Depiction of the Great Montana Cattle Range.* Lincoln: University Press of Nebraska, 1981.

———. *Mourning Dove: A Salishan Autobiography.* Edited and with an introduction by Jay Miller. Lincoln: University Press of Nebraska, 1990.

"Mourning Dove: Remember This." Said It: Feminist News, Culture, and Politics 1–4 (June 1999). Available online. URL: http://www.saidit.org/archives/june99/remember.html. Downloaded on March 3, 2007.

Troy, Judy. *Mourning Dove's Stories.* New York: Scribner's, 1993.

Mr. Vigillus
See MURRAY, JUDITH SARGENT

Mukherjee, Bharati
(1940–   )   *novelist, short story writer*

In her urbane, semiautobiographical fiction, Bharati Mukherjee writes about the cross-cultural experiences, both positive and negative, of South Asians, especially women, who have emigrated to the United States. "While changing citizenship is easy," asserts Mukherjee, "swapping cultures is not."

Born on July 17, 1940, into a middle-class Bengali Brahmin family in Calcutta, India, Mukherjee was educated in Europe and then in India, where she attended a convent school run by Irish nuns. She received a bachelor's degree with honors from the University of Calcutta in 1959, followed by a master's degree in English and ancient Indian culture at the University of Baroda in 1961, the same year she left for America. She continued her studies at the University of Iowa, earning a master's in fine arts degree in creative writing and a doctorate in English and comparative literature.

While at the University of Iowa, Mukherjee met, and in 1963 married, novelist Clark Blaise. They moved to Canada, where they lived with their two sons from 1966 until 1980. For the first time in her life, recalls Mukherjee, she felt like a "brown woman in a white society." In 1972 she published her first novel, *The Tiger's Daughter,* whose central character is an intelligent Indian-American woman who, having left her husband, returns to her native Calcutta in search of her past and her selfhood. Mukherjee's second novel, *Wife* (1975), continued to explore the same theme of reconciling two disparate cultures: a Bengali young woman who emigrated to a fringe immigrant ghetto in New York City ends up performing a violent act of self-assertion.

Mukherjee turned to nonfiction by collaborating with Blaise on an autobiographical journal, *Days and Nights in Calcutta* (1977), based on their year-long stay in India, after having lived in Canada for a decade. The couple also cowrote a book about the investigation of the tragic 1985 bombing of an Air India airliner, and together wrote a screen adaptation (1991) of *Days and Nights in Calcutta.*

After moving to the United States and becoming a naturalized citizen in 1980, Muhkerjee published her first collection of short stories, *Darkness,* in 1985. It focused on the rather bleak immigrant experiences of South Asians from varied backgrounds. However, her next collection of stories, *The Middleman and Other Stories* (1988), was more upbeat, highlighting the adventurous aspects of the immigrant experience. It was critically acclaimed for its "beautifully crafted" characters and won the 1988 National Book Critics Circle Award.

Muhkerjee expanded "Jasmine," one of the stories from *The Middleman,* into a novel by the same name, *Jasmine* (1989). It was about a young widowed Indian girl who leaves her small village, where she was condemned to a life of boredom and sexism, and invents new identities for herself in America. At last she feels free, happy, and satisfied. Like the protagonist, Mukherjee told *Publishers Weekly* in 1989 that she feels imbued by "an intensity of spirit and quality of desire" that exists in the United States. In the first chapter of *Jasmine* the character says:

> That stench [in Hasnapur, India] stays with me. I'm twenty-four now, I live in Baden, Elsa County, Iowa, but every time I lift a glass of water to my lips, fleetingly I smell it. I know what I don't want to become.

Mukherjee wrote two more novels about the perilous collision of cultures. Puritanical America meets Mughal Indian ways of life in *The Holder of the World* (1993), a *New York Times* Notable Book described by the novelist AMY TAN as an "amazing literary feat and a masterpiece of storytelling." *Leave It to Me* (1997), a sometimes humorous tale in which the Greek myth of Electra coexists with the Indian myth of Devi, also was named a Notable Book by the *New York Times.* "I'm the kind of writer who in the very first draft really doesn't know what adventures the characters will get into. . . . The endings have definitely come to me in dreams . . . and often take me by surprise," explained Mukherjee in *Writers Dreaming.*

Her entire body of fiction is characterized by variations on the themes of immigration, displacement, and the re-creation of identifies, says Leela Kapai in *Asian American Short Story Writers.* Mukherjee's recent novels include *Desirable Daughters* (2002), a suspenseful portrait of a traditional Brahmin family that focuses on one of three daughters who discovers she cannot break totally with her ancient Indian traditions, and its sequel, *The Tree Bride* (2004), described by *Publishers Weekly* as Mukherjee's "best work to date, fusing history, mysticism, treachery and enduring love." The storyteller's ability to give voice to a wide range of individuals outside the mainstream, asserts Kapai, "remains uncontested and establishes her as a pioneer charting unknown territories."

Bharati Mukherjee, who has taught at numerous colleges and universities and holds a distinguished professorship at the University of California, Berkeley, says she does not want to confine herself to a "narrow, airless, tightly roofed arena" by defining herself as a "hyphenated, Third World woman writer." She is, rather, an American writer of fiction who documents firsthand the myriad complex facets of the immigrant experience.

Further Reading

Kapai, Leela. "Bharati Mukherjee." In *Asian American Short Story Writers,* edited by Guiyou Huang, 203–213. Westport, Conn.: Greenwood Press, 2003.

Kerns-Rustomji, Roshni. "Bharati Mukherjee." In *The Heath Anthology of American Literature,* 5th ed., edited by Paul Lauter and Richard Yarborough, 2,693–2,694. New York: Houghton Mifflin, 2006.

Mukherjee, Bharati. *Leave It to Me.* New York: Knopf, 1997.

———. *The Middleman and Other Stories.* New York: Grove Press, 1988.

———. *The Tree Bride.* New York: Hyperion, 2004.

Mukherjee, Bharati, and Clark Blaise. *Days and Nights in Calcutta.* New York: Doubleday, 1977.

Nelson, Emmanuel S. *Bharati Mukherjee: Critical Perspectives.* New York: Garland, 1993.

Rustomji-Kerns, Roshni. "Expatriates, Immigrants and Literature: Three South Asian Women Writers." *Massachusetts Review* (Winter 1988–89): 655–665.

Murray, Judith Sargent (Constantia, The Gleaner, Mr. Vigillus)

(1751–1820) *essayist, poet, playwright*

A prominent early American feminist and playwright, Judith Sargent Murray was best known as one of the leading female essayists of the late 18th century.

Born on May 1, 1751, in Gloucester, Massachusetts, the eldest daughter of a wealthy seafaring merchant, Judith Sargent, unlike most young women at that time, was relatively well educated. Her civic-minded father encouraged his intellectually gifted daughter to study with her brother's tutor, and to share her brother's Latin, Greek, and mathematics books as he prepared to attend Harvard University. In 1769, 18-year-old Judith married John Stevens, a ship's captain with a penchant for gambling, and soon began writing verse.

In 1779 Murray composed her first essay, "On the Equality of the Sexes," a cogent feminist statement in which she argued that, in order to become self-sufficient and productive, young women should have the same access to formal education as young men. The ideal republican woman, she

wrote, should not only be a "sensible and informed" mother and wife, but also capable of intellectual and economic independence. The essay was not published until 1790, when it appeared in the *Massachusetts Magazine.*

Using the pseudonym Constantia, Murray published her poems in several literary magazines. In 1784 her essay "Encouraging a Degree of Self-Complacency, Especially in Female Bosoms," a passionate plea for women's rights, appeared in *Gentleman and Lady's Town and Country Magazine.* Women, she insisted, were destined for more than just "contemplating . . . the mechanism of a pudding, or the sewing of the seams of a garment." She also warned young women not to rush into marriage too young, as she had done, and to join her in "a new era in female history."

In 1788, two years after her first husband died in the West Indies, where he had fled to escape his debts, Judith Sargent Stevens married John Murray, a minister and founder of the Universalist Church in America. The couple, who had two children, only one of whom survived infancy, moved to Boston, where Murray wrote about the virtues of Universalist teachings while continuing to publish her poetry. She completed a series of about 100 essays, which were very popular and appeared from 1790 to 1794 in the *Massachusetts Magazine.* Most of them concerned the condition of women or the need to be patriotic by supporting the newly formed republic; they were signed "The Gleaner" and included a sentimental quasi-novel written by Murray's male persona, Mr. Vigillus, a kindly, sensitive man who is raising an adopted daughter.

One of the first American women to promote theater, Murray also wrote two plays to "expand the quantity, as well as the quality" of women's literature. *The Medium, or Virtue Triumphant* (1795) was the first American play staged in Boston and was followed a year later by *The Traveller Returned.* Neither play was successful.

In order to raise money to take care of her daughter and her husband, who was ill, Murray in 1798 put together *The Gleaner,* a three-volume collection of her essays, plays, and biographical sketches of notable women. She offered the volumes under a subscription plan headed by George Washington, one of her admirers. *The Gleaner* was critically acclaimed, and hundreds of readers, about a third of whom were women, signed up.

A year after her husband's death in 1815, Murray edited and published his autobiography. She left Massachusetts, where she had spent her life, and moved to Mississippi to live with her married daughter. Judith Sargent Murray died in Natchez on July 6, 1820. In 1984, an archive of 2,000 letters, documents, and poems—recounting her travels and her meetings with leading figures of the early republic, and often reflecting her insistence on women's intellectual and spiritual capacities—were recovered; they are currently held at the Mississippi Department of History.

In 1996 historian and feminist Bonnie Hurd Smith founded the Judith Sargent Murray Society to promote the writer's life, work, and significance. Smith serves as the Society's director and in 2002 initiated The Letters Book Project, the goal of which is to transcribe and publish each of Murray's 20 descriptive letter books. In 2005 Smith transcribed a collection of letters dated from 1796 to 1799, titled *The Letters I Left Behind, Judith Sargent Murray Papers, Letter Book 10,* with a foreword by the Reverend Gordon Gibson, who discovered the epistolary treasure trove more than 160 years after Murray's death.

Despite very difficult circumstances, Murray remained "a determined and tireless champion of women's equality," said Smith, in an article that appeared in the *Christian Science Monitor* (March 29, 2000), adding that the renowned essayist and playwright is "someone whose place in history must be restored."

Further Reading

Field, Verna Bernadette, *Constantia: A Study of the Life and Works of Judith Sargent Murray.* Orono: University of Maine Press, 1931.

Murray, Judith Sargent. *The Letters I Left Behind, Judith Murray Papers, Letter Book 10.* Transcribed and with an introduction by Bonnie Hurd Smith. Salem, Mass.: Judith Sargent Murray Society in conjunction with the Curious Traveller Press, 2005.

———. *Selected Writing of Judith Sargent Murray.* Edited by Sharon M. Harris. New York: Oxford University Press, 1995.

Roberts, Cokie. *Founding Mothers: The Women Who Raised Our Nation,* 252–254. New York: HarperCollins, 2004.

N

Naylor, Gloria
(1950–) *novelist*

The award-winning novelist Gloria Naylor writes about strong-willed African-American women, and the men they love, who—in spite of crushing poverty and racism—find support, friendship, and hope within the black community.

Born in New York City on January 25, 1950, according to her mother Gloria always had a "vivid imagination." She was also religious and worked as a missionary for the Jehovah's Witnesses while attending Brooklyn College, where she received a bachelor of arts degree in English in 1981. Naylor went on for a master's degree in Afro-American studies from Yale University in 1983, a year after she published her first and most critically acclaimed book, *The Women of Brewster Place: A Novel in Seven Stories,* which garnered the American Book Award for best fiction in 1983.

Using an omniscient narrator to weave together seven interlinked narratives of black women from diverse backgrounds and experiences, who end up living on the same block in a derelict urban neighborhood, Naylor creates complex, believable, and ultimately heroic characters. "I think of *The Women of Brewster Place* as a love letter to the black women

of America—a celebration of their strength and endurance," Naylor commented in *Contemporary Novelists.* The author's melodic, rich prose brings the residents of Brewster Place to life:

> They are hard-edged, soft-centered, brutally demanding, and easily pleased, these women of Brewster Place. They came, they went, grew up, and grew old beyond their years. Like an ebony phoenix, each in her own time and with her own season had a story.

The best-selling novel, which was adapted into a television miniseries in 1989, ends with an act of community solidarity among the beleaguered women.

Naylor described her second novel, *Linden Hills* (1985), an angrier and more cerebral book, as an allegorical "cautionary tale" and "an example of the drastic results if a people forsake their ethnocentric identity under the pressure to assimilate into a mainstream society and seek its rewards." Inspired by a 14th-century work, Dante Alighieri's *Inferno,* the plot concerns members of a middle-class black suburban community who are punished ("taken from Upper Hell to Lower Hell," said Naylor) for trying to imitate their upwardly mobile white neighbors.

Two more novels followed—*Mama Day* (1988), a mythical love story that alludes to William Shakespeare's *The Tempest* and whose central character is imbued with magical powers; and *Bailey's Cafe* (1992), a collection of interrelated stories about misfits who gather together to grapple, vociferously, with their personal and socioeconomic problems. It was adapted by Naylor for the stage in 1994, who a year later edited a collection of short stories by black writers titled *Children of the Night.*

After a 16-year hiatus Naylor returned to the characters of Brewster Place. In *The Men of Brewster Place* (1998), a sequel to her earlier book, the men are given a chance to redeem themselves by apologizing (albeit too late, in many instances) for having acted abusively, violently, or selfishly. Some critics found that *The Men of Brewster Place* lacking the "sweeping, musical prose" and strong emotional ties of *The Women of Brewster Place,* while others noted that the coupling of the two books provided a valuable social commentary on life in an urban black ghetto.

In a book review that appeared in the *African American Review* in spring 2001, Maxine Lavon Montgomery wrote that "there is something peculiarly Southern about Gloria Naylor's fiction—and this despite her birth in New York City. Careful consideration of place—whether it is a dilapidated, rat-infested housing project situated on a dead-end street or a magical island paradise off the Georgia coast—and the uniquely individual folk inhabiting such locales are the hallmarks of Naylor's carefully crafted words. Her deft rendering of peoples, places, and customs invites comparison to that of the best American local colorists who have brought national, and in some instances international, attention to little-known regions of the country."

In 2005 Naylor published *1996,* a fictionalized memoir about having been a victim of covert government surveillance and spying in 1996.

Naylor, who lives in New York City, has received Guggenheim and National Endowment for the Arts fellowships, and has taught at several colleges and universities, including Cornell, Brandeis, and Yale. An important American storyteller and con-temporary novelist, Gloria Naylor said in an interview in *Publishers Weekly* that she does not agree with the "historical tendency to look upon the output of black writers as not really American literature."

Further Reading

Gates, Henry Louis, and K. A. Appiah, eds. *Gloria Naylor: Critical Perspectives, Past and Present.* New York: Amistad, 1993.

Naylor, Gloria. *The Men of Brewster Place.* New York: Hyperion, 1998.

———. *1996.* Chicago: Third World Press, 2005.

———. *The Women of Brewster Place: A Novel in Seven Stories.* New York: Viking Press, 1982.

Wilson, Charles E. *Gloria Naylor: A Critical Companion.* Westport, Conn.: Greenwood Press, 2001.

➤ Nin, Anaïs
(1903–1977)   *diarist, novelist*

Anaïs Nin is considered one of the most celebrated and remarkable diarists of modern times. Her writings represented, as she explained it, "visualizations of an inner necessity" in which she explored, in detail and as a woman and an artist, her psyche and her personal experiences.

Born on February 21, 1903, in Paris, France, Anaïs Nin grew up surrounded by internationally renowned artists and musicians who were friends or associates of her father, a respected Cuban pianist and composer, and her mother, a French-Danish singer. But when she was 10, Anaïs's father, whom she both adored and feared, deserted his family, never to return. Her mother decided to emigrate to the United States with her young children.

During the long voyage to New York City, the 11-year-old Anaïs began writing the journal that eventually would become a seven-volume publication that spanned 50 years and that is regarded as her most acclaimed work. "I hate New York," she confessed in an entry written in 1914. "I find it too big, too superficial, everything goes too fast. It is just *hell.*" Anaïs turned to her diary for companionship and as a way to record her innermost feelings. At age 16 she dropped out of school, which she claimed neither interested nor stimulated her; instead, she read avidly, and worked as an illustrator, dancer, and fashion and artist's model. No matter what she did, she faithfully recorded it in her diaries.

In 1926, having married a prosperous banker, Hugh Guiler, who made it financially possible for her to pursue a literary career, Nin returned to Paris. (She had two husbands—Guiler in New York City and Rupert Pole, an artist and park ranger, in Los Angeles.) "Why did I not remain merely a diarist? Because there was a world beyond the personal which could be handled through the art form, through fiction," she noted in an essay.

Nin became an active member of the bohemian literati, befriending the surrealist poet Antonin Artaud, novelist Lawrence Durrell, and the controversial American writer Henry Miller, who like Nin was an early champion of the sexual revolution. In 1932 Miller and a few others helped establish a press in Paris that published Nin's first book, a critical study of the English novelist D. H. Lawrence. She admired and was greatly influenced by Lawrence's rejection of naturalism and rationalism in favor of a more sensory, intuitive approach to writing.

While in France, Nin also published her first volume of fiction, a long, surrealistic prose poem entitled *The House of Incest* (1936). "It is the seed of all my work, the poem from which the novels were born," she wrote. In 1939, with the outbreak of World War II, Nin and Guiler returned to New York City. She began intensive psychoanalysis with the well-known psychiatrist Otto Rank and later briefly set up a practice with him.

When Nin returned to her writing, having founded in New York a small avant-garde press for limited editions, her work was profoundly influenced by what she had discovered during her exploration of psychotherapy. In novels such as *Winter of Artifice* (1939), she delved into her unconscious, adhering to the dictum of another analyst, Carl Jung: "Proceed from the dream outward." Nonetheless in the second volume of her diary she admitted: "I want to run away from too much consciousness, too much awareness. At night, I seek dancing, friendships, nature, forgetfulness, music, or sleep."

Her press proved to be unsuccessful, so Nin turned to established publishing companies, and her work began to receive favorable reviews. When *Under a Glass Bell,* a collection of surrealistic short stories, appeared in 1944, the influential critic Edmund Wilson praised Nin for her lyrical "half stories, half dreams" that take place within a world of "feminine perception and fancy." *Cities of the Interior* (1959), a sequence of novels based on fictionalized accounts of her personal experiences, and illustrated by her husband under the name Ian Hugo, included a controversial series of erotica, *A Spy in the House of Love,* written from a female point of view. Still, Nin's work remained largely unknown until 1966, with the publication of the first volume of *The Diary of Anaïs Nin.* The heavily edited (she eventually filled more than 200 manuscript volumes) but very candid diaries brought her international recognition, as well as renewed interest in her previous work.

The seven-volume *Diary,* published between 1966 and 1978, comprises Nin's chronological journey of self discovery, with a focus on her relationships with men and her quest for personal freedom. Because of its popularity, Nin was often asked to lecture, and she became a spokeswoman for the emerging women's liberation movement. Feminists in the 1960s and early 1970s admired Nin for writing honestly about her "erotic awakening" and her insistence that women need to take command of their own lives. But in later years feminists became increasingly critical of Nin, perhaps because she unabashedly believed in femininity. As novelist ERICA JONG noted, Nin was a "seductress in a time when all seduction is presumed to be rape." Nin also refused to repudiate Freud and his beliefs, and was not disparaging of the "dead white male" writers and artists who often are perceived as comprising the Western canon. Yet her work, particularly the *Diary,* continues to have an enthusiastic readership among young women.

Unexpurgated versions of her diaries, which included descriptions of Nin's affairs with her psychiatrists and with Henry Miller and his wife June, were not published until after her death. In 1974, Nin was elected to the National Institute of Arts and Letters. A year later, *A Woman Speaks: The Lectures, Seminars, and Interviews of Anaïs Nin,* an edited pastiche of her central ideas and themes, was issued, followed by the final two edited volumes of her *Diaries.*

Anaïs Nin died on January 14, 1977, in Los Angeles. Later that year, two volumes of erotica, written for a dollar a page in the early 1940s, became best sellers. Nin, whose bigamous marriage to Guiler and Pole became public knowledge when Pole died in 2006, had finally achieved widespread acceptance, largely because of a work she initially had written for herself—the journal she began on a ship bound for New York from Barcelona in 1914. But Nin believed that "the personal life deeply lived always expands into truths beyond itself."

Further Reading

Hinz, Evelyn J. *The Mirror and the Garden: Realism and Reality in the Writings of Anaïs Nin.* New York: Harcourt Brace Jovanovich, 1973.

Knapp, Bettina L. *Anaïs Nin.* New York: Frederick Ungar, 1978.

Nin, Anaïs. *Anaïs Nin Reader.* Edited by Philip K. Jason. Athens, Ohio: Swallow Press, 1973.

———. *Anaïs Nin Reads: Excerpts from the Diaries* [sound recording]. New York: HarperCollins, 1993.

———. *The Diary of Anaïs Nin, 1931–1977,* 7 vols. New York: Harcourt, Brace and World / Harcourt Brace Jovanovich, 1966–1980.

Salvatore, Anne T., ed. *Anaïs Nin's Narratives.* Gainsville: University Press of Florida, 2001.

◈ Norman, Marsha
(1947–) *playwright, novelist*

Marsha Norman, a master at dramatizing quotidian life, is best known for her 1983 Pulitzer Prize–winning play *'night, Mother.* The Tony Award–winning playwright contends that she always writes about the same thing: ordinary characters who endure in spite of personal crises and failed familial relationships.

A native of Louisville, Kentucky, Marsha Norman was born on September 21, 1947, received a bachelor's degree from Agnes Scott College in 1969, and earned a master's degree from the University of Louisville in 1971. Before becoming a dramatist, she taught emotionally disturbed children and was a book reviewer and editor for the *Louisville Times.*

Norman's first three plays premiered at the Actors Theatre of Louisville, where she served as playwright-in-residence for two years. Her off-Broadway debut, *Getting Out* (1978), was an acclaimed psychological drama about a woman who has spent much of her adolescence in prison and, after being released, finds herself confused about supposedly being completely rehabilitated. Praised by critics for its powerful dialogue, emotional honesty, and "frighteningly true" language, it garnered, among other notable awards, the Outer Critics Circle Award for best new playwright. Norman had two actresses, on the stage at the same time, depicting the two sides of the character's personality. In 1994 it was adapted for television as a teleplay.

Third and Oak (1978) was a spare drama comprised of two short, dark but comedic one-act plays about lonely people who frequent an all-night laundromat and a pool hall. While it too favorably impressed drama critics, Norman's next work, *Circus Valentine* (1979), received negative reviews. "It was devastating," she recalled in *Newsday.* "But the most wonderful result of failure was that ultimately . . . I survived. That they had said everything awful that could be said, and I *still* wanted to write."

Norman struck gold with her fifth play, *'night, Mother,* which received the prestigious Pulitzer Prize for drama in 1983, as well as numerous other honors and citations. The two-character drama, which opened on Broadway in 1983, centers on a mother and her bitterly unhappy daughter who spend a tense night engaging in painful, angry dialogue, interspersed with trivial concerns, after the daughter casually announces that she is going to kill herself: "There's just no point in fighting me over it, that's all. Want some coffee?" The provocative play struck a chord with audiences and critics alike.

Traveler in the Dark (1984) was unusual for Norman in that its protagonists were mostly men. An esteemed surgeon unsuccessfully operates on a childhood friend and proclaims that although he wants God to exist, "I don't want it to be me." Two years later Norman wrote the screenplay for *'night, Mother.* The Hollywood movie was compared unfavorably to the celebrated play, in part because the play's structure—two characters talking in a room—was more suitable to the stage than to the screen. By 1986, the play version had been produced in 32 foreign countries. Explaining its

Marsha Norman wrote the provocative play *'night Mother.*
(AP/Wide World Photos)

appeal, Norman told the *New York Times:* "We all lose our children. . . . You think for a lifetime they belong to you, but they are only on loan."

Turning to another literary genre, in 1987 Norman published her first novel, *The Fortune Teller,* a love and mystery story with a psychic dimension in which Norman once again probed a complex mother-daughter relationship.

The next year, Norman returned to writing drama, with an experimental regional piece that had biblical allusions and feminist overtones. *Sarah and Abraham* was first staged at Louisville's Festival of New American Plays and later was produced in New Brunswick, New Jersey. In 1991 she wrote the book and lyrics for the Tony Award–winning Broadway musical *The Secret Garden,* which was adapted from Frances Hodgson Burnett's memorable children's book.

Marsha Norman, who has been married three times and has two children, was one of seven playwrights, including WENDY WASSERSTEIN and NTOZAKE SHANGE, invited to write one-act plays inspired by Shakespeare's sonnets. *Love's First* opened for a limited engagement at New York City's Public Theater in July 1998. Since 1994 Norman has been a faculty member at the Juilliard School in New York City, where she teaches drama. She penned the script for *The Audrey Hepburn Story* (2000), a made-for-television movie, staged *Last Dance* (2003), a play she set in southern France, and wrote the book for the award-winning Broadway musical production of *The Color Purple,* based on the novel by ALICE WALKER, which opened in Manhattan in December 2005. Pleased to be considered among a handful of emerging major woman dramatists, Norman noted that it is a time of "great exploration of secret worlds, or worlds that have been kept very quiet."

Further Reading

Bigsby, Christopher. "Marsha Norman." In *Contemporary American Playwrights,* 210–251. New York: Cambridge University Press, 2000.

Norman, Marsha. *Collected Plays.* New York: Smith and Kraus, 1998.

Simon, John. "Southern Comfort: *Last Dance.*" *New York Magazine,* 16 June 2003, p. 102.

Spencer, Jenny S. "Norman's *'night Mother:* Psychodrama of Female Identity." *Modern Drama* 30, no. 3 (September 1987): 364–375.

Norris, Kathleen Thompson
(1880–1966)   *novelist*

The author of more than 80 novels and numerous magazine stories and newspaper articles, Kathleen Norris rarely won the praise of literary critics but nonetheless was immensely popular with America's women readers for more than half a century. Her books sold over 10 million copies, making her one of the most commercially successful writers of the early- and mid-20th century.

Kathleen Norris was born on July 16, 1880, in San Francisco, California, into an upwardly mobile Irish-American family. She was the eldest daughter of a bank manager and devoutly Catholic mother. Tragedy struck the Norris family in 1919 when both parents died within a few months of each other, leaving 19-year-old Kathleen and her older brother to support their four younger siblings. After working at a series of jobs that included bookkeeping and teaching, Kathleen tried her hand at journalism. Among her first published writings were articles on the devastating San Francisco earthquake of 1906. She earned $12.50 for her first published magazine article.

In 1909 Kathleen married Charles G. Norris, also a writer and the younger brother of well-known novelist Frank Norris. The couple soon moved to New York City and enjoyed a long and loving marriage that lasted until Charles's death in 1954. They had a son who became a physician and two daughters who died in infancy, and adopted four other children.

Norris's marriage eased her financial responsibilities and enabled her to concentrate on writing fiction. Her first novel, *Mother,* appeared in 1911 and was highly successful. Like many of her novels, it drew heavily on Norris's Irish-American upbringing in San Francisco. Among those who praised the novel was President Theodore Roosevelt, according to C. D. Merriman, who wrote an article about the novelist in 2005 for The Literary Network.com. "Kathleen Norris was one of the highest paid female writers in America," asserts Merriman, adding that her novel *Certain People of Importance* (1922) was a best seller, was critically acclaimed, and turned her into a celebrity. Sixteen of Norris's novels were adapted for the screen, including the film *My Best Girl,* released in 1927.

Although some critics labeled her work superficial and sentimental—her romances all had happy endings—Norris provided millions of women readers with what one critic called "high-voltage" romance that chronicled the desires and experiences of ordinary people. Norris made her books authentic and believable by accurately describing the cosmetics, costumes, dinner parties, and other everyday details of the lives of her heroines. The scenes and conversations that captivated her readers often unfolded in the author's imagination while she played solitaire. Norris summed up her somewhat simplistic literary formula for success, which never violated her strict Catholic upbringing, as: "Get a girl in all kinds of trouble and then get her out."

In 1945 Norris shifted to another medium when she wrote scripts for a popular radio soap opera series, *Bright Horizons.* As with her novels, she succeeded in having the scripts reach "the very heart of American women and that's where I want to be."

While Norris placed her fictional heroines in traditional roles, her political opinions and activities often were unconventional. She was a feminist and opponent of capital punishment, as well as an ardent pacifist who strongly opposed America's entry into World War II and advocated disarmament and a halt to nuclear testing after the war.

Norris wrote two autobiographies about her lengthy life, *Control* (1925) and *Family Gathering* (1959). She continued writing until she was nearly 80 years old, despite crippling arthritis, and died on January 18, 1966, in San Francisco. A role model for many of her female readers, Kathleen

Norris offered them this advice: "Life is easier than you would think: all that is necessary is to accept the impossible, do without the indispensable, and bear the intolerable. In spite of the cost of living, it's still popular."

Further Reading

Merriman, C. D. "Kathleen Thompson Norris." *The Literary Network*. Available online: URL: http://www. online-literature.com/kathleen-norris. Downloaded on January 23, 2007.

Norris, Kathleen Thompson. *The Best of Kathleen Norris.* New York: Hanover House, 1955.

———. *Family Gathering*. Garden City, N.Y.: Doubleday, 1959.

———. *Mother*. New York: Grosset and Dunlap, 1911.

Obituary. *New York Times,* 19 January 1966.

Rexroth, Kenneth. "Mrs. Norris' Story." *New York Times Book Review,* 6 February 1955, p. 22.

❧ Norton, Andre (Andrew North, Allen Weston)

(1912–2005) *science fiction/fantasy writer, young adult book writer, short story writer*

Andre Norton, a groundbreaking, award-winning author of science fiction and fantasy, as well as of historical fiction and mystery novels, wrote more than 130 novels and nearly 100 short stories, many for young readers, and edited numerous science fiction anthologies. During her prolific 70-year career, she stressed universal themes such as alienation and self-realization and was praised for her storytelling skills, her carefully crafted portraits of alien heroes and heroines, and her attention to detail when characterizing futuristic settings.

Alice Mary Norton was born on February 17, 1912, in Cleveland, Ohio, where she lived with her elder sister, her mother, and her father, a rug salesman. When Alice was two, her mother began reciting poetry and reading to her. "By the time I was four, she was reading *Little Women* [by LOUISA MAY ALCOTT], and I could follow," recalled Norton in a 1996 interview in *Tangent* magazine. This reading, along with weekly family trips to the library, represented the beginning of Norton's appreciation of literature and, she explained, "a sense of wonder when a book becomes alive to the reader." While attending Collingwood High School in Cleveland, she wrote short stories for the school newspaper. By her senior year had produced a novel that, after revisions, would become her second published book, *Ralestone Luck* (1938).

Norton hoped to become a history teacher when she enrolled at the Flora Stone Mather College of Western Reserve University (now Case Western Reserve University), but she was forced to drop out after her freshman year because of financial restraints brought on by the Great Depression. She signed up for evening courses at Cleveland College and continued to write adventure stories that were published under the pseudonym Andre Norton, because her publisher thought that her predominantly adolescent male readership would prefer that. Norton's first-published historical fantasy novel for young adults, *The Prince Commands,* was released when she was 22, in 1934, the same year she legally changed her name from Alice to Andre. Years later many of the teenage boys who eagerly awaited her books were surprised to learn that Andre was a brown-haired, green-eyed young woman. Norton used the pen name Andrew North, mostly for the popular Solar Queen series, about a tramp space freighter, which included *Plague Ship* (1956) and *Voodoo Planet* (1959). She also occasionally used the pseudonym Allen Weston.

To help support her family, in 1932 Norton took a job as assistant children's librarian for the Cleveland Public Library. She stayed at the library, working at various branches, for 18 years. During that time she became an expert in juvenilia, but because she lacked a college degree she never received a promotion. In 1941 she moved to Maryland, where she bought and managed a bookstore called Mystery House, but the business failed. For a short time she worked at the Library of Congress in Washington, D.C., and then returned to the Cleveland Public Library until 1950.

Despite her demanding jobs, Norton never stopped writing fiction that reflected her interest in both history and science fiction. Her first science fiction story, "People of the Carter," appeared in the first issue of *Fantasy Book* in 1947. By 1950 she had produced nine novels, many of which she set in a particular historic period. For example, she set *Follow the Drum* (1942) in colonial Maryland, *Huon of the Horn* (1951) takes place in the time of Charlemagne, and *Stand to Horse* (1956) uses the Apache wars as a backdrop. Norton's folklore-style stories are filled with telepathic characters and animals imbued with magical powers, aided by magical gems or amulets instead of sophisticated computer-based contraptions. Norton disapproved of depending too much on technology. In an interview in 1983 with Charles Pitt, the author of *Dream Makers,* she asserted that the human race "made a bad mistake at the beginning of the Industrial Revolution. We leaped for the mechanical things." Instead, she believed in providing her readers with "intriguing ideas that are never completely wrapped up at the end of the book, thus leaving something to be filled in by the reader's own imagination," according to Barry McGhan, commenting in *Riverside Quarterly.*

Norton often wrote about alienated or orphaned characters and heroes searching for, and discovering, a place to belong. Above all else her fiction evokes a sense of wonder, allowing her readers to visualize exciting and strange universes for themselves. "An author should not write down to their audience," Norton said to John L. Coker III in *Tangent* magazine. She never patronized young readers and believed in providing them with a sense of hopefulness: "A lot of children's stories these days, while being well-written, are downbeat. They have no hope, and the protagonist is someone that you wouldn't like, and they are no better off at the end of the story than at the beginning," she stated.

After returning to and then leaving her position at the Cleveland Library, in part because of health-related issues, in 1950 she became a manuscript reader at Gnome Press, a publisher of science fiction. In just a single year at Gnome she published six adventure novels, edited an anthology, and began writing her first science fiction novel. In the 1950s science fiction had become increasingly popular. An editor at Ace Books recognized that not only adolescents but adults might be interested in the burgeoning genre. In 1954 he published Norton's first sci-fi novel, originally called *Star Man's Son, 2250 A.D.* (1952), written for young readers, with a new title: *Daybreak–2250 A.D.,* and marketed it to adult readers. The book, which featured a mutant hero who, along with his cat, a kindred spirit with which he communicates telepathically, searches for a radiation-free city after being thrown out of a postwar society, sold well and was a critical success, putting Norton at the forefront of sci-fi for grown-ups.

By 1958, when Norton left Gnome Press to become a full-time writer, 23 of her novels had been published. Norton often populated her stories, based on solid research, with unconventional protagonists: She introduced Native American heroes (*The Beast Master,* 1959), the first African-American character in the genre (*Storm and Warlock,* 1960), and the first female science fiction heroine (*Ordeal Otherwhere,* 1964). Her acclaimed fantasy series, the *Witch World* chronicles, includes 30 titles and features strong women from a matriarchal, semifeudal society on a planet reachable through metaphysical gateways and run by witches who derive their power from mind-enhancing jewels. Notably, the fast-moving series attracted a large female audience. It was followed by other sagas, such as the popular Beast Master and Star Ka'at fantasy series.

In 1966 Norton moved to Florida and then to Murfreesboro, Tennessee, a suburb of Nashville, where she continued to produce books at an astonishing rate. However, as her health deteriorated, she collaborated more frequently with other writers. She also edited fantasy and science fiction anthologies, such as *Renaissance Faire* (2005). In 1999 Norton founded High Hallack (the name of the country in Witch World), a retreat and research library for science fiction, fantasy, horror, and mystery writers, located near her home in Murfreesboro. "There are several writers' retreats in existence," she explained, "but they won't admit genre writers." After Norton became ill and could no longer run the underfunded library, High Hallack closed its doors in 2004.

Among her many awards and honors, Norton was the first woman inducted to the Science Fiction and Fantasy Writers' Hall of Fame (1997). She was the first woman to become a Gandalf Grand Master of Fantasy (1977) and to receive the Nebula Grand Master Award for Lifetime Achievement (1984) from the Science Fiction Writers of America, the same group that in 2005 bestowed its first Andre Norton Award for excellence in the field of writing for young adults. Norton also received the prestigious World Fantasy Convention Life Achievement Award in 1998. The last novel she wrote without a collaborator, *Three Hands for Scorpio,* was published in 2005 shortly after her death. "The late grand mistress of sci-fi and fantasy delivers yet another adventure . . . that constitutes a good introduction to her strengths," noted *Booklist.*

Andre Norton, dubbed by *Life* magazine the "Grand Dame of Science Fiction and Fantasy" and praised as a "superb storyteller with a pace all her own" by the *New York Times,* died of congestive heart failure on March 17, 2005, at her home in Murfreesboro, at the age of 93, surrounded by close friends, caretakers, and her cat. Upon request she was cremated along with a copy of her first and last novels. URSULA K. LE GUIN, a contemporary science fiction writer, described Norton as "a major person in the field of imaginative literature," adding that the sometimes critically overlooked author, who had legions of fans, was a "kind, shy, brilliant, and generous woman" who had a profound influence on future generations of science fiction and fantasy writers.

Further Reading

Bleiler, Richard, ed. *Supernatural Fiction Writers.* New York: Scribners, 2003.

Norton, Andre. *Daybreak—2250 A.D.* New York: Ace Books, 1954.

———. *The Gates to Witch World.* New York: Tor Books, 2001.

———. *Three Hands of Scorpio.* New York: Tor Books, 2005.

——— (under the pseudonym Andrew North). *Voodoo Planet.* New York: Ace Books, 1959.

———, and Jean Rabe, eds. *Renaissance Faire.* New York: DAW Books, 2005.

Wollheim, Betsy, and Sheila Gilberts, eds. *DAW Thirtieth Anniversary Fantasy Anthology.* New York: DAW Books, 2002.

Oates, Joyce Carol (Rosamond Smith)
(1938–) *novelist, short story writer, essayist*

A major American literary figure in the 20th century, Joyce Carol Oates is a prolific, award-winning writer who has mastered several genres. Dubbed "the dark lady of American letters," Oates portrays the tumultuous moral and social conditions and the violent upheavals that define contemporary America.

Joyce Carol Oates was born on June 16, 1938, into an Irish Catholic, working-class family in Lockport, a small town in upstate New York that is the model for "Eden Country," the rural setting of many of her novels. She was raised on her grandparents' farm and attended a one-room schoolhouse. An intelligent, curious, bookish, and solitary child, Joyce was, in her words, "nearly always alone, and drawn to loneliness." Nonetheless, in her journal she recorded, years later, that she was not unhappy: "I begin to see as I grow older how very fortunate I was in my early years: a mother, a father, a grandmother who loved me very much. And rural surroundings . . . beautiful in their simple way," she wrote.

After attending Syracuse University on a scholarship, where in 1960 she graduated and in the same year was inducted into Phi Beta Kappa, in 1961 Oates received a master's degree in English from the University of Wisconsin. That same year she married a fellow graduate student, Raymond Smith, with whom she would found the Ontario Review Press and publish the *Ontario Review.*

Oates began to submit and publish her short stories in notable national literary magazines such as *Epoch,* and in 1963 her first collection of stories, *By the North Gate,* appeared. In it she explores social themes that would dominate her work: violence, mental instability, criminality, and isolation. From the start she wrote serious fiction. As she explained in one of her collection of essays, *New Heaven, New Earth: The Visionary Experience in Literature* (1974), the novelist's obligation was to "do no less than attempt the sanctification of the world!"

In her first novel, *With Shuddering Fall* (1964), set in the fictitious Eden County, one of the protagonists is raped and badly beaten before returning to her family. Criticized for portraying an excess of violence and pain, Oates responded, "the more violent the murders in Macbeth, the more relief one can feel at not having to perform them. . . . Great art is cathartic; it is always moral."

Joyce Carol Oates has been called "the dark lady of American letters."
(AP/Wide World Photos)

be a murderer." The third novel in the trilogy, *them* (1969), which explores inner-city poverty, racism, and violence in Detroit during the 1960s, won the National Book Award for fiction in 1969; Oates, at 31, was one of the youngest writers ever to receive the award.

Oates also excelled at realistic, compelling short fiction. "Where Are You Going, Where Have You Been," a feminist allegory, cautionary tale, and coming-of-age story about the sexual awakening of an adolescent girl, was published in 1970 in Oates's collection *The Wheel of Love* (1970). It became one of her most popular and most anthologized short stories. Twice, in 1970 and 1986, Oates received the O. Henry Special Award for Continuing Achievement. Although her reputation as a novelist is controversial—not all of her novels are well received—she is almost universally considered one of the preeminent masters of the short story. Her work has appeared more frequently in the two annual prize anthologies *Best American Short Stories* and *Prize Stories: The O. Henry Awards,* than that of any other author in either series. "Stories," she wrote in 1999, "come to us as wraiths requiring precise embodiments."

For Oates, fictional characters must act and confront, not avoid, life and reality, no matter what the consequences. In *Do with Me What You Will* (1973), the heroine finally gives up her almost psychotic state of passivity by leaving her husband for a lover. Turning to more experimental forms, in *The Assassins: A Book of House* (1975), Oates dabbled with stream of consciousness, and in *Childhood* (1976), she incorporated shifting voices and interior monologues to represent successive generations. All of Oates's works are carefully structured.

Her next novel, *Bellefleur* (1980), was a sprawling five-part gothic saga about a family. A commercial and critical success, and a popular best seller, it traverses thousands of years, and incorporates the fantastic and the real. In the 1980s Oates wrote a series of postmodern gothic novels that would reflect various epochs in American history: a grotesque, comic parody of a romance novel, *A*

Her second novel (she has written more than 40), *A Garden of Earthly Delights,* is a surrealistic tale published in 1967, the same year she was awarded a Guggenheim fellowship, and is the first of a trilogy of books conceived as a critique of the materialism and self-destructive nature of 20th-century America. In *Expensive People* (1968), the harrowing story of matricide in the affluent suburbs, the narrator is a young killer, and he tells, in an emotionless manner, his own murderous story. The chilling novel begins: "I was a child murderer. I don't mean child-murderer, though that's an idea. I mean child murderer, that is, a murderer who happens to be a child, or a child who happens to

Bloodsmoor Romance; a gothic horror novel, *The Crosswicks Horror;* a detective story, *Mysteries of Winterthurn;* a "family memoir," *My Heart Laid Bare;* and, in 1994, an entire volume of short stories subtitled *Tales of the Grotesque,* in which she dramatized macabre, horrific events of everyday life. Oates described writing the quintet, which encompassed eight decades of American history and some 2,600 pages of prose, as "intriguing."

Oates has written in various styles and genres on subjects as diverse as feminism, the poetry of D. H. Lawrence, mystery, and history, and authored a book-length critical essay espousing her philosophy on sports, *On Boxing* (1987). As of 2005 she had penned eight novels under the pseudonym Rosamond Smith because, she said, "I wanted to escape from my own identity," and has published more than a dozen volumes of poetry and two dozen plays, one of which, *The Perfectionist,* won a nomination from the American Theatre Critics Association for best new play in 1994. Simultaneously, she has continued writing novels.

You Must Remember This (1987), like many of her later novels, was a return to the intense psychological realism of Oates's early novels, such as her 1971 critically acclaimed *Wonderland.* Oates calls her 1993 novel *Foxfire: Confessions of a Girl Gang* a kind of "dialect between romance and realism," and like her other works of that period it features female protagonists and feminist concerns. On the other hand, *Black Water* (1993), a Pulitzer Prize finalist, was a fictionalized account of Senator Edward Kennedy's fatal plunge at Chappaquiddick in 1969, told from the point of view of the drowning woman, at a future time. And *Zombie* (1995), another short novel, was suggested by the case of serial killer Jeffrey Dahmer; it reveals the author's continued horrific-comedic fascination with the criminal mind and with lonely, lost souls.

In his *New York Times* review of *We Were the Mulvaneys* (1996), David Gates wrote: "What keeps us coming back to Oates Country is . . . her uncanny gift of making the page a window, with something happening on the other side that we would swear was life itself." In the 1998 novel *My*

Heart Laid Bare, Oates returns to an old-fashioned family saga, with a touch of gothic. In it, through her characters she examines social turmoil, destiny, and death. In 1998 she also published *The Collector of Hearts: New Tales of the Grotesque.* Although she has been attacked for writing fiction that is too violent and pessimistic, Oates claims that the act of writing is in itself an optimistic act. "I think of [writing] primarily as a gesture of sympathy." Violence, she believes, stems not from personal circumstances but from external, everyday conditions.

By 2005 Oates had more than 100 works in print, and she continues to produce at least three new books each year. Oates once commented that while she is asked frequently *how* she writes so much, she is rarely asked *why.* She also continues to garner honorary doctorate degrees—from Syracuse and Northwestern Universities in 2000—and a bevy of awards and honors. *Blonde* (2000), which Oates described as exploring the "riddle and curse . . . the inner, poetic, and spiritual life" of Marilyn Monroe, through a fictional treatise, was a 2001 finalist for the Pulitzer Prize and the National Book Award. In 2003 she won the Common Wealth Award for Distinguished Service in Literature and the Kenyon Review Award for Literary Achievement, followed in 2004 by a Fairfax Prize for Lifetime Achievement in the Literary Arts.

In 2005 Oates received the Prix Femina, a prestigious French award for the best foreign novel, for *The Falls* (2004), a harrowing story in which Niagara Falls plays a major role as the dramatic backdrop and an apt metaphor for the wild forces that play havoc with the inner struggles of her protagonists. The book, from its shocking beginning, deftly explores the complexity of the American family in the mid-20th century. "While there is intense love, whether erotic or parental," explains Oates, about families, in a BookBrowse.com interview, "it is likely to become possessive and stifling, provoking rebellion. Upsets may occur, even painful misunderstandings and separations, yet the essential love remains, and might again flourish, more temperately." Oates is fearless and unsparing in entering the minds and deeds of her characters, no matter where this might lead her or the reader.

Also in 2005 her story "The Cousins" was included in *The Best American Short Stories 2005* (she had penned another short story collection, *I Am No One You Know,* in 2004), and she edited and introduced *The Best American Mystery Stories 2005*. In the same year Oates published *Missing Mom,* a haunting novel about absence and its effects on others; *Sexy,* a young adult book; and a nonfiction collection, *Uncensored: Views and (Re)views,* a compilation of prose essays and reviews whose goal, wrote Oates, is "to call attention solely to books and authors that merit such attention." She also candidly included a discussion on her own writing process.

In her collection of mystery and suspense stories *The Female of the Species* (2006), Oates "adroitly shows how one bad decision leads to a host of others, and how those choices can change a woman from a mistress to a murderer," writes Hillary Frey in the *New York Times Book Review.* "Even as Oates's unrepentant, selfish characters repel you, their tales hold you hostage."

Displaying her versatility and ability to produce, Oates had at least seven other books planned for publication in 2006 and 2007, including novels, an anthology of short fiction and another of women cartoonists, a book of verse, a young adult novel, and a children's book. Two of these books already have been published in 2006: *High Lonesome,* a collection of stories, and *Black Girl / White Girl,* a controversial novel about race relations. In 2007 Oates produced another provocative novel, *The Gravedigger's Daughter.* In a review of *Missing Mom* for the *New York Times,* critic Stacey D'Erasmo asserts, "In her novels, plays, poetry, essays, thrillers (under the nom de plume Rosamond Smith) and critical analyses not only of others but of herself, Oates has a strong predilection for bearing down until she draws blood. Everything, over the vast terrain of Oatesiana, ultimately comes down to this basic element, sign of life and, often, of brutal force."

Joyce Carol Oates has taught English at the University of Detroit and the University of Wind-

sor in Ontario, Canada. Elected to the National Academy and Institute of Arts and Letters and a recipient of the Bobst Award for Lifetime Achievement in Fiction, she and her husband live in Princeton, New Jersey, where she is the Robert S. Berlind Distinguished Professor of the Humanities at Princeton University.

Further Reading

Cologne-Brookes, Galvin. *Dark Eyes on America: The Novels of Joyce Carol Oates.* Baton Rouge: Louisiana State University Press, 2005.

Friedman, Ellen G. *Joyce Carol Oates.* New York: Frederick Ungar, 1980.

Johnson, Greg, ed. *Joyce Carol Oates: Conversations, 1970–2006.* New York: Ontario Review Books (dist. by W. W. Norton), 2006.

Oates, Joyce Carol. *Bellefleur.* New York: Dutton, 1980.

———. *Black Girl/White Girl.* New York: HarperCollins, 2006.

———. *The Falls.* New York: HarperCollins, 2004.

———. *The Female of the Species: Tales of Mystery and Suspense.* New York: Harcourt, 2006.

———. *High Lonesome: Selected Stories, 1966–2006.* New York: Ecco/HarperCollins, 2006.

———. *them.* New York: Vanguard, 1969.

Souther, Randy. "Celestial Timepiece—Resources for Joyce Carol Oates's Work." Available online. URL: http://jco.usfca.edu/. Downloaded on May 22, 2007.

O'Brien, Howard Allen
See RICE, ANNE

O'Connor, Mary Flannery
(1925–1964)   *novelist, short story writer*

Flannery O'Connor combined gothic, grotesque, and religious elements with apocalyptic violence and southern, deadpan humor in her prize-winning short stories and novels. Despite her small body of work, she is considered one of America's leading fiction writers and has been compared in stature to EMILY DICKINSON and Nathaniel Hawthorne.

Born on March 25, 1925, in Savannah, Georgia, the only child of devout Catholic parents,

Mary Flannery O'Connor was 15 when her much-loved father died of disseminated lupus, the same disease that would claim her own life 25 years later.

A precocious, lively child, she enjoyed writing in her journal and composing stories and essays, as well as playing with her pet fowl, especially the deformed ones. She helped raise quails, chickens, and peacocks, the latter of which figured prominently in several of her stories, such as "The Displaced Person." When a local newspaper photographer documented one of her pet chickens walking backward, the young O'Connor considered it "the highpoint of her life" and the beginning of her obsession with the grotesque.

A sociology major at Georgia College, O'Connor edited the school newspaper and wrote fiction for the literary magazine before graduating in 1945. Her undergraduate writing won her a fellowship to the Writers' Workshop of the University of Iowa, and in 1946 she sold her first story, "The Geranium" to *Accent* magazine. A year later she was granted a master of fine arts degree in literature.

O'Connor began writing her first novel, *Wise Blood*, while at Yaddo, a writers' retreat in New York State, where she met and befriended the poet Robert Lowell, who had converted to Catholicism. She moved to New York City in 1949, and then to Connecticut, where she lived with friends for two years. She was delighted when several chapters of her novel-in-progress were published in national literary quarterlies. But at age 25, O'Connor suffered a serious attack of lupus, and in 1951 she returned, permanently, to her mother's dairy farm near Milledgeville, Georgia. There she raised peafowl, painted, and wrote about doomed and maimed characters and the power of God's grace in a fallen, temporal world.

Weakened by the crippling disease and effects of the drugs intended to slow its progress, she rarely left the farm. "I have never been anywhere but sick," she explained in her posthumously published collection of essays, *Mystery and Manners: Occasional Prose* (1969). "In a sense sickness is a place, more instructive than a long trip to Europe, and it's always a place where there's no company, where nobody can follow." While she loved the slow pace and friendliness of the South, as an unmarried woman who wrote about violence and religion, when she was not helping her mother run a farm, and as a staunch Catholic in the predominantly Protestant deep South, O'Connor was, as she put it, "both native and alien."

When *Wise Blood* appeared in 1952, it was acclaimed, if not universally understood, by critics. Most praised the author's lucid, precise style, and her powerful, vivid portrayal of southern gothic characters such as Hazel Motes, a soldier who had lost his faith. He returned home as a would-be founder of a "church without Christ, where the blind stay blind, the lame stay lame and them that's dead stays that way." Motes meets a street preacher who pretends to be blind, and has an affair with the preacher's seductive teenage daughter. In a bizarre twist, Motes blinds himself as an act of redemption and then awaits his death, and salvation, in darkness and solitude. O'Connor considered *Wise Blood* funny and in its introduction asserted that "all comic novels that are any good must be about matters of life and death."

In "A Good Man Is Hard to Find," the title story in her first collection by the same name, the protagonist is an escaped convict known as The Misfit, who equates himself with Jesus but questions his own faith and ends up murdering an elderly woman whom he encounters on vacation with several members of her family. "'I never was a bad boy that I remember of,' The Misfit said in an almost dreamy voice, 'but somewheres along the line I done something wrong and got sent to the penitentiary, I was buried alive.'" Before he fatally shoots the old woman, she accepts The Misfit by calling him "one of her babies, one of her children." For O'Connor, the acceptance of grace was the guiding force of both her life and her fiction, although she never allowed a trace of religious sentimentality to slip into her work. In another popular story from *A Good Man Is Hard to Find* (1955), "The Displaced Person," which was adapted as a television drama in 1979, an outsider, whose symbolic double is a peacock, is the main character.

O'Connor's second novel, *The Violent Bear It Away* (1959), centers on another fugitive from Christ—a country boy who drowns his cousin instead of baptizing him. After being raped, he recognizes what he has done and becomes a "prophet." As in most of O'Connor's fiction, a violent action leads to a purifying act. Her posthumously released collection of short stories, *Everything That Rises Must Converge* (1965), includes what is considered one of her finest stories, "Revelation," about a maimed country girl and her relationship with her complacent, selfish mother.

A few literary critics charged O'Connor with bringing too much violence, harshness, and grotesquerie into her writing. She professed amusement at these attacks and refused to change her mordant style or soften her characters, whether religious hucksters or crippled visionary farm hands. "I am interested in making up a good case for distortion, as I am coming to believe it is the only way to make people see," she responded.

O'Connor's talents were recognized during her brief lifetime. She received honorary degrees at St. Mary's College at Notre Dame and Smith College, grants from the National Institute of Arts and Letters and the Ford Foundation, three O. Henry awards, and the *Kenyon Review* Fellowship in Fiction. Although she needed braces to walk and was often in pain, O'Connor continued to write for at least two hours a day, no matter what, because, she said, "I have to write to discover what I am doing." In an essay from *Mystery and Manners: Occasional Prose* (1969), she claimed that "if a writer is any good, what he makes will have its source in a realm much larger than that which his conscious mind can encompass and will always be a greater surprise to him than it can ever be to his reader."

The Flannery O'Connor-Andalusia Foundation was incorporated in 2001 to encourage and promote an increased understanding of the life, time, surroundings, and accomplishments of Flannery O'Connor. Located near Milledgeville, Georgia, on the bucolic estate-farm complex where O'Connor once lived and worked, Andalusia provides public access to scholars, teachers, students, and general visitors who want to learn more about the author and her impressive body of work.

Flannery O'Connor died on August 3, 1964, at age 39, in Milledgeville. In 1971 she posthumously received the National Book Award for *The Complete Stories*. A prolific correspondent, in 1979 a selection of O'Connor's letters was published under the title *The Habit of Being;* it garnered a National Book Critics Circle Award. A classic film adaptation of *Wise Blood,* directed by John Huston, was released in 1980. Robert Lowell once described O'Connor's characters as "wholeheartedly horrible and almost better than life. I find it hard to think of a funnier or more frightening writer."

Further Reading

Edmondson, Henry T. *Return to Good and Evil: Flannery O'Connor's Response to Nihilism.* Lanham, Md.: Lexington Books, 2002.

Ficket, Harold, and Douglas R. Gilbert. *Flannery O'Connor: Images of Grace.* Grand Rapids, Mich.: Eerdmans, 1986.

Friedman, Melvin J., and Beverly Lyon Clark, eds. *Critical Essays on Flannery O'Connor.* Boston: G. K. Hall, 1985.

O'Connor, Flannery. *Collected Works* (includes novels and stories). Edited by Sally Fitzgerald. New York: Library of America, 1988.

———. *Mystery and Manners: Occasional Prose.* Edited by Sally Fitzgerald and Robert Fitzgerald. New York: Farrar, Straus, 1969.

O'Gorman, Farrell. *Peculiar Crossroads: Flannery O'Connor, Walker Percy, and Catholic Vision in Postwar Southern Fiction.* Baton Rouge: Louisiana State University Press, 2004.

Simpson, Melissa. *Flannery O'Connor: A Biography.* Westport, Conn.: Greenwood Press, 2005.

✑ O'Flaherty, Katherine

See CHOPIN, KATHERINE O'FLAHERTY

✑ Olds, Sharon
(1942–) *poet*

One of the preeminent voices in contemporary American poetry, Sharon Olds has written seven volumes of highly descriptive, personal, and sometimes shockingly explicit verse about physical and metaphysical pleasure and pain.

Born on November 19, 1942, in San Francisco, California, where she was raised, Olds received a bachelor's degree from Stanford University in 1964 and a doctorate from Columbia University in 1972. Her poems have appeared in national literary journals and magazines such as the *New Yorker, Paris Review,* and *Poetry,* as well as in numerous anthologies and textbooks, and her works have been translated into Italian, Chinese, French, and Russian.

Olds's first collection of verse, *Satan Says* (1980), lyrically explored the poet's varied roles as mother, daughter, and lover, and her varied emotions, from anger and terror to love and ecstasy. A critic for the *American Book Review* noted that the poems in *Satan Says* depict a "psychic world as turbulent, sensual, and strange as a world seen under water." Several, such as "The Language of the Brag," celebrate childbirth:

> I have lain down and sweated and shaken and passed blood and feces and water and slowly alone in the center of a circle I have passed the new person out. . . .

Her second book, *The Dead and the Living* (1984), which garnered the Lamont Poetry Selection from the Academy of American Poets and the National Book Critics Circle Award, sold 50,000 copies and was lauded for its lyrical acuity and ebullient language, and for its accurate observations, both private and universal. Olds often writes movingly about family life and strife, especially the violent details of her childhood, as well as about sexuality.

In *The Gold Cell* (1987), Olds touched upon a variety of topics: a man perched on a rooftop in New York City who decides not to kill himself, the poet's first sexual encounter, Alcatraz, and the death of her alcoholic father. In the *New York Times* in 1998, Olds was described as "one of the country's best-known poets [who] writes about life

inside a physical body: the pleasure, the sufferings, the various life-giving angles and fluids."

Olds's other collections of verse include *The Matter of This World: New and Selected Poems* (1987), *The Sign of Saturn* (1991), *The Father* (1992), and *The Wellspring: Poems* (1996), and *Blood, Tin, Straw* (1999). In 1998 she received the Walt Whitman Citation of Merit (her writing has often been compared to Walt Whitman's) and was named the official New York State Poet, a two-year appointment that includes teaching in public schools and giving readings across the state.

Olds's volume of verse *The Unswept Room* (2002) was nominated for a National Book Award. A *Booklist* reviewer noted that it "gives rise to some stunningly visceral poems about suffering and death that are rendered as unsparingly and transcendently as the most explicitly and demanding of religious paintings and charged with a fierce holiness." *Critical Survey of Poetry* asserts that Olds's signature poems are autobiographical lyrics, many of them charged with eroticism, violence, or both.

Strike Sparks: Selected Poems, 1980–2002, a collection of 117 of Olds's finest poems drawn from her seven published volumes, includes verse that moves beyond the personal but also features Olds's more familiar themes as she "carries the reader through rooms of passion and loss," writes novelist Michael Ondaatje, in describing her affecting poetry. Published in 2004, *Strike Sparks* won the National Books Critics Circle Award. Olds's work has been anthologized in more than 100 collections and translated into seven languages. Olds is a popular, accessible American poet, and most of her volumes have undergone multiple printings. "Poets are like steam valves, where the ordinary feelings of ordinary people can escape and be shown," she once explained.

Never one to shy away from controversy, Olds declined to attend the National Book Festival in September 2005 as the guest of First Lady Laura Bush, because, as Olds wrote to Mrs. Bush, she would be taking food from the hand of the First Lady "who represents the Administration that unleashed this . . . undeclared and devastating war [the Iraq War that started in 2003] and that wills its continuation."

Sharon Olds, who believes that poetry has the power to heal and to enhance life, perhaps even to save children from the impending apocalypse, resides in New York City, where she is associate professor of English at New York University and directs the graduate program in creative writing. The recipient of several grants and fellowships, she has taught poetry at Columbia and Brandeis Universities and at Goldwater Hospital for the severely handicapped on Roosevelt Island in New York, where she founded a writers' workshop.

Further Reading

Jason, Philip K., ed. *Critical Survey of Poetry, Second Revised Edition,* 2,817–2,822. Pasadena, Calif.: Salem Press, 2003.

Matson Suzanne, "Talking to Our Father: The Political and Mythical Appropriations of Adrienne Rich and Sharon Olds." *American Poetry Review* 18 (1989).

Olds, Sharon. *The Dead and the Living.* New York: Knopf, 1983.

———. *Satan Says.* Pittsburgh: University of Pittsburgh Press, 1980.

———. *Strike Sparks: Selected Poems, 1980–2002.* New York: Knopf, 2004.

———. *The Unswept Room.* New York: Knopf, 2002.

Ostriker, Alicia S. *Stealing the Language: The Emergence of Women's Poetry in America.* Boston: Beacon Press, 1986.

∾ Oliver, Mary
(1935–) *poet, essayist*

Mary Oliver writes accessible, popular verse that is also critically acclaimed. Her highly personal encounters with the natural world seem to resonate with legions of readers, in part because of her carefully crafted, meditative, and precise but lyrical imagery. In addition to winning a Pulitzer Prize for *American Primitive* in 1984, Oliver, who has been writing poetry for nearly five decades and has published nearly 20 books, received a National Book Award in 1992 for *New and Selected Poems.*

Oliver was born in Cleveland, Ohio, on September 10, 1935. "Her childhood profoundly influences her poetry," asserts Rosemary Winslow in *A Critical Survey of Poetry,* referring especially to Oliver's troubled relationship with her father, which was never reconciled. In the poem "Rage," the poet describes a scene in which a child is the victim of incest and delineates the damaging, long-standing effects of that traumatic experience. However, Oliver never took on a victim persona, as did the confessional poets SLYVIA PLATH and ANNE SEXTON. "Oliver's poetry is remarkable for its limited focus on herself as a personality while showing a path out of terror and sorrow to acceptance, safety, joy, and freedom," notes Winslow. "Her vision is ecstatic, arising from silence, darkness, deep pain and questioning."

After attending Ohio State University for one year, followed by a year at Vassar College before she dropped out, Oliver wrote to the sister of EDNA ST. VINCENT MILLAY, since she was influenced and impressed by Millay's body of work. She was invited to visit Millay at Steepletop, her farmstead in upstate New York, which she did on several occasions, serving as a secretarial assistant to Millay's sister. Oliver moved to New York City, spent a year in England, and then returned to America in 1964. Her first collection of verse, *No Voyage and Other Poems,* was published in 1965. Other books of poetry followed, including the Pulitzer Prize–winning *American Primitive* (1983), composed of 50 visionary, luminous poems; *New and Selected Poems, Volume One* (1992), for which she won a National Book Award; *The Leaf and the Cloud* (2000); and *New and Selected Poems, Volume Two* (2005), which contained 32 new poems. In 2006 a CD of the poet reading her verse, *At Blackwater Pond,* was released, as well as another well-received volume of poems titled *Thirst.* "My work is loving the world," wrote Oliver in an introduction to *Thirst,* "which celebrates the splendor and redemptive power of nature."

She also has produced collections that combined poetry and essays, such as *Owls and Other Fantasies: Poems and Essays* (2003) and *Blue Iris:*

Poems and Essays (2004); chapbooks (small books containing poems or tracts); and nonfiction titles including *Rules for the Dance: A Handbook for Writing and Reading Metrical Verse* (1998); *Winter Hours* (1999), a collection of poems, prose poems, and nine essays on topics ranging from turtle eggs to the poetry of Robert Frost; and *Long Life: Essays and Other Writings* (2004). Many of her prose pieces focus on the craft of writing or on poets who have influenced her work and who, like she, celebrate nature or look to it for inspiration, such as Walt Whitman and William Blake. Oliver believes that it is important to read and gain insight from other poets, especially the romantic writers such as John Keats and Percy Bysshe Shelley.

Oliver is an "indefatigable guide to the natural world, particularly to its lesser-known aspects," writes contemporary poet MAXINE KUMIN in *Women's Review of Books*. In some of her poems, for example in "Moccasin Flowers," when Oliver refers to "the pink lungs of the bodies" of flowers as they open and blossom, before dying and melding with trees, the nature imagery and human imagery merge in a kind of divine spiritual moment. "It is one of the perils of our so-called civilized age that we do not yet acknowledge enough, or cherish enough, this connection between soul and landscape," wrote Oliver in *Aperture* magazine.

Among her numerous honors, Oliver has won a Lannan Foundation Literary Award for Poetry, an Achievement Award from the American Academy and Institute of Arts and Letters, and the Poetry Society of America's Shelley Memorial Award. She also has received Guggenheim and National Endowment for the Arts (NEA) fellowships and has taught at universities and colleges throughout the United States, including Case Western Reserve as Mather Visiting Professor, Sweet Briar College in Virginia as Banister Writer-in-Residence, the University of Cincinnati, and Bennington College in Vermont, where she currently holds the Catharine Osborn Foster Chair for Distinguished Teaching. According to Dwight Garner in the *New York Times Book Review* (February 18, 2007), Oliver is "far and away this country's best-selling poet."

Further Reading

Oliver, Mary. *American Primitive*. New York: Little, Brown 1983.

———. *New and Selected Poems, Volume Two*. Boston: Beacon Press, 2005.

———. *Thirst: Poems*. Boston: Beacon Press, 2006.

———. *Winter Hours: Prose, Prose Poems, and Poems*. Boston: Houghton Mifflin, 1999.

Sewall, Marilyn, ed. *The Crisis of Spirit: 300 Poems in Celebration of Women's Spirituality*. Boston: Beacon Press, 2000.

Winslow, Rosemary. "Mary Oliver." In *Critical Survey of Poetry, Second Revised Edition,* edited by Philip K. Jason, 2,822–2,826. Pasadena, Calif.: Salem Press, 2003.

Olsen, Tillie Lerner
(1913–2007)   short story writer, essayist

The author of *Tell Me a Riddle,* a collection of critically acclaimed short stories about the breakdown of personal relationships, Tillie Olsen writes frequently about the aspirations and disappointments of the working class, and about women who are denied the opportunity to express themselves.

Tillie Lerner was born on January 14, 1913, on a tenant farm in Omaha, Nebraska, to politically active Jewish Russian immigrant parents. A prolific reader, Tillie was self-taught and dropped out of high school in 11th grade. "Public libraries were my college," she later said, "[along with] work, motherhood, struggle, and literature."

At a young age Tillie read *Life in the Iron Mills,* an obscure 19th-century account of factory workers written by REBECCA HARDING DAVIS. (In 1973 Olsen was instrumental in getting the book back into print and wrote the afterword for the new edition.) She identified with working class issues and in 1930 was imprisoned for trying to organize packinghouse workers in Omaha and Kansas City.

In 1932 Olsen began writing a semiautobiographical novel that eventually would evolve into *Yonnondio*. After moving to San Francisco, California, she became involved in the city's fierce maritime labor strike of 1934 and was arrested. That same year, while she was in jail, a chapter of *Yonnondio* appeared in the *Partisan Review.*

In 1936 she married Jack Olsen, a printer and fervent unionist, and gave up working on *Yonnondio* in order to raise the couple's four daughters. "In the twenty years I bore and reared my children, the simplest circumstances for creation did not exist," Olsen recalled in one of her essays.

As her children got older, Olsen returned to writing and in 1953 penned one of her best-known and most anthologized short stories, "I Stand Here Ironing." A mother's lament about lost opportunities that was included in *Best American Short Stories of 1957,* it was one of four stories in Olsen's first and most widely praised book, *Tell Me a Riddle,* which was published in 1961, when Olsen was nearly 50. The volume's title story demonstrated Olsen's commanding use of language and received

Short-story writer Tillie Olsen is pictured here in 1980.
(AP/Wide World Photos)

the first prize O. Henry Award of 1961. In it an elderly, terminally ill woman attempts to understand what went wrong in her marriage:

> For forty-seven years they had been married. How deep back the stubborn, gnarled roots of the quarrel reached, no one could say—but only now, when tending to the needs of others no longer shackled them together, the roots swelled up visible, split the earth between them, and the tearing shook even to the children, long since grown.

Olsen finally saw the publication of *Yonnondio: From the Thirties* in 1974. It was well received, although some critics found the saga too depressing. A midwestern family, not unlike Olsen's, attempts against all odds to cope with the Great Depression, first as miners and then as tenant farmers. A critic for the *Washington Post Book World* called *Yonnondio* "the best novel to come out of the so-called proletarian movement of the thirties," in spite of the unrelenting misery it portrays. Although Olsen never avoided confronting the "pain of reality" in her work, she also felt that her socialist Jewish background provided her with "an absolute belief in the potentiality of human beings."

In 1978 Olsen published *Silences,* a collection of critical essays and speeches, several of which criticized restrictions placed on women writers who also raised and supported their families. Of her own almost 15-year "silence" between publishing *Tell Me a Riddle* and *Yonnondio,* she wrote bitterly of "nearly remaining mute and having let writing die over and over again in me."

In 1980, *Tell Me a Riddle* was adapted into an Academy Award–winning movie, and a year later a dramatic version of "I Stand Here Ironing" was produced in New York City. Olsen edited a reader about the mother-daughter relationship, followed in 1989 by "an exploration in photographs," another collection about mothers and daughters that included a tribute to her own mother.

Olsen taught writing at numerous colleges and universities and received several honorary degrees and fellowships. Her works have been translated into 11 languages and her short stories have appeared in more than 100 anthologies. For many years she lived in a third-floor walk-up apartment in San Francisco, a city that designated May 18, 1981, as "Tillie Olsen Day." A writer, teacher, activist, and mother, Olsen encouraged young women writers to explore and exploit their creativity and talent.

In 1994 Tillie Olsen won the honored Rea Award for the Short Story. In citing her work, juror MARY GORDON said:

> With her collection, *Tell Me a Riddle,* Tillie Olsen radically widened the possibilities for American writers of fiction. The stories have the lyric intensity of an Emily Dickinson poem and the scope of a Balzac novel. She has forced open the language of the short story, insisting that it include the domestic life of women, the passions and anguishes of maternity, the deep and gnarled roots of a long marriage, the hopes and frustrations of immigration, the shining charge of political commitment. Olsen's voice has both challenged and cleared the way for all those who come after her.

Olsen died, at 94, in Oakland, California, on January 1, 2007. She was eulogized as a chronicler of the working class and widely respected short story writer.

Further Reading

Frye, Joanne S. *Tillie Olsen: A Study of the Short Fiction.* Boston: Twayne, 1995.

Holley, Joe. "Tillie Olsen: Her Fiction Explored Fraying Seams of Blue-Collar Life." *Boston Globe,* 5 January 2007, p. C5.

Olsen, Tillie. *Silences.* New York: Delacorte Press/Seymour Lawrence, 1978.

———. *Tell Me a Riddle.* Philadelphia: Lippincott, 1961.

———. *Yonnondio: From the Thirties.* New York: Delacorte, 1974.

Pearlman, Mickey, and Abby H. Werlock. *Tillie Olsen.* Boston: Twayne, 1991.

Rosenfelt, Deborah Silverton. "Tillie Olsen." In *The Columbia Companion to the Twentieth-Century American Short Story,* edited by Blanche H. Gelfant, 423–429. New York: Columbia University Press, 2000.

➴ Ozick, Cynthia
(1928–)   *short story writer, novelist, essayist*

Cynthia Ozick, who has been critically acclaimed for her powerful and imaginative use of language in both her fiction and essays, writes forcefully about Judaism's rich and complex intellectual, religious, and historical heritage. The *New York Times Book Review* called Ozick a "narrative hypnotist . . . and the best American writer to have emerged in recent years."

Born on April 17, 1928, in New York City, to religious Russian immigrant parents who owned a pharmacy in the Bronx, Cynthia Ozick attended public schools in a section of the Bronx where it was, as she recalled, "brutally difficult to be a Jew." Early on she displayed a passion for reading and writing. "As soon as I was conscious of being alive, I knew I was a writer," she commented in 1983.

Ozick received a bachelor's degree cum laude with honors in English from New York University in 1949, and the following year she earned a master's from Ohio State University, where she wrote her thesis on American novelist Henry James, whose fiction she greatly admired.

In 1952 she married a lawyer, Bernard Hallote, and she gave birth to their daughter, Rachel, in 1965. That same year she began publishing a series of poems in *Judaism* and other national literary magazines. Influenced by her uncle, a renowned Hebrew poet, after a short stint as an advertising copywriter and teaching at New York University, Ozick became, as she put it, an "unnatural writing beast." She spent seven years on a never-published philosophical novel modeled after the style of Henry James, and almost that long on her first novel, *Trust,* which was published in 1966 to favorable reviews. A long, witty, intricate book, it touched on several of Ozick's favorite themes—Jewish ethos, idolatry versus Jewish values, duplicity, and self-discovery.

Five years later Ozick published *The Pagan Rabbi, and Other Stories* (1971), a collection that was nominated for a National Book Award and won the Jewish Heritage Award in 1972. In the title story, a rabbi who identifies with the Jewish Dutch philosopher Benedict de Spinoza, hangs himself, having reached a kind of pantheistic ecstasy. He waxes poetically, in his last testament: "The molecules dance within all forms . . . and within the atoms dance still profounder sources of divine vitality. There is nothing that is Dead."

Ozick's next short story collection, *Bloodshed and Three Novellas* (1976), was also well received. The unifying theme was the protagonist's rediscovery of the importance of his or her Jewish identity, based on ancient mystical and primal forces. In "Bloodshed," one of the characters contemplates suicide because God has allowed the Holocaust to happen; he is rescued by a Holocaust survivor who explains that "despair must be earned." Ozick's consciousness as a writer, asserts Ellen Pifer in *Contemporary American Women Writers* (1985), has been formed by the history and traditions, as well as by the suffering, of the Jewish people.

In 1982, with the publication of another volume of short fiction, *Levitation: Five Fictions,* Ozick's literary reputation was firmly established. In one of the stories, "genuine" Jewish characters levitate away from "pseudo-Jews" at a New York literary party, again demonstrating the author's mastery at combining satirical surrealism with tragic realism.

Ozick penned two more noteworthy novels: *The Cannibal Galaxy* (1983), which took on the problems of modern Jewish assimilation, and *The Messiah of Stockholm* (1987), a lyrical, complex tale which one reviewer described as "juxtaposing Kafkaesque abstractions with Waugh-like comedy."

Having written more than 100 essays and reviews, Ozick turned to another genre at which she excelled, and published three collections of influential essays, *Art and Ardor* (1983), *Metaphor and Memory* (1989), and *Fame and Folly: Essays* (1996).

In "The Shawl," perhaps Ozick's most celebrated short story, which first appeared in the *New Yorker* in 1980, the central character, Rosa Lubin, witnesses a concentration camp guard murder her baby. Rosa appears in the sequel, a novella, that takes place 30 years later, as a "madwoman and a scavenger" in a Miami hotel. Appearing in and linking both stories, the shawl of the title represents sustenance, destruction, and hope—a means of magically conjuring Rosa's child back to life. Ozick has stated that her intention in *The Shawl: A Story and Novella* (1989) was to render the horrors of the Holocaust and "not to be merciful" to its deniers. She adapted the story into a successful play that was produced off-Broadway in New York City in 1996.

After a 10-year hiatus, Ozick returned to fiction with *The Puttermesser Papers* (1997), a collection of previously published stories that she turned into a novel. The tale revolves around Ruth Puttermesser, a bored intellectual and rationalist who studies Jewish textual traditions and conjures up a golem (someone created by magical art) to get her elected as mayor of New York City. She also casts herself as George Eliot, one of Ozick's favorite novelists, and ultimately winds up in heaven. Critics and readers alike admired Puttermesser, the protean antiheroine. It was a National Book Award finalist and named one of the top 10 books of 1997 by the *New York Times Book Review, Publishers Weekly,* and the *Los Angeles Times Book Review.*

Ozick went on to produce her fourth and "best collection of essays to date," according to the *Boston Globe. Quarrel and Quandary* (2000) includes 19 essays on topics ranging from Fyodor Dostoyevsky and Franz Kafka to GERTRUDE STEIN and W. G. Sebald, and it won Ozick a National Book Critics Circle Award. She then returned to fiction with *Heir to the Glimmering World* (2004), which she set in "sparse and weedy northeast Bronx," where Ozick herself grew up, during the depression era. The novel interweaves the stories of a strange group of richly drawn characters, including the feisty, smart, orphaned heroine, 18-year-old Rose Meadows, who works for an obsessive Jewish refugee scholar and helps take care of his invalid wife and their children. "Ozick is an intellectual magpie," writes critic Sarah Coleman in the *San Francisco*

Chronicle, "and ultimately, it's hard to resist a novel that bristles with as much life as this one."

In 2006 she produced *The Din in the Head,* a collection of essays about writers she admires and their work, from Leo Tolstoy to SYLVIA PLATH, whom Ozick describes as being "both Emily Dickinson and Betty Crocker." Ozick manages to balance moral discernment with levity. "The light a genuine novel gives out is struck off by the nightmare calculations of art: story, language (language especially), irony, comedy, the crooked lanes of desire and deceit," wrote Ozick in *Who We Are: On Being (and Not Being) a Jewish American Writer.*

Ozick, who lives in New Rochelle, New York, has been the recipient of numerous awards and fellowships, including four first prize O. Henry Awards, an American Academy and National Institute of Arts and Letters Award, and 11 honorary doctorate degrees. In 1998 she won the National Magazine Award for a *New Yorker* essay, "Who Owns Anne Frank?," in which she chastised writers for attempting to remove Anne Frank's Jewishness, which was central to Frank's life, from the famous autobiography. In 2000 she received the Lannon Literary Award for fiction.

A premier translator of Yiddish poetry, Ozick is also a staunch and vociferous defender of Israel. She also believes that women need "equal access to the greater world" but rejects the separatist classification of "woman writer." Instead, she sees herself, and wants to be judged, as a "writer," who also proudly defines herself as a "Jewish writer."

Nonetheless, Ozick contributes importantly to the larger American literary tradition. As a writer, she explained in an essay in *Who We Are:*

I feel responsible only to the comely shape of a sentence, and to the unfettered imagination, which sometimes leads to wild places via wild routes. At the same time I reserve my respect for writers who do not remain ignorant of history . . . who do not choose to run after trivia, who recognize that ideas are emotions, and that emotions are ideas; and this is what we mean when we speak of the insights of art.

In the *New York Review of Books,* literary critic. A. Alvarez asserted that "there is seemingly nothing [Ozick] cannot do. . . . She is a stylist in the best and most complete sense, in language, in wit, in her apprehension of reality and her curious, crooked flights of imagination."

Further Reading

Friedman, Lawrence S. *Understanding Cynthia Ozick.* Columbia: University of South Carolina Press, 1991.

Lowin, Joseph. *Cynthia Ozick.* Boston: Twayne, 1988.

Ozick, Cynthia. *A Cynthia Ozick Reader.* Edited by Elaine M. Kauvar. Bloomington: Indiana University Press, 1996.

———. *The Din in the Head.* New York: Houghton Mifflin, 2006.

———. *Heir to the Glimmering World.* New York: Houghton Mifflin, 2004.

———. *The Pagan Rabbi, and Other Stories.* New York: Knopf, 1971.

———. *Quarrel and Quandary.* New York: Knopf, 2000.

———. *The Shawl: A Story and Novella.* New York: Knopf, 1989.

Rubin, Derek, ed. *Who We Are: On Being (and Not Being) a Jewish American Writer,* 19–23. New York: Schocken Books, 2005.

Wisse, Ruth R. "American Jewish Writing, Act II." *Commentary* 61, no. 6 (June 1976): 40–45.

P

Paley, Grace Goodside
(1922–2007) *short story writer, poet*

In spite of her relatively slender body of work, Grace Paley was considered one of America's premier short story writers. With simplicity, wit, and compassion, she portrayed characters from everyday life on the streets of New York City.

Grace Goodside was born on December 11, 1922, in New York City, the daughter of secular Jewish immigrant parents, both of whom had been exiled from tsarist Russia because of their socialist political beliefs. "My parents believed in an ethical, idealistic way of life," she recalled, "and in storytelling—in Yiddish, English, and Russian."

In 1938, at age 16, Grace enrolled at Hunter College. She also took courses at New York University and the New School for Social Research, where she studied poetry with W. H. Auden, who encouraged her to write the way people speak. After dropping out of school, Paley worked as a typist to support herself. In her spare time she read, and was influenced by, the works of Virginia Woolf, James Joyce, GERTRUDE STEIN, and Charlotte Brontë.

At 19 she married a cinematographer, Jess Paley, with whom she had two "copper-haired, brown-eyed children." While living in army camps during the early years of their marriage, Paley began observing ordinary people whose lives were "both common *and* important." In later years, she would fictionalize them.

After moving to New York City's Greenwich Village, where she spent most of her life, and with her children no longer infants, the 33-year-old Paley began writing stories. They appeared in prestigious publications such as the *New Yorker* and the *Atlantic Monthly*. Her first book of stories, *The Little Disturbances of Man* (1959), was widely acclaimed for its rich and lively use of language, and for her funny, sympathetic, but unsentimentalized characters, especially women, who led "morally aware and engaged lives." Like Faith Darwin, a central protagonist who reappears in all three collections, Paley divorced her husband, raised her children, and increasingly committed herself to social change and community activism.

In 1970, Paley won the National Institute of Arts and Letters Award for short fiction. After a hiatus of 15 years, she returned to short fiction with the publication of *Enormous Changes at the Last Minute* (1974). The 15 stories, Paley said, were about "daily life—death, desertion, loss, divorce, failure, love." In "Conversation with My

Father," the narrator juxtaposes her father's somber, tragic demeanor to her own lighter, less analytical, more life-affirming views. In spite of himself, the father survives:

> [His] life was not ruined, nor did he have to die. Shortly before the baby's birth, he fell hard on the bathroom tiles, cracked his skull, dipped the wires of his brain into his heart's blood . . . but he was smart as ever, and able to begin again with few scruples to notice and appreciate.

The writer E. L. Doctorow said that Paley expresses "a whole life in one line."

A lifelong political activist, during the Vietnam War Paley was arrested for unfurling a banner protesting the war on the White House lawn. She also met with North Vietnamese leaders in Hanoi in 1969 and wrote the preface to *Peacemeal,* the Greenwich Village Peace Center cookbook. Asked why she had never written a novel, she replied: "Art is too long and life is too short."

Paley, who was elected to the American Academy and Institute of Arts and Letters in 1980, published the first of two volumes of poetry, *Leaning Forward* in 1985, the same year her third book of stories, *Later the Same Day,* appeared to glowing reviews. In 1989, Governor Mario Cuomo declared Paley the first official New York State Writer. Another collection of poems and prose pieces, *Long Walks and Intimate Talks* (1991), brought her further acclaim.

In 1988, she and her second husband, activist Bob Nichols, moved from New York City to a two-story cabin in rural Vermont, where she continued to write, support feminism and world peace, and spend time with her grandson. An anthology of her classic stories, *The Collected Stories,* was a finalist for the 1994 National Book Award. In a profile in *Vanity Fair* (1998), Alexis Jetter described the then-75-year-old Paley as an "angelic-looking grandmother with revolution in her blood" and "America's mistress of the short story." *Just as I Thought* (1998), a medley of political essays and family memoirs, was published to mixed reviews. Commenting on the book and its author, fiction

writer MAXINE HONG KINGSTON noted that Paley's "practical, steady work in her actions and in her art is vital to the continuing of civilized life. . . . Hers is a life of integrity, and her work is to heal divisions of souls and country."

Demonstrating her versatility, Paley, who won the Lannon Literary Award for fiction in 1997, started the new millennium by publishing a collection of poems titled *Begin Again* (2000). "Her poems retain the winning openness . . . and the political commitments her fiction flaunts," said a reviewer for *Publishers Weekly.* "They also contain deep insight." Paley's verse appeared in the *New Yorker* in December 2005. The first line of the poem "Anti-Love Poem" read, "Sometimes you don't want to love the person you love." Interested in supporting women writers, especially those who were once well known but have become largely forgotten, in 2004 she penned the introduction to a story collection by writer FANNIE HURST, published by The Feminist Press.

Meanwhile, Paley continued to write short fiction. "Compassionate, her stories are nonetheless truthful," commented writer Joan Leegant in *The Jewish Reader: A Guide for Book Groups.* "They have almost always relied on the intimacy created by a strong voice, usually first person, that makes you instantly want to perk up and listen. . . . Love, loss, and the excruciating way the two are forever entwined are nearly always at the core of Grace Paley's work. . . . Her characters embrace life in all its heady complexity."

On August 22, 2007, Paley, who had been battling breast cancer, died at her home in Vermont.

Further Reading

Jetter, Alexis. "State of Grace." *Vanity Fair,* March 1998, pp. 220–266.

Leegant, Joan. "Collected Stories by Grace Paley." The Jewish Reader/National Yiddish Book Center. Available online. URL: http://yiddishbookcenter.org/story.php?n=10090. Downloaded on January 23, 2007.

Lidof, Joan. "Clearing Her Throat: An Interview with Grace Paley." *Shenandoah* 32 (1981): 3–26.

Paley. Grace. *Begin Again: Collected Poems.* New York: Farrar, Straus and Giroux, 2000.

———. *The Collected Stories.* New York: Farrar, Straus and Giroux, 1994.

———. *Just as I Thought.* New York: Farrar, Straus and Giroux, 1998.

Wirth-Nesher, Hana. "Pronouncing America, Writing Jewish: Paley and Others." In *Call It English: The Languages of Jewish Literature,* 2–31. Princeton, N.J.: Princeton University Press, 2005.

∾ Paretsky, Sara
(1947–) *mystery writer*

Sara Paretsky is best known for her noteworthy series of mystery novels featuring the private detective V. I. Warshawski, a tough but compassionate feminist sleuth. The *Christian Science Monitor* called Paretsky "the best of the emerging group of women writing private eye novels of quality."

Born on June 8, 1947, in Ames, Iowa, Sara Paretsky received a bachelor's degree from the University of Kansas in 1967, married Courtenay Wright, a professor, in 1976, and earned master's and doctorate degrees from the University of Chicago in 1977. She and Wright live in Chicago and have three sons.

Before turning to mystery writing, Paretsky was a middle manager for a large, multinational insurance company in Chicago. It was during that time that she invented a female private investigator who was "doing what I was doing, which was trying to make a success in a field traditionally dominated by men."

In Paretsky's "V. I. Warshawski mysteries, the heroine-narrator is an attractive, intelligent, cultured, hard-boiled, half-Polish, half-Italian detective who unravels murders, deceit, and corruption in organized crime, the church, and the medical profession. Paretsky has stated that she tries to dispel some of the "typical sexual stereotypes in literature" by creating a female private eye who was neither predatory nor helpless, and who remained interested in social causes and friends while winning dangerous cases.

In the first book to introduce the Warshawski character, *Indemnity Only* (1982), a corporate vice president asks her, "What does the V stand for?" To which Warshawski replies, "My first name." By offering only her initials, she hoped to be treated seriously, like male detectives who go by their last names. Well received, in 1992 the novel was adapted into a Hollywood film starring Kathleen Turner. It was followed by the publication of *Deadlock,* the winner of the 1995 Award from Friends of American Writers.

Over breakfast at a conference in 1986, Paretsky, an active member in the male-dominated Mystery Writers of America, organized Sisters In Crime (SinC), an international organization for professional female crime writers (although men have joined) with members such as the popular mystery writer SUE GRAFTON. The group sent a letter to the *New York Times* pointing out that in 1985, of the 88 mysteries that the *Times* had reviewed, only 14—or 16 percent—were written by women.

In *Bitter Medicine* (1987), one of Paretsky's more overtly feminist works, Warshawski investigates the death of a friend and the murder of a doctor, and the connection to violent demonstrations staged by an antiabortion group. *Ms.* magazine named Paretsky one of its "1987 Women of the Year" for her feminist writing and activism. *Bloodshot* (1988), which won the Silver Dagger award from the Crime Writers' Association, brings Warshawski back to her childhood neighborhood on Chicago's South Side, where her friend has mysteriously drowned:

> In my sleep that night I saw Caroline again as a baby, her face pink and blotchy from crying. My mother stood behind me telling me to look after the child. When I went to work at nine the dream lay heavy in my head, cloaking me in lethargy. The job I'd agreed to do filled me with distaste.

By the end of the 1990s, Paretsky had edited three anthologies of mystery fiction by women and written several more V. I. Warshawski books: *Burn Marks* (1990); *Guardian Angel* (1992), which a *New York Times* critic considered "the richest and most engaging yet of Paretsky's fast-paced thrillers"; *Tunnel Vision* (1994); *Windy City Blues* (1995); and

Ghost Country (1998). In 2002 Paretsky won the Crime Writers' Association's coveted Cartier Diamond Dagger lifetime achievement award in the genre of crime writing. Her next novel, *Blacklist* (2003), garnered the Crime Writers' Association's Gold Dagger for fiction. Jurors called the novel "a powerful piece of Chicago gothic that engages with the important issues of our time." *Fire Scale* (2005) is another offering in the long-running V. I. Warshawski series, which, said a critic in *Washington Post Book World,* has only grown richer and more ambitious with age. In 2007 Paretsky published a collection of essays about the need for dissent called *Writing in an Age of Silence.*

In an interview in *Newsweek,* Sara Paretsky explained why she continues to use V. I. Warshawski as a protagonist in her stories: "The things I want to say about law, society, women, seem to come naturally in her voice. There are women just beginning to be aware, who need strong role models."

Further Reading

Ashley, Mike, ed. *The Mammoth Encyclopedia of Modern Crime Fiction.* New York: Avalon Publishing, 2002.

Champion, Laurie, and Rhonda Austin. *Contemporary American Women Fiction Writers.* Westport, Conn.: Greenwood Press, 2002.

Paretsky, Sara. *Bitter Medicine.* New York: Morrow, 1987.

———. *Blacklist.* New York: Putnam, 2003.

———. *Fire Scale.* New York: Putnam, 2005.

———. *Three Complete Novels* (*Indemnity Only, Blood Shot,* and *Burn Marks*). New York: Wings, 1995.

Reddy, T. Maureen. *Sisters in Crime: Feminism and the Crime Novel.* New York: Continuum, 1988.

∾ Parker, Dorothy Rothschild

(1893–1967) *critic, short story writer, poet*

In a writing career that spanned almost half a century, Dorothy Parker laced her essays, short stories, poetry, and conversation with a wry, rapier wit that made her one of the most quotable literary figures of her time. While much of her best work appeared in national magazines such as *Vanity Fair* and the

Flamboyant Dorothy Parker was known for her acerbic wit.
(AP/Wide World Photos)

New Yorker, many of her most famous comments were spontaneous one-liners.

Dorothy Parker was born on August 23, 1893, the fourth child of Henry Rothschild, a prosperous garment manufacturer in New York City, and Eliza Marsten Rothschild, a former school teacher of Scottish descent. Dorothy's childhood was unhappy: her mother died when she was five, and Dorothy did not get along with her siblings or, after her father remarried, with her stepmother. She once described herself as "a plain disagreeable child with stringy hair and a yen to write poetry." As an adult, however, she was quite attractive, and even vain; for example, despite being severely nearsighted, she refused to wear her thick eye-glasses in the presence of men.

Parker's first job was playing piano in a dance school, but in 1916 she was hired by *Vogue* magazine. A year later, she married Edwin Parker—they would divorce 11 years later—and became drama critic at *Vanity Fair,* a position she held until 1926. During that time she became a founding member, along with Robert Benchley and Robert Sherwood, of a lionized and legendary literary circle known as the Algonquin Round Table. The group regularly met for lunch at a large, circular table within the Algonquin Hotel in New York. Known for their brilliant, cutting, and often hilarious repartee and sardonic humor, members of the Algonquin Round Table eventually included such New York City notables as George S. Kaufman, Alexander Woolcott, Harold Ross (founder of the *New Yorker*), and the writer EDNA FERBER.

Parker began contributing short stories and reviews to the *New Yorker* in 1926; her association with the prestigious magazine lasted three decades. One of her stories, "Big Blonde," won the O. Henry Memorial Award in 1929, while several others aptly depict the nightlife of New York City's sophisticated set in the 1920s. The morose title of her first published book of verse, *Enough Rope* (1926), evoked her first (in 1923), of several, suicide attempts. (The title borrows from the old proverb "Give a thief enough rope and he'll hang himself.") The volume was well received, as were three other poetry collections: *Sunset Gun* (1928), *Death and Taxes* (1931), and *Not Deep as a Well* (1936).

In 1933 Parker married the handsome bisexual actor and writer Alan Campbell. Punctuated by a three-year divorce between 1947 and their remarriage in 1950, as well as by several separations, the marriage lasted until Campbell's death in 1963. The couple moved to Hollywood, where they collaborated on several screenplays, including the script for "A Star is Born" (1937), which was nominated for an Academy Award. Parker received a second Academy Award nomination for *Smash-Up: The Story of a Woman* (1947), written jointly with Frank Cavett. By the 1940s, however, Parker's longtime problem with excessive drinking had evolved into full-blown alcoholism. Nonetheless, in the 1950s she managed to produce several important works, including a

play, *Ladies of the Corridor* (1953), coauthored with Arnaud d'Usseau.

Parker's stormy personal life was matched by her controversial association with left-wing causes, which began in the 1920s and eventually led to her being forced to testify, along with hundreds of other prominent American literary and artistic figures, before of the House Un-American Activities Committee in 1951. She denied being a Communist and refused to incriminate her colleagues.

Weakened and debilitated by alcoholism, Parker died on June 7, 1967, after three failed suicide attempts. According to *Bobbed Hair and Bathtub Gin: Writers Running Wild in the Twenties* (2004), Parker bequeathed the bulk of her estate to the Reverend Dr. Martin Luther King, Jr. For someone who protested the execution of Italian immigrants Sacco and Vanzetti and was outspoken in her political beliefs, her decision is understandable, although considered surprising at the time. "In her public life, Parker transformed the 19th-century role of the nurturing woman who guides the family in the private sphere into the role of the intellectual colleague who makes her convictions known to the world at large, thereby shaping 20th-century public opinion," wrote Wendy Martin, professor of American Literature at Claremont Graduate University, in an essay about Parker published in 2000.

In 1994, a film, *Mrs. Parker and the Vicious Circle,* which was directed by Alan Rudolph and starred Jennifer Jason Leigh, was released. The film detailed Parker's relationships with other members of the Algonquin Round Table and focused particularly on her friendship with Robert Benchley. A subsequent documentary, *Would You Kindly Direct Me to Hell?: The Infamous Dorothy Parker,* was based in part on the 1994 film but discussed her full biography in depth.

Today, Dorothy Parker is remembered for her sharp-edged wit and descriptive short stories. As the distinguished literary critic Edmund Wilson noted, "[Parker] has put into what she has written a voice, a state of mind, an era, a few moments of human experience that nobody else has conveyed."

Further Reading

Fitzpatrick, Kevin C. *A Journey into Dorothy Parker's New York*. Berkeley, Calif.: Roaring Forties Press, 2005.

Kinney, Arthur. *Dorothy Parker*. Boston: Twayne, 1978.

Meade, Marion. *Bobbed Hair and Bathtub Gin: Writers Running Wild in the Twenties*. New York: Doubleday, 2004.

Parker, Dorothy. *Complete Stories*. New York: Penguin, 1995.

———. *The Portable Dorothy Parker, Penguin Classics Deluxe Edition*. Edited by Marion Meade. New York: Penguin, 2006.

～ Parrish, Mary Frances

See FISHER, MARY FRANCES KENNEDY

～ Perillo, Lucia

(1958–) *poet, essayist*

The recipient of a John D. and Catherine T. MacArthur Foundation so-called genius award in 2000, as well as several other prestigious prizes, Lucia Perillo has been widely commended for her four books of poetry. The MacArthur Foundation described the poet's work as "marked by an urban speed and a narrative style driven by characterization and drama." In her deeply felt work, she keenly, irreverently, and fearlessly observes a multitude of experiences, both highly personal and universal.

Perillo was born in 1958 and grew up in the suburbs of New York City. After graduating with a bachelor of arts degree from McGill University in 1979, where she majored in wildlife management, she worked for the U.S. Fish & Wildlife Services at the Denver Wildlife Research Center and at the San Francisco Bay National Wildlife Refuge. While in California she took evening writing classes at San Jose State. One of her teachers, Robert Hass, later became a U.S. poet laureate. "I'd had a friend in college who was a writer, who'd stay up all night to write," recalled Perillo. "It seemed very glamorous."

In 1984 Perillo enrolled in graduate school at Syracuse University, where she earned a master's degree in creative writing. She studied with the widely read poet Tess Gallagher, among others. "I've always had a lot of beginner's luck," said Perillo. Her first published poem won a prize, as did her first published book, *Dangerous Life* (1989), which, in manuscript form, earned the Samuel French Morse Poetry Prize from Northeastern University and the Norma Farber First Book Award from the Poetry Society of America for the best "first book" of 1989. Perillo deserved early recognition, according to her peers. For example, LORRIE MOORE, the esteemed contemporary fiction writer, calls Perillo's work "breathtaking and bold in its range and reference and feeling. . . . It is full of energy yet with an eye for the holy and serene."

As much as she enjoyed writing, Perillo relished spending time in the natural world. She worked seasonally as a park ranger at Mount Rainier National Park and in 1987 moved to Olympia, Washington, where she had been offered a teaching position at Saint Martin's College, a small school affiliated with a Benedictine monastery. Meanwhile, Perillo was struggling with multiple sclerosis, which had been diagnosed in the mid-1980s. Unfortunately, working outdoors became increasingly difficult for Perillo, but she continued to spend as much time as possible surrounded by nature. In 1991 she began teaching in the creative writing program at Southern Illinois University in Carbondale, Illinois. She commuted to Olympia, located at the southern tip of Puget Sound, where her husband, James Rudy, worked as a stage technician and where she spent her summers.

In an article about Perillo in Southern Illinois University's magazine *Perspectives*, Marilyn Davis describes the poet's verse as "vivid, metaphor-rich . . . at once lyrical and conversational, controlled and emotional. . . . Candor about her own experiences and limitations [from her chronic illness] has been a hallmark of Perillo's writing." However, Perillo asserts that she "fictionalizes in equal amounts" when including autobiographical information in her verse, "but it's hard to convince other people about that, especially family members."

Although she is best known as a Northwest poet, Perillo also has written short fiction and essays and received an Illinois Arts Council grant in nonfiction in 1993. Her essays and reviews have been published in the *Chronicle of Higher Education* and the *Chicago Tribune,* and her nonfiction has appeared in *Quarterly West* and the *New England Review.* Even more impressive, her verse has been published in prestigious magazines such as the *New Yorker* and the *Atlantic,* as well as in numerous literary magazines such as the *Paris Review,* which in 2004 published two of her poems, and the *Kenyon Review.* It has been reprinted in both the *Pushcart* and *Best American Poetry* anthologies.

In 1996 Perillo's second and most personal book of verse, *The Body Mutinies,* won the Revson Foundation Poetry fellowship from PEN; the Kate Tufts Discovery Poetry Award from Claremont University, for a book by a poet of "genuine promise"; the Balcones Prize from Austin Community College; and the Verna Emery Poetry Prize from Purdue University. In commenting on *The Body Mutinies,* which she had reworked several times, Perillo noted that it took her three years to find a publisher, perhaps in part because she decided to mention frankly the effects of multiple sclerosis in the book, although she admitted that she was concerned that writing about something as personal as her illness might "overwhelm" her readers.

Perillo's next book, *The Oldest Map with the Name America: New and Selected Poems* (1999), received the sixth annual Chad Walsh Poetry Award. The same year, her fiction was reprinted in the 1999 volume of *The Pushcart Prize: Best of the Small Presses.* Perillo's multifarious themes vary extensively, including the harsh realities of nature, violence against women, the psychological and physical effects of illness, and pop culture. The poet seems equally at home writing, with her trademark wry humor, about hot dogs, rock climbing, nudism in America, going to the moon, or her large nose, which she describes as being built from random parts "like a mythical creature—a gryphon or sphinx." "No subject, it seems, is too mundane or too exotic for Perillo's engaging poems," asserted a critic in the *New Yorker.*

In the spring of 2000 Perillo received a MacArthur Foundation fellowship for "exceptional creativity, record of significant accomplishment, and potential for still greater achievement." The illustrious fellowship enabled Perillo to take an extended leave from Southern Illinois University as associate professor of creative writing in order to live with her husband in Olympia, and to devote more time to her craft and health-related issues. She continues to be honored for her small but significant body of work: Perillo's book *Luck Is Luck* was named a finalist for the *Los Angeles Times* Book Prize, was included in the New York Public Library's list of "books to remember" from 2005, and won the 2006 Kingsley Tufts Poetry Award. Perillo is the first Kate Tufts winner also to receive the Kingsley Award, the largest prize given for midcareer poetry. *Luck Is Luck* gives readers stories that show the familiar in unfamiliar ways, according to Robert Wrigley, professor of English at the University of Idaho. "It manages to be simultaneously light hearted and moving, a very elusive quality, but captured by Lucia Perillo," said Wrigley.

Perillo has been praised for her sense of humor and sense of adventure, and for producing exquisitely wrought, intellectually complex poems. As she becomes a more mature poet, Perillo said in her interview in 2000 with Marilyn Davis, she hopes to recapture some of the early energy that she had. "I didn't know what I was doing, but I had a lot of drive behind those [early] poems." But poetry still seems glamorous to her, she said, "when it's working properly—but it's usually not working. . . . What I want to accomplish now is more ambitious."

Further Reading

Davis, Marilyn. "Writing at Full Tilt: Lucia Perillo." *Perspectives:* Southern Illinois University, Carbondale. Available online. URL: http://www.siu.edu/~perspect/00_fall/perillo.html. Downloaded on January 23, 2007.

"Lucia Perillo." PoetsWest. Available online. URL: http://www.poetswest.com/directory3.htm P. Downloaded on January 23, 2007.

Marshall, Tod, ed. *Range of the Possible: Conversations with Contemporary Poets.* Spokane, Wash.: Eastern Washington University Press, 2002.

Perillo, Lucia. *Luck Is Luck.* New York: Random House, 2005.

———. *The Oldest Map with the Name America: New and Selected Poems.* New York: Random House, 1999.

Stein, Kevin, and G. E. Murray, eds. *Illinois Voices: An Anthology of Twentieth-Century Poetry.* Champaign, Ill.: University of Illinois Press, 2001.

∾ Petry, Ann Lane
(1908–1997)   *novelist, short story, young adult book writer*

Although not as well known as some other black writers, Ann Petry was the first African-American woman to write a national best seller. Published in 1946, *The Street,* which sold about 2 million copies, unflinchingly tells the story of a disadvantaged black woman from Harlem and the social, racial, and economic problems she and her young son face. Petry also wrote short stories and nonfiction books for young adults about experiences that affect and shape the lives of both blacks and whites.

Ann Lane Petry was born on October 12, 1908, upstairs from her father's drugstore, in Old Saybrook, Connecticut. Her heritage included four generations of African-American New Englanders and a penchant for storytelling. The tales she heard from or about her relatives, from a grandfather who was a runaway slave and aunts who were conjurers and root-workers, "were part of [my] education," she later recalled. There were only two African-American families in the small seacoast town, and Ann's father, one of the first registered black pharmacists in Connecticut, fought racially motivated attempts to drive him out of Old Saybrook. He went on to become a successful proprietor of two drug stores, where he served as the pharmacist. Petry's mother, who encouraged Ann's love of reading and writing, worked in a variety of jobs, including as a licensed chiropodist, a barber,

and an owner of a linen business. The Lanes were a close-knit, happy, middle-class family who came from a long line of chemists and pharmacists. Even so, in an article titled "My Most Humiliating Jim Crow Experience," Petry recalled how, at the age of seven, during a Sunday school beach outing, the guard demanded that the class leave because, as he put it, "niggers" were not allowed on the beach. Petry's teacher did not come to her defense.

While a student at Old Saybrook High School, Ann wrote short stories and one-act plays. But after graduating, she opted to attend the Connecticut College of Pharmacy, matriculating with a degree in pharmacy in 1931. For several years she worked in the family's drugstores in Old Saybrook and nearby Lyme, spending her spare time writing stories. While a pharmacist, she carefully observed the customers, some of whom she later would portray as characters, particularly in the "drugstore" stories published in *Miss Muriel and Other Stories* and the character of the druggist Doc, in her novel *Country Place.*

In 1938 Petry gave up her pharmaceutical position to marry George D. Petry, a mystery writer. The couple moved to Harlem, an uptown section of New York City, and for the first time Petry sampled bustling urban life. She got a job selling advertisements and then as a copywriter for the *Amsterdam News,* a highly regarded African-American newspaper. In 1941 she was hired by *People's Voice,* a Harlem-based militant newspaper, to write feature-length articles on provocative topics such as inner-city police brutality and sexual harassment and to edit the women's page and write a society column. At the same time Petry became involved in Harlem-related community projects. The seeds of her famous future novel *The Street* were planted while she was working at a Harlem elementary after-school program, where she helped design programs for troubled children. She also helped organize Negro Women Inc., a legislative group for working-class women. In her spare time, she took creative writing classes at Columbia University, signed up for painting and piano lessons, and acted with the American Negro Theatre, enabling her to learn more about dialogue and pacing—important tools for an aspiring writer.

Petry's first published short story, "On Saturday the Siren Sounds at Noon," whose venue was the streets of Harlem, appeared in 1943 in *The Crisis,* a literary magazine featuring talented young black writers. "Like a Winding Sheet," a story about the insidious relationship between domestic violence and racism in Harlem, also appeared in *The Crisis* and was included in the collection *The Best American Short Stories, 1946.* Meanwhile, "On Saturday the Siren Sounds at Noon" caught the attention of an editor at Houghton Mifflin Publishing Company, and he encouraged her to work on a novel. Based on the first five chapters of *The Street,* Petry was awarded Houghton Mifflin's prestigious literary fellowship in 1945. The monetary award enabled her to work without interruption, full time, as a professional writer. *The Street* was published to great acclaim a year later.

A scathing social commentary on African-American life and social injustice in New York City, *The Street,* set in the 1940s, presents a graphic portrait of a poverty-stricken, ambitious single mother, Luti Johnson, who lives in Harlem, tries valiantly to ameliorate conditions for herself and her eight-year-old son, but is defeated in the end. Petry "revealed a world in which the individual with the most integrity is not only destroyed but is often forced to become an expression of the very society against which [she] is rebelling," wrote reviewer Thelma Shinn in *Critique: Studies in Modern Fiction.* For that reason, Petry has been compared to the renowned author of *Native Son,* Richard Wright: They were both African Americans known for their naturalistic protest writing and explorations of the humanity of individuals.

Country Place, Petry's second and more melodramatic novel, was published in 1947. According to Hilary Holladay, Petry's biographer, *Country Place* is as "unflinching in its portrayal of a white New England town as *The Street* is in its portrayal of a Harlem ghetto. . . . Although it lacks *The Street's* depth of characterization, *Country Place* reveals Petry's continuing fascination with troubled communities." In 1948, uncomfortable with her growing notoriety, Petry moved back to Old Saybrook and a

year later had a daughter, Elisabeth Ann. Petry penned one more novel, *The Narrows* (1953), considered by some critics as her most finely crafted work. Like *Country Place,* it is set in a New England town resembling Old Saybrook. *The Narrows* tells the story of a college-educated African-American man and a wealthy white woman who have a love affair in a small town in the 1950s. The book powerfully attests to interracial class conflicts and, as one critic put it, "with characters made out of love, whole histories were evoked in a page."

Petry also wrote four acclaimed books for children and young adult readers. *Harriet Tubman* (1955) is a vividly rendered, uplifting biography of the courageous slave who escaped and helped transport more than 300 slaves to freedom. In praising the artistry of another young adult book by Petry, *Tituba of Salem Village* (1964), based on the 1692 Salem witch trials and about a young Indian slave from Barbados who has been accused of witchcraft, children's book writer MADELEINE L'ENGLE, in a *New York Times Book Review,* pointed out that at the end of the story "we are left with a feeling of hope, and of the ultimate triumph of good over evil." In *Horn Book* magazine in 1965, Petry explained that she tried to make her protagonists come alive for young readers, to make history speak across the centuries in the voice of people: "Look at them, listen to them. . . . Look at them and remember them. Remember for what a long, long time black people have been in this country, have been a part of America: a sturdy, indestructible, wonderful part of America, woven into its heart and into its soul."

Petry's last work, a collection of 13 short stories titled *Miss Muriel and Other Stories,* came out in 1971. The genre lent itself to the author's precise, rhythmic, rich prose, her astute eye for details, and her unerring ear for dialogue. "Like her novels, Petry's short fiction deals with devastating fissures in insular communities," writes her biographer, Hilary Holladay. "The tension in these stories often results from distrust among people who cannot conquer their own or anyone else's prejudices of race and gender."

249

The Street, with its prescient commentary on the dynamics of race and gender in America, was reissued in 1985 and hailed as a masterpiece of African-American fiction by a new generation of readers. Petry received numerous honors, including citations from the United Nations Association and the city of Philadelphia, and honorary degrees from the University of Connecticut and Mount Holyoke College. She continued to write well into her 70s and in 1986 a short story, "The Moses Project," appeared in *Harbor Review.*

Ann Petry died on April 28, 1997, in a convalescent home in Old Saybrook, not far from where she spent her childhood. An early feminist and visionary, she brought to her compelling fiction the perspective of two worlds: middle-class, mostly white, small-town New England and working-class, black, inner-city New York. A realist and an optimist, Petry believed that although African Americans, especially women, were unjustly oppressed, they nonetheless could survive.

Further Reading

Ervin, Hazel Arnett, ed. *Contributions in Afro-American and African Studies, #209: Ann Petry's Short Fiction: Critical Essays.* New York: Praeger, 2004.

Heutsche, Anne. "Ann Lane Petry." In *Black Women in America,* edited by Darlene Clark Hine, 473–474. New York: Oxford University Press, 2005.

Holladay, Hilary. *Ann Petry.* New York: Twayne, 1996.

———. *The Street.* Boston: Houghton Mifflin, 1946.

McKenzie, Marilyn Mobley. "Ann Petry." In *African American Writers,* edited by Valerie Smith, 613–627. New York: Charles Scribner's, Sons, 2001.

Petry, Ann. *Harriet Tubman: Conductor on the Underground Railroad.* New York: Harper, 1955.

———. *Miss Muriel and Other Stories.* Boston: Houghton, 1971.

∾ Piercy, Marge

(1936–) *poet, novelist, science fiction writer*

Marge Piercy, a prolific and influential writer and ardent feminist, fuses the personal with the political in her award-winning fiction and verse.

Piercy was born on March 31, 1936, to working-class, uneducated parents—her mother was a Jewish housewife and her Welsh father repaired heavy machinery—in a predominantly black section of Detroit, Michigan. She recalls growing up poor, yet "rich in legends," reveling in the stories and myths her mother and grandmother passed on to her. "My mother," Piercy said in 1984, "made me a poet."

The first in her family to attend college, Piercy graduated from the University of Michigan in 1957 and in 1958 earned a master's degree from Northwestern University. She began publishing poetry in small literary magazines during the 1960s, while she was an activist in the civil rights, anti-Vietnam War, and early women's liberation movements. Her first book of poems, *Breaking Camp,* was published in 1968, and her first novel, *Going Down Fast,* followed a year later, after publishers had rejected her first six novels.

Small Changes (1973) was one of her first novels to explore the oppression of women and the inner and outer lives of women on the verge of feminist consciousness. The two main protagonists came from different social strata, but both struggled with male domination in a sexist society. Piercy stated that she wrote *Small Changes,* which was critically acclaimed, to create the fictional equivalent of attending a consciousness-raising support group for "women who would never go through that experience."

Her next novel, the best–selling *Woman on the Edge of Time* (1976), espoused feminist theories through a different genre, science fiction. In it, a woman time-travels away from an oppressive world to an egalitarian utopia. After co-authoring *The Last White Class: A Play about Neighborhood Terror* with Ira Wood (who would become her third husband in 1982), Piercy in 1980 returned to realistic fiction with *Vida,* which chronicled the end of the anti-Vietnam War movement and was praised for the "power with which the loneliness and desolation of the central characters are portrayed."

Equally well known as a poet and as a novelist, in the introduction to *Circles in the Water* (1982),

Piercy explained that she wanted the poems to "speak to and for" her female readers, in order to "give dignity to our pain, our anger, our lust, our losses." In a later collection, *In My Mother's Body* (1985), Piercy records, in a moving sequence of poems, her connection with her mother, including her mother's death.

Braided Lives (1982), which critics considered among her finest and most original novels, related the story of a young woman's painful coming-of-age during the 1950s. In 1987, Piercy wrote a best seller, *Gone to Soldiers,* a World War II saga that interwove the stories of 10 characters from different wartime capitals, including a French female resistance fighter who led Jewish children to safety and a valiant American pilot.

In a science fiction novel entitled *He, She and It* (1991), Piercy returned to her Jewish roots, which she also explores in some of her recent poetry. The story depicts a divorced scientist and her grandmother, an inventor, who live together in a spiritually satisfying Jewish community in the 21st century. Published in England as *Body of Glass* in 1992, it won the Arthur C. Clarke Award for best science fiction novel.

In addition to 17 novels, which include *City of Darkness, City of Light* (1996) and *Storm Tide* (1998), and 17 books of poetry, Piercy has edited collections of essays on the craft of poetry and a volume of selected poems by contemporary American women poets, as well as a memoir. Piercy, who lives on Cape Cod, Massachusetts, and teaches a number of poetry workshops, received several literary awards, including a National Endowment for the Arts (NEA) Award. In 1997, she and the writer Ira Wood, her third husband, cofounded a small publishing company, the Leapfrog Press, which in 1999 published a volume of Piercy's new and old poems. While some critics have dismissed her work as too polemical, writer ERICA JONG wrote in the *New York Times Book Review* that Marge Piercy is "an immensely gifted poet and novelist whose range and versatility have made it hard for her talents to be adequately appreciated critically."

The recipient of four honorary doctorates and several poetry awards, such as the Paterson Poetry Prize for *The Art of Blessing the Day: Poems with a Jewish Theme* (1999), Piercy has produced 40 books as of 2007. Among her latest publications is a novel, *The Third Child* (2003), which *Publishers Weekly* described as "a biting, contemporary take on *Romeo and Juliet* and an acidic commentary on political culture," and a critically well-received book of verse titled *Colors Passing through Us* (2003). In her review of *Colors* for *Booklist,* Donna Seeman wrote, "This major American writer is as subversive in her wit as she is cosmic in her perceptions and political in her convictions."

Two more books followed: *The Crooked Inheritance: Poems* (2006) and *Pesach for the Best of Us: Making the Passover Seder Your Own* (2007), a collection of recipes, poems, and blessings about this Jewish holiday.

In 2001 Marge Piercy penned a memoir, *Sleeping with Cats,* in which she recalls her life, beginning in working-class Detroit where she was raised and ending with her tending her garden and cats at her home on Cape Cod. She continues to write about what matters to her most: women, nature, Jewish rituals, love, and politics. "Remembering is like one of those old-fashioned black-and-white tiled floors," writes Piercy. "Wherever I stand or sit, the tiles converge upon me. So our pasts always seem to lead us directly to our present choices. We turn and make a pattern of the chaos of our lives so that we belong exactly where we are."

Further Reading

Kress, Susan, "In and Out of Time: The Form of Marge Piercy's Novels." In *Future Females: A Critical Anthology,* edited by Marlene S. Barr, 109–122. Bowling Green, Ohio: Bowling Green State University Popular Press, 1981.

Piercy, Marge. *Circles on the Water: Selected Poems of Marge Piercy.* New York: Knopf, 1983.

———. *The Crooked Inheritance: Poems.* New York: Knopf, 2006.

———. *Early Grrrl.* Wellfleet, Mass.: Leapfrog Press, 1999.

———. *Gone to Soldiers.* New York: Summit, 1987.

———. *Sleeping with Cats: A Memoir.* New York: William Morrow, 2001.

———. *Small Changes.* New York: Doubleday, 1973.

———. *The Third Child.* New York: HarperCollins, 2003.

Walker, Sue. "Marge Piercy." In *Dictionary of Bibliography: American Novelists since World War II,* edited by James R. Giles and Wanda Giles, 240–251. Farmington Hills, Mich.: Gale, 2000.

∾ Plath, Sylvia
(1932–1963) *poet, novelist*

One of the preeminent modern American poets, Sylvia Plath's accomplished, Pulitzer Prize–winning but controversial poetry was not fully appreciated or critically recognized until after her tragic suicide at the age of 30.

Sylvia Plath was born on October 27, 1932, in Boston, Massachusetts, to middle-class German immigrants. Her father was an entomologist and professor of biology at Boston University; her mother was a high school teacher who encouraged her willowy, shy, precocious daughter to write. Sylvia published her first poem in the *Boston Traveller* when she was eight years old, the same year she suffered a terrible trauma: her father—whom she both adored and feared—died from complications brought on by an amputated gangrenous leg. Writing stories and poetry became her only, "new way of being happy."

Sylvia's grandparents moved in to help take care of her and her brother, and the family moved from Winthrop, a seaside town near Boston that Sylvia had loved, to Wellesley, a wealthy suburb, where she excelled at the public high school and began to publish stories in popular periodicals such as *Seventeen.* She was determined to become a writer and not a housewife. In her journal, in which she wrote almost daily until her death, the 17-year-old confessed: "I am afraid of getting older. I am afraid of getting married. Spare me from cooking three meals a day—spare me from the relentless cage of routine and rote. I want to be free. . . . I want, I think, to be omniscient. . . ."

While a scholarship student at Smith College, Plath won several of the college's literary prizes and *Mademoiselle* magazine's college fiction contest. In 1953, *Harper's* magazine published three of her poems, and that summer Plath was invited to serve as guest editor for *Mademoiselle,* an honor that thrilled the ambitious young writer. But when she returned from New York City, she suffered from serious nervous breakdown (depression was endemic on her father's side of the family). She attempted suicide and spent several months in a mental hospital, undergoing therapy and electroshock treatments. "A time of darkness, despair, disillusion—so black only as the inferno of the human mind can be . . . [and] then the painful agony of slow rebirth and psychic regeneration," she wrote of this episode.

Fortunately, Plath was able to return to Smith in her senior year. In 1955 she graduated with highest honors, summa cum laude, in English, and won a Fulbright scholarship to study at Cambridge University. In her journal, she confided: "I am so hungry for a big smashing creative burgeoning burdened love." Shortly thereafter, at Cambridge she met, and in 1956 married, the attractive young English poet Ted Hughes. Both were accomplished poets who, as Plath described it, "wanted the world's praise, money & love." Initially, the handsome "perfect couple" shared a creative, passionate, and supportive personal and professional partnership.

They returned to the United States, where she taught at Smith, and was considered an excellent English instructor. Nonetheless, she turned down an academic career and moved with Hughes to Boston, "living on a shoestring for a year writing to see what we could do in favor of writing." Much of Plath's early poetry was rejected by literary magazines. However, Hughes's first collection of verse won him a major literary prize. During their early years together, Plath typed, edited, and promoted his work, while failing to develop her own voice as a poet. But she sat in on Robert Lowell's poetry writing seminar at Boston University, and met George Starbuck and ANNE SEXTON, whose verse inspired and influenced her. In 1957 she won *Poetry* magazine's Bess Hokin Award.

In late 1959, the couple returned to England and settled in London. Plath wrote what she considered much better poems, and in 1960 gave birth to a daughter, Frieda. In 1960, her first volume of poetry, *The Colossus,* which she had written under the influence of poet Theodore Roethke, while at the Yaddo writers' colony in New York State, was published in England; the American version was released in 1962. Critics praised her imaginative, direct verse, that was sometimes witty and at other moments somber. In England, at least, Plath was considered a formidable new talent. She also wrote a radio play that was aired by the British Broadcasting Corporation (BBC) in 1962. *Three Women: A Poem for Three Voices* was a finely crafted piece about her three conflicted voices—those of wife, mother, and artist.

Plath and her family moved to a manor house in the Devonshire countryside, but by that time her marriage was falling apart; Hughes was having an affair with another poet's wife (who later committed suicide by gassing herself and the child she had had with Hughes). After recovering from a miscarriage, Plath had a second child, Nicholas, in 1962. Hughes soon moved out, and Plath filed for divorce. In December she and the children moved to a flat in London where, in spite of feeling isolated and bitter, she wrote some of her best and most intense verse. Many of those ferociously angry, feverish poems, written with unsparing clarity at the rate of two or three a day, would appear, posthumously, in *Ariel* (1965).

Feeling positive about her literary achievement, if not about her life, in a letter to her mother Plath proclaimed: "I am a writer. . . . I am a genius of a writer. . . . I am writing the best poems of my life; they will make my name." She was right: two of her best-known and most anthologized poems, from *Ariel,* were written during that turbulent period. In "Lady Lazarus," she referred to previous suicide attempts and did not rule out another, asserting that she had a "calling" for taking her own life. In *The Savage God: A Study of Suicide,* A. Alvarez noted that with the poems in *Ariel,* Plath made poetry and death inseparable: For her, dying was an art, and she felt she did it very well, referring to her suicide attempts.

Some reviewers, such as George Steiner, lauded her confessional poetry—so called because of the confessional nature of her exposing her innermost and often violent emotions and feelings—as "bitter triumphs" that prove "the capacity of poetry to give to reality the greater permanence of the imagined." Others found her morbid, violent poems cruel and distasteful.

One month before her death, *The Bell Jar* (1963), Plath's only novel, was published in England under a pseudonym. After its publication in the United States, under her own name, in 1972, it became a best seller and is today considered a classic in American literature; it is often compared to J. D. Salinger's *The Catcher in the Rye.* A fictionalized autobiographical account of her adolescent mental breakdown and suicide attempt, in the last pages of the novel the protagonist asks: "How did I know that someday—at college, in Europe, somewhere, anywhere—the bell jar, with its stifling distortions, wouldn't descend again?"

On February 11, 1963, during one of London's bleakest and coldest winters, Plath had been cooped up, ill, without a telephone, and with two needy infants. She set out mugs of milk near her children's cribs, blocked off the kitchen with towels, and turned on the gas oven—the "bell jar" had descended for the final time. "Somehow her death is part of the imaginative risk," wrote Robert Lowell, who described her later poems as "controlled hallucination." On the heels of the success of *Ariel* and *The Bell Jar,* Plath's death at age 30 brought her considerable fame, first in England and, during the next 20 years, in America. She became something of a cult figure among adolescent women, while her poetry, often about feeling betrayed and powerless, foreshadowed feminist writing in later years.

After her death, Hughes, as executor of Plath's estate, edited and published three collections of her later work: *Crossing the Water: Transitional*

Poems (1971), *Winter Trees* (1971), and *Collected Poems* (1981), which in 1982 was awarded a Pulitzer Prize. After years of refusing to discuss his controversial marriage, in his best-selling final book of poems, *Birthday Letters* (1998), Hughes, who was poet laureate of England, published an emotional response to the poems in *Ariel* that had graphically characterized his infidelity. He died in 1998.

The Unabridged Journals of Sylvia Plath: 1950–1962 was released in 2000. Transcribed from 23 journals and journal fragments, the never-before-published personal writings, edited by the assistant curator of rare books at Smith College, where Plath had been an undergraduate and later lectured, provide new insight into the poet's life, work, and psyche. For example, on April 23, 1959, Plath scribbled: "The 'dead black' in my poem may be a transference from the visits to my father's grave."

The publication of the unabridged journals was followed in 2003 by a flurry of new books about Plath, in part to commemorate the 40th anniversary of her death. These include *Giving Up: The Last Days of Sylvia Plath; Her Husband: Hughes and Plath, Portrait of a Marriage;* and *Wintering: A Novel of Sylvia Plath,* all produced in 2003. *Sylvia Plath: A Biography,* by Connie Ann Kirk, followed a year later. In addition, a biopic Hollywood movie, *Sylvia,* starring Gwyneth Paltrow in the title role, came out in 2003, the same year a one-woman play, *Edge,* with Angelica Tom portraying Plath, was performed off-Broadway in New York City.

Sylvia's Plath's haunting verse endures because of her mastery of language and her willingness to use poetry to express the need, as Diane Wood Middlebrook wrote in 1998, for "love, work and—above all—recognition in a man's world."

Further Reading

Axelrod, Steven. "Sylvia Plath." The Literary Encyclopedia. Available online. URL: http://www.litencyc.com/php/speople.php?rec=true&UID=3579. Downloaded on March 5, 2007.

Kirk, Connie Ann. *Sylvia Plath: A Biography.* Westport, Conn.: Greenwood Press, 2004.

Malcolm, Janet. *The Silent Woman: Sylvia Plath and Ted Hughes.* New York: Knopf, 1994.

Middlebrook, Diane. *Her Husband: Hughes and Plath, Portrait of a Marriage.* New York: Viking Press, 2003.

Plath, Sylvia. *The Bell Jar.* New York: HarperCollins, 1996.

———. *The Collected Poems* (includes *The Colossus and Other Poems* and *Ariel*). Edited by Ted Hughes. New York: Harper and Row, 1981.

———. *The Unabridged Journals of Sylvia Plath: 1959–1962.* Edited by Karen V. Kukil. New York: Random House, 2000.

Stevenson, Anne. *Bitter Fame: Life of Sylvia Plath.* Boston: Houghton Mifflin, 1989.

Porter, Katherine Anne (Callie Russell)
(1890–1980)   *short story writer, novelist*

Katherine Anne Porter overcame a hardscrabble background to win a Pulitzer Prize and the National Book Award for her short fiction. Yet she did not earn widespread popularity or financial success until the publication, late in her career, of *Ship of Fools* (1962), her only novel, which critics generally agreed fell short of the brilliance she had demonstrated earlier in her short stories and novellas.

"My life has been incredible," Katherine Anne Porter wrote to her brother in 1957. "I don't believe a word of it." In fact, it was risky for anyone to take Porter at her word when she spoke about her life: she was deeply ashamed of her humble background and often fictionalized it, even as she drew from her real-life experiences to create the fiction that made her famous.

The fourth child of Harrison Boone Porter and Mary Alice Jones Porter, Callie Russell Porter was born on May 15, 1890, in a log cabin in Indian Creek, Texas. Among the many tales Porter told about her family was that her father was descended from the frontier hero Daniel Boone and that she enjoyed a culturally rich childhood, filled with books. In reality, she grew up in poverty, her formal education ended in her early teens, and she married a railroad clerk when she was 16, an unhappy union that was the first of four unsuccessful marriages.

Between 1914 and 1916 Porter "made her dash into that wilder world," moving to Chicago, divorcing her husband, and legally changing her name to Katherine Anne Porter. She landed journalism jobs, first in Chicago and then in Denver, and barely survived the influenza epidemic of 1918–19, an experience that formed the basis of "Pale Horse, Pale Rider," one of her most highly regarded stories.

Porter's sojourns in Mexico during the 1920s provided the raw material for some of best short fiction, including "Maria Concepcion," her first published story, which appeared in *Century* magazine in 1922. In 1930 she achieved critical acclaim with a volume of stories, *Flowering Judas*. Its appearance marked the beginning of a 15-year period during which Porter published what critics consider to have been her most accomplished

Katherine Anne Porter, 82, discusses a future writing assignment.
(AP/Wide World Photos)

work, including the collections *Flowering Judas and Other Stories* (1935), an expanded version of the earlier volume; *Pale Horse, Pale Rider: Three Short Novels* (1939); and *The Leaning Tower and Other Stories* (1944).

Porter's personal life was marred by failed marriages and love affairs. She once wrote that "My own habit of writing fiction has provided a wholesome exercise to my natural, incurable tendency to try to wrangle the sprawling mess of our existence in the bloody world into some kind of shape." It took a great deal of wrangling before Porter finally produced a novel, *Ship of Fools*. The popular book, which chronicled the interrelationships of almost 50 ocean liner passengers, all "caught between the two worlds of yesterday and today," had its origins and setting in Porter's 1931 ocean voyage from Mexico to Germany. She began the novel in 1940 and worked on it intermittently for more than two decades. When *Ship of Fools* finally appeared in 1962, it was received enthusiastically; but later it met with decidedly mixed reviews. One critic noted that the novel "could make a good movie, but that's one thing that's wrong with it." In fact, it was turned into a highly successful movie in 1965.

Whatever the critical response to *Ship of Fools*, it brought Porter wealth and heightened recognition. In 1965 her earlier collections, along with several additional stories, appeared as *The Collected Stories of Katherine Anne Porter*. In 1966 she garnered both the Pulitzer Prize and National Book Award for her short fiction. Among the critics who lavished praise on her was the U.S. poet laureate, Robert Penn Warren, who commented that some of her stories were "unsurpassed in modern fiction." Always looking for a good story, in 1972 she traveled to Cape Canaveral to cover an Apollo moon mission for *Playboy* magazine.

After a long, productive life, Katherine Anne Porter, whose literary output after the mid-1960s was limited by declining health, died in Silver Spring, Maryland, on September 18, 1980. She has not been forgotten: The Katherine Anne Porter Society sponsors scholarly meetings and conferences and issues a newsletter; the Katherine Anne Porter

Museum, located in Kyle, Texas, where the author spent 10 years of her childhood, is open to the public; and a play titled *Passenger on the Ship of Fools* that scrutinized Porter's shifting sense of self from an impoverished childhood to recognition as a master of modern American short fiction was performed in April 2002 at the University of Texas at Austin. In addition, several recent biographical and critical studies illuminate new aspects of Porter's life and work, and in 2006 Porter was featured on a U.S. postage stamp as part of the Literary Arts stamp series.

Further Reading

Flora, Joseph M., and Lucinda H. Mackethan, eds. *The Companion to Southern Literature.* Baton Rouge: Louisiana State University Press, 2002.

Porter, Katherine Anne. *The Collected Stories of Katherine Anne Porter.* New York: Harcourt, Brace, 1965; reissue edition, Harcourt Brace and Company, 1979.

———. *Ship of Fools.* Boston: Little, Brown, 1962.

Titus, Mary. *The Ambivalent Art of Katherine Anne Porter.* Athens: University of Georgia Press, 2005.

Unrue, Darlene Harbour. *Katherine Ann Porter: The Life of an Artist.* Jackson: University Press of Mississippi, 2005.

∽ Portillo Trambley, Estela

(1936–1998)   *playwright, short story writer*

The first Chicana to publish a book of short stories, *Rain of Scorpions,* and to write a musical comedy, *Morality Play,* Estela Portillo Trambley focused on feminism and ethnicity, as well as on more universal themes, in her award-winning work.

Born on January 16, 1936, in El Paso, Texas, Estela Portillo recalled growing up in a very poor family, "pero la pobreza nunca derriba el espíritu [but poverty never defeats the spirit]." When she was only 17, Estela married Robert D. Trambley; the couple had six children. Recognizing the importance of an education, she enrolled at the University of Texas, graduating in 1957 and earning a master's degree in English in 1977.

For 14 years, while raising her children, Portillo Trambley worked as a high school English teacher in El Paso and from 1970 to 1975 was resident dramatist at El Paso's community college. She was also a radio talk show hostess and produced a Chicano cultural television series.

After her only son died as an infant, she turned to writing and in 1971 published her first play—and what many critics consider her best work—*The Day of the Swallows.* In it she dramatized the story of a lesbian Chicana who will do anything, including cutting out a boy's tongue, to keep the judgmental community from knowing her secret. At the end of the play, guilt-ridden and anguished (her lover has left her), she dresses in a wedding gown and drowns herself. "Drama involves the players and the audience outside of myself," Portillo Trambley once commented. "It is a more precarious challenge [than writing fiction], because one works with [other] people."

In 1972, Portillo Trambley won the prestigious Quinto Sol Award for her literary contribution to Chicano literature. Her next work, *Morality Play,* the first musical comedy written and produced by a Chicana, used a 15th-century morality play format to portray the triumph of Hope, Faith, and Charity over Evil. First produced in 1974, in El Paso's Chamizal National Theatre, it was followed by *Black Light,* a tragedy about Chicano displacement and pride that featured Mayan music and dance. She wrote four more plays, *El Hombre Cosmico, Sun Images, Isabel and the Dancing Bear,* and *Sor Juana,* all of which were staged at Chamizal National Theatre.

In 1975 Portillo Trambley's collection of well-received stories, *Rain of Scorpions and Other Writings,* appeared. In the title story, a group of young Chicano boys, who are suffocating in the town's barrio (Spanish-speaking district), descend into a cave in search of a mythical underground garden of paradise. A rainstorm triggers an avalanche of mud above them and hoards of scorpions are released into the Spanish-speaking ghetto. In spite of the squalor and poison surrounding them, the boys discover that paradise can be found in a spiritual place within themselves. In *Chicano Literature,* Laverne Gonzalez described the themes running through the "imagistic and, at times, symbolic stories" in *Rain of Scorpions* as "oppressiveness, personal crises, thwarted aspirations, deceptions, and female exploitation." While the author is sympathetic toward her hapless characters, continued Gonzales, she does not provide them with easy solutions.

In 1986 Portillo Trambley tried her hand at writing a novel. *Trini,* which was lauded by several reviewers, depicted the story of a Tarahumara Indian woman who refuses to give up her traditional spirituality but crosses the border to give birth to her child in America.

In an interview in *Chicano Authors* in 1980, Estela Portillo Trambley, a grandmother of eight who promoted bilingual theater and Chicano fine arts programs in El Paso when she was not writing, said that she separated politics from literature because "when you inject politics into it you limit its life. . . . All good literature is based on the human experience which is nonpolitical. Use literature as a political tool and it becomes provincial, time bound. . . ."

Portillo Trambley was inducted into the El Paso Woman's Hall of Fame in 1986 and named Author of the Pass by the *El Paso Herald Post* in 1990. Five years later she held the Presidential Chair in Creative Writing at the University of California, Davis. The publication of *Sor Juana and Other Plays* in 1983 had brought her considerable critical acclaim. "The culmination of her pursuit of strong women is represented in her exploration of the 18th-century poet and essayist Sor Juana Inés de la Cruz," wrote Nicolás Kanellos in *Who's Who of Hispanic Authors of the United States.* "In both her prose and drama, she develops strong women who resist the social roles that have been predetermined for them because of their sex." However, she repudiated the more radical rhetoric of some Chicano contemporaries and emphasized the influence of European and American classics on her writing. On December 29, 1998, at 72, Estela Portillo Trambley died. Her papers are housed in the Nettie Lee Benson Latin American Collection at the University of Texas in Austin.

Further Reading

Garza, Robert J., ed. *Contemporary Chicano Theatre* (includes *The Day of the Swallows*). Notre Dame, Ind.: University of Notre Dame Press, 1976.

Gonzalez, Laverne, "Estela Portillo Trambley." In *Chicano Literature,* edited by Julio A. Martinez and Francisco A. Lomeli, 316–322. Westport, Conn.: Greenwood Press, 1985.

Ikas, Karin Rosa. *Chicana Ways: Conversations with Ten Chicana Writers.* Reno: University of Nevada Press, 2002.

Kanellos, Nicolás. *Who's Who of Hispanic Authors of the United States,* no. 157. Westport, Conn.: Greenwood Press, 2003.

Portillo Trambley, Estela. *Rain of Scorpions and Other Stories.* Tempe, Ariz.: Bilingual Press, 1992.

———. *Sor Juana and Other Plays.* Tempe, Ariz.: Bilingual Press, 1983.

———. *Trini.* With a foreword by Helena Maria Viramontes. New York: Feminist Press, 2005.

Powell, Dawn
(1897–1965) *novelist, short story writer*

Although her work was praised by critics and admired by writers in both the United States and England, Dawn Powell's satirical novels never garnered a wide readership during her lifetime. Yet a quarter century after her death, the quality of her superbly crafted fiction, which included 15 novels, won her a dedicated new audience.

Dawn Powell was born in the small town of Mt. Gilead, Ohio, on November 28, 1897, the second of three daughters. Her childhood was unhappy. Her father was a salesman who was often away and her mother died at an early age. The children were shunted from one relative to another until their father's remarriage. But Dawn did not get along with her stepmother, who burned all the stories the young girl had written. Eventually she ran away from home with 30¢ in her pocket.

Powell distinguished herself as a writer and actress at Lake Erie College, where she earned a bachelor of arts degree in 1918. (In 1960, her alma mater awarded her an honorary doctorate degree.) After graduating, Powell moved to New York City, where she married Joseph Gousha, who worked in

Dawn Powell's work is enjoying a resurgence
in popularity.
(AP/Wide World Photos)

the advertising industry. The couple's only child
suffered from what probably was a combination of
cerebral palsy and schizophrenia and was institutionalized for most of his life. Powell and Gousha
lived together in bohemian Greenwich Village
until his death in 1962, despite Powell's ongoing
affair with a magazine editor that lasted until she
died. According to her friends, Powell loved both
men, who greeted each formally but politely when
they happened to meet.

Powell was known for her merciless satire. Her
novels often targeted the bourgeoisie, which may
have limited their popularity. "You both confuse
and anger people if you satirize the middle class,"
she acknowledged. "It is considered jolly and good-
humored to point out the oddities of the poor or
of the rich but I go outside the rules with my stuff
because I can't help believing that the middle class

is funny, too." But she was unwilling to compromise in order to spare her readers' feelings. "True
wit should break a wise man's heart," she maintained. "It should rest on a pillar of truth and not
on a gelatin base, and the truth is not so shameful
that it cannot be recorded."

Powell's early novels, including *Dance Night*
(1930), her personal favorite, were set in her native
Ohio. The focus in the six Ohio novels was on
characters who wanted to escape from dreary small
midwestern towns. In the mid-1930s, beginning
with *Turn, Magic Wheel* (1936), Powell switched
settings from the Midwest to urban New York
City; her later novels, such as *My Home Is Far
Away* (1944), which one critic called a masterpiece,
and *The Locusts Have No King* (1948), were populated by the heterogeneous characters of Greenwich Village—from shrewish career women and
philandering businessmen to unscrupulous writers
or publishers and self-serving patrons of the arts.
Yet as Tim Page, her biographer, pointed out, at
her core Powell "may be described as a wordly,
determinedly clear-sighted, deeply skeptical
romantic—but a romantic all the same."

Although many of Dawn Powell's books were
out of print when she died of cancer on November
15, 1965, several of her novels were reissued beginning in 1989 and sold well. In 1998, Page published the first biography of her, and he was
instrumental in having her work reprinted. According to Page, the reason Powell was not better
known in the past was because her "dark, mordant
attitude toward the world . . . rankled."

Tim Page also edited Powell's diaries (1995) and
her letters (1999). In a review in the *New York
Times* of *The Selected Letters of Dawn Powell, 1913–
1965,* short story writer LORRIE MOORE noted:

> So current and alive is Powell's epistolary voice,
> even in the earliest letters, that one is tempted to
> suggest that what we now think of as the contem-
> porary American voice—in journalism and the
> arts—is none other than hers: ironic, triumphant,
> mocking and game; the voice of a smart, chipper,
> small-town Ohio girl newly settled in New York
> just after the First World War. . . . What they

[Powell's letters] offer is . . . a portrait of a hard-working, resilient female artist and professional.

In 2001 The Library of America reissued Powell's novels in two volumes, 1930 to 1942 and 1944 to 1962, enabling a new generation of readers to rediscover "our best comic novelist," as the writer Gore Vidal dubbed her.

Further Reading

"Dawn Powell: Highlights of a Life." Ohioana Authors. Available online. URL: http://www.ohioana_authors. org/powell/highlights.php. Downloaded on March 5, 2007.

Page Tim. *Dawn Powell: A Biography.* New York: Henry Holt, 1998.

Powell, Dawn. *Dawn Powell's Novels, 1930–1942; Dawn Powell's Novels, 1944–1962.* Edited by Tim Page. New York: Library of America, 2001.

———. *The Diaries of Dawn Powell, 1931–1965.* Edited and with an introduction by Tim Page. South Royalton, Vt.: Steerforth Press, 1995.

———. *The Locusts Have No King.* New York: Yarrow Press, 1990.

———. *The Selected Letters of Dawn Powell, 1913–1965.* Edited by Tim Page. New York: Henry Holt and Company, 1999.

➳ Proulx, Annie (E. Annie Proulx, Edna Annie Proulx)
(1935–   )   *short story writer, novelist*

Prize-winning novelist and short story writer Annie Proulx is renowned for her spare yet finely crafted prose, her memorable, quirky characters, and her strikingly beautiful but isolated settings in New England, Canada, and Wyoming. About her writing career, Proulx has said, "I came to writing late, and I'm racing against the clock to get everything down. My head is jammed with stories; they are pushing to get out."

Born Edna Annie Proulx on August 22, 1935, in Norwich, Connecticut, the best-selling author goes by Annie Proulx, although for many years, until 1997 when her story "Brokeback Mountain" was published in the *New Yorker,* she used the initial of her first name, calling herself E. Annie Proulx. Her father, an up-and-coming textile entrepreneur with French-Canadian roots, moved his family frequently, always searching for better opportunities. Annie, the eldest of five sisters, was smitten with wanderlust at an early age. Her mother, whose English ancestors had lived in Connecticut for 350 years, was a gifted amateur painter and naturalist. "From my mother I learned to see and appreciate the natural world, to develop an eye for details, and to tell a story," recalled Proulx. "And from my maternal grandmother (who washed and ironed all her paper money) I picked up some facility in shaping a story, and the exercise of the imagination."

After graduating from Dearing High School in Portland, Maine, Proulx attended Colby College but soon dropped out to marry H. Ridgely Bullock in 1955. The couple had a daughter, Sylvia, who was raised by Bullock once he and Proulx were divorced. (After Bullock's death in 1993, Proulx and her daughter became reacquainted.) Two more marriages resulted in divorce and produced three sons. "It gradually dawned on me that I am not well-suited for marriage," Proulx wrote on her Web site. She then completed her undergraduate education at the University of Vermont, where she studied history and graduated cum laude and Phi Beta Kappa in 1969.

In 1973 Proulx earned a master's degree in history from Sir George Williams (now Concordia) University in Montreal and two years later passed her doctoral oral exams. Opting for a more secure career in freelance journalism instead of academia, she never completed her Ph.D. dissertation. In order to support herself and her three sons, she wrote several how-to books, such as *Plan and Make Your Own Fences and Gates, Walkways, Walls and Drives* (1983). From 1975 to 1988 she wrote non-fiction articles for popular magazines, assignments she described as "tedious non-fiction," on disparate subjects: weather, apples, mice, African beadwork, cider, and mountain lions. Nonetheless, she managed to focus on her creative writing and published two short stories a year in *Gray's Sporting Journal.*

She also spent two years writing for and editing a newspaper in rural Vermont, *Behind the Times,* that she had helped found, all the while continuing to write short stories on the side. Her short fiction began to appear regularly in *Esquire,* and one of the magazine's editors suggested that Proulx compile her stories. Her first collection, *Heart Songs and Other Stories,* set in backwoods towns in Vermont and featuring small-town characters described by critic Kenneth Rosen of the *New York Times Book Review* as "shy, battered, depleted," came out in 1988. (It was reissued, with two additional stories, in 1995.)

Well into her 50s, and with the assistance of a Vermont Council on the Arts fellowship (1989), a National Endowment for the Arts (NEA) grant (1991), and a Guggenheim fellowship (1992), E. Annie Proulx published her debut novel, *Postcards* (1992), a multigenerational, poignant story about the Blood family and their New England farm. The book garnered critical acclaim, especially for Proulx's skills as a first-rate storyteller depicting the collapse of the small farm in post–World War II America, and received a PEN/Faulkner Award for Fiction.

Proulx's second and best-known novel, *The Shipping News* (1993), won both the Pulitzer Prize for fiction and the National Book Award for fiction. Set in a desolate seaside town in Newfoundland, it was especially notable for its haunting sense of place and its authentic, stylized language. The disturbing novel revolves around Quoyle, a love-starved, second-rate journalist and widowed father who moves with his two daughters and aunt to a remote harbor town in an attempt to reclaim the family's land and re-create a home. Proulx visited Newfoundland's Great Northern Peninsula 10 times to do research for the book. During her first visit, a fishing trip with a friend, she reacted "viscerally" to the area. "I have a habit of falling immediately and deeply in love with places," she has said, adding that the harsh climate, grim history, hard lives, and generous, warm characters of the outport fishermen and their families deeply interested her. *The Shipping News,* which the *Chicago Tribune Book World* called "that rare creation, a lyric page turner," became a best seller and in 2001 was adapted as a Hollywood film starring Kevin Spacey.

Accordion Crimes (1996), her next novel, comprises a series of interconnected stories about the American immigrant experience and music in North America, when an accordion ends up with different owners from varied ethnic backgrounds over the duration of a century. It also required extensive research and traveling, which Proulx described as "a slow drift through the territory under examination taking notes . . . hiking the terrain, studying maps and weather."

After editing *Best American Short Stories of 1997,* Proulx published *Close Range: Wyoming Stories* (1999), about the history, violence, and challenging hardships of life in Wyoming. Proulx had moved permanently to Wyoming in 1994, noting in an interview that there was "much about the place that moved her deeply." Five years later she produced a second volume of Wyoming stories, *Bad Dirt,* and it too was populated by resilient, idiosyncratic characters. In one of the stories, "Pairs of Spurs," Proulx comments that Wyoming's unwritten motto is "take care of your own damn self." Her most celebrated story, "Brokeback Mountain," appeared in *Close Range,* having originally been published in the *New Yorker* on October 13, 1997. When it came out in the prestigious literary magazine, "it was so startling and powerful that for many people, the experience of reading it remains a vivid, almost physical memory," wrote Karen Durbin in the *New York Times.*

"Brokeback Mountain" won a 1998 O. Henry Short Story Award and was adapted into a controversial, landmark movie directed by Ang Lee. It became a major, multi-award–winning film, including several Academy Awards in 2006. "When I first read the story, it gripped me," said Lee in a *New York Times* article in 2005. "It's a great American love story, told in a way that felt as if it had never been done before." According to Proulx, "Brokeback Mountain" is the tragic story of two

An award-winning story by Annie Proulx inspired the controversial, critically acclaimed film *Brokeback Mountain*.
(AP Images/Daniel Ochoade Olza)

poor, inarticulate teenagers who have left home and both found summer work herding sheep, and then find themselves, much to their surprise, fiercely attracted to each other. They go on to share a 20-year, clandestine, unresolved but profound homosexual relationship. "The work of imagining, thinking, picturing, describing how things would have been for two 19-year-old rough, uneducated young men in 1963 Wyoming was slow, difficult and arduous. . . . Years of accumulated observation went into the story," commented Proulx. It took the author roughly twice as long to write the evocative short story as it normally takes her to complete a novel.

Annie Proulx has received numerous honors for her storytelling artistry, including, for *The Shipping News*, the *Irish Times* International Fiction Prize and the *Chicago Tribune* Heartland Award; the National Magazine Award for excellence in fiction for "Brokeback Mountain"; inclusion of "The Half-Skinned Steer" in *Best American Short Stories of the Century*, edited by John Updike; and the *New Yorker* Book Award for Best Fiction in 1999. In addition to writing and traveling, Proulx's interests include hunting, fishing, canoeing, wood-lore, homemade bread, knots, and adult literacy. She also says that she likes cold, sharp seasonal changes and weather extremes. One thing she does not like is teaching creative writing courses: "The best way to learn to write is to read—widely, deeply, omnivorously," she asserts.

Further Reading

Durbin, Karen. "Cowboys in Love . . . with Each Other: *Brokeback Mountain*." The *New York Times*, September 4, 2005, Film section, pp. 9, 15.

Proulx, Annie E. *The Shipping News*. New York: Simon & Schuster, 1993.

Proulx, Annie. *Bad Dirt: Wyoming Stories* 2. New York: Scribner, 2004.

Proulx, Annie, Larry McMurtry, and Diana Ossana. *Getting Movied: Story, Screenplay, and Essays*. New York: Scribner, 2005.

Winter, Jessica. "The Scripting News: *Brokeback* Writers on the Road from Page to Screen." *Village Voice*. Available online. URL: http://www.villagevoice.com/film/0548, winter,70454,20.html. Downloaded on March 5, 2007.

Quindlen, Anna

(1953–   ) *novelist, journalist, nonfiction book writer, children's book writer*

Anna Quindlen is a best-selling novelist, a popular syndicated columnist, and an insightful essayist. Winner of the 1992 Pulitzer Prize for commentary, she writes forcefully about politics but also about more personal, familial issues that often have universal and controversial implications. Critics have praised Quindlen for her ability to demonstrate through her writing the profound effect public events can have on ordinary lives.

The eldest of five children, Anna Quindlen was born on July 8, 1953, in Philadelphia. Her father was a management consultant and her mother, Prudence, stayed at home. Anna grew up in a close-knit, Catholic, Irish-Italian family in Drexel Hill, Pennsylvania, and enjoyed what she described as an "extremely happy childhood." A precocious child and an avid, early reader, she turned to literature as a means of challenging herself. "In books I have traveled, not only to other worlds, but into my own," she recalled in *How Reading Changed My Life*. "[Through literature] I learned who I was and who I wanted to be, what I might aspire to, and what I might dare to dream about my world and

myself." Then, Anna's life was irrevocably changed: She was 19 when her mother died, and Anna would later write about how her mother's tragic death forever changed her life.

A year before graduating with a bachelor of arts degree from Barnard College in New York City in 1974, Quindlen began working as a reporter for the *New York Post*. She stayed at that position for two more years before joining the esteemed *New York Times* as a general assignment reporter and then as a city hall reporter. In 1978 she married attorney Gerald Krovatin, her college sweetheart. The couple has three children: Quin, Christopher, and Maria. In 1981 the *New York Times* offered Quindlen her own biweekly column, "About New York," making her only the third woman in the paper's history to write a regular column for its influential op-ed page. It was then, she explained in an interview in *Editor & Publisher*, that she developed a voice of her own without using the first person. That feminist, more intimate voice was radically different from the male-centered commentary that dominated most major newspapers at that time.

Promoted to deputy metropolitan editor of the *Times* in 1983, Quindlen relinquished the demanding position two years later, having given birth to her first child and opting to spend more time with her young son. In addition, she still harbored hopes of writing a novel. In 1986 the executive editor of the *New York Times* convinced her to write a weekly freelance column, which Quindlen called "Life in the 30s." Using her finely honed observation skills and unaffected writing style, Quindlen wrote about her personal family-related experiences as a married working mother in the 1980s and related them to larger, news-oriented themes. "Life in the 30s" struck a nerve with the baby-boomer generation (those born between 1946 and 1964) and was widely read and widely syndicated. John Allemang of the Toronto *Globe and Mail* described Quindlen as "the unofficial voice that news most obviously lacks, the personal columnist who finds her truths in the little things." In 1988 Random House published a collection of selected "Life in the 30s" columns titled *Living Out Loud.*

Quindlen's next biweekly column, "Public & Private," appeared on the op-ed page of the *New York Times* for five years, from 1990 until 1995. In 1992 the trenchant opinion pieces earned Quindlen a Pulitzer Prize for commentary. The Pulitzer judges lauded the journalist's "compelling column covering a wide range of personal and political thoughts." Quindlen's name was mentioned for a deputy editorship at the *Times,* but she had something else in mind: She still wanted to write a novel. "I went into newspapers originally to support my fiction habit," she said. "There's a steady paycheck in reporting, and there simply isn't one in fiction." When she was not taking care of her children or grinding out newspaper columns, she worked on her novel.

In 1991, *Object Lessons,* Quindlen's first novel, was published. A coming-of-age story of an Irish-Catholic family in crisis during one summer in the mid-1960s, told through the eyes of a preadolescent narrator in emotional turmoil, it became a best seller. Novelist ANNE TYLER called *Object Lessons* "intelligent, highly entertaining, and laced with acute perceptions about the nature of day-to-day daily life." Quindlen continued writing columns and, switching genres, produced a children's

book, *The Tree That Came to Stay,* in 1992. It was followed five years later by another book for young readers, *Happily Ever After.* A second collection, *Thinking Out Loud,* composed of a selection of her "Public & Private" columns, was released in 1994 and, noted Quindlen, commented on social and political events from an "underrepresented and valuable female viewpoint."

In 1995 Quindlen left the *New York Times* to work full time on her fiction. "When I quit the *New York Times* to be a full-time mother, the voices of the world said I was nuts," she commented in a commencement speech at Mount Holyoke College in 1999. "When I quit again to be a full-time novelist, they said I was nuts again. But I am not nuts, I am happy. I am successful on my own terms." Quindlen then wrote a second best-selling novel, *One True Thing* (1995), the wrenching story of the relationship between a daughter and her mother, who is dying from cancer. The daughter unwittingly becomes her mother's caretaker, and a new, loving bond between them is formed. Claire Messud, writing in the *Times Literary Supplement* in 1995, asserts that *One True Thing* is so strong because Quindlen "prefers emotional accuracy to literary elegance." In 1998 the book was adapted successfully as a film starring Meryl Streep.

Quindlen's third novel, *Black and Blue* (1998), about spousal abuse and the harrowing effects of domestic violence on the members of one family, was also critically acclaimed. That same year, the author published a memoir, *How Reading Changed My Life,* that explored her lifelong love of reading. In addition to her journalism and fiction, Quindlen offers advice about childrearing. "What the books [by child specialists] taught me, finally, and what the women on the playground taught me, and the well-meaning relations—what they taught me, was that they couldn't really teach me very much at all," wrote Quindlen in a column called "On Being Mom" for *Newsweek.* "Even today I'm not sure what worked and what didn't, what was me and what was simply life. . . . I wound up with the three people I like best in the world, who have done more than anyone to excavate my essential humanity. That's what the books never told me."

In 1999 Quindlen returned to journalism as a biweekly columnist for *Newsweek* magazine. In addition to writing "Last Word," Quindlen continues to produce nonfiction titles such as *A Short Guide to a Happy Life* (2000), a collection of essays on how to enjoy life, and to publish more fiction. *Blessings* (2002) is the story of love and redemption as secrets and lies are revealed by and about Lydia Blessing, a reclusive, elderly character, and members of her family. "I think all families have secrets," Quindlen once commented.

Another collection of essays that combine political commentary with personal reflections, *Loud and Clear* (2004), offers "razor-sharp musings," according to *Publishers Weekly.* Originally written for *Newsweek* and the *New York Times,* the essays tackle small and large subjects ranging from Catholicism (raised a Catholic, Quindlen is critical of the Church's more conservative doctrines) and women's health issues to absentee fathers and the war in Iraq. A travel book about literary London, *Imagined London: A Tour of the World's Greatest Fiction City* (2004), and *Being Perfect* (2005), another best-selling collection of practical advice, were followed by Quindlen's latest novel, *Rise and Shine* (2006), the story of a television journalist whose professional career is ruined because of an indiscre-

tion in her personal life. *Rise and Shine* is Quindlen's fifth novel to make the hardcover *New York Times* best seller list. She is a fellow of the American Academy of Arts.

Anna Quindlen has received several honorary doctorates, including from Dartmouth and Smith colleges, and has been invited to deliver numerous commencement speeches. At Mount Holyoke College in Massachusetts, she admonished the female graduating class to "give up on being perfect and begin the work of becoming yourself."

Further Reading

Carlton, Royce. "Anna Quindlen." Available online. URL: http://www.roycecarlton.com/speakers/quindlen.html. Downloaded on May 22, 2007.

Quindlen, Anna. *Being Perfect.* New York: Random House, 2005.

———. *Black and Blue.* New York: Random House, 1998.

———. "Commencement Speech, Mount Holyoke College." Gifts of Speech. Available online. URL: http://gos.sbc.edu/q/quindlen.html. Downloaded on January 23, 2007.

———. *Rise and Shine.* New York: Random House, 2006.

∾ Quintasket
See MOURNING DOVE

R

Rampling, Anne
See RICE, ANNE

Rand, Ayn (Alice Rosenbaum)
(1905–1982) *novelist*

Ayn Rand's two blockbuster novels, *The Fountain-head* and *Atlas Shrugged,* won her millions of fans and made her one of the 20th century's best-selling American authors. At the same time, to a small coterie of devotees, Rand's fiction established her as a philosopher of an uncompromising brand of rugged individualism, whose stormy temperament mirrored the heroic characters that dominated her fiction.

Ayn Rand was born Alice Rosenbaum in St. Petersburg, Russia, on February 2, 1905, just weeks after the outbreak of the 1905 Revolution. Precociously intellectual, she declared herself an atheist in her early teens and graduated from the University of Leningrad at the age of 19. The Bolshevik Revolution of 1917, which resulted in Russia's becoming the world's first communist state and under whose tyranny she lived for almost a decade, turned her into a bitter foe of collectivist regimes and ideologies. She also deeply despised religion and what she contemptuously called "mysticism."

In 1926, Alice Rosenbaum left Russia for the United States, where she ultimately took the name Ayn Rand. She lived briefly in Chicago before moving to Hollywood, where she found work in the movie industry as an extra and junior script writer. In 1929, she married Charles Francis O'Connor, a mediocre actor and artist. Notwithstanding her admiration for independent people of "genius"—she unhesitatingly placed herself in that category—Rand nonetheless deeply loved O'Connor and remained devoted to him until his death in 1979.

Rand's first novel, *We the Living* (1936), a scathing critique of the suffocating nature of life under communism in the Soviet Union, appeared to unenthusiastic reviews and disappointing sales. Seven years later, *The Fountainhead* (1943) brought Rand both critical acclaim and, eventually, commercial success. The *New York Times* reviewer compared the novel to Thomas Mann's masterpiece *The Magic Mountain* and noted that Rand had written "a hymn in praise of the individual." The central theme in the book, as personified in the protagonist Howard Roark, an innovative architect, is a defense of egoism and individualism.

Rand characterized the novel's, heroine, Dominique Francow, as "herself in a bad mood."

In 1957, Rand reached the pinnacle of critical and popular success with the publication of *Atlas Shrugged*. In her magnum opus, an individualist utopian community, hidden in Rocky Mountain Valley, struggles against the collectivist-dominated world surrounding it. The saga's lengthy list of characters includes Dagny Taggert, described by one critic as "the most heroic female protagonist in American fiction," and John Galt, Rand's ultimate individualist hero. Galt's 60-page speech provides the book's philosophic core, and took the author two years to write. That philosophy is summed up much more succinctly in the motto adopted by Galt's community: "I swear by my life and my love of it that I will never live for the sake of another man nor ask another man to live for mine."

After 1957 Rand abandoned fiction and instead promoted her philosophy, known as objectivism, in a series of nonfiction works, and as a lecturer. She continued to stress that only strict laissez-faire capitalism allowed individuals to reach their potential and society as a whole to prosper. Among admirers influenced by her views were Alan Greenspan, an economic advisor to several American presidents and head of the U.S. Federal Reserve System during the 1990s, and Margaret Thatcher, British prime minister from 1979 to 1990.

Ayn Rand died in New York City on March 6, 1982. Since her death, hundreds of thousands of copies of her novels have continued to sell each year. The Ayn Rand Institute sponsors numerous educational programs, journals and publications, and conferences. For example, in 2006 a nine-day Objectivist Summer Conference was held in Boston, attracting Ayn Rand specialists and acolytes worldwide. Several of Rand's novels have been adapted to the screen, including in 1999 *The Passion of Ayn Rand,* starring Helen Mirren in an award-winning performance. An entire industry has grown around the controversial philosophy of objectivism, and its movement has fractured along partisan lines. More than 100 years after her death, Ayn Rand continues to affect culture, politics, and philosophy in contemporary America.

Further Reading

Britting, Jeff. *Ayn Rand: A Biography.* New York: Overbrook Press, 2004.

Gladstein, Mimi Reisel. *The Ayn Rand Companion.* Westport, Conn.: Greenwood Press, 1984.

Kelley, David. *The Contested Legacy of Ayn Rand.* Edison, N.J.: Transaction, 2000.

Mayhew, Robert, ed. *Essays on Ayn Rand's* We the Living. New York: Lexington Books, 2004.

Rand, Ayn. *Atlas Shrugged.* New York: Random House, 1957.

———. *The Fountainhead.* New York: Bobbs-Merrill, 1943.

———. *Philosophy: Who Needs It.* New York: Bobbs-Merrill, 1971.

Smith, Tara. *Ayn Rand's Normative Ethics: The Virtuous Egoist.* New York: Cambridge University Press, 2006.

Rawlings, Marjorie Kinnan
(1896–1953)   *children's book writer, novelist*

Best known for her Pulitzer Prize–winning novel *The Yearling,* Marjorie Kinnan Rawlings set her most accomplished work in Florida's rural backwood wilderness, where she had spent most of her life.

Born on August 8, 1896, Marjorie Kinnan grew up in Washington D.C., where her mother encouraged her early interest in storytelling and writing; Marjorie won her first writing contest when she was 11. But her happy childhood came to an abrupt end when she was 16, with the death of her father.

The Kinnans moved to Madison, Wisconsin, where in 1918 Marjorie graduated Phi Beta Kappa from the University of Wisconsin, having majored in English. A year later she married Charles Rawlings, a writer, and moved with him to upstate New York. She worked at a variety of jobs—publicist, editor, syndicated verse writer, and journalist at the Louisville *Courier-Journal* and the Rochester *Journal-American.*

In 1928, the couple moved to a 72-acre farm and citrus grove in Cross Creek, an isolated area in north central Florida that Rawlings would immortalize in many of her books. She felt a deep kinship with the poor but fiercely independent local white "crackers," as she referred to them, and with them appreciated the region's "beauty and grace" and its "remoteness from urban confusion."

In 1930 Rawlings sold a collection of stories to *Scribner's* magazine. Three years later she won the prestigious O. Henry Memorial Short Story Award for "Gal Young Un," another Florida-based tale. Her first novel, *South Moon Under,* published in 1933, was notable for its "wholly alive, richly drawn" characters—three generations of moon-

shiners who lived and worked, often violently, in Florida's scrub country. That same year Rawlings divorced her husband and devoted herself full time to her writing. "I stay at my typewriter for eight hours every day when I'm working and keep as free as possible for all distractions for the rest of the day," she explained.

Her second novel, *Golden Apples* (1935), based on a trip to England and featuring an English protagonist, was poorly received. Rawlings returned to writing about Florida's rugged hammock country in her next and most popular novel, *The Yearling* (1938). The story poignantly recounts the coming of age of Jody Baxter, who adopts Flag, a semi-tame pet fawn. After coping with natural disasters and the near-death of his father, Jody must face killing his yearling in order to preserve his family's livelihood—their crops. The novel ends with Jody facing the impact of his loss:

> He found himself listening for something. It was the sound of the yearling for which he listened, running around the house or stirring on his moss pallet in the corner of the bedroom. . . . He did not believe he should ever again love anything, man or woman or his own child, as he had loved the yearling. He would be lonely all his life. But a man took it for his share and went on.

Considered Rawling's finest achievement, *The Yearling* was awarded the 1939 Pulitzer Prize in fiction. In spite of its mature themes, it remains a best seller among children's book and is widely assigned to elementary and junior high school students. In 1946 it was adapted into an Academy Award-winning movie.

In 1941 Rawlings married Norton Sanford Baskin and moved with him to St. Augustine, Florida. She published a critically acclaimed memoir, *Cross Creek* (1942), that combined autobiographical anecdotes with lyrical observations about nature: "Because I had known intimately a river, the earth pulsed under me. . . . For myself, the Creek satisfies a thing that had gone hungry and unfed since childhood days."

Marjorie Kinnan Rawlings, author of *The Yearling,* is pictured here in 1937.
(AP/Wide World Photos)

After winning another O. Henry Award for "Black Secret," and losing a lawsuit brought against her for invasion of privacy, in 1947 Rawlings bought a summer home in the Hudson valley area of New York, where she set her final novel, *The Sojourner* (1953). It was unsuccessful, perhaps because readers identified Rawlings so closely with Florida, even though she never defined herself as a regionalist.

Rawlings received several honorary doctorate degrees and in 1939 was elected to the National Institute of Arts and Letters. An alcoholic who worked hard and played hard, she died at 57, on December 14, 1953, and was buried near her beloved Cross Creek. In her memoir, Marjorie Kinnan Rawlings explained: "It is more important to live the life one wishes to live, and to go down with it if necessary, quite contently, than to live more profitably but less happily."

An unpublished autobiographical first novel entitled *Blood of My Blood,* first written in 1928 and lost for many years until it was discovered after the author's death, was published in 2002. According to *Publishers Weekly,* Rawling's debut novel, which delineates her complicated, combative relationship with her mother, presents an "illuminating look at the background and maturation of a writer who went on to pen an American classic [*The Yearling*]. . . . This seminal work constitutes a useful document for those interested in delving further into Rawling's unusual life."

Further Reading

Bigelow, Gordon E. *Frontier Eden: The Literary Career of Marjorie Kinnan Rawlings.* Gainesville: University of Florida Press, 1966.

Commire, Anne, ed. *Yesterday's Authors of Books for Children,* 218–224. Detroit, Mich.: Gale, 1977.

Rawlings, Marjorie Kinnan. *Blood of My Blood.* Edited by Anne Blythe Meriwether. Gainesville: University Press of Florida, 2002.

———. *Cross Creek.* New York: Scribner's, 1942.

———. *The Yearling.* New York: Scribner's, 1938.

Tarr, Roger L., ed. *The Private Marjorie: The Love Letters of Marjorie Kinnan Rawlings to Norton S. Baskin.* Gainesville: University Press of Florida, 2004.

∾ Rice, Anne (Howard Allen O'Brien, A. N. Roquelaire, Anne Rampling)
(1941–) *novelist*

America's premier female fantasist, the prolific author Anne Rice writes gothic novels about the bizarre and supernatural, as well as more conventional historical novels, and erotica. Whether vampires or witches, her characters explore the nature of good and evil and are driven by very human needs.

Born Howard Allen O'Brien in New Orleans, Louisiana, on October 4, 1941, Anne (she changed her name when she was six) was raised in a large, working-class Irish Catholic family. Her mother, she recalled, nurtured her "fantasies of the imagination," while her father exposed her to classical music and literature, as well as to New Orleans' run-down, ghoulish cemeteries. At a young age Anne began reading gothic fiction and telling ghost stories.

At age 15, a year after her mother died from alcoholism, Anne's father moved his family, including his new wife, to Texas. In 1961, Anne married her high school sweetheart, Stan Rice, a poet and painter with whom she shared a "passionate, stormy love." They moved to San Francisco, California, where Rice received undergraduate and master's degrees at San Francisco State College.

After the couple's six-year-old daughter Michele died from a rare blood disease, Rice turned to writing. It was, she noted, a "catharsis." In 1976 she published the first, and best known, of seven novels in the Vampire Chronicles series. *Interview with the Vampire,* which was lauded by most, although not all, critics for its sensual, humanist, and philosophical elements, sold more than 7 million copies. In it, Louis, a vampire, tells his life story to a young reporter. "Through Louis's eyes," Rice explained, "everything became accessible." She was even able to imagine the vampire's first kill: "The sucking mesmerized me, the warm struggling of the man was soothing to the tension of my hands; and there came the beating of the drum again, which was the drumbeat of his heart." *Interview*

Fantasist Anne Rice writes gothic tales about good and evil.
(AP/Wide World Photos)

with the Vampire established Rice as an important contemporary novelist and fantasist.

After the birth of her son, Christopher, she tried her hand, successfully, at historical fiction, producing two novels in the genre: *The Feast of All Saints* (1980) and *Cry to Heaven* (1982). But she returned to her earlier subject in *The Vampire Lestat* (1985). "I wanted to go back to the supernatural theme, to write about the vampires and their concerns, and I remember having a dream . . . that said, 'Go where the pain and the intensity and the fear is,'" she recalled in *Writers Dreaming.*

Rice published another best-selling vampire book, *The Queen of the Damned* (1988), about the "Mother of all Vampires." A year later she moved

back to New Orleans, where, according to Rice's biographer, Katherine Ramsland, she was able to "transform a dark place into one illuminated by maturity."

Between 1983 and 1985, under the pseudonym A. N. Roquelaire, Rice wrote three books of erotica based loosely on the adventures of Sleeping Beauty. She intended the tales of "discipline, love and surrender" to be "erotic and nothing else, [because] nothing about sex is evil or to be ashamed of." Using the pen name Anne Rampling, she also produced two novels that combined contemporary erotic and romantic themes.

Under her own name, Rice wrote a fictional trilogy about a family of witches, beginning with

271

The Witching Hour (1990), that she set in her own, apparently haunted, antebellum mansion. Rice saw herself as "a divided person with different voices, like an actor playing different roles."

She again returned to The Vampire Chronicles with *The Tale of the Body Thief* (1992), in which Lestat, tired of his immortality, tries to take his life, but fails. As in much of her work, Rice makes Lestat, the victimizing vampire, more interesting, sympathetic, and complex than his victims.

In 1996, Rice wrote *Servant of the Bones,* a non-vampire novel in which the narrator, a Jewish spirit born in ancient Babylon, relates his millennia-long life story to a college professor. Although she rejected Catholicism, Rice considers herself an "armchair theological scholar."

The Vampire Armand (1998), the sixth installment of The Vampire Chronicles, whose protagonist is an eternally young man, was followed by another best-selling gothic novel, *Violin* (1998). In it, the death-haunted heroine, Triana, hears a virtuoso ghost playing the violin outside her window. Entranced, she follows the demon back to the 18th century, where she meets Paganini and Beethoven, and eventually gets control of the ghost's instrument. Like many of Rice's female characters, Triana is independent and courageous. She is also very much like the "Queen of the Gothic"—Anne Rice, who continued her New Tales of the Vampires series with *Pandora* (1998), a well-received tale set in ancient Rome. It was followed in 1999 by *Vittorio the Vampire,* the mesmerizing story of a Renaissance-born Italian vampire. Typical of Rice's oeuvre, blood, history, demons, and vampires come together in a fabulist saga.

Rice's 27th novel, *Christ the Lord: Out of Egypt* (2005), was a critically acclaimed *New York Times* best seller. The first-person account fictionalizes the early years of Jesus, when he was about seven and was attempting to understand his origins and fate. Rice was brought up in the Roman Catholic Church, left it for 30 years, and returned to the church in 1998. The well-researched *Christ the Lord* is a major departure for the author, who is better known for her sanguine vampire tales. But

she makes the transition well, writes *New York Times* book critic Janet Maslin: "Rice delivers the only shock effects still available to her, after a career-length cavalcade of kink: piety and moderation. . . . The restraint and prayerful beauty of *Christ the Lord* is apt to surprise her usual readers and attract new ones."

In 2005 Rice harshly criticized the response to Hurricane Katrina's aftermath in her old hometown of New Orleans (she now lives in the San Diego area). "During this crisis you [America] failed us," wrote Rice in the *New York Times* about the catastrophe. "You looked down on us; you dismissed our victims; you dismissed us."

Further Reading

Epel, Naomi. *Writers Dreaming.* New York: Vintage, 1993.

Ramsland, Katherine. *Prism of the Night: A Biography of Anne Rice.* New York: Dutton, 1991.

Rice, Anne. *Christ the Lord: Out of Egypt.* New York: Knopf, 2005.

———. *Vampire Chronicles.* New York: Random House, 1990. (Contains three novels in the series.)

———. *Vittorio the Vampire: New Tales of the Vampires.* New York: Knopf, 1999.

Roquelaire, A. N. *The Sleeping Beauty Novels.* New York: New American Library, 1991.

Rich, Adrienne Cecile
(1929–)   *poet, essayist*

A highly regarded American poet and feminist theorist, award-winning Adrienne Rich has written more than 20 volumes of verse, several influential collections of essays, and a ground-breaking study of motherhood. Believing that "the search for justice and compassion is the great wellspring for poetry in our time," Rich's compelling work is both personal and political.

Born on May 16, 1929, in Baltimore, Maryland, Adrienne Cecile Rich is the daughter of a professor of pathology at Johns Hopkins Medical School; her mother had given up a promising musical career to raise the couple's two daughters. Rich recalled a childhood filled with books (her heroines were the Brontë sisters and EMILY DICK-INSON) and a domineering father "who encouraged me to read and write," especially poetry. At a young age, Adrienne began writing formal, carefully crafted verse.

After attending a girls' school with a strong female faculty, Rich graduated from Radcliffe College in 1951, where she "did not see a woman teacher for four years." That same year, she won the distinguished Yale Younger Poets Prize for her first collection, *A Change of World.* Her early work was influenced by male poets such as W. H. Auden, who in his preface to her prize-winning book praised Rich's elegance, clarity, formality, and restrained emotion.

After traveling through Europe on the first of two Guggenheim fellowships, Rich in 1953 married Alfred Conrad, a Harvard economist. The couple lived in Cambridge, Massachusetts, and over a four-year period Rich gave birth to three sons. In her celebrated autobiographical essay "When We Dead Awaken: Writing as Revision," Rich expressed her confusion during that period:

> About the time my third child was born, I felt that I had either to consider myself a failed woman and a failed poet, or to try to find some synthesis by which to understand what was happening to me. What frightened me most was the sense of drift, of being pulled along on a current which called itself my destiny, but in which I seemed to be losing touch with whoever I had been. . . .

Her second book, *The Diamond Cutters* (1955), was praised, again, for its finely crafted but staid, formal diction and its restrained emotional content. Rich did not publish another book for almost 10 years, but when she did, her verse was much more lyrical and less controlled. *Snapshots of a Daughter-in-Law* (1963) received mixed reviews. Some critics found several of its poems to be too personal or too bitter, but most critics agreed that Rich had produced overall an original, powerful collection. With this collection, she intended to use her "verbal privilege," as she put it, as a way of speaking for women who were unable to express

their anger, pain, and frustration. In the title poem, Rich uses quotations from Dickinson, Mary Wollstonecraft, and Simone de Beauvoir to illustrate other women who have "spoken out." She also reconfigures other famous excerpts from literature so that their strong words can be juxtaposed with the everyday existence and the social and emotional plights of the modern woman.

After moving with her husband and children to New York City, Rich taught at an inner-city remedial English program and became increasingly involved in the civil rights and anti–Vietnam War movements. In 1966, *Necessities of Life: Poems,*

Adrienne Rich displays one of her many poetry prizes.
(AP/Wide World Photos)

1962–65, was nominated for the National Book Award. With each successive volume, Rich both charted her own personal growth and mirrored the growing consciousness of contemporary American women. She also began experimenting with form. To add a further sense of need and urgency to her poems, Rich employed fragmented sentences and irregular spacing and varied the metrical lengths of each line.

The Will to Change (1971) was a bold, lyrical plea for society to change itself. As the title of the collection implies, "change" is something that a person can initiate, a far cry from the acceptance of change as fate, as was implied in the title of her first collection, *A Change of World.* In 1970 Rich changed her own life by leaving her husband, who committed suicide later that year.

Her next collection, *Diving into the Wreck,* was published in 1973. Some critics derided it for its apparent male-bashing: Helen Vendler, for example, in *Parnassus: Poetry in Review,* wrote, "the poem 'Rape' from *Diving into the Wreck* seems to bestow on all men the image of the sadistic rapist portrayed in the work. This poem, like some others in the volume, is a deliberate refusal of the modulations of intelligence in favor of propaganda." Despite the criticism, *Diving into the Wreck* won the National Book Award in 1974. Rich refused the award but accepted it jointly with co-nominees ALICE WALKER and AUDRE LORDE on behalf of all women who are silenced; she donated all of the prize money to the Sisterhood of Black Single Mothers.

In 1976 Rich published a seminal feminist study, *Of Woman Born: Motherhood as Experience and Institution.* She used anthropological studies, historical research, literature, and her personal history to explore, delineate, and demystify motherhood. After giving up a professorship at Rutgers University in the late 1970s, Rich moved to western Massachusetts with her partner, the Jamaican writer Michelle Cliff, with whom she coedited the lesbian-feminist journal *Sinister Wisdom.* "Every lesbian has been forced to walk past the distorting mirrors of homophobia before she could get down

to the real problems of her work," Rich claimed in the foreword to *Working It Out: 23 Women Writers, Artists, Scientists and Scholars Talk about Their Lives and Work* (1977), an anthology of essays edited by Sara Ruddick and Pamela Daniels. Around that time, she also engaged seriously with her Jewish heritage (her father was Jewish, her mother a southern Protestant) and helped found a Jewish feminist journal, *Bridges.* In an essay in *Nice Jewish Girls: A Lesbian Anthology,* Rich expressed the hope that one day, every aspect of her identity would be interconnected.

Throughout her writing, according to Wendy Martin, author of *An American Tryptych: Anne Bradstreet, Emily Dickinson, Adrienne Rich,* Rich, in particular, tries to translate the inner mind of women: "[She] attempts to portray female-centered or gynecocratic consciousness, which is comprehensive, cooperative and collective, empathetic and sensory."

Rich continued to produce well-received poetry collections, including *An Atlas of the Difficult World* (1991), a 13-part epic poem about America, its politics, and its landscape, which has been compared in content and style to Walt Whitman's *Leaves of Grass.* It received the *Los Angeles Times* Book Prize and was a finalist for the National Book Critics Circle Award. The poems in her collection *Dark Fields of the Republic* (1995) are less angry and more compassionate, but no less forceful, than her earlier verse. Rich seems more concerned about finding solutions to America's problems than in complaining about them. Another collection of poems, *Midnight Salvage,* was published in 1999.

Rich has taught at numerous colleges and universities and is the recipient of many prestigious poetry awards. She was cowinner of the Poetry Society of America's 1992 Frost Silver Medal for distinguished lifetime achievement, and since 1990 has been a member of the Department of Literature of the American Academy of Arts and Letters. Rich received a MacArthur fellowship in 1994. Five years later she was the recipient of the 1999 Lannan Foundation Achievement Award. In 2003 Rich was awarded the Bollington Prize for poetry. *The School among the Ruins: Poems 2000–2004* won the National Book Critics Circle Award and was selected as a best poetry pick of 2004 by *Library Journal,* which described Rich as "one of a handful of major American poets whose every new work is a cause for excitement." The collection also garnered the 2006 San Francisco Poetry Center Award. In 2006 she received the National Book Foundation's annual medal for distinguished contribution to American letters for her "incomparable influence and achievement as a poet and essayist."

Rich, who has been writing and publishing verse for more than 50 years, has a following that seems to value the powerful way she combines art and political conviction in her poetry. When asked about the costs of speaking honestly and openly, Rich replied in an interview in 1991, "What would be the cost of *not* doing it? This is how I cope, this is how I survive."

The Canadian novelist Margaret Atwood once noted that Adrienne Rich is "not just one of America's best feminist poets, or one of America's best woman poets, she is one of America's best poets."

Further Reading

Barnett, Catherine. "Adrienne Rich." In *World Poets,* edited by Ron Padgett, 373–382. New York: Charles Scribner's Sons, 2000.

Halpern, Nick. "'This is what is possible': Adrienne Rich." In *Everyday and Prophetic: The Poetry of Lowell, Ammons, Merrill and Rich,* 184–229. Madison: University of Wisconsin Press, 2003.

Martin, Wendy. *An American Tryptych: Anne Bradstreet, Emily Dickinson, Adrienne Rich.* Chapel Hill: University of North Carolina Press, 1983.

Rich, Adrienne. *Adrienne Rich's Poetry and Prose: A Norton Critical Edition.* Edited by Barbara Charleswoth Gelpi and Albert Gelpi. New York: W. W. Norton, 1993.

———. *Art of the Possible: Essays and Conversations.* New York: W. W. Norton, 2001.

———. *Midnight Salvage: Poems, 1995–1998.* New York: W. W. Norton, 1999.

———. *Of Woman Born: Motherhood as Experience and Institution.* New York: W. W. Norton, 1976.

———. *The School among the Ruins: Poems 2000–2004.* New York: W. W. Norton, 2004.

Templeton, Alice. *The Dream and the Dialogue: Adrienne Rich's Feminist Poetics.* Knoxville: University of Tennessee Press, 1995.

Richardson, Elaine Potter
See Kincaid, Jamaica

Rinehart, Mary Roberts
(1876–1958)   *mystery writer, novelist*

Mary Roberts Rinehart achieved success as a writer of mysteries that combined murder, glamour, humor, romance, and happy endings, selling over 10 million copies of her books during her lifetime. She also enjoyed success in other literary genres, including short fiction, romance novels, and plays.

Mary Roberts Rinehart was born on August 12, 1876, in Allegheny (today is North Side), Pennsylvania. Her father, a sewing machine salesman, shot himself when Mary was 19, while she was attending nursing school. In 1896, two months short of her 20th birthday, she married Stanley M. Rinehart, a physician. By 1901, she was the mother of three sons.

Rinehart became a professional writer out of necessity rather than by intent. Once describing herself as "fiercely a mother," she devoted herself to raising her children. Even after she had become a notable writer, she continued to give her family primacy of place in her life. Although she published several short stories, poems, and articles while her sons were young, she considered writing more a hobby than a profession.

That changed after a stock market crash decimated the family's fortunes. Twelve-thousand dollars in debt, Rinehart turned to writing as a practical way of reviving the family finances. She produced a novel, *The Man in the Lower Ten* (1906), in less than a month, for serialization in *All-Story* magazine. That was followed by *The Circular Staircase,* which, after magazine serialization, was published in 1908 as her first, and some critics say her best book. It was Rinehart who coined the memorable phrase "The butler did it."

Mary Roberts Rinehart wrote best-selling mysteries.
(AP/Wide World Photos)

Rinehart began a long period of enormous productivity. Over a span of 40 years, she published on average a book a year. Eleven of her novels became top-10 best sellers, and she was paid top fees by popular magazines, reaching $65,000 in the 1930s, for serializing her novels. Aside from mysteries such as *The Door* (1930) and *The Yellow Room* (1945), and romances like *The Street of Seven Stars* (1914), Rinehart wrote humorous stories about a middle-aged unmarried woman named "Tish"; the stories were featured in the *Saturday Evening Post* for three decades.

Rinehart also did very well as a playwright. One of her dramas was *The Bat,* a mystery, cowritten with Avery Hopwood, which some critics assert provided the inspiration for Bob Kane's famous comic book character Batman. In addition to writing fiction, Rinehart spent time as a journalist covering the battlefield during World War I and wrote a well-received autobiography, *My Story* (1931).

Despite her financial success—she published many of her books with a company owned by two of her sons—Rinehart had her share of hardships. Her husband died in 1932. One of her employees on her estate in Maine tried to murder her in 1947. She was diagnosed with breast cancer the same year and demonstrated that she was well ahead of her time by writing publicly about her experiences. In 1948, her Maine estate burned to the ground in a forest fire.

Mary Roberts Rinehart, regarded as perhaps the most notable practitioner of the "Had-I-But-Known" mystery genre, suffering from a heart ailment, died on September 22, 1958 in New York City. Many of her mystery novels, in new editions, continue to sell well. A biography of the author published in 1994, *Had She but Known,* by mystery writer Charlotte MacLeod, helped reintroduce Rinehart's work to a new generation of readers. Additionally, a volume of four of her best-known suspense novels, including *The Circular Staircase,* appeared in 2002, demonstrating that America's Agatha Christie, as some critics have called Rinehart, continues to hold an important place in the literature of mystery and crime.

Further Reading

Cohn, Jan. *Improbable Fiction: The Life of Mary Roberts Rinehart.* Pittsburgh: University of Pittsburgh Press, 1980.

MacLeod, Charlotte. *Had She but Known: A Biography of Mary Roberts Rinehart.* New York: Warner Books, 1994.

Murphy, Bruce F. *The Encyclopedia of Murder and Mystery.* New York: St. Martin's Press, 2001.

"North Side: Mary Roberts Rinehart." Carnegie Library of Pittsburgh. Available online. URL: http://www.clpgh.org/exhibit/neighborhoods/northside/NOR_N108.html. Downloaded on March 5, 2007.

Rinehart, Mary Roberts. *The Best Mysteries of Mary Roberts Rinehart: Four Complete Novels by America's First Lady of Mystery.* Pleasantville, N.Y.: Readers Digest Books, 2002.

———. *My Story: A New Edition and Seventeen New Years.* New York: Rinehart, 1948.

∾ Roberts, Nora (J. D. Robb)

(1950–) *romance novelist, historical fantasy writer, mystery writer*

A multiple best-selling author of more than 165 books, Nora Roberts is one of America's most prolific novelists. As of 2007, there were more than 280 million copies of her books in print. She is not only popular but also critically praised for her compelling, entertaining, and well-written page-turners. Roberts is the recipient of several awards, including the Lifetime Achievement Award from Romance Writers of America.

Born on October 10, 1950, in Silver Spring, Maryland, the only daughter and youngest of five children, Nora Roberts attended public and Catholic schools before working briefly as a legal secretary and clerk. At 18, she married Ronald Aufdem-Brinke. They had two sons, Daniel and Jason, and moved to rural Keedysville, Maryland. "I became a kind of earth mother," she told *People* magazine in 1997. When not baking bread, canning, sewing, or growing vegetables, she read romance novels. "For that period of my life—a bad marriage, endless days with small children—they [the novels] were a kind of sanity."

In 1979, while holed up in her home with her two young sons during a week-long, unrelenting snow storm, she began to feel desperate. "When school was canceled every morning that week, I'm not ashamed to admit I wept," she recalls. The 29-year-old homebound housewife with a vivid imagination tried her hand at writing a romance novel. Although her first manuscript, which she wrote down longhand in a spiral notebook using a no. 2 pencil, was rejected, along with others she submitted, in 1981 she sold her first book, *Irish Thoroughbred,* to Silhouette, a new (and in later years the most celebrated) romance publishing company. In the following year, she produced five books and has continued writing romance suspense, category romance, and futuristic mystery novels, as hardcovers or original paperbacks, often at a rate of several per year. "I always have stories running around in my head," she explains. "Once I start putting them down on paper, I just keep going; I just keep writing." Roberts had discovered a satisfying and lucrative career. Romance titles make up 55 percent of all paperback fiction sales, generating more than $1 billion in sales each year, according to *USA Today* (2006).

Roberts was divorced in 1983. Two years later she married Bruce Wilder, a carpenter she had hired to build bookshelves. The couple co-owns a bookstore. Her marriage to Wilder, she says, has been a very happy one. "I am living proof that what I write about can happen in real life," she once declared. Her plots, while steamy, are populated with characters who lead real lives, including strong, intelligent, sensual women. Many of her books have contemporary settings, whether a hidden undersea world or an arson unit, although some are historical romances. Roberts does not count on firsthand knowledge for her writing and is not ashamed of using the Internet for her research. "I know they say write what you know," she said in an interview in 1998 with *Publishers Weekly,* "but I write about what I want to know," namely, women and men who react to love, loss, and their emotions.

Beginning in 1998, with *Holiday in Death,* Roberts took the pseudonym J. D. Robb to pen a series of detective romantic novels set in the future, including the popular Eve Dallas novels. They combine police drama, science fiction, and classic romance. The well-received J. D. Robb title *Origin in Death* (2005), for example, takes place in 2059 and features a tough female New York City police lieutenant, science fiction elements, and affairs of the heart.

After winning a year-long plagiarism lawsuit that began in 1997 against fellow romance writer Janet Dailey, Roberts donated her compensation to the Literacy Volunteers of America and other literary-related nonprofit organizations. Also in 1997, she had six *New York Times* best sellers, breaking her own record. Roberts, considered the "Queen of Romance Novels," keeps getting better, asserted a reviewer in *Publishers Weekly.* "And she shows no sign of abating. . . . When Roberts puts her expert finger on the pulse of romance, legions of fans feel the heartbeat."

To fledgling writers, Roberts offers this advice: Make time for your writing and do not make excuses. As for her own writing process, she says the characters have to draw her in. "If they don't compel me to tell their story, I can't believe the reader would be interested." Once her protagonists have taken on lives of their own, "it's wise to let them go on their own ways."

In 1986 Roberts became the first author inducted into the Romance Writers of America Hall of Fame. She was the keynote speaker at its 1994 national conference in New York and in 2003 won its Rita Award for best romantic suspense novel. Several of her fast-paced, entertaining novels have been optioned and made into films, such as *Sanctuary* (1997), which aired in 2001 as a television movie. *Montana Sky* (1996), her 100th published novel, was bought by Tristar in one of the highest-paid options for a television two-hour movie. Murder and romance figure prominently in the story, which revolves around three half-sisters who inherit their father's huge Montana ranch but first must live together for one year or forfeit the estate. Romanticized settings often are integral to Roberts's plots, although some can be historically specific. For example, in *Blue Smoke* (2005), another *New York Times* best seller, the story opens in Baltimore, Maryland, in 1985: "Catarina Hale's childhood ended on a steamy August night a few hours after the Orioles demolished the Rangers at Memorial Stadium, kicking their Texas butts—as her dad said—nine to one."

Roberts's books have been translated in more than 25 countries, reaching 24 million readers worldwide. In February 2006 she sold film rights for six more of her books. Her online newsletter is read by more than 80,000 members—her "fantastic fans," as she calls them. Nora Roberts lives in Keedysville, Maryland, where she enjoys gardening and spending time with her family. But mostly, she writes. Her latest hardcover, *Born in Death,* was released in 2006, followed by *Innocent in Death* (2007). "Even though the boys are grown men and living on their own, it's basically the same [as when they were young children]: I write. It's my job and it's one that I really love," she says. According to Ginia Bellafonte, writing about Roberts in an article in the *New York Times* (August 23, 2006), Roberts "remains one of the top-selling novelists of the last decade and the most prolific Romance writer of all times."

Further Reading

Quinn, Judy. "Nora Roberts: A Celebration of Emotion." *Publishers Weekly* (February 23, 1998): 46.

Roberts, Nora. *Blue Smoke.* New York: Putnam, 2005.

——— (under the pseudonym J. D. Robb). *Innocent in Death.* New York: Putnam, 2007.

———. *Irish Thoroughbred.* New York: Silhouette Books, 1981.

———. *Montana Sky.* New York: Putnam, 1996.

White, Claire, E. "A Conversation with Nora Roberts." *Writers Write: The Internet Writing Journal.* Available online. URL: http://www.writerswrite.com/journal/jun98/roberts.htm. Downloaded on January 23, 2007.

∾ Robinson, Marilynne
(1943–)   *novelist, essayist*

There was a 23-year lapse between the time Marilynne Robinson won a Hemingway Foundation/PEN Award for her first novel, *Housekeeping,* and the publication of her second work of fiction, *Gilead,* her meditative and luminous Pulitzer Prize–winning book. In between she produced an exposé of Great Britain's role in environmental pollution and a collection of essays on modern thought and society. Despite her relatively small output, Robinson has had a significant influence on contemporary American literature.

Born on November 26, 1943, in Sandpoint, Idaho, Marilynne Robinson recalls, at a young age, reading on her own "as soon as I could, and being overwhelmed again and again—if not by what the books actually said, by what they suggested, what they helped me to imagine." She attended Brown University, graduating in 1966, and received a doctorate in English from the University of Washington in 1977. Robinson was influenced by the works of Ralph Waldo Emerson, Henry David Thoreau, Walt Whitman, and EMILY DICKINSON and "by their explorations of consciousness," she said in an interview in 2004.

While writing her doctoral dissertation at Brown, she began working on her first novel, *Housekeeping.* Published in 1981, it was hailed by the *New York Times* as "one of the most original and striking novels of its time," and earned its author, in addition to the 1982 Hemingway/PEN Award, the Richard and Hinda Rosenthal Award from the American Academy and Institute of Arts and Letters, and a nomination for a Pulitzer Prize. Accepted by the first agent who read it and bought by the first editor who read it, *Housekeeping* is the haunting tale of two young sisters who, following the suicide of their mother and several unsuccessful guardianship placements, end up living with their eccentric aunt—a drifter rather than a housekeeper—in rural Idaho in the mid-1900s. The novel, which was adapted as a Hollywood film starring Christine Lahti in 1987, has a quirky, hallucinatory quality, and it not surprising when one of the sisters remarks, "I have never distinguished readily between thinking and dreaming." Robinson's poetic, precise imagery of the Northwest reflects her understanding of the natural world, but she is equally adept at depicting emotionally based themes such as adolescent angst, transience, and the fleeting nature of happiness.

Robinson changed genres and turned to nonfiction, publishing articles, essays, and book reviews in notable periodicals such as *Harper's, Paris Review,* and the *New York Times Book Review.* While on a sabbatical in England in 1989, she wrote a controversial book about environmental destruction resulting from the British nuclear waste reprocessing plant Sellafield, whereby tons of nuclear waste was dumped into the Irish Sea on a daily basis. *Mother Country: Britain, the Welfare State and Nuclear Pollution* was a finalist for the National Book Award. Her next publication, *The Death of Adam: Essays on Modern Thought* (1998), covered a range of religious, historical, and cultural topics,

such as John Calvin's intellectual legacy. Robinson admires Calvin and has commented that America is a religious country, but "it's the extremes that have taken over the public discussion." The novelist KATHLEEN NORRIS praised *The Death of Adam* as "a rigorous but invigorating . . . bracing collection of truly contrarian essays . . . [that provides a] valuable contribution to American life and letters."

Although her nonfiction was well received, fans and literary critics wondered if Robinson was a one-time novelist, like HARPER LEE. *Gilead,* her long-awaited, widely acclaimed, serious and meditative second novel, proved that was not the case. Set in 1956 in the form of a letter written from John Ames, an ailing 76-year-old Congregational minister, to his young son, *Gilead* delineates the Ames family's remarkable multigenerational story: Gilead is the Iowan town where Ames and his father and grandfather, all ministers, lived and preached. The book also serves as a mouthpiece for John Ames's profound metaphysical observations. *Gilead* is paced slowly and the tone is reflective, lyrical, and calm, yet at the same time powerful. In terms of plot, not much happens in the book, which primarily is about spiritual life and "faith in action," as a *Village Voice* reviewer described it.

Mary Houlihan, a *Chicago Sun-Times* critic, wrote that "the satisfying core of the novel is the preacher's observations on his life and the world that has evolved in the small, forgotten town of Gilead. As Ames faces his own mortality, his writings ache with life in all its abundance of emotional understanding and misunderstanding." In an interview with *Religion and Ethics News Weekly* about *Gilead* in 2005, Robinson commented that she has always had "great interest in Scripture and theology. . . . Having been a church member for many years, I am very aware of how much pastors enrich people's experience, people for whom they are significant." *Gilead* won the 2004 National Book Critics Circle Award for Fiction and the 2005 Pulitzer Prize for fiction. It also was chosen by the *New York Times Book Review* as one of the 10 best books of 2004.

Robinson, who has been praised for her effective character development and almost mystical yet accessible writing style, advises aspiring novelists to stay close to what they feel is their compulsion for writing. "Don't try to calculate—if you do, your writing will be false and tired. Getting published is a long shot, but it's easier if you speak with your own authentic voice," she has said. Robinson also suggests that aspiring authors write the book they want to read, respecting their readers, and waiting for inspiration. "I have to have a narrator whose voice tells me what to do," she explains, "whose voice tells me how to write the novel." For Robinson, writing is like prayer, "seeing beyond what is initially obvious or apparent."

Marilynne Robinson lives in Iowa City with her husband and two sons and teaches writing courses at the University of Iowa Writers' Workshop. She has also taught at several other academic institutions, including the University of Kent in England, Amherst College, and the University of Massachusetts. Robinson serves as a deacon at the Congregational Church to which she belongs and enjoys listening to hymns and liturgical music. Language, she has said, is itself music.

Further Reading

Daniel, Missy. "Interview with Marilynne Robinson." Religion and Ethics News Weekly. March 18, 2005. Available online. URL: http://www.pbs.org/wnet/religionandethics/week829/interview.html. Downloaded on January 23, 2007.

Keillor, Garrison. "Literary Notes: Marilynne Robinson." The Writer's Almanac with Garrison Keillor. November 26, 2006. Available online. URL: http://writersalmanac.publicradio.org/programs/2006/11/20/index.html. Downloaded on March 6, 2007.

Robinson, Marilynne. The Death of Adam: Essays on Modern Thought. Boston: Houghton Mifflin, 1998.

———. Gilead. New York: Farrar, Straus and Giroux, 2004.

———. Housekeeping. New York: Farrar, Straus and Giroux, 1981.

———. Mother Country: Britain, the Welfare State and Nuclear Pollution. New York: Farrar, Straus and Giroux, 1989.

Roquelaire, A. N.
See RICE, ANNE

Rose, Wendy (Bronwen Elizabeth Edwards)
(1948–) *poet*

Wendy Rose writes powerful poetry, sprinkled with spirit-based imagery, about dispossession, often derived from her own experiences as a mixed-blood American Indian. She also addresses feminist, ecological, and anthropological concerns in her multifaceted verse. Born Bronwen Elizabeth Edwards (she later changed her name to Wendy Rose) on May 7, 1948, in Oakland, California, far from the reservation life of her ancestors, Rose was raised as an urbanized Native American. Her father was a full-blood Hopi from Arizona; her mother was mixed-blood—mostly Scottish and Irish, but also Miwok, an Indian tribe from an area near Yosemite National Park in California.

Rose published her first collection of poetry, *Hope Roadrunner Dancing* (1973), before attending the University of California at Berkeley, where she earned a bachelor's degree in 1976 and a master's in 1978, having studied anthropology and archaeology. In her first book, she expressed the profound sense of isolation that comes with being a mixed-blood American Indian separated from her tribal roots and alienated from white society. "I have always felt misunderstood and isolated—whether with Indians or with non-Indians," she said. Dispossession and the search for community would become recurring themes throughout her work, as well as, according to Indian writer PAULA GUNN ALLEN, "the centrality of the feminine power of universal being."

In her third volume, *Academic Squaw* (1977), she angrily addressed academia's refusal to consider American Indian literature a serious and important part of the American literary canon. In *Lost Copper* (1980), which was nominated for a Pulitzer Prize, Rose writes that "freeing the song / from the music / is my poet's task: the words / must be flaked /

from the matrix" in order to foster a greater understanding about Native American culture.

Rose universalizes the plight of her own people in *The Halfbreed Chronicles and Other Poems* (1985) by focusing on members of other groups that have been marginalized or dislocated, including an Auschwitz survivor, Japanese Americans, and the "Ugliest Woman in the World" in a circus. In *Winged Words: American Indian Writers Speak* (1990), Rose asserted that being a "half-breed" is not only based on biology. "[Rather] it's a condition of history, a condition of context, a condition of circumstance. . . . We are in fact all half-breeds in this world today."

Rose has continued to write critically acclaimed verse. A reviewer in *World Literature Today* called *Going to War with All My Relations* (1994) a "significant achievement by an important poet." In a poem about the Anishinabe Occupation, she seemingly attempts to viscerally connect with her tribal ancestors:

I let my tongue lick
your bones back together
. . .
I light the fire
to heat your lips.
I touch your spirit
that was never in danger.

Her next collection, *Bone Dance: New and Selected Poems, 1965–1993,* was influenced by her anthropological studies and touches on global issues, while *Now Poof She Is Gone* (1994) grapples with personal relationships and the poet's tiring struggle with a hostile world:

Permafrost woman
melts in the sun.
Her adobe skin
and heart sealed tight
from trespass as well
as from the nourishing rain,
she tries to paint away
the lies with white clay,
so exhausted
she cannot stop.

In Rose's most recent collection, *Itch Like Crazy* (2002), the poems deal mostly with long-buried private family secrets as well as more public ones related to tragic aspects of American history. The new book also pays tribute to her American Indian and European ancestors. "Rose's verse combines pieces from her own background, glimpses of modern American life, and bits from Indian tradition to weave a tapestry of contemporary indigenous poetry that is unsurpassed in its realism and beauty," writes C. B. Clark in *The Heath Anthology of American Literature* (2005). "Her poetry offers a slice of contemporary American Indian existence in the United States, bringing back to the late twentieth century the sacredness and balance of the ancients among the American Indians," concludes Clark.

An accomplished visual artist as well as a poet, Rose was the editor of the *American Indian Quarterly* and has taught at the University of California, Berkeley, and at California State College in Fresno. She currently teaches at Fresno City College. Whether writing, drawing, or teaching, Wendy Rose attempts to depict Native Americans as multidimensional "living, working artists," rather than as "literate fossils."

Further Reading

Allen, Paula Gunn. *The Sacred Hoop: Recovering the Feminine in American Indian Traditions.* Boston: Beacon Press, 1986.

Clark, C. B. "Wendy Rose." In *The Heath Anthology of American Literature,* edited by Paul Lauter, 3,143–3,152. Boston: Houghton Mifflin, 2005.

Colteli, Laura, ed. *Winged Words: American Indian Writers Speak,* 120–133. Lincoln: University of Nebraska Press, 1990.

Rose, Wendy. *Bone Dance: New and Selected Poems, 1965–1993.* Tucson: University of Arizona Press, 1994.

———. *Going to War with All My Relations: New and Selected Poems.* Flagstaff, Ariz.: Entrada Press, 1993.

———. *Itch Like Crazy.* Tucson: University of Arizona Press, 2002.

⌁ Rosenbaum, Alice

See RAND, AYN

❧ Ross, Ishbel Margaret (Ishbella Ross, Ishobel Ross)
(1895–1975) *journalist, biographer*

During the 1920s and 1930s, Ishbel Ross earned a reputation as one of the best reporters in the highly competitive world of New York City journalism. She also excelled as a writer of popular biographies of notable women, including several women, such as Mary Todd Lincoln, who lived their lives in the shadow of their famous husbands.

Ishbel Margaret Ross was born on December 15, 1895, in the highlands of northern Scotland. She recalled that during her early childhood she was "determined to be a writer" and that she "used to haunt the libraries and read anything I could get my hands on." Ross emigrated to Canada at age 20, where she worked as a reporter for the *Toronto Daily News*. In 1919 she moved to New York City and landed a job at the pretigious *New York Tribune* (later the *Herald Tribune*). As she explained it, "I had no trouble at all getting a job because so many of the men reporters were still in the Army."

Ross quickly made the most of her good fortune. She covered stories that ranged from routine dance marathons and the inaugurations of three presidents to two of the most notorious murders of the time: the Hall-Mills double murder, whose victims were a prominent Episcopal pastor and his mistress, and the 1932 kidnap-murder of the infant son of Charles A. Lindbergh and Anne Morrow Lindbergh. Ross met her future husband, the prominent *New York Times* reporter Bruce Rae, while covering the Hall-Mills trial.

Ross and Rae, who often competed by reporting on the same stories for their respective newspapers, apparently kept their professional rivalry out of their marriage by never discussing those stories at home. The couple had one daughter, who was subject to recurring bouts of mental illness. In 1962, Bruce Rae died.

In the mid-1930s, Ross gave up the daily grind of journalism in order to raise her daughter, while writing fiction from home. Despite one best seller, her first book, Ross was not successful as a novelist.

However, she found her niche as a historical writer and especially as a biographer of a diverse group of women. Her subjects ranged from "Rebel Rose," the Confederate spy Rose O'Neal, to Clara Barton, the founder of the American Red Cross. Ross specialized in biographies of presidents' wives, including the wives of Presidents Grant, Coolidge, Lincoln, and Wilson, as well as a biography of the "First Lady of the South," Varina Howell Davis, the wife of Confederate president Jefferson Davis. Ross often pointed out the difficulties facing "First Ladies." In *The President's Wife: Mary Todd Lincoln* (1973), Ross wrote that Mrs. Lincoln endured enormous personal sorrows while being lashed at by political storms surrounding her husband. In the concluding chapter of the book, Ross commented: "No President was ever more blindly loved than Abraham Lincoln. No President's wife was ever the victim of more misunderstanding and abuse."

Ishbel (also known as Ishobel) Ross died on September 21, 1975, after a fall from her apartment window in New York City. Police speculated that Ross might have committed suicide, a suggestion questioned by those who knew her well. One of her nonfiction books, *Ladies of the Press: The Story of Women in Journalism by an Insider,* originally published in 1936, was reissued in 1974. In 1988 Ross's daughter Jess Dixon published her mother's diary, *Little Grey Partridge: First World War Diary of Ishobel Ross Who Served with the Scottish Women's Hospitals Unit in Serbia.* Numerous contemporary anthologies about women journalists or biographers include entries about Ross.

Further Reading
Belford, Barbara. *Brilliant Bylines: A Biographical Anthology of Notable Newspaperwomen in America.* New York: Columbia University Press, 1986.

Danky, James P., and Wayne A. Wiegand, eds. *Women in Print: Essays on the Print Culture of American Women from the Nineteenth and Twentieth Centuries.* Madison: University of Wisconsin Press, 2006.

Ouditt, Sharon, ed. *Women Writers of the First World War: An Annotated Bibliography.* New York: Routledge, 2000.

Ross, Ishbel. *Charmers and Cranks: Twelve Famous American Women Who Defied Conventions.* New York: Harper and Row, 1965.

———. *Ladies of the Press: The Story of Women in Journalism by an Insider.* North Stratford, N.H.: Ayer Company Publishing, 1974.

———. *The President's Wife: Mary Todd Lincoln.* New York: G. P. Putnam's Sons, 1973.

～ Rowlandson, Mary White
(ca. 1635–1711) *nonfiction writer*

Mary Rowlandson wrote one of America's earliest best sellers, *The Sovereignty and Goodness of God* (1682), the first "captivity narrative" published by a woman during the colonial period. In it she dramatically chronicled her harrowing experiences at the hands of American Indians.

Mary White was born in England and emigrated with her father to Salem, Massachusetts, in 1638. The Whites moved to the western frontier village of Lancaster, Massachusetts, and in 1656 she married the town's first minister, Joseph Rowlandson, and became his "devout helpmate."

In February 10, 1676, Lancaster was attacked and burned down by the Wampanoags. Rowlandson, whose husband was away at the time, was captured, along with her three children. During the long trek to an Indian camp, one of her daughters died of starvation and the cold; Rowlandson, wounded and exhausted, noted in *The Sovereignty of Goodness and God* that "Sarah departed from life like a lamb." There was so little food, she wrote, that "the discovery of six acorns and two chestnuts was regarded as a rich prize."

Thanks to her domestic and needlework skills, Rowlandson was given as a servant to a woman chief, known as a sunksquaw, and her husband, a leader in the attack on Lancaster. A tribesman gave Rowlandson a Bible, and that became her salvation.

After 11 weeks of captivity, Rowlandson was ransomed for about $80 and released. Several weeks later, her two children were rescued, and the traumatized family moved to Boston. In 1677 they settled in Wethersfield, Connecticut, where the next year she wrote her memorable book; that same year, 1678, her husband died. Published in 1682, *The Sovereignty and Goodness of God: Being a Narrative of the Captivity and Restauration of Mrs. Mary Rowlandson* [*sic*] immediately gained popularity in England as well as in the colonies, going through 15 editions before 1800 and serving as a prototype of the captivity narrative. Although later narratives dished up sensationalized, anti-Indian propaganda, Rowlandson's early work was a straightforward document, very much influenced by her Puritan background: "God was with me, in a wonderful manner, carrying me along and bearing up my spirit . . . that I might see more of his Power," she wrote about her suffering, adding "it is good for me that I have been afflicted."

Although Rowlandson rendered a detailed account of surviving in a "lively semblance of hell," and described the brutal slaying of 12 settlers in Lancaster as a "company of sheep torn by wolves," she believed that her incarceration was morally instructive and even mentioned being treated, on occasion, with kindness. She also discovered that the desire to live is supremely powerful. In spite of her disgust, she ate hoof and horse liver, and described them as "sweet and savory to [her] taste."

Mary White Rowlandson, a skilled observer of her times who was able to record her grueling experiences for posterity, died on January 5, 1711, in Wethersfield. The *Sovereignty and Goodness of God* has been reissued in more than 30 editions. The granite ledge known as Redemption Rock, located in Princeton, Massachusetts, where Rowlandson's famous release from captivity took place, became an historic site, open to the public, in 1953 when it was donated by Senator John Hoar's descendents to The Trustees of Reservations. The inscription reads, "Upon this rock May 2nd 1676 was made the agreement for the ransom of Mrs. Mary Rowlandson of Lancaster between the Indians and John Hoar of Concord. King Philip was with the Indians but refused his consent."

283

Further Reading

"About Mary Rowlandson." *Women's History*. Available online. URL: http://womenshistory.about.com/library/bio/blbio_mary_rowlandson.htm. Downloaded January 23, 2007.

Breitwieser, Mitchell R. *American Puritanism and the Defense of Mourning: Religion, Grief, and Ethnology in Mary White Rowlandson's Captivity Narrative*. Madison: University of Wisconsin Press, 1990.

"Mary White Rowlandson." In *American Captivity Narratives,* edited by Gordon M. Sayer, 137–176. Boston: Houghton Mifflin, 2000.

Rowlandson, Mary White. *The Sovereignty and Goodness of God: The True Story of the Captivity of Mrs. Mary Rowlandson among the Indians*. Tucson, Ariz.: American Eagle Publications, 1966.

Toulouse, Teresa A. "American Puritanism and Mary White Rowlandson's Narrative." In *Challenging Boundaries: Gender and Periodization,* edited by Joyce W. Warren and Margaret Dickie, 137–158. Athens: University of Georgia Press, 2000.

∾ Rukeyser, Muriel
(1913–1980)   *poet, essayist*

Muriel Rukeyser's award-winning verse spanned five decades, as did her social activism. An accomplished poet who infused her work with emotionally forceful, life-affirming imagery, Rukeyser was also a translator, biographer, and essayist, and a writer of children's books.

Born on December 15, 1913, in New York City, where she grew up in an affluent but conventional household, Muriel Rukeyser was a precocious child who by age 13 had decided to become a writer. She attended Vassar College, Columbia University, and aviation school. She was fascinated by technology and science and did not consider poetry and science to be in opposition to one another.

While a student at Vassar, she helped found an alternative literary magazine, *Student Review,* which sent the 19-year-old to cover the racially explosive Scottsboro trial, in which several black youths in Alabama were accused of raping two white girls. Rukeyser was arrested and described her experiences in an angry poem, "The Trial." For

the rest of her life she wrote passionate, but non-tendentious, poetry about the injustices that existed throughout the world. She later traveled to Hanoi to protest the Vietnam War and went to South Korea to demonstrate against the imprisonment of poet Kim Chi-Ha.

Rukeyser's first book of poems, *Theory of Flight* (1935), published when she was 22, won the Yale Series of Younger Poets Prize. "Breathe-in experience, breathe-out poetry," she wrote, and went on to produce 20 volumes of poetry, including *Waterlily Fire* (1962), selections from her first 20 books, and *Out of Silence* (1992), selections from later works. Published posthumously, the latter collection triggered a resurgence in her popularity.

Rukeyser's poetry has been compared to that of Walt Whitman, in part because, like his, it is fresh, optimistic, and celebatory, without sinking into

Accomplished poet Muriel Rukeyser poses for a 1972 photograph.
(AP/Wide World Photos)

sentimentality. Rukeyser was essentially a modern poet "of possibility," in the tradition of America's great transcendentalists, commented Louise Kertesz in *The Poetic Vision of Muriel Rukeyser*.

In the 1940s, Rukeyser moved to the San Francisco Bay Area in California, where she led a poetry workshop. Two years later, having married briefly, she had a son, William, whom she raised herself. Although a devoted mother, she continued in her role as "poetic witness" and reminded her readers that it is important to speak out against the "horrors" of war, whether in Europe or in Vietnam. *The Life of Poetry,* a popular, wide-ranging philosophical essay on the meaning of poetry, and other related and nonrelated concerns, appeared as a book in 1949, and has been reissued several times.

In 1950 Rukeyser moved back to New York City and taught at Sarah Lawrence College. She wrote lyrical biographies of scientists Willard Gibbs and Thomas Hariot, and one about politician Wendell Willkie, using poetry, prose, and documents. She returned to verse with *Body of Walking* (1958), a well-received collection that also included translations of poetry by the Mexican writer Octavio Paz. She also produced a prize-winning translation of Swedish poet Gunnar Ekelof's work. Rukeyser then wrote her first and only novel, *The Orgy* (1965), which a critic described as "a long [autobiographical] prose poem in the shape of a novel."

Reviewing *Breaking Open* (1973), writer ERICA JONG praised Rukeyser for her "humor, bawdiness, lyrical sweep, political commitment, compassion, and great moral force," noting that "for all her political passion, she always remembers the . . . humor of everyday interactions."

Rukeyser, who helped jump-start the careers of young female poets such as ALICE WALKER, admired women who, like herself, "believe and resist forever." In *The Speed of Darkness,* she asked, rhetorically, what would happen if even a single woman was candid about her life. Her answer: "The world would split open." Having been brought up in a secular Jewish household, she "sought the truth" by reclaiming her Jewish identity and writing about a martyred first-century rabbi, Akiba, who

was distantly related to her mother and whose heroism she greatly admired. Her poetry appears in *Gates of Prayer,* the Jewish reform movement's prayer book.

Although some critics dismissed Rukeyser's work as "the stuff of bathos" and too simplistic, she was the recipient of several important poetry awards, including the first Harriet Monroe Memorial Award. She also received Guggenheim and American Council of Learned Societies fellowships and the 1977 Shelley Memorial Award in recognition of a lifetime contribution to poetry.

After suffering from debilitating strokes, Muriel Rukeyser, whom fellow poet ANNE SEXTON called the "mother to everyone," and whose varied, energetic poetry spanned more than 40 years, died on February 12, 1980, in New York City. "Throughout her life, her poetry evoked extreme reactions," commented Maida Solomon in an essay on Rukeyser published in 2004 in *Notable American Women: A Biographical Dictionary Completing the Twentieth Century.* "Rukeyser wrote of the dark and bright sides of humanity, of oppression and empowerment. . . . She gave voice to a pithy humor, particularly at the end of her life. The power and keenness of her insights as well as her lyrical poetry are only beginning to be fully recognized."

Further Reading

Dayton, Tim. *Muriel Rukeyser's "The Book of the Dead."* Columbia: University of Missouri Press, 2003.

Kertesz, Louise. *The Poetic Vision of Muriel Rukeyser.* With a foreword by Kenneth Rexroth. Baton Rouge: Louisiana State University Press, 1980.

Rukeyser, Muriel. *The Collected Poems of Muriel Rukeyser.* Edited by Janet F. Kaufman and Anne F. Herzog, with Jan Heller Levi. Pittsburgh: University of Pittsburgh Press, 2005.

———. *The Life of Poetry.* With a new foreword by Jane Cooper. Ashfield, Mass.: Paris Press, 1998.

———. *A Muriel Rukeyser Reader* (poetry and prose). Edited by Jan Heller Levi. New York: W. W. Norton, 1994.

Thurston, Michael. "Muriel Rukeyser." Modern American Poetry. Available online. URL: http://www.english. uiuc.edu/maps/poets/m_r/rukeyser/rukeyser.htm. Downloaded on March 6, 2007.

S

Sanchez, Sonia (Wilsonia Benita Driver)
(1934–   ) *poet, playwright, children's book writer*

An award-winning poet known for her innovative use of language, Sonia Sanchez is also an educator, playwright, and author of children's books. Sanchez's writing style has an improvisational, free-wheeling quality, with minimal punctuation and irregular syntax. She collaborates with musicians to record her verse and employs nontraditional formats such as haiku and tanka (unrhymed verse forms of Japanese origin), urban black English, sonnets, and ballads. Her work often is peppered with angry, deeply felt personal and politicized imagery.

Sonia Sanchez was born Wilsonia Benita Driver in Birmingham, Alabama, on September 9, 1934. Her father, Wilson L. Driver, was a jazz musician. As an adult, Sanchez would record her poetry with jazz and blues musicians, mixing verse with prose and personal reflections. The musicality of poetry has always been important to her. Sonia's mother, Lena Driver, died when Sonia was a year old, and Sonia was brought up by her beloved paternal grandmother, whom she called "mama." Sanchez would later recall that, in the difficult years after

her grandmother's death, while drifting from one caretaker and relative to another, listening to and writing fragments of poetry were the only things that kept her afloat. "It is a love of language that has propelled me, that love of language that came from listening to my grandmother speak Black English," said Sanchez in the *African American Review.*

Having grown up as an African American in Alabama, Sanchez experienced racism. "Each one of us was the finished product of an American dream, nightmarish in concept and execution," she said. In 1943 Sanchez and her older sister, Pat, moved to Harlem, an uptown section of Manhattan in New York City, to reside with their father and his third wife. Living in a cramped, crowded dwelling and feeling isolated, Sanchez again turned to writing as a way to escape her surroundings. She enrolled at Hunter College, where in 1955 she earned her bachelor's degree in political science. Four years later Sanchez took graduate-level courses at New York University and studied with the notable poet LOUISE BOGAN, who encouraged Sanchez to commit to writing as a professional career. Having befriended political activists in Greenwich Village, then a bohemian section of New York City, she joined three other radical young poets, who called themselves the Broadside Quarter, and served as the group's leading voice.

In the 1950s and 1960s, Sanchez became involved with the burgeoning civil rights movement and the Black Arts movement, a group of artists and writers who created politically engaged works about the African-American cultural and historical experience, often referred to as the artistic sister of the better-known Black Power movement. "I write because I must," Sanchez declared, "and if you write from a black experience, you're writing from a universal experience as well." In 1957 Sanchez had met the celebrated civil rights leader Martin Luther King, Jr., who believed in nonviolence as a way to achieve equality for African Americans, but over time she became more militant, basing her identity on her African-American heritage.

Increasingly, Sanchez's poetry and plays (she became a playwright in the 1960s) reflected her radical political and social viewpoints. Sanchez was married briefly to Albert Sanchez, a Puerto Rican immigrant, and decided to retain his surname after they divorced. In 1968 she married poet and activist Etheridge Knight; the couple had three children before divorcing. She admired the Black Muslim separatist leader Malcom X, having met him while working in Harlem, and in 1971 became a member of the Nation of Islam. After five years she resigned from the militant organization, mostly because of its repression of women. Blending combative ghetto imagery with unconventional grammar, language, and structure, she wrote passionately about the oppressive, violent history of African Americans, especially the experiences of black women. Her most critically acclaimed early collections of verse include *Homecoming* (1969), offering a new type of poetry infused with urban Black English conversations she heard on the streets of Harlem; *We a BaddDDD People* (1970); and *Love Poems* (1973).

Sanchez's later poems are more stridently feminist yet at the same time seem subtler in tone. In *A Blues Book for Blue Black Magical Women* (1973), Sanchez focuses on woman's role in society, one that "does not prepare young black women, or women period, to be women," she said in an interview in *Black Writers at Work*. At the same time that she was producing provocative poetry, she was also successfully producing plays. *Sister Sonji* (1969), for example, was staged in 1972 at the Shakespeare Festival Public Theater in New York City.

In 1976 Sanchez moved to Philadelphia. She reacted to a tragic incident that occurred in the city in 1985, when police bombed a residential building that housed the politically radical group Move and ended up destroying a city block and killing children as well as adults, by writing "Elegy: For Move and Philadelphia." *Homegirls & Handgrenades* (1984), a collection of semiautobiographical prose-style poems, won the 1985 American Book Award for poetry from the Before Columbus Foundation, while *Under a Soprano Sky* (1987) demonstrates "both the fact that Sanchez perfectly honed her skills at repetition, hyperbole, and invective, and that she has become more captivated by the sounds of language and the use of metaphor and imagery," wrote professor Joyce Ann Joyce of Chicago State University.

In Sanchez's 13th volume, *Wounded in the House of a Friend* (1995), the poet writes pointedly about rape, adultery, and racism. Nonetheless, the overall tone is hopeful. "[Sanchez] is compassionate, proud, angry, and determined as she writes about both betrayals both private and public," comments Donna Seaman in her review of *Wounded* in *Booklist* (March 1, 1995). "She forces us to confront these bewildering and horrifying tragedies that take place behind closed doors and scar and scorch the American psyche . . . but she offers hope and heroes. She celebrates quiet victories." In 1997 Sanchez published *Does Your House Have Lions?*, a 70-page lyrical poem about her brother's battle with AIDS and his painful reconciliation with his estranged family. It was nominated for a National Book Critics Circle Award and was followed by two collections that largely focused on the experiences of black women: *Shake Loose My Skin: New and Selected Poems* (1999) and *Ash* (2001).

Sanchez also has edited anthologies of short stories by African-American authors, including *Three Hundred and Sixty Degrees of Blackness Comin at You* (1973), a collection of poetry written by her students in a creative writing class she led in Harlem, and has edited and written books for children, such as *The Adventures of Fathead, Smallhead, and Squarehead* (1973). Since 1977, she has been affiliated with Temple University in Philadelphia, where she was the first Presidential Fellow, in 1987, and as a professor of English held the Laura Carnell Chair in English before her retirement in 1999. Sanchez has also taught, among other institutions, at Downtown Community School in New York City; San Francisco State College, where she was an early advocate for black studies; Amherst College; the University of Pennsylvania; and the University of Pittsburgh, where she was the first professor to offer a seminar in literature by black women. In addition, she has lectured at more than 500 universities and colleges and delivered poetry readings throughout the world. She was a columnist for the *American Poetry Review* in 1977 and for the Philadelphia *Daily News* in 1982.

Described by *Library Journal* as one of America's more overlooked older poets and by Gloria Hull in *Shakespeare's Sisters: Feminist Essays on Women Poets* as one of the most underappreciated poets writing today, Sanchez nonetheless has garnered numerous honors and awards, including the 2001 Robert Frost medal, given by the Poetry Society of America for "a distinguished lifetime service to American poetry"; a PEN Writing Award; the Lucretia Mott Award; a National Education Association Award; and the 2004 Harper Lee Award for lifetime achievement of a distinguished Alabaman. Also in 2004, she recorded *Full Moon of Sonia*, a groundbreaking compact disc composed of her eclectic poetry set to a wide range of music, patterned after a poem she published in *Under a Soprano Sky*. Sanchez has been a guest poet on albums featuring such celebrities as singer Diana Ross.

Sonia Sanchez currently lives in Philadelphia. She remains a fierce activist who embraces feminism even more than other political issues. "The world is a better place because of Sonia Sanchez," wrote poet MAYA ANGELOU. "She is a lion in literature's forest. When she writes, she roars, and when she sleeps, other creatures walk gingerly."

Further Reading

Bonair-Agard, Roger. "'Review of *Full Moon of Sonia*,' by Sonia Sanchez." *Black Issues Book Review* 7, no. 2 (March–April 2005): 33.

Joyce, Ann Joyce. *Ijala: Sonia Sanchez and the African Poetic Tradition*. Chicago: Third World Press, 1996.

Medina, Tony, and Louise Reyes Rivera, eds. *Bum Rush the Page: A Def Poetry Jam*. With an introduction by Sonia Sanchez. New York: Crown Publishing, 2001.

Sanchez, Sonia. *Full Moon of Sonia*. CD. Via International Artists, 2004.

———. *Homegirls & Handgrenades: Poems*. New York: Thunder's Mouth Press, 1984.

———. *Shake Loose My Skin: New and Selected Poems*. Boston: Beacon Press, 1999.

———. *Under a Soprano Sky*. Trenton, N.J.: Africa World Press, 1987.

∾ Santiago, Esmeralda
(1948–) *memoirist, novelist, screenwriter*

The author of a critically lauded, best-selling trilogy of memoirs, Esmeralda Santiago chronicles her tumultuous childhood, from living in poverty in rural Puerto Rico to her role as surrogate mother to her younger siblings in the slums of New York City. She deftly captures the complexities, joys, and sorrows of the immigrant experience and the Americanization process.

Born on May 17, 1948, in Santurce, Puerto Rico, Esmeralda Santiago moved when she was 13 from her tropical native land to urban New York City. The strongest memories of her life in Puerto Rico were the peripatetic years when her family moved frequently, sometimes living in the rural barrio (a Spanish-speaking district) of Macun, where her father, Pablo Santiago Diaz, known as Papi, came from. He was a laborer and poet who had fathered Esmeralda and her siblings but refused to marry her mother, Ramona Santiago, a seamstress by trade, whom Esmeralda refers to as Mami. The couple had a common-law marriage instead, which was by turns happy and passionate or destructive and turbulent. After one particularly bad argument, Mami moved her children to Santurce, a larger, wealthier community and a suburb of San Juan. Santiago recalls that she and her siblings were taunted in their relatively upscale neighborhood for being ignorant peasants. It was the first of many times in her life that she was made to feel stupid.

In 1961 Mami moved her family to Brooklyn, a borough of New York City. For the most part, in spite of the difficulties, Santiago felt safe in Puerto Rico, where she knew her neighbors and was lulled gently to sleep by the sound of tree frogs chirping in the mango groves. New York City, on the other hand, was enormous and impersonal. Santiago could not wait to visit her homeland but was disappointed when she did: "I was told I was no longer Puerto Rican because my Spanish was rusty, my gaze too direct, my personality too assertive," she wrote in *When I Was Puerto Rican.* "Yet in the United States, my darkness, my accented speech, my frequent lapses into confused silence between English and Spanish identified me as foreign, non-American." In addition, her family moved frequently from one run-down tenement (shabbily built urban apartment building) to another: "In the twenty-one years I lived with my mother, we moved at least twenty times. . . . We learned not to attach value to possessions because they were as temporary as the walls that held us for a few months, as the neighbors who lived down the street, as the sad-eyed boy who loved me when I was thirteen," she explained in *Almost a Woman.*

But Santiago was determined to integrate and become successful. In junior high school in Brooklyn, because her English was poor, she was placed in a low-performance class although she was very bright. She worked hard at improving her skills and applied to the highly competitive School for Performing Arts High School in Manhattan, where she was accepted. After graduating, she worked full time at a variety of jobs while taking night courses at a community college. Then Santiago moved to Texas to be with her lover, a controlling Turkish filmmaker 17 years her senior, with whom she shared a destructive eight-year affair. "There is such a sense of helplessness and hopelessness when you are in these relationships," she told the *Dallas Morning News.*

When Santiago was accepted at Harvard University, on full scholarship, she moved to Boston. In 1976 she graduated magna cum laude, having majored in film, and finally found the strength to end the emotionally abusive relationship with her boyfriend. (She would later help found one of the first shelters in the Boston area for battered women and their children.) In 1978 she married Frank Cantor, a filmmaker. The couple has two children and cofounded Cantomedia, a film and production company that has won several awards in documentary filmmaking.

In the early 1980s Santiago's career revolved around producing and writing documentary and educational films. She began publishing essays in periodicals such as the *New York Times* and *House and Garden,* produced two screenplays, and wrote several short stories. Santiago received a master of fine arts degree in fiction from Sarah Lawrence College in 1992. Soon thereafter a publisher's representative, having seen one of her personal accounts about her childhood in Puerto Rico, suggested she write a book. Her debut memoir, *When I Was Puerto Rican* (1993), was hailed by critics as an important contribution to contemporary Latino literature. "Santiago's portraits are clear-sighted, the Puerto Rican ambience rich, and her immigrant experience is artfully and movingly told," said a reviewer in *Publishers Weekly.* The finely crafted memoir focuses on the author's early years in Puerto Rico and ends with her move, at 13, to New York City.

America's Dreams (1996), Santiago's sole novel, was sandwiched between her two memoirs. It is, asserts Edna Rodriguez-Mangual in *Latino and Latina Writers,* like the memoirs, the story of a marginalized woman repressed by patriarchy and colonization. *America's Dream* comes to life through its narrator, America Gonzalez, a tenacious woman who, determined that her daughter escape her own fate (domestic abuse and motherhood at 14), leaves Puerto Rico, where she had worked as a hotel maid, and becomes a nanny and housekeeper for a wealthy family in upstate New York. The novel "takes its place along other major works by Latina writers such as SANDRA CISNEROS," according to *Women's Review of Books.*

In 1998 Santiago coedited, with Joie Davidow, *Las Christmas: Favorite Latino Authors Share Their Holiday Memories,* which included 25 remembrances of the family-oriented holiday, Latino-style. Picking up where *When I Was Puerto Rican* left off, the sequel, *Almost a Woman* (1998), portrays the author's coming-of-age post-immigration experiences, as she became the caretaker of her 10 younger siblings and helped them and her mother adjust to the new culture and language. Santiago poignantly captures her adolescent angst at being illegitimate and sharing a bed with her sister, as well as her romantic misadventures.

Santiago received the Alex Award from the American Library Association for *Almost a Woman* and the Latina of the Year in Literature award from *Latina* magazine, both in 1999. *Almost a Woman* was adapted in 2001 as a film for the Public Broadcasting System's "Masterpiece Theatre" and won the prestigious George Foster Peabody Award for excellence in broadcasting. Santiago says she dreams in Spanish, writes in English, sprinkles Spanish throughout her books, and has translated a few of her books into Spanish so they can be read in Spanish-speaking countries. Her books have been published in seven languages.

In 2000 she coedited, again with Joie Davidow, *Las Mamis: Favorite Latino Authors Remember Their Mothers.* The critically acclaimed anthology of essays by celebrated Latin-American and Hispanic-America authors includes an entry by Santiago titled "First Born." It begins when the writer's teenage mother gives birth to her and goes on to describe, lovingly but with ambivalence, Mami's arduous life as a single mother who experienced many failures in terms of both relationships and economic endeavors but never gave up. "Through

the years," writes Santiago, "her life has served as both an example of what we should avoid and what we should aspire to. It is her generous spirit, courage, creativity, and dignity that I, her first-born, try to emulate, her lessons written on every page of my life."

Santiago's third installment of memoirs was released in 2004. In *The Turkish Lover,* which *Booklist* described as a tale of "liberation, desperation, and the crippling grip love," the author admits to escaping her strong-willed mother only to end up in a long-lasting, unhealthy relationship. It was followed a year later by Santiago's first children's book, *A Doll for Navidades,* published in both Spanish and English, and it drew from the author's memories of lush, sunny Christmastime in Puerto Rico. "I collect memories, colors." Santiago told a *Los Angeles Times* reporter. "And I carry my collections everywhere I go."

When asked about her sense of accomplishment, Santiago, who lives with her family in a small town in upstate New York, replied, "It's important to function well with a strong sense of self, and success will follow." In addition to storytelling, Santiago, who is the recipient of three honorary degrees and the winner of the Girl Scouts of America National Woman of Distinction Award (2002), enjoys opera and theater, the paintings of Francisco Goya, salsa dancing, and volunteering for worthy causes. She believes she was put on this earth to "write these memoirs . . . to give a voice to those overlooked lives within the American dream, documenting them while validating her own to help others."

Further Reading

Lopez, Adriana. "When I Was Esmeralda." *Criticas,* November 15, 2005. Available online. URL: http://www.criticasmagazine.com/article/CA6280819.html. Downloaded on January 23, 2007.

Rodriguez-Mangual, Edna. "Esmeralda Santiago." In *Latino and Latina Writers,* edited by Alan West-Duran, 985–1,002. New York: Charles Scribner's Sons, 2004.

Santiago, Esmeralda. *America's Dream.* New York: Harper-Collins, 1996.

————. *The Turkish Lover.* Cambridge, Mass.: Da Capo Press, 2004.

————. *When I Was Puerto Rican.* New York: Vintage Books, 1993.

Santiago, Esmeralda, and Joie Davidow, eds. *Las Mamis: Favorite Latino Authors Remember Their Mothers.* New York: Knopf, 2000.

Sarton, May (Eleanore Marie Sarton)
(1912–1995)   *poet, novelist, diarist, essayist*

In a prolific career that stretched from 1929 to the mid-1990s, May Sarton, despite being overlooked by major literary critics for many years, won a devoted coterie of admirers and, ultimately, a wide audience. Many readers found her candid, deeply personal writings inspiring, consoling, and comprehensible; some, however, found them excessively self-absorbed and sentimental.

May Sarton was born Eleanore Marie Sarton in Woodelgem, Belgium, on May 3, 1912, the only child of an eminent historian of science and an English artist and designer. The family fled Belgium at the outbreak of World War I, living briefly in England before arriving in the United States in 1916. The Sartons settled in Cambridge, Massachusetts, where May attended private school. She claimed never to suffered from not having gone to college, asserting that "this way I'm ignorant but I'm fresh."

Sarton portrayed herself as living alone for many years in New Hampshire and Vermont. In 1973 she moved to coastal York, Maine, where she resided in a clapboard house near the ocean, in what she called "self-imposed loneliness," for the rest of her life. That claim, however, recently has been debunked by biographer Margot Peters, who writes that Sarton, in fact, was "incapable of spending more than a few consecutive days in her own company."

Sarton published 15 books of poetry, 19 novels, and 13 memoirs and journals, but always considered herself a poet. As she put it, "The only thing I enjoy is poems. When you're a poet you're a poet first. When it comes, it's like an angel." In *Journal of a Solitude,* she observed that "poetry always seems to me so much more a true work of the soul than prose." Written in forms ranging from blank and free verse to sonnets, her poems touched on numerous subjects, from summer music and the pleasures of gardening to her father's death and love. Yet it was Sarton's journals, in which she chronicled in meticulous detail the life of a solitary woman writer, that became her most popular works.

Sarton addressed a variety of social and personal issues in her writing, including sexuality and feminism. In her novel *Mrs. Stevens Hears the Mermaids Singing* (1965), whose central character is a female poet and a lesbian, Sarton in effect made public her own sexual preference. However, she did not want to be categorized solely as a lesbian or feminist writer, nor did she pound away militantly at provocative sexual themes in her work. Her method was different and more subtle. As she wrote in *Journal of a Solitude,* "I have been trying to say radical things gently so that they may penetrate without shock."

In her last years, with her health failing, Sarton, who had lectured extensively and received a dozen honorary doctorate degrees, wrote about growing old and facing death. She died of breast cancer on July 16, 1995. Her last journal, *At Eighty-two: A Journal* (1995), was published posthumously. In 2002, Susan Sherman edited a second volume of letters titled *May Sarton: Selected Letters, 1955–1995.* It offers 200 copiously annotated letters, culled from thousands, including selections from poets Louise Bogan and Muriel Rukeyser, Sarton's longtime friends. The letters traverse Sarton's years of maturity and recognition and culminate in her gradual decline and death. "Sarton is one of the great letter writers of our time," *Library Journal* affirmed. Her work continues to enjoy a loyal following. As critic Sheila Ballantyne noted, Sarton is a "seeker after truth with a kind of awesome energy for renewal."

Further Reading

Peters, Margot. *May Sarton: A Biography.* New York: Knopf, 1997.

Sarton, May. *Collected Poems: 1970–1973.* New York: W. W. Norton, 1974.

———. *Journal of a Solitude.* New York: W. W. Norton, 1973.

———. *May Sarton: Selected Letters, 1955–1995.* Edited by Susan Sherman. New York: W. W. Norton, 2002.

———. *Mrs. Stevens Hears the Mermaids Singing.* New York: W. W. Norton, 1965.

Seaman, Elizabeth Jane Cochrane
See BLY, NELLIE

Sedges, John
See BUCK, PEARL COMFORT SYDENSTRICKER

Sedgwick, Catharine Maria
(1789–1867) *novelist, short story writer, children's book writer*

Catharine Maria Sedgwick, best-selling author of *Hope Leslie: Or, Early Times in the Massachusetts* (1827) and other popular novels, is considered one of the most prominent American woman writers of the first half of the 19th century. During her 40-year career of writing novels, short stories, children's books, travelogues, journals, and biographies, she helped create a new form of American literature, combining American historical events with romantic themes.

Sedgwick, the sixth of seven surviving children, was born on December 28, 1789, in Stockbridge, Massachusetts. She came from an established, wealthy colonial family on her maternal side but more humble roots from her father's side: They were rural New England farmers and tavern keepers. Catharine loved her mother, Pamela Dwight Sedgwick. However, her mother suffered from lengthy bouts of depression and was often too sickly to participate in daily activities. Catharine and her siblings were raised by a black servant and caretaker, Elizabeth Freeman, whom they fondly called Mumbet. When Sedgwick was 18, her mother died, and her father remarried shortly

thereafter. Although her father was away frequently, Sedgwick had a good relationship with the hard-working lawyer, who served in both houses of Congress and was Speaker of the House as well as Massachusetts Supreme Court chief justice. He died in 1813, and Sedgwick became even closer to her siblings, especially to her four brothers, one of whom, recognizing his sister's literary talents, encouraged her to write professionally.

After attending grammar school in Stockbridge and Mrs. Bell's School in Albany, New York, Sedgwick completed her formal education at Payne's Finishing School in Boston: She always placed value on the importance of good manners. Reading was encouraged; both the girls and boys were introduced to William Shakespeare, David Hume, and Miguel de Cervantes at a young age. In addition, Sedgwick was given private instruction in several languages. She believed that character was formed "at home," during childhood. She was the only sibling of her large family who never married, although she received at least two proposals, but she did not seem to regret her decision and told a niece that "so many I have loved had made a shipwreck of happiness in marriage or have found it a dreary joyless condition."

Although she was brought up a Calvinist, Sedgwick rejected her childhood religion in favor of the Unitarian Church, which—under the leadership of William Ellery Channing—advocated religious tolerance and fostered social reform. A few of her relatives objected to Sedgwick's becoming a Unitarian, and one aunt went so far as to warn her that she would be punished "after this world" for her blasphemy. Their admonishments led Sedgwick to write a pamphlet denouncing religious intolerance which, when expanded, became the basis for her first full-length novel, *A New-England Tale: Or, Sketches of New-England Character and Manners,* published anonymously in 1822. In this fast-paced morality tale, the protagonist, a young, orphaned Quaker living in rural New England, rebels, with the help of a variety of colorful, eccentric characters, against her repressive Calvinist aunt and other pious but cruel relatives. One of the first true

American novels—not based on British themes, characters, or settings—*A New England Tale* became a best seller in America and England. In addition to its unusual portrayal of a strong-willed female character, the book demonstrated Sedgwick's skills as a regional writer to capture the natural beauty and local costumes of western Massachusetts and the verdant, pastoral Berkshires.

Redwood (1824), her second novel, revolves in part around a Shaker community and the role religion plays in everyday home life. The American domestic novel had its beginnings in works such as *Redwood.* The characters include an outspoken unmarried woman, a Vermont farmer, and a respectable Southern gentleman. Like *A New England Tale, Redwood,* which was translated into German, Swedish, Italian, and French, sold very well, and Sedgwick was compared favorably to her better-known male contemporaries such as William Cullen Bryant, who was a close friend; Washington Irving; and James Fenimore Cooper, author of *The Last of the Mohicans.* They, along with writers Nathaniel Hawthorne, who called Sedgwick "our most truthful novelist," and Ralph Waldo Emerson, attended her tea parties, which became an important gathering place for young and established writers. Paul Ryan Schneider, in *The Oxford Companion to Women's Writing,* asserts that Sedgwick was successful in creating active, vibrant female characters who were far more interesting and effective than those offered by contemporary male writers such as Cooper.

With the publication of *Hope Leslie* (1827), Sedgwick became the most famous American writer of her day. The widely read novel, about a conflict between English colonists and American Indians, featured romance and adventure. One of the characters, Faith Leslie, who is captured by Native Americans and marries an Indian, repudiates an offer to rejoin the Puritan community. (A distant relative of Sedgwick's named Eunice Williams was said to have been captured by American Indians in her childhood and to have stayed with them as an adult.) Other important characters in the novel include the freethinking, rebellious hero-

Catharine Sedgwick was a popular early American novelist who defended the status of unmarried women.
(Library of Congress, Prints and Photographs Division, LC-U 5162-113381)

ine Hope Leslie, who challenges the restrictions imposed on women by repressive Puritan leaders. Madawisca, a smart and compassionate American Indian who survived a massacre by white men, saves Hope's fiancé when he is attacked by Mohawks, losing her arm in the process.

Hope Leslie was striking for its sympathetic portrayal of Native American religious beliefs and customs and of strong, independent-minded women. "Sedgwick's fiction," writes Barbara A. Bardes in *The Heath Anthology of American Literature,* "repeatedly emphasized the political and personal need for liberty and independence." Many of her female characters are courageous and "imbued with the independent spirit of the times," as Sedgwick describes a female protagonist in *Redwood* who opts to remain single. "Sedgwick was a writer who considered political and ethical questions through marketable, often fast-paced literature, in the process producing some of the most spirited women in fiction," writes Erica Bauermeister in *500 Great Books by Women: A Reader's Guide.*

Both *Hope Leslie* and *The Linwoods: Or, "Sixty Years Since" in America* (1835), set during the Revolutionary War, combined historical events with a romantic, fictionalized plot. They were followed by *Letters from Abroad to Kindred at Home* (1841), a travelogue recording the experiences of the writer's 15-month European trip. In the last novel she produced, *Married or Single?* (1857), written when she was 68, Sedgwick attempted to "drive away the smile . . . at the name of 'old maid,'" negating negative stereotypes of spinsters and advocating the rights of women to refuse marriage if it means giving up their self-respect. Nonetheless, the heroine marries at the end of the novel.

Sedgwick went on to publish short fiction, from the 1820s to the 1850s, including the short story collection *Tales and Sketches* (1835), and six books for children. She also was known for her popular didactic novels that emphasized the importance of education, strong family ties, and domestic virtues such as proper manners. Most of her didactic novels, including *Home, The Poor Rich Man and the Rich Poor Man,* and *Live and Let Live,* all written between 1835 and 1837, went through more than a dozen editions. Although she wrote voluminously, she found time to volunteer actively in a variety of social causes and founded the Society for the Aid and Relief of Poor Women as well as the first free school in New York City, attended mostly by children of Irish immigrants. She also was involved in promoting prison reform and became the first director of the Women's Prison Association of New York.

Catharine Maria Sedgwick died, at 78, in West Roxbury, Massachusetts, on July 31, 1867, at the home of a favorite niece. She was buried next to her beloved childhood caretaker, Mumbet, in Stockbridge, her birthplace. While celebrated as a premier writer in her lifetime, she was largely forgotten until her body of work was rediscovered and reexamined in the 1970s. In 1997, a group of scholars founded the Catharine Maria Sedgwick Society to provide greater visibility and legitimacy to Sedgwick scholarship and publications. For example, the society participated in a 2005 symposium held at Fordham University in New York City called "Antebellum American Women Writers and the City," and in 2007 the society celebrated its 10th anniversary with a special symposium held in Stockbridge, Sedgwick's hometown. Sedgwick's fiction, popular with readers and critics alike, helped define the burgeoning American literary tradition.

Further Reading

Coontz, Stephanie. *Marriage, a History from Obedience to Intimacy.* New York: Viking, 2005.

Damon-Bach, Lucinda, and Victoria Clement, eds. *Catharine Maria Sedgwick: Critical Perspectives.* Boston: Northeastern University Press, 2003.

Fetterley, Judith. "Oh My Sister! My Sister! The Rhetoric of Catharine Sedgwick's *Hope Leslie.*" *American Literature* 70, no. 3 (September 1998): 491–516.

Sedgwick, Catharine Maria. *Hope Leslie: Or, Early Times in the Massachusetts.* 2d ed. New Brunswick, N.J.: Rutgers University Press, 1987.

———. *A New-England Tale; Or, Sketches of New-England Character and Manners.* Edited and with an introduction by Susan K. Harris. 2d ed. New York: Penguin, 2003.

ꙮ Settle, Mary Lee
(1918–2005) *novelist, memoirist*

Mary Lee Settle, a writer of historical fiction best known for *The Beulah Quintet,* an interconnected, five-book, three-century saga, was a prolific novelist whose subject matter ranged from miners in Appalachia to expatriates in Turkey. She produced 23 books in several genres, many of which were drawn from memories of her West Virginia roots or based on years of research and travel. Settle, the founder of the PEN/Faulkner Award, has been critically lauded for her craftsmanship and emphasis on precision.

Born on July 29, 1918, in Charleston, West Virginia, Mary Lee Settle was the daughter of Joseph and Rachel Tompkins Settle. Her father was a coal mine owner and civil engineer responsible for the safety of mine workers. Settle attended grade school in Montgomery, West Virginia, and middle and high school in Charleston. She studied at Sweet Briar College in Virginia from 1936 to 1938 before moving to New York City to pursue a career in modeling and acting: She was said to have auditioned for the role of Scarlett O'Hara in the movie *Gone with the Wind,* although it went to Vivien Leigh, but she was a successful model. "I took for granted the kind of looks that other women envied and that I treated with a slight contempt," she recalled. In 1939, she married an Englishman, Rodney Weathersbee. The couple moved to Canada and had a son, Christopher. After leaving her young son with her parents in West Virginia, Settle left for England to serve in their war effort.

During World War II Settle joined the Women's Auxiliary of the British Royal Air Force and then transferred to the Office of War Information in London as a writer. After the war she returned to Manhattan and in 1945 was named assistant editor of *Harper's Bazaar* magazine, but she quickly gave up her coveted position to write fiction. Settle and Weathersbee were divorced in 1946, the same year she married the poet Douglas Newton. That marriage ended in divorce 10 years later.

In 1954, Settle produced her first novel, *The Love Eaters,* about a theater company, followed in 1955 by *The Kiss of Kin.* Her breakthrough came with the publication of *O Beulah Land,* the first in the Beulah Quintet series, in 1956. The series chronicles the history of three families who have a common ancestor. The historical novel takes the families from Cromwellian England in the 1640s to the development of contemporary West Virginia in the 1980s. The books reflect the author's meticulous knowledge of her southern mountain heritage, with its "feudal coal culture," as she called it, and her compassion for the people as they struggled for freedom in the New World. In an intro-

duction to *O Beulah Land,* Settle explained that to inform her work, she "let the past become a present, let it fall beyond intelligence into reliving, which is true sensuous recall, where dreams come from with all their fears and future hopes of things long past."

O Beulah Land begins, wrote Settle in *Bloodroot,* a collection of autobiographical essays by female writers from Appalachia, with

an image of a woman stripped down to survival, lost and mindless with fear, moving toward the east through the Endless Mountains, now called the Alleghenies. Her name is Hannah Bridewell. The time is 1754. She glimpses and remembers a small valley, the first sight of Beulah. Hunger for land of one's own, safe from exile, is the guiding force of the time.

The novel ends "with the last colonial year before the American Revolution." The other four books in the quintet, *Know Nothing, Prisons, The Scapegoat,* and *The Killing Ground,* were written between 1960 and 1982. Settle described in *Contemporary Authors* how she got the idea for writing the five-book saga: "I had a picture of one man hitting another in a West Virginia drunk tank one Saturday night, and the idea was to go all the way back to see what lay behind that blow. At first I went back all the way to 1755; then I realized that wasn't far enough, and I went back further still."

Settle also produced books in other genres, including a memoir of her years in the Women's Auxiliary Air Force, *All the Brave Promises: Memories of Aircraft Woman Second Class 2146391* (1966). She wrote it, she said, "almost as a protest against the romanticism about the Second World War." According to Alan Pryce-Jones of *Commonweal* magazine, it is one of the few good books to come out of World War II. Settle considered *The Clam Shell* (1971) her only autobiographical novel; it is based on her Sweet Briar College years. She also published two children's books, a young adult account of the celebrated Scopes "monkey" trial, several novels peripheral or unrelated to the Beulah Quintet, and short stories that appeared in periodicals such as the *Paris Review* and *Harper's Magazine*. Her short fiction was included in the 1957 *O. Henry Prize Story Collection*.

Although she did not define herself as an academic, Settle was associate professor at Bard College from 1965 until 1976 and in 1978 a visiting lecturer at the University of Virginia in Charlottesville. That same year she married William Littleton Tazewell, an American columnist and historian, and received the 1978 National Book Award for fiction for *Blood Tie* (1977), a visually striking novel with a contemporary setting, about expatriates living in Turkey, where Settle had resided for two years in the 1970s. She believed strongly in recognizing and financially rewarding her fellow writers, and therefore helped create the PEN/Faulkner award, whose winners are selected by their peers and which, since its establishment in 1980, has grown into the monetarily largest major fiction award. Settle was also a founding member of the Fellowship of Southern Writers. The recipient of two Guggenheim fellowships, in 1983 she received the Janet Heidinger Kafka prize in fiction for *The Killing Ground* and the Lillian Smith Award for *Choices* (1995).

Settle has been praised for the painstaking accuracy of her historical novels. She would spend months immersed in libraries in America and abroad reading letters, original documents, and personal accounts from the period about which she was writing in order to capture perfectly both the facts and emotional truth of that particular time period. She accomplished this without taking notes, instead internalizing the information so it would sound more natural. As one of her editors noted, Settle believed that the key to understanding these people, and thus her characters, was in their words.

Turkish Reflections: A Biography of a Place, a memoir published in 1991, was part travelogue, part history, part personal reflections. "I had consciously to develop a visual sense [she was partially blind due to a childhood illness] and that psychic awakening was to me like seeing for the first time," she explained. Her most recently published works include *Addie* (1998), drawn from poignant memories of her mother and grandmother; another historical novel, *I, Roger Williams: A Fragment of an Autobiography* (2001), written from the founder of Rhode Island's point of view when he was an old man; and *Spanish Recognitions: The Roads to the Present* (2004), a travel memoir based on solo car trips she made to Spain while in her 80s. "I was looking forward to discovery, not to being tied to that deadening word itinerary," said Settle.

In 1994 Settle received an award from the Academy of Arts and Letters. "Her novels penetrate the American experience with rare depth and immediacy," asserted critic Richard Dyer in the *Boston Globe*. He went on to describe the author as "colorful and outspoken, who lived a life in which adventure alternated with the kind of reflective solitude that a writer's art demands." When asked by the *Boston Globe* in 2001 why she thought her books were not fashionable, Settle replied, "I don't write books about being vaguely unhappy in Connecticut, nor do I belong to the Island School, the island being Manhattan."

Mary Lee Settle received the Library of Virginia Lifetime Achievement Award in 2002. She died at the age of 87 of lung cancer on September 27, 2005, in Charlottesville, where she had made her home, not far from the hardscrabble region of southern Appalachia she had written about so fervently in her major work. She also spent 17 years living and working in countries such as England, Greece, and Turkey and traveling to faraway destinations such as Kurdistan, Africa, and Hong Kong. At the time of her death Settle was writing an appreciation of Thomas Jefferson, focusing on his youth. Brian Rosenberg, in the *Virginia Quarterly Review*, called Settle "one of the more interesting, yet overlooked of modern American novelists."

Further Reading

Dyer, Joyce, ed. *Bloodroot: Reflections on Place by Appalachian Women Writers*, 244–246. Lexington: University of Kentucky, 1998.

Gates, Anita. "Mary Lee Settle, 87, Author of 'Beulah' Novels, Is Dead." *New York Times*, 29 September 2005, sec. A.

Settle, Mary Lee. *All the Brave Promises: Memories of Aircraft Woman Second Class 2146391.* New York: Delacorte, 1966.

———. *Blood Tie.* Boston: Houghton Mifflin, 1977.

———. *O Beulah Land.* New York: Viking, 1956.

———. *Spanish Recognitions: The Roads to the Present.* New York: W. W. Norton, 2004.

Sexton, Anne Gray Harvey
(1928–1974)   *poet*

Anne Sexton was a Pulitzer Prize–winning "confessional" poet who wrote intensely personal verse, with bold, forceful imagery, often about her experiences with mental illness and the struggle between her life-affirming creativity and her suicidal tendencies.

Anne Gray Harvey was born in Newton, Massachusetts, on November 9, 1928. She grew up in affluent suburbs of Boston and spent seaside summers in Maine but had an emotionally troubled adolescence. Her mother, she recalled, was competitive and self-absorbed, while her father was an abusive alcoholic. Her only refuge was her loving great-aunt, "Nana," who lived with the Harveys but who ended up in a mental institution.

At age 19, having dropped out of college, Anne impulsively eloped with Alfred "Kayo" Sexton, a wool salesman. Vivacious and attractive (she worked briefly as a fashion model), Sexton tried to adjust to life as a suburban housewife and mother. However, after the birth of her second daughter in 1955, she suffered a major nervous breakdown. She began drinking heavily and taking strong sedatives prescribed for her depression. Unable to cope with her stormy marriage and her own uncontrollable rage, often directed at her young children, Sexton repeatedly attempted to kill herself.

In 1957, a psychiatrist suggested that she try describing what she was "feeling and thinking and dreaming." Sexton discovered she enjoyed writing and was good at it; she was soon producing two or three sonnets a day and experienced a "rebirth at twenty-nine." She took a poetry workshop at the Boston Center for Adult Education, where she met another "suburban housewife poet," MAXINE KUMIN, who would become a lifelong friend. A year later she joined a graduate seminar at Boston University taught by Robert Lowell. One of her classmates was SYLVIA PLATH, another talented, unstable poet with whom she is often compared. After Plath committed suicide, Sexton wrote a poem about envying her friend for having succeeded at dying. But Sexton also lived life fully and engaged in several extramarital love affairs, including—according to her biographer Diane Wood Middlebrook—one with her psychiatrist.

With Lowell's encouragement, Sexton published her first volume of poetry. *To Bedlam, Part Way and Back* (1960), as its title implied, was about the terrifying journey into madness or near-

Poet Anne Sexton poses for a photograph on the day she won a Pulitzer Prize for *Live or Die.* (AP/Wide World Photos)

madness, and the difficult trip back from it. The book received wide critical attention, although mixed reviews, and Sexton was dubbed a "confessional" poet, a label that suited her candid, autobiographical writing style.

Her next volume, *All My Pretty Ones* (1962), received *Poetry* magazine's Levinson Prize and was nominated for a National Book Award. From 1961 to 1963, Sexton served as a scholar at the Radcliffe Institute for Independent Study, where she befriended Tillie Olsen, a writer who like herself had no college degree but whose work was widely admired by women.

When Sexton's best known collection, *Live or Die,* won a Pulitzer Prize in 1967, the "mad housewife poet" became a respected member of Boston's literati. Although she wrote arresting verse about suicide, humiliation, and death, she ended *Live or Die* on an upbeat note, with reasons to live rather than to die. In her work, as in her life, she often explored the conflict between the creative and self-destructive selves.

Sexton's poems appeared regularly in periodicals and magazines such as the *Quarterly Review of Literature* and the *New Yorker,* and she won numerous poetry awards, fellowships, and prizes. She liked her celebrity status and in 1968 set her poetry to music by forming a rock-and-roll band that performed a 17-song/poem repertoire. She also led a poetry workshop at the same Boston-area mental institution where she had been confined.

In 1969, her one-act play, *45 Mercy Street,* a psychodrama about incest and dysfunctional family relationships, was produced off-Broadway. When not obsessed with madness or love, Sexton wrote fierce, graphic verse celebrating female sexuality and anatomy. The poet Muriel Rukeyser praised her for allowing the women in her poems to become "the center, after many years of silence and taboo."

Five more collections appeared in rapid succession, including an arresting volume of *Love Poems* (1969), *Transformations* (1971), a revisionist version of Grimm's fairy tales produced as a free-form opera, and *The Death Notebooks,* which was pub-lished in 1974, the same year she finally ended her tumultuous marriage.

In 1972 Sexton became a professor of creative writing at Boston University and also taught at Colgate University. Although busy writing and teaching, she continued to be plagued by severe depression. During a three-week frenzy in January 1973, she wrote 39 poems, published posthumously in 1975 as *The Awful Rowing toward God,* "with two days out for despair and three days out in a mental hospital."

On October 4, 1974, Anne Sexton, the 45-year-old accomplished but anguished poet, flamboyantly draped herself in her mother's fur coat, poured herself a drink, pulled her car into the garage of her Weston home, closed the door, and died from carbon monoxide poisoning. In "Wanting to Die," she all too aptly described the special language and the personal pull of suicide as a solution and a means to an end.

"When I'm writing, I know I'm doing the thing I was born to do," Sexton once said. By the end of the 1980s, nearly a half-million volumes of her poetry had sold in America. In 1994 her daughter, Linda, wrote a revealing memoir about her relationship with her mother. *Women's Letters* (2005) included a missive from Anne Sexton to Linda, who was 16 years old at the time: "Life is not easy. It is awfully lonely. I know that. Now you too know it. . . . But I've had a good life—I wrote unhappy—but I lived to the hilt. You too, Linda— Live to the HILT! To the top. I love you, 40-year-old Linda."

Further Reading

Gill, Jo, ed. *Modern Confessional Writing: New Critical Essays.* New York: Routledge, 2006.

Grunwald, Lisa, and Stephen J. Adler, eds. *Women's Letters: America from the Revolutionary War to the Present.* New York: Dial Press, 2005.

Middlebrook, Diane Wood. *Anne Sexton: A Biography.* Boston: Houghton Mifflin, 1991.

Sexton, Anne. *The Complete Poems.* With a foreword by Maxine Kumin. Boston: Houghton Mifflin, 1981.

Sexton, Linda Gray. *Searching for Mercy Street: My Journey Back to My Mother.* Boston: Houghton Mifflin, 1994.

~ Shange, Ntozake (Paulette Linda Williams)
(1948–) playwright, poet, novelist, children's book writer

The author of the award-winning Broadway play and best seller *for colored girls who have considered suicide / when the rainbow is enuf* (1975), Ntozake Shange writes with brio about black women who have been abused or abandoned by men and society but who nonetheless survive and come to believe in a better future.

The oldest of four children, Paulette Linda Williams was born on October 18, 1948, in Trenton, New Jersey. Her middle-class parents, a surgeon and a social worker, filled their home with books, music, and laughter: "Laughter from the kitchen, Laughter up the stairs. . . . My mother had . . . something in her soul that let her know what touch or hug a body needed," Shange later recalled in an essay about her mother.

When Paulette was eight, she moved to St. Louis, Missouri, where her parents socialized with notable jazz musicians such as Charlie Parker and Miles Davis. But when she suggested that *she* become a jazz musician or a war correspondent, the response was, "no good for a woman." She attended a German-American school that did not welcome black children, and increasingly she escaped into her books. At age 13, Paulette returned to New Jersey, where she finished high school.

After a brief, failed marriage and exposure to the growing racial tensions of the 1950s and 1960s, as well as to what she perceived as a sexist society, she became depressed and attempted suicide several times. Eventually she turned her rage against society rather than herself, and earned a bachelor's degree, with honors, from Barnard College (1970) and a master's degree from the University of Southern California (1973).

In 1970, influenced by the Civil Rights movement, she gave herself an African name: "Ntozake" (EN-to-ze-ke), which in Zulu means "she who comes with her own things," and "Shange" (Shong-ge), which means "who walks like a lion." Having discovered a rich African-American literary heritage, she decided to become a writer. As a form of rebellion, she used nonstandard, idiosyncratic syntax and spellings.

When not writing, Shange performed as a dancer or actress, taught at several colleges, and choreographed poems. In California, her choreopoem (a combination of music, dance, and poetry) about rape, abuse, abandonment, and self-actualization, *for colored girls who have considered suicide / when the rainbow is enuf,* a tribute to black women, was first dramatized at a woman's bar near Berkeley. She moved to New York City, where in 1975 it was produced off-Broadway. In 1976 *for colored girls* made it to Broadway and was an instant and longlasting hit, garnering several prizes, including Obie and Outer Critics Circle awards. It also became a best-selling book. Shange had succeeded at her goal: to portray, as Elizabeth Brown-Guillory wrote in *Black Women in America,* "[black] women in a state of pain, rage, anguish, or disillusionment." Although some critics felt that it unfairly "lynched" black men by focusing on their violent behavior, Shange responded: "My job as an artist is to say what I see."

A prolific and versatile writer, Shange then published two novellas and three novels, the first of which was *Sassafrass, Cypress & Indigo* (1977), several collections of well-received poetry, and five more dramas, beginning with another choreopoem, *Spell #7* (1979). She also adapted Bertolt Brecht's *Mother Courage and Her Children* (1980) into an off-Broadway production that won an Obie Award, and in 1984 published a collection of essays about her work.

The recipient of Guggenheim and National Endowment for the Arts (NEA) fellowships, a Medal of Excellence from Columbia University, and the National Black Theatre Festival's Living Legend Award, Shange continued to teach performance art and African literature in Philadelphia, Pennsylvania, where she and her daughter lived. Her other work includes a novel, *Liliane: Resurrection of a Daughter* (1994); a collection of poetry, *I Live in Music* (1994); and *If I Can Cook / You Know God Can* (1998), a literary, anecdotal cookbook that celebrates the African-American culinary experience.

In recent years Shange has produced several books for children, such as *Float like a Butterfly* (2002), a picture book about the famous boxer Muhammad Ali; *Daddy Says* (2003); and *Ellington Was Not a Street* (2004), a story that recalls, in the format of a poem, Shange's childhood home and the close-knit group of innovative, visionary black men, including Paul Robeson, Dizzy Gillespie, and Duke Ellington, who gathered there.

In her introduction to *for colored girls,* Ntozake Shange, explained, optimistically, that she was "on the other side of the rainbow." Her works, says Brown-Guillory, empower women to take responsibility for their lives by learning to love themselves and to challenge their oppressors.

Further Reading

Brown-Guillory, Elizabeth. "Ntozake Shange." In *Black Women in America,* edited by Darlene Clark Hine, 1,026–1,029. Brooklyn, N.Y.: Carlson Publishing, 1993.

Lester, Neal A. *Ntozake Shange: A Critical Study of the Plays.* New York: Garland, 1995.

Shange, Ntozake. *for colored girls who have considered suicide / when the rainbow is enuf.* New York: Macmillan, 1976.

———. *Ellington Was Not a Street.* New York: Simon & Schuster, 2004.

⌒ Shreve, Anita
(1946–) *novelist*

In a period of 11 years, Anita Shreve penned 10 critically acclaimed, compelling novels, five of which became best sellers. She writes about love—"a devalued subject to be writing about these days," she has asserted. Shreve infuses her stories with mystery and murder, and her characters pay a considerable toll for falling in, or out of, love. Many of her protagonists are intelligent, attractive women who find themselves, much to their surprise, uncertain about their romantic relationships.

Shreve was born the eldest of three daughters on October 7, 1946, in Dedham, Massachusetts, a middle-class suburb of Boston. Her father was an airline pilot, her mother a homemaker. As a child, Shreve was a voracious reader: Playwright Eugene O'Neill and novelist EDITH WHARTON were among her favorite authors. Shreve spent her childhood summers on the coasts of Massachusetts and Maine, climbing sand dunes and gazing at the cold, inky-blue ocean. The rugged yet beautiful New England coastline often appears as an austere backdrop for her novels. "The sea is an absolutely dizzyingly wonderful metaphor," said Shreve in an article that appeared on September 20, 1998, in the *Boston Globe Magazine.* "I could be a writer for the rest of my life and not exhaust the descriptions of the sea and the metaphor. In nearly all my books, I've used it."

After attending Tufts University, where she studied writing with the poet MAXINE KUMIN, Shreve graduated in 1968 with a degree in English. For five years she taught high school English in the Boston area, writing short fiction in her spare time. "Past the Island, Drifting," a short story published in a small literary journal, won a coveted O. Henry Prize in 1975.

Seeking something more adventurous than teaching but more financially rewarding than writing short fiction, Shreve became a journalist. She spent three years in Kenya, Africa, where she helped establish a magazine and where she met her future husband, John Osborn, a graduate student. She returned to America in the late 1970s, married Osborn, had two children, and worked as a freelance writer for periodicals that varied from *Seventeen* magazine and *Newsweek* to the *New York Times Magazine.* In 1985 she copublished two books with Dr. Lawrence Balter about infancy and early childhood, while continuing to write journalistic articles. She expanded one of them, about the plight of working mothers, into the book *Remaking Motherhood: How Working Mothers Are Shaping Our Children's Future* (1987). It was followed two years later by *Women Together, Women Alone,* which also was based on an article that appeared originally in the *New York Times Magazine.*

With the advance from her second nonfiction book, Shreve set out to write a novel. "I said to myself, 'You're either going to do it now, or it's not going to happen.'" As opposed to reportage, she loved the idea of the "rush of freedom that [she] could make it up." The result was her debut novel, *Eden Close* (1989), a gothic tale about violence (the protagonist is blinded by a shotgun blast from a home intruder), rape, and the healing power of friendship. Other novels, all critically successful, quickly followed. These included *Strange Fits of Passion* (1991), another portrait of violence against women, in this case a lifetime of domestic abuse that leads to murder; *Where or When* (1993), a story of unrequited love and risk taking; and *Resistance* (1995), a *New York Times* best seller, revolving around a World War II American bomber who crashes in Belgium and ends up falling in love with a Belgian housewife.

The Weight of Water (1997), developed from a short story titled "Silence at Smuttynose," is based on the true story of a double murder in 1873 off the New Hampshire coast on the Isles of Shoals and simultaneously on a modern-day marriage that is dissolving. Lauded for its eloquent prose and historically and emotionally shifting plotlines, in 1998 it earned Shreve a PEN/L. L. Winship Award and the New England Book Award for Fiction from the New England Booksellers' Association. It also was selected as a finalist for Great Britain's Orange Prize. "Shreve makes us see how, acted on by tumultuous feelings, we may choose to pretend we are not accountable," noted critic Rebecca Radner in the *San Francisco Chronicle*. Shreve is a master at exploring how lives and destinies are interconnected.

Another best-selling title about deception and disaster, *The Pilot's Wife* (1998), was chosen by television celebrity Oprah Winfrey as an Oprah's Book Club selection, which resulted in a precipitous increase in sales and propelled Shreve to national recognition. The novel presents a dual-life portrayal of a seemingly happy marriage, until the central character discovers that her recently deceased husband had a mistress overseas with whom he shared another life. When asked in 2001 by *The Writer* about the complex arena of love, Shreve replied, "Love is a wonderful place in which to place characters. It's something extraordinary that happens to ordinary people. It's often, as well,

a terrific testing ground for moral character." *The Pilot's Wife* sold more than 2 million copies in paperback. Shreve's next novel was *Fortune's Rocks* (2000), a coming-of-age tale that takes place at the turn of the 20th century. The story delineates the emotional repercussions of an unexpected affair between a 15-year-old and her father's friend, a 41-year-old married physician, that results in a child. Shreve's characters are, as she describes them, "ordinary people in extraordinary circumstances" who often do not encounter happy endings.

"It's a kind of prequel and a sequel," explains Anita Shreve, referring to *The Last Time They Met* (2001), the story of two people who harbor a lifelong passion for each other even though they meet only a few times. Thomas Janes, a character from *The Weight of Water*, reappears in this book as a widowed poet. "The idea for *The Last Time They Met*, the conceit of the book, is contained within a couple of sentences in *The Weight of Water*, in a reference to Janes's life's work," said Shreve in an interview. In *Sea Glass*, produced a year later in 2002, readers may recognize the decaying beach house, which plays a central role in the novel, because it also appeared in *The Pilot's Wife* and *Fortune's Rocks*. That house, explained Shreve to the *London Independent*, was based on one she saw fleetingly in Maine and could not forget. It may have inspired her, but it is also "straight out of my imagination. It's just another character," she said. Two of her novels have been adapted into screenplays: *The Pilot's Wife* aired as a television movie and *The Weight of Water* as a Hollywood feature film.

A portrait of a Victorian-era American marriage told in flashback, *All He Ever Wanted* is another work of historical fiction. It came out in 2003 and was followed a year later by *Light on Snow*, which reached the *New York Times* best seller list and chronicles a New England winter, during which time a girl and her father, who had suffered terrible personal losses two years earlier, find an abandoned baby. "Shreve's characters are sympathetic, without being pitiable," writes a reviewer in *Publishers Weekly*. Shreve's next novel, *A Wedding in December* (2005), focuses on seven former classmates who meet, following September 11, 2001, after 27 years. In 2007 she penned *Body Surfing*, a novel about rootlessness and dislocation. "The pull of history has been a strong theme in my life as a novelist," the author has said.

Anita Shreve, whose books are written in longhand in the corner of the living room of her turn-of-the-century home in western Massachusetts, contends that her goal as a writer is to tell a good story and have a beautiful command of the language. She admits to being driven and "can't imagine not writing. It's my work. You don't stop just because you've finished a book," she explained during an interview in 2002. "A novel is a collision of ideas," she wrote in an author's note to *Sea Glass*. "Three or four threads may be floating around in the writer's consciousness, and at a single moment in time, these ideas collide and produce a novel." Shreve, who has two children and three stepchildren divides her time between Massachusetts and New Hampshire. "I spend the majority of my writing life imagining other people's lives," she has remarked. "Writing itself is about experiencing the unlived life in many senses."

Further Reading

Fox, Sue. "Anita Shreve: A Fortune Found in the Seas." *London Independent,* March 30, 2002. Available online. URL: http://www.findarticles.com/p/articles/mi_qn4158/is_20020330/ai_n12602314. Downloaded on January 23, 2007.

Roche, B. J. "Anita Shreve's Life Stories." *The Boston Globe Magazine,* September 20, 1998. Available online. URL: http://cache.boston.com/globe/magazine/1998/9-20/featurestory1. Downloaded on January 23, 2007.

Shreve, Anita. *Body Surfing.* Boston: Little, Brown, 2007.

———. *Eden Close.* New York: Harcourt, 1989.

———. *Sea Glass.* Boston: Little, Brown, 2002.

———. *A Wedding in December.* Boston: Little, Brown, 2005.

———. *The Weight of Water.* Boston: Little, Brown, 1997.

∿ Silko, Leslie Marmon
(1948–) *novelist, poet, essayist*

In her work, Leslie Marmon Silko, whom the *New York Times Book Review* called "the most accomplished Indian writer of her generation," explores the primal connection between the land and Native Americans and the importance of passing on American Indian culture and a sense of community to future generations.

Born on March 5, 1948, in Albuquerque, New Mexico, of mixed ancestry—Laguna Pueblo, Mexican, and Caucasian—Leslie Marmon Silko grew up hearing Indian stories and folklore. "Traditionally everyone, from the youngest child to the oldest person, was expected to listen and to be able to recall or tell a portion [of the story]. Thus the remembering and retelling were a communal process," explained Silko in *The Woman That I Am.*

Educated at Bureau of Indian Affairs schools until she attended high school, Silko graduated summa cum laude from the University of Mexico in 1969. She entered law school but decided instead to become a writer. Although she published a collection of richly conceived semiautobiographical poems, *Laguna Woman* (1974), it was not until her first novel, *Ceremony* (1977), appeared that she was recognized as an important literary figure. The story of a traumatized mixed-blood man who returns to his Indian reservation following World War II and encounters a wise man who helps him to restore harmony in his life, *Ceremony* was critically acclaimed. Merging western and tribal techniques, Silko created characters who learned to value continuity; as one of them says: "Only growth keeps the ceremonies strong." In *The Sacred Hoop,* the American Indian writer PAULA GUNN ALLEN contends that Silko's emphasis in *Ceremony*—"environmental integrity and pacifism"—along with witchcraft, developed out of an Indian perspective that is "fundamental to the fabric of pueblo life and thought."

In 1981 Silko published *Storyteller,* a volume of short fiction and poetry. "Yellow Woman," a frequently anthologized story in which the protagonist is abducted by a cattle ranger whom she believes to be a spirit, ends with her return home: "I decided to tell them that some Navajo had kidnapped me, but I was sorry that old Grandpa wasn't alive to hear my story because it was the Yellow Woman stories he liked to tell best."

It was another decade before Silko published her next book, an epic novel and morality tale, *Almanac of the Dead* (1991), which spanned five centuries and portrayed an array of colorful characters, including an Indian psychic who transcribes the history of her people and in the process foretells the future of "all the Americas." In describing why she wrote *Almanac of the Dead,* Silko said she was trying to give history a character. "It was as if native spirits were possessing me, like a spell."

In *Yellow Woman and a Beauty of the Spirit* (1996), a collection of essays about contemporary American Indian life, Silko examines the role of literature and language in Native American heritage, as well as the role of the U.S. government in perpetuating crimes against the American Indians. "One of the reasons I felt I must write the essays was to remedy this country's shocking ignorance of its own history," Silko wrote, adding that until the "real" story is known, there can be no justice, "and without justice, there can be no peace." Silko's third novel, *Gardens in the Dunes* (1999), explores the legend of the garden paradise and the plant kingdom.

In 2000 Leslie Marmon Silko won the Lannan Literary Award in fiction, the same year *Conversations with Leslie Marmon Silko,* a collection of 16 interviews reflecting her interest in the interfacing of American Indian and Western cultures, as well as in history, psychology, spirituality, and literature, was published. In his critical study, *Silko: Writing Storyteller and Medicine Woman* (2004), Brewster E. Fitz explores the relationship between the spoken story and the written word, revealing how it carries over from the author's upbringing and plays out in her writings, ultimately creating a new vision of Pueblo culture that weaves together the oral and the written tradition.

Silko is the recipient of a National Endowment for the Arts (NEA) grant and a prestigious Catherine T. MacArthur Foundation fellowship. She is divorced and lives in Tucson, Arizona, with her two sons, where she teaches English at the University of Arizona, writes, and works on film scripts.

Further Reading

Allen, Paula Gunn. *The Sacred Hoop: Recovering the Feminine in American Indian Traditions.* Boston: Beacon Press, 1986.

Arnold, Ellen L., ed. *Conversations with Leslie Marmon Silko.* Jackson: University Press of Mississippi, 2000.

Fitz, Brewster E. *Silko: Writing Storyteller and Medicine Woman.* Norman: University of Oklahoma Press, 2004.

Green, Rayna. *That's What She Said: Contemporary Fiction and Poetry by Native American Women.* Bloomington: Indiana University Press, 1984.

"Leslie Marmon Silko." American Indian Resources: Backgrounds to Native American Literature. Available online. URL: http://www2005.lang.osaka-u.ac.jp/~krkvls/laguna.html. Downloaded on March 6, 2007.

Silko, Leslie Marmon. *Ceremony.* New York: Viking, 1977.

———. *Gardens in the Dunes.* New York: Simon & Schuster, 1999.

———. *Yellow Woman and a Beauty of the Spirit: Essays on Native American Life Today.* New York: Simon & Schuster, 1996.

Simon, Kate (Kaila Grobsmith)
(1912–1990)   *travel writer, memoirist*

Kate Simon, one of America's best-known travel writers, who according to the *New York Times Book Review* turned "one of the dullest forms of literature [into] a brilliant work of art," was also praised for her insightful three-part autobiography.

Born Kaila Grobsmith on December 5, 1912, in Poland's Warsaw ghetto, Kate (her Americanized name) emigrated to America with her mother and brother; she later described her arrival in *A Wider World* (1986):

> She was a four-year-old vessel of apprehension and hope, sped along Ellis Island with bundles and bears and shawls by her mother. . . . There, at the gate to America, stands the tall, handsome father . . . who is God: not the bearded angry old Punisher, but the giver of fresh milk. . . .

Simon would also recall, in her highly praised memoir *Bronx Primitive: Portraits in a Childhood* (1982), that life in the New World was both difficult and rewarding. Her strict, authoritarian father, a Jewish shoemaker, was disappointed that his daughter did not become a concert pianist. Her mother, on the other hand, encouraged her to become well educated and not to marry until she had a career, because "with a profession . . . you're free."

After graduating from a first-rate public high school, at age 15 Kate became a live-in babysitter for a family who introduced her to left-wing politics and bohemian culture. She went on to earn a bachelor's degree at Hunter College in 1935, worked for several publishing companies, and reviewed books for the *New Republic* and the *Nation.*

Not long after her husband, Dr. Stanley Goldman, died in 1942, her only child, Alexandra, died at the age of 22. Devastated, she married the publisher Robert Simon, but the troubled marriage ended in divorce. Kate Simon turned to writing and discovered she had a natural gift for informative, colorful travel articles.

Her career was launched with the publication of her first book, *New York Places and Pleasures: An Uncommon Guidebook* (1959), a best seller that has been revised four times. Rich in detail, urbane but unpretentious, it is considered one of the finest New York City travel guides. "Come home," Simon implored in the preface. "The city is as outrageous, capricious, ugly and dramatic as ever."

Between 1965 and 1978, Simon wrote travel books on Mexico, Paris, London, Italy, Rome, and England. *Publishers Weekly* described them as "distinctly personal guides of rare good taste and discernment." In 1978 Simon focused on a single street in *Fifth Avenue: A Very Social History,* an exploration of New York City's famous avenue and its affluent inhabitants, from the Astors to the Rockefellers.

Simon also wrote three memoirs, which were lauded for their candor, humor, and lack of sentimentality. *Bronx Primitive* (1982), which was selected as one of the best books of the year by the *New York Times* and received a National Book Critics Circle Award, recalled the author's early years in her poor immigrant neighborhood, where various ethnic groups staked out their territory: "Except for a few entertaining, itinerant drunks, unaccented English was the alarm for the wary silence and the alert poise of the hunted," wrote Simon.

The next volume, *A Wider World* (1986), portrayed Simon's rebellious, Depression-era adolescence, when she dabbled with romance, travel, and, on the darker side, underwent an abortion. Simon turned to nonfiction in 1988 with *A Renaissance Tapestry: The Gonzaga of Mantua* (1988), a vivid account of the Italian Renaissance and a family that had ruled a province of the Lombardy region in Italy for four centuries.

On February 5, 1990, at age 77, Simon died in the city she had described so intimately and with such passion, New York. *Etchings in an Hourglass,* the third volume in her autobiographical series, which covered her adult life, was published posthumously in 1990. A book reviewer for *Time* magazine noted that whether describing Rome or growing up in the Bronx, Simon was one of those rare writers who is "preternaturally incapable of writing a dull sentence."

Further Reading

"Kate Simon." Niobrara County Library: Ordinary Lives. Available online. URL: http://www.niobraracounty library.org/wch/series012/bronx.php. Downloaded on March 6, 2007.

Obituary. *New York Times,* February 5, 1990.

Simon, Kate. *Bronx Primitive: Portraits in a Childhood.* New York: Viking Press, 1982.

———. *New York Places and Pleasures: An Uncommon Guidebook.* Rev. ed. New York: Harper and Row, 1971.

∽ Smith, Anna Deavere
(1950–) *playwright*

Hailed by *Newsweek* (1993) as "the most exciting individual in American theater," Anna Deavere

Smith, an African-American actress, educator, and distinguished playwright, has written and performed in provocative one-woman plays that explore controversial contemporary events from multiple points of view.

Born on September 18, 1950, in Baltimore, Maryland, the daughter of a coffee merchant and an elementary school principal, Anna Deavere Smith moved to San Francisco, California, where she took acting courses and where in 1976 she received a master of fine arts degree from the American Conservatory Theatre. She has also taught acting there, as well as at Yale, Carnegie-Mellon, and New York universities, and has been Ann O'Day Maples Professor of the Arts at Stanford University.

In 1983 Smith produced her first play, *On the Road,* in Berkeley, California. A year later, *Aye, Aye, Aye, I'm Integrated* was staged off-Broadway. Since 1985, Smith has created a series of theatrical works entitled *On The Road: The Search for American Character.* Each play in the series is based on an actual current event and on verbatim interviews, conducted by the playwright, that represent varied points of view.

Fires in the Mirror: Crown Heights, Brooklyn and Other Identities (1991), Smith's first one-woman show, based on her own interviews, chronicled the clash between Hasidic Jews and African Americans in Crown Heights, Brooklyn. The play generated lively discussions wherever it was performed and earned an Obie Award. It was also the runner-up for the 1993 Pulitzer Prize. In it, Smith impersonated multiple characters: the *New York Times* called the actress "the ultimate impressionist; she does people's souls." *Fires in the Mirror* depicted reactions to an incident which began when a black child was killed in a car accident, triggering the murder of a Jewish rabbinical student by an angry black mob.

In her next critically acclaimed but equally controversial play, *Twilight: Los Angeles 1992* (1994), Smith played 40 characters—rich and poor, men and women, blacks and white, Korean and Latino—based again on verbatim interviews. She "became" the characters through her use of body language and voice modulation. "I believe that character lives in how a person speaks as well as in what they say, and in the inability to speak as well as in moments of fluid articulation," explained the soft-spoken performer. *Twilight,* which was staged on Broadway in New York and in Los Angeles and received two Tony Award nominations, examined civil unrest in Los Angeles following the 1992 Rodney King verdict in Los Angeles; King, an African American, was videotaped being beaten by four white police officers who were initially acquitted. "The purpose of the work is to create a dialogue and to use the ambiance and techniques of the theater to inspire discussion about the events of our time," Smith wrote in "The Shades of Loss," a statement about her work. "I tell stories and give examples and let [the audience] make up their mind. . . . What I want people to ask is, 'What can I do?'"

For the 35th anniversary season of the Alvin Ailey American Dance Theater, Smith collaborated in 1994 with Judith Jamison on a ballet entitled *Hymn,* which premiered in New York. In 1996, the MacArthur Foundation awarded her a fellowship, saying Smith had created a new form of theater—"a blend of theatrical act, social commentary, journalism and intimate reverie." A year later, Harvard University named Smith director of its new Institute on the Arts and Civic Dialogue, an annual summer program whose goal is to explore ways in which the arts can enhance public discussion of vital social issues.

House Arrest: Fire Edition, by Smith, premiered in Washington, D.C., in 1998. Characterizing our national identity as embodied by the American presidency, both past and present, the play features a multiracial, multicultural cast and is, again, based on interviews by a playwright who, according to the notable black scholar Henry Louis Gates, Jr., "invented an art form, one that she has perfected."

Anna Deavere Smith has taught at Carnegie-Mellon, Yale, and Stanford universities and has appeared in several Hollywood films, including *Philadelphia* and *The American President,* as well as on the popular television series *The West Wing*. In 2005 she was a guest at Oprah Winfrey's Legends Ball, honoring a select group of extraordinary African-American women. A year later she was chosen as an Alphonse Fletcher Senior Fellow for "work that contributes to the improvement of race relations in American society."

Turning to another genre, Smith offers her advice as a seasoned playwright in *Letters to a Young Artist* (2006). Two key qualities of an artist, she writes, are presence and inquisitiveness. "Being an artist of any kind—whether you're just a guardian of the human spirit or whether you're trying to create art that is meaningful in the world—is about being insatiably curious," contends Smith, whom *Newsweek* called "the most exciting individual in American theater."

Further Reading

Fucillo, Rita Angella, ed. *Playbill* (November 1996). Boston: Northeast Playbill Inc., 1996.

Smith, Anna Deavere. *Fires in the Mirror: Crown Heights, Brooklyn, and Other Identities.* New York: Anchor Books, 1993.

———. *Letters to a Young Artist: Straight-Up Advice on Making a Life in the Arts—For Actors, Performers, Writers, and Artists of Every Kind.* New York: Anchor Books, 2006.

———. *Twilight: Los Angeles, 1992.* New York: Anchor Books, 1994.

∾ Smith, Rosamond

See OATES, JOYCE CAROL

∾ Sontag, Susan

(1933–2004)   *essayist, critic, novelist, screenwriter*

A major cultural critic of the American modernist movement, Susan Sontag was a prolific, versatile, and controversial writer, a fearlessly independent thinker, and a self-described intellectual generalist.

Born on January 16, 1933, in New York City, Susan Sontag spent her early childhood living with

Writer and intellectual Susan Sontag poses in her apartment in New York City.
(AP/Wide World Photos)

her grandparents while her parents, fur exporters, resided in China. After her father's death in 1938, her mother returned to America and took her two daughters to Arizona, in part because of Susan's severe asthma. After her mother's remarriage to Nathan Sontag in 1946, they moved to Los Angeles, California.

Susan was a solitary, studious, and precocious child, who at an early age was attracted to European writers and culture. She later described feeling like "the resident alien" in a "facsimile of family life." While attending North Hollywood High School, she read a copy of *Partisan Review*, which would publish her celebrated essay "Notes on Camp" in 1964, and became "literature-intoxicated." She graduated from high school at age 15 and received a bachelor's degree in philosophy from the University of Chicago when she was 18, a year after marrying Philip Reiff, a sociologist; in 1952, the couple had a son, David. Sontag earned double master's degrees from Harvard University, in English and philosophy.

After further studies at Oxford University and the University of Paris, and divorcing Reiff in 1958, Sontag moved back to New York, where she worked briefly as a contributing editor at *Commentary*, a popular intellectual magazine. She became an established freelance writer, publishing 26 essays between 1962 and 1965, and teaching philosophy and English at several colleges and universities. *The Benefactor* (1963), her first novel, which was experimental and picaresque in form, recounted the story of a European man who looks back on his life and cannot separate his surrealistic dreams from reality. It was well received, although some reviewers found the author's style too dense.

Sontag earned her reputation as a champion of popular culture and the avant-garde with the publication of her first collection of essays, or "case-studies for an aesthetic," as she preferred to call them, *Against Interpretation, and Other Essays* (1966). Boldly advocating a "new sensibility," she introduced Americans to important European writers and intellectuals and suggested the importance of form over content, and experience over meaning. Topics in the critically acclaimed volume ranged from "The Anthropologist as Hero" to "Happenings: An Art of Radical Juxtaposition."

Sontag published a second novel, *Death Kit* (1967), followed by *Trip to Hanoi* (1968), an autobiographical essay based on her visit to North Vietnam, in which she examined the interrelationship between politics and art. In *Styles of Radical Will* (1969), another eclectic volume of essays, Sontag argued for the inclusion of pornography as a literary genre, earning her the label "the Dark Lady of the Intellectuals."

Again demonstrating impressive artistic versatility, Sontag wrote and directed three experimental films: *Duet for Cannibals* (1969) and *Brother Carl* (1971), both of which were filmed in Sweden,

and *Promised Lands,* a documentary about Israel's Yom Kippur War. (Although Jewish, Sontag was raised in an assimilated, secular household.)

In 1973, she published a landmark essay, "The Third World of Women," in *Partisan Review,* in which she staunchly defended feminism, even though many feminists disagreed with her stance on pornography and her political conservatism in certain areas. After battling breast cancer and seeking treatment in France, Sontag produced a best-selling collection of essays, *On Photography* (1977), which analyzed photography, including its predatory nature, and the ways in which it has affected our way of looking at the world. It won a National Book Critics Circle Award. *Illness as Metaphor* (1978) was an attempt to demystify disease and was based on sources that ranged from Greek and medieval writings to the work of Leon Trotsky. Sontag denounced blaming and punishing victims of cancer for having caused their own illness.

In 1978, Sontag also published a collection of semiautobiographical short stories, *I, etcetera* (1978). Her stories appeared in prominent magazines such as the *Atlantic Monthly* and the *New Yorker.* Her next collection of essays, *Under the Sign of Saturn* (1980), included articles on two famous German filmmakers; analyses of her mentors, writers Walter Benjamin and Antonin Artaud; and a rejection of her earlier view that style is more important than content.

Sontag became involved in a dispute with left-wing intellectuals in 1982 when the normally private writer, who had earlier traveled to Hanoi to protest America's involvement in the Vietnam War, spoke publicly against communism at a rally in support of the Solidarity labor movement in Poland. She infuriated the crowd of New York writers by claiming that communism was nothing more than "successful fascism, if you will." An independent thinker, Sontag once commented that she did not like party lines [because] "they make for intellectual monotony and bad prose."

In 1985 Sontag switched gears and directed Milan Kundera's play *Jacques and His Master.* She then returned to the essay form with another best-selling collection, *AIDS and Its Metaphor* (1989). After receiving a five-year fellowship from the MacArthur Foundation, one of numerous grants, fellowships, honorary doctorates, and awards she has garnered, Sontag wrote a play, *Alice in Bed,* that was staged in Germany in 1991. A year later she published her most critically acclaimed novel, *The Volcano Lover: A Romance* (1992), an engaging retelling of a scandalous late-18th-century love affair between Admiral Lord Nelson and Emma Hamilton, the wife of Sir William Hamilton.

In 1993 Sontag traveled to war-besieged Bosnia to direct a production of Samuel Beckett's *Waiting for Godot* in Sarajevo. "I don't want to be a tourist here," she explained. "I want to give something, to contribute." In 1999 she wrote another historical novel, *In America.* The complex portrait of America on the cusp of modernity won the 2000 National Book Award for Fiction but resulted in accusations of plagiarism, which Sontag denied. Her last non-fiction work, *Regarding the Pain of Others* (2002), was another influential collection of essays on the importance of imagery, especially in terms of how war and devastation are viewed and perceived.

Sontag's books have been translated into 32 languages. She received the 2001 Jerusalem Prize, the 2003 Prince of Asturias Prize for Literature, and the 2003 Peace Prize of the German Book Trade. She once said that all her work says the same thing: "Be serious, be passionate, wake up." Sontag shared a 15-year intimate relationship with photographer Annie Leibovitz, who included a series of striking, evocative pictures of Sontag, some chronicling her illness, in *A Photographer's Life* (2006).

Film critic, filmmaker, movie lover (at the end of her life, even though she was very ill, Sontag went to the movies almost every day), essayist, novelist, playwright, and the "Dark Lady" of American intellectual life for over four decades, Sontag died of cancer at age 71 in New York City on December 28, 2004.

Susan Sontag, who remained committed to "high" and "low" culture and criticism, has been lauded and vilified by her peers, who have either praised her as a brilliant contemporary American

literary figure and critic or debunked her as a trendy pop icon. In "One Culture and the New Sensibility," an essay in *Against Interpretation,* Sontag answered her detractors: "What we are getting is not the demise of art, but a transformation of the function of art."

Further Reading

Bernstein, Richard. "Susan Sontag, as Image and as Herself." *New York Times,* January 26, 1989, p. C17.

Rollyson, Carl, and Lisa Paddock. *Susan Sontag: The Making of an Icon.* New York: W. W. Norton, 2000.

Sayres, Sohnya. *Susan Sontag: The Elegiac Modernist.* New York: Routledge, 1990.

Sontag, Susan. *At the Same Time: Essays and Speeches.* With a foreword by David Rieff. New York: Farrar, Straus and Giroux, 2007.

———. *Illness as Metaphor* and *AIDS and Its Metaphors.* New York: Doubleday, 1990.

———. *Regarding the Pain of Others.* New York: Farrar, Straus and Giroux, 2002.

———. *A Susan Sontag Reader.* With an introduction by Elizabeth Hardwick. New York: Farrar, Straus and Giroux, 1982.

∾ Stafford, Jean
(1915–1979)   *short story writer, novelist*

Although she was a successful novelist early in her career, Jean Stafford's literary reputation rests primarily on her finely crafted short stories, of which she published more than 40. She won the 1955 O. Henry Prize for what is probably her best-known short story, "In the Zoo"; *The Collected Stories of Jean Stafford* (1969) earned her the 1970 Pulitzer Prize in fiction.

Jean Stafford was born in Corvina, California, on July 1, 1915, the youngest of four children. Her father, an unsuccessful writer of pulp Western fiction who lost the wealth he had inherited when Jean was a young girl, uprooted the family to Boulder, Colorado. Very shy, pretty, witty, and smart, Jean attended the University of Colorado on a scholarship, graduating with both bachelor and master's degrees in 1936, less than a year after her closest friend at college committed suicide in her presence, an event that haunted Stafford for the rest of her life.

Between 1937 and 1940, Stafford studied in Germany on a fellowship, taught at Stephens College in Columbia, Missouri, and enrolled briefly in a doctoral program at the University of Iowa, before deciding she "hated academia." In 1940, she married the poet Robert Lowell, one of the prominent Boston Lowells. Their tumultuous marriage lasted until 1948, during which time Stafford established herself as a writer. Lowell, meanwhile, won a Pulitzer Prize in 1947 for *Lord's Weary Castle,* a collection of poems he dedicated to his wife. Stafford's second marriage, to a *Life* magazine writer, Oliver Jensen, ended after three years. A third marriage, to A. J. Liebling, a columnist for the *New Yorker* magazine, lasted from 1959 until Liebling's death in 1963. Their relationship, although not without its problems, at least provided Stafford with some degree of happiness, although she was plagued by worsening physical and mental health problems and by alcoholism.

In 1944, she published her first novel, *Boston Adventure,* the story of a lonely young immigrant who attempts to escape her dreary life by working for a wealthy Bostonian. It was a critically acclaimed best seller. *The Mountain Lion* (1947), set in Colorado, chronicles the lives of a brother and sister alienated from their surroundings; it is loosely based on the painful adolescent experiences shared by Stafford and her brother. Although it did not sell well, many critics considered it her best work. Her third novel, *The Catherine Wheel* (1952), also deals with a protagonist who feels alienated, in this case a moribund middle-aged woman who cares for a 12-year-old boy.

Stafford's short stories, which have been praised for their stylistic brilliance, were published in numerous well-regarded magazines and periodicals, including the *New Yorker, Harper's Bazaar,* and *Sewanee Review.* Influenced by the fiction of Anton Chekov, Henry James, and Mark Twain, Stafford's stories were traditional in form and carefully and precisely crafted. They rarely needed editing, which was important to Stafford, who once

observed, "Overediting is a mistake. They say Dickens needed an editor; if he had had one, he wouldn't have existed."

Stafford often wrote about alienated or marginalized adolescents, mostly female but also male protagonists, such as in a short story about an orphaned American Indian boy who arrives at an orphanage in Oklahoma during an epidemic. She created a world that a *New York Times* critic once described as "bleakly inhibited . . . into which sunlight and fresh air seldom penetrate." None of her short fiction portrayed that world better than "In the Zoo," which appeared in the *New Yorker* in 1953. In it, two elderly sisters who, meeting at a zoo where they observed a blind polar bear, recall their painful childhoods living in a foster home. One of the two sisters proclaims that life is "essentially a matter of being done in, let down, and swindled." Stafford specifically rejected being labeled a woman writer, preferring to focus on universal themes such as loneliness and disappointment.

Mary Ann Wilson, a professor of English at the University of Louisiana, in a scholarly essay on Stafford published in 2000, asserts that during her distinguished career, Stafford produced a small but brilliant canon of short stories whose settings and themes echo her geographical rootlessness.

> Stylistically, she alternates between the colloquial, folksy diction of Mark Twain and the elegant, refined prose of Henry James, often mixing the two for comic effect. . . . Irony abounds in her tales of lost loves, shattered dreams, and missed opportunities, and this characteristic detached authorial stance gives the author the distance and objectivity she advised young writers to adopt.

By the 1960s, Jean Stafford's most productive years were behind her. She did not complete a novel after 1952 and had written her best story a decade or more before she won her Pulitzer Prize in 1970. Stafford, whose short fiction has enjoyed something of a resurgence since the mid-1980s, died of cardiac arrest on March 26, 1979, in White Plains, New York. Her body was cremated and her ashes placed next to A. J. Liebling's grave. To the astonishment of friends, Stafford left almost her entire estate to Josephine Monsell, her housekeeper.

Further Reading

Roberts, David. *Jean Stafford: A Biography.* Boston: Little, Brown, 1988.

Stafford, Jean. *The Collected Stories of Jean Stafford.* New York: Farrar, Straus and Giroux, 1969.

———. *The Mountain Lion.* New York: Harcourt, Brace, 1947.

Wilson, Mary Ann. *Jean Stafford: A Study of the Short Fiction.* New York: Twayne, 1996.

———. "Jean Stafford." In *The Columbia Companion to the Twentieth-Century Short Story,* edited by Blanche H. Gelfant, 515–519. New York: Columbia University Press, 2000.

Yardley, Jonathan. "A Diamond in a Rough Life." *Washington Post,* 12 February 2007, p. C01.

Steel, Danielle (Danielle Fernande Dominique Schuelein-Steel)
(1947–) *novelist*

One of the most popular authors in the history of America, as of 2007 Danielle Steel has sold more than 560 million copies of her books worldwide. According to the *Guinness Book of World Records,* one or more of her books have been on the *New York Times* hardcover and paperback best seller list for more than 390 consecutive weeks, and 21 of her novels have been adapted as films for television.

Born Danielle Fernande Dominique Schuelein-Steel on August 14, 1947, in New York City, Danielle Steel came from a self-proclaimed dysfunctional family. Her father, a German-Jewish immigrant, and her mother, who came from a Portuguese-American background, were divorced when Danielle was seven. She lived with her father, who traveled extensively and was "fun but not fatherly. . . . I had a very adult childhood," she recalled, "attending formal social functions and dinner parties with my parents." Lonely and isolated, she turned to writing stories and by her late teens was writing poetry to offset these feelings. Studious and serious, she graduated early, at age 15, from Manhattan's exclusive Lycée Francais de

New York. She hoped to pursue a career in fashion by studying at Parsons School of Design but had to undergo surgery when she was 16 to have an ovary removed. This was in addition to coping with a stomach ulcer and hepatitis. She left Parsons and in 1963 enrolled at New York University, studying French and Italian.

Two years later, soon after turning 18, Steel married Claude-Eric Lazard, a wealthy French banker eight years her senior whom she had dated throughout her adolescence. She dropped out of New York University four months shy of graduating and gave birth to a daughter. Although Steel enjoyed motherhood and was employed by a pioneering small public relations firm, where she did well, she felt that something was missing in her life: She converted from Roman Catholicism and became a Christian Scientist. And she took the advice of one of her clients, who recognized her talent as a writer, and hired a literary agent.

By the time she was 20 years old, she was separated from her husband, commuting between New York City and San Francisco (her two favorite American cities), and had completed her first novel, *Going Home,* in San Francisco, which took her three months to write. It was published in 1973. She also published poems and articles in women's magazines such as *Cosmopolitan* and *Ladies' Home Journal.* After deciding to settle in San Francisco, Steel met and married a convicted felon while he was in jail, but she ended the relationship two years later. The day after her divorce was finalized, she remarried, this time to a recovering heroin addict who had a prison record. She was married a total of five times. Her family would expand to include nine children—her own, stepchildren, and foster children. "I didn't delegate raising the children to the [hired help]," she said in *Family Circle* magazine. She also said that her children were what mattered most to her in life.

Steel worked as a copywriter for an advertising company and supplemented her income by teaching creative writing at a high school in San Francisco. In her spare time she continued to write fiction. Her second manuscript was rejected, as were her next four books and a screenplay. But *The Promise,* published in 1978, became a paperback best seller by 1979, and Steel was offered a contract to write three more books. Her career as a novelist began to take off. Steel has written all of her books on a 1946 Olympia manual typewriter, the same one she uses today. She sometimes works close to 20 hours per day when completing a first draft, ending up with swollen hands and bruised fingers, and she often works on several books at the same time—researching one, writing another, and editing the third. The "Queen of Romance Novels," as she has been dubbed, Steel places her characters—usually glamorous, powerful, professional, but romantic heroines—in contemporary or meticulously researched historical settings. Steel spends two to three years researching and developing a project and then writes at a furious pace.

In addition to her novels, she has published the Max and Martha series of storybooks for young readers, which she wrote originally to comfort her own young children as they struggled emotionally with difficult issues. Another juvenile series about real-life situations followed, with titles such as *Freddie's First Night Away* and *Freddie's Accident* (both 1991). In addition, many of her novels have been adapted into critically acclaimed television movies, including the miniseries *Jewels,* which aired in 1992 and earned two Golden Globe nominations.

Steel is also the author of a volume of poetry and two nonfiction books, *Having a Baby* and *His Bright Light.* In 1994, after an unauthorized biography about Steel by two *People* magazine staff writers was released, previously unknown details about the author's turbulent personal life were revealed. Suddenly her readership knew about her troubled marriages and the death of her 19-year-old son, Nicholas Traina. Steel responded by penning a memoir, *His Bright Light* (1998), a candid account of Nick's desperate attempt to deal with a lifelong bipolar disorder and his tragic death by suicide. *His Bright Light* became a best-selling title on the *New York Times* nonfiction list. Meanwhile, Steel's fiction continued to dominate the *New York Times,* the *Wall Street Journal,* and comparable best seller lists around the world. In 2005 *Toxic Bachelors* and *Miracle* both became best sellers, as have all of her novels.

In 2002 Steel was decorated by the French government (she has a residence in France and spends a part of each year there with her family) as a "Chevalier" of the distinguished Order of Arts and Letters for her lifetime contribution to world culture. She was awarded the second-highest rank of the order. A year later she opened an art gallery in San Francisco, where she lives, in order to promote the paintings and sculptures of emerging artists. She runs two foundations, one named in honor of her late son, The Nick Traina Foundation, which funds organizations dealing with mental illness. The other nonprofit organization assists the homeless. Steel has won numerous awards for her personal work with mentally ill adolescents and children. She also served as the national chairperson for the American Library Association.

Steel's books, which tackle universal themes such as illness, self-discovery, midlife crises, love, and the ways characters handle and are transformed by these life-changing experiences, have been translated into 28 languages and are available in 47 countries. Although literary critics often disparage her body of work as being too predictable and melodramatic, she remains one of the most popular authors writing today. Danielle Steel continues to write two or three novels a year, including *Coming Out* and *The House,* both published in 2006. The latter is her 66th book, in which the restoration of an old mansion provides the backdrop of a "typical Steel fairy tale," as *Booklist* describes it. In 2007 Steel published another best seller titled *Sisters.* In fact, according to her Web site, every book Steel has written has become a best seller. A believer in happy endings, Danielle Steel contends that "if you see the magic in a fairytale, you can face the future."

Further Reading

Bane, Vickie L., and Lorenzo Benet. *The Lives of Daniel Steel: The Unauthorized Biography of America's #1 Best-Selling Author.* New York: St. Martin's Press, 1994.

"Danielle Steel." who2: Encyclopedia of Famous People. Available online. URL: http://www.who2.com/daniellesteel.html. Downloaded on January 24, 2007.

Steel, Danielle. *His Bright Light*. New York: Delacorte Press, 1998.

———. *The House*. New York: Delacorte Press, 2006.

———. *Martha's New Daddy*. New York: Delacorte Book for Young Readers, 1989.

———. *Sisters*. New York: Delacorte Press, 2007.

Stein, Gertrude
(1874–1946) *novelist, playwright, memoirist*

One of America's best-known and least understood modernist writers, Gertrude Stein wrote 40 books in several genres, most of them highly experimental; among them is a best-selling memoir, *The Autobiography of Alice B. Toklas*. While living in Paris, she discovered, influenced, and supported avant-garde writers and artists, many of whom became much more famous than Stein.

The youngest child in a large, middle-class, German-Jewish immigrant family, Gertrude Stein was born on February 13, 1874, in Allegheny, Pennsylvania. Her father, a cold, domineering man, moved his family to Vienna and Paris before settling them in Oakland, California, a city about which Stein famously remarked, "There is no there there." Precocious Gertrude frequented the public library and discussed literature, philosophy, and art with her brother Leo, who became her mentor and closest friend.

After Stein's parents died, during her adolescence, her eldest brother, Michael, became the breadwinner and provided his siblings with a permanent income. Stein lived briefly with an aunt in Baltimore, Maryland, before attending the Harvard Annex, the precursor to Radcliffe College. She graduated magna cum laude in philosophy in 1897, having studied with and been influenced by the noted psychologist William James.

She went on to study neurology and the controversial new "women's medicine" (obstetrics) at Johns Hopkins Medical School. But after a disappointing relationship with a female student (she described the failed lesbian love affair in *Things as They Are*, a story published posthumously in 1950), and having lost interest in medicine, she dropped out of school.

In 1903 Stein moved to Paris to join her brother Leo, who had become a painter, and lived with him at 27 rue de Fleuris. Their Montparnasse apartment became a gathering place for avant-garde painters. Under Leo's tutelage, Stein learned about modern art and how to collect it. She befriended such unknown young artists as Pablo Picasso and Henri Matisse, and acquired their works when no one else was taking them seriously.

During the 1920s, Stein's Saturday salon also attracted a group of fledgling American writers such as F. Scott Fitzgerald and Ernest Hemingway, whose writing style and language Stein influenced. She called the young expatriates the "Lost Generation," because they seemed aimless and rootless. Stein, an imposing figure who said she preferred to look and be treated like a man, and who always dressed in black, often sat surrounded by and conversing with a veritable Who's Who of visitors, including Thornton Wilder, Richard Wright, Jean Cocteau, and Edith Sitwell.

Gertrude Stein was an influential modernist writer and patron of the arts.
(AP/Wide World Photos)

In 1907, Alice B. Toklas, an aspiring writer and musician from California, arrived in Paris. Within a short time Toklas became Stein's lifelong lover, personal secretary and business manager, housekeeper, and the undisputed "wife" in their relationship. The couple never attempted to hide their lesbianism and in 1910 were "officially married." In 1913, Leo, who increasingly disliked living as a threesome, Picasso's cubism, and the "Godalmighty rubbish" his sister was writing, moved out of their flat, and after 1920 he never saw or spoke to his sibling again.

The Making of Americans, on which Stein worked from 1906 to 1911, but which was not published until 1925, was a voluminous, fictionalized account of "the progress" of an American family that formed "not so much a history of Americans as a full description and analysis of many human beings, including Gertrude Stein and the reader and all the reader's friends," according to writer KATHERINE ANNE PORTER. *Three Lives* (1909), which many critics consider her best work, was a collection of three short stories about lower-class women who, like Stein, were alienated from mainstream society. Stein claimed the book, with its repetitious use of syntax, was influenced by post-impressionist painting and was "the first definite step away from the nineteenth and into the twentieth Century in literature."

With each new publication, whether poetry or prose, Stein attempted to create a "continuous present" through repetition and disjointed idioms. However, as one critic pointed out, "the concrete meaning was inaccessible to the reader." Even Stein's publisher had little idea what her books were about. "They always quote it," Stein replied to those who parodied and ridiculed her work. "A sentence has not really any beginning or middle or ending because each part is its part is its part," she explained in *Narration* (1935). An often-quoted example comes from her poem "Sacred Emily": "Rose is a rose is a rose is a rose."

Tender Buttons: Objects, Food, Rooms (1914), was comprised of prose poems that combined descriptions of elements, such as food, with medi-

tative musings. Stein considered these "verbal collages" similar to what her friends Pablo Picasso and Georges Braque were attempting to create visually with cubism. As Linda Simon explained in *Jewish Women in America,* Stein attempted in this and other later works to "revitalize language by stripping words of their historical and cultural connotations," in the same way the cubists did on their canvases.

From 1916 to 1919, Stein and Toklas served as volunteers with the American Friends of the French Wounded, delivering hospital supplies in a remodeled Ford truck. Stein then tried her hand at an operatic libretto, *Four Saints in Three Acts* (1927), which was set to music by her friend Virgil Thomson; it boasted an all-black cast, the first opera production ever to do so. In spite of repetitious lyrics and a purposefully monotonous, monotonal musical score, it contained the memorable line, "Pigeons on the grass alas." Stein once explained that she disliked punctuation because it interfered with what was "going on."

Stein wrote a stylistically accessible but irreverent memoir titled *The Autobiography of Alice B. Toklas* (1933) that in fact was not an autobiography, but rather was written by Stein from Toklas's point of view. It quickly emerged as a best seller. Stein, suddenly popular, returned to America for a well-publicized lecture tour. But she was disappointed that her first, and only, major literary success was for what she regarded as her least hermetic work. Nonetheless, in 1999, the Modern Library declared it as one of the top 100 best nonfiction books written in English during the 20th century. She proceeded to write books of criticism; a second volume of memoirs, *Everybody's Autobiography* (1937); a widely praised study of Picasso; a book for children; and an homage to her adopted city, *Paris, France* (1940).

During World War II, Stein and Toklas, who were both Jewish, left Paris and moved to the French countryside. Villagers with ties to the pro-German Vichy regime nonetheless shielded them from the Nazis. Although she claimed that politics were irrelevant, and that she was proud of her heritage, Stein was accused of having been a collaborator; she had openly defended Marshal Henri Pétain, premier of France's Vichy government from 1940 to 1944, whom she compared to George Washington, and she never spoke out against the persecution of Jews. After the war, the couple returned to Paris, where Stein published a third book of memoirs, *Wars I Have Seen* (1945). Shortly before her death, she completed an opera based loosely on the life of Susan B. Anthony, *The Mother of Us All* (1947), again set to music by Virgil Thomson.

Gertrude Stein, who according to the *New Yorker* was "the first true voice of modern literature," died on July 27, 1946, in an American hospital in Paris. Dana Cairns Watson, in her study *Gertrude Stein and the Essence of What Happens* (2004), points out that Stein recognized both the repressive quality of conventional order, as demonstrated by and carried in language, and the fact that individual free will can exist in language and thereby enable social change. "In the play of literary aesthetics," writes Watson, "Stein saw a liberating force."

Both hailed as the "Mama of Dada" and derided as the "Mother Goose of Montparnasse," Stein, a self-declared genius, will be remembered mostly for nurturing the genius in several internationally recognized artists and writers. On her deathbed, Stein was said to have asked, "What is the answer?" When Toklas, who would convert to Catholicism, write a cookbook, and die in poverty 21 years later, did not reply, Stein continued, "In that case, what is the question?"

Further Reading

Hoffman, Michael J., ed. *Critical Essays on Gertrude Stein.* Boston: G. K. Hall, 1986.

Malcolm, Janet. "Strangers in Paradise—Stein and Toklas." *New Yorker,* 13 November 2006, pp. 54–61.

Pierpoint, Claudia Roth. "Gertrude Stein: The Mother of Confusion." In *Passionate Minds: Women Rewriting the World,* 33–50. New York: Knopf, 2000.

Stein, Gertrude. *The Autobiography of Alice B. Toklas.* New York: Harcourt, 1933.

———. *Writings 1903–1932; Writings 1932–1946,* two vols. Edited by Catherine R. Stimpson and Harriet Chessman. New York: Library of America, 1998.

Wagner-Martin, Linda. *Favored Strangers: Gertrude Stein and Her Family.* New Brunswick, N.J.: Rutgers University Press, 1995.

Watson, Dana Cairns. *Gertrude Stein and the Essence of What Happens.* Nashville, Tenn.: Vanderbilt University Press, 2004.

Stowe, Harriet Elizabeth Beecher
(1811–1896) *novelist*

Abraham Lincoln supposedly described Harriet Beecher Stowe as "the little lady who made the big war," referring to her momentous antislavery novel, *Uncle Tom's Cabin* (1852), the nation's first best seller and one of the most influential books of the 19th century.

Born in Litchfield, Connecticut, on June 14, 1811, Harriet Elizabeth Beecher was one of nine children. Her father, a respected Congregational minister, constantly emphasized the importance of sin and salvation; life was rather grim for the Beechers. When Harriet was five, her sweet, intelligent mother died of tuberculosis. She loved but feared her father, who provided her with a strict Calvinist education and proclaimed her a "genius" when she was eight. He also noted that she was as "odd as she is intelligent and studious." At 13, Harriet attended the Hartford Female Academy founded in 1823 by her sister Catherine Beecher. At 16 she began teaching at the academy. She believed in redemption through Christian benevolence (she disliked Calvinism's rigidity and harshness) and held that women were the spiritual redeemers of men, who by necessity were more involved in the material world.

In 1832, after marrying Harriet Porter, Reverend Beecher moved his family to Cincinnati, Ohio, where he served as president of Lane Theological Seminary. Harriet Beecher listened to the young seminary students discussing antislavery literature and ideas. Living near the slaveholding state of Kentucky, she met both abolitionist and fugitive slaves, and was horrified by the latter's tales of bondage. Four years later she met and married Calvin Ellis Stowe, a theology teacher at the seminary

Harriet Beecher Stowe wrote the celebrated antislavery novel, *Uncle Tom's Cabin.*
(AP/Wide World Photos)

who was a kind man but poorly paid and, like his wife, prone to bouts of depression.

Stowe began publishing articles and stories in newspapers and magazines, while at the same time raising seven children, who were born between 1836 and 1850. She needed a diversion from what she called the "daily death" of housekeeping chores. But even more important, she had to provide income for her expanding family. In 1843 her first collection of magazine stories, *The Mayflower,* was published.

In 1850 she moved to Brunswick, Maine, where her husband had obtained a position at Bowdoin College. One Sunday, while sitting in a pew at Brunswick's First Parish Church, Stowe claims she had a "tangible vision to her mind:" an image of a white man forcing two slaves to beat to death an elderly black man. She hurried home and, "guided by a divine power," began writing *Uncle Tom's Cabin.* She started with the last chapter of the novel—a compelling description of the brutal death of Tom, the elderly slave, at the hands of his sadistic white master, Simon Legree. She worked on the story day and night, finding the book "much more an intense reality to her than any other earthly thing." Some of her information about slavery came from discussions with female housekeepers in Ohio, whose relatives had been beaten and raped by their slave masters. Having lost an infant son during a cholera epidemic, Stowe said she could identify with "what a poor slave mother may feel when her child is torn from her."

Uncle Tom's Cabin, or Life among the Lowly, which was serialized before it was published as a book in 1852, was the first American novel to portray a black man as the hero. Stowe's goal, she explained, was to create a story that would "make the whole nation feel what an accursed thing slavery is." Although *Uncle Tom's Cabin* was enormously popular, stirring antislavery sentiment and becoming the first American novel to sell more than a million copies, it also incurred acrimony from slavery's supporters and sympathizers, who bitterly condemned the novel and its author.

Stowe, whose book made her an international celebrity, had sold the copyright to *Uncle Tom's Cabin* for $300, enough to buy a silk dress. Nevertheless, she became wealthy from the royalties. In 1852, the Stowes moved to a comfortable home in Andover, Massachusetts, where they remained for 12 years. She angrily answered her critics in *The Key to Uncle Tom's Cabin* (1854), and after a triumphal European trip at the invitation of the Glasgow, Scotland, Antislavery Society, she produced another antislavery novel, *Dred: A Tale of the Dismal Swamp* (1856). It sold well but did not have the dramatic appeal of her first book, and she never again wrote about slavery. In 1862 Stowe had the honor of meeting President Abraham Lincoln, at which time he mentioned the extraordinary influence of *Uncle Tom* on the emancipation movement.

Stowe continued to financially support her husband and several of her children, including an alcoholic son. At the rate of almost one per year, she produced nine novels, including two well-received regional historical novels set in New England—*The Minister's Wooing* (1859) and *The Pearl of Orris Island* (1862); children's fiction; domestic manuals; and collections of short stories, poetry, and essays. In 1863, the Stowes returned to Hartford, Connecticut, not far from where the writer Mark Twain lived, but they were forced to sell their rambling Victorian house to pay mounting debts.

In 1870, Stowe, who had greatly admired the verse of the English poet Lord Byron, wrote a controversial exposé of Byron's sexual infidelities and incest entitled *Lord Byron Vindicated;* women at that time were not supposed to know or write about such subjects. She also wrote sentimental fiction with heroines who saved their "fallen" husbands and sons by providing them with spiritual inspiration. Her last novel, the semiautobiographical *Poganuc People,* appeared in 1878.

After the death of her husband in 1886, Stowe, who increasingly suffered from senility, tended her garden and divided her time between Connecticut and a Florida orange plantation she had purchased. She continued to write an occasional children's story and hymn, as well as an autobiography.

Considered one of the foremost American woman writers and humanitarians of the 19th century, Harriet Beecher Stowe died in Hartford on July 1, 1896, at age 85. Millions of people around the world mourned her passing, and in 1910, she was elected to the Hall of Fame, formerly known as the Hall of Fame for Great Americans—a memorial hall of statues built in 1899 on the Campus of New York University. *Pink and White Tyranny: A Society Novel,* one of Stowe's lesser-known works, originally published in 1871, was reissued in 2004. Reflecting Stowe's concern for social problems, *Pink and White Tyranny* shows off Stowe's considerable talent as a light humorist. Also in 2004 Cindy Weinstein edited a volume of essays on Stowe that provides fresh perspectives on *Uncle Tom's Cabin* as well as on the author's long-lasting impact on the American literary tradition. As the English poet Elizabeth Barrett Browning remarked about Stowe, "She above all women (yes, and men of the age) has moved the world—and *for good.*"

Further Reading

Ammons, Elizabeth, ed. *Critical Essays on Harriet Beecher Stowe.* Boston: G. K. Hall, 1980.

Kohn, Denise, Sarah Meer, and Emily B. Todd, eds. *Harriet Beecher Stowe and European Culture.* Iowa City: University of Iowa Press, 2006.

Rugoff, Milton. *The Beechers: An American Family in the Nineteenth Century.* New York: Harper and Row, 1981.

Stowe, Harriet Beecher. *The Key to Uncle Tom's Cabin.* New York: Arno Press, 1968.

———. *Pink and White Tyranny: A Society Novel.* Rockville, Md.: Wildside Press, 2004.

———. *Uncle Tom's Cabin.* New York: Oxford University Press, 1998.

Weinstein, Cindy, ed. *The Cambridge Companion to Harriet Beecher Stowe.* New York: Cambridge University Press, 2004.

Tan, Amy Ruth
(1952–) *novelist, children's book writer*

Amy Tan has written seven books, including best-selling, critically successful novels—*The Joy Luck Club, The Kitchen God's Wife,* and *The Hundred Secret Senses*—in which she powerfully depicts the cultural differences between the older generation of traditionally raised Chinese women and their modern, Chinese-American daughters.

Amy Ruth Tan was born on February 19, 1952, in Oakland, California, two-and-a-half years after her parents came to America from China. In *Home to Stay: Asian American Women's Fiction,* Tan recalled: "My parents believed strongly in education and good English skills as the stepping stones to success in America. I was led to believe from the age of six that I would grow up to be a neurosurgeon by trade and a concert pianist by hobby."

Instead, Amy preferred reading and writing, and she won her first literary contest when she was eight. After her brother and father died of brain tumors, she moved with her mother from their "diseased house" to Montreux, Switzerland, where she completed high school. Upon returning to California, Tan attended San Jose State University as a scholarship student, receiving a bachelor's degree in 1973. A year later she married Lou DeMattei, a tax attorney, and completed a master's degree in linguistics at San Jose State.

Before becoming a full-time writer, Tan was a language consultant to programs for disabled children in Oakland, the managing editor of *Emergency Room Reports,* and, from 1983 to 1987, a freelance technical writer who worked 90 hours per week. Feeling dissatisfied and exhausted, she quit her job and tried her hand at fiction. Her short stories appeared in such periodicals as the *Atlantic Monthly, Lear's,* and *McCall's.*

In 1987, Tan traveled to China with her husband and mother. "It was," she recalled, "just as my mother said: As soon as my feet touched China, I became Chinese." While there, she met her half sisters, the daughters her mother had been forced to leave behind when she fled to America in 1949.

Tan's first novel, *The Joy Luck Club* (1989), came from discoveries during her "roots" trip to China, oral histories passed on by her mother and other relatives, and her own ambivalence about her Chinese background. Set in the late 1980s, it is the tale of a young woman and her late Chinese mother's three Chinese immigrant friends, members of the Joy Luck mah jong club in San Francisco, who relate their arduous, tragic life stories.

Amy Tan's novels depict traditional Chinese mothers and their Americanized daughters.
(AP/Wide World Photos)

It is also about their Americanized daughters, who are torn between respecting and resenting their old-fashioned mothers. In one of *Joy Luck*'s passages, an elderly Chinese woman describes her first-generation daughter as "[growing] up speaking only English and swallowing more Coca-Cola than sorrow." Writing the book, Tan said in an interview, helped her discover "how very Chinese I was." *The Joy Luck Club,* a best seller and finalist for the National Book and the National Book Critics Circle awards, was adapted as a popular American movie and produced as a play in China in 1993 and in New York City in 1999.

Tan's next novel, *The Kitchen God's Wife* (1991), was based on a series of conversations the author had with her mother, who was concerned that

readers thought *The Joy Luck Club* was a true story about her. Using historical events, it is narrated from a mother's perspective and portrays her harrowing childhood and wartime experiences in China.

Meanwhile, Tan continued to write short fiction and essays. In 1991, one of her essays was selected by writer JOYCE CAROL OATES for inclusion in *Best American Essays.*

Her third novel, *The Hundred Secret Senses* (1995) is set in San Francisco and a remote village in southern China and, unlike her other books, has a supernatural component. The central protagonist, a young American girl named Olivia, is introduced to her adult half sister from China and is subjected to her so-called communication with the secret spirit world of her ancestors. Olivia rudely dismisses her half sister's claims, but 30 years later, during a trip to rural China, she discovers that the "ghost stories" related to her long ago were based on reality. In *The Bonesetter's Daughter* (2001), her next best-selling novel, Tan's concern for "what memory keeps and what it elects to hide is that single source, allowing her characters subtly to illuminate one another's perspectives," writes reviewer Nancy Willard in the *New York Times.* "And what marvelous characters she gives us."

Turning to nonfiction, Tan published *The Opposite of Fate: A Book of Musings* (2003), a collection of the author's favorite previously published essays and articles. In one of the entries, Tan suggests that the best of fiction can "enlarge us by helping us notice small details in life." In another essay, Tan attempts to explain why she writes:

Because I once thought I couldn't, and I now know I can. Because I have qualities in my nature shaped by my past—a secret legacy of suicide, forced marriages, and abandoned children in China; an eclectic upbringing that included no fewer than 15 residences; a distorted view of life shaped by two conflicting religions, the death of my father and brother in a year's time, and the murder of my best friend. These elements and others in my life have combined to make me feel that writing provides the sort of freedom and danger, satisfaction and discomfort, truth and contradiction that I can't find anywhere else in life.

Tan, who has sold more books than any other Asian-American writer, received the Common Wealth Award for Literature in 2005, the same year she published *Saving Fish from Drowning,* a satirical novel about culture clashes, identity, genocide, fate, and war, narrated from beyond the grave. In the book she juxtaposes social comedy with the horrific political situation taking place today in Burma. "Humor and fiction are among the most potent ways to address serious problems," explains Tan. "Comedy is one of the most expedient ways to get people to understand nasty matters." In her most recent project, she is collaborating on an opera based on *The Bonesetter's Daughter,* while she continues to perform, in spite of suffering from sometimes debilitating Lyme disease, in a writers' vintage rock garage band called the Rock Bottom Remainders.

Describing, in *Writers Dreaming,* the process of writing, Tan explained: "I often play music as a way of blocking out the rest of my consciousness, so I can enter into this world and let it go where it wants to go, wherever the characters want to go. It takes me into some surprising places."

Tan, whose work has been translated into 36 languages, has been lauded by *Newsweek* "one of the prime storytellers writing fiction today . . . with a rare power to touch the heart." Amy Tan, who has also written two well-received children's books, *The Moon Lady* (1992), which won the American Library Association's award for best book for young adults, and *The Chinese Siamese Cat* (1994), lives in San Francisco and New York, with her husband and pets.

Further Reading

Bowen, Richard. *Mei Mei, Little Sister: Portraits from a Chinese Orphanage.* With an introduction by Amy Tan. San Francisco: Chronicle Books, 2005.

Epel, Naomi, ed. *Writers Dreaming: Twenty-Six Writers Talk about Their Dreams and the Creative Process.* New York: Vintage, 1993.

Tan, Amy. *The Hundred Secret Senses.* New York: G. P. Putnam's Sons, 1995.

———. *The Joy Luck Club.* New York: G. P. Putnam's Sons, 1989.

———. *The Kitchen God's Wife.* G. P. Putnam's Sons, 1991.

———. *The Opposite of Fate: A Book of Musings.* New York: G. P. Putnam's Sons, 2003.

———. *Saving Fish from Drowning.* New York: G. P. Putnam's Sons, 2005.

Watanabe, Sylvia and Carol Bruchac, eds. *Home to Stay: Asian American Women's Fiction.* Greenfield Center, N.Y.: Greenfield Review Press, 1990.

Tarbell, Ida Minerva
(1857–1944)   *journalist, biographer*

A prominent fixture in the American world of letters for half a century, Ida Tarbell was a well-regarded journalist and biographer. Her expose of the multimillionaire industrialist John D. Rockefeller, *The History of the Standard Oil Company* (1904), was a pioneering work of muckraking journalism, while her biographies, such as *The Life of Abraham Lincoln* (1900), were well-researched popular successes.

Ida Minerva Tarbell was born on November 5, 1857, in Erie County, Pennsylvania. Her father was a carpenter who adapted his skills to become a successful manufacturer of wooden oil tanks after "black gold" was discovered in the region in 1859. Tarbell attended Allegheny College, where she was the only female in the freshman class. She graduated in 1880 with a degree in biology and received a master's degree in 1883. After a brief stint teaching, in 1882 Tarbell began her writing career at *The Chautauquan,* where she worked for eight years, eventually becoming managing editor of the magazine.

Tarbell wanted to broaden her horizons and in 1891 left for Paris, France, to study history. She supported herself by writing articles for American magazines, including the newly-founded *McClure's Magazine,* whose staff she joined after returning to the United States in 1894. Beginning in 1895, Tarbell wrote a series of articles on the life of Abraham Lincoln for *McClure's* that proved to be very popular; the format was based on an earlier series she had written for *McClure's* on the life of Napoleon Bonaparte. Tarbell's articles on Lincoln were published as a two-volume biography in 1900. When Tarbell died 44 years later, it still was considered one of the standard works on the American president. She eventually wrote eight books on various aspects of Lincoln's life and career.

Tarbell's reputation as a muckraking journalist dates from a series of articles that *McClure's* published beginning in November 1902. They were turned into a two-volume book, *The History of the Standard Oil Company,* in 1904. Tarbell's exposure of John D. Rockefeller's predatory business practices, among whose victims had been her father, fed the growing national sentiment against Standard Oil and other trusts that increasingly dominated American economic life and that resulted in the 1911 Supreme Court decision that broke up

Journalist Ida M. Tarbell is pictured here in 1937.
(AP/Wide World Photos)

Rockefeller's behemoth. In later years, however, Tarbell's views changed and she became more pro-business, as demonstrated by her sympathetic 1925 biography of the steel magnate Elbert H. Gary.

After more than a decade, Tarbell left *McClure's* and joined a group of colleagues to purchase *American Magazine,* where she worked until 1915. Deeply upset by World War I, Tarbell actively supported President Woodrow Wilson's unsuccessful attempt to get the United States to join the League of Nations. Her most significant postwar publication was her a well-received autobiography, *All in a Day's Work* (1939).

One of the more controversial aspects of Tarbell's career was her opposition to the women's suffrage movement. Tarbell strongly supported the struggle of poor and working class women to improve their conditions, but she just as strongly advocated traditional roles for middle-class women. Although she never married and her career as a writer was central to her life, she insisted that society was best served by women marrying and having children.

Tarbell, who is best remembered for her classic expose of the oil industry, died of pneumonia on January 6, 1944, in Bridgeport, Connecticut. In 1999, *The History of the Standard Oil Company* was named by New York University's journalism department as one of the top 10 works of journalism in the 20th century.

Shortly before her death, Tarbell was asked by a young history professor, "If you could rewrite *The History of Standard Oil,* what would you change?" "Not one word, young man," she replied firmly, "Not one word." Tarbell continues posthumously to receive honors for her contribution as a leading force in American journalism. On October 7, 2000, she was inducted into the National Women's Hall of Fame in historic Seneca Falls, New York; the Pennsylvania State House declared November 4, 2000, "Ida Tarbell Day" in Pennsylvania; and on September 14, 2002, the United States Postal Service issued a stamp commemorating and recognizing the talents of Tarbell and three other female journalists.

Further Reading

Brady, Kathleen, *Ida Tarbell: Portrait of a Muckracker.* New York: Seaview/Putnam, 1984.

"Ida M. Tarbell." The Tarbell Page at Pelletier Library of Allegheny College, maintained by Helen McCullough. Available online. URL: http://tarbell.allegheny.edu/index.html. Downloaded on January 24, 2007.

Tarbell, Ida M. *All in a Day's Work.* New York: Macmillan, 1939.

———. *The History of the Standard Oil Company.* Edited by David M. Chambers. New York: Harper and Row, 1966.

———. *More Than a Muckracker: Ida Tarbell's Lifetime in Journalism.* Edited and with an introduction by Robert C. Kochersberger, Jr. Knoxville: University of Tennessee Press, 1994.

Teasdale, Sara Trevor
(1884–1933) *poet*

Sara Teasdale, a well-regarded, popular poet in the early 20th century, wrote lyrical, unsophisticated but polished verse about love, nature, and in later years, death. Hailed for its craftsmanship and classical technique, Teasdale's mature verse was less sentimental and more modern than her earlier work.

The unplanned, youngest child of middle-aged parents, Sara Trevor Teasdale was born in St. Louis, Missouri, on August 8, 1884. Shy, sensitive, and frail, she grew up in an affluent Victorian family, where, according to biographer William Drake, she was "a prisoner of good breeding . . . smothered with anxious care and attention to an irrational degree." Sara was educated by tutors until she was nine and then completed her studies at private schools. She was a voracious reader and began writing poetry at an early age, publishing her first poems in 1902 in the *Potter's Wheel,* a magazine which she and a group of her friends produced. In 1905, Teasdale traveled with her mother to Europe. Her favorite country was England, and she would return there frequently.

In 1907, Teasdale's first collection, *Sonnets to Duse and Other Poems,* was published and criti-cally noticed. It included sonnets inspired by her admiration of the actress Eleanora Duse, who Teasdale's friend, poet AMY LOWELL, also paid homage to in her verse. In 1911, she visited New York City and fell in love with it, from its subway system to its bright lights. Her next collection, *Helen of Troy and Other Poems* (1911), contained several poems about New York City landmarks such as Central Park, Union Square, and the Metropolitan Museum, as well as verse featuring classical allusions.

After ending a passionate relationship with the married poet Vachel Lindsay, Teasdale in 1914 married Ernest Filsinger, a foreign trade expert, and dedicated herself to poetry, writing four books in six years. *Rivers to the Sea* appeared in 1915 to favorable reviews and included one of Teasdale's best-known and most anthologized poems, "I Shall Not Care." In 1916, she moved to New York City, permanently. The following year, her burgeoning talent was recognized: *Love Songs* (1917) received the Poetry Society's Award and the Columbia Poetry Prize, the forerunner of the Pulitzer Prize. Praised for its remarkable lyricism and restrained but effective imagery, a critic in the *New York Times Book Review* commented that Teasdale is "first, last, and always a singer."

Dark of the Moon (1926), a collection of autumnal poems that was critically well received, reflected the poet's own sadness, as she coped with an unhappy marriage and the death of friends and family. She was cheered up somewhat in 1926 when she met Margaret Conklin, a college student who became her companion. In 1929 Teasdale was divorced from her husband and two years later learned that Vachel Lindsay, had committed suicide. For the final time she traveled to England, where she visited the favorite places of her mentor, British poet Christina Rossetti, about whom she was writing a biography. Returning home, ill and acutely depressed, at 48 Sara Teasdale committed suicide by taking an overdose of sleeping pills; she died on January 19, 1933.

Despite her Victorian upbringing, Teasdale had attempted to focus on her craft and literary profession; she took her role as a woman and as an artist seriously. The poet LOUISE BOGAN called Teasdale's last, posthumously published book, *Strange Victory* (1933), "the final expression of a purely lyrical talent and a poetic career remarkable for its integrity throughout." *The Collected Poems of Sara Teasdale,* originally published in 1937, has been through 25 reprintings. In 1994 the poet was inducted into the St. Louis Walk of Fame. Dr. David Hades, a professor of English at Washington University, accepted on behalf of Teasdale. One of her biographers, he pointed out, noted that Teasdale spoke for "women emerging from the humility of subservience into the pride of achievement."

Further Reading

Drake, William. *Sara Teasdale: Woman and Poet.* San Francisco: Harper and Row, 1979.

"Poems by Teasdale." Poetry Archive. Available online. URL: http://www.poetry-archive.com/t/teasdale_sara.html. Downloaded on March 7, 2007.

Shoen, Carol B. *Sara Teasdale.* Boston: Twayne, 1986.

Teasdale, Sara. *Collected Poems of Sara Teasdale.* New York: Macmillan. Reissued with an introduction by Marya Zaturenska, 1966.

———. *Mirror of the Heart: Poems by Sara Teasdale.* Edited by William Drake. New York: Macmillan, 1984.

∼ Thompson, Dorothy
(1894–1961) *journalist*

As a correspondent and staff reporter in Europe and the first woman to head a major American news bureau overseas, Dorothy Thompson was a pioneer among American women journalists. In the United States, her syndicated column "On the Record" made her for many years one of the most widely read and respected journalists and commentators on international affairs.

Dorothy Thompson was born on July 9, 1894, in Lancaster, New York, the eldest child of Peter Thompson, a Methodist minister, and Margaret Grierson Thompson, who died when Dorothy was eight. When her father remarried, Dorothy fought with her stepmother and was sent to live with rela-tives in Chicago, Illinois. After graduating from Syracuse University in 1914, Thompson worked for the Woman Suffrage party before sailing in 1920 for Europe, with $150 in her pocket and no journalistic experience, to fulfill her ambition: she planned to become a foreign correspondent.

A series of successful freelance articles won Thompson a position as a staff writer for the *Philadelphia Public Ledger.* In 1924, she was appointed bureau chief in Berlin, Germany, for the *Ledger* and the *New York Evening Post;* both publications were owned by the newspaper magnate Cyrus H. K. Curtis. Meanwhile, Thompson had married Hungarian writer Josef Bard, who she subsequently divorced in 1927. A year later she published her first book, *The New Russia,* a collection of her newspaper articles, and married Sinclair Lewis, who in 1930 became the first American writer to win the Nobel Prize in literature. The marriage produced a son, Michael, before ending in divorce in 1942 (in large part because of Lewis's alcoholism). A third marriage in 1943 to Czech painter and sculptor Maxim Kopf was more successful and fulfilling, and lasted until Kopf's death in 1958.

Thompson resigned her position with the Curtis newspapers just before she married Lewis, but she continued to work in Europe until the mid-1930s. In late 1931 she interviewed the Nazi Party leader Adolf Hitler, and made one of the worst mistakes of her professional career: she called Hitler, the future dictator of Germany, a man "of startling insignificance." Once Hitler came to power in 1933, Thompson became an unrelenting clarion warning readers of the threat his regime represented; in 1934 she was expelled from Germany on Hitler's orders. After returning to America, Thompson continued her campaign against the Nazis in "On the Record," which by 1936 was appearing three times a week in the *New York Herald Tribune.* In addition, Thompson denounced the Munich agreement (in which Britain and France caved in to Hitler's demands to dismantle Czechoslovakia), savaging British Prime Minister Neville Chamberlain for exercising "responsibility without reasoning" and comparing him to the naive character Alice in *Alice in Wonderland.*

When World War II broke out in 1939, Thompson braved America's isolationist sentiment and strongly urged intervention on behalf of the Allies. By then her column was running in more than 170 newspapers with 8 million readers, while a monthly article she wrote for *Ladies'Home Journal* magazine reached 3 million readers, and her radio broadcasts for the National Broadcasting Company (NBC) reached 5 million listeners. Thompson was at the height of her career. On June 12, 1939, she was the subject of a *Time* magazine cover story that listed her as the second most influential woman in the United States, after Eleanor Roosevelt.

In 1940 Thompson's support of Franklin Roosevelt caused a break with the *Tribune;* thereafter her flagship outlet became the *New York Post.* However, her influence waned after World War II. She alienated many supporters during the late stages of the war by opposing the Allied policy of unconditional surrender because, she claimed, without creditable evidence, there was extensive anti-Nazi sentiment in Germany. In 1947, the *Post* dropped her column because of her intense opposition to the creation of the state of Israel. Four years later she helped found the pro-Arab American Friends of the Middle East, an organization funded in part by Arabian American Oil Company (ARAMCO), the consortium of American companies producing oil in Saudi Arabia, and, secretly, by the CIA.

After the death of her third husband in 1958, longtime journalist Dorothy Thompson gave up her column, "On the Record," but continued writing for the *Ladies Home Journal.* She died of a heart attack on January 30, 1961, in Lisbon, Portugal. In a *Los Angeles Times* review of Peter Kurth's biography *American Cassandra,* Thompson is referred to as "perhaps the most influential woman journalist of the century." According to the review, the popular movie *Woman of the Year,* starring Katharine Hepburn, was an "explicit satire on Thompson's exploits and notoriety. The fact that Dorothy Thompson is so little remembered today

is itself a satire on celebrity, because in the interwar years, she was one of the best known women in America."

Further Reading

Cairns, Kathleen A. *Front-Page Women Journalists, 1920–1950.* Lincoln: University of Nebraska Press, 2003.

Halper, Donna L. *Invisible Stars: A Social History of Women in American Broadcasting.* New York: M. E. Sharpe, 2001.

Kurth, Peter, *American Cassandra: The Life of Dorothy Thompson.* Boston: Little, Brown, 1990.

Thompson, Dorothy. *The Courage to Be Happy.* Boston: Houghton Mifflin, 1957.

———. *Let the Record Speak.* Boston: Houghton Mifflin, 1939.

Widner, James. "Radio Days—Dorothy Thompson." Radio News. Available online. URL: http://www.otr.com/thompson.shtml. Downloaded on March 7, 2007.

Truth, Sojourner (Isabella Hardenbergh Van Wagenen)
(ca. 1797–1883) *autobiographer*

An influential early feminist, abolitionist, and orator, Sojourner Truth is remembered for her life story, *The Narrative of Sojourner Truth* (1850), which she dictated to a neighbor. It is one of America's most illuminating personal accounts about slavery by a female freed slave.

The daughter of Baumfree and Mau-Mau Bett, both slaves, Isabella, or Belle as she was called, was born around 1797, in Hurley, New York. She was owned by Colonel Charles Hardenbergh, of Dutch descent, and, as property, took his last name. After being separated from her parents when she was nine, she worked for four different households. Her second master beat her for speaking Dutch instead of English. Although she was illiterate, Belle was intelligent and quickly memorized what was read aloud to her, including the Bible and newspapers.

In 1810, Belle was purchased by a farmer, John Dumont, and served as his field hand, maid, cook, and wet nurse. She was married off to an older slave, Thomas, for whom she had little affection; she had five children with him, one of whom died in infancy. In 1826, a year before New York State freed its slaves, she escaped from Dumont, who had deceived her, and was protected by a kind antislavery Quaker family, the Van Wagenens. When she learned that Dumont had illegally sold one of her sons into slavery in Alabama, she convinced an attorney to help her file a lawsuit for the return of her child. It would not be the last time that Sojourner Truth would fight for her rights and win.

In 1829, she moved with her family to New York City, where she cleaned houses and became involved with pentecostal evangelists. In 1843, she renamed herself Sojourner Truth, based on her belief that God commanded her to preach the truth about slavery and tolerance. She left New York and moved to Northampton, Massachusetts, where she joined a utopian association and listened to speeches by abolitionists, including William Lloyd Garrison and Frederick Douglass. It was Garrison who persuaded Truth to write about her 30 years in bondage, which she did by dictating her autobiography to a neighbor, Olive Gilbert, who edited the transcript. *The Narrative of Sojourner Truth* (1850) is considered one of America's most important documents about slavery from a woman's point of view.

A popular, effective orator with a commanding presence—she was nearly six feet tall—and a deep, low voice, Truth, dressed piously in simple Quaker attire, traveled across the country, speaking out against slavery and inequality. "Chillun, I talk to God, and God talks to me," she told large crowds, who responded to her mystical illusions, biblical metaphors, and riveting gospel songs. "This unlearned African woman," wrote an observer from Iowa, "had a magnetic power over an audience [that was] perfectly astounding." Truth once commented that although she could not read, she could "read people." She used her speeches to sell copies of the *Narrative,* and after four years was able to pay off the mortgage on her Northampton home.

Truth met and befriended early feminists Lucretia Mott and Elizabeth Cady Stanton. In 1851, she addressed the Women's Rights Convention in Akron, Ohio, where Frances Gage, who was presiding over the convention, recorded Truth's passionate defense of women's rights—her celebrated "A'rn't I a Woman?" speech. However, it is unclear how reliable Gage was in recalling what Truth actually said. The journalistic account that appeared in the *Anti-Slavery Bugle* was much more accurate but less flamboyant than Gage's version, which purported Truth as rhetorically asking:

> Nobody ever helps me into carriages, or over mud puddles or gives me any best place, and ar'n't I a woman? . . . I have borne thirteen children and seen them almost all sold off into slavery, and when I cried out with my mother's grief, none but Jesus heard—and ar'n't I a woman?

In 1857, Truth sold her Northampton property and moved to Battle Creek, Michigan, where she remained until her death. She continued preaching about women's rights and the evils of slavery, and during the Civil War she helped recruit black troops for the Union army and collect contributions for black volunteer regiments. HARRIET BEECHER STOWE, author of the best-selling antislavery novel *Uncle Tom's Cabin,* profiled Truth in the *Atlantic Monthly* in 1863, noting that she could not recall "anyone who had more of that silent and subtle power which we call personal presence."

On October 29, 1864, Truth was invited to meet with President Abraham Lincoln, who praised her for her work assisting freed slaves. In 1867, at the first American Equal Rights Association Convention, she told her audience, "I have done a great deal of work; as much as a man, but did not get so much pay . . . I want women to have their rights." She also warned that newly-freed black women needed their rights, or black men would become "masters over the women, and it will be just as bad as before."

From 1870 to 1874, she worked diligently, with some success, to get the United States Congress to set aside parcels of land in the West for former slaves. "The law is with you; get behind it!", she reminded freed slaves and women. In 1875, the third edition of her slave narrative was published, and included letters to and articles about her.

Sojourner Truth, a legend in her own time, traveled and lectured well into her 80s, until her health deteriorated. She died at home in Battle Creek, on November 26, 1883. Frederick Douglass, himself an escaped slave who campaigned against slavery, had greatly admired Truth and praised her "remarkable independence and courageous self-assertion."

In 1997 a community-wide, yearlong celebration of the 200th anniversary of Truth's birth was held in Battle Creek. It culminated in a conference of eminent scholars in women's studies who led a weeklong symposium on Sojourner Truth. As a follow-up to the bicentennial activities, the Sojourner Truth Institute of Battle Creek was established in 1998 to "expand the historical and biographical knowledge of her life's work and carry on her mission by teaching, demonstrating and promoting projects that accentuate the ideals and principles for which she stood." In November 2005 the Institute sponsored a program that featured talks by several of Truth's descendents and performances of her songs and speeches. The social reformer's words seem as relevant today as when they were first written over a century ago.

Further Reading

Felder, Deborah G. "Sojourner Truth." In *The 100 Most Influential Women of All Time*, 69–72. New York: Carol Publishing, 1996.

Levert, Suzanne. "Sojourner Truth," The Home of the American Civil War. *Encyclopedia of the Civil War*. Available online. URL: http://www.civilwarhome.com/truthbio.htm. Downloaded on January 24, 2007.

Painter, Nell Irvin. *Sojourner Truth*. New York: W. W. Norton, 1996.

"Sojourner Truth." The Sojourner Truth Virtual Institute of Battle Creek. Available online. URL: http://www.sojournertruth.org/Default.htm. Downloaded on January 24, 2007.

Truth, Sojourner, and Olive Gilbert. *Narrative of Sojourner Truth*. Edited and with an introduction by Margaret Washington. New York: Vintage, 1993. (Includes "Ar'n't I a Woman" speech.)

Tsukiyama, Gail
(1957–   )   *novelist, short story writer*

A gifted storyteller, Gail Tsukiyama has written five popular, critically well-received novels that reflect her multicultural upbringing and quietly but powerfully portray the plight of Chinese women. Her writing style is controlled and straightforward but also richly descriptive, especially when she delineates complicated familial relationships. "Writing chose me," Tsukiyama once said. "It came out of the need to learn about my heritage."

Born in San Francisco on September 13, 1957, to a Chinese mother from Hong Kong and a Japanese father from Hawaii, Tsukiyama grew up immersed in several cultures. She started writing, mostly poetry, as a teenager. Initially a film major at San Francisco State University, where she received bachelor's and master's degrees, she realized writing was closer to what she wanted to do than film, so she switched to English, with a concentration in creative writing. Her master's thesis was a volume of poetry, but she was drawn to fiction and began to write short stories.

Tsukiyama then turned to producing a novel. Her debut novel, *Women of the Silk* (1991), became an unexpected best seller, praised by *Library Journal* for its "great sensory detail, allowing the reader to touch, taste, and feel the world Tsukiyama creates." The story, which begins in rural China in 1926 before the rise of communism, revolves around a group of female silk factory workers who forge a sisterhood. The central character, Pei, is sold into the silk trade by her poverty-stricken parents and is forced, like the other women, to work from dawn until dusk, enduring horrific conditions. Courageously, the group forms a workers' union and organizes a strike. By the end of the novel, "the sisterhood had scattered, but she (Pei) would remember it always," writes Tsukiyama, who considers herself an examiner of "early Chinese feminists."

Gail Tsukiyama's popular debut novel, *Women of the Silk,* focused on Chinese female factory workers and their struggles.
(Jerry Bauer)

She presents the challenging lives of Asian women realistically but with dignity and sensitivity.

The Samurai's Garden (1995), Tsukiyama's next novel, is set in the 1930s during the Japanese invasion of China. In the book, which exemplifies the differences between Chinese and Japanese culture, an ailing 20-year-old Chinese artist is cared for by a Japanese housekeeper who is also a "samurai of the soul," a man devoted to doing good and finding beauty in the world. *Night of Many Dreams* (1998), the author's third novel, is a coming-of-age story about two sisters growing up in Hong Kong during World War II and how their strong family bonds sustain them and provide spiritual sustenance. *The Language of Threads,* published in 1999, is a sequel to *Women of the Silk* in that Tsukiyama returns to Pei, the memorable protagonist from the earlier novel, as she begins her life anew and alone in Japanese-occupied Hong Kong. Having carefully researched the "silk sisterhood" that took place in China between 1830 and 1930, Tsukiyama said in an interview that recognizing what these Chinese female workers went through in

order to create lives for themselves and earn their own livings has given her a greater sense of who she is.

In 2000 Tsukiyama was named chair of the fiction panel for the prestigious Kiriyama Pacific Rim book award, having served as a judge for two years previously. She received another honor in 2002 when was she was among only 50 authors chosen by the Library of Congress to participate in the first National Book Festival. In addition, many of her short stories have been anthologized and translated, and she has won an Academy of American Poets Award.

Tsukiyama's novel *Dreaming Water* (2002) portrays a complex mother-daughter relationship after the daughter, Hana, is diagnosed with Werner's syndrome, a disease that makes a person age at twice the rate of a healthy individual. Her mother, Cate, a widow, cares for her daughter while still grieving for her husband, a Japanese-American with his own complex past. In *Dreaming Water* "Tsukiyama creates a bond between Cate and Hana that mothers and daughters will know as almost a physical need, so deeply entwined are they in each other's lives," according to *USA Today.* "They anticipate each other's pain; one will unexpectedly laugh or suddenly cry, and the other one responds in kind. The reader, too, laughs and aches under the spell of such graceful writing."

Gail Tsukiyama, who resides in El Cerrito, California, has taught creative writing at San Francisco State University and is currently book review editor for the online magazine *Pacific Rim Voices.* She also has been a guest speaker on writing at the Hong Kong International Literary Festival, the Vancouver International Writers and Readers Festival, and the Maui Writers Conference. Among her favorite contemporary female authors are LOUISE ERDRICH, ANNIE PROULX, and BARBARA KINGSOLVER. Although in many ways she is as "American as apple pie," as Tsukiyama puts it, "all the Chinese traditions from my mother's side of the family are within me, and have somehow found expression through my books."

Further Reading

Siciliano, Jana. "Author Profile: Gail Tsukiyama." Bookreporter. Available online. URL: http://www.bookreporter. com/authors/au-tsukiyama-gail.asp. Downloaded May 28, 2007.

Tsukiyama, Gail. *Dreaming Water.* New York: St. Martin's Press, 2002.

———. *Women of the Silk.* New York: St. Martin's Press, 1991.

∾ Tuchman, Barbara Wertheim
(1912–1989) *nonfiction writer*

The winner of two Pulitzer Prizes, Barbara Tuchman was a popular historian whose subject matter ranged from the 14th century to the Vietnam War. She was recognized as a master of the art of historical narrative and excelled at writing clearly, compellingly, and gracefully about complex historical events.

Barbara Tuchman was born on January 12, 1912, in New York City, into a life of comfort, privilege, and high culture. Her father, Maurice Wertheim, a successful banker, was also a philanthropist, art collector, prominent Jewish community leader, and owner of the liberal political magazine, the *Nation.* Her mother, Alma Morganthau Wertheim, was the daughter of the noted diplomat Henry Morganthau, who served in the Woodrow Wilson administration, and the sister of Henry Morganthau, Jr., secretary of the treasury under President Franklin D. Roosevelt. Barbara was educated at Radcliffe College, where she studied history and literature. After graduating in 1933, she volunteered with the American Council of the Institute of Foreign Relations, spending a year in Tokyo before becoming a staff writer and foreign correspondent at the *Nation.* While at the magazine, she covered the Spanish civil war, an assignment that generated her first book, *The Lost British Policy: Britain and Spain since 1700* (1938). In 1940, she married Lester R. Tuchman, a physician; the couple had three daughters. During World War II, with her husband serving overseas, Tuchman worked in New York for the Office of War Information.

Tuchman is best known for six of her 11 books, all of which sold well and were critical successes. *The Zimmermann Telegram* (1958), about Germany's World War I attempt to provoke war between the United States and Mexico, was her first best seller. Far more ambitious was the Pulitzer Prize–winning *The Guns of August* (1962), in which she covered the background and beginning of World War I and the origins of the horrendous battlefield stalemate that dominated the Great War. *The Proud Tower: A Portrait of the World before the War, 1890–1914* (1966) examined the long-term social and political factors that led to World War I. *Stilwell and the American Experience in China, 1911–1945* (1971), a biography of the American military officer who served in China for more than three decades, won Tuchman her second Pulitzer Prize. *A Distant Mirror: The Calamitous Fourteenth Century* (1978), chronicled a period ravaged by plagues and wars, which Tuchman likened to the 20th century. And *The March of Folly: From Troy to Vietnam* (1984) was an analysis and comparison of disastrous blunders by political leaders from ancient times through the 1970s.

Reviewers commented on Tuchman's lucid writing style, her ability to tell a story in dramatic and engaging fashion, and her thorough research. At the same time, while Tuchman was indisputably a popular writer, a tension existed between her and traditional academic historians. She maintained that they produced overly detailed and impenetrable tomes that could not hold the attention of a general audience. Historians, she argued, should create an interesting narrative which should have "a beginning, middle, and an end. Plus an element of suspense to keep the reader turning the pages." Academic historians, who often praised certain aspects of her work, such as her ability to make history come alive, criticized what they considered her omissions, misinterpretations, and sweeping theories and generalizations. Reviewing a reissued edition of *Practicing History: Selected Essays,* first published in 1981, Edward James Mills III, in the *International Social Science Review* (2001), wrote that he has always been in awe of Tuchman's "ability to write history and make it readable." In the collection's section titled "The Craft," Mills was struck by the importance she placed on history being readable. This may help explain, said Mills, Tuchman's "enormous popular support and the animus towards her that I have encountered in some academic circles."

Barbara W. Tuchman died of a stroke in Greenwich, Connecticut, on February 6, 1989. At the time of her death, her last book, *The First Salute,* a study that viewed the American Revolution from an international perspective, was enjoying its 17th week on the *New York Times* best seller list. "The unrecorded past is none other than our old friend, the tree in the primeval forest which fell without being heard," Tuchman wrote in 1964 in an essay entitled "Can History Be Served Up Hot?"

Further Reading

Brody, Seymour. "Barbara Wertheim Tuchman." Jewish Virtual Library. Available online. URL: http://www. jewishvirtuallibrary.org/jsource/biography/tuchman. html. Downloaded on March 7, 2007.

Felden, Deborah G. "Barbara Tuchman." In *The 100 Most Influential Women of All Time,* 251–254. New York City: Citadel Press, Carol Publishing, 1996.

Mills, Edward James, III. "A Book Review of Barbara W. Tuchman's *Practicing History." International Social Science Review* (Fall–Winter, 2001).

Tuchman, Barbara. *The Guns of August.* New York: Macmillan, 1962.

———. *The March of Folly: From Troy to Vietnam.* New York: Knopf, 1984.

———. *Practicing History: Selected Essays.* New York: Knopf, 1981.

———. *Stilwell and the American Experience in China, 1911–1945.* New York: Macmillan, 1966.

⤳ Tyler, Anne
(1941–) *novelist, short story writer*

Anne Tyler has published more than 15 novels, including *Breathing Lessons,* which garnered a Pulitzer Prize in 1989. In her fiction, Tyler depicts the lives of ordinary, somewhat eccentric, middle-class Americans, who, as Tyler explains it, "manage to endure."

Although she was born in Minneapolis, Minnesota, on October 25, 1941, and grew up in a Quaker community near Raleigh, North Carolina, Anne Tyler is strongly identified with Baltimore, Maryland, where she has set most of her novels and has lived with her family since 1967. Anne began writing fiction at an early age, and at 16 enrolled at Duke University. She was encouraged to write by one of her professors, the novelist Reynolds Price, who became her mentor. After graduating Phi Beta Kappa in Russian studies, she worked as a Russian bibliographer at Duke's library.

In 1963, she married Taghi Modarressi, an Iranian-born child psychiatrist and writer, and had two daughters. Tyler's goal has remained the same: to write books and raise her children. "I know this makes me seem narrow, but in fact, I *am* narrow. I like routine and rituals and I hate leaving home," she explained in *The Writer on Her Work.* It is not surprising, therefore, that familial themes dominate her fiction.

Tyler has published more than fifty short stories in magazines ranging from *Seventeen* to the *New Yorker,* and is a prominent book reviewer. In 1964, she published her first novel, *If Morning Ever Comes,* which received largely negative reviews. In an interview, Tyler stated that her first two novels "should be burned." During the 1970s, she wrote mostly about characters torn between wanting to belong to, and to escape from, their families. *Celestial Navigation* (1974), Tyler's personal favorite, was praised for its intricate structure, while *Searching for Caleb* (1976), which chronicles three generations of a Baltimore family, was recommended by the fiction writer John Updike. In the *New Yorker* magazine, he compared Tyler to such esteemed Southern writers as Flannery O'Connor, Carson McCullers, and Eudora Welty. Like Welty, whom she greatly admires, Tyler has a keen eye for details and compellingly renders quotidian life in pure, direct language.

Morgan's Passing (1980) won the Janet Heidinger Kafka Prize for fiction and was nominated for an American Book Award. The award-winning, best-selling, tragicomic *Dinner at the Homesick Restaurant* (1982) charts the evolution of the Tulls, two brothers and a sister, who come from an abusive, dysfunctional family and who, before going forward, must face a past that did not include sharing happy family meals together. *The Accidental Tourist* (1985), possibly Tyler's finest novel and winner of a National Book Critics Circle Award, is peopled with quirky but endearing and believable characters. The protagonist, Macon Leary, who has suffered the loss of a son and his marriage, ultimately realizes that one may "choose what to lose." In 1988, it was successfully adapted as an Academy Award–winning movie starring Kathleen Turner, Geena Davis, and William Hurt.

For her portrayal of the strengths and weaknesses of a 28-year marriage in *Breathing Lessons* (1988), Tyler won a Pulitzer Prize in 1989, although some critics felt that this book was not her best work. In *Ladder of Years* (1995), a character who wonders why celery is not called "corduroy plant," which would be "much more colorful." On an impulse, she walks away from her marriage and three children and for a short time takes on a new identity and a new life in a strange town, before returning to her family. *A Patchwork Planet* (1998) is another novel about dislocated outsider, whom the author treats with compassion and understanding.

A Patchwork Planet was followed by *Back When We Were Grownups* (2001), *The Amateur Marriage* (2004), and her 17th novel, *Digging to America* (2006), the story of two families who meet by chance and their increasingly intertwined and improvised lives. In a review of the book for the *Boston Globe,* Gail Caldwell wrote, "Tyler's is a world defined by valiant efforts at connection; that more than a few of them fail is what keeps her out of the realm of sentimentality. She assumes that bad things happen to good people, but what interests her is how the good endures—how it manages to avoid being strong-armed into weary cynicism or snuffed out altogether." Tyler, called by the *New Yorker* (June 2006) "our consummate chronicler of the bewilderments of family life," believes in connections and companionship of all sorts, because everyone has the potential to be interesting. "Most people are not very average and ordinary, if you look carefully enough." We are, Tyler asserts, surrounded by unsung heroes in our everyday lives.

Although Tyler creates female characters who are complex, strong, and intelligent, she has been criticized by some feminists for placing them in traditional roles, and for avoiding sexual and political issues. Biographer Elizabeth Evans points out that Tyler is more interested in endurance and reconciliation than in alienation and isolation. "She wants her fiction to be *readable*—that is, to be understood."

The contemporary novelist GAIL GODWIN noted in the *New York Times Book Review* that Tyler's fiction is filled with displaced persons who persist stubbornly in their own destinies. "She has such a way of transcribing their peculiarities with such loving wholeness that when we examine them we keep finding more and more pieces of ourselves."

Further Reading

Bail, Paul. *Ann Tyler: A Critical Companion.* Westport, Conn.: Greenwood Press, 1998.

Evans, Elizabeth. *Anne Tyler.* New York: Twayne, 1993.

Petry, Alice Hall. *Understanding Anne Tyler.* Columbia: University of South Carolina Press, 1990.

Tyler, Anne. *Anne Tyler: Four Complete Novels* (includes *Dinner at the Homesick Restaurant*). New York: Avenel, 1990.

———. *Anne Tyler: A New Collection* (includes *The Accidental Tourist and Breathing Lessons*). New York: Wings, 1991.

———. *Digging to America.* New York: Knopf, 2006.

———. *A Patchwork Planet.* New York: Knopf, 1998.

Uchida, Yoshiko
(1921–1992) *children's book writer, memoirist, folklorist*

A widely respected and popular author of Japanese-American juvenile fiction and nonfiction, Yoshiko Uchida often wrote about her own childhood experiences. She wanted her books to help Asian-American children become more aware of their history and culture and to understand the "traditions, hopes, and values of the early immigrants."

Born on November 24, 1921, in Alameda, California, to Japanese parents who emigrated to California, Yoshiko was raised in Berkeley, California, where her mother, a poet, encouraged her to read, write, and steep herself in American and Japanese culture. She penned her first book when she was 10. After completing high school, where she longed to be accepted as an American but was excluded from the social activities of her white peers, she enrolled at the University of California at Berkeley. She received a bachelor's degree, cum laude, in 1942, but the diploma was delivered to her at an internment camp.

After Japan bombed the American naval base at Pearl Harbor, causing America to enter World War II, President Franklin D. Roosevelt authorized the imprisonment of 120,000 Americans of Japanese descent of the West Coast. On May 1, 1942, the Uchidas were sent to the Tanforan race-track, an internment camp in San Mateo, California, that housed 8,000 Japanese Americans in its stables and barracks. Uchida taught second graders and was paid $16 a week. Later that year, she and her family were moved to Topaz, a barren, dusty camp located in Utah's desert, where they slept on army cots without mattresses. In her autobiography for young adults, *The Invisible Thread* (1991), she recalled: "The Japanese endured with dignity and grace, and it is that spirit which has made me especially proud of my heritage."

Assisted by the National Japanese Student Relocation Committee, Uchida was released in 1943, having obtained a graduate fellowship at Smith College, where she subsequently received a master's degree in education. While working as a secretary in New York City and teaching at a Quaker elementary school in Pennsylvania, Uchida continued to write short fiction and articles. In 1952–53 she studied in Japan as a Ford Foundation fellow, collecting traditional folktales that she would later incorporate in two of her award-winning children's books, *The Magic Listening Cap* (1955) and *The*

Sea of Gold (1965). Her experience in Japan, she wrote, was as positive and restorative as the uprooting and imprisonment had been negative and depleting. "I wasn't really totally American, and I wasn't totally Japanese. I was a mixture of the two, and it could never be anything else," Uchida once explained.

Noticing a dearth of books about Asian-American children, Uchida wrote her first, well-received juvenile book, *The Dancing Kettle and Other Japanese Folk Tales* (1949, reissued in 1986), a collection of 14 Japanese folktales passed on to Ushida during her childhood that she adapted for American readers. *New Friends for Susan* (1951), *The Full Circle* (1957), *The Promised Year* (1959), and *Rokubei and the Thousand Rice Bowls* (1962) were among her other acclaimed early work, which mostly characterized Japanese children.

In the late 1960s, Uchida began writing about the Japanese-American experience. In 1971, she fictionalized her internment and relocation experiences in *Journey to Topaz: A Story of the Japanese-American Evacuation* and *Journey Home* (1978). *A Jar of Dreams* (1981) was a sensitively wrought depression-era story about two Japanese-American children who are subjected to brutal bigotry. Its sequel, *The Best Bad Thing*, was named an American Library Association Notable Children's Book in 1983. *The Happiest Ending* (1985) completed the trilogy, in which, as Uchida explained in her autobiography *The Invisible Thread*, she attempted to convey the "strength of spirit as well as the sense of purpose, hope, and affirmation that sustained the early Japanese immigrant families."

She also wrote adults books, including a study of the Japanese folk artist Kanjiro Kawai, a memoir entitled *Desert Exile: The Uprooting of a Japanese-American Family* (1982), and a novel, *Picture Bride* (1987).

Yoshiko Uchida's lively, gracefully crafted work has been widely anthologized and translated. She died on June 21, 1992, at her home in Berkeley, California. In *Desert Exile,* Uchida described why she enjoyed writing for and speaking with school-aged children: "I tell them of my pride in being a Japanese American today, but I also tell them I celebrate our common humanity, for I feel we must never lose our sense of connection with the human race." Her goal was also to give young Asian Americans a sense of their past and to reinforce their self-esteem and self-knowledge. "At the same time, I want to dispel the stereotypic image still held by many non-Asians about the Japanese and write about them as real people," she said on the international Web site *Voices from the Gaps*. "I hope to convey the strength of spirit and the sense of hope and purpose I have observed in many first-generation Japanese."

Further Reading

Commire, Anne, ed. *Something about the Author: Authors of Books for Young People,* 147–157. Detroit, Mich.: Gale, 1988.

Grice, Helena. "Yoshiko Uchida." In *Dictionary of Literary Biography, Vol. 312: Asian American Writers,* edited by Deborah Madsen, 304–309. Farmington Hills, Mich.: Gale, 2005.

Uchida, Yoshiko. *Desert Exile: The Uprooting of a Japanese-American Family.* Seattle: University of Washington Press, 1982.

———. *The Invisible Thread: A Memoir.* New York: Simon & Schuster, 1991.

———. *Journey Home.* New York: Atheneum, 1978.

———. *Journey to Topaz.* New York: Scribner's, 1975.

Vogel, Paula
(1951–)   *playwright*

Paula Vogel is the author of the bittersweet comedy *How I Learned to Drive,* one of the most honored contemporary plays and the winner of the 1998 Pulitzer Prize for drama. She also wrote several other critically acclaimed plays—comedies written from the perspective of a gay feminist, including *The Oldest Profession* and *Baltimore Waltz.* Her work is punctuated with provocative images and unabashed humor as she takes on controversial topics such as incest, the AIDS epidemic, pornography, and domestic violence. Vogel looks at dark subjects lightly, candidly, and irreverently.

Born on November 16, 1951, in Washington, D.C., Paula Anne Vogel came from a working-class family. Her parents divorced when she was 11, which led to a "very painful adjustment," said Vogel. She and her older brother Carl stayed with their mother, and she only got to know her father, who had remarried, later in life, when Carl was dying of the AIDS virus. Paula's interest in the theater world blossomed as an adolescent, when she recalls "stumbling into drama class" while a high-school sophomore and feeling at home; she ended up stage managing several productions. Vogel then

attended Bryn Mawr College on a scholarship but left when they reduced her scholarship and ended up graduating in 1974 with a bachelor of arts degree in theater with honors from Catholic University in Washington, D.C. Initially her attempts at playwriting were unsuccessful: Her earliest plays were rejected by the Eugene O'Neill National Playwright's Conference, and based on plays she submitted, she was not accepted into the Yale School of Drama. But she discovered other young playwrights like herself and they formed a support group, reading each other's work and sharing innovative playwriting exercises, some of which cropped up in her early plays.

Vogel continued graduate studies in theater arts at Cornell University, in Ithaca, New York, where her first three plays, *Meg, The Last Pat Epstein Show before the Reruns,* and *Desdemona,* were produced in the late 1970s. Also while at Cornell she lectured in women's studies and theater arts. Teaching and drama remained lifelong interests. Vogel moved to New York City, the heart of the drama world, and became artistic director at the Theater with Teeth in the early 1980s and then, for two years, production supervisor at Lincoln Center. Since 1985 she has been on the faculty of Brown University, teaching and directing the graduate playwriting program. "She is a great teacher and a great model," commented director Oskar Eustis, who worked with Vogel when he was chair of the Brown University/Trinity Consortium. "She says to students, 'Everything in your personal life is your subject matter, and everything in the library of world theater is yours to plunder and work with and reappropriate.' And those two things don't contradict each other."

In 1986, *And Baby Makes Seven* (1984), an inventive play in which a homosexual man and two lesbians, who are a couple, become the parents of a child but also have three imaginary children, opened in San Francisco and then off-Broadway in New York, briefly, because it was a box-office failure. It was followed by *The Oldest Profession* (1988), which explored, humorously, how society views and treats elderly prostitutes. Her first hit, *The Baltimore Waltz* (1992), opened in New York and was performed widely in regional theaters. Vogel wrote the play in memory of her brother, a gay activist who, according to Vogel, was more damaged by homophobia (he was beaten up) than by AIDS, the disease that killed him. *Baltimore Waltz* won the 1992 Obie Award for best play. "The ferocious comedy," wrote Tish Dace in *Contemporary Dramatists*, "playful and poignant and written in lieu of a panel for the AIDS memorial quilt, veers quickly from nightmarish satire to medical quackery, to bereavement to a magical waltz." Two more plays followed: *Hot 'n' Throbbing* (1994), a penetrating portrait of domestic violence, and *The Mineola Twins* (1996), a mordant political satire set in suburban Long Island and first performed in 1999 in Juneau, Alaska.

Vogel's best-known work is *How I Learned to Drive* (1997), which won a Pulitzer Prize for drama and numerous other honors, including Obie, Drama Desk, New York Drama Critics, Outer Critics Circle, and Lucille Lortel awards. It was produced 50 times in 1998, the year Vogel received the Pulitzer Prize, and continues to be staged frequently nationally and internationally, including a lengthy off-Broadway run. Inspired by Vladimir Nabokov's novel *Lolita,* Vogel's disturbing play tells the story of a young woman called Little Bit who is seduced, starting when she is 11 years old and continuing until she was 18, by an older relative, Uncle Peck, while he teaches her to drive. "*How I Learned to Drive* is about healing, forgiving, and moving on," commented Vogel, during a television interview in 1998. "I sometimes feel that being in that kind of mind set of victimization causes almost as much trauma as the original abuse." The *New York Times* describes the play, which progresses in a series of flashbacks and flash forwards in the mind of Little Bit, the narrator, as a "lovely, harrowing guide to a crippling persistence of one woman's memories."

In 2003, *The Long Christmas Ride Home,* about a troubled family with three siblings whose past and present collide in the back seat of a car as it spins out of control on a snowy Christmas Eve, opened in New York City. "Vogel's language [in this play] is at its most poetic, eloquent, and elegiac," wrote a *New Haven Register* critic, "and its vivid imagery rivals the prose style of any great American short story writer." In 2004 *The Oldest Profession* was revived in New York City by the Signature Theater Company, as was her play *The Baltimore Waltz.* In 2005 *Hot 'n' Throbbing* premiered in New York City, concluding the Signature Theater Company's season, which was devoted exclusively to Vogel's work and where she had served as playwright-in-residence. Vogel has been recognized increasingly for combining, with brio and honesty, dark subject matter with a sense of whimsy, compassion, and optimism. According to *Contemporary Dramatists,* as a playwright Vogel has a "keen ear for her characters' colloquial speech, an intuitive understanding of their honor, pride, and enjoyment in their work, and subtlety in dramatizing their deprivations, ambitions, conflicts, and mutual nurturing."

Vogel, the Adele Kellenberg Seaver Professor of English in the literary arts program at Brown University, was married in Massachusetts in 2004 to her longtime companion, Anne Fausto-Sterling, a professor of biology and gender studies at Brown. Vogel has received numerous fellowships, including those from the National Endowment for the Arts (NEA), the MacDowell Colony, Bunting, Yaddo, McKnight, and the Guggenheim foundation. In 2006 Vogel was named a fellow at the Academy of Arts and Sciences and penned another play, *A Civil War Christmas*. "We have no popular playwright who has pushed the boundaries of the form more than Vogel," contends Eustis, the artistic director of the Public Theater in New York City. Her plays continue to be staged and to earn awards, in part because Paula Vogel sees theater as a way to create community and as a medium for democracy. "To me, entertainment and political subject matter go hand in hand," she explains. In 2006 *How I Learned to Drive* won two Jesse Richardson Theatre Awards, based on a production of the play staged by Performance Works on Granville Island in Vancouver, British Columbia, in Canada.

Further Reading

"A Prize-Winning Playwright." The News Hour with Jim Lehrer, Public Broadcasting System. Available online. URL:http://www.pbs.org/newshour/bb/entertainment/jan–june98/play_4–16.html. Downloaded on January 24, 2007.

Vogel, Paula. *The Long Christmas Ride Home.* New York: Theatre Communications Group, 2004.

———. *The Mammary Plays* (*The Mineola Twins; How I Learned to Drive*). New York: Theatre Communications Group, 1998.

Van Wagenen, Isabella Hardenbergh

See Truth, Sojourner

Walker, Alice Malsenior
(1944–) *novelist, poet, essayist*

A prominent figure of contemporary African-American literature and an avid civil rights activist and feminist, Alice Walker is a versatile and prolific writer who won the Pulitzer Prize and the American Book Award for her best-selling, best-known novel, *The Color Purple.*

Like many of her fictional characters, Alice Malsenior Walker was the daughter of black sharecroppers from the rural South. Born on February 9, 1944, in Eatonton, Georgia, she was the eighth child of a sharecropping farmer and his hard-working wife. But no matter how difficult their situation, Walker recalled, her mother never lost her belief that things would turn out right "if *you* were right."

Walker was valedictorian of her high school graduating class and attended Spelman College on a rehabilitation scholarship—a childhood accident had left her badly scarred and blinded in one eye. In 1965 she received a bachelor's degree from Sarah Lawrence College, where one of her teachers, the poet MURIEL RUKEYSER, had encouraged her to submit her verse for publication. In 1967 Walker married Melvyn Leventhal, a civil rights lawyer.

The interracial couple moved to Jackson, Mississippi, and in 1969 they had a daughter, Rebecca Walker, a writer who is known for her provocative memoir, *Black White, and Jewish* (2002). The marriage ended in 1977.

The poems in Walker's first book, *Once* (1968), reflected her burgeoning commitment to the civil rights movement and the acute depression she had suffered during her college years. Writing poetry, she later remarked, was a way to celebrate each day with the knowledge that she had not committed suicide. For Walker, inner peace could come only through self-knowledge, self-pride, and familial ties. "Family relationships," she once wrote, "are sacred."

The Third Life of Grange Copeland (1970), Walker's first novel, chronicled three generations of poor black sharecroppers in Georgia and was based largely on her parents' oppressive experiences. It also exposed the terrible ways in which blacks sometimes treated each other. *Revolutionary Petunias and Other Poems,* another book of verse, was nominated for the National Book Award in 1973. The same year, she published her first collection of short fiction, *In Love and Trouble: Stories of Black Women,* which won an American Academy and Institute of Arts and Letters

Award. The 13 stories in this collection depicted the anguish of African-American female characters dominated and defined by the cruel men in their lives, but who found the spiritual strength to survive. Later in 1973, Walker traveled to Eatonville, Florida, where novelist Zora Neale Hurston, whom Walker greatly admired, had been buried. She placed a headstone on the neglected grave. She also wrote an essay based on her search for Hurston's grave site in 1974 and in 1979 edited a collection of Hurston's writings, helping to restore her "foremother" to her rightful place as an important and influential African-American literary figure.

Alice Walker's popular third novel, *The Color Purple,* won the Pulitzer Prize.
(AP/Wide World Photos)

Walker's next novel, *Meridian* (1976), which portrayed the turbulent times of activists who worked in the South during the 1960s, has been cited as one of the best novels of the civil rights movement. In 1982, Walker published her most controversial and famous book, *The Color Purple.* Written in epistolary (letters) form, the novel included vivid descriptions of rape, incest, bisexuality, lesbianism, and "black-on-black" violence and abuse. It recounted the tragic but ultimately triumphant life story of Celie, a young victimized black woman. A year after it appeared, *The Color Purple* garnered the Pulitzer Prize in fiction and the National Book Award, and in 1985 it was adapted as a major motion picture. Walker's longtime best seller transcended racial and gender issues, although it, as with much of her work, was criticized by some black men for "male bashing."

Walker returned to her own roots with *In Search of Our Mothers' Gardens: Womanist Prose* (1983), a book-length collection of essays and memoirs inspired by her mother's capacity to create beautiful gardens in spite of her wretched living conditions. Walker coined the term "womanist" to define someone who fully appreciates women's culture, emotions, and character.

Another novel, *Possessing the Secret of Joy* (1992), related the chilling tale of a tribal African woman who lived in America but was traumatized by having undergone genital mutilation (female circumcision), a common practice in certain areas of Africa. Walker further explored female circumcision in a 1993 documentary film, *Warrior Marks,* which she coproduced and narrated. *By the Light of My Father's Smile* (1998), which exposed how America's puritanical values suppress women's sexuality, and whose characters included angels and a tarot-reading dwarf, was compared unfavorably by reviewers to her earlier fiction.

Other books by Walker include *Sent by Earth: A Message from the Grandmother Spirit* (2002), the writer's reaction, through political commentary and poetry, to the 9/11 attacks on the World Trade Center and the Pentagon; *Absolute Trust in the Goodness of the Earth: New Poems* (2003), Walker's sixth volume of verse; a novel *Now Is the Time to Open Your Heart* (2004), about a woman's spiritual adventure; a children's book, *There Is a Flower at the Tip of My Nose Smelling Me* (2006); and a nonfiction work, *We Are the Ones We Have Been Waiting for: Light in a Time of Darkness* (2006).

"Walker paid a personal and professional price for eschewing the orthodoxy of race and sex, primarily following the uproar attending the publication of *The Color Purple*," wrote *Booklist* in its review of Evelyn White's biography (2004) of Alice Walker. In 2005, a musical adaptation of *The Color Purple*, with a book by the eminent playwright MARSHA NORMAN, opened on Broadway in New York City. Walker's inspiring family saga garnered 11 Tony nominations, and the actress LaChanze, who played the indomitable Celie, won an award for best actress.

Walker, who lectures nationwide, lives in northern California, where she cofounded a small publishing house, Wild Trees, to help promote little-known African-American women writers. Most of her work has focused on the plight of the black American woman who, Walker contends, is "one of America's greatest heroes."

Further Reading

Bracks, Lean'tin L. *Writings on Black Women of the Diaspora: History, Language and Identity.* New York: Garland, 1997.

Tate, Claudia, ed. "Alice Walker." In *Black Women Writers at Work,* 175–187. New York: Continuum, 1983.

Walker, Alice. *The Color Purple.* New York: Harcourt, 1982.

———. *Her Blue Body Everything We Know: Earthling Poems, 1965–1990.* New York: Harcourt, 1991.

———. *In Search of Our Mothers' Gardens: Womanist Prose.* New York: Harcourt, 1983.

———. *Now Is the Time to Open Your Heart.* New York: Random House, 2004.

———. *We Are the Ones We Have Been Waiting for: Light in a Time of Darkness.* New York: New Press, 2006.

White, Evelyn C. *Alice Walker: A Life.* New York: W. W. Norton, 2004.

Winchell, Donna Haisty. *Alice Walker.* New York: Twayne, 1992.

Walker, Margaret Abigail
(1915–1998)   *poet, novelist*

Margaret Walker is best known for her only novel, *Jubilee,* which took her 30 years to write, and her poem "For My People," one of a thousand, which she composed, with the exception of the last stanza, in 15 minutes. Both works, and her efforts as a creative writer, scholar, and teacher since the 1930s, have been inseparable from her militant commitment to promoting the African-American struggle for equality and civil rights.

Margaret Abigail Walker was born on July 1, 1915, in Birmingham, Alabama, one of four children of Sigismund Walker, a Methodist minister and college graduate, and Marion Dozier Walker, a music teacher; education was stressed in the Walker home. Margaret began college in New Orleans, Louisiana, at the age of 15 and, urged by renowned black poet Langston Hughes, transferred to Northwestern University, where she graduated in 1935. While at Northwestern, Walker met the famous civil rights activist W. E. B. DuBois, who published her poetry in *Crisis,* the magazine of the NAACP (National Association for the Advancement of Colored People), affording her, at the age of 18, national exposure.

After a futile seven-month search for a job—it was during the Great Depression—Walker joined the Chicago Writers' Project, which was sponsored by the Works Progress Administration (WPA), a New Deal agency. During her three years in Chicago, Illinois, Walker's ethical Christian beliefs about social justice fused with radical and Marxist ideas that were popular with several intellectuals she encountered, among them the black novelist Richard Wright. In 1940, Walker earned a master's degree in creative writing from the University of Iowa, having submitted a collection of poems, *All My People,* as her master's thesis. In 1942, the collection brought Walker to national prominence, when it won her the Yale Younger Poets Series Award. She was the first black woman to receive the prestigious award.

Walker's first academic job, at Livingstone College in North Carolina, earned her $135 a month. In 1943, Walker married Firnist James Alexander, but retained her maiden name. The couple had four children and were married 37 years, until Alexander's death in 1980. In 1949, Walker accepted a position at Jackson State College in Mississippi, where she taught until she retired from teaching in 1979. In the 1960s she established the first black studies program in the South at Jackson State.

Despite financial hardship—she was earning less than $6,000 a year at Jackson State as late as 1960, a sum on which she had to support her four children and war-disabled husband—Walker returned to the University of Iowa and earned her Ph.D. in 1965. Her doctoral dissertation was the novel *Jubilee*, a chronicle of a black family during the Civil War era, which she completed after three decades. The book was based both on what Walker learned as a child from her maternal grandmother and extensive scholarly research. Although it received mixed reviews, *Jubilee* had its fervent admirers who considered it a landmark for depicting history from an African-American perspective.

In addition to *Jubilee*, Margaret Abigail Walker, who died in Chicago on November 30, 1998, published five books of poetry, a scholarly biography of Richard Wright, and several other books, as well as essays that focus on a broad range of topics, including feminist concerns—in particular the role of black women in American life.

During her final public appearance in 1998, at the Gwendolyn Brooks Writers' Conference in Chicago, Walker, whose accolades included six honorary degrees, was inducted into the African American Literary Hall of Fame. In a profile for *Modern American Poetry*, Tomeiko Ashford, assistant professor of English at Florida State University, noted that "Walker continued to write, tour, lecture, and give readings until her death. Among the most formidable literary voices to emerge in the 20th century, Margaret Walker will be remembered as one of the foremost transcribers of African American heritage."

Further Reading

Berke, Nancy. *Women Poets on the Left: Lola Ridge, Genevieve Taggard, Margaret Walker*. Gainesville: University of Florida Press, 2001.

Braxton, Joanne M., and Andraee Nicola McLaughlin, eds. *Wild Women in the Whirlwind: Afro-American Culture and the Contemporary Literary Renaissance*. New Brunswick, N.J.: Rutgers University Press, 1990.

Evans, Mari, ed. *Black Women Writers (1950–1980): A Critical Evaluation*. New York: Anchor/Doubleday, 1982.

Graham, Maryemma, ed. *Conversations with Margaret Walker*. Jackson: University Press of Mississippi, 2002.

Walker, Margaret. *How I Wrote Jubilee and Other Essays on Life and Literature*. Coauthored by Maryemma Graham. New York: The Feminist Press, 1990.

———. *Jubilee*. Boston: Houghton Mifflin, 1965.

———. *This Is My Century: New and Collected Poems*. Athens: University of Georgia Press, 1989.

Warren, Mercy Otis
(1728–1814)   *playwright, historian*

Placed by familial ties at the vortex of the political storm that intensified into the American Revolution, Mercy Otis Warren made her own impact on the course of events in the 1770s as the author of satirical plays that supported the patriot cause. She is best known, however, for *History of the Rise, Progress, and Termination of the American Revolution* (1805), one of the most important narratives during the period that gave birth to the United States. She is considered one of the most important American women of the revolutionary era.

Mercy Otis was born on September 25, 1728, in Barnstable, Massachusetts, the third child (of 13) and eldest daughter of Colonel James Otis, a self-educated farmer, merchant, attorney, and politician, and Mary Allyne Otis, whose great-great grandfather had signed the Mayflower Compact. Tutored along with her older brothers, Mercy received a sound education that included the classics, as well as John Dryden, John Milton, and William Shakespeare. She was particularly close to her brilliant but erratic oldest brother, James, Jr., who in the 1760s was one of the leading militants in Massachusetts opposing British colonial policies, and whose *Rights of the British Colonies Asserted and Proved* became an important statement of the colonists' case against the British.

In 1754 Mercy Otis married James Warren, another leader in the colonial struggle who became a general in George Washington's army. The couple had a long, happy marriage that lasted until James Warren's death in 1808. They had five sons, three of whom predeceased their parents.

It was through her brother and father that Mercy Otis Warren became involved in politics and won the respect of many of the outstanding figures of the American Revolution, from John and Samuel Adams of Massachusetts to George Washington. Like her friend ABIGAIL ADAMS, a famous letter writer and the wife of John Adams, Mercy Otis Warren produced a body of influential writing. However, while Abigail Adams wrote letters to her husband, exerting her influence privately through him, Warren published incendiary political plays, albeit anonymously, that directly impacted on public opinion during a turbulent time.

Warren's first play, *The Adulateur,* appeared in 1772. Set in the mythical country of Upper Servia, its villain was the vengeful Rapatio, easily recognizable to readers as Thomas Hutchinson, the pro-British Tory governor of Massachusetts. Other Tory villains, representing Hutchinson's associates, were characters with names such as Dupe, Meagre, and Gripeall; the play's heros, Brutus and Cassius, clearly were meant to represent Sam Adams and James Otis. In 1773, Warren's *The Defeat* again savaged Hutchinson and helped destroy his political career. It was followed in 1775, two weeks before the famous Battle of Lexington, by *The Group,* the name Warren gave to the Tories who were at that time administering Boston. Her satirical plays were meant to be read rather than performed. She had, in fact, never seen a theatrical performance; her skills as a dramatist came primarily from reading works by Shakespeare and Molière.

During the debate over the Constitution in the late 1780s, James and Mercy Warren (James, incapacitated by mental illness, died in 1783) sided with the opponents of ratification. In a pamphlet published anonymously in 1788, *Observations on the New Constitution, and on the Federal and State Conventions,* Mercy Warren raised several objections to the proposed constitution, including its lack of a bill of rights. The Warrens believed the document favored the wealthy at the expense of the common people, and therefore violated the democratic spirit of the revolution.

In 1790, Warren took a major step when she published *Poems, Dramatic and Miscellaneous.* Comprised of many of her favorite early writings, the collection was her first work published under her own name, Mrs. M. Warren. The book was dedicated to the newly inaugurated president of the United States, George Washington. Warren's Republican (anti-Federalist/Jeffersonian) views were evident in her major work, on which she labored for two decades, the three-volume *History of the Rise, Progress, and Termination of the American Revolution.* Aside from expressing her political agenda, it is notable for the remarkable personal profiles it provides of the major leaders on both sides of the revolutionary struggle. According to numerous historians, Warren was the outstanding female intellectual of her generation.

Mercy Otis Warren died on October 19, 1814, in Plymouth, Massachusetts, where she was buried on the old Burial Hill of the Pilgrims, next to her husband.

Further Reading

Davies, Kate. *Catharine Macaulay and Mercy Otis Warren: The Revolutionary Atlantic and the Politics of Gender.* New York: Oxford University Press, 2006.

"Mercy Otis Warren." Web Exhibition of the Battle of Bunker Hill. Massachusetts Historical Society. Available online. URL: http://www.masshist.org/bh/mercybio.html. Downloaded on January 24, 2007.

Warren, Mercy Otis. *History of the Rise, Progress, and Termination of the American Revolution, interspersed with Biographical and Moral Observations.* 3 vols. Boston: Ebenezer Larkin, 1805.

———. *The Plays and Poems of Mercy Otis Warren: Facsimile Reproductions.* Delmar, N.Y.: Scholars Facsimiles and Reprints, 1980.

Zagarri, Rosemarie. *A Woman's Dilemma: Mercy Otis Warren and the American Revolution.* Wheeling, Ill.: Harlan Davidson, 1995.

∿ Wasserstein, Wendy
(1950–2006) *playwright*

Wendy Wasserstein wrote provocative, urbane, humorous plays about accomplished contemporary women struggling to define themselves in postfeminist America. In 1989, she won a Pulitzer Prize for her best-known play, *The Heidi Chronicles.*

The youngest of four children of Jewish immigrant parents, Wendy Wasserstein was born on October 18, 1950, in Brooklyn, New York, and moved to Manhattan when she was 12. Influenced by her flamboyant mother, an aficionado of dance and theater, Wendy attended Broadway plays and musicals and took ballet and tap classes. A natural-born comedian, she kept her classmates in stitches with her witty one-liners, but beneath the surface she was also deeply serious. "Funny," she once commented, "is a very complicated issue."

In 1971, Wasserstein received a bachelor's degree from Mount Holyoke College, followed in 1973 by a master's degree in creative writing from the City College of New York, where noted writers Israel Horovitz and Joseph Heller were among her teachers. While a graduate student, she wrote her first play, *Any Woman Can't,* a farce about a young woman who gets married after a disappointing tap dance audition. It was produced off-Broadway in 1973 and, like her later work, attempted to portray the full range of a woman's experiences. Wasserstein felt most male dramatists—even those she greatly admired, such as Anton Chekhov—had failed to do that.

While attending the Yale University School of Drama, where she earned a master's of fine arts degree in 1976, Wasserstein befriended playwright Christopher Durang, with whom she cowrote a musical parody, *When Dinah Shore Ruled the Earth.* Her first critically acclaimed play, *Uncommon Women and Others,* was produced off-Broadway in New York City in 1977 and won an Obie Award. It focused on affluent, college-educated women who were influenced by the emerging women's movement but worried about combining careers with motherhood. The play was televised in 1978

Wendy Wasserstein wrote witty, urbane plays about contemporary women.
(AP/Wide World Photos)

and revived on Broadway in 1994. Critics hailed it for its mature treatment of contemporary women's issues, in spite of being a comedy. "Serious issues and serious people can be quite funny," Wasserstein explained in the *New York Times.*

Other plays about urban modern women followed, including *Isn't It Romantic* in 1981. But it was *The Heidi Chronicles,* Wasserstein's first play to open on Broadway, that brought her popular and critical acclaim and earned her a Pulitzer Prize in drama in 1989. She also became the first woman to receive the Tony Award for Best Play. *The Heidi Chronicles* depicts the life of Heidi Holland, an intelligent, independent, but increasingly disillusioned art history professor who came of age during the idealistic 1960s and finds herself alone as she approaches middle age in the 1980s. Praised for its "gentle wit" and "tremendous emotional voltage," it dealt insightfully with feminist issues, although Wasserstein resisted being labeled a "feminist" playwright, calling herself a "humanist" instead. The climax is an impromptu confession Heidi makes at a high school alumni luncheon: "It's just that I feel stranded. And I thought the whole point was that we wouldn't feel stranded I thought the point was we were all in this together." The play ends with Heidi adopting a baby, which is something Wasserstein, who was unmarried, had also considered doing. Instead, she gave birth to a daughter, Lucy Jane, in 1999.

In addition to writing three musicals, comedy skits for television, and essays for *New York Woman* magazine, Wasserstein has published a collection of humorous essays, *Bachelor Girls* (1991), and a children's book. She considered her next comedy hit, *The Sisters Rosensweig,* which was produced at New York City's Lincoln Center in 1992, her most optimistic and overtly Jewish work. *An American Daughter* (1997), a political satire set in Washington, D.C., examined why several women who were nominated for government office were forced to withdraw their nominations or resign. This was unusual territory for Wasserstein, who described herself as a quintessential "New York playwright liberal," and the play received mixed reviews. Wasserstein also wrote several screenplays, including John Cheever's *The Sorrows of Gin,* adapted for television in 1979, and in 1998 a film adaptation of Stephen McCauley's novel *The Object of My Affection.* Her last work, the play *Third,* about an independent, strong but emotionally needy female college professor whose feminist convictions are tested by a student, was staged in New York City in 2005, selling out its run at Lincoln Center.

Wendy Wasserstein died from lymphoma on January 30, 2006, at age 55. In her honor, the lights on Broadway were dimmed the night after her death. Her first and only novel, *Elements of Style,* described favorably by the *New York Times* as

"chick-lit with a chill and a pedigree . . . both a blithe, funny feat of escapism and a sobering reminder of the inescapable," was published posthumously. "Wasserstein was known for being a popular, funny playwright, but she was also a woman and a writer of deep conviction and political activism," said André Bishop, artistic director of Lincoln Center Theater. "In Wendy's plays women saw themselves portrayed in a way they hadn't been onstage before—wittily, intelligently and seriously at the same time. We take that for granted now, but it was not the case 25 years ago. She was a real pioneer."

Considered by the *New York Times* as one of America's most talented young playwrights, Wendy Wasserstein commented that her goal was to entertain but also to use the theater to "shake things up a little bit. I want to make people think."

Further Reading

Isherwood, Charles. "Wendy Wasserstein Dies at 55; Her Plays Spoke to a Generation." *New York Times,* January 31, 2006, sec. A.

Wasserstein, Wendy. *Elements of Style.* New York: Knopf, 2006.

———. *The Heidi Chronicles and Other Plays.* San Diego: Harcourt Brace Jovanovich, 1990.

———. *The Sisters Rosensweig.* New York: Harcourt Brace, 1993.

Whitfield, Stephen J. "Wendy Wasserstein, and the Crisis of Jewish Identity." In *Women of Valor: Contemporary Jewish Identity,* edited by Jay L. Halio and Ben Siegel, 116–146. Newark: University of Delaware Press, 1997.

ᴕ Wells-Barnett, Ida Bell
(1862–1931) *journalist*

Ida Wells-Barnett's career as a journalist grew out of and was tied to her passionate commitment to the African-American struggle for civil rights. More than any other writer, she brought the issue of the lynching of black people in the South to national and international attention.

Ida Bell Wells was born a slave on July 16, 1862, in Holly Springs, Mississippi, the eldest of eight children. Her father was the son of his white owner, by one of his female slaves; her mother probably was part American Indian. The family lived reasonably well in the Reconstruction South because her father, acknowledged by the white plantation owner as his son, was trained as a carpenter and was able to earn a living as free man.

Ida attended Rust College, one of the few schools set up in the South to educate former slaves. Her relatively secure and happy childhood ended abruptly in 1878, when her parents and youngest brother died in a yellow fever epidemic. At the age of 16, determined to earn a living and keep the remaining members of her family together, Ida became a teacher in a local one-room school.

In 1883, Wells moved to Memphis, Tennessee, where she taught in a nearby town while continuing her studies at Fisk University. The next year, while traveling to her job by train, she was forcibly removed from a first-class car and made to ride with other blacks in a shabby car reserved for smokers. Wells sued the railroad and was awarded $500, although the verdict was reversed in 1887 by the Tennessee Supreme Court. That same year, Wells published her first newspaper article, about her suit against the railroad. She quickly earned a reputation as a notable African-American journalist. In 1891 she became editor and part owner of the *Free Speech and Headlight* in Memphis and was fired from her teaching position because of her crusading articles that criticized conditions in the city's black schools.

In 1892, Wells wrote a scathing series about the lynching of three young black men in Memphis, followed by a general expose on the lynching of blacks. She debunked the "old thread-bare lie that Negro men assault white women," an excuse frequently used in defense of lynchings. The reaction—her newspaper's offices were destroyed and her life was threatened—forced Barnett-Wells to relocate. Eventually she settled in Chicago.

Wells soon became internationally recognized. In 1892, she published her first antilynching pamphlet, *Southern Horrors: Lynch Law in All Its Phases.* The next year she toured England to publicize the

issue of lynching and was invited back in 1894; her efforts contributed to the founding of the British Anti-Lynching Committee. In 1895, Wells published *A Red Report: Tabulated Statistics and Alleged Causes of Lynching in the United States, 1892–1893–1894.* This devastating expose was all the more powerful because it relied on the *Chicago Tribune,* a pillar of the white establishment press, for its statistics. Wells's other major work, *Mob Rule in New Orleans* (1900), was an account of the city's race riots in 1900.

Ida B. Wells became Ida Wells-Barnett in 1895 when she married Ferdinand L. Barnett, a prominent Chicago lawyer and founder of the *Conservator,* the city's first black newspaper. The two civil rights activists were considered among the most influential black couples in the country. They had four children and, because Wells-Barnett firmly believed a mother should be at home while her children were growing up, for many years she cut back on her journalistic and political activities. She did, however, continue to work, sometimes attending lectures or meetings with a nursing baby.

During her later years, Wells-Barnett often found herself at odds with more moderate black leaders and organizations they controlled, such as the NAACP (National Association for the Advancement of Colored People). Personality conflicts with fellow militants such as W. E. B. DuBois also contributed to her isolation, although at times she cooperated with white suffragists in their struggle to win women the right to vote and by doing so, integrated the suffrage movement. In an award-winning book about Wells published in 2001, Patricia Ann Schechter shows how, in addition to her brazen antilynching crusade, the religiously inspired pioneering journalist held an important place in America's early reform movements for civil rights, woman suffrage, and social justice for African Americans, even though she often was marginalized or misunderstood.

Ida B. Wells-Barnett died in Chicago on March 21, 1931. In 1940, Chicago named a housing project in her honor; 10 years later the city named her one of 25 outstanding women in its history.

The United States Postal Service issued a stamp in her honor in 1990.

Further Reading

"Jim Crow Stories: Ida B. Wells." The Rise and Fall of Jim Crow. WNET/New York, Public Broadcasting System. Available Online. URL: http://www.pbs.org/wnet/jimcrow/index.html. Downloaded on January 24, 2007.

Schechter, Patricia Ann. *Ida B. Wells-Barnett and American Reform, 1880–1930*. Chapel Hill: University of North Carolina Press, 2001.

Wells-Barnett, Ida B. *Crusade for Justice: The Autobiography of Ida B. Wells*. Edited by Alfred M. Duster. Chicago: University of Chicago Press, 1970.

———. *The Selected Works of Ida B. Wells-Barnett*. Compiled and with an introduction by Trudier Harris. New York: Oxford University Press, 1991.

~ Welty, Eudora
(1909–2001)   *short story writer, novelist*

In a career that spanned six decades, Eudora Welty used what she called "the complexities of the everyday" that she observed and experienced in her native Mississippi, and her fascination with regional folktales, anecdotes, and legends, to create fiction that probes the "endlessly new, mysterious, and alluring" inner life of people and their search for identity and meaning.

Eudora Welty was born in Jackson, Mississippi, on April 13, 1909, the eldest of three children of parents who had come to the deep South from Ohio and West Virginia. Eudora's mother passed on a love of books and learning to her only daughter, while her father, a successful life insurance executive, could afford to send her to Mississippi State College for Women and the University of Wisconsin, where she earned a bachelor's degree, and then to the Columbia Graduate School of Business in New York City. Welty loved New York City; she described it as her "cornucopia," with its theaters, museums, concert halls, and Harlem jazz clubs. But she was unable to find work, and in 1931 she returned home. When her father died suddenly, she remained in Jackson, and the Tudor-style house her father had built became her permanent home. She never married.

In 1933 Welty took a job as a publicity agent with the federal government's Works Progress Administration (WPA). The position afforded her the opportunity to travel throughout Mississippi and exposed her to the dreadful poverty of her native state, made even worse by the Depression. Welty took hundreds of photographs of the people she met, some of which were published in 1971 in *One Time, One Place: Mississippi in the Depression: A Snapshot*. But, more important, she discovered "the real germ of my wanting to become a real writer, a true writer."

Welty's first published story, "Death of a Traveling Salesman," appeared in 1936 in a small magazine called *Manuscript*. During the next two years, the *Southern Review*, one of whose editors was the noted poet, novelist, and critic Robert Penn Warren, published six of Welty's short stories. Her first collection, *A Curtain of Green*, appeared in 1941, with an introduction by fiction writer KATHERINE ANN PORTER, who wrote, "there is even in the smallest story a sense of power in reserve which makes me believe firmly that, splendid beginning that this is, it is only the beginning." A novella and a second collection of short stories were followed in 1946 by *Delta Wedding*, Welty's first novel. Focusing on the numerous human interactions that take place at everyday events such as weddings, reunions, and funerals, *Delta Wedding* received mixed reviews. On a positive note, the critic in the *New York Times Book Review* commented that Welty's book "shares the excellencies of her short stories with all the advantages of a wider pattern," and added that the novel, while set in the deep South, "is true to human life as you will find it at considerable distance from the Mississippi Delta."

In 1949, Welty produced another collection, *The Golden Apples*, an outstanding example of the genre called the short story cycle, whose interrelated stories cover 40 years and include a local cast of wanderers and residents in the town of Morgana, Mississippi. The volume's centerpiece, "June

Recital," is the poignant story of an unmarried piano teacher whose life is a canvas of disappointment and frustration. Welty called *The Golden Apples,* with its mix of comedy and tragedy and its blending of myth and realty, "in a way . . . closest to my heart of all my books." In the mid-1950s she published another short story collection and a novel, *The Ponder Heart,* which was adapted as a Broadway play in 1956. But the burden of caring for her ill mother, who died in 1966, sapped her of much of her energy, and between 1955 and 1970 she published only a few minor works.

In 1972 Welty published *The Optimist's Daughter,* a novel that won the Pulitzer Prize in fiction, and in 1984 she achieved a new measure of popular success with *One Writer's Beginnings,* three autobiographical sketches based on a lecture series she had delivered at Harvard University the previous year. *One Writer's Beginnings* sold more than 100,000 copies and remained on the *New York Times* best seller list for 47 weeks.

After being criticized for not taking a public stand against segregation in the South, Welty wrote an essay in 1965 entitled "Must a Novelist Crusade?" In it she contended that a writer "works neither to correct nor to condone, not at all to comfort, but to make what's told alive." Welty felt that her private life was her own business and insisted that her work be judged on its literary merits, not on any other basis. To that end, she was highly successful. Aside from the Pulitzer Prize, she won numerous awards including four O. Henry Awards, the William Dean Howells Medal, and the National Institute of Arts and Letters Gold Medal for fiction. An honor she seemed especially to cherish was strictly unofficial; it came in 1943 in the form of a letter from a fellow Mississippian, the esteemed novelist William Faulkner, after he read *The Robber Bridegroom,* Welty's first novella. "You're doing all right," he told the young author. Today the framed letter hangs in the same room where Welty worked and continued to do "all right" for the next half century.

Eudora Welty, who in 1998 became the first living writer to have her collected works included in the prestigious Library of America Series, died on July 22, 2001, at age 92. In *Eudora Welty: A Biography* (2005), Suzanne Marrs—a professor of language and literature at Millsaps College in Mississippi, the author of a critical study of Welty's work, and the writer's longtime friend—portrayed Welty not as reclusive and solitary but rather as an avid traveler who enjoyed an active social life, including two significant romantic relationships.

In a *Boston Globe* review of Marrs's biography, Chris Navratil wrote that "Welty was a tremendous force in 20th-century literature. She approached fiction with an astonishingly fresh eye to form and with an exacting ear for language (particularly for dialect) and with a passion to explore far-ranging subject matter." He also noted that while she traveled extensively, it was in her hometown of Jackson that she "found solace and inspiration and was at her most productive." In 2006 Welty's home in Jackson, simply referred to as "1119 Pinehurst" by the author and having been restored by the Eudora Welty Foundation and the State of Mississippi, opened to the public and became a National Historic Landmark. It was where Eudora Welty had penned virtually all of her writing.

Further Reading

"Eudora Welty." The Mississippi Writers Page. Available online. URL: http://www.olemiss.edu/depts/english/ms-writers/dir/welty_eudora/index.html. Downloaded on March 7, 2007.

Marrs, Suzanne. *One Writer's Imagination: The Fiction of Eudora Welty.* Baton Rouge: Louisiana State University Press, 2002.

———. *Eudora Welty: A Biography.* New York: Harcourt, 2005.

McHaney, Pearl Amelia, ed. *Eudora Welty: The Contemporary Reviews.* New York: Cambridge University Press, 2005.

Welty, Eudora. *The Collected Stories of Eudora Welty.* New York: Harcourt Brace Jovanovich, 1980.

———. *Eudora Welty: Complete Novels.* New York: Library of America, 1998.

———. *One Writer's Beginnings.* Cambridge, Mass.: Harvard University Press, 1984.

≈ West, Dorothy
(1907–1998)   *short story writer, novelist*

The last surviving member of the Harlem Renaissance, Dorothy West, while primarily a short story writer, was best known for two novels that appeared almost 50 years apart: *The Living Is Easy* (1948) and *The Wedding* (1995).

Dorothy West was born in Boston, Massachusetts, on June 2, 1907, the only child of Isaac West, an ex-slave who became a successful businessman, and Rachel West. The Wests belonged to Boston's small emerging black middle class—Dorothy spoke with a rich Yankee accent—and were among the first blacks to buy property and summer on Martha's Vineyard, a resort island off the coast of Massachusetts. Another notable feature of Dorothy West's family, a result of having both white and black ancestors, was its virtual rainbow of skin and hair colors, "pink and gold and brown and ebony," as she put it. West, in contrast with many black intellectuals, frequently said, "Color is important, but class is more important."

After graduating from Boston's prestigious Girls' Latin School, West attended Boston University and then moved to New York City to attend Columbia University School of Journalism. In 1926, her first significant publication, a short story called "The Typewriter," appeared in *Opportunity,* the National Urban League's magazine, and was included in *The Best Short Stories of 1926.* West participated in the Harlem Renaissance, a cultural revival among African Americans centered in New York's Harlem neighborhood during the 1920s.

Although she was considered a minor Harlem Renaissance figure, West was friendly with many of its leading representatives, including writers Langston Hughes, Richard Wright, and ZORA NEALE HURSTON. In 1932, West, Hughes, and 20 other black intellectuals went to the Soviet Union to make a film about the oppression of blacks in the United States. The film was never made, but West stayed in the Soviet Union for nine months, returning to America when her father died. In 1934, after the Depression forced an end to the Harlem Renaissance, West tried to recapture its vitality by founding the magazine *Challenge*. It succumbed to financial problems in 1937 and its successor, *New Challenge,* survived for only one issue.

Beginning in 1940, West regularly published short stories in the *New York Daily News.* In 1947 she left New York and moved to a cottage on Martha's Vineyard that her father had bought years earlier; she lived there for the remainder of her life. In 1948, West published *The Living Is Easy,* a semiautobiographical novel that critiqued what she perceived as the false values of upwardly mobile middle-class blacks. She also wrote a column for the local newspaper, the *Vineyard Gazette.* Meanwhile, she labored for years on *The Wedding,* a novel that focused on snobbery and materialism among light-skinned, middle-class blacks in the 1950s. West abandoned the project in the 1960s because she was afraid it would not be well received by militant activists such as the Black Panthers. "I wanted to write about people like my father, who were ambitious," she commented. "But people like him were anathema to the Black Panthers, who said all black people are victims." The book finally was completed with the encouragement of former First Lady Jacqueline Kennedy Onassis, who was also a summer resident of Martha's Vineyard and a book editor. Generally considered West's finest work, *The Wedding* was published in 1995, shortly after Mrs. Onassis's death, and was dedicated to her memory. In 1998 Oprah Winfrey produced a TV adaptation of *The Wedding* starring Halle Berry. A best seller, its theme was clearly stated by the heroine in the book's last line, "Color was a false distinction; love was not." West also published *The Richer, the Poorer* (1995), a collection of 30 stories and essays.

In the 1930s, Dorothy West was rumored to be romantically involved with Langston Hughes and to have received several marriage proposals from him, but she never married. A woman of enormous grace and vitality, she died in Boston on August 16, 1998, at age 91.

349

Further Reading

Barnes, Paula C. "Dorothy West." In *New Voices on the Harlem Renaissance,* edited by Paula C. Barnes and Australia Tarver, 99–124. Cranbury, N.J.: Rosemont Publishing, 2006.

Jones, Sharon L. "A Closet Revolutionary: The Politics of Representation in the Fiction of Dorothy West." In *Rereading the Harlem Renaissance,* 117–148. Westport, Conn.: Greenwood Press, 2002.

McDowell, Deborah E. "Conversations with Dorothy West." In *The Harlem Renaissance Re-examined,* edited by Victor A. Kramer, 265–282. New York: AMS Press, 1987.

Miller, E. Ethelbert. "Dorothy West 1907–1998: A Tribute to the Long Legacy of *The Kid.*" Poets & Writers. Available online. URL: http://www.pw.org/mag/West.htm. Downloaded on March 7, 2007.

West, Dorothy. *The Dorothy West Martha's Vineyard: Stories, Essays and Reminiscences: Writings from the Vineyard Gazette, 1960s to 1990s.* Edited by James R. Saunders and Renae N. Shackelford. Jefferson, N.C.: McFarland and Company, 2001.

———. *The Richer, the Poorer: Stories, Sketches and Reminiscences.* New York: Doubleday, 1995.

———. *The Wedding.* New York: Doubleday, 1995.

∾ Wharton, Edith Newbold Jones
(1862–1937) *novelist, short story writer, memoirist*

An accomplished, versatile writer, Edith Wharton produced more than 40 volumes of fiction, nonfiction, poetry, and critical essays. She was best known for novels that depicted New York City's upper-crust high society between the 1870s and 1920s, such as the Pulitzer Prize–winning *The Age of Innocence.* She also wrote *Ethan Frome,* an acclaimed, tragic love story set in rural New England, published while she was an expatriate novelist residing in France.

Born and bred into an affluent, aristocratic family of British and Dutch ancestry, on January 24, 1862, in New York City, Edith Newbold Jones was raised in the sheltered, decorous, and restricted world of upper-class New York society. Shy and intelligent, she was educated by tutors and spent much of her childhood in Europe or reading books from her father's well-stocked library. "I was," she

recalled, "enthralled by *words.* . . . Wherever I went, they sang to me like the birds in an enchanted forest." Her two goals as an adolescent were to be the best-dressed woman in New York, like her mother, and to be a writer. By age 16, she had written and privately published a volume of poetry, but her life as a debutante revolved mostly around society parties and dances.

At 23, she married Edward (Teddy) Robbins Wharton, a prominent Boston banker who was kind but mentally unstable and more interested in sports than in literature. Although they traveled in the same social circles, the Whartons shared very little else. Over the years they drifted apart, finally divorcing in 1912. Increasingly, Wharton escaped from unhappiness and boredom by writing. She began publishing verse and short stories in magazines such as *Scribner's* and *Harper's,* and in 1897 collaborated with an architect on *The Decoration of Houses,* in which the expression of personal, individualized taste was encouraged—a radical concept

Edith Wharton wrote 46 books, including the tragic love story *Ethan Frome.*
(AP/Wide World Photos)

at that time. (The social critic Edmund Wilson later called Wharton "not only one of the great pioneers, but also the poet of interior decoration.")

In 1898 Wharton suffered a major nervous breakdown. Nonetheless she was able to publish *The Greater Inclination* (1899), a collection of short fiction that contained some of her most memorable short stories. From that point on, she would write, on the average, a book a year until she died in 1937. The Whartons moved from their summer home in Newport, Rhode Island, to Lenox, Massachusetts, where they built The Mount, an elegant estate replete with lush gardens that Wharton helped design. She soon published her first novel, *The Valley of Decision* (1902), which examined the moral decline of 18th-century Italy and was lauded for its craftsmanship and form. But her close friend and mentor, the American novelist Henry James, with whom she has often been compared, recommended that next time, she should "Do New York!" She heeded his advice, and with the publication of *The House of Mirth* (1905) Wharton's reputation as a prominent writer of American fiction soared. The best-selling novel focused on "a group of pleasure-loving New Yorkers, mostly as dull as they [were] immoral . . . ," as she described the characters, and how their rigid set of social rules crushed, literally, a nonconformist, Lily Bart—she committed suicide—whom they treated like one of their discarded decorative objects.

In 1906, having moved to France, Wharton had a passionate but ultimately unsatisfactory three-year love affair with journalist Morton Fullerton; meanwhile, Teddy Wharton had a nervous breakdown and was sent to a sanitorium in Switzerland. Wharton continued writing poetry, gardening, and architecture books; travel articles; fiction; and ghost stories, including the chilling collection *Tales of Men and Ghosts* (1910). After her divorce, she settled permanently in France, where she befriended and entertained illustrious artists and literati.

In 1911, Wharton published *Ethan Frome,* a haunting novella which many critics consider her finest work. Using a first-person narration and

lucid, polished prose, the love story and tragic morality tale is set in bleak, lower-middle-class, rural New England. One of Wharton's biographers, Louis Auchincloss, described her "firm, crisp, smooth, direct, easily flowing style" as the perfect instrument of a "clear, undazzled eye, an analytic mind, and a sense of humor alert to the least pretentiousness."

Wharton's personal favorite among her own works was *The Custom of the Country* (1913), a fiercely critical novel of manners about New York society in which one of the characters claims it is the "custom of the country . . . that the average American looks down on his wife. . . ." A few years later she published her most commercially successful book, which in 1921 won the Pulitzer Prize. *The Age of Innocence* (1920) was based on childhood memories, her own socially acceptable but unhappy marriage, and her belief in the importance of upholding fundamental values. Although Wharton candidly delineated the vulgarity and superficiality of Old New York society, she also acknowledged that its "standards of honor and conduct" contributed to America's "moral wealth."

During World War I, a patriotic Wharton helped organize relief programs in Paris for Belgian refugees. For her assistance, she was awarded the Legion of Honor by the French government. She returned briefly to the United States to become the first female recipient of an honorary doctorate degree from Yale University. She was also the first woman to receive the National Institute of Arts and Letters's Gold Medal, and was elected to the American Academy of Arts and Letters.

Eight novels and novellas followed *The Age of Innocence,* including *The Marne* and *A Son at the Front,* which were based on her war experiences. In 1934 she published her autobiography, *A Backward Glance.* Wharton, who was nominated for, but did not receive, a Nobel Prize in recognition of her status as "the most distinguished American writer of her generation," was described by Henry James as "the angel of desolation and devastation, the historic ravager." Her books have been translated into Italian, German, and French, and several have been adapted successfully as dramatizations and films.

At the end of her life, Edith Wharton returned to, as Auchincloss put it, the "rich field of her childhood memories" in her last, unfinished, post-humously published novel *The Buccaneers* (1938), which a number of critics believed would have ranked among the best of her work. Wharton, the first woman to win a Pulitzer Prize in fiction, died of a stroke at age 75 on August 11, 1937, at her villa in France, and was buried in Versailles.

The Edith Wharton Society was founded in 1983 to foster Wharton scholarship through national and international conferences and a biannual peer-reviewed journal, *The Edith Wharton Review.* In 2005 Wharton's extensive library, comprising 2,600 volumes that she had collected, read, and cherished, was returned from England, where a British bookseller in a small Yorkshire village had owned the massive collection, to Wharton's estate, The Mount, in Lenox, Massachusetts. The collection will be made available to literary scholars and Wharton aficionados worldwide. Hermione Lee, a Wharton scholar at Oxford University, called the library "a form of writer's autobiography," reflecting Wharton's life. "Her whole social milieu, her private affairs, and her literary career can be discerned from her collection," wrote Lee.

Further Reading

Auchincloss, Louis. *Edith Wharton, A Woman in Her Time.* New York: Viking Press, 1971.

———, ed. *The Edith Wharton Reader.* New York: Scribner's, 1965.

Cowell, Alan. "After a Century, an American Writer's Library Will Go to America." *New York Times,* December 15, 2005, sec. B.

Lee, Hermione. Edith Wharton. New York: Knopf, 2007.

Ohler, Paul. *Edith Wharton's Evolutionary Conception: Darwinian Allegory in Her Major Novels.* New York: Routledge, 2006.

Wharton, Edith. *A Backward Glance* (autobiography). New York: Appleton-Century, 1934.

———. *The Edith Omnibus* (includes *The Age of Innocence, Ethan Frome,* and *Old New York*—four short novels). New York: Scribner's, 1978.

~ Wheatley, Phillis
(ca. 1753–1784)   *poet*

Born in Africa, brought to America and sold into slavery as a young girl, and plagued by frail health for most of her short life, Phillis Wheatley nonetheless became the first significant black American writer and one of the most respected poets of her time. *Poems on Various Subjects, Religious and Moral* (1773) was the first book of poetry, and probably the first book of any kind, published by an African American.

Phillis Wheatley, who was born in West Africa around 1753, was kidnapped and brought on a slave ship to Boston in 1761. As Wheatley would later write, she was "snatch'd from Afric's fancy'd happy seat." A prominent Boston merchant, John Wheatley, bought the sickly girl, who was dressed in rags, to be the personal servant of his wife, Susanna. The Wheatleys, a deeply religious family, were struck by Phillis's remarkable intelligence. Although she was expected to perform certain domestic chores, she was provided with her own room and an education that was remarkable for its time. With Mrs. Wheatley as her primary tutor, protector, and friend, Phillis studied the Bible, learned Latin, and read British literature, including the poetry of Alexander Pope and John Milton, her favorite, and the classical works of Homer, Terence, Ovid, and Virgil.

Like her owners, Phillis Wheatley was devoutly religious, and her Christian faith and enthusiasm for America infused her writings. Her first poem was published in 1767, but she gained wide public recognition in 1770 with her poem "An Elegiac Poem, on the Death of that Celebrated, Divine, and Eminent Servant of Jesus Christ, the Reverend and Learned George Whitefield." Wheatley was identified as "a Servant girl of 17 Years of Age, Belonging to Mrs. J. Wheatley, Boston—And has been but 9 years in the Country from Africa." Several other poems were published by 1773, when Wheatley sailed to England, where *Poems on Various Subjects, Religious and Moral,* the first book of verse by an African American, was published in

London. Some copies, which were also sold in Boston, appeared with a foreword signed by 18 prominent colonial figures, including Massachusetts Governor Thomas Hutchinson and John Hancock, affirming that a 20-year-old slave had, indeed, written the poems that appeared in the book. Wheatley was feted and honored in London. It was the high point of her life.

Wheatley received her freedom shortly after returning to Boston in the fall of 1773, but she continued to live with her former owners. However, beginning in 1774, when Susannah Wheatley died, Phillis Wheatley's fortunes took a turn for the worse. In October 1775, having enthusiastically embraced the revolutionary cause, she wrote a poem praising George Washington and sent it to the embattled general. He replied in February 1776 by inviting "a person so favored by the muses" to visit him at his Cambridge headquarters. But the American Revolution took its toll, and eventually the Wheatley family was scattered. In 1778, Phillis Wheatley married a free black man named John Peters. The marriage brought her little but poverty and hardship. None of the couple's three children survived for more than a few years.

Wheatley has been criticized for not condemning the evils of slavery, but in fact she did at times refer to its negative aspects. In one of her later poems, she denounced Christian slaveholders:

> But how presumptuous shall we hope to find
> Devine acceptance with the Almighty mind
> While yet o deed ungenerous they disgrace
> And hold in bondage Afric's blameless race.

While Wheatley was a celebrated poet in her time, most contemporary critics agree that she was not an outstanding one. Yet the magnitude of her literary achievement, given her circumstances, remains impressive. In *The Trials of Phillis Wheatley: America's First Black Poet and Encounters with the Founding Fathers* (2003), based on his 2002 Thomas Jefferson Lecture in the Humanities at the Library of Congress, the eminent scholar Henry Louis Gates, Jr., confirms and celebrates Wheatley's long-lasting literary significance. Gates examines the pivotal roles that Jefferson, a slave-owning politician, and Wheatley, a slave and literary prodigy, played in shaping the black literary tradition.

Phillis Wheatley died in Boston, suffering from cold and malnutrition, on December 5, 1784. Her last surviving child, who also died that day, was buried with her.

Further Reading

Abcarian, Richard, and Marvin Klotz, eds. "Phillis Wheatley." In *Literature: The Human Experience, 9th edition,* 473–474. New York: Bedford/St. Martin's, 2006.

Berkin, Carol. *Revolutionary Mothers: Women in the Struggle for America's Independence.* New York: Knopf, 2005.

Carretta, Vincent, ed. *Complete Writings by Phillis Wheatley.* New York: Putnam, 2001.

Gates, Henry Louis, Jr. *The Trials of Phillis Wheatley: America's First Black Poet and Encounters with the Founding Fathers.* New York: Basic Civitas Books, 2003.

Robinson, William H. *Phillis Wheatley and Her Writings.* New York: Garland, 1984.

Wheatley, Phillis. *The Poems of Phillis Wheatley.* Revised and enlarged edition. Edited and with an Introduction by Julian D. Mason, Jr. Chapel Hill: University of North Carolina Press, 1989.

Wilder, Laura Elizabeth Ingalls
(1867–1957)   *children's book writer*

Laura Ingalls Wilder is remembered for her popular, engaging books for children that comprised the acclaimed, best-selling "Little House" series (1932–43), which she began writing while in her 60s. They were based on Wilder's riveting experiences growing up among the early pioneers in America's frontier West.

One of four daughters, Laura Elizabeth Ingalls was born on February 7, 1867, in a log cabin on the edge of woods, near Pepin, Wisconsin. During the 1870s and 1880s, Laura and her family lived in six different Midwestern states. In spite of the many hardships they endured, including traveling by covered wagon through icy waters and over swollen rivers, and coping with malaria, plagues, drought, blizzards, and near-starvation, Wilder fondly recalled a "wonderful childhood." She artfully described her life on the frontier in the Little House series, which have offered millions of young readers a captivating but realistic picture of American pioneer life.

Wherever they settled, whether in a sod dugout or at a railroad camp, the Ingalls's house was, she wrote, filled with "love and music." Her father was an accomplished fiddler; her mother, a cultured woman, stressed the importance of education, family, and proper manners. Although Laura had her father's adventurous spirit, she also enjoyed reading. "I went to little red schoolhouses all over the west and never graduated from anything," Wilder once said. "The only reason I can think of being able to write at all was that father and mother were great readers and I read a lot at home with them."

After Laura's mother issued a "no further" edict, the Ingalls stopped traveling and set up a homestead in De Smet, in an area that became South Dakota. At age 15, Laura taught at a country school 12 miles from her home, boarding with a disagreeable family and braving blizzards to return home on weekends, where she would entertain, through her imaginative stories, her blind sister, Mary. On August 25, 1885, Laura married Almanzo James Wilder, a homesteader and horse trainer. The first year of their marriage was fraught with problems. Their crops failed and Almanzo became partially, though never permanently, paralyzed from a bout with diphtheria. In 1886 they had a daughter, Rose, but they lost an infant son, as well as their house, which had burned to the ground in a fire. After moving numerous times, they bought a small farm and a one-room cabin with no windows in Mansfield, Missouri. They built up the farm and lived there for the rest of their lives.

Wilder began writing for the *Missouri Ruralist,* a country journal, and published articles in *McCall's* and *Country Gentleman.* Her daughter, Rose Wilder Land, who had married, divorced, and become a journalist and novelist, encouraged her mother to record her childhood remembrances and later helped her edit and shape her manuscripts. In 1932, Wilder published her first book, *Little House in the Big Woods,* a tale about her experiences: "Once upon a time, sixty years ago, a little girl lived in the Big Woods of Wisconsin, in a little gray house made of logs." So began her childhood saga, although as Janet Spaeth pointed out in her study of Wilder's works, the author's goal was "to retain the larger truth that she wanted to convey— the pioneer experiences in America." Wilder never patronized her young readership: She wrote her entertaining tales from the point of view of a child, using honest, unsentimental, direct prose.

The second Little House book, *Farmer Boy* (1933), was based on Almanzo's boyhood experiences on a farm in northern New York State in the 1860s. With her next book, the best-selling *Little House on the Prairie* (1935), Wilder returned to her girlhood and depicted the Ingalls's journey, by covered wagon, to a little house on the prairie in Kansas. Five more books in the series followed, including *On the Banks of Plum Creek* (1937), in which a grasshopper plague completely destroys the family's wheat harvest and livelihood:

The grasshoppers walked steadily over the house. They walked over the stable. They walked over Spot until Pa shut her in the stable. They walked into Plum Creek and drowned, and those behind kept on walking in and drowning until dead grasshoppers choked the creek and filled the water and live grasshoppers walked across on them.

The eighth book in the series, *These Happy Golden Years* (1943), recounts Wilder's adolescent years as a teacher and ends with her marriage at age 18: Laura separates from her parents and begins her own frontier life. At 76, Wilder had completed her widely read Little House series, although some consider *The First Four Years,* which Wilder never edited or planned to publish, and which appeared posthumously in 1971, the last volume. In 1954, the American Library Association established the Laura Ingalls Wilder Award, with Wilder as their first recipient. Her books have since been translated into more than 20 languages and were adapted for a popular weekly television series, *Little House on the Prairie,* which aired from 1974 to 1982.

"The proliferation of Wilder scholarship has been remarkable in the 1990s," asserts Susan N. Maher in a book review that appeared in *The Lion and the Unicorn* (2000), a journal devoted to literature for children published by the Johns Hopkins Press. "Fortunately the quality of this literature is high, in contrast to some of the questionable products [*Little House* items such as dolls and cookbooks]." Maher also points out that "despite scholarly ambivalence toward Wilder's patriarchal family, her representation of Native Americans, and her political beliefs, a plethora of insightful, critical studies marks the continued centrality of Laura Ingalls Wilder in American children's literature."

Beyond the Prairie: The True Story of Laura Ingalls Wilder premiered as a television movie in 2000 and, despite the discrepancies between Wilder's real life and what was presented as factual in the movie, it was nominated for an Emmy Award. In 2005 a new television version of the celebrated series, *Laura Ingalls Wilder's Little House on the Prairie,* debuted. According to *TV Reviews,* critics and audiences alike responded favorably to the six-hour miniseries. However, it was not as successful as the original 1970s series.

Laura Ingalls Wilder, the sturdy farm wife with a frontier education, who had become one of the most respected, beloved, and best-selling children's writers of the 20th century, died on February 10, 1957, at the age of 90, in Mansfield, Missouri. The home she and Almanzo had built has since been turned into a public museum. In her work, as in her life, Wilder proved that "it is still best to be honest and truthful; to make the most of what we have; to be happy with simple pleasures and to be cheerful and courageous when things go wrong."

Further Reading

Maher, Susan Naramore. Review of *Becoming Laura Ingalls Wilder: The Woman behind the Legend,* by John E. Miller, and *Constructing the Little House: Gender, Culture, and Laura Ingalls Wilder,* by Ann Romines. *The Lion and the Unicorn* 24, no. 1 (January 2000): 162–168.

Miller, John E. *Becoming Laura Ingalls Wilder: The Woman behind the Legend.* Columbia: University of Missouri Press, 1998.

Spaeth, Janet. *Laura Ingalls Wilder.* Boston: Twayne, 1987.

Wilder, Laura Ingalls. *The Little House Series* (nine books, boxed edition, reissued). Illustrated by Garth Williams. New York: Harper and Row, Publishers, 1953.

∾ Williams, Paulette Linda
See SHANGE, NTOZAKE

∾ Wilson, Harriet E. Adams
(ca. 1827–ca. 1870)   *novelist*

The inadvertent discovery in 1983 of Harriet E. Adams Wilson's autobiographical novel *Our Nig* (1859), by the black studies scholar and critic Henry Louis Gates, Jr., led to the realization that Wilson was the first black female novelist in America and, according to Gates, "one of the first major innovators of American fictional narrative form." *Our Nig* was also unusual in that the villainous characters are not southern slaveholders but northerners who professed to be abolitionists.

Harriet E. Adams was probably born in Milford, New Hampshire, around 1827. Very little is known about her life, other than details gleaned from *Our Nig,* a few public documents, and new information reported by Barbara White in *American Literature* in 1993. As an indentured servant (someone bound to work for another for a specified period), Harriet was hired out when she was six to Nehemiah Hayward and his wife Rebecca Hutchinson, who came from a wealthy, prominent family in Milford and whose relatives were well-known abolitionists. Nonetheless, Wilson based the cruel "she-devil" character, Mrs. Bellmont, in *Our Nig,* on Rebecca Hutchinson Hayward. It is Mrs. Bellmont and her daughter who beat and overwork the novel's heroine, Alfrado, an orphaned mulatto abandoned by her white mother.

Adams left the Haywards, ill and exhausted, when she was 18; she began to work for other white families. One woman taught her millinery skills and provided her with reading material. In 1851 she married Thomas Wilson, a lecturer who pretended he was a fugitive slave and railed against slavery's horrors. Thomas Wilson soon abandoned his wife and their newborn son, George Mason, who was born in 1852 in a disease-infested pauper's farm. Impoverished and too sick to work, Wilson gave her son up to white foster parents and, confined to bed, turned to writing as a way of earning enough money to keep him from being sent back to the pauper's farm. Published on September 5, 1859, *Our Nig* ends with a direct plea to Wilson's "colored brethren" to buy the book to help her support herself and her child. Sadly, her seven-year-old son died six months after the book came out. His death certificate officially established his mother's racial identity—some literary critics had assumed the author of *Our Nig* was a white male. Harriet E. Adams Wilson was listed in the Boston City Directory in 1863, but after that her name disappeared from the public record.

Wilson's third-person fictional narrative, the full title of which was *Our Nig; or, Sketches from the Life of a Free Black, in a Two-Story White House, North, Showing That Slavery's Shadows Fall Even There,* was largely ignored for more than a century. In the early 1980s, Gates came across a copy of it in a bookstore in New York City. Recognizing its significance, he helped see that it was reissued in 1983. The African-American novelist ALICE WALKER later recalled, "I sat up most of the night reading and pondering the enormous significance of Harriet Wilson's novel *Our Nig.* It is as if we'd just discovered Phillis Wheatley—or Langston Hughes." Although typical of the novels of the time, with its long-suffering female heroine, *Our Nig* has been praised for being less contrived and more original and inventive than most other conventional sentimental novels of that period. In addition, it offers a riveting portrait of a black indentured servant mistreated by a Northern family that espoused abolitionist views: "Mrs. Bellmont and Mary [her daughter] commenced beating her inhumanly; then propping her mouth open with a piece of wood, shut her up in a dark room without any supper." Alfrado stands up to her mistress and, like Wilson, leaves New Hampshire (Wilson lived in Boston from 1856 until 1863), learns a trade, and briefly achieves a sense of independence and happiness. But she is abandoned by her husband, a fugitive slave, and becomes ill, destitute, and unable to take care of her newborn child.

Although it is difficult to ascertain exactly what extent *Our Nig* was based on Wilson's own life and what she fabricated, she wrote a well-crafted story and created her own plot structure to narrate her troubling saga. Alice Walker, pondering what would have happened to Harriet E. Adams Wilson had she been granted "a body of her own, a room of her own, and a love of her own," speculated that she would have assumed the stature of such well-known black male novelists as Paul Laurence Dunbar and Charles Chestnutt.

In April 2003, the Harriet Wilson Project was formed in Milford, New Hampshire, the birthplace of the "mother of the African-American novelist tradition," as Henry Louis Gates, Jr., has called Wilson. The project's goal is to raise awareness about the life and literary and historical accomplishments of Harriet Wilson through statewide and local discussions of her work and the creation of a memorial statue to honor the indentured servant-turned-novelist. When the memorial statue was completed in 2006, Wilson became the first person of color in New Hampshire history to have a monument in her likeness.

Further Reading

Curtis, Davis Ames, and Henry Louis Gates, Jr. "Establishing the Identity of the Author of *Our Nig.*" In *Wild Women in the Whirlwind: Afra-American Culture and the Contemporary Renaissance,* edited by Joanne Braxton and Andree McLaughlin, 48–69. New Brunswick, N.J.: Rutgers University Press, 1990.

"Harriet Wilson." The Harriet Wilson Project. Available online. URL: http://www.harrietwilsonproject.org/. Downloaded on January 24, 2007.

White, Barbara. "*Our Nig* and the She-Devil: New Information about Harriet Wilson and the Bellmont Family." *American Literature* 65, no. 1 (March 1993): 19–51.

Wilson, Harriet E. Adams. *Our Nig; or, Sketches from the Life of a Free Black*. With an introduction by Henry Louis Gates, Jr. 3d ed., reprinted from the 1859 edition. New York: Vintage, 2002.

∾ Wofford, Chloe Anthony
See MORRISON, TONI

∾ Wylie, Elinor Morton Hoyt
(1885–1928)   *poet, novelist*

During a brief period of eight years, from 1921 to 1928, Elinor Wylie produced four books of poems and four novels that turned her from a relatively unknown writer into an important American literary figure. Although her reputation declined after the 1950s, her work has enjoyed a renewed level of interest and appreciation since the 1980s.

Elinor Morton Hoyt was born on September 7, 1885, in Somerville, New Jersey, into a prominent but troubled family. Her mother was a controlling hypochondriac, while her father, who held important posts in the administrations of Presidents William McKinley and Theodore Roosevelt, remained remote from his family. Of Elinor's four siblings, a brother and sister committed suicide, and another brother attempted suicide. Elinor's appearance—her striking, ethereal beauty and elegant style—stood in marked contrast to her own problems, including chronic high blood pressure, frequent migraine headaches, and a deeply-rooted sense of insecurity that even the considerable acclaim she received as a writer during the 1920s could not help alleviate.

Married three times, Wylie never found personal happiness. In 1905, with President Theodore Roosevelt in attendance, she wed Philip Hichborn, the son of an admiral. But five years later she abandoned him and her three-year-old son in favor of Horace Wylie, a wealthy lawyer who was already married and had four children of his own. Ostra-

cized by their peers, the couple lived in England until 1915, three years after the unstable Hichborn committed suicide. They returned to the United States and, once Horace was finally divorced, married in 1916. Wylie's attempts to have a child with Horace ended in several miscarriages and a stillbirth.

Horace Wylie believed strongly in his wife's literary talent and encouraged her to write. During their marriage, she published her first major poetry collection, *Nets to Catch the Wind* in 1921 (in 1912 a small collection of early poems had been printed privately and anonymously in England).

It was an immediate success and contained some of her best poetry, including "Velvet Shoes," which has since become her most widely anthologized poem. By the early 1920s, Wylie's admirers included luminaries such as the novelists Sinclair Lewis and John Dos Passos and the critics Edmund Wilson and Carl Van Doren. Another ardent fan was William Rose Benét, the brother of Stephen Vincent Benét, the well-known poet and editor of the prestigious *Saturday Review of Literature*. In 1923, two years after separating from Horace, Wylie married Benét but kept her second husband's name. That same year, Wylie published a second successful volume of poetry, *Black Armour,* and her first novel, *Jennifer Lorn: A Sedate Extravaganza,* a romance set in 18th-century England and France. It also enjoyed popular and critical success. Wylie's second novel, which some critics consider her best, was *The Venetian Glass Nephew* (1925), a fantasy romance set in 18th-century Venice. It tells the story of a young woman who falls in love with a man who has been created, magically, out of glass; she volunteers to be turned into glass herself in order to love the artificial man. In Wylie's first two novels, the heroine is a wife who is destroyed because she is subordinated to the demands of others.

As a poet, Wylie attempted to perfect what she called her "small clean technique." She confined her finely crafted poems to a few simple themes and composed them using short stanzas and lines. Often those themes reflected her own personal frustrations, including her inability to respond passionately to her husbands and lovers. She expressed her acute bitterness especially well in "This Hand," a poem published in *Black Armour*. Although Wylie's poems were praised during her lifetime, after her death some critics found them lacking in depth.

Wylie's two later novels reflect her obsession with and admiration for the English romantic poet Percy Bysshe Shelley. She devoted the books *The Orphan Angel* (1926) and *Mr. Hodge and Mr. Hazard* (1928) to him, and one biographer has suggested that she transferred to Shelley "the affection, care, and devotion she withheld from her three husbands." Yet Wylie's work as a whole represents much more than a reflection of her personal problems. As one critic pointed out in 1986, "Her technical mastery enabled her to create precise images of great beauty." Another critic observed in *Dictionary of Literary Biography* that "Without a doubt the poems and novels of Elinor Wylie can stand on their own, even if we do not know the tortured woman beneath the silvery-cool facade of physical beauty."

In 1928, having separated from Benét, Wylie was planning to leave the United States and settle in England. By then she had fallen in love with a wealthy married Englishman, Henry de Clifford Woodhouse, who became the subject of a sequence of 19 critically acclaimed sonnets that were included in her fourth poetry volume, *Angels and Earthly Creatures* (1929), which appeared shortly after her death.

Elinor Wylie died of a stroke in New York City on December 16, 1928, while working on the typescript of *Angels and Earthly Creatures*. Only a few select friends and family members were at her funeral. The poet EDNA ST. VINCENT MILLAY placed a laurel wreath atop her peer's beautifully coiffed hair. Wylie was buried near her father, in Wilkes-Barre, Pennsylvania. The epigraph on her gravestone consisted of two lines, one from the New Testament and the other a line of verse by the romantic poet who so commanded her passion, Percy Bysshe Shelley.

Further Reading

Farr, Judith. *The Life and Art of Elinor Wylie*. Baton Rouge: Louisiana State University Press, 1983.

Hively, Evelyn Hemlick. *A Private Madness: The Genius of Eleanor Wylie*. Kent, Ohio: Kent State University Press, 2003.

Olsen, Stanley. *Elinor Wylie: A Life Apart*. New York: Dial Press, 1979.

Wylie, Elinor. *Collected Poems of Elinor Wylie*. New York: Knopf, 1932.

———. *Collected Prose of Elinor Wylie*. New York: Knopf, 1933.

———. *Selected Works of Elinor Wiley*. Edited by Evelyn Helmick Hively. Kent, Ohio: Kent State University Press, 2005.

~ Yamamoto, Hisaye

(1921–)   *short story writer, essayist*

Hisaye Yamamoto was one of the first Japanese-American writers to gain national recognition after World War II. Blending compassion, wit, and subtle irony, Yamamoto often writes about Nisei (second-generation Japanese-American) women, like herself. Most of her short stories, she says, deal with the "interaction of the Japanese tradition with the American experience."

The daughter of Japanese immigrant farmers, Hisaye Yamamoto was born in Redondo Beach, California, in 1921, and spent most of her childhood in small Southern California communities. "I had early contracted the disease of compulsive reading," she noted in an autobiographical essay. As a teenager, she wrote short stories and poetry, sometimes under the pseudonym Napoleon. She received her first rejection slip when she was 14 and her first acceptance from a major literary journal at age 27. In between, she was always writing. In an early poem, Hisaye described her skin as "sun-gold," her cheekbones as "proud," and her hair "touched with the dusky bloom of purple plums."

Soon after Japan bombed Pearl Harbor on December 7, 1941, and the United States was catapulted into World War II, the Yamamotos were forced to move to an internment camp for Japanese Americans. Hisaye's family was assigned to the Colorado River Relocation Center in Poston, Arizona, and remained there until 1944, when she and her two brothers were sent to work in Massachusetts. Hisaye became a cook for a wealthy widow and described her amusing experiences in "The Pleasure of Plain Rice" (*Rafu Shimpo,* 1960). After her 19-year-old brother was killed in combat in Italy, while serving with the U.S. Army, Yamamoto and her siblings returned to Poston. She formed important, long-lasting friendships at the camp and set several of her most haunting and successful stories at relocation centers. Many of her characters are brave or frightened women who suffer long-term effects of incarceration. The "Camp Experience," asserts Yamamoto, "is an episode in our collective life which wounded us more painfully than we realize."

While at Poston, Yamamoto became a columnist for the relocation center's newspaper. After her family was liberated in 1945, she took a job as a reporter for the *Los Angeles Tribune,* an African-American weekly and one of the few newspapers that would hire anyone who looked Japanese. In

1948, she published "The High-Heeled Shoes," a story about sexual harassment, in *Partisan Review,* a prominent literary magazine. Her short fiction and essays, on subjects that ranged from interracial marriage to the relationship between a Nisei woman and an Inuit man who corresponds with her from prison, also appeared in *Harper's Bazaar* and *Kenyon Review.*

In 1950, Yamamoto received a fellowship from the John Hay Whitney Foundation, enabling her to write full time for a year. More accolades followed: one of her best-known stories, "Yoneko's Earthquake," about Japanese-American tenant farmers, was selected for inclusion in *The Best American Short Stories, 1952.* Three other stories were chosen for the annual listing of "Distinctive Short Stories" in *Best American Short Stories.* From 1953 to 1955 she volunteered, with her adopted son, in a Catholic Worker rehabilitation farm in New York. She married Anthony DeSoto in 1955, returned with him to Los Angeles, and had four more children. In 1986 she won the prestigious American Book Award for Lifetime Achievement from the Before Columbus Foundation.

Yamamoto's only published book, *Seventeen Syllables and Other Stories* (1988), is a collection of 15 stories that span her 40-year literary career. It includes her most widely anthologized story, "Seventeen Syllables," which originally appeared in *Partisan Review.* Based loosely on her mother, the tale revolves around a repressed Issei (Japanese immigrant) who writes haiku in the evenings after having completed her chores. She wins a haiku contest, but her husband, a farmer who has no interest in poetry or art, destroys the prize by setting it on fire. The woman's horrified daughter observes that her mother, "was very calm" as she watched "the dying fire . . . until there remained only a feeble smoke under the blazing sun."

In her introduction to *Seventeen Syllables and Other Stories,* which received the Award for Literature from the Association for Asian American Studies, King-Kok Cheung, a professor of English and Asian-American studies at the University of Califor-

nia in Los Angeles, compares Yamamoto's best stories to the "masterpieces of GRACE PALEY, FLANNERY O'CONNOR, and Katherine Mansfield." Cheung points out that Yamamoto confronts religious, familial, and moral issues in her fiction, but is "never dogmatic or moralistic in her judgement." When she is not writing, Hisaye Yamamoto stays busy by taking care of her "family, flowers, and friends."

The late Amy Ling, who had been a professor in the department of English and the Asian American studies program at the University of Wisconsin, in an essay about Yamamoto published in 2000, wrote:

> Because of her own trauma of imprisonment as an adolescent, Yamamoto takes a particularly sympathetic stance toward others whom society has cast aside as 'undesirables.' With her keen, nonjudgmental eye and her large compassion for all of human variety, Yamamoto forces her reader to reconsider such categories as sanity and insanity, good and evil, weakness and strength, value and worthlessness. . . . Using understatement, emotional restraint, condensation, and indirection, her stories show us the arbitrariness of racial, sexual, and class divisions and hierarchies, and challenge us to expand our capacity for love.

Further Reading

"Hisaye Yamamoto." *20th Century American Women Writers.* Available online. URL: http://faculty.ccc.edu/wr-womenauthors/pinkver/yamamoto.htm. Downloaded on March 7, 2007.

Ling, Amy. "Hisaye Yamamoto." In *The Columbia Companion to the Twentieth-Century American Short Story,* edited by Blanche H. Gelfant, 596–600. New York: Columbia University Press, 2000.

McDonald, Dorothy Risuko, and Katharine Newman. "Relocation and Dislocation: The Writings of Hisaye Yamamoto and Wakako Yamauchi." *MELUS* 7, no. 3 (Fall 1980): 21–38.

Schweik, Susan. *So Deeply Cut: American Women Poets and the Second World War.* Madison: University of Wisconsin Press, 1991.

Yamamoto, Hisaye. *Seventeen Syllables and Other Stories.* With an introduction by King-Kok Cheung. New Brunswick, N.J.: Rutgers University Press, 1998.

～ Yezierska, Anzia
(ca. 1880–1970)   *novelist, short story writer*

In her short stories and novels, Anzia Yezierska vividly portrayed turn-of-the-century Eastern European Jewish immigrant women who lived in New York City in poverty and despair but who longed to assimilate and take more control of their lives. Yezierska's autobiographical fiction was popular in the 1920s and again beginning in 1975, when her classic feminist novel, *Bread Givers* (1925), was reissued.

Born in a mud hut in the Russian-Polish village of Plotsk, around 1880, Anzia Yezierska was the youngest of seven children. She emigrated to America when she was about 10 and lived with her impoverished family in a crowded tenement apartment on New York City's Lower East Side. Her father was an old-fashioned, pious Talmudic scholar who depended on his wife and children for money. A bright, curious child, Anzia was forced to drop out of public school and work full-time in sweatshops and as a domestic for wealthy families. Determined to escape the dreariness of the ghetto, she studied English at night and eventually was able to attend Columbia University's Teachers College as a scholarship student in domestic science.

After a brief marriage that was annulled, Yezierska in 1911 married Arnold Levitas, a high school teacher. The following year, the couple had a child, Louise. Unable to cope with familial responsibilities, she left her second husband in 1916 and sent her daughter to live with him. Louise Levitas Henriksen, who later become Yezierska's biographer, described her mother as "an emotional volcano"— smart, impassioned, and courageous, but also moody and egotistical.

In 1913, Yezierska began to write short stories, not in her native tongue, Yiddish (the language of European Jewry), but in her own form of English that sounded like Yiddish—the way her immigrant characters really spoke. In 1915, her first short story, "Free Vacation House," appeared in *Forum.* Its spirited protagonist was a poor Russian-Jewish woman forced to put up with a condescending German-Jewish social worker who provided "scientific charity," as Yezierska put it, to newly arrived immigrants. During the next decade many of her stories would appear in respected magazines and journals.

Yezierska audited a graduate seminar in social and political thought at Columbia University in 1917 led by the philosopher John Dewey. "I want to make from myself a person!" she told him. Dewey read and was impressed by her work, and became enamored with his red-headed, passionate young student. She considered Dewey a brilliant "Yankee" who "opened the wings of her soul." But their affair was never consummated, and the relationship ended in disappointment for both of them. Nonetheless, Yezierska was deeply affected by the relationship and based several of her fictional characters on Dewey. She gained national recognition when one of her stories, "The Fat of the Land," was included in Edward J. O'Brien's *Best Short Stories of 1919,* and with the publication in 1920 of her first acclaimed collection of short stories about Jewish immigrant life, *Hungry Hearts.* Movie producer Samuel Goldwyn brought her to Hollywood to write the screenplay, which was adapted as a silent film in 1922. Dubbed "Queen of the Ghetto" by the press, Yezierska hated Hollywood and called it a "fish-market in evening clothes." She felt like "a tortured soul with a bank account," according to historian Alice Kessler-Harris, "because her muse lay in the ghetto and without it she could not write." Within a year, she returned to New York.

Yezierska wrote her first novel, *Salome of the Tenements* (1923), basing the plot on the marriage of her immigrant Jewish friend to an upper-class Protestant "real" American. That same year, she published another well-received collection of short fiction, *Children of Loneliness,* in which the protagonist declared, "My one story is hunger." Most of her female characters are feisty and fiercely determined to acculturate, but are thwarted by economic, social, and sexual barriers; still, they do not give up on the American dream. Yezierska's best-known and most fully-realized novel, *Bread Givers*

361

(1925), subtitled *A Struggle between a Father of the Old World and a Daughter of the New,* is a poignant, largely autobiographical indictment of her father's authoritarianism. The *New York Times Book Review* praised its "raw, uncontrollable poetry and powerful, sweeping design." By the 1930s, however, publishers were no longer interested in Yezierska's immigrant tales, and some critics found her work "too Jewish." In the early 1930s, she worked for the Work Projects Administration (WPA) Writers' Project, cataloging trees in Central Park.

Yezierska's fictionalized autobiography, *Red Ribbon on a White Horse* (1950), recounted her early life on the Lower East Side of New York and her desire to escape the "black curse of poverty." However, when it suited her, she omitted certain essential details about herself, such as having had a child. Her last published story, "Take up Your Bed and Walk," written from the perspective of an elderly Jewish woman, appeared in the *Chicago Jewish Forum* in 1969, a year before she died in Ontario, California, on November 21, 1970, at age 90. Five years later, *Bread Givers* was reissued.

One of the first American Jewish fiction writers to become popular, and to depict deftly the Jewish immigrant experience from a woman's point of view, Anzia Yezierska had, as one of her characters said, "wandered between two worlds that are at once too old and too new to live in." However, with renewed interest in her writings, her works live on. Included in *500 Great Books by Women: A Reader's Guide,* Yezierska's acclaimed novel *Bread Givers* was reprinted in a third edition in 2003. *Bread Givers,* asserted the distinguished American literary critic, social commentator, and historian Irving Howe, "is one of the authentic and touching testaments of the struggle of Jewish immigrants, especially Jewish women, to find their way in the new world."

Further Reading

Bolton-Fasman, Judy. "*Bread Givers* by Anzia Yezierska." The Jewish Reader, April 2004. Available online. URL: http://yiddishbookcenter.org/story.php?n-10146. Downloaded on March 7, 2007.

Henriksen, Louise Levitas. *Anzia Yezierska: A Writer's Life.* New Brunswick, N.J.: Rutgers University Press, 1988.

———. *How I Found America: Collected Stories by Anzia Yezierska.* New York: Persea, 1991.

———. *The Open Cage: An Anzia Yezierska Collection.* Edited and with an introduction by Alice Kessler-Harris. New York: Persea, 1979.

———. *Red Ribbon on a White Horse.* New York: Scribner's, 1950.

Konzett, Delia C. *Ethnic Modernisms: Anzia Yezierska, Zora Neale Hurston, Jean Rhys, and the Aesthetics of Dislocation.* New York: Palgrave Macmillan, 2002.

Yezierska, Anzia. *Bread Givers.* With a revised introduction by Alice Kessler-Harris. 3d ed. New York: Persea, 2003.

Z

Zitkala Sa (Gertrude Simmons Bonnin, Zitkala Să; Zitkala Sha)
(1876–1938) *short story writer, essayist*

A notable author and American Indian rights activist, Zitkala Sa (Gertrude Simmons Bonnin) was one of the first Native Americans to write about her life without the assistance of non-Indians. Her stories and essays reflect both her pride in her Sioux heritage and, because of her exposure to non-Indian education and customs, a sense of displacement.

Gertrude Bonnin was born on February 22, 1876, on South Dakota's Yankton Sioux Reservation, to a full-blooded Yankton Nakota (Sioux) mother and a white father whom she never knew. Her mother was remarried, to John Haysting Simmons, and Gertrude took his surname. At the age of eight, in spite of her mother's admonishing her to be wary of the "heartless paleface," Gertrude left the reservation to attend White's Indiana Manual Labor Institute, a Quaker-sponsored missionary school for Indians in Wabash, Indiana. Beaten and punished for speaking anything other than English, Gertrude realized that her mother had been right about distrusting the missionaries. But she quickly picked up English and became an excellent student. However, as she recalled in an essay in the *Atlantic Monthly*, when she went back to the reservation she was "neither a wild Indian nor a tame one." Nonetheless, she returned to White's school and earned a diploma.

At age 19, Simmons attended Earlham College in Richmond, Indiana, where she excelled as an orator; she won a state-wide competition in spite of racist taunts from other students. She also studied the violin and enrolled in education courses. After graduating in 1897, she taught at the Carlisle Industrial Boarding School in Pennsylvania, a prototype of schools set up for American Indians. But Simmons felt that the administration patronized its American Indian students by offering them a limited vocational curricula instead of the academic subjects available to white students. She left Carlisle and studied music at the New England Conservatory of Music in Boston, Massachusetts. At the 1900 Paris Exposition, she performed a violin solo with the Carlisle Indian Band.

While in Boston, Simmons began to hone another of her skills: writing. She published a series of well received autobiographical essays and short stories under the pseudonym Zitkala Sa ("red bird" in the Yankton language), in the *Atlantic Monthly* (1900 and 1902) and *Harper's Magazine* (1901).

Mostly she focused on her childhood experiences, such as time spent with her mother in a wigwam, or excursions "into the natural gardens where the voice of the Great Spirit is heard. . . ."

In 1901, she published her first book, *Old Indian Legends,* a collection of Nakota Iktomi (Trickster) stories. By translating the American Indian tales and myths that had been passed on to her into English, Zitkala Sa hoped to preserve them for future generations. She returned to the Yankton Reservation and in 1902 married Raymond T. Bonnin, a Nakota who worked for the Indian Service (which later became the Bureau of Indian Affairs). The Bonnins had a son, Raymond Ohiya, in 1903, and were assigned to the Uintah and Ouray Reservation in Utah, where they both were employed by the Indian Service. In 1911, Zitkala Sa joined a group of educated Indians to form the Society of American Indians (SAI). This marked the beginning of her lifelong activism as an Indian reformist.

In 1913, Zitkala Sa collaborated with the composer William Hanson in writing an opera, *Sundance,* which utilized authentic, traditional Yankton rituals, dance, and melodies. But increasingly she devoted herself to promoting Indian causes, such as restricting the use of peyote, which she contended was a twin evil for Indians, along with alcohol. In 1916, Zitkala Sa was elected secretary of the Society of American Indians, and the Bonnins moved to Washington, D.C. She became an effective lobbyist who helped change several Indian-related federal policies and attitudes toward Native Americans. She lectured throughout the country and for two years edited the society's periodical, *American Indian Magazine.* She also supported women's suffrage and in 1921 persuaded the wealthy leadership of the General Federation of Women's Clubs to establish an Indian Welfare Committee to help improve housing, education, and health care. At meetings, Zitkala Sa purposely wore Yankton attire, including a buckskin dress.

In 1921, her early short stories and vignettes were collected and published in *American Indian Stories* (1921). Appalled by the theft of oil-rich Indian lands in Oklahoma, which sometimes led to murdering Indian landowners, in 1924 Zitkala Sa coauthored a report entitled *Oklahoma's Poor Rich Indians, an Orgy of Graft and Exploitation of the Five Civilized Tribes, Legalized Robbery.* Two years later she helped found another Native American rights organization, the National Council of American Indians, and served as its president until she died in Washington, D.C., on January 26, 1938. She was buried in Arlington Cemetery, not because of her myriad achievements, but because her husband had been an army captain.

One of the most important Indian reformers of the 20th century, as a writer Zitkala Sa used her non-Indian education to help empower her tribal people by portraying, from a woman's point of view, their traditions, beliefs, and concerns.

In 2003, a new collection of Zitkala Sa's compelling stories and nonfiction writings was published, including background information about the author, selections from "Old Indian Legends" (retellings of oral story traditions), selections from *American Indian Magazine,* and a selection of Zitkala Sa's poetry and essays. Editors Cathy Davidson and Ada Norris note that Zitkala Sa "makes significant changes to the traditional tales in order to address key political and social issues . . . specifically, land infringement, challenges to tribal sovereignty, and the effects of missionary boarding schools on Yankton or Sioux culture more generally." Applying her own difficult personal experiences to larger issues such as assimilation and identity, Zitkala Sa forces readers to face the complexities of the tragic American Indian experience.

Further Reading

Hafen, P. Jane. "Zitkala Să." In *Encyclopedia of North American Indians,* edited by Frederick E. Hoxie, 708–710. Boston: Houghton Mifflin, 1996.

Henderson, Renee Melissa. "Gertrude Simmons Bonnin, Zitkala-Sa." Voices from the Gaps. Available online. URL: http://voices.cla.umn.edu/vg/Bios/entries/bonnin_

gertrude_simmons_zitkalasa.html. Downloaded on January 24, 2007.

Sonneborn, Liz. "Gertrude Simmons Bonnin." *A to Z of American Indian Women, Revised Edition,* 20–24. New York: Facts On File, 2007.

Zitkala-Sa. *American Indian Stories, Legends, and Other Writings.* Edited and with an introduction and notes by Cathy N. Davidson and Ada Norris. New York: Penguin, 2003.

———. "Impressions of an Indian Childhood." *Atlantic Monthly* 85 (January 1900): 37–47.

———. *Old Indian Legends.* Lincoln: University of Nebraska Press, 1985.

RECOMMENDED SOURCES ON AMERICAN WOMEN WRITERS

Allen, Paula Gunn. *The Sacred Hoop: Recovering the Feminine in American Indian Traditions.* Boston: Beacon Press, 1986.

Amoia, Alba, and Bettina L. Knapp, eds. *Multicultural Writers since 1915.* Westport, Conn.: Greenwood Press, 2004.

Anderson, Lorraine, ed. *Sisters of the Earth: Women's Prose and Poetry about Nature.* 2d ed. New York: Vintage Books, 2003.

Antler, Joyce. *The Journey Home: Jewish Women and the American Century.* New York: The Free Press, 1997.

Austenfeid, Thomas Carl. *American Women Writers and the Nazis: Ethics and Politics in Boyle, Porter, Stafford, and Hellman.* Charlottesville: University of Virginia Press, 2000.

Bailey, Brooke. *The Remarkable Lives of 100 Women Writers and Journalists.* Holbrook, Mass.: Bob Adams, 1994.

Barr, Marleen S. *Feminist Fabulation: Space/Postmodern Fiction.* Iowa City: University of Iowa Press, 1992.

Bataille, Gretchen M., ed. *Native American Women: A Biographical Dictionary.* New York: Garland, 1991.

Baum, Charlotte, et al., eds. *The Jewish Woman in America.* New York: Dial Press, 1975.

Belford, Barbara. *Brilliant Bylines: A Biographical Anthology of Notable Newspaperwomen in America.* New York: Columbia University Press, 1986.

Bell, Bernard W. *The Afro-American Novel and Its Tradition.* Amherst: University of Massachusetts Press, 1987.

Benbow-Pfalzgraf, Taryn, ed. *American Women Writers: A Critical Reference Guide from Colonial Times to the Present.* 2d ed. Detroit, Mich.: St. James Press, 1999.

Benstock, Sheri, ed. *The Private Self: Theory and Practice of Women's Autobiographical Writings.* Chapel Hill: University of North Carolina Press, 1988.

Bigsby, Christopher. *Contemporary American Playwrights.* New York: Cambridge University Press, 2000.

Blair, Virginia, et al., eds. *The Feminist Companion to Literature in English.* New Haven, Conn.: Yale University Press, 1990.

Bloom, Harold, ed. *American Women Poets.* New York: Chelsea House, 1986.

Botshon, Lisa, and Meredith Goldsmith, eds. *Middlebrow Moderns: Popular American Women Writers of the 1920s.* Boston: Northeastern University Press, 2003.

Bracks, Lean'tin L. *Writings on Black Women of the Diaspora: History, Language and Identity.* New York: Garland, 1997.

Braxton, Joanne, and Andree N. McLaughlin. *Wild Women in the Whirlwind: Afra-American Culture and the Contemporary Literary Renaissance.* New Brunswick, N.J.: Rutgers University Press, 1990.

Brown, Janet. *Taking Center Stage: Feminism in Contemporary American Drama.* Metuchen, N.J.: Scarecrow Press, 1991.

Bruce-Novoa, Juan D., ed. *Chicano Authors: Inquiring by Interview.* Austin: University of Texas Press, 1980.

Burt, Daniel S., ed. *The Chronology of American Literature.* Boston: Houghton Mifflin, 2004.

Cahill, Susan, ed. *Women Write: A Mosaic of Women's Voices in Fiction, Poetry, Memoir and Essay.* New York: New American Library, 2004.

———. *Writing Women's Lives: An Anthology of Autobiographical Narratives by Twentieth-Century American Women Writers.* New York: HarperCollins, 1994.

Cairns, Kathleen A. *Front-Page Women Journalists.* Lincoln: University of Nebraska Press, 2003.

Cane, Aleta Feinsod, and Susan Alves, eds. *The Only Efficient Instrument: American Women Writers and the Periodicals, 1837–1916.* Iowa City: University of Iowa Press, 2004.

Champion, Laurie, and Rhonda Austin, eds. *Contemporary American Women Fiction Writers.* Westport, Conn.: Greenwood Press, 2002.

Chin, Marilyn, and Victoria M. Chang, eds. *Asian American Poetry: The Next Generation.* Urbana-Champaign: University of Illinois Press, 2004.

Christian, Barbara. *Black Women Novelists: The Development of a Tradition, 1892–1976.* Westport, Conn.: Greenwood Press, 1980.

Coltelli, Laura. *Winged Words: American Indian Writers Speak.* Lincoln: University Press of Nebraska, 1990.

Corbett, William. *Literary New England: A History and Guide.* Winchester, Mass.: Faber and Faber, 1993.

Dance, D. Cumber, ed. *Fifty Caribbean Writers.* Westport, Conn.: Greenwood Press, 1986.

Davidson, Cathy N., and Linda Wagner-Martin, eds. *The Oxford Companion to Women's Writing in the United States.* New York: Oxford University Press, 1995.

Davis, Charles T., and Henry Louis Gates, Jr., eds. *The Slave's Narrative.* New York: Oxford University Press, 1984.

DeShazer, Mary K., ed. *The Longman Anthology of Women's Literature.* New York: Longman, Addison-Wesley, 2001.

Drake, William. *The First Wave: Women Poets in America, 1915–1945.* New York: Macmillan, 1987.

Duncan, Patti. *Tell This Silence: Asian American Writers and the Politics of Speech.* Iowa City: University of Iowa Press, 2004.

Dyer, Joyce, ed. *Bloodroots: Reflections on Place by Appalachian Women Writers.* Lexington: University of Kentucky Press, 1998.

Epel, Naomi. *Writers Dreaming: Twenty-six Writers Talk about Their Dreams and Creative Process.* New York: Vintage, 1993.

Erdrich, Heidi E., and Laura Tohre, eds. *Sister Nations: Native American Women Writers on Community.* Minneapolis: University of Minnesota Press, 2002.

Evans, Mari, ed. *Black Women Writers (1950–1980): A Critical Evaluation.* New York: Doubleday, 1984.

Faust, Langdon Lynne, ed. *American Women Writers: A Critical Reference Guide from Colonial Times to the Present.* New York: Frederick Ungar, 1979.

Ferguson, Margaret, and Jon Stallworthy, eds. *The Norton Anthology of Poetry, 4th ed.* New York: W. W. Norton, 1996.

Flora, Joseph H., and Lucinda H. Mackethan, eds. *The Companion to Southern Literature.* Baton Rouge: Louisiana State Press, 2002.

Gates, Henry Louis, Jr., and Neely Y. McKay, eds. *The Norton Anthology of African American Literature.* 2d ed. New York: W. W. Norton, 2004.

Gelfant, Blanche H., ed. *The Columbia Companion to the Twentieth-Century Short Story.* New York: Columbia University Press, 2000.

Gilbert, Sandra M., and Susan Gubar, eds. *The Norton Anthology of Literature by Women: The Traditions in English.* New York: W. W. Norton, 1996.

Green, Rayna. *That's What I Said: Contemporary Fiction and Poetry by Native American Women.* Bloomington: Indiana University Press, 1984.

Grunwald, Lisa, and Stephen J. Adler, eds. *Women's Letters: America from the Revolutionary War to the Present.* New York: Dial Press, 2005.

Halio, Jay L., and Ben Siegel, eds. *Women of Valor: Contemporary Jewish American Women Writers.* Newark: University of Delaware Press, 1997.

Halper, Donna L. *Invisible Stars: A Social History of Women in American Broadcasting*. New York: M. E. Sharpe, 2001.

Heredia, Juanita, and Bridget Kevane, eds. *Latina Self-Portraits: Interviews with Contemporary Women Writers*. Albuquerque: University of New Mexico Press, 2000.

Hogeland, Lisa Maria, and May Klages. *The Aunt Lute Anthology of U.S. Women Writers*. San Francisco: Aunt Lute Books, 2004.

Hongo, Garrett, ed. *The Open Boat: Poems from Asian America*. New York: Anchor/Doubleday, 1993.

Howe, Florence, and Ellen Bass, eds. *No More Masks! An Anthology of Poems by Women*. Garden City, N.Y.: Anchor, 1973.

Howorth, Lisa, ed. *The South: A Treasury of Art Literature*. New York: Hugh Lauter Levin Associates, 1993.

Huggins, Nathan Irvin, ed. *Voices from the Harlem Renaissance*. New York: Oxford University Press, 1976.

Hull, Gloria T. *Color, Sex, and Poetry: Three Women Writers of the Harlem Renaissance*. Bloomington: Indiana University Press, 1987.

James, Edward, T., ed. *Notable American Women*. Cambridge, Mass.: Belknap Press of Harvard University Press, 1971.

Johnson, Sarah Anne, ed. *Conversations with American Women Writers*. Lebanon, N.H.: University Press of New England, 2004.

Kalaidjian, Walter, ed. *The Cambridge Companion to American Modernism*. New York: Cambridge University Press, 2005.

Kanellos, Nicolás, ed. *Hispanic Literature of the United States*. Westport, Conn.: Greenwood Press, 2003.

Kerbel, Sorrel, ed. *Jewish Writers of the Twentieth Century*. New York: Routledge, 2003.

Kilcup, Karen L., ed. *Native American Women's Writing, 1800–1924*. Malden, Mass.: Blackwell Publishing, 2000.

Knight, Denise D., ed. *The Writers of the American Renaissance*. Westport, Conn.: Greenwood Press, 2003.

Lehman, David, ed. *The Oxford Book of American Poetry*. New York: Oxford University Press, 2006.

Lim, Shirley Geok-lin, et al., eds. *The Forbidden Stitch: An Asian American Women's Anthology*. Corvallis, Oreg.: Calyx, 1989.

Lindsay, Claire. *Locating Latin American Women Writers*. New York: Peter Lang, 2003.

Ling, Amy. *Between Worlds: Women Writers of Chinese Ancestry*. New York: Pergamon, 1990.

Madison, D. Soyini. *The Woman That I Am: The Literature and Culture of Contemporary Women of Color*. New York: St. Martin's, 1994.

Magil, Frank N., ed. *Great Women Writers: The Lives and Works of 135 of the World's Most Important Women Writers*. New York: Henry Holt, 1994.

Manning, Carol, ed. *Female Tradition in Southern Literature*. Bloomington: University of Illinois Press, 1993.

Marshall, Carmen Ross. *Black Professional Women in Recent American Fiction*. Jefferson, N.C.: McFarland and Company, 2003.

Martin, Wendy, ed. *More Stories We Tell: The Best Contemporary Short Stories by North American Women*. New York: Pantheon, 2004.

Mazolf, Marion. *Up from the Footnote: A History of Women Journalists*. New York: Hastings House, 1977.

Munt, Sally, ed. *New Lesbian Criticism: Literary and Cultural Readings*. New York: Columbia University Press, 1992.

Nelson, Emmanuel S., ed. *Contemporary Gay American Poets and Playwrights*. Westport, Conn.: Greenwood Press, 2003.

Ostriker, Alicia S. *Stealing the Language: The Emergence of Women's Poetry in America*. Boston: Beacon Press, 1986.

Pearl, Nancy. *Book Lust: Recommended Reading for Every Mood, Moment, and Reason*. Seattle, Wash.: Sasquatch Books, 2003.

Perry, Donna. *Women Writers Speak Out*. New Brunswick, N.J.: Rutgers University Press, 1993.

Petter, Henri. *The Early American Novel*. Columbus: Ohio State University Press, 1971.

Pierpoint, Claudia Roth. *Passionate Minds: Women Rewriting the World*. New York: Knopf, 2000.

Powers, Retha, and Kathy Kiernan, eds. *This Is My Best: Great Writers Share Their Favorite Books*. San Francisco: Chronicle Books, 2004.

369

Prenshaw, Peggy Whitman, ed. *Women Writers of the Contemporary South.* Jackson: University Press of Mississippi, 1984.

Pryse, Marjorie, and Hortense J. Spillers, eds. *Conjuring: Black Women, Fiction, and Literary Tradition.* Bloomington: Indiana University Press, 1985.

Reddy, Maureen T. *Sisters in Crime: Feminism and the Crime Novel.* New York: Continuum, 1988.

Richey, Elinor. *Eminent Women of the West.* Berkeley, Calif.: Howell-North Books, 1975.

Roberts, Cokie. *Founding Mothers: The Women Who Raised Our Nation.* New York: William Morrow, 2004.

Roses, Lorraine E. *The Harlem Renaissance and Beyond: 100 Black Women Writers, 1900–1945.* New York: Macmillan, 1989.

Rubin, Derek, ed. *Who We Are: On Being (And Not Being) a Jewish American Writer.* New York: Schocken Books, 2005.

Sanchez-Gonzalez, Lisa. *Boricua Literature: A Literary History of the Puerto Rican Diaspora.* New York: New York University Press, 2001.

Sawaya, Francesca. *Modern Women, Modern Work: Domesticity, Professionalism, and American Writing, 1890–1950.* Philadelphia: University of Pennsylvania Press, 2003.

Schlipp, Madelon Golden, and Sharon M. Murphy. *Great Women of the Press.* Carbondale: Southern Illinois University Press, 1983.

Schlueter, June, ed. *Modern American Drama: The Female Canon.* London, England: Fairleigh Dickinson Press, 1990.

Schweik, Susan. *So Deeply Cut: American Women Poets and the Second War.* Madison: University of Wisconsin Press, 1991.

Shorris, Earl. *Latinos: A Biography of the People.* New York: W. W. Norton, 1992.

Sinnott, Susan. *Extraordinary Hispanic Americans.* Chicago: Children's Press, 1991.

Slater, Elinor, and Robert Slater. *Great Jewish Women.* Middle Village, N.Y.: Jonathan David, 1994.

Solotaroff, Ted, ed. *Alfred Kazin's America: Critical and Personal Writings.* New York: HarperCollins, 2003.

Sonneborn, Liz. *A to Z of American Indian Women, Revised Edition.* New York: Facts On File, 2007.

Stauffer, Helen Winter, and Susan J. Rosowski. *Women and Western American Literature.* Troy, N.Y.: Whitson, 1982.

Sterling, Dorothy, ed. *We Are Your Sisters: Black Women in the Nineteenth Century.* New York: W. W. Norton, 1984.

Sternburg, Janet, ed. *The Writer on Her World.* New York: W. W. Norton, 1980.

Swanson, Jean, and David James. *By a Woman's Hand: A Guide to Mystery Fiction by Women.* New York: Berkeley Prime Crime, 1996.

Tate, Claudia, ed. *Black Women Writers at Work.* New York: Continuum, 1983.

Telgen, Diane, and Jim Kemp, eds. *Latinas! Women of Achievement.* Detroit, Mich.: Visible Ink Press, 1996.

Ware, Susan, ed. *Notable American Women: A Biographical Dictionary Completing the Twentieth Century.* Cambridge, Mass.: Belknap Press of Harvard University Press, 2005.

Watanabe, Sylvia, and Carol Bruchac, eds. *Home to Stay: Asian American Women's Fiction.* Greenfield Center, N.Y.: Greenfield Review Press, 1990.

Weatherford, Doris. *American Women's History.* New York: Prentice Hall, 1994.

West-Duran, Alan, ed. *Latino and Latina Writers.* New York: Charles Scribner's Sons, 2004.

Wilkinson, Brenda. *Black Stars: African-American Women Writers.* New York: John Wiley and Sons, 2000.

Wirth-Nesher, Hana. *Call It English: The Language of Jewish American Literature.* Princeton: Princeton University Press, 2005.

Wiser, William. *The Great Good Place: American Expatriate Women in Paris.* New York: W. W. Norton, 1991.

Wilson, Vincent, Jr. *The Book of Distinguished Women.* Brookeville, Md.: American History Research Associates, 1983.

Wong, Shawn, ed. *Asian American Literature.* New York: HarperCollins, 1996.

Zia, Helen. *Asian American Dreams: The Emergence of an American People.* New York: Farrar, Straus and Giroux, 2000.

Web Sites

American Women Writers, 1890–1929: Modernism and Mythology http://www.geocities.com/Wellesley/7327/modernism.html

Anthology of Modern American Poetry http://www.english.uiuc.edu/maps/index.htm

Archive of Nineteenth-Century U.S. Women's Writings http://www.facstaff.bucknell.edu/gcarr/19cUSWW

A Celebration of Women Writers http://digital.library.upenn.edu/women

Society for the Study of American Women Writers http://www.lehigh.edu/~dek7/SSAWW

Women Writers of the 20th Century http://womenshistory.about.com/od

ENTRIES BY LITERARY GENRE

Autobiographer

Angelou, Maya
Antin, Mary
Brooks, Gwendolyn
Dillard, Annie Doak
Fisher, Mary Frances
    Kennedy
Graham, Katharine
Jacobs, Harriet Ann
Truth, Sojourner
Welty, Eudora
Yezierska, Anzia

Biographer

Bowen, Catherine Drinker
Buck, Pearl Comfort
    Sydenstricker
Goodwin, Doris Helen
    Kearns
Hale, Sarah Josepha Buell
Lowell, Amy Lawrence
Ross, Ishbel Margaret
Tarbell, Ida Minerva

Children's/Young Adult Book Writer

Alcott, Louisa May
Allen, Paula Gunn
Angelou, Maya
Brown, Margaret Wise
Clifton, Lucille Sayles

Danticat, Edwidge
Hoffman, Alice
Le Guin, Ursula Kroeber
L'Engle, Madeleine
Lurie, Alison
Mohr, Nicholasa Golpe
Norton, Andre
Petry, Ann Lane
Quindlen, Anna
Rawlings, Marjorie Kinnan
Sanchez, Sonia
Sedgwick, Catharine Maria
Shange, Ntozake
Tan, Amy Ruth
Uchida, Yoshiko
Wilder, Laura Elizabeth
    Ingalls

Detective/Mystery Writer

Cornwell, Patricia
Grafton, Sue Taylor
Oates, Joyce Carol
Paretsky, Sara
Rinehart, Mary Roberts
Roberts, Nora

Diarist/Journal Writer

Dunbar-Nelson, Alice
    Ruth Moore
Nin, Anaïs
Sarton, May

Editor

Child, Lydia Maria Francis
Fauset, Jessie Redmon
Fuller, Sarah Margaret
Gilman, Charlotte Perkins
Graham, Katharine
Hale, Sarah Josepha Buell
Hardwick, Elizabeth
McMillan, Terry

Essayist

Allen, Paula Gunn
Antin, Mary
Bogan, Louise
Bombeck, Erma Louise Fiste
Boyle, Kay
Didion, Joan
Dillard, Annie Doak
Ehrenreich, Barbara
Flanner, Janet
Fuller, Sarah Margaret
Gordon, Mary Catherine
Hansberry, Lorraine Vivian
Hardwick, Elizabeth
Hogan, Linda Henderson
Jackson, Helen Maria
    Fiske Hunt
Kingsolver, Barbara
Levertov, Denise
Lorde, Audre Geraldin

Lurie, Alison
Morrison, Toni
Murray, Judith Sargent
Oates, Joyce Carol
Oliver, Mary
Olsen, Tillie Lerner
Ozick, Cynthia
Perillo, Lucia
Rich, Adrienne Cecile
Robinson, Marilynne
Rukeyser, Muriel
Sarton, May
Silko, Leslie Marmon
Sontag, Susan
Walker, Alice Malsenior
Wasserstein, Wendy
Yamamoto, Hisaye
Yezierska, Anzia
Zitkala Sa

Food/Travel Writer

Fisher, Mary Frances Kennedy
Simon, Kate
Wharton, Edith Newbold Jones

Horror Fiction Writer

Rice, Anne

Journalist

Barnes, Djuna
Bly, Nellie
Bombeck, Erma Louise Fiste
Bonfils, Martha Winifred
    Sweet Black
Carson, Rachel Louise
Didion, Joan
Ehrenreich, Barbara
Ferber, Edna
Flanner, Janet
Fuller, Sarah Margaret
García, Cristina
Herbst, Josephine Frey
Quindlen, Anna
Ross, Ishbel Margaret
Tarbell, Ida Minerva

Thompson, Dorothy
Wells-Barnett, Ida Bell

Letter Writer

Adams, Abigail Smith
Alcott, Louisa May
Bishop, Elizabeth
Dickinson, Emily Elizabeth

Literary Critic

Bogan, Louise
Fuller, Sarah Margaret
Glück, Louise Elisabeth
Hardwick, Elizabeth
McCarthy, Mary Therese
Parker, Dorothy Rothschild
Sontag, Susan
Stein, Gertrude

Memoirist

Clifton, Lucille Sayles
Erdrich, Karen Louise
Goodwin, Doris Helen
    Kearns
Gordon, Mary Catherine
Hellman, Lillian Florence
Herbst, Josephine Frey
Jong, Erica Mann
Kingston, Maxine Hong
Kumin, Maxine Winokur
Lorde, Audre Geraldin
McCarthy, Mary Therese
Miller, Sue
Santiago, Esmeralda
Settle, Mary Lee
Simon, Kate
Stein, Gertrude
Uchida, Yoshiko
Wharton, Edith Newbold Jones

Nature Writer

Austin, Mary Hunter
Carson, Rachel Louise
Dillard, Annie Doak

Nonfiction Book Writer

Carson, Rachel Louise
Child, Lydia Maria Francis
Cornwell, Patricia Daniels
Ehrenreich, Barbara
Fuller, Sarah Margaret
Gilman, Charlotte Perkins
Godwin, Gail Kathleen
Hamilton, Edith
McCarthy, Mary Therese
Quindlen, Anna
Rowlandson, Mary White
Tuchman, Barbara Wertheim
Warren, Mercy Otis

Novelist

Alcott, Louisa May
Allen, Paula Gunn
Alvarez, Julie
Arnow, Harriette Louisa
    Simpson
Auel, Jean Marie Untinen
Austin, Mary Hunter
Bambara, Toni Cade
Barnes, Djuna
Bombeck, Erma Louise Fiste
Boyle, Kay
Brooks, Gwendolyn
Brown, Rita Mae
Buck, Pearl Comfort
    Sydenstricker
Cather, Willa Sibert
Child, Lydia Maria Francis
Chopin, Katherine O'Flaherty
Chute, Carolyn
Danticat, Edwidge
Davis, Rebecca Harding
Didion, Joan
Doolittle, Hilda
Erdrich, Karen Louise
Fauset, Jessie Redmon
Ferber, Edna
Fisher, Mary Frances Kennedy
Flanner, Janet

Foster, Hannah Webster
Freeman, Mary Eleanor Wilkins
Gaitskill, Mary
García, Cristina
Gilman, Charlotte Perkins
Glaspell, Susan Keating
Godwin, Gail Kathleen
Gordon, Mary Catherine
Grafton, Sue Taylor
Hardwick, Elizabeth
Harper, Frances Ellen Watkins
Herbst, Josephine Frey
Hoffman, Alice
Hogan, Linda Henderson
Hurst, Fannie
Hurston, Zora Neale
Jackson, Helen Maria Fiske Hunt
Jackson, Shirley
Jen, Gish
Jewett, Theodora Sarah Orne
Jong, Erica Mann
Kincaid, Jamaica
Kingsolver, Barbara
Kingston, Maxine Hong
Kumin, Maxine Winokur
Lahiri, Jhumpa
Larsen, Nella
Lazarus, Emma
Lee, Nelle Harper
Le Guin, Ursula Kroeber
L'Engle, Madeleine
Loos, Anita
Lurie, Alison
Marshall, Paule
McCarthy, Mary Therese
McCullers, Lula Carson Smith
McDermott, Alice
McMillan, Terry
Miller, Sue
Mitchell, Margaret Munnerlyn
Mohr, Nicholasa
Moore, Lorrie
Morrison, Toni

Mourning Dove
Mukherjee, Bharati
Naylor, Gloria
Nin, Anaïs
Norman, Marsha
Norris, Kathleen Thompson
Oates, Joyce Carol
O'Connor, Mary Flannery
Ozick, Cynthia
Petry, Ann Lane
Piercy, Marge
Plath, Sylvia
Porter, Katherine Anne
Powell, Dawn
Proulx, Annie
Quindlen, Anna
Rand, Ayn
Rawlings, Marjorie Kinnan
Rice, Anne
Rinehart, Mary Roberts
Roberts, Nora
Robinson, Marilynne
Santiago, Esmeralda
Sarton, May
Sedgwick, Catharine Maria
Settle, Mary Lee
Sexton, Anne Gray Harvey
Shange, Ntozake
Shreve, Anita
Silko, Leslie Marmon
Sontag, Susan
Stafford, Jean
Steel, Danielle
Stein, Gertrude
Stowe, Harriet Elizabeth Beecher
Tan, Amy Ruth
Tsukiyama, Gail
Tyler, Anne
Walker, Alice Malsenior
Walker, Margaret Abigail
Welty, Eudora
West, Dorothy
Wharton, Edith Newbold Jones

Wilson, Harriet E. Adams
Wylie, Elinor Morton Hoyt
Yezierska, Anzia

Playwright

Barnes, Djuna
Ferber, Edna
Glaspell, Susan Keating
Hansberry, Lorraine Vivian
Hellman, Lillian Florence
Henley, Elizabeth Becker
Johnson, Georgia Douglas Camp
Loos, Anita
McCullers, Lula Carson Smith
Millay, Edna St. Vincent
Murray, Judith Sargent
Norman, Marsha
Portillo Trambley, Estela
Rinehart, Mary Roberts
Sanchez, Sonia
Shange, Ntozake
Smith, Anna Deavere
Stein, Gertrude
Vogel, Paula
Warren, Mercy Otis
Wasserstein, Wendy

Poet

Allen, Paula Gunn
Alvarez, Julia
Angelou, Maya
Bishop, Elizabeth
Bogan, Louise
Bradstreet, Anne Dudley
Brooks, Gwendolyn
Brown, Rita Mae
Chin, Marilyn
Cisneros, Sandra
Clampitt, Amy
Clifton, Lucille Sayles
Dickinson, Emily Elizabeth
Doolittle, Hilda
Dove, Rita Frances
Dunbar-Nelson, Alice Ruth Moore

Erdrich, Karen Louise
Glück, Louise Elisabeth
Hale, Sarah Josepha Buell
Harper, Francis Ellen
　　Watkins
Hogan, Linda Henderson
Howe, Julia Ward
Jackson, Helen Maria Fiske
　　Hunt
Johnson, Georgia Douglas
　　Camp
Jong, Erica Mann
Kumin, Maxine Winokur
Lazarus, Emma
Levertov, Denise
Lorde, Audre Geraldin
Lowell, Amy Lawrence
Millay, Edna St. Vincent
Moore, Marianne Craig
Murray, Judith Sargent
Olds, Sharon
Oliver, Mary
Paley, Grace Goodside
Parker, Dorothy Rothschild
Perillo, Lucia
Piercy, Marge
Plath, Sylvia
Rich, Adrienne Cecile
Rose, Wendy
Rukeyser, Muriel
Sanchez, Sonia
Sarton, May
Sexton, Anne Gray Harvey
Shange, Ntozake
Silko, Leslie Marmon
Teasdale, Sara Trevor
Walker, Alice Malsenior
Walker, Margaret Abigail
Warren, Mercy Otis
Wheatley, Phillis
Wylie, Elinor Morton Hoyt

Science Fiction/Historical Fantasy Writer

Butler, Octavia Estelle
Le Guin, Ursula Kroeber

Norton, Andre
Piercy, Marge
Roberts, Nora

Screenwriter

Brown, Rita Mae
Henley, Elizabeth Becker
Hoffman, Alice
Loos, Anita
McMillan, Terry
Parker, Dorothy Rothschild
Santiago, Esmeralda
Sontag, Susan

Short Story Writer

Bambara, Toni Cade
Boyle, Kay
Butler, Octavia Estelle
Cather, Willa Sibert
Chopin, Katherine
　　O'Flaherty
Chute, Carolyn
Cisneros, Sandra
Danticat, Edwidge
Davis, Rebecca Harding
Dove, Rita Frances
Dunbar-Nelson, Alice
　　Ruth Moore
Erdrich, Karen Louise
Ferber, Edna
Freeman, Mary Eleanor Wilkins
Gaitskill, Mary
Gilman, Charlotte Perkins
Godwin, Gail Kathleen
Gordon, Mary Catherine
Harper, Frances Ellen Wat-
　　kins
Hurst, Fannie
Jackson, Shirley
Jen, Gish
Jewett, Theodora Sarah Orne
Kincaid, Jamaica
Kingsolver, Barbara
Kumin, Maxine Winokur

Lahiri, Jhumpa
Larsen, Nella
Loos, Anita
Marshall, Paule
McCullers, Lula Carson
　　Smith
McDermott, Alice
Miller, Sue
Mohr, Nicholasa Golpe
Moore, Lorrie
Mourning Dove
Mukherjee, Bharati
Norton, Andre
Oates, Joyce Carol
O'Connor, Mary Flannery
Olsen, Tillie Lerner
Ozick, Cynthia
Paley, Grace Goodside
Parker, Dorothy Rothschild
Petry, Ann Lane
Porter, Katherine Anne
Portillo Trambley, Estela
Powell, Dawn
Proulx, Annie
Sedgwick, Catharine Maria
Stafford, Jean
Tyler, Anne
Welty, Eudora
West, Dorothy
Wharton, Edith Newbold
　　Jones
Yamamoto, Hisaye
Yezierska, Anzia
Zitkala Sa

Slave or Captivity Narrative Writer

Jacobs, Harriet Ann
Rowlandson, Mary White
Truth, Sojourner
Wilson, Harriet E. Adams

Travel Writer

Simon, Kate

ENTRIES BY REGION/SUBJECT MATTER/BACKGROUND/STYLE

Abolition Movement

Child, Lydia Maria Francis
Jacobs, Harriet Ann
Truth, Sojourner
Wilson, Harriet E. Adams

American Revolution

Adams, Abigail Smith
Warren, Mercy Otis
Wheatley, Phillis

Ancient Greece and Rome

Hamilton, Edith

Appalachia

Arnow, Harriette Louisa
Simpson

China

Buck, Pearl Comfort
Sydenstricker

Civil Rights

American Indian Rights
Allen, Paula Gunn
Jackson, Helen Maria Fiske
Hunt
Mourning Dove
Silko, Leslie Marmon

African-American Rights (See also Abolition Movement)
Hansberry, Lorraine Vivian
Harper, Frances Ellen Watkins

Women's Rights
Fuller, Sarah Margaret
Gilman, Charlotte Perkins
Jong, Erica Mann
Sontag, Susan
Truth, Sojourner
Wells-Bernett, Ida Bell

Civil War

Howe, Julia Ward
Mitchell, Margaret
Munnerlyn

Deep South

Henley, Elizabeth Becker
Lee, Nelle Harper
McCullers, Lula Carson Smith
O'Connor, Mary Flannery
Welty, Eudora

Expatriate Background

Barnes, Djuna
Flanner, Janet
Stein, Gertrude
Wharton, Edith Newbold
Jones

Florida

Rawlings, Marjorie Kinnan

Folklorists

Austin, Mary Hunter
Hurston, Zora Neale
Mourning Dove
Uchida, Yoshiko
Zitkala Sa

Gothic Writers

Alcott, Louisa May
Barnes, Djuna
Jackson, Shirley
Oates, Joyce Carol
Rice, Anne
Wharton, Edith Newbold
Jones

Harlem Renaissance/Black Arts Movement

Dunbar-Nelson, Alice
Ruth Moore
Fauset, Jessie Redmon
Hurston, Zora Neale
Larsen, Nella
Petry, Ann Lane
Sanchez, Sonia
West, Dorothy

Immigrant or Cross-Cultural Experiences

American Indian

Allen, Paula Gunn
Erdrich, Karen Louise
Mourning Dove
Rose, Wendy
Silko, Leslie Marmon
Zitkala Sa

Asian American

Chin, Marilyn
Jen, Gish
Kingston, Maxine Hong
Tan, Amy Ruth
Tsukiyama, Gail
Uchida, Yoshiko
Yamamoto, Hisaye

Cajun/Creole

Chopin, Katherine O'Flaherty

Caribbean

Alvarez, Julia
Danticat, Edwidge
García, Cristina
Kincaid, Jamaica
Marshall, Paule

Eastern European/Russian Jewish

Antin, Mary

Lazarus, Emma
Yezierska, Anzia

Hispanic American

Cisneros, Sandra
Mohr, Nicholasa Golpe
Portillo Trambley, Estela
Santiago, Esmeralda

Indian/South Asian

Lahiri, Jhumpa
Mukherjee, Bharati

Irish American

McDermott, Alice
Quindlen, Anna

Louisiana Bayou

Chopin, Katherine
O'Flaherty

Modernists

Barnes, Djuna
Doolittle, Hilda
Lowell, Amy Lawrence
Stein, Gertrude

New England

Chute, Carolyn
Dickinson, Emily Elizabeth
Freeman, Mary Eleanor Wilkins

Jewett, Theodora Sarah Orne
Kumin, Maxine Winokur
Lowell, Amy Lawrence
Sedgwick, Catharine Maria

Southern Gothic Writers

Henley, Elizabeth Becker
McCullers, Lula Carson
Smith
O'Conner, Mary Flannery

Southwest/Midwest/Frontier

Austin, Mary Hunter
Cather, Willa Sibert
Didion, Joan
Kingsolver, Barbara
Wilder, Laura Elizabeth
Ingalls

Transcendentalism

Alcott, Louisa May
Dickinson, Emily Elizabeth
Fuller, Sarah Margaret

Virginia/West Virginia

Cornwell, Patricia Daniels
Davis, Rebecca Harding
Settle, Mary Lee

ENTRIES BY YEAR OF BIRTH

1600s

Bradstreet, Anne Dudley
Rowlandson, Mary White

1700–1749

Adams, Abigail Smith
Warren, Mercy Otis

1750–1799

Foster, Hannah Webster
Hale, Sarah Josepha Buell
Murray, Judith Sargent
Sedgwick, Catharine Maria
Truth, Sojourner
Wheatley, Phillis

1800–1829

Child, Lydia Maria Francis
Fuller, Sarah Margaret
Harper, Frances Ellen Watkins
Howe, Julia Ward
Jacobs, Harriet Ann
Stowe, Harriet Elizabeth
    Beecher
Wilson, Harriet E. Adams

1830–1849

Alcott, Louisa May
Davis, Rebecca Harding
Dickinson, Emily Elizabeth

Jackson, Helen Maria Fiske
    Hunt
Jewett, Theodora Sarah Orne
Lazarus, Emma

1850–1859

Chopin, Katherine O'Flaherty
Freeman, Mary Eleanor Wilkins
Tarbell, Ida Minerva

1860–1869

Austin, Mary Hunter
Bly, Nellie
Bonfils, Martha Winifred
    Sweet Black
Gilman, Charlotte Perkins
Hamilton, Edith
Wells-Barnett, Ida Bell
Wharton, Edith Newbold
    Jones
Wilder, Laura Elizabeth Ingalls

1870–1879

Cather, Willa Sibert
Dunbar-Nelson, Alice Ruth
    Moore
Glaspell, Susan Keating
Lowell, Amy Lawrence
Rinehart, Mary Roberts
Stein, Gertrude
Zitkala Sa

1880–1889

Antin, Mary
Doolittle, Hilda
Fauset, Jessie Redmon
Ferber, Edna
Johnson, Georgia Douglas
    Camp
Moore, Marianne Craig
Mourning Dove
Norris, Kathleen Thompson
Teasdale, Sara Trevor
Wylie, Elinor Morton Hoyt
Yezierska, Anzia

1890–1899

Barnes, Djuna
Bogan, Louise
Bowen, Catherine Drinker
Buck, Pearl Comfort
    Sydenstricker
Flanner, Janet
Herbst, Josephine Frey
Larsen, Nella
Loos, Anita
Millay, Edna St. Vincent
Parker, Dorothy Rothschild
Porter, Katherine Anne
Powell, Dawn
Rawlings, Marjorie Kinnan
Ross, Ishbel Margaret
Thompson, Dorothy

1900–1909

Arnow, Harriette Louisa
   Simpson
Boyle, Kay
Carson, Rachel Louise
Fisher, Mary Frances Kennedy
Hellman, Lillian Florence
Mitchell, Margaret Munnerlyn
Nin, Anaïs
Petry, Ann Lane
Rand, Ayn
Welty, Eudora
West, Dorothy

1910–1919

Bishop, Elizabeth
Brooks, Gwendolyn
Brown, Margaret Wise
Graham, Katharine
Hardwick, Elizabeth
Jackson, Shirley
L'Engle, Madeleine
McCarthy, Mary Therese
McCullers, Lula Carson Smith
Norton, Andre
Olsen, Tillie Lerner
Rukeyser, Muriel
Sarton, May
Settle, Mary Lee
Simon, Kate
Stafford, Jean
Tuchman, Barbara Wertheim
Walker, Margaret Abigail

1920–1929

Angelou, Maya
Bombeck, Erma Louise Fiste
Clampitt, Amy
Kumin, Maxine Winokur
Lee, Nelle Harper
Le Guin, Ursula Kroeber
Levertov, Denise
Lurie, Alison

Marshall, Paule
O'Connor, Mary Flannery
Ozick, Cynthia
Paley, Grace Goodside
Rich, Adrienne Cecile
Sexton, Anne Gray Harvey
Uchida, Yoshiko
Yamamoto, Hisaye

1930–1939

Allen, Paula Gunn
Auel, Jean Marie Untinen
Bambara, Toni Cade
Clifton, Lucille Sayles
Didion, Joan
Godwin, Gail Kathleen
Hansberry, Lorraine Vivian
Lorde, Audre Geraldin
Mohr, Nicholasa Golpe
Morrison, Toni
Oates, Joyce Carol
Oliver, Mary
Piercy, Marge
Plath, Sylvia
Portillo Trambley, Estela
Proulx, Annie
Sanchez, Sonia
Sontag, Susan

1940–1949

Brown, Rita Mae
Butler, Octavia Estelle
Chute, Carolyn
Dillard, Annie Doak
Ehrenreich, Barbara
Glück, Louise Elisabeth
Gordon, Mary Catherine
Grafton, Sue Taylor
Hogan, Linda Henderson
Jong, Erica Mann
Kincaid, Jamaica
Kingston, Maxine Hong
Miller, Sue
Mukherjee, Bharati

Norman, Marsha
Olds, Sharon
Paretsky, Sara
Rice, Anne
Robinson, Marilynne
Rose, Wendy
Santiago, Esmeralda
Shange, Ntozake
Shreve, Anita
Silko, Leslie Marmon
Steel, Danielle
Tyler, Anne
Walker, Alice Malsenior

1950–1959

Alvarez, Julia
Chin, Marilyn
Cisneros, Sandra
Cornwell, Patricia Daniels
Dove, Rita Frances
Erdrich, Karen Louise
Gaitskill, Mary
García, Cristina
Goodwin, Doris Helen Kearns
Henley, Elizabeth Becker
Hoffman, Alice
Jen, Gish
Kingsolver, Barbara
McDermott, Alice
McMillan, Terry
Moore, Lorrie
Naylor, Gloria
Perillo, Lucia
Quindlen, Anna
Roberts, Nora
Smith, Anna Deavere
Tan, Amy Ruth
Tsukiyama, Gail
Vogel, Paula
Wasserstein, Wendy

1960–1969

Danticat, Edwidge
Lahiri, Jhumpa

CREDITS

INDEX

Boldface numbers indicate entries.
Italic numbers indicate illustrations.

397